"From mindfulness to income inequality to urban planning, Sadavoy and Zube's ambitious tome is a must read for all behavior analysts! These essays are filled with ideas on how to incorporate compassion into our work, and how the science of behavior can be applied to a wide range of critical social issues. If you want to know what Love has to do with it, and how behavior analysis can indeed change the world, this is a great place to start."

Bridget A. Taylor, *PsyD, BCBA-D, Alpine Learning Group*

"The field of behavior analysis has waited a long time for a book like this, almost too long, but it's right on time. The content serves as the beginnings to an actionable methodology for anyone ready to embrace the science of behavior analysis as a powerful vehicle for positive social change. Threaded together by themes of compassion, humility, and justice, this book arrives as a call to action for all of us to reflect on our own values and beliefs and how they inform our work as practitioners of behavior analysis. Undoubtedly, this is an essential reading for everyone in our field and at all levels."

Nasiah Cirincione-Ulezi, *EdD, BCBA, CEO & founder, ULEZI, LLC*

"Skinner's vision of behavior analysis was that it was a generic science that would one day be seen to be relevant for all human behavior. Clearly that vision has not been realized. Behavior analysis has flourished under one tail of the normal distribution but it has not often ventured very far out and underthe dome of that distribution. At least that is how the field is viewed by most people outside of it. Needed are demonstrations that make good on Skinner's vision and this book fits the bill perfectly. The expanse of its conceptual diversity is unmatched by any behavior analytic books I have in my extensive collection. The book is timely without being trendy and could ultimately serve as a go to resource for persons interested in behavior analytic perspectives on contemporary, cultural, and professional issues."

Patrick C. Friman, *PhD, ABPP, vice president of Behavioral Health, Boys Town; clinical professor of Pediatrics, UNMC*

A SCIENTIFIC FRAMEWORK FOR COMPASSION AND SOCIAL JUSTICE

A Scientific Framework for Compassion and Social Justice provides readers with an in-depth understanding of the behavior analytic principles that maintain social justice issues and highlights behavior analytic principles that promote self-awareness and compassion.

Expanding on the goals of the field of applied behavioral analysis (ABA), this collection of essays from subject-matter experts in various fields combines personal experiences, scientific explanations, and effective strategies to promote a better existence; a better world. Chapters investigate the self-imposed barriers that contribute to human suffering and offer scientific explanations as to how the environment can systematically be shaped and generate a sociocultural system that promotes harmony, equality, fulfilment, and love.

The goal of this text is to help the reader focus overwhelming feelings of confusion and upheaval into action and to make a stand for social justice while mobilizing others to take value-based actions. The lifelong benefit of these essays extends beyond ABA practitioners to readers in gender studies, diversity studies, education, public health, and other mental health fields.

Jacob A. Sadavoy, QBA, BCBA, has 20 years of behavior analytic experience improving socially significant outcomes in schools, centers, businesses, hospitals, and homes in more than 15 different countries.

Michelle L. Zube, MA, BCBA, has been in the field of behavior analysis for over 15 years consulting for schools and businesses both locally and internationally. She believes in the utility of the science and its broader applications for meaningful and sustainable change.

A SCIENTIFIC FRAMEWORK FOR COMPASSION AND SOCIAL JUSTICE

Lessons in Applied Behavior Analysis

Edited by Jacob A. Sadavoy and Michelle L. Zube

Routledge
Taylor & Francis Group

NEW YORK AND LONDON

First published 2022
by Routledge
605 Third Avenue, New York, NY 10158

and by Routledge
2 Park Square, Milton Park, Abingdon, Oxon, OX14 4RN

Routledge is an imprint of the Taylor & Francis Group, an informa business

Library of Congress Cataloging-in-Publication Data
Names: Sadavoy, Jacob A., editor. | Zube, Michelle L., editor.
Title: A scientific framework for compassion and social justice: lessons in applied behavior analysis/ edited by Jacob A. Sadavoy, Michelle L. Zube.
Description: 1 Edition. | New York: Routledge, 2021. | Identifiers: LCCN 2020048558 (print) | LCCN 2020048559 (ebook) | ISBN 9780367676193 (hardback) | ISBN 9780367676186 (paperback) | ISBN 9781003132011 (ebook)
Subjects: LCSH: Compassion. | Behavioral assessment. | Social justice.
Classification: LCC BF176.5 .S35 2021 (print) | LCC BF176.5 (ebook) | DDC 155.2/8—dc23
LC record available at https://lccn.loc.gov/2020048558
LC ebook record available at https://lccn.loc.gov/2020048559

ISBN: 978-0-367-67619-3 (hbk)
ISBN: 978-0-367-67618-6 (pbk)
ISBN: 978-1-003-13201-1 (ebk)

Typeset in Baskerville
by Apex CoVantage, LLC

In Loving Memory of . . .

Feda Almaliti, a champion of compassion,
Ruth Bader Ginsburg, a champion of justice,
& Jose Martinez-Diaz, a champion of applied behavior analysis.

The world misses your leadership.
Thank you for enriching today to make the future better for all of us.

CONTENTS

ACKNOWLEDGEMENTS

All royalty proceeds will be distributed evenly between three not-for-profit organizations that are endorsed by the authors because of their passionate commitment to making the world better for the marginalized population they serve.

PFLAG ~ envisions a world where diversity is celebrated and all people are respected, valued, and affirmed inclusive of their sexual orientation, gender identity, and gender expression.

Gathering for Justice ~ seeks to build a movement to end child incarceration while working to eliminate the racial inequities that permeate the justice system.

Empowerment Collective ~ envisions a world where women are empowered to be leaders in their communities advocating for improved human rights, in control of their own lives, their own rights, and free to make their own decisions.

Jacob A. Sadavoy wishes to acknowledge and thank the subject-matter essayists for their thoughtful, inspired, and practical contributions. This collection is special because of each of you. Robin Sadavoy, thank you for your artistic prowess, Grace and Amanda for your publishing support, mom and dad, Sava, Helen Smolack (you are missed greatly), and of course, Michelle Zube, for your brilliance, passion, and being such an extraordinary collaborator.

Michelle L. Zube wishes to acknowledge my family for their unwavering support, my dear friend and colleague Jacob Sadavoy for always pushing the envelope, and for my soon to be ... I hope to have made the world even a slightly better place for you and generations to come.

This text was created from the certainty that we possess both the ability and responsibility to address social injustice utilizing a science informed, behavior analytic approach to address systemic challenges that plague society. The topics within are not exhaustive of all injustices. It is a starting point, a call to action, for us to be cause in the matter of our behavior and the behavior of others, in an effort to create a culture and community where all humans are loved for who they are and who they aren't.

socialjusticeaba.com

INTRODUCTION
Metta-Contingencies

Michelle L. Zube

Why behavior analysis? From the outset, the goal of behavior analysis was to develop a scientific approach to account for the broad and complex behaviors of humans. The history of behavior analysis, albeit a short one in comparison to other fields, has proven to be vast in its utility across a variety of people and settings. Shifts in the field towards Organizational Behavior Management (OBM), Acceptance and Commitment Therapy/Training (ACT/ ACTr), Clinical Behavior Analysis, and Prosocial are clear indications of the efficacy of behavior analysis to impart change to society at large.

The idea of behavior analysts working towards social change is nothing new. First published in 1978 as the *Behaviorists for Social Action Journal, Behavior and Social Issues (BSI)* has addressed topics such as social justice, human rights, and sustainability for over forty years. According to Mattaini (2006), *"Behavior and Social Issues* is committed to expanding the possible contributions of behavior science to social justice and human rights, recognizing that justice and rights and their contraries are grounded in human action" (p. 1). The oldest Special Interest Group (SIG) in the Association for Behavior Analysis: International (ABAI) is Behaviorists for Social Responsibility (BFSR). Over the years, other groups formed (i.e, Radical Political Behaviorists, Behaviorists for Social Action) and journals published (e.g., Behavior Analysis and Social Action [BASA]). Luke and colleagues (2017) biblometric analysis of behavior analysis applications to social justice yielded results showing 3,889 citations from BSI articles however, the publication is "lesser known journal in behavior analysis, given the range of topics addressed, it appears to fill an important and underserved niche in both the discipline and society" (Luke et al., 2017 p. 126).

We are in a time when the unrest of our micro and macro environments can not be ignored. Despite the prodigious globalization we have undergone, the omnipresence of abuses of human rights remains (Mattaini, 2006). Behavior analysts have the tools and the scientific framework to facilitate meaningful and lasting socially significant change. Biglan (2015) stated:

> the advances in our practical understanding of human behavior put us in a position to create a world where we have not only previously unimaginable creature comforts, but also the psychological flexibility and loving interpersonal relations that can enable us to evolve societies that nurture human well-being and the ecosystems on which we depend.
>
> (p. 12)

The collaborative effort of the contributors of this book supports a global and societal transformation with a unifying message for hope and action. We must collectively be responsible and accountable for our behaviors; what we do, say, and think matters. The global and collateral effects of our collective behaviors have brought us to these challenging times. With the knowledge and resources we possess, we can unravel the failed processes and systems and replace them with empirically sound and effective procedures to ensure equality for all people, everywhere.

Behavior analysis is rooted in contingencies such that the concept of contingency is central in any discussion about learned behavior and in its application to problems of social significance (Lattal, 1995). Marr (2006) referred to the concept of contingency as "one big card to play" as contingencies "can address a multitude of phenomena" (p. 58). Contingencies function to maintain and change behaviors that facilitate patterns of behavior across individuals, interactions with others, across groups, and larger networks of people.

B.F. Skinner, the father of behavior analysis, predicated the science on the effects of consequences on behavior such that some consequences would increase behavior (reinforcement) while others would decrease behavior (punishment). Skinner published a number of works (Skinner, 1948, 1953, 1974, 1971) detailing his vision of a society where people would develop their potential and work for the greater good of others by selection of consequences (Biglan, 2015). Skinner laid the conceptual and theoretical foundation for behavior analysts to begin to employ behavior analytic principles into the evolution of cultures and cultural practices (e.g., Glenn, 2004; Malott & Glenn, 2006; Houmanfar et al., 2010) in an effort to urge behavior analysts to begin to facilitate meaningful change for global problems (e.g., Cihon & Mattaini, 2019). Marr (2006) stated, ". . . without the application of a science of behavior to set up conditions for applying effective techniques from whatever source, very little can be accomplished, as Skinner noted more than 50 years ago" (p. 65).

The goal of this text is to start a comprehensive conversation, to guide us on how we can begin to listen, observe, and mitigate injustices and global crises with the principles of behavior analysis. To embark upon a mission in which we seek to change systemic problems it is critical to understand the interlocking behavior contingencies under which these problems exist and function within and across various levels of our environment. An in-depth analysis of contingencies is complex and far exceeds the breadth of this introduction; however, it lends itself to a conceptual understanding of how all behaviors, their consequences, and the context in which they occur have systemic implications.

Skinner (1981) suggested that selection by consequences is a robust phenomenon that is applicable across various levels of analysis. Skinner proposed that natural selection and operant selection might be joined by a cultural-level of selection in a comprehensive description of the dynamics of change observed in the world around us (Krispin, 2016).

The selection process is what contributes to learning. Learning refers to the history of these contingencies, or specific consequences, that an individual has come into contact with over the course of a lifetime that shapes their behavior. Glenn (2004) offered that:

> Learned behavior is the substructure of human cultures, and the transmission of learned behavior powers the evolution of human cultures. Human behavior produces cumulative change in human environments, and continually changing environments require continuing behavioral adjustments. Successful adjustments can become embedded in cultural practices and transmitted to later generations.
>
> (p. 133)

Humanity has come so far and yet in many ways we have not evolved; made the appropriate behavioral adjustments, or embedded and transmitted cultural practices that ensure a quality of life for all humans, everywhere. To be able to find a solution, we must understand the complex dynamics of how we as individuals and collective groups of people operate in and among the various levels of our ever changing environments.

This understanding begins with the relationship between cultural materialism (the science of culture), and behavior analysis (the science of behavior). These fields diverge at the level of scientific analysis in that behavior analysis focuses on the relationship between the behavior of organisms and environmental events, while cultural materialism is focused on the relationship between cultural practices and the environment where those practices take place.

The unit of analysis in behavior analysis is the contingency of reinforcement whereas cultural practices "refers to similar patterns of behavioral content, usually resulting from similarities in environments" (Glenn 2004, p. 140). Other terms to describe these practices include: "metabehavior" (Mawhinney, 1995) and "macrobehavior" (Glenn, 2004). Unlike the individual unit of analysis, these cultural practices typically involve the behavior of several individuals interacting in a system of organization. The term "macrocontingency" (Glenn, 2004) is also used to describe the relation between "a cultural practice and the aggregate sum of consequences of the macrobehavior constituting the practice." In essence, it is the result of many people engaging in various forms of a behavior. The cumulative effects of macrocontingencies can be problematic for the people within a culture because effects of the practice will be more beneficial for some and not for others. Cultural practices vary in behavioral complexity and can be understood as "a set of interlocking contingencies of reinforcement in which the behavior and behavioral products of each participant function as environmental events with which the behavior of other individuals interacts. This is the behavioral view of a cultural practice" (Glenn, 1988, p. 167).

These interlocking behavior contingencies are referred to as metacontingencies "The prefix meta- together with the root contingencies is intended to suggest selection contingencies that are hierarchically related to, and subsume, behavioral contingencies" (Glenn, 2004, p. 144). Metacontingencies are the ongoing interlocking behavioral contingencies that function together to produce outcomes which inform the ongoing occurrence of IBCS resulting in the cumulative effect of interrelated behavior. "Together with behavioral contingencies, metacontingencies account for cultural selection and evolutionary change in organizations" (Glenn & Malott, 2004, p. 100). These contingencies are influential across all of the domains in which we seek systemic and meaningful change.

Busch and colleagues (2019) explicate the function of metacontiengies in their conceptual analysis *The untapped potential of behavior analysis and interprofessional care*. Here they discuss how the principles of behavior analysis can contribute to interprofessional care by providing an analysis by which behaviors can be better predicted and influenced. In this case, interprofessional collaboration serves as the metacontingency. The authors offer that extending functional contextualism, with the underlying goal to predict and influence behaviors, a framework for values driven interprofessional collaboration and improved outcomes for clients. In this case, the client functions as the product.

To illustrate this point, Busch and colleagues provide a representation of an extrapolation of metacontingency with respect to an interprofessional practice on a mental health team (Figure 0.1). Several coordinated behaviors are shown to occur between professionals within mental health care settings; these can be described as interlocking behavioural contingencies.

For instance, "the identification of available housing by a social worker may prompt a vocational skills assessment by an occupational therapist while simultaneously reinforcing the stabilization efforts of the behaviour analyst and psychiatrist, the assessment and treatment behaviors of nursing staff, and the engagement in therapeutic programming by the patient (rewarding/cuing exchanges depicted by solid black arrows [p. 5])." They purport,

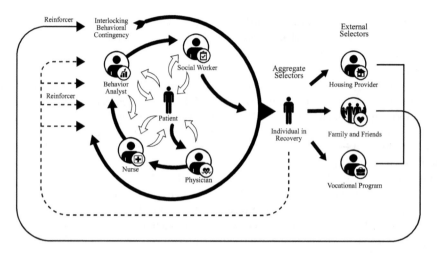

Figure 0.1 Metacontingency depicting the interlocking behavioural contingency of a kitchen brigade and the selection of its aggregate effect by external selectors.
Source: (Adapted from Busch et al., 2019).

"interlocking behavioral contingencies that produce better patient outcomes and movement through the system, would reinforce the collaborative efforts of the interprofessional team, while increasing the probability of selection by housing providers, vocational programs, family and social networks (external selectors [p. 6])."

We can generalize this concept across various settings, groups of people, and societal issues. Patient can easily be replaced by student, government official, victim, or rainforest, to name a few. It is becoming increasingly apparent through research and daily life that our actions are synergistic. According to Dr. Steven Hayes, "the benefits of this science-based approach to transforming society can extend well beyond prevention of individual psychological and behavioral problems. At this point, we can use a wealth of accumulated knowledge to evolve to a society where people cooperate and care for each other" (as cited in Biglan, 2015, p. 3).

So how did we get here? Where were the breakdowns in our organizations? How did we come to a point of cultural evolution where we live in a society in which the well-being of all members are not considered? How do we breed compassion and foster the development of caring for others? There may be several means to this end however, Biglan (2009) suggests that increasing psychological flexibility is a "means of facilitating diverse beneficial developments in cultural evolution" (p. 15). Psychological flexibility is the overarching goal of Acceptance and Commitment Therapy. It is "the ability to contact the present moment more fully as a conscious human being and to change, or persist in, behavior when doing so serves valued ends" (Biglan et al., 2008, p. 142). The antithesis of flexibility is experiential avoidance which are behaviors that circumvent the discomfort of uncomfortable private events leading to an unwillingness or lack of acceptance of the present experience.

Biglan discusses how the unwillingness or inability of people to care for one another contributes to many societal problems (e.g., conflict, crime, prejudice, aggression). ACT has demonstrated its efficacy across hundreds of studies some of which have led to increased psychological flexibility across a number of problems such as prejudice (Kenny & Bizumic,

2016), substance abuse (Lee et al., 2015), and mental health conditions (Bardeen & Fergus, 2016; Dindo et al., 2019).

The use of mindful approaches can reduce interpersonal and group conflict (e.g., police misconduct, harassment, religious and racial intolerance) as conflicts are based on the thought and feelings of one individual and how they deal with others (e.g., racial bias). Biglan suggests that the more psychologically flexible individuals are, than attending to the well-being of others would become a shared value in and among groups. "Such a shared value seems fundamental in evolving a society in which the practices of government, business, education, and civic life ensure that the society meets the basic needs of each person. Businesses would increasingly act in ways that benefit the society as well as their bottom line. Governments would evaluate their impact on human well-being."

What Biglan offers, as others will in this text, is that the way to increase psychological flexibility is to infuse ACT into organizations at all levels (e.g., governments, schools, public policy). Similarly the Prosocial process (Atkins, Wilson, & Hayes, 2019), which aims to increase the efficacy of group dynamics through the use of ABA, ACT, OBM, and Ostrom's 8 Core Design Principles (Ostrom, 1990), can be a beacon of light to ameliorate societal challenges.

To this end, I offer a third definition: Metta-contingencies. Metta (Maitrī: Sanskrit; Pali: mettā) meaning loving kindness, benevolence, goodwill, amity, and non-violence. Metta-contingencies refers to those in which universal love and compassion are the ties that bind us together in a collective consciousness with one another and Mother Earth. It is only through greater understanding of our actions, the implications of our behavior, and how a prosocial model to increase the efficacy of group dynamics will we begin to abolish the systems and practices that prevent us from being fully human.

In 1969, Skinner offered, "A more likely solution to achieving a better world may lie in arranging better contingencies in our current environments to move us toward that goal" (Skinner, 1969, p. 97). In 2006, Marr warned us that in our efforts to better understand and control social behavior, we are not only entering into a territory that has been saturated by other professions but we have also arrived late to offer our help. Marr suggests that in order for behavior analysts to be involved in social/cultural work, we must learn about the relevant social sciences, the problems, address, and the methods used to address them. Marr suggests, "as behavior analysts, have at least as much to learn as to teach" (p. 60).

Similarly, during Dr. Mattaini's 2019 presidential address at the annual Applied Behavior Analysis International (ABAI) conference, he discussed the limitations of the field of behavior analysis with regards to societal change. He suggested that behavior analysts begin to use a transdisciplinary approach to cultural analysis with a focus on macrobehaviors (Cihon & Mattaini, 2019). We do not have another 50 years to wait to start creating contingencies that will improve our current environments. Glenn (2004) proposed that, "The only way to do something about the cumulative effects of macrobehavior is to find ways to alter the behavior of as many individual participants as possible" (p. 147). This is our mission.

REFERENCES

Atkins, P. W., Hayes, S. C., & Wilson, D. S. (2019). *Prosocial: Using evolutionary science to build productive, equitable, and collaborative groups.* Context Publishing.

Bardeen, J. R., & Fergus, T. A. (2016). The interactive effect of cognitive fusion and experiential avoidance on anxiety, depression, stress and posttraumatic stress symptoms. *Journal of Contextual Behavioral Science, 5*, 1–6. http://doi.org/10.1016/j.jcbs.2016.02.002

Biglan, A., Hayes, S. C., & Pistorello, J. (2008). Acceptance and commitment: Implications for prevention science. *Prevention Science: The Official Journal of the Society for Prevention Research, 9*(3), 139–152. https://doi.org/10.1007/s11121-008-0099-0094

Biglan, A. (2009). Increasing psychological flexibility to influence cultural evolution. *Behavior and Social Issues, 18*, 15–24. https://doi.org/10.5210/bsi.v18i1.2280

Biglan, A. (2015). *The nurture effect : How the science of human behavior can improve our lives and our world.* New Harbinger Publications.

Busch, L. P. A., Porter, J., & Barreira, L. (2019). The untapped potential of behaviour analysis and interprofessional care. *Journal of Interprofessional Care*, 1–8. https://doi.org/10.1080/13561820.2019.1633292

Cihon, T. M., & Mattaini, M. A. (2019). Editorial: Emerging cultural and behavioral systems science. *Perspectives on Behavior Science, 42*, 699–711. https://doi.org/10.1007/s40614-019-002

Dindo, L., Brandt, C. P., & Fiedorowicz, J. G. (2019). Cross-sectional relations between psychological inflexibility and symptoms of depression and anxiety among adults reporting migraines or risk factors for cardiovascular disease. *Journal of Contextual Behavioral Science, 13*, 1–6. https://psycnet.apa.org/doi/10.1016/j.jcbs.2019.06.001

Glenn, S. S. (1988). Contingencies and metacontingencies: Toward a synthesis of behavior analysis and cultural materialism. *The Behavior Analyst, 11*(2), 161–179. https://doi.org/10.1007/BF03392470

Glenn, S. S. (2004). Individual behavior, culture, and social change. *The Behavior Analyst, 27*(2), 133–151. https://doi.org/10.1007/BF03393175

Glenn, S. S., & Malott, M. E. (2004). Complexity and selection: Implications for organizational change. *Behavior and Social Issues, 13*(2), 89–106. https://doi.org/10.5210/bsi.v13i2.378

Houmanfar, R., Rodrigues, N. J., & Ward, T. (2010, May).Emergence and metacontingency: Points of contact and departure. *Behavior and Social Issues, 19*(1), 53–78. https://doi.org/10.5210/bsi.v19i0.3065

Kenny, A., & Bizumic, B. (2016). Learn and ACT: Changing prejudice towards people with mental illness using stigma reduction interventions. *Journal of Contextual Behavioral Science, 5*(3), 178–185. https://psycnet.apa.org/doi/10.1016/j.jcbs.2016.06.004

Krispin, J. V. (2016). What is the Metacontingency? Deconstructing claims of emergence and cultural-level selection. *Behavior and Social Issues, 25*, 28–41. https://doi.org/10.5210/bsi.v25i0.6186

Lattal K. A. (1995). Contingency and behavior analysis. *The Behavior Analyst, 18*(2), 209–224. https://doi.org/10.1007/BF03392709

Lee, E. B., An, W., Levin, M. E., & Twohig, M. P. (2015). An initial meta-analysis of Acceptance and Commitment Therapy for treating substance use disorders. *Drug & Alcohol Dependence, 155*, 1–7. https://doi.org/10.1016/j.drugalcdep.2015.08.004

Luke, M. M., Roose, K. M., & Rakos, R. F. et al. (2017). The history and current status of *Behavior and Social Issues*: 1978–2016. *Behav. Soc. Iss., 26*, 111–127. https://doi.org/10.5210/bsi.v26i0.7728

Malott, M. E., & Glenn, S. S. (2006). Targets of intervention in cultural and behavioral change. *Behavior and Social Issues, 15*(1), 31–56. https://doi.org/10.5210/bsi.v15i1.344

Marr, M J. (2006, March). Behavior analysis and social dynamics: Some questions and concerns. *Behavior and Social Issues, 15*(1), 31. 10.5210/bsi.v15i1.345

Mattaini, M. A. (Ed.). (2006). Editorial: Human rights, pragmatic solidarity, and behavior science. *Behavior and Social Issues, 15*(1), 1–4. https://doi.org/10.5210/bsi.v15i1.382

Mawhinney, V. T. (1995). Metabehaviors as discriminative stimuli for planned cultural evolution. *Behavior and Social Issues, 5*(1), 35–44. https://doi.org/10.5210/bsi.v5i1.217

Ostrom, E. 1990. *Governing the commons: The evolution of institutions for collective action.* Cambridge University Press.

Skinner, B. F. (1948). *Walden two.* Macmillan.

Skinner, B. F. (1953). *Science and human behavior.* Macmillan

Skinner, B. F. (1969). *Contingencies of reinforcement: A theoretical analysis.* Appleton-Century-Crofts.

Skinner, B. F. (1971). *Beyond freedom and dignity.* Alfred A Knopf.

Skinner, B. F. (1974). *About behaviorism.* Alfred A Knopf.

Skinner, B. F. (1981/1986). Selection by consequences. *Science, 213,* 501–504. http://dx.doi.org/10.1126/science.7244649

1

ACCEPTANCE AND COMMITMENT TRAINING

Acting to Support Compassion-Focused Applied Behavior Analysis

Jonathan Tarbox and Kristine Rodriguez

INTRODUCTION

The world is changing rapidly, global culture is in flux, and yet centuries-old inequities persist. The field of applied behavior analysis (ABA) is situated squarely within the purpose of *serving humanity*. This is evident to us, as the vast majority of researchers and practitioners in ABA have dedicated our careers to helping empower families living with autism and other developmental disabilities. While this dedication to serving humanity seems obvious to us in the field of ABA, it seems it has not been entirely obvious to others that we lead with our hearts. What's more, there is a growing yearning inside the field of ABA to connect with other humans in more complete and fundamental ways.

In this chapter, we will make the case for embracing compassion in the field of ABA and discuss ways to use Acceptance and Commitment Training (ACT) to empower us to live compassion in our daily research and practice.

This chapter begins with the belief that humans treating other humans with love, compassion, and dignity is among the highest moral imperatives. Many have argued that compassion is a near-fundamental value, across millennia, across cultures, and across all major world faith traditions, including Christianity, Buddhism, Judaism, Hinduism, and Islam (Strauss et al., 2016). To lay the groundwork, we will briefly touch upon how empathy and compassion can be viewed as behavioral repertoires.

ROOTS OF EMPATHY AND COMPASSION

Compassion has been defined as taking action to benefit others and is supported by empathy (Eisenberg & Miller, 1987); however, very little behavioral research has been published on empathy. In one of the few available behavioral conceptual accounts of empathy, Vilardaga (2009) suggests that empathy consists of perspective-taking behavior, referred to as deictic relational framing, involving the operant behavior of relating oneself to the other in terms of similarity. For example, "The RBT I am supervising is the same as me, in that we both work with children with autism in the ABA field." Expanding on Vilardaga's RFT account of empathy, we have recently suggested that empathy may be strengthened if perspective-taking behavior is directed at shared values (Persicke, 2020). Empathy is likely strengthened when I see similarities between myself and you, in terms of something that matters a great deal to me, such as my values, my religion, my life's purpose, etc.

The RFT literature predicts that empathy and compassionate behavior can be strengthened through repeated practice, across many different exemplars, until generalization occurs. If I want to strengthen my empathizing behavior, I should actively practice noticing, talking about, and writing about the ways in which I am the same as others, in terms of values. For example, I might practice identifying ways in which:

- I and specific people of different racial/ethnic backgrounds might be the same (e.g., we are all humans, we all want the best for our families, etc.)

- I and people of different religions might be the same (e.g., we both care deeply about our faith, we both care about our right to practice our faith, etc.), and
- I and people of different professions might be the same (e.g., we both care deeply about making a difference, etc.)

When looked at through a behavioral lens, empathy is not a personality trait or mental state, it is a skill to be practiced until fluency and generalization occurs.

Very little has been written about compassion from a behavior analytic perspective. However, Bridget Taylor and Linda LeBlanc have recently called for developing compassionate repertoires in ABA (2019; 2020). Among the many important messages of these recent papers is that compassion converts empathy into *behavior* aimed at alleviating the suffering of others. Put plainly, who we are in our heads doesn't touch the world. It's not about our intent; it's about the impact we have through our behavior. If we are serious about moving toward a more compassionate future in ABA, then we will all need to demonstrate behavior change in our daily jobs, through small overt behaviors that care for and nurture our clients and colleagues in new and meaningful ways.

Seeing the need for greater compassionate behavior is the easy part; the work of actually practicing empathy and compassion can be difficult and uncomfortable. Below, we describe strategies from the ACT literature that we can use to support our empathy and compassion-building work.

ACCEPTANCE AND COMMITMENT TRAINING

Originally designed as a behavior analytic approach to talk therapy, ACT has flourished as a *training* approach outside of talk therapy for more than a decade (Tarbox et al., 2020). For an excellent overview of ACT, read *A Liberated Mind* (e.g., Hayes, 2020). Below, we discuss how components of ACT can be harnessed to support our compassionate behavior.

Values

Values are what we care deeply about and they give our lives meaning and purpose. Values are unique to each individual person but behavior analysts commonly report values such as, "making the world a better place" and "helping our clients achieve their highest potential," among others. In behavioral perspective, values can be thought of as augmentals or verbally mediated motivating operations, which can give meaning to our behavior (Little et al., 2020). To contact your values, try putting down this book and just write for a few minutes about what you care about most, personally and professionally.

To use values to strengthen your compassion skills, first reflect on what you just wrote and ask yourself if compassion fits in anywhere. You may have identified compassion as something you care about most, for example, *I care about being a compassionate helper at work*. If compassion did not show up in your values reflection, are there any ways you can imagine that behaving more compassionately might help serve one of the values you did identify? For example, if you identified *supporting families living with autism* as one of your values, does it follow that behaving more compassionately might serve that value?

Committed Action

Committed action is the ACT component aimed directly at socially meaningful overt behavior change. To take committed action toward the value of building compassionate behavior, start by identifying small, achievable, measurable, overt behaviors and set a goal for yourself. For example, if you notice that your clients' caregivers might wish to feel more heard by you, perhaps commit to dedicating the first five minutes of each caregiver meeting to just listening to their concerns, without trying to fix or change them. Or if you want to work on being more compassionate with the staff you supervise, perhaps commit to sharing one small way in which you empathize with the difficulty they are experiencing at your next supervision meeting (e.g., "I remember how stressed out I was when I was a new behavioral technician. I get where you are coming from; it's a totally normal human reaction."). After identifying the specific goal, make a commitment to someone you respect. Then do the behavior and collect data on yourself. Once a week or so, reflect on your progress and adjust as needed.

Acceptance

Engaging in the self-reflection necessary for empathetic perspective-taking can be uncomfortable because it necessitates seeing how others see us, perhaps sometimes as "cold and uncaring ABA people." Engaging in new patterns of overt compassionate behavior may be uncomfortable, too, because it may require vulnerability. Acceptance skills, also often called "willingness" skills, consist of making room for the full range of emotions and thoughts that show up, including discomfort. From a behavioral perspective, it seems to consist of the behavioral repertoire of moving *toward* experiencing aversive emotions and thoughts, when doing so helps one choose committed action toward values. To practice building your acceptance skills, try to remember a time when a parent, client, or other professional judged you as being uncaring. See if you can remember the look of the place where it happened and the feeling in your stomach and chest. If you are like most humans, you are going to immediately want to stop thinking about this. To practice your acceptance skills, try just sitting with those feelings and thoughts for a bit longer. If you notice yourself trying to explain or rationalize them away, that's okay, just try to bring your attention back to how it actually felt, then and now. As you practice these acceptance skills more and more, you might notice that you are able to experience discomfort for longer. Ultimately, you might find that your answer to this question gradually becomes more affirmative: Would you be willing to feel this discomfort again, if it was the price you need to pay to more fully enact your values of treating others with compassion?

Defusion

At this point, your mind is likely telling you plenty of convincing reasons not to do what this chapter is recommending (e.g., "it's too fluffy," "it's not behavior analytic," etc.). The human mind, that is, our repertoire of private verbal behavior, is very good at this. From the age of about four or five, we become able to derive cause-and-effect rules about *should* and *shouldn't*. The purpose of defusion training is to help us build more flexible, values-based repertoires of responding to our own thoughts, in the interest of opening up more space for values-based action.

A behavior analytic perspective on thoughts is that they can influence behavior in the same way that overt verbal rules can, by verbally describing an imagined future. We can then respond to those verbal rules as though they are literally true. For example, it is likely common to have thoughts like, "I have to be professional, I can't show weakness," in our jobs. If we notice that we may be following this rule in an overly rigid way, for example, by never showing or acknowledging emotions with our clients, then the rule may be getting in the way of our value of conducting ourselves with greater compassion.

A defusion procedure that many find helpful is called Thanks Mind. To practice Thanks Mind, take a minute to list a few reasons your mind is telling you why you aren't going to be able to do this compassionate behavior stuff. Now try saying one of those reasons out loud and then immediately add a sarcastic, "Wow, thanks mind! I really appreciate how you are always there to help me out when I'm trying to be more compassionate!"

A second handy defusion exercise is Or Not and it involves simply adding ". . . or not" to the end of whatever thought is telling you to put off or avoid executing your commitments to compassionate behavior. For example, "If I listen to this RBT complain, it's just going to reinforce their complaining behavior . . . *or not*," or "I just don't have the energy to call this mom right now and listen to her concerns . . . *or not*." Defusion exercises do not aim to disprove your unhelpful thoughts. They are merely providing more flexible, varied ways to react to our own thoughts, especially when those thoughts encourage us to avoid.

Present Moment Attention

We all have an incredible capacity to think about stuff other than what is actually happening in front of us. The capacity to reconsider the past and to anticipate the future is incredibly powerful and can be adaptive, when done in the right context. Unfortunately, it is very human to spend way too much time paying attention to something other than the present.

Present moment training involves training the behavior of paying attention more to what is happening here and now and less to thoughts about the past or future. Furthermore, it involves learning to self-manage our own attending behavior and redirect it back to the here and now, much as we track and redirect our own attention back to the road when we are driving and get distracted. How is this relevant to compassion? Fundamentally, humans want to be seen and heard. If we want to behave more compassionately when interacting with others, it is absolutely critical that we are paying attention to the people we are interacting with and that, when we notice our attention wander, we redirect it back to the people we are interacting with. To get good at this, make a commitment to really be present next time you interact with someone at work, whether it's a client, a parent, or staff member. Really lean in and listen when they speak. Put down or turn off all electronics and notice where your attention is. When you notice yourself thinking of something else, kindly thank your mind for being unhelpful and bring your attention back to the person you are interacting with.

Self-as-Context

Humans tend to learn and hold onto verbal rules about who we are and these rules can influence our behavior in unhelpful ways, especially if we cling to them too rigidly. For example, try filling in the following sentence with the very first words that come to mind: "I am a behavior analyst, so I HAVE to _____." Even for highly compassionate folks, rigid verbal behavior about who we are can get in the way of doing what we care about. For example, if our first thought when learning about racial injustice is, "I'm not racist," and we respond to this thought rigidly, then we may be less likely to do the work needed to contribute to equity. Similarly, if, when we hear that a client's parent perceives us as cold or uncaring, and our first thought is, "That's bullshit, I probably care too much!", and we respond to that thought as though it is literally true, we may be less likely to consider multiple possible strategies for healing our relationship with that client.

Self-as-context training is about creating more flexible, varied, and values-oriented repertoires of perspective-taking. The goal is to train the ability to see ourselves in multiple, flexible ways, that are sensitive to the context and the feedback that our environment is giving us. To put this into practice, next time you are *very sure you are right* about something and the thought includes the frame "I am," just try one of the defusion strategies on that thought. Other commonly used self-as-context strategies include imagining your thoughts and emotions as weather, sometimes a storm, sometimes sunny and beautiful. Then shift perspective and imagine you are the sky and practice just noticing your thoughts and emotions battling for space in your mind's sky, without having to engage or change them.

THE ACT MATRIX

The ACT Matrix is a powerful self-management tool that helps us organize our values, our uncomfortable thoughts and feelings, our avoidant behaviors, and our committed actions all on one page (see Polk and colleagues' 2016 how-to manual for in-depth coverage of the matrix). Like all ACT skills, to get good at the ACT Matrix requires practice across multiple examples and settings. Figure 1.1 contains an example from Taylor, LeBlanc, and Nosik (2019). Imagine a client's parent has left three angry voicemails on your phone. How do you

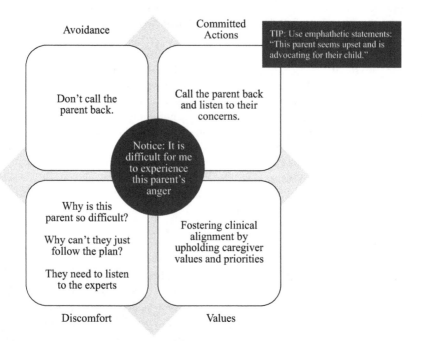

Figure 1.1 A sample ACT matrix for increasing compassionate behavior with a parent.

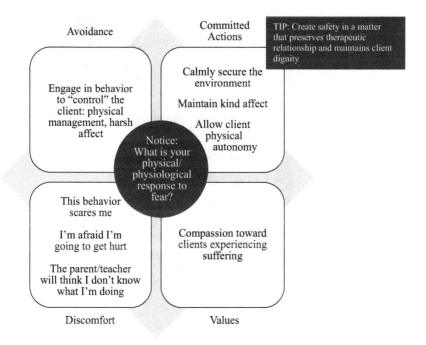

Avoidance   Committed
                   Actions

TIP: Create safety in a matter that preserves therapeutic relationship and maintains client dignity

Engage in behavior to "control" the client: physical management, harsh affect

Calmly secure the environment

Maintain kind affect

Allow client physical autonomy

Notice: What is your physical/ physiological response to fear?

This behavior scares me

I'm afraid I'm going to get hurt

The parent/teacher will think I don't know what I'm doing

Compassion toward clients experiencing suffering

Discomfort   Values

Figure 1.2 A sample ACT matrix for demonstrating compassion in the presence of dangerous behavior.

model compassion and address their concerns when it feels aversive to interact with them? In the bottom right quadrant, list your values that could be relevant to the situation. In the bottom left, list your thoughts and feelings that might get in your way. In the top left quadrant, list some of the avoidant behaviors you might engage in. Most importantly, in the top right, list a small committed action that you are willing to engage in that will move you toward the value that you listed in the bottom right.

Next, imagine a client who is engaging in dangerous behavior that makes you feel afraid for your safety. How do you respond (physically and with your voice and expressions) in a way that communicates compassion for the client who is experiencing distress? Again, take a trip around the four quadrants of the matrix and try listing various words and see how they land for you. The matrix isn't about "judging" yourself. It's about practicing noticing what we care about and how we can take small steps away from avoidance and toward values.

Finally, imagine a colleague is experiencing discrimination in the workplace. How can you act meaningfully as an ally? Especially for white folks who do not yet have a substantial history of taking action toward social justice (which is most of us), thoughts and feelings are going to show up that will give us plenty of reasons to do and say nothing. The matrix is a way to get honest with ourselves about our barriers and begin to take small steps toward a more just future.

Being Pragmatic

Lest this chapter be misinterpreted as suggesting that everyone needs to engage this labor-intensive work of compassion every time, with every person they interact with, or else they

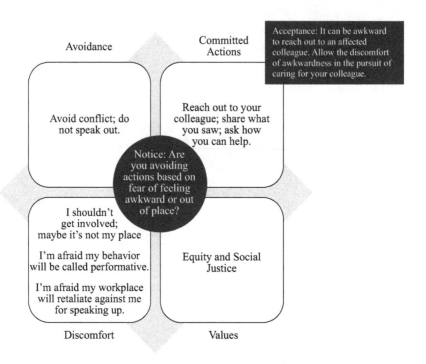

Figure 1.3 A sample ACT matrix for facing discrimination in the workplace.

are "not a compassionate person." We think it's important to keep in mind that this chapter provides just one set of tools that may be useful in some contexts. Many other skills, including self-advocacy, are equally important in professional and personal life. For example, for someone experiencing sexual or racial harassment, working on compassion for their harasser is certainly not the first priority. But when the time and context are right for working on compassion, we hope that the tools offered here will be useful.

CONCLUSION

Life is too short to wait until later to treat others with kindness, love, and compassion. Our science gives us incredible power to change behavior and we believe that committing to a foundation of compassion will help us wield that power more wholeheartedly. By practicing perspective-taking, we can strengthen our empathy and by practicing ACT skills in small but meaningful ways, we can empower ourselves to empower others. Like any behavior change, the path will not be easy, but it's a path we are committed to.

REFERENCES

Brodhead, M. T., Quigley, S. P., & Wilczynski, S. M. (2018). A call for discussion about scope of competence in behavior analysis. *Behavior Analysis in Practice, 11*(4), 424–435. https://doi.org/10.1007/s40617-018-00303-8

Decety, J., & Jackson, P. L. (2004). The functional architecture of human empathy. *Behavioral and Cognitive Neuroscience Reviews, 3*, 71–100. https://doi.org/10.1177/1534582304267187

Eisenberg, N., & Miller, P. A. (1987). The relation of empathy to prosocial and related behaviors. *Psychological Bulletin, 101*, 91–119. https://doi.org/10.1037/0033-2909.101.1.91

Hayes, S. C. (2020). *A liberated mind: How to pivot toward what matters*. Avery.

LeBlanc, L. A., Taylor, B. A. & Marchese, N. V. (2020). The training experiences of behavior analysts: Compassionate care and therapeutic relationships with caregivers. *Behav Analysis Practice, 13*, 387–393. https://doi.org/10.1007/s40617-019-00368-z

Little, A., Tarbox, J., & Alzaabi, K. (2020). Using acceptance and commitment training to enhance the effectiveness of behavioral skills training. *Journal of Contextual Behavioral Science, 16*, 9–16.

Persicke, A. (2020). *A relational frame theory account of the establishment of empathic responding* (Doctoral dissertation). The Chicago School of Professional Psychology.

Polk, K. L., Schoendorff, B., Webster, M., & Olaz, F. O. (2016). *The essential guide to the ACT Matrix: A step-by-step approach to using the ACT Matrix model in clinical practice*. New Harbinger Publications.

Strauss, C., Taylor, B. L., Gu, J., Kuyken, W., Baer, R., Jones, F., & Cavanagh, K. (2016). What is compassion and how can we measure it? A review of definitions and measures. *Clinical Psychology Review, 47*, 15–27.

Tarbox, J., Szabo, T. G., & Aclan, M. (2020). Acceptance and commitment training within the scope of practice of Applied Behavior Analysis. *Behav Analysis Practice*. https://doi.org/10.1007/s40617-020-00466-3

Taylor, B. A., LeBlanc, L. A., & Nosik, M. R. (2019). Compassionate care in behavior analytic treatment: Can outcomes be enhanced by attending to relationships with caregivers?. *Behav Analysis Practice, 12*, 654–666. https://doi.org/10.1007/s40617-018-00289-3

Vilardaga, R. (2009). A relational frame theory account of empathy. *International Journal of Behavioral Consultation and Therapy, 5*(2), 178–184. http://dx.doi.org/10.1037/h0100879

2

AGEISM

Reconsidering Aging: An Examination of Contextual
Factors and the Construct of Old Age

Claudia Drossel and Rachel VanPutten

INTRODUCTION

The *Oxford English Dictionary* (OED) defines ageism as "prejudice or discrimination on the grounds of a person's age; age discrimination" (2020). The first use of the term was recorded in 1969, when a psychiatrist, R.N. Butler, M.D., gave an interview to Carl Bernstein of the Washington Post (Bengtson, 2014). According to Butler, reluctance to be close to adults aged 65 and older was one of the major barriers to establishing affordable housing within neighborhoods. Ageism represents the result of a complex interaction of rule-governed behavior (myths and distortions influencing individuals' attitudes and beliefs) with other forms of stimulus control (negative visual media images, negative olfactory experiences related to substandard health services) that then lead to systemic and institutionalized contingencies segregating older adults. One quick glance at birthday cards for sale, with their thinly veiled derision about aging as a waning of social or interactional power, tells the story about our complicated relationship with accumulating life years. Indeed, if one were to follow birthday card recommendations, birthdays are a reminder to conserve youth or battle age mostly through consumption such as shopping, visiting spas, and taking in special treats. While aging is a lifelong process that affects everybody, there are currently no social contingencies in place that alert laypeople and providers of any age to the blatant ageism present in their personal or professional lives, including their perpetuation of ageist practices. The first step to creating and actively promoting such social contingencies is to question the meaning of "aging" and "old age." The next steps, outlined below, are self-reflection and advocacy for change in both personal and public spheres.

FIRST STEPS

"Old Age" as a Social Construct

"Aging" denotes the developmental process of growing, maturing, coming of age, and becoming old (OED, 2020). The human lifespan is finite, and sociocultural contingencies cleave lifespan into childhood, adolescence, adulthood, and advanced age. In the mid-19th century, industrialization and the necessity to protect children as well as adult workers generated contingencies for a new form of time measurement – keeping track of age (Baselice, et al., 2019). Labor rights introduced decision-making heuristics or biases based on a certain age (Baars, 2012). Today, these age-based heuristics or biases have entered our knowledge as "facts of life." The debates surrounding the social construction and inception of these heuristics and biases are forgotten. Examples include: the Fair Labor Standards Act of 1938 (Lumpkin, 1939), which limited the labor of children in the U.S. who were younger than age 16; age 18 as the time point at which to assume the legal rights and responsibilities of adulthood, now accepted by most states in the U.S.; 21 as the age that permits purchase and consumption of alcohol; age 26 by which to cease coverage as a dependent child on a parent's healthcare policy (the Affordable Care Act implemented in 2014); and mandatory retirement ages from 60 to 70 in some countries. These time points are cultural artifacts, socially constructed with consensus of verbal communities. At the same time, arbitrary or politically negotiated rules produce real-world contingencies and consequences, from risky "coming-of-age"-binges of alcohol in the U.S.A. (Fillo et al., 2020) to potential cessation of health services delivery when adult children outgrow parental insurance coverage (Kozloff & Sommers, 2017; see also Rubenstein & Bishop, 2019).

Such social construction with substantial consequences also applies to "old age." In the United States, as in other Western countries, 65 typically denotes the threshold to old age. This is not a coincidence: Social security plans – introduced in the German government under Bismarck in 1889 – covered workers who were at least 70 years old. Because actuarial data on mortality and morbidity had been imprecise, the age for social security eligibility was lowered to 65 in 1910, when the average life expectancy was 45 years for men and 48 years for women, ascertaining that financial demands would not overwhelm the public system. Only a small fraction of workers lived long enough to benefit. While life expectancy has increased considerably since then, the putative threshold for transitioning from midlife into retirement and thus old age has not kept pace. If the actuarial logic from 1910 were applied today, and social security eligibility were set to an age at which about 4 to 5% of individuals of an age cohort were alive, speaking of "retirement age" would be restricted to those over 95 years of age. One in four adults aged 65 today will live beyond 90 years of age (Arias & Xu, 2019). Laypeople's social conception of aging is out of step with the process. The mid-60s are the presumed benchmark for entering the "golden years," and for many people, nearly 30 years of living remains.

Aging and Disability

Life events are manifold and, as they happen, adults' paths diverge – even if they shared initial childhood social and physical environments. For this reason, adults in later life constitute a heterogeneous population that differs along many dimensions, among them cohort effects (e.g., Korean War, Civil Rights Movement, Vietnam era, HIV/AIDS epidemic, digital revolution), employment, health status, and lifestyle factors. Aging and disability are often confounded, yet results from a national survey (Okoro et al., 2018) suggest that about a quarter of adults older than 18 report a disability. Conversely, while the risk for chronic diseases (e.g., hypertension, diabetes, arthritis, or chronic lung or heart disease) increases with age, many people have no chronic conditions until very late in life. According to 2016 Behavioral Risk Factor Surveillance System (BRFSS) data analyzed by Okoro and colleagues, sensory loss, mobility issues, and need for assistance with activities of daily living constitute the most common disabilities among adults aged 65 and older. Yet, contrary to common myth, disability related to cognitive impairment is most prevalent in the age group of 18 to 44-year-olds. Myths about the predominance of cognitive impairment in late-life populations obscure the effects of education and public health efforts that have resulted in decreasing rates of dementia (Langa et al., 2017).

The occurrence of disability during one's lifetime is a result of a complex interaction of factors related to exposures to adverse events in prenatal and childhood nutritional and epidemiological environments (e.g., war, famine); adult exposures (e.g., to substances or occupational hazards); adult health behaviors (e.g., sleep or exercise); and access to advanced medical or behavioral health services, including preventive or chronic care (Payne, 2018). Contextual factors play such a great role that declines in the prevalence of disabilities are associated with decreasing poverty. Systemic disenfranchisement, impoverishment, and exploitation aggregate life experiences that raise cumulative risk for poor health and disability. Like disability, aging cannot be discussed meaningfully without reference to the individual's lifetime contexts, including reference to the contexts that society arranges for individuals in late life.

Ageism and Health Behaviors

Engagement in activities is important throughout the lifespan. Yet, one of the adverse effects of chronometry or age-grading is the circumstance that institutional contingencies – structures that scaffold or promote engagement – fall away as people reach retirement age. Individuals must be knowledgeable about the effects of contingencies on health behaviors to become effective self-managers (see also Epstein, 1997) and maintain their physical and socio-emotional well-being by implementing scheduled activities. Any inadvertent withdrawal from meaningful activities – perhaps because of a need for caregiving, loss of a partner or friend, a move to a new setting, or employment-related separation of family members – can lead to depression, loneliness, and social isolation, all of which are associated with increased morbidity and mortality risks (Blazer, 2020). Thus, empirically supported behavioral health interventions to reduce late-life depression typically consist of systematic problem-solving (Kirkham et al., 2016) and behavioral activation (Polenick & Flora, 2013), to teach the relationship between mood and engagement in activities. Depressogenic physical and social environments arise from ageist practices, yet their effects on behavior are attributed to age and perpetuate further age-related myths and segregation.

From a behavioral perspective, public health systems arrange contingencies that point to the importance of lifestyle or systemic choices by implementing health promotion and disease prevention models (e.g., monetary incentives for communities to provide walkable neighborhoods and public transportation, distance from home to groceries with fresh fruits and vegetables, monetary incentives to consumers for adhering to early detection procedures such as: colonoscopies, mammograms, or to regular vaccination schedules and dental hygiene). Many societies that view healthcare as a right rather than a privilege institute preventive programming to limit long-term costs. Such public health programming acknowledges that lifestyle-related chronic conditions (e.g., hypertension, diabetes, or obesity) slowly emerge from a primrose path of a myriad of accumulated choices in midlife and earlier. Often attributed to "age" and viewed as inevitable and costly, lifestyle-related chronic conditions represent failures of public health systems designs.

Ageism not only affects thinking about healthcare, but also individuals' engagement in health services. For example, a person who believes that discomfort, aches, and pains are inevitable as one ages may misattribute medical problems to "age" and forego proper assessment and detection of potentially serious medical conditions. Behavioral health recommendations and solvable problems may be neglected, and preventable conditions may turn into health emergencies or catastrophes.

Healthcare professionals are not exempt from ageist practices (Wyman et al., 2018). While almost all primary care physicians as well as behavioral health specialists work with older adults, most have not received specialty training. Consequently, age may overshadow diagnostic procedures. For example, providers may misattribute a patient's complaints to "age" and undertreat known conditions; or they may fail to order necessary tests to rule out new disease processes or drug-induced iatrogenic illnesses. In midlife and beyond, sexual functioning may not be assessed, leaving addressable problems untreated. Octogenarians and older might be considered intractably frail when rehabilitative measures (e.g., physical therapy, occupational therapy, etc.) could reestablish increased independence in basic and instrumental activities of daily living.

Ageism and Cognitive Loss

Lack of adequate training also affects the quality of long-term health services (e.g., advanced nurse practitioners, registered nurses, certified nursing assistants, or home health aides), particularly for adults who need assistance because of difficulties attending, remembering, problem-solving, or reasoning. Notably, such difficulties are not part of aging but a sign of a disease involving neurodegenerative processes. These processes may be progressive, stable, or reversible. Initially, individuals or families may have difficulties obtaining diagnostic workups: Ageist notions may result in providers' attribution of cognitive difficulties to age rather than disease processes yet to be pinpointed. When diagnoses have been established (e.g., Alzheimer's, vascular dementia, Lewy bodies disease, frontotemporal lobar degeneration), unreported – and thus untreated – pain or discomfort, poorly managed chronic conditions, or undetected sensory loss may lead to behavioral changes that then are viewed as part of the neurodegenerative disease process. This also applies to individuals with neurodevelopmental disorders, who may not have had access to basic strategies for health promotion and disease prevention, whose failure to report adverse physical conditions may be interpreted as an absence of those conditions, or whose emerging behavioral problems in adulthood might be misattributed to aging. Providers not schooled in differentiating verbal and non-verbal behavior or unaware of the potential of medical conditions to disrupt operant behavior, are at risk of ignoring tertiary prevention strategies and the management of reversible factors contributing to functional decline.

In institutional settings serving people with moderate to severe dementia, staff may interpret residents' verbal barriers to reporting their rich personal histories as "forgotten identities" – as if the person's preferences and values, accumulated over a lifetime of larger behavioral patterns and small, meaningful habits, have been altogether erased (Kitwood, 1997; Powell, 2019). Failure to consider the person's extensive personal history (including a verbal history of considerable breadth and depth) results in a phenomenon termed "elderspeak" – the condescending infantilization of older adults through changes in tone, pitch, and loudness, and the gratuitous use of first names and terms of endearment unwarranted by the provider-service recipient relationship (e.g., "honey," "sweetheart"). Studies have demonstrated that inappropriate social interactions contribute to the withdrawal of individuals with cognitive loss (Williams et al., 2009). Knowing a person's premorbid or historical strengths and weaknesses, providing needed medical care, ascertaining continuity with lifelong preferences and values (e.g., for personal care or cultural/ethnic dietary choices), understanding cognitive loss as faulty stimulus control affecting both verbal and non-verbal behavior, and arranging prosthetic physical and social supports to maintain engagement in activities, prevents behavioral changes associated with cognitive loss and increases the quality of life (McCurry & Drossel, 2011).

NEXT STEPS

Implications

None of the strategies mentioned above – from public health design to dementia services – come without a cost. Indeed, high-quality programming and services to maintain or reestablish skills require significant resources (Kane & Kane, 2015). When addressing how to generate contingencies that support quality of life across physical, behavioral, and social domains throughout the lifespan, personal and societal values come to the fore.

All of us, we hope, will one day belong to the population of older adults. In line with economic choice theories that emphasize the influence of delay and uncertainty over choice patterns, starting in midlife our temporal perspective gradually shifts from years-lived-so-far to years-left-to-live. Adults in late life are generally more resilient and equanimous than their younger counterparts: Carstensen and colleagues (1999) predicted that with age, adults become more selective in how and with whom they spend their time. In other words, as the end of life edges into view, the time horizon permits less flexibility considering potential delay and uncertainty, and discounting curves shift. Consequently, the "now" takes on greater significance within social interactions. Today, the degree to which people can implement their preferences and spend their later years accordingly is a matter of privilege. Well-off and relatively healthy adults may seek meaningful employment or volunteer opportunities in late-life or a lifestyle focusing on social activities, leisure, and well-being with like-minded friends. At the same time, individuals from disenfranchised or marginalized communities are likely to have fewer choices in selecting environments that match their preferences.

A discussion emerged in the United States in the late summer of 2020 about the grievability of those who have died from coronavirus disease 2019 (COVID-19) (see Butler, 2020, for the construct of "grievability"). Mortality risk from COVID-19 and other viruses slowly increases with age until about age 55, then rises faster and concentrates within the higher age brackets. Mirroring the section "Aging and Disability" above, recent studies of age-related mortality distributions across countries have suggested that not only age but also systemic factors, such as living conditions and access to health services and their quality amplified by aspects of diversity, contribute to the disparity in case fatality rates. Caught in the debates about how to best prevent further economic losses from pandemic lockdowns, yet expecting a worsening of infection rates amid a potentially contentious election, family members bury their loved ones, who mostly died alone to protect others, in a social vacuum. Mass deaths remain unmourned and, in some instances, unrecognized given the lack of contact between members from privileged and disenfranchised or marginalized communities. Are social contingencies such that the population of adults aged 60 and older is considered worthy of support, or is this population already deemed lost and thus expendable (Butler, 2020)? Is this population grievable? An exploration of ageism appears pressing, as ageism within personal and public spheres is ineffective at best and at worst poses a threat to individuals' and public health.

While investment in social policies has reduced late-life poverty since the 1950s, a focus on lived preferences and values and the degree to which these are differentially supported by social environments is only emerging now. What scaffolding is necessary to promote aging in place with quality of life in a time of increasing social inequalities? What reforms are necessary to generate residential environments that promote not only safety but also skills maintenance and rehabilitation (see de Mazières et al., 2017)? To start drawing attention to ageist practices, reeducation is important.

Aspirational Goals

Professional associations, such as the American Psychological Association, have established guidelines for behavioral health services involving older adults (2014). These guidelines and the

Pikes Peak Model for Training in Professional Geropsychology (Knight et al., 2009) advocate for the mobilization of a workforce centered first and foremost around behavioral science. To build such a workforce, training and practice guidelines recommend examining one's preconceptions and assumptions about aging while reading the empirical literature, challenging cultural myths, and recognizing when we inadvertently participate in discriminatory or questionable practices. Behavior analysts are in a unique position to build a verbal community of peers committed to exploring ageism in their personal and professional spheres.

RESOURCES

Notably, many of the resources suggested below are not in the language of behavior analysis; however, they purport its humanist spirit and an emphasis on contingency analyses, including provider skills and competencies.

Recommendations for Providers

American Psychological Association (2014). Guidelines for psychological practice with older adults. *American Psychologist, 69*(1), 34–65. https://doi.org/10.1037/a0035063
American Psychological Association (2020). Bias-free language guidelines. In *Publication manual of the American Psychological Association* (7th ed.), pp. 131–152. https://doi.org/10.1037/0000165-000.
Ayalon, L., & Tesch-Römer, C. (Eds.) (2018). *Contemporary perspectives on ageism.* Springer. https://doi.org/10.1007/978-3-319-73820-8
Knight, B. G., Karel, M. J., Hinrichsen, G. A., Qualls, S. H., & Duffy, M. (2009). Pikes peak model for training in professional geropsychology. *American Psychologist, 64*(3), 205–214. https://doi.org/10.1037/a0015059
Lundebjerg, N. E., Trucil, D. E., Hammond, D. E., & Applegate, W. B. (2017). When it comes to older adults, language matters: *Journal of the American Geriatric Society* adopts modified American Medical Association style [Editorial]. *Journal of the American Geriatrics Society, 65*(7). https://doi.org/10.1111/jgs.14941

Online Toolkits for Writers

https://www.frameworksinstitute.org/toolkit/gaining-momentum/
https://www.geron.org/programs-services/reframing-aging-initiative

Articles and Books that Raise Awareness

Aronson, L. (2019). *Elderhood: Redefining aging, transforming medicine, reimagining life.* Bloomsbury Publishing.
Baars, J. (2012). *Aging and the art of living.* Johns Hopkins University Press.
Cruikshank, M. (2013). *Learning to be old: Gender, culture, and aging* (3rd ed.). Rowman & Littlefield Publishers.
de Mazières, C. L., Morley, J. E., Levy, C., Agenes, F., Barbagallo, M., Cesari, M., de Souto Barreto, P., Donini, L. M., Fitten, J., Franco, A., Izquierdo, M., Kane, R. A., Martin, F. C., Onder, G., Ouslander, J., Pitkälä, K., Saliba, D., Sinclair, A., . . . Rolland, Y. (2017). Prevention of functional decline by reframing the role of nursing homes? *Journal of the American Medical Directors Association, 18*(2), 105–110. https://doi.org/10.1016/j.jamda.2016.11.019
Friend, T. (2017, November 20). Why ageism never gets old. *The New Yorker.* https://www.newyorker.com/magazine/2017/11/20/why-ageism-never-gets-old
Irving, P. H. (with Beamish, R.). (Ed.). (2014). *The upside of aging: How long life is changing the world of health, work, innovation, policy, and purpose.* John Wiley & Sons.

Hall, D. (2014). *Essays after eighty*. Houghton Mifflin Harcourt.

Jacoby, S. (2011). *Never say die: The myth and marketing of the new old age*. Pantheon Books.

Kane, R. L., & West, J. C. (2005). *It shouldn't be this way: The failure of long-term care*. Vanderbilt University Press.

Kitwood, T. (1997). *Dementia reconsidered: The person comes first*. Open University Press.

Pinkser, J. (2020, January 27). When does someone become "old"? *The Atlantic*. https://www.theatlantic.com/family/archive/2020/01/old-people-older-elderly-middle-age/605590/

Skinner, B. F., & Vaughan, M. E. (1997). *Enjoy old age: A practical guide*. WW Norton & Company (Original work published in 1983).

Professional Associations

American Psychological Association, Division 20 (Adult Development and Aging); Association for Contextual Behavioral Science, Aging in Context Special Interest Group; Association of Behavior Analysis International, Behavioral Gerontology Special Interest Group; Gerontological Society of America; Psychologists in Long-term Care

Additional In-text References (not listed in Resources)

Arias, E., & Xu, J. Q. (2019). United States life tables, 2017. *National Vital Statistics Reports, 68*(7). National Center for Health Statistics. https://stacks.cdc.gov/view/cdc/79487

Baselice, V., Burrichter, D., & Stearns, P. N. (2019). Debating the birthday: Innovation and resistance in celebrating children. *The Journal of the History of Childhood and Youth, 12*(2), 262–284. https://doi.org/10.1353/hcy.2019.0023

Bengtson, V. (2014). From ageism to the longevity revolution: Robert Butler, pioneer. *The Gerontologist, 54*(6), 1064–1069. https://doi.org/10.1093/geront/gnu100

Blazer, D. (2020). Social isolation and loneliness in older adults—a mental health/public health challenge. *JAMA Psychiatry*. https://doi.org/10.1001/jamapsychiatry.2020.1054

Butler, J. (2020). *The force of nonviolence: An ethico-political bind*. New York: Verso Books.

Carstensen, L. L., Isaacowitz, D. M., & Charles, S. (1999). Taking time seriously: A theory of socioemotional selectivity. *American Psychologist, 54*(3), 165–181. https://doi.org/10.1037/0003-066X.54.3.165

Epstein, R. (1997). Skinner as self-manager. *Journal of Applied Behavior Analysis, 30*(3), 545–568. https://doi.org/10.1901/jaba.1997.30-545

Fillo, J., Rodriguez, L., Neighbors, C., & Lee, C. (2020). Intrapersonal and interpersonal pathways linking 21st birthday celebration beliefs, intentions, and drinking behavior. *Addictive Behaviors, 110*, Article 106526. https://doi.org/10.1016/j.addbeh.2020.106526

Kane, R. L., & Kane, R. A. (2015). The long view of long-term care: Our personal take on progress, pitfalls, and possibilities. *Journal of the American Geriatrics Society, 63*(11), 2400–2406. https://doi.org/10.1111/jgs.13659

Kirkham, J. G., Choi, N., & Seitz, D. P. (2016). Meta-analysis of problem solving therapy for the treatment of major depressive disorder in older adults. *International Journal of Geriatric Psychiatry, 31*(5), 526–535. https://doi.org/ 0.1002/gps.4358

Kozloff, N., & Sommers, B. D. (2017). Insurance coverage and health outcomes in young adults with mental illness following the Affordable Care Act dependent coverage expansion. *The Journal of Clinical Psychiatry, 78*(7), e821–e827. https://doi.org/10.4088/JCP.16m11357

Langa, K. M., Larson, E. B., Crimmins, E. M., Faul, J. D., Levine, D. A., Kabeto, M. U., & Weir, D. R. (2017). A comparison of the prevalence of dementia in the United States in 2000 and 2012. *JAMA Internal Medicine, 177*(1), 51–58. https://doi.org/10.1001/jamainternmed.2016.6807

Lumpkin, K. (1939). The child labor provisions of the fair labor standards act. *Law and Contemporary Problems, 6*(3), 391–405. https://heinonline.org/HOL/P?h=hein.journals/lcp6&i=404

McCurry, S., & Drossel, C. (2011). *Treating dementia in context: A step-by-step guide to work with individuals and families.* American Psychological Association (APA) Books.

Okoro, C., Hollis, N., Cyrus, A., & Griffin-Blake, S. (2018). Prevalence of disabilities and health care access by disability status and type among adults – United States, 2016. *Morbidity and Mortality Weekly Report, 67*(32), 882–887. https://doi.org/10.15585/mmwr.mm6732a3

Payne, C. (2018). Aging in the Americas: Disability-free life expectancy among adults aged 65 and older in the United States, Costa Rica, Mexico, and Puerto Rico. *The Journals of Gerontology: Series B, 73*(2), 337–348. https://doi.org/10.1093/geronb/gbv076

Polenick, C., & Flora, S. (2013). Behavioral activation for depression in older adults: Theoretical and practical considerations. *The Behavior Analyst, 36*(1), 35–55. https://doi.org/10.1007/BF03392291

Powell, T. (2019). *Dementia reimagined: Building a life of joy and dignity from beginning to end.* Penguin Random House.

Rubenstein, E., & Bishop, L. (2019). Is the autism boom headed for Medicaid? Patterns in the enrollment of autistic adults [*sic*] in Wisconsin Medicaid, 2008–2018. *Autism Research, 12*(10), 1541–1550. https://doi.org/10.1002/aur.2173

Williams, K. N., Herman, R., Gajewski, B., & Wilson, K. (2009). Elderspeak communication: Impact on dementia care. *American Journal of Alzheimer's Disease and Other Dementias, 24*(1), 11–20. https://doi.org/10.1177/1533317508318472

Wyman, M. F., Shiovitz-Ezra, S., & Bengel, J. (2018). Ageism in the health care system: Providers, patients, and systems. In L Ayalon & C Tesch-Römer (Eds.), *Contemporary perspectives on ageism* (pp. 193–212). Springer. https://doi.org/10.1007/978-3-319-73820-8_13

3

ABA: AN EVOLUTION

Rooted in Compassion: How B.F. Skinner Planted the Seeds of
Social Justice for Behavior Analysis and How We Have
Grown Over the Past 70 Years

Sarah Trautman

INTRODUCTION

According to Skinner (1948):

> Either we do nothing and allow a miserable and probably catastrophic future to overtake us,
> or we use our knowledge about human behavior to create a social environment in which we
> shall live productive and creative lives and do so without jeopardizing the chances that those
> who follow us will be able to do the same.

(p. xvi)

Being a behavior analyst has always made me feel like I have spent my career doing something that matters. I chose a profession that focuses on addressing issues of social significance (Baer, Wolf & Risley, 1968). Behavior analysts have made incredible contributions that have improved the lives of persons living with autism and developmental disabilities (Foxx, 2008), have helped persons with Tourette's use habit reversal procedures to decrease or eradicate their tics (Azrin & Peterson, 1988), and improved business practices for organizations (Lattal, 2014) using the best of our science.

I have attended innumerable conferences over the last 20 years where I have been endlessly told that behavior analysis can SAVE THE WORLD! Now, who is not down with THAT?? But, the question remains even 20 years later . . . Are we doing it? This is something that I have been thinking about a lot lately given the context of when I am writing this.

It's September 2020 and the world is in the midst of a once-in-a-lifetime pandemic which has upended all of our lives. We have had to abruptly modify how we do EVERYTHING. In the United States, we are collectively trying to find the safest ways to provide behavior analytic services as "essential workers," whether from our homes via telehealth (also known as "Zoom ABA"), or in clinics, schools or our clients' own households. Many of us are also trying to support our own children's distance learning, which involves frequent requests for help, epic meltdowns, and lots of hugs and snacks (I don't even want to think about my kids' next visit to the dentist – "Sarah, were you aware that ALL of your children's teeth have rotted in the last 6-months?"). Oh, and we are trying to not lose our own shit on a daily basis, too (true story: I do this at least four out of seven days per week).

As a result of the pandemic, behavior analysts in practice are engaging in incredible amounts of professional development (*is TikTok an effective way to teach tacts?*) to continue to meaningfully support the vulnerable persons that most of them work with. Behavior analysts nationwide are attempting to continue to provide quality essential services, while juggling all the aforementioned COVID-related daily, safety issues.

Similarly, behavior analysts in academia have largely moved their classes online (read: teaching from home sporting a formal top paired with athleisure or pajama bottoms) for the foreseeable future. Professors and faculty members are busy carving out time for daily wellness/

mental health checks for their students and colleagues, in addition to their regular academic instruction (now occurring largely via Zoom), working hard to ensure meaningful research and publishing is still occurring, wondering when they will ever get to present their work IRL (this means in real life, old timers) since all of their universities have restricted travel until like 2047 AND are juggling all of the aforementioned COVID-related daily issues!

And just when we all thought that 2020 couldn't get any worse, we have had the horrifying, yet critical, task of finally acknowledging our American history of systemic racism, as we watched George Floyd's murder and heard his infamous final words, "I can't breathe," pasted all over our FB feeds, Twitter accounts, and news media.

As behavior analysts, we are in the midst of having raw, honest, and painful discussions about who we are, what we do, and how we can continue to do better work to help solve human problems of social significance. It's like behavior analysis was given one of those magnifying mirrors that estheticians use to see every blemish or impurity on our face. NO ONE wants to really see what their face looks like that close up. But EVERYONE wants to show off their amazing fresh, glowing skin after a facial. But here is some hard truth, you cannot get to the glowing skin part without first having to look into the magnifying mirror and get nasty extractions. Behavior analysis needs to be willing to hold the mirror up to our face and acknowledge that the extractions are essential to get to the great stuff. We can create a field that is more representative of ALL of us and that values our diverse backgrounds and perspectives. We can acknowledge the stuff we have done that was wrong, celebrate the stuff we have done right, AND continue to do work that positively impacts not just the individual clients whom we serve, but also their families and communities.

Yes, most of our field has been built upon research conducted by and about white people. According to Pritchett and colleagues (2020), "applied behavior analysis was developed within a Western hegemonic structure. It is a discipline that operates within a larger structure that is racist, sexist, and ableist." I agree with Pritchett and colleagues regarding the hegemonic structure that our field has been built upon. However, I do not believe this means that we should discard all of the work that has been done in our field by the dominant group (read: white dudes). According to Robert Heinlein (1973), "A generation which ignores history has no past – and no future." Understanding the history of our field and its practices is important because, for better or worse, what we've done has shaped what we do, or don't do, now.

A tool that can help us better understand our past, as well as our present, is the concept of philosophical doubt. According to Cooper, Heron & Heward (2020):

> The attitude of philosophic doubt requires the scientist to continually question the truthfulness of what is regarded as fact. Scientific knowledge must always be viewed as tentative. Scientists must be willing to set aside their most cherished beliefs and findings and replace them with the knowledge derived from new discoveries. Good scientists maintain a healthy level of skepticism. Although being skeptical of others' research may be easy, a more difficult but critical characteristic of scientists is that they remain open to the possibility – as well as look for evidence – that their own findings or interpretations are wrong.
>
> (p. 6)

Another way of conceptualizing this idea is, "Don't throw the baby out with the bathwater." Just throw out the gross bath water, get that baby a fresh Notorious RBG onesie, and continually remain open to new ideas that challenge what we think and inform what we do.

The rest of this chapter will be devoted to examining **SOME** of the most important works that have provided a framework for our field's approach to addressing compassion and social justice, as I was only allotted 2,500 words by the editors of this text. This is why I bolded and italicized the word "SOME" above. Do not send me hate mail (or you can, but I'll probably ignore it).

So, take a seat in your proverbial DeLorean (if you don't get this pop culture reference you were clearly born after 1985 and thus I suggest you watch "Back to the Future" ASAP because it is and will forever be a pop culture classic) and let's take a trip back in time to look at the evolution of our field as it relates to compassion and social justice.

IT ALL STARTED WITH *WALDEN TWO*

If B.F. Skinner were still living, we would likely describe him as "woke." Maybe even "woke AF." Why? Because Skinner understood that issues related to social justice and human well-being could be effectively addressed using the science of behavior analysis. OK, so you might be asking yourself, *Why should I care about a book that was written almost 100 years ago?*

In a nutshell, *Walden Two* (published in 1948) is a novel narrated by the primary character, Professor Burris, who works with some WWII veterans to create an intentional community that is modeled after Henry David Thoreau's Walden Pond. The culture and community governance is based on the idea that human behavior is a product of its environment (sound familiar, LOL). The members of the Walden Two community are encouraged "to view every habit and custom with an eye to possible improvement" using a "constantly experimental attitude toward everything" (Skinner, 1948, pp. 18 and 25).

I do not have enough space and time to provide you, dear reader, with a thorough analysis of *Walden Two*. But guess what? A bunch of other really smart people have already written about this exact subject. I highly recommend getting your hands on and devouring the reference I list in the "Geek Your Heart Out" section at the end of this chapter.

Ok, back to *Walden Two*. There are two primary reasons that you should care about this book:

1. *Walden Two* was Skinner's first extension of his science, system and philosophy to issues of social justice and human well-being (Altus & Morris, 2009).

2. *Walden Two* provided an incredible amount of inspiration for behavior analytic practices (Altus & Morris, 2009). Another way of conceptualizing the importance of this book can be illustrated using the following analogy – *Walden Two* is to behavior analysis as Run DMC is to hip-hop (btw, "It's Tricky" is still my all-time Run DMC fave).

So, what other publications have helped to shape the work our field does in the areas of compassion and social justice over the last 80-years?

Skinner's book: *Science & Human Behavior* (1953) aka The Foundation of our Field aka It's all about Operant Conditioning

Why this book matters: To use a modern colloquial term this book had people "shook." Skinner introduced and discussed a variety of behavioral principles that ended up providing the foundation for much of our science. Concepts like operant conditioning (chapter 5), shaping (chapter 6), the distinction between function and topography (chapter 8), private events (chapter 17), AND MORE!

Geek Bonus: Read Catania and Harnad's (1988) article *"The Selection of Behavior: The Operant Behaviorism of BF Skinner: Comments and Consequences"* for a deeper dive of some of Skinner's most well-known articles, commentaries on the articles and Skinner's response to the commentaries!

Baer, Wolf, & Risley's (1968) article: *Some Current Dimensions of Applied Behavior Analysis* aka When Three Behavior Analysts Dropped the Mic on EVERYONE

Why article matters: The seven dimensions of applied behavior analysis were proposed by Baer, Wolf & Risley in response to the increase of applied work being done in behavior analysis to provide "stimulus controls..for behavior-analytic conduct in the world of application" (Baer et al., 1987). You can, hopefully, recite the seven dimensions of ABA by heart. But just in case you forgot they are – applied, behavioral, analytic, technological, conceptual, effective, and capable of appropriately generalized outcomes. I don't think it's speaking in hyperbole to say that this article has helped to shape the research and practice of applied behavior analysis more than any other.

   Geek Bonus: Baer, Wolf & Risley wrote a follow-up to their initial article in 1987 – *Some still-current dimensions of applied behavior analysis*. It is a worthwhile read and a great reminder that "effectiveness for the future will probably be built primarily on system – wide interventions and high – quality failures, as we continue to bring theory to the point of designs that solve problems" (1987, p. 325).

Mont Wolf's (1978) article: *Social Validity: The Case for Subjective Measurement or How Applied Behavior Analysis is Finding its Heart* aka Why We Should Care about How Other People Feel (I know, I wrote the f-word, get over it)

Why this article matters: Mont Wolf created the concept of social validity as a result of early work he conducted at a group home called Achievement Place, which would serve as the foundation for the teaching-family model. Wolf and the other creators of the teaching-family model believed "that the opinions of youths, parents, referral agents, and others were important and valid and it was up to researchers to routinely solicit their views and take them seriously" (Fixsen, 2019). In a nutshell, Wolf helped to create a framework for behavior analysts to ask important questions in terms of who decides something is a problem, who decides what interventions are acceptable, and how are problems solved. Wolf laid the foundation for our ethical conduct as it relates to WHAT we do and HOW we do it.

Murray Sidman's book: *Coercion and its Fallout* aka "Why Crap like the Death Penalty DOESN'T WORK"

Why this book matters: The goal of Sidman's book was to "indicate a critical kind of change that will have to take place in our social interactions if we are ever to do something constructive about the miseries we currently inflict on each other" (1991, p. 9). This book was a clear rejection of our society's use of coercion (read: punishment) as a primary tool to change problem behavior. So what's a more effective, scientifically validated method to create long-terms behavior change? Come on guys, I sincerely hope you already know this . . . POSITIVE REINFORCEMENT!

Steve Hayes, Kirk Strosahl and Kelly Wilson's book: *Acceptance and Commitment Therapy* aka "How Behavior Analysis Can Truly Decrease Human Suffering"

Why this book matters: Acceptance and Commitment Therapy (ACT) has been an effective treatment for persons suffering from anxiety, addiction, depression, chronic pain, and for parents of children diagnosed with developmental disabilities (Pull, 2009). ACT has radically shifted how people can view their own suffering by better understanding how to develop an acceptance of experiences that are out of one's control coupled with strategies to develop actions to live a valued life. In other words, ACT helps people understand that things happen in life that suck. But just because SOME things suck doesn't mean ALL of your life has to suck. So, learn some strategies to better understand what sucks, how you can live with the suck and, most importantly, identify values that help keep you focused on what DOESN'T suck about your life.

Tony Biglan's book: *The Nurture Effect* aka "A Highlight Reel of Behavioral Science" & ABA (this was too witty for me to come up with, this is ALL Dr. Derek Reed. He also wrote an incredible review of this book which I quote below)

Why this book matters: When someone else writes something so perfect that you can't possibly think of a better way to state what the perfect words already captured, you use those perfect words. Thus, I give you the perfectly written words of my homie, Dr. Derek Reed, regarding the importance of *The Nurture Effect* (2015),

> Take Baer, Wolf, and Risley's dimensions of behavior analysis (1968), sprinkle in Wolf's social validity (1978), garnish with Hayes' ACT (2004) while taking it to scale using Seekins and Fawcett's recommendations (1989) and you get *The Nurture Effect*. If that's not a recipe for a behavior analytic homerun, I clearly don't understand behavior analysis. Anthony Biglan has cooked up this recipe - adding his own public health and prevention science zest - throughout his career. The resulting compendium of his work is impressive to any social scientist, public health advocate, or epidemiologist . . . We have the science, the data, and the know-how to make big changes to our lives and our world.
>
> (Reed, 2015, p. 310)

Bridget Tayor, Linda LeBlanc and Melissa Nosik's article: *Compassionate Care in Behavior Analytic Treatment* aka "How to Show You Really Care in Clinical Settings"

Why this article matters: This is one of my fave articles of all time and I reference it at least one time per month. Why? If we are fundamentally involved in a natural science whose purpose is to focus on behaviors of social significance to help alleviate the suffering of others, isn't it imperative that we can identify and build relationship skills with the people whom we are working with? Wouldn't it be great if we had a behavior analytic way to operationalize compassion? I already knew that Taylor, LeBlanc, and Nosik were incredible people. This article just made me love them even more.

Geek Bonus: Maithri Sivaraman wrote a great review about this article in 2019. My favorite quote from her review is the last sentence – "The universality of compassion and empathy in all roles that behavior analysts pursue makes a compelling rationale for our attention and inquiry" (Sivaraman, 2019). It's a review that's definitely worth your time.

SO, WHERE DO WE GO FROM HERE?

I hope that I have provided some compelling evidence that BF Skinner's book *Walden Two* ignited our field's passion for addressing issues related to social justice and compassion, and that we have produced a significant body of work over the 70 years since that has built upon the idea that behavior analysis can fundamentally make the world a better place.

Given the current state of, well, everything, I believe it is clear that we still have a ways to go before we can claim that we are actually saving the world with Behavior Analysis. In fact, I don't think we should try to make this claim at all. The idea that we are going to save the world means that there's an endpoint to our work and that we are the only ones that have all the answers. I do not believe that is true. I would like to suggest that we reframe how we approach our work in a way that acknowledges that we are on a collective journey as humans to live a good life and to do good for others in the brief period of time we each occupy the earth.

B.F. Skinner's last act in his life was to ask his daughter to pass him a glass of water, from which he took a sip and said, "Marvelous" – his last word on earth. My deepest desire for all of us is to be able to reflect on the work we have done and be able to say the same – that it has all been "Marvelous."

GEEK YOUR HEART OUT – A.K.A. REFERENCES AND OTHER GREAT STUFF YOU SHOULD READ

Altus, D. E., & Morris, E. K. (2009). B. F. Skinner's utopian vision: Behind and beyond *Walden Two*. *The Behavior Analyst, 32*(2), 319–335. https://doi.org/10.1007/BF03392195

Azrin, N. H., & Peterson, A. L. (1988). Habit reversal for the treatment of Tourette syndrome. *Behaviour Research and Therapy, 26*(4), 347–351. https://doi.org/10.1016/0005-7967(88)90089-7

Baer, D. M., Wolf, M. M., & Risley, T. R. (1968). Some current dimensions of applied behavior analysis. *Journal of Applied Behavior Analysis, 1*, 91–97.

Baer, D. M., & Wolf, M. M. (1987). Some still-current dimensions of applied behavior analysis. *Journal of Applied Behavior Analysis, 20*(4), 313–327. https://doi.org/10.1901/jaba.1987.20-313

Biglan, A., (2015). *The nurture effect: How the science of human behavior can improve our lives & our world*. New Harbinger Publications.

Catania, A. C., & Harnad, S. (Eds.). (1988). *The selection of behavior: The operant behaviorism of BF Skinner: Comments and consequences*. Cambridge University Press.

Cooper, J. O., Heron, T. E., & Heward, W. L. (2020). *Applied behavior analysis*. Pearson Education.

Fixsen, D. (2019). *The origins of social validity*. AIRN Active Implementation Research Network ®. https://www.activeimplementation.org/resources/the-origins-of-social-validity/

Foxx, R. M. (2008). Applied behavior analysis treatment of autism: the state of the art. *Child and adolescent psychiatric clinics of North America, 17*(4), 821–ix.

Hayes, S. C., Strosahl, K. D., & Wilson, K. G. (2012). *Acceptance and commitment therapy: An experiential approach to behavior change.* Guilford.

Heinlein, R. A. (Robert Anson), 1907–1988. (1973). *Time enough for love, the lives of Lazarus Long; a novel.* Putnam.

Kuhlmann, H. (2005). *Living Walden Two: B. F. Skinner's behaviorist utopia and experimental communities.* University of Illinois Press.

Lattal, K. (2014). Book review: *Performance management: Changing behavior that drives organizational effectiveness,* fifth edition *Performance Improvement, 53*(10), 38–41. https://doi.org/10.1002/pfi.21445

Leigland S. (2011). Beyond freedom and dignity at 40: Comments on behavioral science, the future, and chance (2007). *The behavior analyst, 34*(2), 283–295. https://doi.org/10.1007/BF03392258

Lovaas, O. I. (1987). Behavioral treatment and normal educational and intellectual functioning in young autistic children. *Journal of Consulting and Clinical Psychology, 55*(1), 3.

Pritchett, M., Ala'i, S., Re Cruz, A., & Cihon, T. (2020, August 19). Social justice is the spirit and aim of an applied science of human behavior: Moving from colonial to participatory research practices. *Behavior Analysis in Practice.* https://doi.org/10.31234/osf.io/t87p4

Pull C. B. (2009). Current empirical status of acceptance and commitment therapy. *Current Opinion in Psychiatry, 22*(1), 55–60. https://doi.org/10.1097/YCO.0b013e32831a6e9d

Reed D. D. (2015). Applied behavioral science goes to scale: A review of Biglan's *The Nurture Effect. The Behavior Analyst, 38*(2), 309–320. https://doi.org/10.1007/s40614-015-0033-6

Sidman, M., & Center, D. B. (1991). Coercion and its fallout. *Behavioral Disorders, 16*(4), 315–317. https://doi.org/10.1177/019874299101600403

Sivaraman, M. (2019). Review of "Compassionate care in behavior analytic treatment: Can outcomes be enhanced by attending to relationships with caregivers?" *Science in Autism Treatment, 16* (1).

Skinner, B. F. (1948). *Walden two.* Macmillan.

Skinner, B. F. (1953). *Science and human behavior.* Macmillan.

Skinner B. F. (1979) *The shaping of a behaviorist.* Knopf.

Skinner, B. F. (1987). *Upon further reflection.* Prentice Hall

Taylor, B. A., LeBlanc, L. A. & Nosik, M. R. (2019). Compassionate care in behavior analytic treatment: Can outcomes be enhanced by attending to relationships with caregivers?. *Behavior Analysis in Practice, 12*, 654–666. https://doi.org/10.1007/s40617-018-00289-3

Wolf M. M. (1978). Social validity: the case for subjective measurement or how applied behavior analysis is finding its heart. *Journal of Applied Behavior Analysis, 11*(2), 203–214. https://doi.org/10.1901/jaba.1978.11-203

4

BEHAVIORAL ECONOMICS

In Health and in Sickness: Irrationality of the Decision-Making Process

Liliane de Aguiar-Rocha

INTRODUCTION

Behavioral economics is a discipline that blends concepts from psychology and economics. It asserts that people's decision-making process is not rational; instead it is full of bias (Voyer, 2015). Understanding the common biases that affect the decision process and devising strategies to optimize decision-making for the benefit of the consumer are the main goals of behavioral economics (Cohen et al., 2016). The healthcare environment is complex, and the decision-making process is often biased both for patients and providers. The use of strategies based on behavioral economics can substantially improve care and support optimal decision-making (Courtney et al., 2014; Volpp, 2016).

One of the most widely known paradigms for interventions associated with behavioral economics is libertarian paternalism (Schrijvers, 2017). A central idea in libertarian paternalism is that the individual's best interest is taken into account when designing choices and defaults while maintaining the possibility of choosing something different (Korobkin, 2016). This idea allows the intervention designer to create systems that promote best outcomes both for the individual and for the designer. In healthcare, behavioral economics supports a patient-centered approach by shaping the choices which makes it easier for patients to make medically desired decisions (Iskowitz, 2018).

In order to understand the applicability of behavioral economics to healthcare, it is important to become familiar with its main strategies. Behavioral economics can help healthcare providers understand the biases involved in how people make decisions. Many strategies derived from the principles of behavioral economics have been effectively used to improve healthcare outcomes (Samson, 2020). Two key concepts in behavioral economics are biases in decision-making and influences from the social environment (Voyer, 2015). Strategies that explore biases in decision-making include the use of defaults and framing. Strategies that explore the influences from the social environment include commitment and the use of social norms.

Biases in decision-making refer to situations involving complex decisions, with novel factors, or that involve trade-offs, such as; deciding on elective surgery, advance directives, in-vitro fertilization, or wearing a mask during a pandemic. These decisions are likely to result in the use of heuristics that can result in less than ideal outcomes for the decision maker (Korobkin, 2016). Some of these heuristics and strategies to prevent them are discussed below.

Framing. When using framing, the choice designer should arrange the information in such a way that loss aversion and present bias are avoided. *Loss aversion* indicates that people are reluctant to take risks, unless it can be off-set by potential important rewards. *Present bias* or *hyperbolic discounting* is a decision-making bias in which individuals tend to discount the future ramifications of their decisions and focus on maximizing present gain. Present bias also leads to the general preference for immediate rewards (even if smaller), when compared to delayed rewards.

Defaults. The defaults strategy is based on the idea that when making decisions, people prefer adhering to the norm rather than deviating from it. Behavioral economics suggests, patients are more likely to agree to the medically desired option that is made the default option, when giving the patient the option to "opt-out" of the default decision.

Social influences. The social environment also influences people's decisions. Individuals tend to compare themselves to others in the social environment to estimate how well or how badly they are doing. When not doing at least as well as the average, most are motivated to change their behavior. This concept is known as *social norms*. Individuals are more likely to change their behavior if they think they owe someone something; this concept is known as *reciprocity*. Voyer (2015) suggested that providers can take advantage of the influence of the social environment; for example, letting people know what the proportion of people who perform at a certain level (e.g., "80% of patients in this clinic arrive on time for their appointments") to inspire them to adjust their behavior accordingly. Additionally, the principle of reciprocity can be used to encourage behaviors that benefit the collective group, such as keeping an area clean or encouraging blood donations (e.g., "If you needed some blood, wouldn't you like it to have it available?"), and even when encouraging citizens to wear a mask (e.g., "if someone has COVID-19 and was asymptomatic, wouldn't you like them to wear a mask when talking to you?").

These principles should be taken into consideration when guiding patients to focus on behavioral change, for example, by breaking long-term goals into short-term increments; or, presenting advantages and disadvantages of different procedures in a concrete way, so losses and gains appear tangible (Voyer, 2015). When these principles are applied to healthcare management, they can result in programs such as opt-out enrollment as opposed to opt-in (making the desired behavior the default).

Strategies derived from behavioral economics have been widely used in government policy-making, banks, and large organizations such as Google, Coca-Cola, and General Electric (Samson, 2020); however, application in healthcare remains in its infancy (Blumenthal & Opel, 2018). Galizzi and Wiesen (2018) reviewed a series of experiments in behavioral economics covering a variety of healthcare issues including: vaccinations, smoke cessation, weight loss, healthcare financing policies, HIV treatment compliance, etc. They demonstrate that there is a wide variety of healthcare matters that can benefit from behavioral economic application. Patients often have difficulty making critical health decisions in situations where they don't understand the information presented to them (Rice, 2013). Developing tools that can support a decision that is in the patient's best interest is essential.

For example, sudden infant death and sleep problems are a common problem in pediatrics that can benefit from a behavior economics-based approach. Stevens and Kelleher (2017) described six strategies, detailed below, based on behavioral economic principles that could be used to promote safe sleep practices for infants: choice overload, social norms, salience, loss aversion, identifiable victim effect, and framing. The principle of *choice overload* argues that too much information at a time may lead to inertia and inaction, therefore, parents should be given brief key information at first. For example, use of the acronym "ABC" (alone, on the back, in the crib) to simplify information and make it easy to remember for new parents. *Social norms* were used to influence parents to put their child to sleep in a safe position by creating a lottery contest on Facebook. Parents who posted a picture of their child sleeping in a safe position earned a lottery ticket for a special prize. Pictures of children in safe positions became more visible and the desirable side of this social norm was highlighted, compelling parents to match the behavior of the norm (i.e., have their child sleep in a safe position). The principle of *salience* recognizes that decision-makers have finite cognitive resources and making the important information salient may aid in making the optimal decision. For example, sleep safe messages can be printed in fitted mattresses sheets, and sleep safe campaigns could use celebrities as speakers (also known as the *messenger effect*). *Loss aversion* (described above) has been used to enhance parents' will to avoid embarrassment by making a public, written commitment to safe sleep practices. Additionally, when hearing about an individual or a personal story, people are more likely to take action rather than hearing general statistics. This is known as the *identifiable victim effect*. Providers may take advantage of this effect by telling their experience with a child lost to unsafe sleep practices. A parent who has had this experience may be amenable to participate in a testimonial video in order to prevent the death of other children. To take advantage of framing, instead of saying, "old sleep practices were incorrect," providers can say that grandparents and older family members "did their best with the information available at the time" and highlight that new information now recommends different sleep practices.

Another area of healthcare that can benefit from behavioral economics interventions is Quality Improvement (QI). Service improvements do not always mean better patient outcomes (Craig, 2018). In order to maximize success and minimize decision biases, it is recommended that intervention designers take into account behavioral economics principles and how they can be applied to both designers and implementers of QI projects. Stevens (2017) discussed ways in which a particular QI intervention, the use of reminders in the electronic health records (EHR), could benefit from tactics derived from behavioral economics. He postulated several strategies to address common clinician concerns manifested during the implementation of those EHR interventions. These concerns varied from perceptions of new clinical guidelines might not be accessible and realistic and might reduce clinician's autonomy. A strategy to counteract these possible barriers could be using defaults (opt-out), social norms, and the IKEA effect (people are more invested on the things they help build). He continues offering solutions to other concerns, for example, a lack of motivation and discomfort with proposed changes could be addressed with reciprocity and framing, respectively.

Stevens (2017) emphasized that behavioral economic strategies should be used every time that individuals consider the need for change to be a high stake. He suggested that future research should determine in which situations the application of behavioral economic strategies would result in better care. He added that it would be beneficial for intervention designers to become acquainted with behavioral economic concepts and other behavior change strategies for innovative ideas on approaching QI processes.

When discussing the QI intervention design process, Vlaev et al. (2016) recommended to start with an all-inclusive analysis of the behavioral problem. They asserted that the MINDSPACE framework (Dolan et al., 2010) can be used to both identify strategies to be used in behavior change as it can help in identifying barriers. MINDSPACE is an acronym that includes nine behavioral economic principles: **M**essenger (who gives the message matters), **I**ncentives (people are biased towards gains), **N**orms (people like to be like others), **D**efaults (people prefer to stay with the default choice rather than changing), **S**alience (novelty and relevance draws attention), **P**riming (subtle cues influence behavior), **A**ffect (emotions have an effect on behavior), **C**ommitments (public promises and a sense of duty influence behavior).

One of the most widely known QI methodologies is Lean, a continuous improvement process that seeks to eliminate waste and add value (https://goleansixsigma.com/what-is-lean/). Lean has a set of key principles from which its tools and practices derive: ensure quality at the source, re-design for steady flow, establish standard of work, engage and respect everyone's enterprise, eliminate waste, install a visual workplace. *Ensure quality at the source* is the principle which asks about the customer's expectation, rather than making assumptions. *Re-design for steady flow*, is the principle that guides workflow design such that it serves customer's demands. *Establish standard work* is a principle that determines how all staff will complete a specific process or task, such that it is consistent. *Engage and respect everyone's expertise* is a principle that suggests that QI projects should consider the knowledge of those on the front line. *Eliminate waste* is the principle that guides continuous review of processes such that waste (from the customer's perspective) is reduced and value is added. Finally, *install a visual workplace* is the principle that suggests that progress towards a goal be displayed visually where all staff can see (Steinfeld et al., 2015). Strategies based on behavioral economic principles can be combined with Lean key principles such that QI implementation can be enhanced. Steinfeld et al. (2015) described four stages of the implementation process: problem identification, development/adoption, implementation/execution, reflection/evaluation. Below are ways in which behavioral economic principles can be combined with Lean practices during each implementation phase.

Problem identification – During this stage, QI interventionists identify which variables affect a problem. These variables can be related to the organization's culture, as it relates to its customers, in our case, patients. Lean recommends the use of the A3 to conduct a root cause analysis and determine areas for improvement (Steinfeld et al., 2015). We propose that QI intervention designers consider the effect of biases in decision-making, such as loss aversion and present bias, as well as the influence of social norms. In order to enhance the probability of staff engagement, intervention designers should consider how to frame the problem such that they will captivate the staff and get buy-in. In addition, intervention designers can take advantage of social norms to boost interest in solving the identified problem.

Development/adoption – This is the stage in which intervention designers assess the feasibility of the intervention, as measured by staff engagement and intervention characteristics. Here, Lean recommends the use of a project charter and the realization of a Rapid Process Improvement Workshop (RPIW); an event that can last up to five days, where front-line staff considered subject matter experts get together with management to design new processes (Steinfeld et al., 2015). In this stage, intervention designers should capitalize on the IKEA effect, as described by Stevens (2017); which suggests that individuals tend to overvalue projects to which they contributed. The RPIW is an example of a strategy which can take advantage of this effect thus, maximizing employee buy-in and fostering the development of champions for the new idea/project. This is also the stage in which a new standard of work can be developed. Designers should consider the use of defaults to maximize the possibility of staff choosing the option that will lead to better outcomes, while still allowing the opportunity for individual choice by using accountable justifications as described in Stevens, 2017.

Implementation/execution – In this stage, QI intervention designers are concerned with training and fidelity. The Lean model suggests an oversight team, coupled with the use of a daily management system that displays measurement of the process and outcomes (Steinfeld et al., 2015). Intervention designers should consider using f social norms and salience during this stage. For example, the visual management board should display outcomes in relation to a norm that is set as the goal, and information that is relevant and can trigger action should be made salient. During training, careful consideration should be given to messenger effects, such that the trainer should be someone who is knowledgeable and well-liked within the organization.

Reflection and evaluation – This is the final stage in a QI project. Here, intervention designers are concerned with the outcomes of the intervention and the fidelity of its implementation. Lean methodology suggests the use of PDCA (Plan, Do, Check, Act) cycles and a vertical check in revision of the A3 tool utilized in the problem identification stage. Intervention designers should be cautious of Ego, the letter E in the Mindspace acronym: Individuals are likely to act in ways to make themselves feel better (Dolan et al., 2010). Intervention designers are also prey to this effect and may not be able to be completely objective when evaluating the outcomes of the project. It is advisable to have a colleague, who was not part of the design team, participate in the evaluation, so that the IKEA effect does not shadow impartiality.

In addition to its use in combination with Lean methodology, providers can take advantage of behavioral economic principles and strategies when addressing some clinical issues, for which behavioral change is necessary. Table 4.1 describes some situations in which behavioral economic principles can be used to enhance outcomes.

FINAL THOUGHTS

Patients and providers are faced with many complex decisions for which their choice is not always rational (Rice, 2013). Strategies based on behavioral economic principles have a place in healthcare. They should be taken into consideration when designing interventions to address behavioral changes in patients, and to address other issues related to the decision-making process. Guus Schrijvers (2017) investigated how behavioral principles could contribute to the actualization of the Triple Aim. He concluded it is plausible that the use of strategies derived from behavioral principles (e.g., defaults, incentives, etc.) could enhance population health, improve the quality of care, and lower costs per capita.

Several examples of behavioral economic principles were discussed thus far attesting to their validity. The problems tackled in these studies were complex and the solutions relatively simple and cost-effective. It is arguable that choice-design using behavioral economic principles are a valuable tool in QI projects and in healthcare management. This chapter presented an example of how these principles can be used to enhance other valuable QI methodologies, such as Lean methodology, and how they can address several common situations in healthcare. Future research should consider the effect of these strategies on the fourth (provider care) and fifth (patient engagement) aims for healthcare improvement.

Table 4.1 Suggested behavioral economic strategies to address specific situations

Situation	Behavior economic principle to be considered and proposed strategy
Patient needs to make radical lifestyle changes (e.g. cardiac patients, blood pressure control issues, management of diabetes).	*Social norm & Loss aversion:* Break long-term goals into short-term increments; present advantages and disadvantages of different procedures in a concrete way, so losses and gains appear tangible.
Patient behavior change will affect more than him or herself (e.g., arriving on time, attending follow ups, blood and organ donations).	*Reciprocity & Social norms and feedback:* Describe how many people would benefit from a patient's behavior change or a different choice. Ask for them to imagine how it would feel to be on the receiving end of the behavior change.
Patient receives a lot of complex information at once (e.g., first well-visit at the pediatrician; when a patient is diagnosed with a chronic condition such as diabetes).	*Salience:* Summarize the most critical information in a concise and objective way, make that information salient from other stimuli by changing font color, using an acronym, or changing the environmental arrangement. *Defaults:* If a choice is necessary, make the choice that is most beneficial to the patient by default, educate the patient about other possibilities and make the opt-out choice available.
Clinicians do not welcome new practice guidelines (e.g., adoption of new clinical pathways or change in the EHR).	*IKEA effect:* Involve key players in the development of new procedures and guidelines, who may become agents of change for the other staff.
There is a need to boost utilization of a particular practice (e.g., vaccination, breast feeding).	*Framing – Loss aversion and present bias:* Train community workers and clinic staff to incorporate loss frames into promotion campaigns targeted to boost utilization. Interventions must be designed so that the benefits are as immediate and as tangible as the costs.
Patient has attempted to change his behavior in the past and failed (e.g., weight management).	*Social norms – Commitment:* Combine a deposit contract with an incentive program for greater effect. Create an incentive program whereby the patient is at risk of losing something (a privilege or a small amount of money). If he/she does not engage in behaviors leading to the goal, and earn the accumulated amount and more once the goal is achieved.

REFERENCES

Blumenthal, B. J., & Opel, D. J. (2018). Nudge or grudge? Choice architecture and parental decision-making. *Hastings Center Report, 48*(2), 33–39. https://doi.org/10.1002/hast.837

Cohen, G. I., Lynch, H. F., & Robertson, C. T. (2016). *Nudging health: Health law and behavioral economics.* John Hopkins University Press.

Courtney, M. R., Spivey, C., & Daniel, K. M. (2014). Helping patients make better decisions: How to apply behavioral economics in clinical practice. *Patient Preference & Adherence, 8*, 1503. https://doi.org/10.2147/ppa.s71224

Craig, L. (2018). Service improvement in health care: A literature review. *British Journal of Nursing, 27*(15), 893–896. https://doi.org/10.12968/bjon.2018.27.15.893

Dolan, P., Hallsworth, M., Halpern, D., King, D., & Vlaev, V. (2010). *MINDSPACE: Influencing behaviour for public policy.* Institute of Government.

Galizzi, M., & Wiesen D. (2018). *Behavioral experiments in health economics.* Oxford University Press. https://doi.org/10.1093/acrefore/9780190625979.013.244

Iskowitz, M. (2018). Healthcare's own undoing project. *Medical Marketing & Media, 53*(9), 6.

Korobkin, R. (2016). Chapter 1- Three choice architecture paradigms for healthcare policy. In Cohen, G. I., Lynch, H. F., & Robertson, C. T. (Eds.), *Nudging health: Health law and behavioral economics.* Johns Hopkins University Press.

Rice, T. (2013). The behavioral economics of health and health care. *Annual Review of Public Health,* (34), 431–447. https://doi.org/10.1146/annurev-publhealth-031912-114353

Samson, A. (2020, June 16). *The behavioral economics guide 2018.* BehavioralEconomics.com. The BE Hub. https://www.behavioraleconomics.com/be-guide/the-behavioral-economics-guide-2018/

Schrijvers, G. (2017). *Integrated care better and cheaper.* Reed Business Information.

Steinfeld, B., Scott, J., Vilander, G., Marx, L., Quirk, M., Lindberg, J., & Koerner, K. (2015). The role of lean process improvement in implementation of evidence-based practices in behavioral health care. *Journal of Behavioral Health Services & Research, 42*(4), 504–518.

Stevens, J. (2017). The promising contributions of behavioral economics to quality improvement in health care. *Pediatric Quality & Safety, 2*(3), 1.

Stevens, J., & Kelleher, K. (2017). The potential of behavioral economics to promote safe infant sleep practices. *Maternal & Child Health Journal, 21*(2), 229–233. https://doi.org/10.1007/s10995-016-2163-2161

Vlaev, I., King, D., Dolan, P., & Darzi, A. (2016). The theory and practice of "Nudging": Changing health behaviors. *Public Administration Review, 76*(4), 550–561.

Volpp, K. G. (2016). Behavioral economics: Key to effective care management programs for patients, payers, and providers. *Population Health Management, 19,* S-5–S-6.

Voyer, B. (2015). "Nudging" behaviours in healthcare: Insights from behavioural economics. *British Journal of Healthcare Management, 21*(3), 130–135.

5

BLACK LIVES MATTER

From Theoretical Conceptualization to Function-Based
Real-Life Application

Denisha Gingles

Black Lives Matter (BLM), the hashtag, began in 2013 as a response to injustice and violence perpetrated on the Black community. As the BLM movement experienced a surge in attention in 2020 (Anderson et al., 2020), conversations regarding systemic racism, potential solutions, and various theoretical interpretations also emerged. With the increase in awareness, one may conclude this specific moment in time necessitated novel responding, unlike any other point in history. This conclusion would be underdeveloped and disingenuous to the longstanding history of injustices committed against Black people and the pre-existing fight for civil rights. Black lives mattered before the year 1619, and certainly before 2020, and will continue to matter in years yet to come. This chapter aims to overview the etiology of BLM, differentiate the concept and the movement, review BLM as a verbal operant, and outline function-based actions to show up for Black lives beyond a brief interval of time.

EVOLUTION OF BLM

The Hashtag, Global Organization, and a Decentralized Movement

Amid a global pandemic (World Health Organization, 2020), Americans found themselves wrestling with consecutive murders of Ahmaud Abery, Breonna Taylor, George Floyd, and Tony McDade. The senseless murder of each person served as a reminder that even during global chaos, Anti-Black racism still held precedence. Amid this chaos, during the most recent uprisings, BLM experienced a steep increase in online attention (Anderson et al., 2020), which may have caused some to deduce BLM as a new campaign. However, BLM is a movement that broke ground well before the 2020 uprisings.

After Trayvon Martin was fatally shot, Alicia Garza wrote a post online expressing grief and a state of loss concerning the acquittal of the man who killed Trayvon.[1] In this post, Garza outlined her intention as an action to affirm Black lives. Patrisse Cullors sequentially provided commentary, stamping #BlackLivesMatter under the written thread, and a new hashtag was born from Garza's moment of public mourning (Cullors, 2019). According to these two BLM organization founders, Garza and Cullors, the hashtag was created to spark a campaign dedicated to fighting anti-Black racism through social media and street organizing (Flaherty, 2016). At its inception, BLM was confined to a pound symbol, used online briefly after the acquittal, and only gaining traction again after the murder of Michael Brown (Freelon et al., 2016). The use of the hashtag by users online after the murder of Michael Brown showed a similar trend revealing increases after other incidents of police violence and gained the most attention after the uprisings that took place starting in June 2020. Suppose one

---

[1]   The name of the man who killed Trayvon Martin is intentionally redacted in this text.

were to solely use social media hashtags to determine the validity of BLM. In that case, they might conclude Black lives only matter when Black people are killed by law enforcement and vigilantes. Those who label Black Lives Matter in their natural environment beg to differ.

The Organization and A Leader-decentralized Movement

Both women who originated the Black Lives Matter hashtag corresponded with Opal Tometi to create a non-profit, 501(c)3 organization. BLM, the organization, has multiple chapters across the world and works to "eradicate white supremacy and build local power to intervene in violence inflicted on Black communities by state and vigilantes," per their mission statement (Black Lives Matter, 2020). As an organization, chapters work on a local level in alignment with the organization's mission. The actions that this global group has publicly taken credit for include: responding to excessive force used by Immigrations and Customs Enforcement (ICE), the murder of Stephon Clark, and humane treatment of migrants and those seeking asylum. Using the data provided by their website, this group's actions do not speak for the more extensive use of Black Lives Matter.

An individual may vocalize Black Lives Matter, use the hashtag, or attach personal meaning to the phrase but do not identify as being part of the organization. This is also an intention of the BLM founders. Black Lives Matter exists as a method for individuals to actualize change in their local communities without being connected to an organizational structure that is run and spoken on behalf of only a few people. This means that any person or group can determine the meaning and actionable steps for themselves and their community. This is what the BLM movement has revealed over time.

BLM AND VERBAL BEHAVIOR

As previously outlined, BLM in history has been regarded as a hashtag, a non-profit organization, and the name of a leader-decentralized social justice movement. Black Lives Matter or "Black lives matter," depending on the speaker and the listener may serve various functions. BLM may still evoke varying levels of responding beyond the three explanations previously provided in the text. B.F. Skinner (1957) outlined a functional analytic approach to language, which may further the analysis of Black Lives Matter as behavior for a particular individual or group. Taking a functional analytic approach to BLM, we may appropriately determine how to respond to the speaker(s), and for the purpose of this chapter, the Black community.

Function of Behavior

Behavior analysts examine behavior as a method to determine the function or, in layman's terms, the "why" for an individual's actions. The four functions of behavior that have been widely accepted in the behavior analytic literature include automatic, access to tangibles, escape, and attention. Automatic functions are those that provide a sensory-related consequence, such as warmth, after putting on a jacket in cold temperature. Access to tangibles is the provision of physical access to items. An example may be access to a generalized conditioned reinforcer such as money. The escape function describes consequences that provide the removal of stimuli from the environment. This could include putting headphones on as a means to avoid unwanted conversations from strangers. And lastly, attention offers some form of momentary awareness or presence of other people, such as saying hi to strangers to engage in conversation. The four functions will be further detailed with verbal operants in connection to the phrase Black Lives Matter.

Black Lives Matter as a Mand

A mand, or for some labeled as a command, demand, or request, is a verbal operant that serves the function of producing a response equivalent or appropriate to the initial verbal stimuli. For example, a person in a crowded, noisy environment may scream (or demand), "shut up!" Consequently, the other individuals in the environment may cease talking, even if only for a brief moment. For the individual, their use of "shut up" served them in the presence of aversive stimuli and the escape of noise served as a negative reinforcer. Therefore in the future, this person may be more likely to use that or a similar phrase to quiet their environment. When considering Black Lives Matter as a mand, we must consider what consequences the individual anticipates based on their learning history. As a means to do this, we can also use the environment as a cue. Using the environment as a cue may inform us of the motivating operation(s) present for the individual that makes a specific consequence more or less valuable. For the person who screamed shut up, the noisy environment is the cue for their particular behavior and a quiet environment is of value. When an individual demands "BLM," motivating operations tell us that stimuli may either be missing from the environment, and the consequence is an appetitive stimulus, or stimuli are heavily represented in the environment, and the consequence is an aversive stimulus. Therefore, BLM may, to an individual, be a mand for attention, access, and/or escape.

BLM to Escape and Avoid

Many protestors who proclaim Black Lives Matter in the social justice movement of 2020 have made their anticipated consequences clear; escape and avoid police brutality (Mohapatra, 2020; Florido & Peñaloza, 2020). Black activists have specifically called for this to be accomplished by defunding the police. This means decreasing the current 180 billion dollar budget spent yearly on police and incarceration in the United States of America (McCarthy, 2020). To attempt a behavioral explanation, defunding police may be considered similarly to differential reinforcement, in which law enforcement agencies are provided with funding exclusively for specific behaviors, and all other behaviors are placed on extinction. Defunding would allow police to reduce response effort and increase fluency only in areas where they best serve the broader community. The reinforcement that would be withheld from law enforcement would then be provided to other agencies such as: parks and recreation, mental health and substance abuse treatment, employment and equitable wages, education, and housing. Using differential reinforcement, the environment may then be enriched and further reduce the need for militarized law enforcement officers and incarceration. And while defunding and abolishing the police are popular asks of individuals who command Black Lives Matter, it is essential to note that a wide array of consequences exist outside of defunding. Other mands for decrease include ending deportations, in which Black people, specifically Haitian people, continue to make up a large percentage of detainments (RAICES, 2020), physical and medical violence against Black women, community violence, and harassment of all groups that experience marginalization, including Black transgender women. Lastly, it could include freedom from all other forms of discrimination and microaggressions.

BLM to Access Tangibles

Like the previous example of demands as a function to escape aversive environmental stimuli revealed, there is also a mand for access to tangible consequences. Using historical data of the civil rights movements, tangible outcomes have been communicated as a mand well before 2020. However, the concrete results Black people have demanded for decades were ignored and intentionally withheld (Constitutional Rights Foundation, 2020). One tangible response the Black community has advocated for includes reparations for chattel slavery and other government abuses that left Black Americans owning none of the wealth in which they provided the country (Coates, 2014). At the time slavery ended, previously enslaved Black ancestors were promised 40-acre plots of land. Lawmakers reneged, and disenfranchisement took a new form through Jim Crow laws, domestic terrorism, mass incarceration, redlining, and police brutality. Other tangible consequences as a response to Black Lives Matter include equitable education, pay, and healthcare and access to housing (Movement for Black Lives, 2020). It also includes painted murals and street names (King, 2020; Mask, 2020) and stopping intentional efforts to repeal Black civil rights (Pettypiece, 2020).

BLM to Access Attention

The last function to be considered is mand for attention. Mands for attention have been followed by large corporations' public statements, individuals sharing information, and street signs that reveal the phrase. Attention may also be gaining recognition for contributions and efforts or providing a platform for an individual. To mand Black Lives Matter with a desire to receive attention from others, it is possible that an individual may also have a personal attachment to the words in which the affirmation of Black Lives Matter may also draw specific meaning for that person (Barnes et al., 2004; Hayes, 1989), and serve as a positive reinforcer.

FUNCTION-BASED RESPONDING OF BLACK LIVES MATTER

A fundamental assumption of behavior analysis is the use of function-based intervention. Once the function(s) of a particular behavior has been identified, an equivalent response should be provided. Considering the requests of Black individuals and those who explicitly mand Black Lives Matter, will also reveal the environmental disparities and excesses and determine consequences that maintain the behavior. Non-function-based outcomes are less effective (Ingram et al., 2015); the responses of individuals who mand Black Lives Matter should receive function-based responses that improve their environment's condition.

For one individual, the use of Black Lives Matter as a mand could be one, two, or all of the functions outlined. For example, while requests for street signs and murals are tangible outcomes, Black Lives Matter as a mand for this consequence could also be a means to access attention. In reverse, attention may be a necessary function of receiving tangible outcomes. Whether Black Lives Matter may serve as one or multiple functions, individuals and the broader society will need to provide function-based responses, especially if the goal is to uplift the community. Failure to respond adequately might essentially communicate that Black lives do not matter.

BEHAVING FOR BLACK LIVES

The most practical responses to Black Lives Matter as a mand are functional responses. Functionally behaving for Black lives would require each person to respond according to the individual's needs instead of determining their own set of non-functional responses and expecting their behavior to be adequate. The consequences necessary to prove Black Lives Matter will not appear in the environment until they are strategically placed there. In order to appear in the environment, people must behave intentionally. While this section of this chapter will not address all necessary behaviors that individuals and groups could emit to meet the desired needs labeled by members of the Black community, it will overview actions that may be taken to address some concerns detailed in this chapter.

Black people must be able to escape discriminatory practices and behaviors and access tangible outcomes. To do this, each person must become an active observer of their own actions and orient towards behaviors that are aversive to individuals in the Black community and further perpetuate systemic issues outlined in this text. Discrete behaviors that may lead to abuses such as police brutality, could be calling 911 to settle non-violent and non-emergency issues. Each person should be willing to engage in replacement behaviors that humanize, as opposed to villainizing Black people, and placing them in a potential situation to be harmed. This would also require each person to consider new operational definitions for certain crimes such as loitering, transpassing, and noise complaints. Consider if the definition and reaction to the offense changes based on the person engaging in it. Additionally protective behaviors such as speaking up when situations arise like someone calling the police to address an incident that could otherwise be solved through community-based intervention (Sakala, 2018). Using community-based interventions also helps to address defunding the police, however, it will require more than simply diverting local calls to community agencies. It will require that community agencies have the proper resources to respond. Many outcomes, such as defunding the police require voting and advocating in some capacity. It is not enough to provide attention to a cause when a tangible action is desired. Each person will need to engage in behaviors such as letter writing and calling their local elected officials, sharing support in their local communities, and speaking at local community board meetings for a reduction of the police budget and increase in alternative agency budgets. They will need to engage in voting behavior should it appear on a ballot.

Another tangible outcome reviewed is reparations. A behavior to engage in initially for those who are not familiar is to receptively identify which groups have received reparations in the United States. Once this has been assessed, discriminate which group(s) have not. Further, read previous proposals to provide reparations to the Black community and share the information, particularly to other non-Black individuals who may be unaware of this demand (Jackson Lee, 2019). And finally, engage with local government to vote on behalf of proposed legislation.

Providing attention to the mand Black Lives Matter may include sharing information of individuals and groups who particularly are advocating for the group. By uplifting those who are requesting particular responses, it has the potential of championing others to also enact behaviors in support of the community. Additionally, it may require appropriate attention to trustworthy information and promoting Black voices in their environment. While Black voices are provided with the desired consequence, also individuals should ensure they do not engage in punitive behaviors such as response interrupting vocal speech and unjustly diminishing their contributions.

Other everyday actions to behave for Black lives include, remaining accountable to mistakes. While it is not possible to create antecedent strategies for every person and in every environment, if mistakes or lack of proper interventions occur, emit flexible behaviors based on direct requests of the community. Rallying for Black lives is not a one-time event. It will require an ongoing commitment (e.g., one letter to an elected official is not enough). There must be repeated actions until the desired consequence is delivered. Lastly, it will require challenging the behaviors of friends, family, organizations, and evoking new behaviors across all environments.

REFERENCES

Anderson, M., Barthel, M., Perrin, A., & Vogels, E. A. (2020, August 28). #BlackLivesMatter surges on Twitter after George Floyd's death. Pew Research Center. https://www.pewresearch.org/fact-tank/2020/06/10/blacklivesmatter-surges-on-twitter-after-george-floyds-death/

Barnes-Holmes, D., Luciano, C., & Barnes-Holmes, Y. (2004). Relational frame theory: Definitions, controversies, and applications I. Special issue of the *International Journal of Psychology and Psychological Therapy*, 4, 177–394.

Black Lives Matter. (2020, June 22). *Home.* https://blacklivesmatter.com/

Coates, T.-N. (2014, May 21). The case for reparations. *The Atlantic.* https://www.theatlantic.com/magazine/archive/2014/06/the-case-for-reparations/361631

Cullors, P. (2019). 6 years strong. Black Lives Matter. https://blacklivesmatter.com/six-years-strong/

Flaherty, J. (2016). *No more heroes: Grassroots challenges to the savior mentality.* AK Press.

Florido, A., & Peñaloza, M. (2020, August 27). As nation reckons with race, poll finds white Americans least engaged. NPR. https://www.npr.org/2020/08/27/906329303/as-nation-reckons-with-race-poll-finds-white-americans-least-engaged?fbclid=IwAR1vmQ2Y_FTCeWD6du9P8OHPl4igJvEjr Csy1G2ODREpVYZVY2t-QRxlPjQ

Freelon, D., McIlwain, C., & Clark, M. (2016). Quantifying the power and consequences of social media protest. *New Media & Society, 20*(3), 990–1011. https://doi.org/10.1177/1461444816676646

Hayes, S. C. (Ed.). (1989). *Rule-governed behavior: Cognition, contingencies, and instructional control.* Plenum Press.

Ingram, K., Lewis-Palmer, T., & Sugai, G., (2015). Function-based intervention planning: Comparing the effectiveness of FBA function-based and non-function-based intervention plans. *Journal of Positive Behavior Interventions*, 7(4) 224–236. https://journals.sagepub.com/doi/10.1177/109830070500 70040401

Jackson Lee, S. (2019, June 19). H.R.40–116th Congress (2019–2020): Commission to study and develop reparation proposals for African-Americans Act. https://www.congress.gov/bill/116th-congress/house-bill/40

King, J. (2016, April 22). The women behind #blacklivesmatter. *The California Sunday Magazine.* https://stories.californiasunday.com/2015-03-01/black-lives-matter/.

King, M. (2020, July 20). "It's not enough": Activists say Black Lives Matter murals are empty gesture. *POLITICO.* https://www.politico.com/news/2020/07/19/black-lives-matter-murals-369091

Mask, D. (2020, July 22). The Black Lives Matter movement is being written into the streetscape. *The Atlantic.* https://www.theatlantic.com/ideas/archive/2020/07/street-naming-more-performative-gesture/614416/

McCarthy, N. (2017, August 7). How much do U.S. cities spend every year on policing? [Infographic]. *Forbes.* https://www.forbes.com/sites/niallmccarthy/2017/08/07/how-much-do-u-s-cities-spend-every-year-on-policing-infographic/

McCarthy, N., & Richter, F. (2020, June 11). Infographic: Police spending per capita in major U.S. cities. Statista Infographics. https://www.statista.com/chart/21963/amount-spent-on-policing-per-person/

Mohapatra, M., Raven, L., Amuchie, N., Sultan, R., Agbebiyi, K., Hamid, S., & Kuo, R. (2020). #8toAbolition. https://www.8toabolition.com/

The Movement for Black Lives. (2020). *End the war on black people – m4bl*. M4BL. https://m4bl.org/end-the-war-on-black-people

Pettypiece, S. (2020, September 17). Trump calls for "patriotic education," says anti-racism teachings are "child abuse." *NBCNews.com*. https://www.nbcnews.com/politics/white-house/trump-calls-patriotic-eduction-says-anti-racism-teachings-are-child-n1240372

RAICES. (2020, July 22). *Black immigrant lives are under attack*. https://www.raicestexas.org/2020/07/22/black-immigrant-lives-are-under-attack/

Reparations for Slavery Reading. Constitutional Rights Foundation. https://www.crf-usa.org/brown-v-board-50th-anniversary/reparations-for-slavery-reading.html

Sakala, L., Harvell, S., & Thomson, C. (2018). *Public investment in community: Driven safety initiatives. Landscape study and key considerations*. Urban Institute. https://www.urban.org/research/publication/public-investment-community-driven-safety-initiatives

Skinner, B. F. (1957). *Verbal behavior*. Appleton-Century-Crofts.

World Health Organization. (n.d.).Home. World Health Organization. https://www.who.int

6

BLAME

Not I: A Behavioral Conceptualization of Perpetrator Blame

Eva Lieberman, Emily Sandoz, and Karen Kate Kellum

According to the FBI, rape is the third most common violent crime committed in the United States (FBI, 2019). Rape is also the most underreported crime in the US (Rennison, 2002). Experts estimate that over 75% of instances of sexual assault that occur are not reported to law enforcement (RAINN, 2017). With the reports received by the police, and the number of unreported assaults, we can safely assume that sexual violence is widespread. Studies conducted over several decades find similar explanations for this disparity in reporting. One of the most consistent findings is that victims cite they don't report sexual violence due to potential negative social reactions (Sable et al., 2006; Khan et al., 2018). Those negative reactions are often expressed as *victim blame*, where in many different ways, observers and perpetrators blame the victim for the assault. Victim blame is also present for victims themselves, where they assign blame to themselves for their own assault.

In cases of sexual violence, observers attribute blame to actors in the situation, both perpetrators and victims (Strömwall et al., 2014; Van Der Bruggen & Grubb, 2014). The misattribution of blame toward victims of sexual violence can negatively impact victims by inducing additional trauma (Campbell et al., 2001). Negative social reactions are often expressed as attributing responsibility of a sexual assault toward the victim of the assault, and there is a negative correlation between victim blame and perpetrator blame (Brems & Wegner, 1994; Strömwall et al., 2014). When victims are attributed more blame, perpetrators are attributed less, which results in improper sentencing and negative effects on victim recovery. This includes post-traumatic stress, problem drinking, and suicidal ideations (Campbell et al., 2001; Ullman, 1999). Social psychologists have delved deeper into factors that influence how blame is attributed, with research on gender of the observer, how much the observer ascribes to rape myths, and observer's previous experience with sexual violence (Grubb & Turner, 2012; Kopper, 1996; Perilloux et al., 2014). A social psychologist might identify those factors as characteristics of the observer. From a behavioral perspective, however, we might consider the learning history implied and, in some cases, controlled by the interaction of these characteristics with their environment.

Research on blame from a social psychology perspective has primarily focused on victim blame. The literature often explores how observer characteristics and victim characteristics impact how people attribute blame, mostly to victims. This perspective commonly neglects to investigate how these same characteristics may influence how blame is attributed toward perpetrators of sexual violence. This may be because the phenomenon of blame is not specifically defined, and examining a broad group of behaviors as one generalized phenomenon presents a challenge to assessment. In the social literature, when blame is discussed, researchers seem to be referring to when someone is blamed. The term "blame" is often used interchangeably with responsibility and fault (e.g., Amacker & Littleton, 2013; Donde, 2017). There is not a place in the literature where there is an explicit distinction between the naming of the behavior of "blame" and other behaviors like attributing fault or responsibility. This is especially problematic within sexual violence research and when examining perpetrator blame. Not only does this reveal a potential gap in the literature, but without an explicit definition of the behavior of blaming, psychologists tend to differ in their measurement, assessment, and evaluation of how we attribute blame to those perpetrators of sexual violence.

Examining the phenomenon of perpetrator blame from a behavior analytic perspective presents an important opportunity to understand this behavior functionally. Approaching perpetrator blame as a behavior exhibited in the presence of particular antecedents and consequences that bear functions consistent with a specific learning history allows us to examine differences in attributions of blame in terms of their controlling conditions. This kind of contextual investigation into blame as behavior not only allows for consideration of what influences misattributions, but also has direct implications for behavior change.

Operationalizing the behavior of "blaming" as a psychological term requires that we first understand under what conditions researchers use the word "blame" (Skinner, 1945). Traditionally, blame is assessed through self-report (e.g., Donde, 2017; Perilloux et al., 2014). Participants answer questions about who they think is to blame, who is at fault, and who is responsible in written scenarios provided by the researchers. In the typical self-report context, then, blame is what people do when we instruct them to blame. This instruction is also behavior that is more or less probable, depending on the context.

In general, blame is when someone attributes the cause of an aversive event to an individual's behaviors. In other words, the antecedent of blaming behavior is an event that the person blaming would typically act to avoid. Aversive events may evoke blaming behavior in the repertoire of a person whose behavior resulted in the aversive event, a person directly impacted by the aversive event, or a person who merely observed the aversive event, directly or indirectly. For example, the point of the game, Jenga, is to initiate the tower falling. The tower falling directly impacts all players, and is the result of one player's behavior. Once the tower falls, other players blame the person who pulled the most recent piece from the tower. In this case, the event is only aversive to the player who caused it. Spilling coffee on a stranger's new shoes is often aversive for both the spiller and the spilled upon, who are likely to engage in blaming behavior. However, this same event is likely not particularly evocative for an observer. Some aversive events are likely to evoke blaming behavior, even in a person with limited involvement in the event. In the case of sexual assault, both the perpetrator and victim engage in blaming behavior, and those who may only contact the event indirectly (e.g. by news report) will also likely blame.

Blaming is not only distinguished by antecedent conditions. Escape or avoidance of additional aversive consequences tends to consequate blaming behavior. These consequences are socially mediated, and just as the aversive antecedent, can occur in a number of different contexts. These consequences can be as common and trivial as being laughed at for knocking over a Jenga tower. They can be unpleasant for those involved, like if you are yelled at for spilling a coffee all over another person. And the consequences of blaming can be aversive to anyone who either directly or tangentially experiences them, such as social ostracization, arrest, or imprisonment. That is, blaming behavior likely occurs after an aversive antecedent event that is functionally similar to contexts in which blaming effectively functioned to avoid or escape aversive socially mediated consequences.

Blaming is only one of many behaviors that may allow the person to avoid or escape socially mediated aversives. For example, running away and hiding after an aversive event could result in avoiding negative social consequences. But running and hiding is not "blame," perhaps because blame is inherently a verbal behavior. In *Verbal Behavior*, Skinner (1957) defines verbal behavior as sensitive to socially mediated consequences, where the listener responds in ways that reinforce the speaker's behavior. The history of negative reinforcement around blaming increases the probability that the speaker, or the person blaming, will continue engaging in the behavior. Skinner further specifies that a verbal behavior does not have to be vocal behavior. In the context of blame, using language to explicitly state blame is fairly straightforward blaming behavior, someone could also point their finger at another person and still engage in the verbal behavior of "blame." The behavior of "blaming" often seems to involve a correspondence between the specific content of the verbal behavior and presumably observed aspects of the antecedent (e.g., It was them who fell the tower, spilled the coffee, or caused the sexual assault). In other words, though blame may take the form of a tact, this behavior does not function as such. By engaging in the behavior of blame, the person blaming may avoid negative social consequences associated with the aversive antecedent. It is important to differentiate that the behavior of "blame" is a verbal behavior consistent with an indirect mand. A direct mand of, for example, saying "don't punish me for this" after an aversive event could also serve to avoid or escape the aversive social consequences, but that would not be blame. Nor is blame a tact. Where a tact is a verbal response to a non-verbal stimulus, and results in socially mediated consequence, tacting is primarily under antecedent control (Skinner, 1957). Tacting is still an operant and is under control of generalized conditioned reinforcement, but they are not specific to the form of the verbal utterance. It is the specific consequential control that differentiates blaming behavior from a tact. While a person may tact the initial aversive event, they then mand in ways that have been consequated by avoidance of specific negative social consequences. Therefore, we can explicitly identify "blame" as an indirect mand – verbal behavior with an aversive antecedent, which serves as an establishing operation for specific negative reinforcement around the avoidance of aversive social contingencies.

A person who exhibits high probability blaming behavior, then, would be assumed to have a history of consequential control supporting the development and maintenance of blaming behavior. This is so common that social psychological theory describes it as a general tendency called Defensive Attribution Theory. From a social psychology perspective, the Defensive Attribution Theory states that people tend to blame in ways that distance them from negative events (Shaver, 1970). This is consistent with the behavioral conceptualization, which implies that blaming is under Defensive Attribution Theory. This is clearly demonstrated in sexual violence research, where observers similar to a perpetrator of an assault tend to blame the perpetrator less and blame the victim more than those dissimilar to the perpetrator (Bell et al., 1994; Dexter et al., 1997). By misattributing blame in these instances, the participants escape from or avoid the aversive event and the socially mediated consequences that accompany the event.

This conceptualization of blame applies to general attributions, but can also be specifically applied when examining blame in cases of sexual violence. For example, individuals' learning histories when blaming a perpetrator stem from a clear dichotomy between victim and perpetrator. The circumstances under which one would use the term "perpetrator" implies that there is a victim. Further, the term "perpetrator" is used in cases of sexual violence when referring to an individual who commits a non-consensual sexual act upon a victim. Just as blaming behavior has an antecedent of an aversive event, naming someone a perpetrator has a specific aversive event of an act of sexual violence. In labeling someone else as a perpetrator, people may also provide relief from socially mediated consequences (e.g., being labeled a perpetrator themselves, or behaving as if they could also be a victim), just as Defensive Attribution Theory would support. In this way, calling someone a perpetrator at all seems to imply some blame while calling someone a victim typically implies that that actor is blameless. Despite these implications, the oxymoron "victim blame" exists, highlighting just how often blame is misattributed in those situations that are even aversive to observers. In this type of interactional event someone causes another person harm, and attributing blame to the perpetrator of the undesirable event is the result of previous patterns of reinforcing attributing blame when other aversive events occur.

When the context is exerting aversive control, an entire response class of avoidance and escape are probable. Blaming quickly and efficiently allows the behaving person to escape both the aversive event and negative socially mediated consequences, even when erroneous. These misattributions often take the form of victim blame, and if the behavior is manding under aversive control, it may be the behavior with the least response cost. This is especially true if the person blaming shares features with the perpetrator, as Defensive Attribution Theory would suggest (Shaver, 1970).

The extant literature seems to suggest that victim and perpetrator blame exist in a zero-sum negative relationship, such that reducing victim blame necessarily involves increasing perpetrator blame. This analysis suggests, however, that perhaps we, as a society, should encourage moving away from blame as a behavior under aversive control and as a means of escape. Instead, the target behavior should be tracking behavior-context relationships, particularly in the context of aversives – appropriately tacting perpetrator behavior and the context in which perpetrator behavior occurred. By shifting the function of blaming behavior from manding under aversive control to tacting under appetitive control, we can start to facilitate and build learning histories that reward appropriate blame, instead of punishing, or just ignoring these misattributions. To make that shift to appetitive control, we can work to reduce the establishing operation for negative reinforcement of social relief simply by non-contingently positively reinforcing the reporting behavior of those who witness or experience sexual violence. Such a report is, at the very least, a tact of the reporter's acute experience, and we should be reinforcing reporting that experience. We propose that shifting blaming to be under appetitive control would create a context for increased accurate reporting of sexual violence, decreased unreported instances of sexual violence, and improved attention, compassion, and flexibility on the part of those that receive such reports.

REFERENCES

Amacker, A. M., & Littleton, H. L. (2013). Perceptions of similarity and responsibility attributions to an acquaintance sexual assault victim. *Violence Against Women, 19*(11), 1384–1407. doi.org/10.1177/1077801213514860

Brems, C., & Wegner, P. (1994). Blame of victim and perpetrator in rape versus theft. *The Journal of Social Psychology, 134*(3), 363–374. https://doi.org/10.1080/00224545.1994.9711741

Campbell, R., Ahrens, C., Sefl, T., Wasco, S., & Barnes, H. (2001). Social reactions to rape victims: Healing and hurtful effects on psychological and physical health outcomes. *Violence and Victims, 16*(3), 287–302. https://doi.org/10.1891/0886-6708.16.3.287

Donde, S. D. (2017). College women's assignment of blame versus responsibility for sexual assault experiences. *Violence Against Women, 23*(14), 1671–1688. doi.org/10.1177/1077801216665481

Federal Bureau of Investigation. (2019, September 30). FBI Releases 2018 Crime Statistics. *FBI.* https://www.fbi.gov/news/pressrel/press-releases/fbi-releases-2018-crime-statistics

Grubb, A., & Turner, E. (2012). Attribution of blame in rape cases: A review of the impact of rape myth acceptance, gender role conformity and substance use on victim blaming. *Aggression and Violent Behavior, 17*(5), 443–452. https://doi.org/10.1016/j.avb.2012.06.002

Khan, S., Hirsch, J., Wamboldt, A., & Mellins, C. (2018). "I Didn't want to be 'that Girl'": The social risks of labeling, Telling, and reporting sexual assault. *Sociological Science, 5*, 432–460. https://doi. org/10.15195/v5.a19

Kopper, B. A. (1996). Gender, gender identity, rape myth acceptance, and time of initial resistance on the perception of acquaintance rape blame and avoidability. *Sex Roles, 34*(1–2), 81–93. https://doi. org/10.1007/bf01544797

Perilloux, C., Duntley, J. D., & Buss, D. M. (2014). Blame attribution in sexual victimization. *Personality and Individual Differences, 63*, 81–86. https://doi.org/10.1016/j.paid.2014.01.058

RAINN. (2017). The criminal justice system: Statistics. https://www.rainn.org/statistics/criminal-justice-system

Rennison, C. A. (2002). Rape and sexual assault: Reporting to police and medical attention, 1992–2000 [NCJ 194530]. *U.S. Department of Justice, Office of Justice Programs, Bureau of Justice Statistics.* http://bjs. ojp. usdoj.gov/content/pub/pdf/rsarp00.pdf

Sable, M. R., Danis, F., Mauzy, D. L., & Gallagher, S. K. (2006). Barriers to reporting sexual assault for women and men: Perspectives of college students. *Journal of American College Health, 55*(3), 157–162.

Shaver, K. G. (1970). Defensive attribution: Effects of severity and relevance on the responsibility assigned for an accident. *Journal of Personality and Social Psychology, 14*(2), 101–113.

Skinner, B. F. (1945). The operational analysis of psychological terms. *Psychological Review, 52*(5), 270.

Skinner, B. F. (1957). *Verbal behavior.* Appleton-Century-Crofts.

Strömwall, L. A., Landström, S., & Alfredsson, H. (2014). Perpetrator characteristics and blame attributions in a stranger rape situation. *The European Journal of Psychology Applied to Legal Context, 6*(2), 63–67. https://doi.org/10.1016/j.ejpal.2014.06.002

Ullman, S. E. (1999). Social support and recovery from sexual assault. *Aggression and Violent Behavior, 4*(3), 343–358. https://doi.org/10.1016/s1359-1789(98)00006-8

Van Der Bruggen, M., & Grubb, A. (2014). A review of the literature relating to rape victim blaming: An analysis of the impact of observer and victim characteristics on attribution of blame in rape cases. *Aggression and Violent Behavior, 19*(5), 523–531. https://doi.org/10.1016/j.avb.2014.07.008

7

BULLYING

Queen Bees, Wannabees, Bee-havior Analysts: Looking at
Bullying through a Behavioral Lens

Ann Beirne

It has often been said that "real life is like high school with money." While many of us may look back on that time in our lives and cringe at our egregious social skills, our unearned self-confidence, and certainly our fashion sense, there is certainly a kernel of truth to this. As any coming-of age movie or teenage romantic comedy tells us, the high school cafeteria is a social structure that consists of encapsulated groups – the jocks, the nerds, the cool kids, etc. We continue to tend to be most comfortable in the groups with whom we have the most in common, where we are included in the bubble, and see ourselves in those inside.

Unfortunately, the stratification of the metaphorical cafeteria table is often not where the similarities end. While we expect bullying to plague the halls of high schools, many of us had hoped that it was a phase of life we would simply outgrow. Like the conversion of Regina George in the movie and musical *Mean Girls*, bullies would simply figure it out.

Both current data and the personal experience of many behavior analysts, however, indicate that bullying is one of the things that persist into our careers. Many companies, large and small, have their own Regina Georges (or perhaps George Reginas).

PROFESSIONAL ETHICS AND PERSONAL MORALITY

Many students of behavior analysis (and even many certified practitioners) believe that ethics should be intuitive – that beyond being a "good person" there is little to be done to ensure ethical practice. There is a persistent view that all that is required for ethical practice of any human service is the drive to help others. Those that behave in unethical ways are inherently lacking any moral compass. It is not just the actions themselves that are unethical, but the people who engage in them. It is far easier to dismiss unethical behavior as the actions of bad people. Nothing like us! The problem with this view is that it fails to address a distinction between professional ethics and personal morality, which inevitably causes confusion in any attempt to promote either (and certainly the attempt to promote both).

Professional ethics are defined by adherence to a set of guidelines as specified by a governing body (Beirne & Sadavoy, 2019). In the case of behavior analysis, our governing body is the Behavior Analyst Certification Board® and the ethical expectations are drafted in the The Ethical Code for Behavior Analysts®. As a document that is written both by and for behavior analysts, this Code specifies the behavioral expectations for ethical practice. It is intended to be as objective as possible, which allows for more consistent enforcement of ethical behavior and maintenance of high standards for the field.

Moral behavior, on the other hand, is far more subjectively defined. In fact, philosophers and sages over the centuries have extensively debated the nature of what it means to be a good person, leaving a great deal of disagreement. While the answers to questions such as, "Have I done all of the good that I can do?" may certainly influence the quality of our work, these are not necessarily questions of ethical practice. Morality is individually determined, although it is influenced by culture.

Culture, as behavior analysts understand it, is characterized by interlocking sets of social contingencies which result in a shared set of behaviors (Glenn, 1988). These behaviors include everything that we commonly associate with the word "culture" – religious practices, idiomatic expressions, and social customs. However, it is also a more far-reaching and inclusive definition, encompassing habits and quirks that are perpetuated within families or workplace practices that are described by saying "That's just the way we do things here." The personal biases that we carry are as much a part of our culture as our favorite holidays. Culture describes the best as well as the worst of us.

Morality, therefore, assumes some mutual understanding of "right" and "wrong" which may be nonexistent. The subjectivity of right/wrong, polite/rude, or professional/unprofessional can cause our personal biases to lead to bullying. Relying exclusively on one's moral compass, rather than adhering to ethical codes, can allow us to make decisions influenced by these biases. The risk here is that we will fall into a trap of engaging in behavior that makes us comfortable rather than allowing our ethics to challenge us to grow. Moral practice may feel good, but the behavior associated with the biases that influence it can potentially be harmful.

Bullying Defined

Definition of workplace bullying is somewhat complicated and there is considerable debate as to the defining features. Though some argue that in order to be considered "bullying" the aggressive behavior in question must be persistent over a long period, others maintain that more intense incidents are often more short-term (Crawshaw, 2009).

Bullying in the workplace is defined as the repeated, unwanted actions against employees or colleagues that humiliate or offend, which may compromise work performance or create a hostile work environment (Zapf et al., 2020). Zapf et al. (2020) cite several specific examples of workplace bullying, including changing work tasks so that their difficulty is increased, exclusion from social events or communication, personal attacks, jokes at the individual's expense, insults, excessive criticism, yelling, or public humiliation.

The costs of workplace bullying are considerable not only personally but financially as well. The punishing nature of these persistent interactions may decrease communication and employee initiative, which exacerbates problems in performance (Zapf et al., 2020). Hollis (2015) also studied the financial impacts of employee disengagement as a direct result of bullying. She writes:

> replacement of some employees can cost as much as 250% of the departing employee's salary . . . Given this figure of 150% of the departing employee's salary for replacement costs, if an employee on a salary of US$50,000 left the organization (the median salary of the participants in this study), the organization spent US$75,000 to replace that person . . . The mean salary for higher education personnel nationally was US$67,000; therefore, the average cost of turnover per employee was US$100,500. If 62% of higher education staff was affected by bullying, and as a result this staff disengaged for 3.9 hr each week, then, for example, a college with 1,900 people on staff was potentially losing more than US$8 million by allowing workplace bullying. A large university with 22,000 on the staff was potentially losing more than US$93 million. A medium-sized school with 1,100 on the staff was potentially losing more than US$4.6 million annually because staff were disengaging from work to strategize or worry about the tactics of a bully.

The personal impact of workplace bullying, however, is not to be overlooked. Attell, Brown, and Treiber (2017) examined the psychological impact of workplace bullying and found that workplace bullying was associated with psychological distress, including anxiety and hopelessness. In addition, this study demonstrated that workplace bullying was a greater issue for women, and persons of color (Attell et al., 2017). Bullying and discrimination are intimately linked.

Given that the features of this definition include that these interactions are unwanted and have a negative impact, there is, admittedly, some subjectivity here. Bullying tends to be defined by its effects on the victim. However, we cannot allow the difficulty of developing an objective definition to dismiss this as an issue. The creation and maintenance of a healthy work environment includes behaviors that can – and should – be well defined.

Preventing Bullying: A Look Outward

The Professional and Ethical Compliance Code® compels us to examine the social contingencies which may shape bullying behaviors, or, at a minimum, allow these behaviors to continue unchecked. Our Core Principles state that our obligations include "Actively identifying and addressing factors (e.g., personal, financial, institutional, political, religious, cultural) that might lead to conflicts of interest, misuse of their position, or negative impacts on their professional activities" (BACB, 2020). Certainly bullying would be among the institutional factors that impact our professional activities and those of others. And, ultimately, this affects our clients.

On an institutional level there are several practices that both small and large companies can promote in order to prevent bullying and avoid discrimination.

Use competency based assessments and use them often.

The use of objective measures to measure job performance prevents more subjective measures from being used in their place. If we are going to expect "professionalism" we must have a clear idea of exactly what that is, and it should have to do with job expectations.

Communicate clearly regarding schedules and expectations.

Are the communicated hours consistent with the behavioral expectations of the workplace? Or are employees expected to demonstrate "dedication" by staying after hours, working through lunch, or answering phone calls or texts on days off? There should be no unspoken understandings – if it is an expectation, it should be well communicated and documented with an employment contract.

Develop reinforcement systems.

We all know that "behavior goes where reinforcement flows" and that punishment is only capable of decreasing behavior, not increasing desired behavior. If employee engagement is the goal, the emphasis should be on consistent reinforcement of fulfillment of well communicated job responsibilities.

Have clear protocols for reporting.

In order to promote an ethical workplace, employees must know where they can go to resolve issues, and that such problems will be heard and appropriately addressed. Not every conflict will be easily resolved, but there must be a mechanism in place to make good faith attempts.

Promote an active learning environment.

Do not assume mutual understanding of corporate practices or cultural differences. Encourage employees to learn more, to communicate their needs, and to ask questions. Make changes to things that aren't working.

Hire a diverse workforce.

Actively recruit employees of color as well as those from the LGBTQ2IA community and other marginalized groups.

Preventing Bullying: A Look Inward

In addition to looking at the cultural structures and contingencies in place at the institutional level, the Ethics Code for Behavior Analysts® requires that we examine our own behavior on the individual level. This involves examining our own biases as well. This is difficult and uncomfortable work, but necessary.

Separate the ethical and unprofessional from the uncomfortable.

We all have workplace habits and behaviors that have been reinforced as well as tacit understanding of what we consider "professional" or "ethical" behavior. Behaviors that are considered "professional" should have to do with the safe and efficient fulfillment of job responsibilities rather than these habitual expectations.

Acknowledge that your own experience is not everyone's experience.

Offensive or discriminatory behavior is often dismissed because "that's just who they are." Or, ironically, "That's not who they are," even if both statements are applied to the same individual engaged in the same behavior. The implication here is "that is/is not who they are *in my experience*." When you hear of another individual's experience, one is likely to be more willing to listen objectively.

Listen to diverse voices (and not just about diversity!).

Include the work of a wide variety of individuals in your research, in your professional development, and on your bookshelf.

Develop a "growth mindset."

There are very few things in life I know for sure, but I do know this: I will screw up. I will make mistakes, and some of those mistakes will hurt people. Accepting this is not resignation. Rather, it empowers me to strive to do better – to make fewer mistakes (or failing that, at least different ones). We do not have to know everything. We must, however, commit to learning more and doing better. It is okay to be wrong, and it is okay (even preferable) to admit it.

BULLYING RESPONSE: THE ETHICAL AND THE PERSONAL

The Behavior Analyst Certification Board® provides some guidance as to appropriate steps if you are the victim of workplace bullying. The Ethics Code states, "Behavior analysts should address concerns about the professional misconduct of others directly with the, when, after assessing the situation, it seems possible that doing so will resolve the issue and not place the behavior analyst or others at undue risk" (BACB, 2020). Though we are encouraged to use a direct approach, it is not mandated.

Determine how to assess.

Several factors can be considered in order to determine the assessment of the situation and determining if an informal resolution is appropriate. One such factor may be the context of the offensive behavior. If the context is more casual and in a social setting, informing the individual may be sufficient to encourage a change in behavior (including, one would hope, a sincere apology). Just as stated by the Code, part of the determination of "appropriateness" should be the likelihood that an informal resolution would be successful. If the incident is part of a more long-standing pattern of behavior, it may be necessary to involve other authorities.

Document.

*Even if you determine th*at an unintentional offense is best addressed informally, it is still necessary to document this. Rather than trust that the behavior will change, introduce some accountability.

Move on.

Not every work environment will be the right one for you, and that is okay. You are not a tree, forced to grow where you are planted. If it isn't the right place, there are other places that might be.

Being an "Upstander": Growth and Discomfort

Philosopher and statesman Edmund Burke once said "The only thing necessary for the triumph of evil is for good men to do nothing." When we witness bullying or harassment, it is crucial to do something, even if this action is imperfect. As a starting point, we might consider the following actions.

Question.

Simply asking why a joke is funny or what may have provoked an offensive comment can often be enough to help a potential bully change their behavior.

Reach out.

Be sure to provide support to the victim of bullying. Offer to assist in documentation and/or encourage your colleague to document the offense. Simply asking, "Are you okay?" can make a world of difference.

Be the change.

Be public in your support of colleagues, your efforts to provide a supportive workplace, and your continued efforts to eliminate your personal biases.

"Get in loser, we're practicing ethically": Final Thoughts

For queen bee Regina George, rule by mockery and cruelty was destined to end badly. As in any teenage fable, the "losers" she befriended eventually thought better of it and she learned the error of her ways. Unfortunately, workplace bullying is rarely so neatly resolved. The costs, both personal costs to individual employees and financial costs to organizations, can make or break institutions. Respect is free, but a lack of respect can be very costly.

Like any set of behaviors, however, we as behavior analysts believe that culture – including corporate culture – can change. It is not a static state, but rather a dynamic one. Learning is always possible. As Maya Angelou said, we do the best that we can until we know better. And when we know better, we do better. It is our obligation, as both ethical professionals and moral ones, to continually strive to do better – for our colleagues, for our clients, and for ourselves.

REFERENCES

Attell, B. K., Brown, K. K., & Treiber, L. A. (2017). Workplace bullying, perceived job stressors, and psychological distress: Gender and race differences in the stress process. *Social Science Research, 65,* 210–221.

Behavior Analyst Certification Board. (2020). *Professional and ethical compliance code for behavior analysts.* Author.

Beirne, A. B., & Sadavoy, J. A. (2019). *Understanding ethics in applied behavior analysis: Practical applications.* Routledge.

Crawshaw, L. (2009). Workplace bullying? Mobbing? Harassment? Distraction by a thousand definitions. *Consulting Psychology Journal: Practice and Research, 61*(3), 263.

Glenn, S. S. (1988). Contingencies and metacontingencies: Toward a synthesis of behavior analysis and cultural materialism. *The Behavior analyst, 11*(2), 161–179. https://doi.org/10.1007/BF03392470

Hollis, L. P. (2015). Bully university? The cost of workplace bullying and employee disengagement in American higher education. *Sage Open, 5*(2). https://doi.org/10.1177/2158244015589997

Zapf, D., Escartin, J., Scheppa-Lahyani, M., Einarsen, S. V., Hoel, H., & Vartia, M. (2020). Empirical findings on prevalence and risk groups of bullying in the workplace. In S. V. Einarsen, H. Hoel, D. Zapf, & C. L. Cooper (Eds.), *Bullying and harassment in the workplace: Theory, research and practice* (3rd ed., pp. 105–162). CRC Press. https://doi.org/10.1201/9780429462528-5

8

BURNOUT & SELF-CARE

Filling your Vessel: Recognizing Burnout and Choosing Self-Care

Crystal Thompson

Let us start off by asking ourselves some questions. How do you define self-care? Is self-care a priority to you? Do you currently have a self-care routine? Have you ever experienced burnout? What causes burnout? What does it feel like to you? At that time, were you practicing self-care?

Self-care is not selfish. Growing up, I often thought that being too concerned about yourself was selfish; and that our energies should go into helping others. For the past several years, I have come to the realization that we have to make taking care of ourselves a priority, in order to live our very best life, and to be the best possible version of ourselves. How can we help others if we are not taking care of ourselves? Simple answer: we cannot.

Being successful in your career may require several years of school, many hours of research and training, attending conferences to learn the latest advancements, meetings with other professionals, and the list goes on. These behaviors are often reinforced by various rewards for putting in the hard work. Of course, we continue to engage in the behaviors that got us the promotion, raise, extra time off, or "Employee of the Month." While these reinforcers are well-deserving, were there sacrifices made to get there? I am not implying that you give less than 100%, but how can you give 100% if you are not at 100%? Speaking specifically to the field of Applied Behavior Analysis, our goal should be giving our very best; give 100% to our clients, their families, and our community. We give so much of our time, energy, and talents to help improve the quality of life for others. Who is ensuring that your own quality of life is improving? In a career that can be time consuming, where do you take time for yourself?

Without taking the necessary time for yourself, you are likely to encounter burnout. Burnout is defined as "a state of emotional, physical, and mental exhaustion caused by excessive and prolonged stress. It occurs when you feel overwhelmed, emotionally drained, and unable to meet constant demands. As the stress continues, you begin to lose the interest and motivation that led you to take on a certain role in the first place" (Smith et al., 2019). Smith and colleagues (2019) discriminate the differences between stress and burnout as they are not the same. Stress is our body's response to the demands of the world (Mayo Clinic, 2019). Stress may be having too much to do and being too engaged; while burnout is the loss of engagement and essentially the loss of emotional connection to activities you once enjoyed. Burnout can occur with your job and your personal life. How do we prevent burnout? While we may not be able to avoid situations that can cause stress, also known as stressors, does learning how to manage stress ultimately contribute to preventing burnout? I believe it does. We encounter stressors daily that sometimes cannot be avoided, but it is how we handle those stressors that will decide if they will cause prolonged stress. In addition to recognizing and having a plan to handle stressors, self-care is vital in order to prevent burnout.

Eleanor Brown said "Rest and self-care are so important. When you take time to replenish your spirit, it allows you to serve others from overflow. You cannot serve from an empty vessel" (Clark, 2017). What happens when we serve from an empty or half full vessel? What if our vessels are already empty before we get started? Is that when burnout happens? Yes. How do we keep our vessels full? Self-care.

Simply put, self-care is taking care of yourself, physically, emotionally, and mentally. Let's pretend we have a house plant we are trying to keep alive. What does it need? You start by giving the plant what it needs to grow – sun, water, some plant food, and maybe a little song or some positive words. Our self-care is not much different. As humans we need physical activity, healthy food, rest, and positivity. We underestimate how important all of these components are to our bodies and mind. As previously mentioned, the "hustle and bustle" is celebrated in today's society. If we are not working on the next project or constantly setting goals, we can be viewed as lazy or unmotivated. Speaking from personal experience, it is perfectly healthy to take time to rest. When mountain climbers reach the summit, they do not immediately go on the next mountain. They take time to enjoy their accomplishment, and rest. Taking a break and resting are not a lack of motivation, but rather a sign of someone who is self-aware and understands that breaks are necessary.

ACHIEVING AND MAINTAINING SELF-CARE

Maintaining Your Physical and Mental Health

A healthy body equals a healthy mind. What we consume is how we fuel our bodies. Consumption is not just about what we eat, but it is anything our body and mind absorbs. It is important to eat the right foods to maintain physical and mental health. A nutritious diet will play a huge role in our emotional and mental well-being. Emotional and mental health helps us to stay focused on the current tasks, and allows us to handle and cope with stressors. Barish-Wreden (2020) states:

> Our guts and brain are physically linked . . . and the two are able to send messages to one another. While the gut is able to influence emotional behavior in the brain, the brain can also alter the type of bacteria living in the gut. According to the American Psychological Association, gut bacteria produce an array of neurochemicals that the brain uses for the regulation of physiological and mental processes, including mood. It's believed 95 percent of the body's supply of serotonin, a mood stabilizer, is produced by gut bacteria. Stress is thought to suppress beneficial gut bacteria.

We are a sum of all of our parts which has to work together and be connected in order to have optimal performance. When we are operating as close to optimal each day, we have a balance and better able to handle what life gives us.

Another component to physical and mental health is getting rest and daily activity. Both of these can be undervalued. Good, adequate rest and some form of physical exercise have countless benefits, such as mental clarity, stress reduction, an improvement in mood, and increased levels of energy (Office of Disease Prevention and Health Promotion, 2020). Lastly, your covert verbal behavior can be one of the most beneficial aspects to maintaining self-care. Our private events (how we talk to ourselves) are just as important as how we talk to others. Imagine constantly hearing other people talk about our failures and pointing out our areas of weakness. It would be nearly impossible to make it through one day! Imagine if you talked to yourself like that on a daily basis, what do you think the outcome would be? Negative self-talk can impede upon your ability to engage in behaviors that are meaningful and bring value to your life. One strategy is to start each day with positive affirmations that include what you hope to accomplish during the day. Even when things go opposite to what you had hoped, remember that you are here for a reason (something you value) and that you are making an impact in someone's life. Another strategy borrowed from Acceptance and Commitment TRaining (ACTr) to deal with negative private events and thoughts comes from the process of cognitive defusion (Szabo & Tarbox, 2018). Cognitive defusion is the process or skill of seeing your thoughts simply as thoughts, and not truths. Using ACTr, one "defuse" (or separate) from thoughts by creating contexts in which their unhelpful functions are diminished. Take a thought like "I'm not good enough," "I am a bad presenter," or "I don't deserve that" and write it down and toss it in the garbage to physicalize "getting rid of the thought"; or conceptualize it on a helium balloon and let it go into the atmosphere. These are techniques that distance you from unhelpful private events (e.g., negative self-talk, self-deprecating thoughts) because that voice inside our head loves to tell us that we are doing everything incorrectly.

Creating Boundaries

According to IPFW/Parkview Student Assistance Program (Selva, 2018), "A boundary is a limit or space between you and the other person; a clear place where you begin and the other person ends . . . The purpose of setting a healthy boundary is, of course, to protect and take good care of you." As behavior analysts we need to ensure that we are not engaging in multiple relationships with clients (Code 1.11) but equally important and often neglected is our responsibility to engage in healthy boundaries to ensure that our service delivery is effective, professional, and ethical (BACB, 2020; Beirne & Sadavoy, 2019). The Code states that it is our professional and scientific responsibility by "actively identifying and addressing the potential negative impacts of their own physical and mental health on their professional activities" (BACB, 2020, p. 4). The author suggests that one should attempt to create boundaries in all areas of your life; including your job. You can create workplace boundaries by doing the following: saying "no" when you are not available, setting a time when you stop checking emails for the day or answering work calls, maintaining a manageable workload, referring clients to other providers when you are unable to perform the job effectively, and managing your time wisely. When you set boundaries at work, you are drawing a very clear line between your work life and personal life. In your personal life, you can set boundaries by avoiding people and situations that are stressors or drain your energy. Some stressors are clearly unavoidable, and we have to learn how to cope with them. Becoming more self-aware and knowing when you need a break or are unable to participate in an activity. When needed, ask for help. Asking for help does not indicate a weakness, it means you recognize that we are meant to work together and other people in our life can be of help. Selva (2018) provides several advantages of having healthy boundaries: good mental and emotional health, avoidance of burnout, influence the behavior of others, developed autonomy, and developed identity.

Doing Something You Love Daily

All this can seem pretty straight forward. But think about your typical day: wake up, do your morning routine (include the kids if you have any), get to work, scarf down lunch, finish work, pick up the kids, have dinner, take the kids to their practices, help with homework, eventually off to bed to do it again the next day. Sometimes your day includes the grocery store, doctor appointments, school work, etc. Where do you fit in time for yourself? It almost seems impossible, right?

In the past when I thought of self-care, I would always picture a bubble bath with flower petals, candles, and easy listening music playing in the background. The reality is, I do not remember the last time I had time to take a bubble bath. Life is busy and can be hard sometimes, but we have to make taking care of ourselves a priority too. This is not selfish, it is necessary. Self-care does not have to be defined as some grand gesture. It can be a simple as listening to your favorite songs on the way to work, a cup of tea in the morning, reading a chapter from your favorite book, sitting in silence, praying, meditating, going to the beach, going on a mini-vacation, having brunch with friends, getting a babysitter for the evening, and going to dinner, and just recently, I have discovered how calming it is to just sit in your car after work watching random YouTube videos. Whatever daily self-care activity you decide to do, make sure you are doing it for yourself.

Burnout can happen to anyone. When it occurs, burnout affects work life and personal life; and can seriously impact your outlook on life. The goal is to prevent burnout from occurring by practicing self-care. Self-care is having self-awareness and knowing what your needs are, creating boundaries, and taking time to do things that you love. Self-care must be practiced on a daily basis. You cannot give your best to others, if you are not giving the best to yourself.

REFERENCES

Barish-Wreden, M. (2020, April 14). *Eating well for mental health*. Sutter Health. https://www.sutterhealth. org/health/nutrition/eating-well-for-mental-health

Behavior Analyst Certification Board. (2020). *Ethics code for behavior analysts*. Littleton, CO: Author.

Beirne, A. B., & Sadavoy, J. A. (2019). *Understanding ethics in applied behavior analysis: Practical applications* (1st ed.). Routledge.

Clark, P. (2017, August 30). *You cannot pour from an empty cup*. Medium. https://www.medium.com/thrive-global/you-cannot-pour-from-an-empty-cup-cd7c0f12f22c

Mayo Clinic. (2019, March 28). *Identify your stress triggers*. Mayo Clinic. https://www.mayoclinic.org/healthy-lifestyle/stress-management/in-depth/stress-manage ment/art-20044151

Office of Disease Prevention and Health Promotion. (2020, September 12). *Get enough sleep*. U.S. Department of Health and Human Services. https://health.gov/myhealthfinder/topics/everyday-healthy-living/mental-health-and-relationships/get-enough-sleep#panel-2

Selva, J. (2018, November 11). *How to set healthy boundaries: 10 examples + PDF worksheets*. PositivePsychology.com. https://positivepsychology.com/great-self-care-setting-healthy-boundaries/

Smith, M., Segal, J., & Robinson, L. (2019, October). *Burnout prevention and treatment*. HelpGuide.org. https://www.helpguide.org/articles/stress/burnout-prevention-and-recovery.htm

Szabo, T. G., & Tarbox, J. (2018, July 20). *Acceptance and commitment training and the scope of practice of BCBAs*. Behavioral Science in the 21st Century. https://bsci21.org/acceptance-and-commitment-training-and-the-scope-of-practice-of-bcbas/

9

COMPASSION

The Role of Compassion in Social Justice Efforts

Linda A. LeBlanc, Denisha Gingles, and Erika Byers

INTRODUCTION

Recent behavior analytic publications have examined the value of compassion in the provision of behavior analytic services (Taylor et al., 2019). There is similar value in behavior analysts examining the role of compassion in ongoing social justice efforts. Our understanding of the role of compassion in social justice begins with an understanding of the definitions of three related terms (i.e., perspective taking, empathy, compassion). That understanding continues with a conceptual analysis of the contingencies, rules, values, and communities that support compassionate action in the context of social justice issues.

TERMS AND DEFINITIONS

Perspective taking includes two components: a) understanding that what another person sees, hears, thinks, feels, or believes may differ from your own experiences, thoughts, or beliefs; and b) predicting that the other person's behavior will be controlled by their own perspective rather than yours (LeBlanc et al., 2003; Sigman & Capps, 1997). Perspective taking is important in social behaviors such as; sharing, turn taking, and empathy (Byers, 2016; DeBernardis, et al., 2014; Iannotti, 1985). Empathy requires perspective taking in that one must perceive the experience of the other person and have some understanding of the emotional response that person is having. An empathetic response is possible even without identical experiences, as we typically draw upon past similar experiences to inform our understanding of others' feelings. Thus, "empathy is the act of being in touch with another's personal experience by relating it to one's own" (Taylor et al., 2019, p. 655). Byers (2016) demonstrated that preschool-aged children observing peers who were denied access to items they had also been denied in the past often manded on behalf of the peer, even though they already had access to the item themselves.

Compassion extends empathetic understanding to action designed to alleviate the suffering of another person (Lown et al., 2014; Taylor et al., 2019). In her essay, *On Compassion*, B. L. Ascher refers to empathy as "the mother of compassion" and indicates that "compassion . . . must be learned and it is learned by having adversity at our windows, coming through gates of our yards, the walls of our towns, adversity that becomes so familiar that we begin to identify and empathize with it" (Cohen, 2016, p. 42). Ascher's writing resonates with us (i.e., the authors) as behavior analysts because it focuses on compassionate behavior as a learned response to the stimulus class of adverse situations, regardless of the person directly experiencing the adversity. This definition of compassion is consistent with the idea that social justice efforts are compassionate acts directed towards those within our human communities who suffer social inequities and injustices.

Behavior analysts suggest that skills such as perspective taking and self-control can be conceptualized as generalized social operants (DeBernardis et al., 2014; Dunkel-Jackson & Dixon, 2016) in that these skills can be applied to different situations without prior instruction in those situations. We argue that compassionate social justice efforts can also be viewed as a generalized social operant. That is, as we learn about and take action on a variety of issues such as human rights, climate change, animal welfare, we begin to see myriad injustices as worthy of compassionate action. However as Ascher suggests, compassion requires that one consistently make contact with adversity which is an aversive experience. When adversity is experienced by others rather than directly, there is an option to escape it in ways that marginalized groups cannot (i.e., deny the existence, focus on other things). We have to understand social justice efforts as a concurrent operant situation in which the reinforcers associated with compassionate action are potentially pitted against negative reinforcers. As behavior analysts, we have the potential to act as a community in line with the words of Coretta Scott King who said, "The greatness of a community is most accurately measured by the compassionate action of its members." At some point in history, the greatness of the behavior analytic community may well be measured by our compassionate actions in the realm of social justice.

COMPASSION IN SOCIAL JUSTICE EFFORTS

Viray and Nash (2014) indicate that the most salient social justice action of all is to feel the suffering of others and try hard to alleviate it. In social justice movements, allies are those who perform acts of compassion based on their empathy for those who are oppressed. Oftentimes allies have also experienced forms of oppression and they draw upon these experiences in understanding the suffering of their fellow humans. This is seen in the Indigenous peoples' participation in the protests for the Black Lives Matter (BLM) movement and in the advocacy and lobbying of feminist leaders for LGBTQ2IA rights. The experience of systemic oppression based on some aspect of their own identity leads them to compassionate acts for others experiencing parallel oppression. Similar to the mands from the preschool children on behalf of their peers (Byers, 2016), the feeling (i.e., empathy) turns into compassionate action (i.e., non-violent protest, legislative change). Compassionate activism is the display of a set of broad behaviors (i.e. a generalized repertoire) in the service of others. Behavior analysts can learn from previous social justice groups and activists and imitate their consistent and committed action towards equity for all marginalized groups.

Social justice activists have long revealed their work as compassionate acts, showing care for others who are not direct members of their family or immediate network. The Black Panther Party (BPP), was founded in 1966 as a response to the assassination of freedom fighter Malcolm X and the murder of an unarmed Black teenager, Matthew Johnson, by the San Francisco Police Department (Duncan, 2018; History.com, 2017). Neither BPP founder, Huey P. Newton or Bobby Seale, experienced these events personally, but their prior learning histories of suffering injustices led them to start a movement of compassion in the service of all oppressed people. The BPP has been labeled as a violent Black extremist organization (Desert Sun, 1969), yet, their work anchors the group as a community- and service-based organization. The BPP fought against injustices of state-sanctioned violence, but also behaved as servant leaders to their community (Pope & Flanigan, 2013) by developing "Survival Programs" and a 10-Point Program that included assistance for the elderly, medically fragile, and those in low-income households (Duncan, 2018). The Panther's compassion towards others was further evidenced through concerted efforts with Puerto Ricans and Dominicans.

Collective grassroots action by Puerto Rican organizers led to the formation of the Young Lords Organization (Ogbar, 2006). From their inception, compassion for others served as the fabric of their movement (Jeffries, 2003). The cold war, women's liberation, and Black freedom were all antecedents to the development of the Young Lords, with the Black Power Movement being the most prominent inspiration (Falion, 2012). The Young Lords worked on independence for Puerto Rico, which was specific to their community, but also targeted issues that impacted all oppressed groups (e.g., police brutality, health care, education, income inequality, and community gentrification). The Young Lords established a 13-point program and platform to achieve tangible outcomes for their communities by offering a breakfast program, childcare, and a poor people's housing project for low to moderate income families that was later rejected by the city of Chicago (1970).

The Young Patriot Organization (YPO), a group of mostly Southern whites who worked to respond to the needs of people in Chicago, was also an activist organization. They created breakfast programs and healthcare clinics (Turner, 1972), organized tenet unions (Moser, 2017), and at times shielded Black men from being subjected and detained by police (Strano, 2009). They organized initially as poor whites fighting against capitalism, but later coordinated actions with leaders of the BPP, establishing their own 11-point plan (n.d.). The YPO found commonality with all groups based on class struggles and exclusion from the larger society and over the course of their activism, served as "actors not allies," for people of color (Sonnie & Tracy, 2012).

Respect, empathy, and compassion led the Young Lords, the BPP, and the YPO to create the first Rainbow Coalition (Jeffries, 2003) to educate others, create food programs and take political action. Together they yelled, "All power to the people!" (Sonnie & Tracy, 2012, p. 19). The work of these three organizations suggests that compassionate activism is not confined to one action, one group, or one issue. Compassionate activism took the form of service-related activities and boldly fighting for the civil rights of others suffering similar oppression. Through compassionate solidarity, they became a larger, more robust force than any could have been in isolation.

SOCIAL JUSTICE WITHOUT COMPASSION

Social Justice efforts that are not compassion-based are problematic because these efforts are controlled by the wrong reinforcers. Compassionate social justice actions should decrease harm to others or change systems that allowed for that harm. A true ally or compassionate social justice activist strives to alleviate the distress of those harmed (i.e., negative reinforcement for others) and their own empathetic distress (i.e., negative reinforcement for self). Saad (2020) gives examples of allyship as "standing up, even when you feel scared" and "transferring the benefits of your privilege to those who lack it" (Saad, 2020). If that is not the function of the allyship, it is performative rather than compassionate. Performative allyship may be automatically reinforced because the person can now think of themselves as "a good person" who is unlike "the bad oppressors" or may be socially positively reinforced by attention from others or a feeling of social belonging or connectedness with others. Unfortunately, these reinforcers may be substitutable for the relief of the oppressed (i.e., the person feels better about themselves and stops even if the social injustice persists). In addition, these reinforcers may be transient such that the reinforcers sustain low-effort behavior (e.g., posting on social media), but not meaningful high-effort behavior (e.g., active protest).

RECOMMENDATIONS FOR INDIVIDUAL AND GROUP COMPASSIONATE SOCIAL JUSTICE ACTIONS

We offer the following recommendations for those who wish to pursue compassionate actions in pursuit of social justice. The first recommendation addresses *individual* motivation, action and reflection. The second recommendation addresses the actions of *groups* in supporting the social justice efforts of their members.

Individual

Individuals pursuing social justice actions should operate with humility by consistently reflecting on the variables controlling their actions (e.g., negative reinforcement for others, social positive attention) (Bell, 2000). This reflection might allow you to identify if your actions are actually compassionate rather than performative throughout the social justice journey. Additionally, reflection on the specific actions may illustrate when your actions may be inadvertently causing immediate or delayed harm to those who are oppressed. Viewing your everyday actions as social justice actions will increase awareness of how your individual actions affect the lives of others and have the potential to reinforce oppressive conditions for marginalized groups. A person might move into an up and coming (i.e., gentrification in progress) neighborhood without realizing that their action may drive up the costs for current residents leading to displacement. An organization might hire a person of color or a trans-gender individual as part of an inclusion and diversity movement without recognizing the effort and burden placed on that person if they have to singularly "represent diversity" in the organization.

Individuals should also develop strategies for strengthening and maintaining their own compassionate social justice repertoires, particularly important when your repertoires are new. Without a plan for sustainable action, good intentions and compassion may be insufficient to maintain social justice actions over time. Compassionate social justice actions are effortful and can lead to what is termed "compassion fatigue." Recruit communities who share your reinforcers to support and reinforce your social justice efforts. Avoid interactions and confrontations with those who would actively, if not intentionally, punish your social justice actions. Pay attention to times when energy is low and feelings of apathy are present (i.e., I no longer have the energy to empathize so I cease to care or even attend to the injustice). Allies who don't directly suffer the oppression can retreat from the movement with few consequences, while those who are oppressed cannot. Layla Saad, anti-racism educator, describes apathy as just as dangerous as intentional acts of oppression (Saad, 2020). When apathy creeps in, name the values that are consistent with your social justice efforts and how your actions support those values describing the long-term social justice objectives as the goal (e.g., I protest against this action so that people of color will be safe from police violence). This description may increase the likelihood of persistent actions when reinforcers are exceptionally distant and experienced by the next generation. Layla Saad (2020), describes her motivation for social justice actions as "a passionate desire to become a good ancestor" (p. 3). Many social justice actions focus on "leaving the world a better place than you have found it" so that there is change and "new possibilities for those who will come after" (p. 3).

Group

Groups that want to support social change initiatives and advance social justice should intentionally view their group as a community of practice. Communities of practice are groups of individuals that share a common mission and a commitment to learning to advance that mission (Wenger & Snyder, 2000). The group should articulate its values (e.g., cultural humility, compassion) and ensure those values are respected by others in the group (LeBlanc et al., 2020). Regardless of the other purposes of the group (e.g., supporting behavior analytic practice), there should be an explicit statement of a purpose to provide support, guidance, perspective, encouragement, and sustaining reinforcement for the social justice efforts of the group members.

A second recommendation is particularly relevant to groups that are not directly disadvantaged by the oppression targeted in their social justice efforts (e.g., white allies to BLM). Those who do not directly experience oppression can feel empathy and can take compassionate action to help with the injustice. However, compassion and empathy do not ensure understanding of the specifics of the experiences of that group. Without consistent efforts to learn from members of the group that have experienced injustice, allies are likely to engage in naive, misguided actions that can increase burden for their social justice partners. Build meaningful relationships and actively seek knowledge and experiences with partner groups in a way that is humble and avoids voyeurism (i.e., observing cultures without actually participating in a caring, committed way).

SUMMARY AND CONCLUSIONS

We encourage behavior analysts to examine the role of compassion in ongoing social justice efforts and to actively take compassionate action to support marginalized groups in society. Perspective taking skills allow us to feel empathy for the plight of others which is the motivation for compassionate action designed to alleviate the suffering of those oppressed by people in positions of social power. Throughout the history of social justice efforts, there is evidence that compassion for others strengthens the movements and leads to expansion of the social change initiatives for many different groups. It is possible to understand and even investigate the contingencies, values, and communities that support compassionate action in the context of social justice issues. We encourage our fellow behavior analysts to value meaningful social justice efforts as compassionate actions consistent with our behavior analytic values and worldview of using the science of human behavior to improve the human condition and minimize coercion (Sidman, 1989; Skinner, 1948).

REFERENCES

Ascher, B. L. (2016). On compassion. In S. Cohen, *50 Essays: A Portable Anthology* (5th ed. pp. 40–43). Bedford.

Bell, D. A. (2002). *Ethical ambition: Living a life of meaning and worth.* Bloomsbury.

Black Panthers. (1966, October 15). Black Panthers ten-point program. Marxists Internet Archive. https://www.marxists.org/history/usa/workers/black-panthers/1966/10/15.htm

Black Panther Greatest Threat to U.S. Security. California Digital Newspaper Collection. (1969). https://cdnc.ucr.edu/cgi-bin/cdnc?a=d.

The Black Panther Party: Challenging police and promoting social change. (2020, August 23). National Museum of African American History and Culture. https://nmaahc.si.edu/blog-post/black-panther-party-challenging-police-and-promoting-social-change

Byers, E. M. (2016). *An analysis of the relation between preschool children's attention to peers and the presence of the behavioral developmental cusp for learning by observation* (Doctoral dissertation). Teachers College.

DeBernardis, G. M., Hayes, L. J., & Fryling, M. J. (2014). Perspective taking as a continuum. *The Psychological Record, 64*(1), 123–131. https://doi.org/10.1007/s40732-014-0008-0

Duncan, G. A. (2018). Black Panther Party. *Encyclopædia Britannica.*

Dunkel-Jackson, S. M., & Dixon, S. S. (2016). Self-control as generalized operant behavior by adults with autism spectrum disorder. *Journal of Applied Behavior Analysis, 49*(3), 705–710. https://doi.org/10.1002/jaba.315

Falion, A. (2012). Pa'lante: The direct action campaigns of the Young Lords Party. https://www.marxists.org/history/erol/ncm-1/direct-action.pdf.

History.com Editors. (2018, August 21). *Black Panthers.* History. https://www.history.com/topics/civil-rights-movement/black-panthers

Iannotti, R. (1985). Naturalistic and structured assessments of prosocial behavior in preschool children: The influence of empathy and perspective taking. *Journal of Developmental Psychology, 21* (1), 46–55. https://doi.org/10.1037/0012-1649.21.1.46

Jeffries, J. (2003). From gang-bangers to urban revolutionaries: *Illinois History,* 264–280. https://doi.org/10.5406/j.ctv80cbdt.16

LeBlanc, L. A., Morris, C., Coates, A., Daneshvar, S., Charlop-Christy, M. H., & Lancaster, B. M. (2003). Teaching perspective-taking skills to children with autism. *Journal of Applied Behavior Analysis, 36*, 253–257. https://doi.org/10.1901/jaba.2003.36-253

LeBlanc, L. A., Sellers, T. P., & Ala'i, S. (2020). *Building and sustaining meaningful relationships as a supervisor and mentor.* Sloan.

Lown, B. A., & McIntosh, S. (2020, August 23). *The Black Panther Party: Challenging police and promoting social change.* National Museum of African American History and Culture. https://nmaahc.si.edu/blog-post/black-panther-party-challenging-police-and-promoting-social-change

Lown, B. A., McIntosh, S., McGuinn, K., Aschenbrener, C., DeWitt, B. B., Chou, C., Durrah, H., Irons, M., & Moser, R. (2017). *Young Patriots, Black Panthers and the Rainbow Coalition.* CounterPunch.org. https://www.counterpunch.org/2017/11/22/young-patriots-black-panthers-and-the-rainbow-coalition/.

Ogbar, J. (2006). Puerto Rico en mi corazón: The Young Lords, Black Power and Puerto Rican nationalism in the U.S., 1966–1972 [Review of Puerto Rico en mi corazón: The Young Lords, Black Power and Puerto Rican nationalism in the U.S.,1966–1972]. XVIII (1), 148–169. The City University of New York. https://marxists.catbull.com/history/erol/ncm-1/corazon.pdf

Pope, R. J., & Flanigan, S. T. (2013). Revolution for breakfast: Intersections of activism, service, and violence in the Black Panther Party's community service programs. *Social Justice Research, 26*(4), 445–470.

Public Broadcasting Service. *A Huey P. Newton Story – Actions – Survival Programs.* PBS. https://www.pbs.org/hueypnewton/actions/actions_survival.html.

Saad, L. F. (2020). *Me and white supremacy: Combat racism, change the world, and become a good Ancestor.* Sourcebooks.

Sidman, M. (1989). *Coercion and its fallout.* Authors cooperative.

Sigman, M., & Capps, L. (1997). *Children with autism: A developmental perspective.* Harvard University Press.

Skinner, B. F. (1948). *Walden Two.* Hackett.

Sonnie, A., & Tracy, J. (2012). Hillbilly nationalists, urban race rebels and black power: Community organizing in radical times. *The Sixties, 5*(2), 251–254. https://doi.org/10.1080/17541328.2012.686028

Taylor, B. A., LeBlanc, L. A., & Nosik, M. R. (2019). Compassionate care in behavior analytic treatment: Can outcomes be enhanced by attending to relationships with caregivers?. *Behavior Analysis in Practice, 12*(3), 654–666. https://doi.org/10.1007/s40617-018-00289-3

Turner, I. R. (1972). Free health centers: A new concept? *American Journal of Public Health, 62*(10), 1348–1353. https://doi.org/10.2105/ajph.62.10.1348

Vilardaga, R. (2009). A relational frame theory account of empathy. *International Journal of Behavioral Consultation and Therapy, 5*(2), 178–184.

Viray, S. & Nash, R. J. (2014). Taming the madvocate within: Social justice meets social compassion. *About Campus: Enriching the Student Learning Experience, 19*(5), 20–27. https://doi.org/10.1002/abc.21170

Wenger, E. C., & Snyder, W. M. (2000). Communities of practice: The organizational frontier. *Harvard Business Review, 78*(1), 139–146.

10

CONNECTEDNESS

Lessons in Cultural Humility, Racial Capitalism,
Racial Colorblindness, Implicit Bias, and Colorism

Miguel E. Gallardo

A BRIEF NOTE ABOUT WHERE I AM POSITIONED IN THESE DISCUSSIONS

Before I express my thoughts, and those of others, in this brief chapter on what cultural humility means to me in the midst of one of the most divisive times in the history of the United States, I want to situate myself for the reader. Everything is culture bound, and nothing is value free. I am influenced by the many social and cultural identities that make up who I am as a human being, how I see the world, and how I talk about what I experience and feel. It is important that the reader understand that my thoughts are value-laden and immersed within my middle-class, lighter-skinned, heterosexual, cisgender, Catholic, Mexican American identities, to name a few. Other identities include being an oppressor, being oppressed, being a husband, a father, a son, a brother, a psychologist, and being privileged in more ways today than I have ever been in my life. This all matters because there are many ways to talk about compassion, social justice, and cultural humility. While there may be many avenues to talk about these human experiences and values, we all appear to be headed in the same direction . . . at least that is my hope. My hope is that we are all trying to work towards being more humanizing towards others. At this moment in time, we are dehumanizing the most vulnerable in our society, for the profit and benefit of few.

WHAT DOES IT MEAN TO BE HUMAN?

As I reflected on the ideas of compassion and social justice, I was struck by how often these two values often end up on different ends of the humanity spectrum, and not always in the same conversation. Unfortunately, it has become akin to speaking out of both sides of our mouths. There has never been a more important time in our history, or at least in my lifetime, when affirming our humanity and connectedness to one another, is paramount to our very existence and future. Simultaneously, there has never been a more salient time in our history when the individualistic tenets that underlay the values espoused here in the United States, have never been more salient.

As I sit and write this brief chapter, we are in the middle of two pandemics, with possibly a third one on its way – the 2020 election. The first, COVID-19, and the second, what some have called a "racism pandemic," have highlighted the racial and ethnic disparities that permeate across every system in the United States, and to a large extent, across the world. Despite evidence to support the existence of racial and ethnic disparities, many of our national leaders have continued to deny the inequitable distribution of resources, access to adequate healthcare, and the denial of other basic necessities, human needs, that many Black, Indigenous, People of Color (BIPOC) search for on a daily basis. During this time, I continue to hear, "We are in this together," yet, it feels like we are drifting farther and farther apart from one another.

The current realities in the United States reflects times in our history that many have tried to move beyond, but not forget, for more just and equitable realities. In my opinion, we are seeing division and divisiveness that mirrors our past. Junger (2014) argues that today we believe we no longer need one another for our survival. As a result, he argues that we have lost a sense of who we are. Whether we are in the middle of pandemics or whether life is back to "normal," there is value in seeing our interconnectedness and interdependence with one another. In the midst of all this, I was reminded of the following quote, "The moral test of a society, or the measure of a society, is based on how it treats its most vulnerable members." Variations of this quote have been attributed to Vice President Hubert Humphrey, Mahatma Gandhi, and Pearl Buck. We are failing our moral test as a society. Additionally, we are also very ahistorical in the United States, and as a result, we continue to repeat our past, which has always been layered with the exploitation of many to the benefit of few.

Aristotle purported that all humans are political animals. There are many interpretations of this statement, but Guremen (2018) interprets this statement to mean, "Human beings need to communicate their sentiments of justice, because they need a multiplicity of communities for a self-sufficient life" (p. 180). In essence, we are social beings and socially embedded in multiple contexts. Aristotle did not intend to mean political in the sense of who is red, blue, conservative, liberal, but to state that the contexts in which we find ourselves influences how we see ourselves, others, and the world. To pretend that we can conveniently close our eyes to the injustice or the aspects of the world around us that is often too painful to acknowledge, that which we do not agree with, or do not understand, is an injustice in and of itself. We have a voice to express our sentiments of what is just and that which is unjust. This includes our roles as service providers. Holding our degrees in one hand and the local newspaper feed in the other, are part and parcel to our work. We have become accustomed to keeping our social commitments optional and our clinical work "safely neutral."

Doherty (2013) states that the task of the mental health provider is to be citizen-therapists. Doherty states, "all clinical problems treated by therapists are thoroughly interconnected with larger public issues, but the public dimensions of psychological problems, and the civic action that could be appropriate to take, don't appear in our treatment manuals" (p. 17). If this is true, and I believe it is, then our work must evolve and include the tenets of human rights beyond what we can see in our "offices." Each client and family bring with them the lived experiences in their lives that must be front and center if we are to truly create better outcomes for our clients. We must make synonymous the concept of social justice with human rights for all.

RACIAL CAPITALISM

Laster Pirtle (2020) states that "Racial capitalism has been the fundamental cause of disease in the world . . ." (p. 1). Robinson (1983) coined the term racial capitalism to illustrate the process of developing social and economic value from a person of a different racial identity. While Robinson stated that any person of any race can engage in racial capitalism, what we have seen throughout our history is a system of economic gain for primarily White and lighter-skinned individuals at the expense and inequality for many BIPOC. Our system of slavery in the United States in founded upon racial capitalism, as is our history of violence, including genocide, Japanese internment camps, anti-immigrant sentiments, and mass incarceration of primarily black and brown communities, to name a few. Racial capitalism impacts access to resources. Those of us with higher SES have access to more accurate knowledge, financial resources, and advantageous social connections/relationships, all of which alleviate the costs of inequitable systems.

Interventions designed to lessen societal inequities, cannot fully get rid of the relationship between racism, poverty, and health because they are replaced by other processes like gentrification and raises in rent, unregulated stores in barrios (neighborhoods), which all leads to instability and homelessness. Racism restricts our freedom. Unfreedoms, or the lack of control BIPOC have over our lives in the United States, whether it be attributed to historical systems of slavery or mass incarceration today, puts us at heighted risks for mental and physical health problems (Alexander, 2020; Phelan & Link, 2018). Racialized capitalist pursuits have left behind the poor, people of color, devaluing our lives so much so that we are dying at disproportionate rates of our populations in society. I am reminded of W.E.B. Du Bois statement, "If there is anybody in this land who thoroughly believes that the meek shall inherit the earth, they have not often let their presence be known" (Hunter, 2005). It is traumatizing to BIPOC, and if our work as service providers is not inclusive of these experiences, then our interventions are limited and may even perpetuate more oppressive practices and unjust behaviors.

DEHUMANIZATION AND TRAUMA . . . THREE SIMPLE WORDS

The dehumanization of BIPOC in the United States is as overt and salient today as it ever has been. Many are having their "awakening" moment through the most recent Black Lives Matter (BLM) movement – three simple words, which many continue to negate and silence. I often wonder if this is a retake or return to what has been, or a critical tipping point for something different moving forward. When the dust settles, where will we be in our treatment of our most vulnerable? Burstow (2003), states, "oppressed people are routinely worn down by the insidious trauma involved in day after day living in a sexist, racist, classist, homophobic, and ableist society . . . hearing racist innuendoes even from one's White's allies" (p. 1296). Research also has demonstrated that the frequency of racial discrimination has been found to predict a posttraumatic stress disorder (PTSD) diagnosis among African Americans and Latinos (Sibrava et al., 2019).

Ethno-racial trauma has been defined as "individual and/or collective psychological distress and fear of danger that results from experiencing or witnessing discrimination, threats of harm, violence, and intimidation directed at ethno-racial devalued groups. This form of trauma stems from a legacy of oppressive laws, policies, and practices" (Chavez-Dueñas, Adames, Perez-Chavez, & Salas, 2019, p. 49). Furthermore, Helms, Nicolas, and Green (2010) categorize police violence against racial and ethnic marginalized persons as a *"direct cataclysmic racial and cultural event"* (p. 68).

These events can range from witnessing police violence against another person and racial microaggressions such as being called a racial slur by a police officer to threat of harm, physical assault, or even murder. As I communicate my thoughts on this, it is important to note that this is not an either/or discussion, this is a both/and narrative. Too often we assume that to point out one critical area of concern, also implies the minimization or denial of the other. We do not do a very good job, as humans, of holding two potentially opposing positions simultaneously. Not all police officers are bad people. Just like not all black individuals are criminals. However, to negate the existence of inequitable and unjust treatment of Black and brown communities within our healthcare and criminal justice systems, further oppresses and dehumanizes our very existence. While many argue that the concept of race does not exist and that we are all human, our lives as humans do not unfold in the same manner. The color of one's skin absolutely does matter and the social implications of race are as present today as they ever have been.

COLOR-BLIND RACIAL IDEOLOGY (CBRI)

For many, the solution to addressing racial issues is to not discuss them. The concept of Color-Blind Racial Ideology (CBRI) Neville, Gallardo, and Sue (2015), is that all people are fundamentally the same, and thus we should ignore racial differences and treat everyone as an individual. Some individuals may truly believe that not discussing race advances racial harmony and equality, by preventing people from being judged by their race (Goff et al., 2013). For others, color-blindness may be a way to ignore racial inequalities and thus preserve the status quo to their own benefit (Saguy et al., 2008). And for others, it is a way to avoid any mention of race to ensure that they do not inadvertently say something offensive and risk being labeled a racist (Apfelbaum, Sommers, et al. 2008). The latter is the one that is most often cited in qualitative interactions with others.

What we know from research is that the more one endorses a CBRI perspective, the more one actually engages in more racially insensitive behavior and appears less friendly (Apfelbaum, Pauker et al., 2008). We need to have these discussions in our classrooms, workplaces, with our colleagues, with our family and friends, and with our clients. When we continue to have many of the same conversations today that we were having 20–30 years ago, and continuing to deal with the same systemic issues, something needs to change.

CULTURAL HUMILITY . . . A HUMAN EXPERIENCE MORE THAN AN ACADEMIC ONE

While the literature on cultural humility has grown over the last two decades (Fisher-Borne et al., 2015; Gallardo, 2013; Gallardo, in press; Mosher et al., 2017; Tervalon & Murray-Garcia, 1998), there are still debates and dialogues about terminology and meaning. Tervalon and Murray-Garcia (1998) first defined cultural humility as a lifelong process of self-reflection, self-critique, continual assessment of power imbalances and developing mutually respectful relationships and partnerships.

More recently, Mosher, Hook, Farrell, Watkins, and Davis (2017) defined cultural humility as (a) a lifelong motivation to learn from others, (b) critical self-examination of cultural awareness, (c) interpersonal respect, (d) developing mutual partnerships that address power imbalances, and (e) an other-oriented stance open to new cultural information. Fisher-Borne, Montana Cain, and Martin (2015) state,

> The major criticisms of cultural competency frameworks include: (a) the focus on comfort with 'others' framed as self-awareness; (b) the use of 'culture' as a proxy for minority racial/ethnic group identity; (c) the emphasis on attempting to 'know' and become 'competent' in understanding another's culture or cultures; and (d) the lack of a transformative social justice agenda that addresses and challenges social inequalities.
>
> (p. 169)

Hindsight is always 20/20. In reflecting on our initial path towards creating just outcomes, we unintentionally may have put the cart before the horse. An emphasis of our cultural competency models has been on the acquisition of knowledge to demonstrate one's ability to understand and implement skills while working with those culturally different from oneself. It has served us well and it has served a purpose for us, but it has also, unintentionally, created unjust outcomes for many. Good well-intentioned providers have unintentionally violated those they intended to serve under the guise of cultural knowledge and skills, while basing their interventions on racial and ethnic variables only.

Cultural humility is about understanding that, regardless of who we are and where we come from, we are all working together. We need to be cautious about ascribing cultural credibility to folks of color simply because they are "of color," and we should not always assume White individuals do not understand. It is, and always has been, about consciousness, not just color. As an example, the BLM movement has highlighted colorism in my own Latinx communities, or the preference for lighter-skinned Latinx individuals. Light-skin preference has been common practice in the Black, indigenous, and other communities of color for generations.

In my own Mexican American communities, those of us with lighter skin, on average, earn more money, are enrolled in the education system for longer periods of time, and live in more diverse neighborhoods than do our darker skinned family members. The BLM movement has brought to light our own anti-black sentiments in very painful ways. My comments on the work that we as BIPOC need to do, does not in any way minimize or negate the work that our White colleagues, friends, and family need to continue to do. In fact, the notion of colorism in my own communities is a direct effect of colonization and White-body supremacist ideologies.

Colorism is not the same as racism. When Black and brown communities are killing one another, we do not benefit, the already existing power structures in society benefit and remain intact. Embedded in racism are power and privilege, neither of which BIPOC have in our current social structures. Cultural humility is not about shaming people, but developing empathy for the other. It is about seeing our interconnectedness to one another and seeing every encounter as an encounter with knowledge and opportunities for personal and professional growth.

When I talk and write about cultural humility, I am often responded to by, "You are not going to change the neo-Nazi, or white supremist's perspectives." I don't totally disagree with this sentiment. However, I want to change the good well-intentioned White individual who does not believe they are racist and who endorses racial color-blindness as a strategy for dealing with these challenging issues. This is possible. I also want BIPOC communities to not assume that we do not have a role to play in creating a more just and peaceful society. We all have blind spots and have come to narrowly define aspects of our world in different ways for different reasons.

IMPLICIT BIAS

Cornel West states, "You have to die before you can live." If we are truly engaging in self-analysis, while also assuming that we are either working for or against the institutional and systemic injustices in society, regardless of where we are situated, then we also understand we have biases. Implicit biases arise through overlearned associations (Kawakami et al., 2000), which can be rooted in early childhood socialization, repeated personal experience, widespread media exposure, or cultural representations of others. Implicit bias often operates at a level below conscious awareness and without intentional control. Research finds that implicit biases are automatically activated for a majority of Americans regardless of age, socioeconomic status, and political orientation (Blair et al., 2013).

Why does this matter? Regardless of our ethnic or racial background, we have biases. We are as influenced by what we are not told as much by what we are told. A critical first step in working towards being culturally humble service providers is acknowledging where we are positioned and situated within these conversations. I did not come out of my mother's womb culturally humble. I have to work as much as the next person to ensure that I do not further oppress. While I still unintentionally oppress at times, I also need to recognize when I do, and repair the rupture, whether it be within my personal life, or within my professional work with colleagues and clients.

WHAT IS OUR ROLE IN HELPING OTHERS?

Viray and Nash (2014) state that to experience the suffering of others and then try hard to lessen that suffering, is the most salient social justice action of all. If there is an authentic and genuine commitment to walking alongside our clients, there is also an acknowledgement that our knowledge and skill sets are limited. We should always find out what is right with our clients and families as a first step in our work. Regardless of where clients come from, what their circumstances are, or the lack of resources they have at their disposal, we must engage in a conversation about the assets that they bring to the encounter with us. Their humanity is tied to ours. Our humanity is tied to theirs.

It is not enough to acknowledge injustice. A mere acknowledgement does not change us or those who we work with. It is important to center our continued self-analysis on personal and professional development and to understand that examining and actively processing our different viewpoints and lived experiences can be empowering. We also need to accept disagreement and challenges as part of our work and growth. It is not always going to look pretty and feel good.

We also need to be aware of our own triggers and attempt to do what Taylor and Fiske (1984) called being Cognitive Misers, or the tendency to rely on simple and time efficient strategies to process new information. This can include assigning new information to already existing categories that are easy for us to process mentally. When we are presented with new information that may be hard for us to hear, we may disagree with, or do not understand, we may employ our cognitive miser strategies. If these strategies are activated, we are no longer in the "space" with our clients and families. We are safely keeping ourselves at a distance and therefore, may be missing important information that might be helpful in our work. What are your cognitive miser strategies? Cognitive miser strategies result in a tendency to not stray far from already established beliefs when considering new information an awareness of our "go to" strategies is critical.

A final thought. In his book, *Just Mercy*, Stevenson (2015), recalls each time he would see his grandmother, she would hug him and pull him in close and tell him,

"You can't understand most of the important things from a distance, Bryan. You have to get close." (p. 14). As you finish reading this chapter, ask yourself, what issues, communities, problems, are you keeping at a safe distance? What do you need to lean into and get closer to? Carlson (2013) states, our new charge must be to "comfort the afflicted and afflict the comfortable" (p. 284). I could not agree more.

REFERENCES

Alexander, M. (2020). *The new Jim Crow: Mass incarceration in the age of colorblindness* (10th ed.). The New Press.

Apfelbaum, E. P., Pauker, K., Ambady, N., Sommers, S. R., & Norton, M. I. (2008). Learning (not) to talk about race: When older children underperform in social categorization. *Developmental Psychology, 44*(5), 1513–1518. https://doi.org/10.1037/a0012835

Apfelbaum, E. P., Sommers, S. R., & Norton, M. I. (2008). Seeing race and seeming racist? Evaluating strategic colorblindness in social interaction. *Journal of Personality and Social Psychology, 95*(4), 918–932.

Blair, I. V., Steiner, J. F., Fairclough, D. L., Hanratty, R., Price, D. W., Hirsh, H. K., Wright, L. A., Bronsert, M., Karimkhani, E., Magid, D. J., & Havranek, E. P. (2013). Clinicians' implicit ethnic/racial bias and perceptions of care among Black and Latino patients. *Annals of Family Medicine, 11*(1), 43–52.

Burstow, B. (2003). Towards a radical understanding of trauma and trauma work. *Violence Against Women, 9*(11), 1293–1317.

Carlson, J. (2013). A life devoted to service. In J. A.Kottler, M. Englar-Carlson, & J. Carlson (Eds.), *Helping beyond the 50-minute hour: Therapists involved in meaningful social Action.* (pp. 277–287). Routledge Press

Chavez-Dueñas, N. Y., Adames, H. Y., Perez-Chavez, J. G., & Salas, S. P. (2019). Healing ethno-racial trauma in Latinx immigrant communities: Cultivating hope, resistance, and action. *American Psychologist, 74*, 49–62.

Doherty, W. J. (2013). The citizen-therapist and social change. In J. A. Kottler, M. Englar-Carlson, & J. Carlson (Eds.), *Helping beyond the 50-minute hour: Therapists involved in meaningful social action* (pp. 15–25). Routledge Press.

Fisher-Borne, M., Montana Cain, J., & Martin, S. L. (2015) From mastery to accountability: Cultural humility as an alternative to cultural competence. *Social Work Education, 34*(2), 165–181.

Fiske, S. T., & Taylor, S. E. (1984). *Social cognition: Topics and social psychology.* McGraw- Hill Ryerson.

Gallardo, M. E. (Ed.). (2013). *Developing cultural humility: Embracing race, privilege and power.* Sage Publications.

Gallardo, M. E. (Ed.). (in press). *Developing cultural humility: Embracing race, privilege and power* (2nd ed.). Cognella Press.

Goff, P. A., Jackson, M. C., Nichols, A. H., & Di Leone, B. A. (2013). Anything but race: Avoiding racial discourse to avoid hurting you or me. *Psychology, 4*(3), 335–339.

Guremen, R. (2018). In what sense exactly are human being more political according to Aristotle? *Philosophy and Society, 29*(2), 153–316.

Helms, J. E., Nicolas, G., & Green, C. E. (2010). Racism and ethnoviolence as trauma: Enhancing professional training. *Traumatology, 16*(4), 53–62.

Hunter, M. (2005). *Race, gender, and the politics of skin tone.* Routledge.

Junger, S. (2014). *Tribe: On homecoming and belonging.* Twelve.

Kawakami, K., Dovidio, J. F., Moll, J., Hermsen, S., & Russin, A. (2000). Just say no (to stereotyping): Effects of training in the negation of stereotypic associations on stereotype activation. *Journal of Personality and Social Psychology, 78*(5), 871–888.

Laster Pirtle, W. N. (2020). Racial capitalism: A fundamental cause of novel coronavirus (COVID-19) pandemic in the United States. *Health Education and Behavior*, 1–5.

Mosher, D. K., Hook, J. N., Captari, L. E., Davis, D. E., DeBlaere, C., & Owen, J. (2017). Cultural humility: A therapeutic framework for engaging diverse clients. *Practice Innovations, 2*(4), 221–233.

Neville, H. A., Gallardo, M. E., & Sue, D. W. (2015). *What does it mean to be color-blind? Manifestation, dynamics, and impact.* American Psychological Association.

Phelan, J. C., & Link, B. G. (2015). Is racism a fundamental cause of inequalities in health? *Annual Review of Sociology, 41*, 311–330.

Robinson, C. J. (1983). *Black Marxism: The making of the black radical tradition.* Zed Books.

Saguy, T., Dovidio, J. F., & Pratto, F. (2008). Beyond contact: Intergroup contact in the context of power relations. *Personality and Social Psychology Bulletin, 34*(3), 432–445.

Sibrava, N. J., Bjornsson, A. S., Pérez Benítez, A. I., Moitra, E., Weisberg, R. B., & Keller, M. B. (2019). Posttraumatic stress disorder in African American and Latinx adults: Clinical course and the role of racial and ethnic discrimination. *American Psychologist, 74*, 101–116.

Stevenson, B. (2015). *Just mercy: A story of justice and redemption*. Scribe Publications.

Tervalon, M. & Murray-Garcia, J. (1998). Cultural humility versus cultural competence: A critical distinction in defining physician training outcomes in multicultural education. *Journal of Health Care for the Poor and Underserved, 9*(2), 117–125.

Viray, S., & Nash, R. J. (2014). Taming the madvocate within: Social justice meets social compassion. *About Campus, 19*(5), 20–27.

11

CORRUPTION

An Integrity Violation Examined from a Behavior Analytic Perspective

Tete Kobla Agbota

INTRODUCTION

Corruption is one of the most critical social problems of the 21st century. The United Nations Convention against Corruption (2003) defines corruption as the abuse of entrusted power or responsibility for personal or organizational gain at the expense of one's social organization. The visible by-products of corruption are: bribing, nepotism, cronyism, patronage, fraud and theft, conflict of interest, misuse and manipulation of information, waste and abuse of resources due to non-compliance of organizational standards and private life misconduct which harms the public's trust in the organization (Huberts et al., 2006). According to the World Bank, businesses and individuals pay over $1 trillion in bribes every year and this practice is persistent despite the fight against bribery (OECD, 2014). This chapter intends to enhance our understanding of corruption by providing: (i) a behavior analytic definition, (ii) examine corruption as an avoidance behavior and (iii) present possible interventions. We offer an operant analysis of corruption, an "explanatory mechanism linking behaviors, antecedents, and consequences to a dynamic continuum that constitutes an organism's history" (Marr, 1997, p. 155). Corruption is a subject matter studied by diverse academic disciplines that offer different theories to explore the phenomenon and each discipline has its conceptual tools. In the first section of this chapter, we present the common definition of corruption and how some social science theories explain corrupt behavior. In the second section, we examine from a behavior analytic perspective, the definition of corruption by using operant and culturant theoretical framework; look at corruption as a social problem and within an ethical dimension. Furthermore, we present the finding of two studies that analyzed corruption as an avoidance behavior while providing examples of possible interventions. We see how Rwanda tackled corruption through several administrative reforms and through the Itorero Civic Education Program to shape the integrity of its population. We end this chapter by calling behavior analysts to devote some of their attention to corruption.

WHAT IS CORRUPTION?

Corruption is often denoted as grand or petty; the distinguishing features are: (i) whether the amount involved in the transaction is small or large, (ii) how often it takes place, and (iii) whether the positions occupied by the officials involved are elective or appointive positions and (iv) whether they are junior or senior officials (Pedersen & Johannsen, 2005).

Grand or political corruption takes place at the policy formulation end of politics, where politicians and senior bureaucrats interact with private sector actors or representatives of foreign governments on big-ticket items like the construction of roads, building of hospitals, purchasing of military equipment, issuance of licenses for fisheries and the extractive industries (Vicente, 2010). Petty corruption also known as administrative corruption, tends to be associated with street-level bureaucrats or junior officers and takes place during the exercising of authority to enforce existing laws and regulations, the collection of taxes, issuance of licenses, allocation of benefits like subsidized housing, government scholarship and job inducement programs (Basu, 2011).

Explaining Corruption – Some Social Science Theories

For the sake of brevity, we group theories that social sciences offer to explain corruption as personality traits of individuals, institutional, and systemic. The personality trait perspective sees corruption as an attribute of human nature. Characteristically, a person may behave corruptly due to personal greed and other manners of self-aggrandizement; the bad or rotten apple theories claim that anyone can behave corruptly to advance their personal interests as exemplified by the neo-classical economic individual model of decision-making (de Graaf, 2007). Klitgaard (1988), asserts corruption is a crime of calculation and not passion and puts forward a formula: corruption equals monopoly plus discretion minus accountability (C=M+D-A). A corrupt individual will undertake a cost-benefit calculation with the following key decision elements: (i) the level of the bribe (i.e., the amount in question), (ii) the probability of detection, (iii) and the severity of the penalty if caught (Van Rijckeghem & Weder, 2001). Behavioral economics, a discipline at the intersection of psychology and economics, shows that logic or rationality alone (cost-benefit calculations) may not explain the decision to engage in or desist from a corrupt behavior, because decisions are sometimes also based on heuristics such as mental shortcuts and false intuitions (Kahneman, 2011). Mir Djawadi and Fahr (2013) suggest that some individuals engage in corruption because they underestimate the risk of being caught or overestimate their own ability to prevent the detection of their venal behaviors.

Irrespective of the type of corruption (petty or grand), the phenomenon denotes either a unit of individual behavior or a social behavior with similar functions, for example: (i) when a person or a corporate body offers a public officer a bribe to access licit or illicit services; (ii) when a public officer demands a payment as a condition to provide licit or illicit services; and (iii) when the interlocking behaviors of a few individuals make it possible for them to flout laws and regulations for personal or organizational gain. The interactions between the briber and bribee may be relatively permanent and recur with the same persons (such as in corrupt closed systems). However, it could be a one-time nonrecurring affair, for example, an encounter between a traffic police officer and a driver who has been unfortunately caught in traffic controls. Most social science theories in their quest to explain behavior start by probing events preceding the actions (antecedents). This approach differs from Skinner's theory of behavior, which begins with what occurs after an action contacts its environment (postcedent), and, as a corollary, the "contact makes available selective effect on later occurrences of equivalent actions, and as well as to their class of actions" (Vargas, 2017, p. 13).

A BEHAVIOR ANALYTIC PERSPECTIVE OF CORRUPTION

In this chapter, we offer an analysis of corruption that is grounded in the ontology and epistemology adopted by behavior analysts. It is an undertaking that investigates "concrete instances of the elements in the three-term contingency-stimuli and responses and, implicitly in many analyses, an organism that receives the stimuli, performs the responses, and has had a specific history of stimulation and responding" (Reese, 1993, p. 67). Goldstein and Pennypacker (1998) is possibly the first work to perform an operant analysis of corruption. However, this body of knowledge is growing gradually with publications (Agbota et al., 2017; Agbota et al., 2019; Dal

Ben et al., 2016; Fernandes et al., 2015) indicating that behavior analysis as a discipline can play a role in understanding one of the critical social issues of humanity.

A Behavior Analytic Definition of Corruption

A corrupt operant is defined as "an illegal verbal or non-verbal behavior of a person who flouts administrative rules and uses his or her control of reinforcers/punishers for personal or organizational gain in connection with the provision or receipt of goods and services"; at the expense of an entity (organization or society) (Agbota et al., 2017, p. 32).

The three-term contingency, as shown in Figure 11.1, has been employed to analyze petty corruption during the public officer-client (citizen) interface. The antecedents for the maladaptive behavior are denoted as *A* in Figure 11.1. These antecedent events such as (i) long case processing queues, (ii) the inability of public officers to locate files or missing files, (iii) arrogant and non-responsive public officers, (iv) excessive regulation, and (v) complicated case processing procedures involving several different officials. The dichotomy of open or

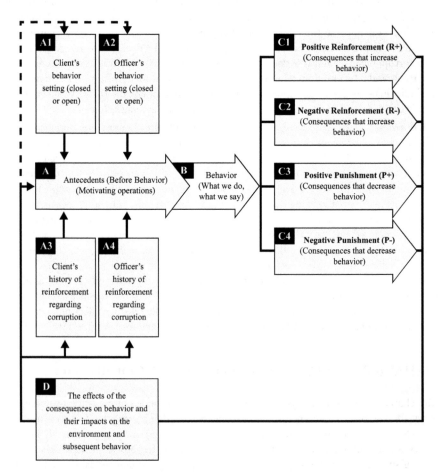

Figure 11.1 Explaining a corrupt behavior – the three-term contingency.
Source: (Agbota, Sandaker, Carvalho, & Couto, 2017, p. 32).

closed setting in *A1* and *A2* is introduced in the model to characterize the choice possibilities in the environment for both the client and the public officer (Foxall, 2010). An open setting gives a client an alternative course(s) of action when confronted with punishing environmental events. A choice among several institutions (agencies), for instance, may imply an open setting for a client. However, a closed setting may leave the client with no alternatives. There is evidence in the literature suggesting that some bureaucrats may create artificial shortages or queues (antecedents) and then exploit these situations to extort bribes (Aktan & Dokuzcesmeler, 2015). Thus, long queues may constitute motivating operations arranged by unscrupulous public officers to elicit a bribe paying behavior.

The asymmetric nature of the setting of public encounters may constitute antecedents for corrupt behavior. The setting of the client, *A1*, is often closed because officialdom has a monopoly when exercising public authority. Some people pay bribes to jump queues during public encounters rather than stay in the queue and fight for a corruption-free case processing. A bribe paying behavior, *B*, has possible consequences. The client is positively reinforced *C1* because they get an application processed more quickly. However, the payment of money could be seen as a punishment (positive or negative) denoted by *C3* and *C4*, respectively. The feedback loop signified by *D* indicates the effects of the consequences on behavior and their impacts on the environment and subsequent behavior. Whether or not bribery and corruption will become part of a behavioral repertoire depends on the individual's history of reinforcement shown as *A3* and *A4* concerning bribe payment or extortion during the officer-client interface.

Corruption as a group phenomenon or a social event is an illegal verbal or nonverbal transaction between at least two people during the provision of goods and services maintained by the joint product of the behavior of the individuals cooperating at the expense of the society. The aggregate product produced by flouting laid rules may or may not have a receiving system (Agbota et al., 2017). To analyze corruption as a group or social activity, we used the first term in the concept of metacontingency, "the recurring interlocking behavioral contingencies (IBCs) having an aggregate product (AP)" (Glenn et al., 2016, p. 13). In corrupt transactions, "the aggregate product itself may have the individual function of reinforcing the behavior of the participating people and of selecting the interlocking contingencies that result in the product" (Glenn et al., p. 16). Figure 11.2 portrays how police officers at road checkpoints in Ghana collaborate to extort a bribe from drivers (Agbota, 2019).

The first police officer's behavior functions as the antecedent for the second police officer's behavior; the second officer's behavior functions as the antecedent for the third officer (the senior officer among them). The third officer who should provide oversight is often part of the corrupt culturant, a unit of social behavior comprising the interlocking behavioral contingencies to produce the aggregate product. The above description is consistent with the assertion of Carvalho and Sandaker (2016) that group cooperation itself may be the object of selection as well as the aggregate product. In the scenario described above, the driver is not part of the culturant but rather the target for the extortion activities of the police.

Corruption Is an Ethical Issue

To sum up, corruption constitutes an integrity violation (Johnston, 2000), hence its conceptualization is an ethical issue (da Hora & Sampaio, 2019). It is condemned as morally

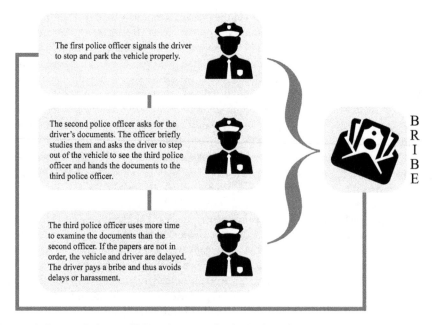

Figure 11.2 Corrupt Culturant (IBCs + Aggregate Product) where the aggregate product equals the selector.
Source: The figure is based on Glenn et al., 2016.

repugnant in many societies, and ethical standards of behavior are instituted by the society to promote the survival of its culture, because unethical behaviors have disruptive or detrimental effects on the culture of the social organization (Martin & Pear, 2014; Skinner, 1971). The ethical element is evident when the consequences of a corrupt operant for the individual and the culture (group/society) are juxtaposed. A corrupt behavior produces a short-term positive reinforcer (s) for the individual. However, the short-term reinforcers are attained at the expense of the long-term aversive consequences necessary for the survival of the culture (da Hora & Sampaio, 2019, p. 4). Such a cultural interpretation of integrity violation highlights the tension between consequences for the individual and the group. Thus, the attempt to explain corruption and find methods in fighting corruption, ought to bear in mind this tension. In the rest of the section, we examine the use of corruption language and intermediaries in corruption transactions.

Corruption as an Avoidance Behavior – The Use of Figurative Language

Corruption is illegal and universally shameful, however both petty and grand forms are persistent in the face of anti-corruption campaigns. Individuals engaged in corrupt practices tend to be discreet and they tend to use imprecise language. Lambsdorff (2002) observed that "Partners in the corrupt transaction may avoid precision to preserve the chances to find better excuses later" (p. 225). The use of corruption vocabulary (a figurative language of metaphors and euphemisms) is a common phenomenon associated with the demand and supply sides of corruption (Agbota et al., 2015). Their study revealed that corruption vocabulary is preferred because it does not offend or embarrass. Furthermore, the polysemous nature of the metaphors leaves open the possibility for both the one soliciting and the one offering a bribe to switch between the language of corruption and the ordinary meaning in the broader verbal community. For example, a public officer who asks for candy during a public encounter, may well be soliciting a bribe; on the other hand, it is not a criminal offense to ask someone for candy. Agbota and colleagues (2015), observed that the use of corruption vocabulary could be understood as a form of avoidance behavior and suggested that this may partially explain the widespread corrupt behavior in Ghana, where the study was conducted.

Corruption as an Avoidance Behavior – The Use of Middlemen in Corrupt Transactions

The use of intermediaries in corruption transactions is a common practice in corrupt transactions. The intermediaries are used to acquire different mandatory permits or certificates to operate businesses, often because of antecedent factors such as (i) lack of understanding of rules and regulations, (ii) to avoid wasting time in long case processing queues, and (iii) unresponsive public officials. Social science literature is replete with analyses of the phenomenon: Le Vine (1975), documents the existence of intermediaries known as *goro boys* in the interface between the Ghanaian bureaucracy and firms and individuals; Husted (1994) describes how *coyotes* help individuals obtain a driver's license in Mexico; Lambsdorff (2002) refers to *tramitadores* assisting individuals to navigate the bureaucracy in El Salvador; and Grisham (2005) describes the *Brazilian despachante* who also act as a bureaucratic facilitator. They are an integral part of Brazilian life. Social science literature often uses theories of social norms, reciprocity, and social network analysis to explain the use of intermediaries in corrupt social behaviors (Callahan, 2005; Jancsics, 2015). Even though the use of intermediaries in corruption transactions has behavioral traits, this theme has not been examined from a behavior analytic perspective.

An operant analysis of corruption reveals interesting findings other than being conduits between clients and public officers. The phenomenon is examined as avoidance behavior (Agbota, 2020). Refer to Figure 11.3 that depicts the antecedent, behavior and consequences of behavior for each of the briber, intermediary, and bribee.

Agbota (2020) shows how the use of intermediaries facilitates corruption not only by reducing the transaction costs but makes unethical behavior less aversive for bribers and bribees. Expressed in another way, intermediaries reduce conflict between corrupt behavior and ethical principles (cognitive dissonance) that may be experienced due to an unethical behavior condemned as morally repugnant. Another finding made by the study is that the intermediary, briber and bribee constitute a closed corrupt behavioral system. In this system, cooperation itself may be the object of selection as well as the aggregate product as shown in Figure 11.4. This avoidance system institutionalizes corruption and makes combating it a difficult task since people who are to provide oversight participate in the interlocking culturants that produce corrupt outcomes. Combating this form of corruption should focus more on methods to destabilize corrupt collusion.

Individual/Firm Antecedent	Intermediary Antecedent	Public Officer Antecedent
• Officialdom has a monopoly in the issuance of permits, which constitutes a closed setting for the individual/firm. It cannot procure licenses from any other private entities and must put up with the cumbersome mandatory procedures and red tape. Thus, individuals and firms spend a considerable amount of time in completing licensing procedures, including visiting multiple government offices at different locations and points in time.	• Seen as a One Shop-Stop • Administrative literate • Seen as having good rapport with public officers	• Has an open setting (officialdom has monopoly of case processing) • Lack of transparency, monitoring or evaluation because oversight participates in corrupt IBCs
	Behavior:	**Behavior:**
Behavior:	• Files applicant on behalf of a client • Does not offer bribe because of an agreed upon sum (fees) with public official	• Processes applicant in record time
• Uses intermediary • Pays bribe (speed money)		**Consequences:**
	Consequences:	• Avoid asking for bribe because of prearranged payable sums
Consequences:	• Monetary reward • Reputation as someone who has connections to clients • Good standing with public officers as someone who brings jobs • Avoids reporting public officer's corrupt behavior • May be recommended to other clients	• Earns extra money • Good standing with intermediary (a reliable and trustworthy network) • Fears not detection and subsequently punishment • Incentive to increase red tape, creating more need for intermediaries
• Procures permit in record time • Saves time and money • Avoids direct encounter with public officer • Loses money		

Figure 11.3 The use of an intermediary in corrupt transactions.

Process for Legal or Illegal Application in a Corrupt Institutional System

1. Applicant:

B1 Contracts Intermediary to file application and gives them money to cover transactional costs.

C1 Applicant has no contact with Public Officer, avoiding hassles and ethical costs associated with the application and processing; procures permit in record time.

C2 Applicant pays money.

2. Intermediary:

B1 Collects documents, contacts the Public Officer to procure permit.

C1 Receives extra income.

C2 Earns reputation with Applicant and Public Officer as someone who can deliver.

3. Public Officer:

B1 Does not request bribe from Intermediary since an agreed-upon sum is understood.

B2 Expedites action on legal or illegal application.

C1 Receives extra income.

C2 Incentivized to manipulate case processing time.

C3 Earns reliable reputation with Intermediary.

Figure 11.4 Corrupt culturant.
Note: Behavior = B; Consequence = C.

CONCLUDING REMARKS

Fighting Corruption – Interventions

One often gets the question, what is your solution to corruption? There is no one silver bullet for fighting corruption. Generally, anti-corruption efforts have been pursued along three trajectories: (i) repression and prevention with legal instruments, (ii) incentives such as omnibus wage increments, and (iii) public education (Johnston, 2000; Matukhno, 2016; Mutonyi, 2002). However, the solution depends on the unit of analysis: corrupt operant or corrupt culturant. Strategies to combat or minimize dishonest operant behavior at the individual level should target the specific behavior and the specific "decision point" the behavior is emitted. Both the use of corrupt languages and intermediaries are often due to (i) cumbersome rules and regulations, (ii) lack of timeliness or long case processing queues, and (iii) unresponsive public officials. The ensuing paragraphs show how Rwanda conducted its anti-corruption fight at the individual and cultural levels.

Rwanda was ranked the 121st corrupt among 163 countries in 2006, scoring 25 over 100 points in Transparency International's Corruption Perception Index (TI, 2007). However, in 2018 it was ranked the 48th out of 180 countries and scored 56 over 100 points (TI, 2018). Today, Rwanda is perceived as one of the most successful examples of fighting corruption. The antecedents of corrupt behavior, have been addressed with interventions like electronic or paperless processing of applications (prevent physical contact), timeliness in case processing – time guarantees, making application processes and procedures less cumbersome, legal avenues to fast track applications at extra cost and the use of multiple agencies/ alternatives to alleviate queues. Baez-Camargo and Passas (2017), attest petty corruption has been effectively eradicated from Rwanda within 12 years. Administrative reforms eliminated opportunities for misconduct. Oversight mechanisms that can control, monitor, and handle issues such as asset declaration by public servants, money laundering, and conflict of interest were implemented (Oyamada, 2017).

Both the corrupt operant and culturant examined in this chapter are choice situations where the individuals or group may emit responses, compliance, or non-compliance with certain rules. Compliance or non-compliance in corrupt behavior is epitomized by the concepts of *self-control (the conflict between larger—later and smaller—sooner individual consequences and ethical self-control)* (the conflict between individual and group consequences) (da Hora and Sampaio, 2019, p. 14). Rwanda has been successful in implementing a cultural intervention that has fostered self-control and ethical self-control, through *reframing or construction of its cultural environment* (Baez-Camargo and Passas, 2017). As part of its good governance and anti-corruption efforts, Rwanda implemented the Itorero Civic Education Program to shape the integrity of its population. A key element in this program comprises instruction in the history of Rwanda that emphasizes traditional cultural values underpinning a strong commitment to public service and good governance in the contemporary setting. The Itorero civic culture is emphasized at home, primary and secondary schools, universities, and workplaces. The Itorero program and the administrative reforms have been an effective contingency for desired behavior (behaving for the good of the culture) and led to the reduction of corruption. The program reinforced the value of good reputation and professionalism in the Rwandan society.

More Behavior Analytic Work on Corruption – The Appeal

Scholarly investigations of corruption from a behavior analytic perspective is underdeveloped, even though behavior analysis as a discipline has conceptual tools that can "help us see the actions of others objectively, assess the effects, and determine the next steps for behavior change" (Daniels & Lattal, 2017, p. 145). The persistence of petty corruption in many other countries is a testimony of our failure to construe corruption as operant and cultural phenomenon, with a strong presence of avoidance behavior. Further, the dynamics of operant and cultural sides of corruption are not well articulated in our efforts to understand and minimize corruption. "Anyone who wants to increase the effectiveness in changing behavior" must pay attention "to the larger effects of behavior on the values we espouse" (Daniels and Lattal, 2017, p. 145). Anti-corruption strategies need to be designed to bring about cultural changes by harnessing contingencies of the social system that are stronger than the competing contingencies at an individual level (Sandaker, 2009). Behavior analysts have the scientific tools to account for corruption and arrange contingencies of reinforcement to get individuals to emit ethically acceptable social behaviors.

REFERENCES

Agbota, T. K. (2019). *Examining petty corruption from a behavioural perspective* (PhD dissertation). Oslo Metropolitan University, Oslo.

Agbota, T. K. (2020). *Behavioral and cultural analysis of the use of intermediaries in corruption transactions.* Paper presented at the ABAI 46th Annual Convention Washington DC. Online.

Agbota, T. K., Sandaker, I., Carvalho d. C. L., and Couto, C. K. (2017). Behavioral and cultural accounts of corruption in the interface between public officer and client. *Brazilian Journal of Behavior Analysis, 13*(1).

Agbota, T. K., Sandaker, I., & Ree, G. (2015). Verbal operants of corruption: A study of avoidance in corruption behavior. *Behavior and Social Issues, 24*, 126–148. https://doi.org/10.5210/bsi.v24i0.5864

Aktan, C. C., & Dokuzcesmeler, B. (2015). Political corruption: An introductory study on terminology and typology. *The International Journal of Social Sciences and Humanity Studies, 7*(1).

Baez-Camargo, C., & Passas, N. (2017). Hidden agendas, social norms and why we need to re-think anti-corruption. https://edoc.unibas.ch/66320/1/20181029113841_5bd6e331c2456.pdf

Basu, K. (2011). Why, for a class of bribes, the act of giving a bribe should be treated as legal. http://mpra.ub.uni-muenchen.de/50335/1/MPRA_paper_50335.pdf.

Callahan, W. A. (2005). Social capital and corruption: Vote buying and the politics of reform in Thailand. *Perspectives on Politics*, 495–508.

da Hora, K. L., & Sampaio, A. A. S. (2019). Units of analysis for corruption experiments: Operant, culturobehavioral lineage, culturant, and macrobehavior. *Perspectives on Behavior Science*, 1–21. https://doi.org/10.1007/s40614-019-00225-y

Dal Ben, R., Calixto, F. C., & Ferreira, A. L. (2016). Are Brazilian behavior analysts publishing outside the box? A survey of general science media. *Behavior Analysis Practice*, 1–9. https://doi.org/10.1007/s40617-016-0152-x

de Graaf, G. (2007). Causes of corruption: Towards a contextual theory of corruption. *Public Administration Quarterly, 31*(No. 1/2 Spring-Summer), 39–86.

Fernandes, D. M., Perallis, C. G., & Pezzato, F. A. (2015). Creativity, Brazilian "jeitinho," and cultural practices: A behavioral analysis. *Behavior Analysis: Research and Practice, 15*(1), 28.

Foxall, G. R. (2010). *Interpreting consumer choice: The behavioral perspective model.* Routledge.

Glenn, S. S., Malott, M. E., Andery, M. A. P. A., Benvenuti, M., Houmanfar, R. A., Sandaker, I, Todorov, J. C., Tourinho, E. Z., & Vasconcelos, L. A. (2016). Toward consistent terminology in a behaviorist approach to cultural analysis. *Behavior and Social Issues, 25*, 11–27. https://doi.org/10.5210/bsi.v25i0.6634

Goldstein, M. K., & Pennypacker, H. S. (1998). From candidate to criminal: The contingencies of corruption in elected public office. *Behavior and Social Issues, 8*, 1–8.

Grisham, J. (2005). *The testament.* Random House.

Husted, B. W. (1994). Honor among thieves: A transaction-cost interpretation of corruption in third world countries. *Business Ethics Quarterly, 4*, 17–27. https://doi.org/10.2307/3857556

Jancsics, D. (2015). Imperatives in informal organizational resource exchange in central Europe. *Journal of Eurasian Studies, 6*(1), 59–68.

Johnston, M. (2000). *Fighting corruption as a systemic problem: Challenges and strategies.* Colgate University.

Kahneman, D. (2011). *Thinking, fast and slow.* Macmillan.

Klitgaard, R. E. (1988). *Controlling corruption.* University of California Press.

Lambsdorff, J. G. (2002). Making corrupt deals: Contracting in the shadow of the law. *Journal of Economic Behavior & Organization, 48*(3), 221–241.

Le Vine, V. T. (1975). *Political corruption: The Ghana case.* Hoover Institution Press.

Marr, J. (1997). Infants' feats of inference: A commentary on Bower and Watson. *The Behavior Analyst, 20*(2), 155–159.

Martin, G., & Pear, J. (2014). *Behavior modification: What it is and how to do it.* Pearson.

Matukhno, N. (2016). How people can tackle corruption: Tools, methods, and approaches.

Mir Djawadi, B., & Fahr, R. (2013). The impact of risk perception and risk attitudes on corrupt behavior: Evidence from a petty corruption experiment. https://ideas.repec.org/p/iza/izadps/dp7383.html

Mutonyi, J. (2002). Fighting corruption: Is Kenya on the right track? *Police Practice and Research, 3*(1), 21–39. https://doi.org/10.1080/15614260290011318

Pedersen, K. H., & Johannsen, L. (2005). *Corruption: Commonality, causes & consequences comparing 15 ex-communist countries.* Department of Political Science, University of Aarhus.

Reese, H. W. (1993). Comments about Morris's paper. *The Behavior Analyst, 16*(1), 67.

Sandaker, I. (2009). A selectionist perspective on systemic and behavioral change in organizations. *Journal of Organizational Behavior Management, 29*(3–4), 276–293.

Skinner, B. F. (1971). *Beyond freedom and dignity.* Penguin.

Transparency International. (2007). Combating corruption in judicial systems – An advocacy toolkit. https://www.transparency.org/en/cpi/2006#.

Transparency International. (2018). Corruption Perceptions Index 2017. https://images.transparencycdn.org/images/2018_CPI_Executive_Summary.pdf.

Van Rijckeghem, C., & Weder, B. (2001). Bureaucratic corruption and the rate Of Temptation: Do wages in the civil service affect corruption, and by how much? *Journal of Development Economics, 65*, 307–331.

Vargas, E. (2017). BF Skinner's theory of behavior. *European Journal of Behavior Analysis, 18*(1), 2–38.

Vicente, P. C. (2010). Does oil corrupt? Evidence from a natural experiment in West Africa. *Journal of Development Economics, 92*, 28–38.

12

CULTURAL RESPONSIVENESS

The Development and Implications of Cultural Responsive
Practices to Behavior Change Programs

Cherelle Maschè Williams

INTRODUCTION

If the goal of behavior change programs is to improve the human condition (BACB, 8/2020), what better science is there to address conditions which impact humanity? Behavior analysis has the potential to make social change if practiced effectively and ethically. This chapter provides insight into the development of skills related to cultural responsiveness and diversity for a behavior analytic autism intervention program however; further applications of findings may provide implications for the use of culturally-informed behavior approaches to address social issues. If behavior analysts can create an informed method of developing cultural responsiveness in programming, decision making, and in interactions with one another and clients, this could have both intra and interdisciplinary applications. Currently, there is a major gap in cultural approaches to behavior change programs despite other fields having made strides within culture awareness and multiculturalism (Beirne & Sadavoy, 2019; Jibaja-Rusth et al., 1994; Norbury & Sparks, 2013; Tanaka-Matsumi, 1996). This may be a direct reflection of how young the field of behavior analysis is when compared to other fields of study. However it could also be a result of cultural responsiveness being too subjective to examine experimentally and operationally define (Taylor et al., 2018). This provides an opportunity for practitioners and researchers to test experimental questions as well as assess the efficacy of the approaches thus far in the field. We must challenge ourselves to do better in order to establish a common language around culture with the intention of improving the human condition for all humans, regardless of their background (Dixon et al., 2018).

Additionally, we must challenge ourselves to integrate into other contexts outside of the delivery of services to individual clients. To improve the human condition, we must consider all potential variables and barriers to quality of life. For example, we must consider the environmental context of the individual in order to improve their condition; if not, we confine ourselves to goals taken directly from developmental or functional assessments. We must expand the assessment process to include ecological and cultural assessments to gain better insights into the potential barriers. Furthermore, there is no formal education or training requirement in culture as it is not currently included on the task list (BACB, 2017) and only recently has cultural responsiveness, diversity, and personal bias been identified as an area of behavior analytic need in the newly created Ethics Code for Behavior Analysts (BACB, 2020). A key question is, how do we improve the human condition without any cultural awareness? Moreover, for those of us who consider ourselves to be culturally aware, what approaches are we taking to reflect this in our practice (Beaulieu et al., 2018)? It is evident that training is required so that behavior change programs are infused with cultural considerations, otherwise the program may be socially significant in the eyes of the practitioner, but not the client.

WHY BEING CULTURALLY RESPONSIVE IS NOT IMPORTANT BUT ESSENTIAL

Behavior change programs are individualized based on the assessment of an individual's skills and behaviors which may impede the development of said skills (BACB, 8/2020). To date, there has not been one standardized cultural assessment for evaluating individuals for behavior change programs; as a result normative data from commonly used assessment tools are North American-centric. This chapter proposes the idea that truly individualized behavior change programs must consider the cultural context of the individual. Often, we learn of great successes and breakthroughs in research and practice within controlled settings, but we also hear about the challenges of generalizing these results into the individual's home environment (Fong et al., 2016). We hear, "he's doing great, but the family is not onboard" or "the client has mastered all the programs, but the family is still having trouble in the home." Such statements shed light on a major challenge for behavior change programs. How do we effectively program for generalization? It is suggested that we start at the beginning of the assessment process.

The type of assessments we choose and the goals we select (based on these assessment results) will set the foundation for the entire program (Sue, 2003). If we do not stop to consider the individual context, such as the family dynamics and cultural influences, we may blindly be applying our science based on practitioner bias (Taylor et al., 2018). What happens when we blindly apply our science? Children are stuck in behavior change programs for years without significant progress and parents lose faith in the treatment process which results in resignation of services and negative social validity. Ultimately, we have fostered the poor reputation of our science as cold, sterile, robotic, and uncompassionate (Schreibman, 2005; Taylor et al., 2018). Many professionals within our field have not received formal cultural training (Beaulieu et al., 2018; Fong et al. 2017). If we are going to make a difference, it starts with recognizing our limitations and improving so we can uphold the science.

The author calls for greater awareness and targets that are informed by practitioners' skills related to cultural responsiveness but, based on survey data, these skills are glaringly underdeveloped and absent which comes at a significant detrimental cost to the quality of the program and connection with the client's environment (Beaulieu et al., 2018). In order to achieve cultural responsiveness with clients and stakeholders, we must develop professionals who value and promote diversity and inclusivity. It is important for behavioral professionals to acknowledge the importance of culture for the delivery of services and our own professional development. It is equally important for us to apply cultural responsiveness within our profession towards colleagues and other related service professionals. Engaging in cultural responsiveness aligns with our ethical standards and core princples (for individualization of programming), embeds compassion, and ensuring competency to perform behavior analytic responsibilities. Therefore, we must adhere to an informed, ethical approach to practice which allows us to better serve our clients, better support our team members, and leads the way for groundbreaking integration of cultural responsiveness. In order to apply a culturally responsive approach to behavior analysis, it is integral for the clinicians and stakeholders to understand and value the culturally responsive approach to behavior change programs. Fong and colleagues (2016) present one of the field's founding fathers, B.F. Skinner's definition of culture as, "variables arranged by other people." That is, humans control contingencies of reinforcement and punishment that affect the behavior and reinforcers and punishers for a person or group of people. Culture may be further defined as "the extent to which a group of individuals engage in overt and verbal behavior reflecting shared behavioral learning histories, serving to differentiate the group from other groups, and predicting how individuals within the group act in specific setting conditions" (Sugai et al. 2012, p. 200). Basically, culture is not innate. We are not born having certain beliefs or values; culture is learned. We adhere to spoken and unspoken rules of our environment early in life which can be a direct experience of our family context.

While each family has its own culture, we can go further to state that every *individual* has their own culture. We must emphasize that each individual is unique to *their* environment which is significant for developing flexibility and readiness to learn how to effectively apply our science within the *context of the individual*. This is a critical component of cultural responsiveness and developing cultural competence. Cultural competence is defined as a set of congruent behaviors, attitudes, and policies that come together in a system, agency or among professionals, and enable that system, agency or those professions to work effectively in cross-cultural situations (Fong et al., 2016). Cultural responsiveness on the other hand represents an inquiry that values differences and variations in culture as things to be nurtured and discovered ongoingly (Miller et al., 2019).

Upon reviewing behavior analytic literature, there are glaring research, academic, and training deficits for behavior analysts in relation to culture and cultural responsiveness. The author synthesized the suggestions from seminal articles on cultural responsiveness (Fong et al., 2016; Fong et al., 2017; Miller et al., 2019) and a replication of Para Cardona and colleagues (2012) in order to determine and measure strengths and challenges in practice. The implications from the results of the author's study are shared as a means to demonstrate how we can take research and apply it to practice within a culturally responsive framework. It is the author's hope that this example will become one of many case studies within the field for others to replicate and assess significant social changes. It is important to note that the effects of *not* engaging in cultural responsiveness are: lack of client progress, decreased family engagement/lack of buy-in, and potential ethical concerns (Fong et al., 2017). The impact of culturally responsive professionals on client outcomes and for organizations include: increased client outcomes, increased family involvement in the treatment process, and increased/maintenance of best practices, and adherence to ethical guidelines. The results of the case study conducted by the author demonstrate all three of the aforementioned outcomes.

Anderson and colleagues (2016) concluded that improved client outcomes were associated with increased use of interpersonal skills. Data from the study also showed improved treatment compliance with providers who skillfully adjusted to the client's needs. Interpersonal skills appeared in literature review across various domains (i.e., psychology, social work) to be one of the most important skills in developing cultural competence (Anderson et al., 2016). Therefore, we must take into consideration the perception of others during service delivery to ensure we demonstrate cultural responsiveness. Cultural responsiveness cannot be demonstrated by simply taking a webinar, attending a conference, or reading a book *without* proper application of this knowledge and making the necessary changes to programming (Parsons et al., 2013). This is integral for taking the interpersonal stance within our approach into practice so that we can modify our behaviors for the individuals we serve. Professionals who are able to accomplish this, will likely see significant increases in both client outcomes and family engagement – which should be areas of focus for a best practice behavior change program.

Imagine a behavior change program that has definite outcomes which leads to faster discharge of clients and facilitates a decrease in waitlist time for clients seeking behavior analytic services? If we implement a cultural humility approach to our practice, we could open doors for many more clients! It is important for us as professionals to seek the knowledge and skills necessary to engage in best practice. Currently, the Behavior Analyst Certification Board® (BACB) does not reference cultural responsiveness or multiculturalism on the task list and has recently added it to the code of ethics (BACB, 2017; BACB, 2020) which is highlighting an awareness that one cannot create a sound, individualized behavior analytic program without culture-informed, environment-centric targets.

There is an onus on supervisees to seek supervision that will achieve both clinical competence and the critical cultural responsiveness skills to provide informed treatment (Beirne & Sadavoy, 2019; Fong et al., 2017). This can be difficult to obtain when many of our supervisors have not had the cultural training or supervision themselves (Beaulieu et al., 2018). Furthermore, the demographic of the field is largely composed of white women. The BACB released the following practitioner demographic information: American Indian/Alaska Native 0.34% Asian 5.77%, Black 6.69%,Hispanic/Latinx 20.55%, Native Hawaiian/ Pacific Islander 0.56%, White 58.78%, No Answer 7.31%. (*Note:* Total % of certificants who responded per category was 53.5% [BCBA/BCBA-D]; 54.2% [BCaBA]; 30.3% [RBT] [BACB, 9/2020]). How can our field address the cultural diversity when the field is not representative of all populations? It is the author's opinion that course sequences feature mandatory diversity and cultural responsiveness training and the ethics code acknowledges the need to practice within one's cultural competence. This is necessary to protect clients from cultural blindness which is rampant in the field. Cultural blindness is apparent in a survey which showed that behavior analysts who have not had formal training in cultural sensitivity and diversity rated themselves as "feeling" culturally competent (Beaulieu et al., 2016). We **must** continue developing cultural approaches to behavior change programs in order to improve and disseminate our science to others.

A REVIEW OF CULTURAL APPROACHES TO PRACTICE

Three key articles from the aforementioned literature review are worthy of notation. Fong and colleagues (2017) highlight the need for behavior analysis to serve consumers with diverse cultural backgrounds has significantly increased. The increase in the demand to serve diverse populations has brought to light the need for culturally responsive behavior analysts. In order to meet these demands, behavior analysts must develop cultural responsiveness training. They purport that there is a need for the development of culturally diverse educational curricula and materials The implication of cultural training within behavior analysis has the potential to provide effective approaches to cultural responsiveness across settings. Fong and colleagues highlight that language barriers, lack of mentor opportunities, microaggressions, tokenism, and adverse campus climates present challenges for developing culturally diverse professionals – especially during the academic training phase. These same challenges may arise within professional training and development. To address these challenges we must develop culture and diversity related curricula, mentoring opportunities, and greater support for minority and culturally diverse populations.

LaFromboise and Rowe (1983), provide a social skills model for developing bicultural competence to address the mental health needs of Native Americans. A training program was developed to reflect cultural sensitivity to the population of Native Americans which included a specific outline for skills that need to be acquired. The one-year study examined 30 tribal groups and agencies and measured conditions in which stereotyping and discrimination are commonly presented (e.g., discriminatory hiring practices). The research-ers adapted training to reflect the Native American traditions of role modeling, appren-ticeship training, and group consensus. These traditions were directly related to social skills training which included instruction, modeling, behavior rehearsal, reinforcement, feedback, skill improvement, and generalization to the natural environment. The study determined which approaches to training were reflective of the Native Americans' traditions which allowed their approach to result in positive gains. LaFromboise and Rowe identified the following prerequisite skills needed for social skills training: discrimination skills in bicultural rights, language styles, social expectations, and social reinforcers were essential in training. They suggest that social skills training reflects cultural sensitivity. It is not enough to just develop knowledge of a particular group, but to directly adjust your approach to meet their traditions and values. This study further suggests the need for additional studies outside of specific populations or groups.

Parra Cardona and colleagues (2012) provide insight for individualized cultural approaches to prevention and intervention. They recommend the consideration of the cultural context of the individual for programming and offer a translational approach in applying prevention and intervention to Latino families. Their literature review found that many programs have been developed or modified specifically for Latino families; however, few have successfully tested the role of cultural values on outcomes. The article provides specific recommendations for integrating the values of Latino families to enrich behavior change programs to be more individualized and socially significant. For example, they found that placing practitioners representative of the family's cultural group resulted in statistically significant improvements in treatment outcomes. This finding demonstrates the problematic nature of the homogeneity of the field based on the BCBA's demographic data shared ear-lier. Parra Cardona and colleagues offer an example of direct testing of cultural approaches to treatment and the effects on outcomes.

CULTURAL RESPONSIVENESS TRAINING: APPROACHES TO COMPREHENSIVE CULTURAL TRAINING

Currently, standard approaches to cultural training involve workshops, conference presen-tations, webinars, or recorded training (Fong et al., 2016). These approaches lack the appli-cation of the skills into practice. We must caution against such approaches alone because they can lead to overgeneralization of the content and often do not assess the acquisition of specific skills or the maintenance of skills over time. These approaches often focus on specific groups or populations rather than on *how* to develop cultural responsiveness which involves interacting cross-culturally – not *just* interactions between specific groups (Miller et al., 2019).

The literature review by the author revealed a lack of sufficient examples of cultural approaches to practice based in science. Skills necessary to embed cultural awareness into practice are: communication skills, persuasion, interpersonal skills, rapport building, social skills, perspective taking, self-awareness skills, and contextual decision making (LaFromboise & Rowe, 1983). These skills were adapted into a curriculum created by the author which targeted specific goals for the acquisition and maintenance of the skills trained. A sample goal includes the ability to accurately tact the experiences of others for the purpose of per-spective taking. This is relevant to interpersonal skills such as the ability to develop a rapport and build relationships with others. The skills selected specifically targeted the development of cultural responsiveness rather than simply providing knowledge content. The training of cultural responsiveness also leads to improved attitudes surrounding cultural diversity and behaviors that are viewed as socially acceptable (Miller et al., 2019). The author argues that a comprehensive approach to training which targets knowledge, skills, and attitudes leads to a comprehensive training program for more culturally responsive professionals.

The model developed by the author includes the content areas of culture and family dynamics, cultural considerations, ethical applications, and local law and agency policy. Training content is able to be adapted to any environment and includes specific objectives: communication skills, social skills, interpersonal skills, and self-awareness skills. These objectives are trained via behavioral skills training/role play. Once the professional has demonstrated mastery of skills in training, ongoing self-monitoring and peer evaluation measures ensure maintenance of the skills over time and creates opportunities for further development and coaching as needed.

In addition to creating a comprehensive training model, steps were taken to evaluate what organizational changes need to occur to further promote a cultural approach to service delivery. These steps included: increased use of values assessments to ensure treatments align with client values, treatment plan audits to specifically identify goals reflected in the client's culture/family context, tracking of individualized parent goals, assessment of data, and the development of a client outcomes tracker. Professionals were not only trained in cultural responsiveness, but the agency was responsible for incorporating cultural responsiveness policies and procedures into their organizational culture. The goal was for culturally responsive training to lead to improved client outcomes and family training that was aligned with the compassionate care pillars of collaboration, empathy, compassion, and positive social interactions (Taylor et al., 2018).

EMPOWERING FAMILIES TRAINING

The author's model was based on The Parent Training Action (PTA) model of Parra Cardone and colleagues (2012) to improve caregiver involvement in the treatment process. In the PTA model, families were assigned a liaison who reflected their specific cultural representation (e.g., Hispanic families were assigned a Hispanic liaison) to facilitate training along with the case manager. They found an increase in family engagement and treatment integrity for families assigned a liaison. The results of this study indicated a need for practitioners who are reflective of the family's culture. The implications of this study do not simply imply that we must pair families with individuals from their culture but to individuals that have the ability to relate (e.g., engage in perspective taking). Given the challenges associated with finding providers who are a match for each family, this part of the intervention was not replicated; however, practitioners who were trained in the comprehensive approach to cultural responsiveness were assigned.

This led the author to develop the Empowering Families Training (EFT) model. EFT ensures families receive culturally sensitive services by individualizing training objectives to the families' specific values following the assessments. Goals are created with the family rather than for them. Baseline data were taken to assess family engagement and client's skills prior to implementation of EFT. Preliminary data were also obtained to determine the effects of the culturally competent team members working on the case. Once family values are assessed, a curriculum is developed to program for areas of need from the parent's perspective and adapted to the learning environment; they are also individualized to meet the specific familial needs of the client for the purpose of contacting reinforcement and for training families at their own pace. Examples of content areas within EFT are: verbal behavior, pairing, reinforcement, and extinction.

Once families receive content training, the team member uses behavior skills training to assess comprehension and begins training the application of the skills. The team member provides ongoing feedback and teaches the family how to monitor themselves outside of sessions. This empowers the family to take charge of their own treatment process and to advocate for approaches that work best for them which mitigates challenges of families not adhering to treatment plans and lack of buy-in. We must remember that we are not experts in their environment. We have to be able to apply our science within the individual family context or risk doing them a disservice.

Many professionals want to increase cultural diversity and inclusion, but do not know how. A peripheral goal of this work was to provide concrete action items for behavior professionals to aid in effective collaboration and provide training to culturally varied families, training based on the individual's environment and not the cultural biases that are devoid of specialized training. The action items are listed below.

Behavior Action Items

- Increase training in cultural competence
  Comprehensive Cultural Competence Series
  - Includes behavior skills training
  - Curriculum outlines specific skills to learn based on research
  - Ongoing analysis and monitoring of employee performance
  - Survey the family to ensure they perceive the team members to be culturally aware and in alignment with their values
  Webinars/workshops/conferences for additional resources
- Audit client treatment plans and curricula
  Ensure treatment plans account for cultural/family contexts for at least 50% of goals
  Consult with family about curriculum goals before signing off to ensure they understand they can provide feedback and adjustments at any point during the treatment process
- Track individualized parent goals
  Create individualized goals based on family values and track data
  Report on progress directly with caregivers and update goals as new barriers arise
- Create client outcome trackers
  Track program progress, family involvement and assessment results
  Provide updates on progress each quarter to ensure positive trends in data

RESULTS OF THESE ACTIONS: EMPOWERING FAMILIES TRAINING CASE STUDY RESULTS

EFT was implemented with Client Z to assess the utility of the action items. Because EFT focuses on family values and creates specific curriculum based on these values and barriers to treatment, there was a focus on increasing cultural competence of clinicians working directly with the family. Client progress (i.e., programs), family engagement (percentage of opportunities), and cultural competence data were tracked following baseline over the period of 9 months. Z was not selected based on any inclusionary criteria. During baseline, X (who had been receiving services for three years) did not engage in any social interactions with the family. After the 9-months, X engaged in social interactions across 50% of opportunities presented. In addition to social gains, X's skill acquisition programs increased by 60% from baseline which met discharge criteria. A social validity questionnaire given to the family, yielded a perfect rating score for a cultural awareness; meaning they perceived their clinicians as reflecting cultural sensitivity within service delivery. X's results were compared to a client not participating in EFT. The comparison indicated significant differences in program mastery, family involvement, and assessment results. The use of a cultural responsive approach to behavior change programs was found to increase client outcomes and improve family training, as suggested by Fong and colleagues (2016) and Parra Cardona and colleagues (2012). The results of this case study suggest that a cultural responsive approach may lead to greater positive outcomes and facilitate earlier discharge of clients.

DISCUSSION

In an attempt to replicate and extend the PTA model within the behavioral field and apply the skills found by Fong et al. (2016) to be effective, the EFT model involves the individual development of curriculum goals rather than providing a specific curriculum to follow. Professionals should align goals with the family values which require skills associated with cultural responsiveness. It is possible for EFT to be implemented without cultural responsiveness training; however, the author recommends cultural responsiveness training occurs prior to and throughout the treatment process for optimal results.

The author found that the development of a comprehensive approach to cultural training and a culturally sensitive model of parent training led to improved outcomes and client satisfaction. It is important to note that this is not the only approach to cultural responsiveness. Preliminary data were obtained from one subject while other case studies are currently in progress. This approach is open to improvements and considerations. Additionally, research in practice lends itself to potential barriers and we must consider extraneous variables when analyzing data, especially with the limited control outside of the lab. EFT is an ongoing work in progress as we continue to evaluate the procedures and application.

Direct observation and data analysis are a significant factor in evaluating the success of this approach. Clinicians often face challenges providing ongoing observations of their clients and continuous analysis of the effects of treatment, and this approach requires an increase in this behavior specifically upon inception services. Some challenges to implementing cultural responsive approaches to behavior change programs are: large caseloads requiring ongoing monitoring, work environments which do not reflect diversity inclusivity, and lack of mentoring opportunities for those who need additional support – especially those who struggle with communication skills and self-awareness (Fong et al., 2016).

The author challenges you to think about what behaviors you would like to see within your organization that will contribute to building cultural competence, humility, and responsiveness. Think about how your agency's core values influence your behaviors. Does your agency value diversity and inclusion? If others are not upholding the core values, ask yourself why and how you can create an environment that is inclusive of others' values/perspectives.

How your agency handles cultural competence within the organization will greatly influence service delivery that is culturally-informed. Challenge your agency to adhere to best practice by sharing these specific action items to promote better outcomes for those you serve as well as lead the way for our science to improve systematic deficits in culture awareness, humility, and equity.

REFERENCES

Anderson, T., McClintock, A. S., Himawan, L., Song, X., & Patterson, C. L. (2016). A prospective study of therapist facilitative interpersonal skills as a predictor of treatment outcome. *Journal of Consulting and Clinical Psychology, 84*(1), 57–66. https://doi.org/10.1037/ccp0000060

Beaulieu, L., Addington, J., & Almeida, D. (2018). Behavior analysts' training and practices regarding cultural diversity: The case for culturally competent care. *Behavior Analysis in Practice, 12*(3), 557–575. https://doi.org/10.1007/s40617-018-00313-6

Behavior Analyst Certification Board. (2020). Ethics code for behavior analysts. Littleton, CO: Author.

Behavior Analyst Certification Board. (2020. August, 28). *About behavior analysis*. BACB. https://www.bacb.com/about-behavior-analysis/

Behavior Analyst Certification Board. (2020, September 15). *BACB certificant data*: BACB: https://www:bacb:com/bacb-certificant-data/

Behavior Analyst Certification Board: (2017). *BCBA/BCaBA task list* (5th ed.). BACB.

Beirne, A. B., & Sadavoy, J. A. (2019). *Understanding ethics in applied behavior analysis: Practical applications*. Routledge.

Dixon, M. R., Belisle, J., Rehfeldt, R. A., & Root, W. B. (2018). Why we are still not acting to save the world: The upward challenge of a post-skinnerian behavior science. *Perspectives on Behavior Science, 41*(1), 241–267. https://doi.org/10.1007/s40614-018-0162-9

Fong, E. H., Catagnus, R. M., Brodhead, M. T., Quigley, S., & Field, S. (2016). Developing the cultural awareness skills of behavior analysts. *Behavior Analysis in Practice, 9*, 84–94.

Fong, E. H., Ficklin, S., & Lee, Y. H. (2017). Increasing cultural understanding and diversity in applied behavior analysis. *Behavior Analysis: Research and Practice, 17*(2), 103–113.

Jibaja-Rusth, M. L., Kingery, P. M., Holcomb, J. D., Bruckner, W. P., & Pruitt, B. E. (1994). Development of a multicultural sensitivity scale. *Journal of Health Education, 25*(6), 350–357. https://doi.org/10.1080/10556699.1994.10603060

LaFromboise, T. D., & Rowe, W. (1983). Skills training for bicultural competence: Rationale and application. *Journal of Counseling Psychology, 30*(4), 589–595. https://doi.org/10.1037/0022-0167.30.4.589

Miller, K. L., Re Cruz, A., & Ala'i-Rosales, S. (2019). Inherent tensions and possibilities: Behavior analysis and cultural responsiveness. *Behavior and Social Issues, 28*(1), 16–36. https://doi.org/10.1007/s42822-019-00010-1

Norbury, C. F., & Sparks, A. (2013). Difference or disorder? Cultural issues in understanding neurodevelopmental disorders. *Developmental Psychology, 49*(1), 45.

Parra Cardona, J. R., Domenech Rodriguez, M., Forgatch, M., Sullivan, C., Bybee, D., Holtrop, K. et al. (2012). Culturally adapting an evidence-based parenting intervention for Latino immigrants: The need to integrate fidelity and cultural relevance. *Family Process, 51*, 56–72.

Parsons, M. B., Rollyson, J. H., & Reid, D. H. (2013). Teaching practitioners to conduct behavioral skills training: A pyramidal approach for training multiple human service staff. *Behavior Analysis in Practice, 6*(2), 4–16. https://doi.org/10.1007/BF03391798

Schreibman, L. (2005). *The science and fiction of autism*. Harvard University Press.

Sue, D. W. (2003). Cultural competence in the treatment of ethnic minority populations. In D. W. Sue (Ed.), Psychological treatment of ethnic minority populations (pp. 4–7). APA Press.

Sugai, G., O'Keeffe, B. V., & Fallon, L. M. (2012). A contextual consideration of culture and school-wide positive behavior support. *Journal of Positive Behavior Interventions, 14*(4). 197–208. https://doi.org/10.1177/1098300711426334

Tanaka-Matsumi, J., Seiden, D. Y., & Lam, K. N. (1996). The Culturally Informed Functional Assessment (CIFA) interview: A strategy for cross-cultural behavioral practice. *Cognitive and Behavioral Practice, 3*(2), 215–233. https://doi.org/10.1016/S1077-7229(96)80015-0

13

CULTURALLY AWARE PRACTICE

Cultural Considerations for Delivering Effective Treatment

Lina Slim and David Celiberti

Substantial evidence indicates there is a significant rise in the worldwide prevalence of autism spectrum disorder (ASD) across all racial, ethnic, and socioeconomic groups (e.g., Maenner et al., 2016). Moreover, this increase co-occurs with mobility of Board Certified Behavior Analysts (BCBA) internationally (BACB, 2020), increasing opportunities for working with culturally and linguistically diverse (CLD) families.

While practitioners of applied behavior analysis (ABA) have the education, training, and clinical skills to treat ASD, education and training in culturally and linguistically sensitive practices is lacking (Dennison et al., 2019; Taylor et al., 2018). Moreover, some ABA practitioners may believe that the principles of behavior analysis are universally applicable regardless of cultural considerations (Brodhead et al., 2016). This is compounded by a lack of self-awareness around one's own personal biases, lack of experience, and knowledge gaps.

The purpose of this chapter is twofold. First, we aim to raise awareness around the importance of understanding diversity in cultural norms, values and practices, and how diversity can impact treatment outcomes. Second, we want to highlight some considerations to the adoption of effective treatments and offer suggestions to address some challenges and reduce the dangerous influences of pseudoscience (i.e., causing harm, poor outcomes, and depletion of resources).

Societal attitudes associated with autism in a community could result in a family choosing harmful, ineffective, or untested treatments. For example, in communities where an autism diagnosis is associated with "stigma," a child's stereotypical behavior often attracts negative attention. Let us imagine that a family that is impacted by such stigma is now faced with two options – reaching out to a behavior analyst or pursuing sessions with a yoga trainer who promises a reduction in all types of stereotypical behaviors through meditation and other exercises. If the behavior analyst is unaware of – or does not consider – the family's context and the external factors that influence treatment decisions, they may recommend goals targeting communication and toilet training based on the child's skill deficits in these areas. If the family is one that avoids confrontation, they may refrain from communicating their displeasure about the behavior analyst's recommendations, and instead opt for sessions with the yoga trainer simply because their priorities appear to be better matched. Similarly, in some families, interaction between opposite genders is not practiced. The mother of a girl with autism from such a family may choose to avoid attending parent training sessions with a male behavior analyst. Moreover, in some communities the role of mothers as primary caregivers is shifting towards assuming professional careers outside their homes, and they may rely on home support aides who may not be fluent in the home language to raise their children (Sopaul, 2019). Having home support aides care for the child with autism may create challenges to treatment implementation and outcomes. Thus, cultural values, norms, family dynamics, and practices are critical to consider during the intervention process as they may influence the adoption and acceptance of effective treatments.

Given the diverse cultures and languages in families, there is no "one size fits all" approach to intervention. More importantly, we need to recognize that each family is a unique entity in itself that comes with their own idiosyncratic behaviors. As practitioners, we must make every effort to learn the family's culture to better understand how their values fit within the broader context in which they live and make decisions from that family's individualized perspective. This cultural sensitivity and awareness of the family's dynamics promotes acceptance, facilitates open communication, fosters trusting relationships, and enhances efforts to select appropriate goals, individualized to meet the child and family's particular needs (Fong et al., 2016).

Family–practitioner dynamics are very complex as the perceptions and assumptions of all members of the team are influenced by their biases and learning histories. To address these personal barriers and improve the family–practitioner relationship, we may want to consider enhancing our clinical skills by developing culturally aware practices. These practices involve (1) mindfully attending to the family's needs and concerns, engaging in active listening without judgment (Bishop et al., 2004; Hayes & Plumb, 2007), (2) objectively analyzing the family's/client's behaviors by relying on data (Sue, 1998), (3) building cultural competency skills through educational and clinical activities (e.g., training, supervision, consultation, and coursework, Brodhead & Higbee, 2012; Fong & Tanaka, 2013), (4) embracing cultural humility by acknowledging one's own limitations and overcoming these limitations by seeking to understand others' cultures and building mutual respect (Hook et al., 2017; Mosher et al., 2016), and (5) being culturally responsive to contextual conditions within which the family operates and making appropriate adaptations (Neely et al., 2019). Displaying cultural humility can be challenging because a person may simply not know what they don't know; they may lack self-awareness regarding their own cultural biases, making adjustments difficult. Our behaviors, biases, assumptions, the ways in which we perceive the world, and the decisions we make are all conditioned and influenced by our learning histories and our experiences. It is important to note that we need to recognize that all families and individuals in general have their own unique subcultures, and as such caution against overgeneralizing, stereotyping, or assuming that all members within a specified culture behave in the same ways. In other words, the "one size does *not* fit all" concept must be applied to every individual and family unit we work with. As such, in this chapter we consider every family unit as being CLD.

The following are some considerations when working with CLD families and some suggestions on how to address the challenges that may arise.

CONSIDERATION #1: CULTURAL NORMS AND VALUES

Our learning histories, biases, and educational/professional cultures influence our behaviors, perceptions, assumptions, and thoughts. We also know that we do not know everything and cannot presume to have the answers to all problems. As such, recognizing that we are imperfect humans and works in progress will help us to accept our own limitations. Being culturally responsive and humble is a dynamic engagement, acknowledging our own limitations, actively seeking to increase our understanding of other's cultures, while recognizing factors that may influence access to effective treatments and health outcomes. Second, we need to display sensitivity and perspective taking by attending to the different ways that others receive and respond to information and adjust our approach to meet the needs of each family.

Identifying motivating and culturally appropriate goals increases the probability that families will accept the selection of goals and implement treatment strategies. When working with families, it is important to capture the family members' motivation to work on goals they consider valuable, ones that will help their child participate in relationships with family members, and with members of the larger community (i.e., school, social, community settings, etc.).

For example, some families will choose to work on goals that help their child participate in social family gathering (e.g., mealtime, prayer time) over goals that focus on academic skills. Other families will prefer to focus on academic goals rather than on addressing toilet training and other daily living activities. While behavior analysts want the recipients of our services to be successful in their natural settings and systems, practitioners need to prioritize functional goals that families will be motivated to implement, even if those may differ from the practitioner's preferences. A practitioner's selection of treatment approaches cannot help but be influenced by his or her own cultural norms and beliefs, but bias in the selection of these treatments can inadvertently compromise safe and effective delivery of services.

To address this challenge, the practitioner should apply active listening, mindful attention, and cultural humility to better understand and respect the families' cultural beliefs and rituals. This will help to establish effective relationships and introduce safe and culturally acceptable treatment options that respect their families' constraints while also respecting the constraints within which families live. In addition, practitioners should monitor and observe the family's verbal and non-verbal responses for signs of discomfort throughout the course of treatment and make adaptations accordingly. It is important to assess and treat every family on an individual basis, select appropriate goals that matter to them and treatment approaches that enhance their particular dynamics, and provide necessary support to cope with stressors from the broader community. These practices will help build a trusting relationship between the practitioner and each family with increased opportunities for buy-in and adoption of effective treatments. Moreover, practitioners should practice cultural responsiveness and sensitivity, a dynamic and ongoing process that promotes a deeper understanding of the family's cultural norms, beliefs, and values, and enhances the practitioner–family relationship.

A practitioner can consult with members of the family unit and community at large to gauge (1) availability and access to resources; (2) the level of support from family members, the community, and educational and health services; and (3) the family's culture, norms, and values such as preferred language, family dynamics and routines, methods and venues of communication, and treatment delivery and approaches. By way of example, in some families grandparents act as primary caregivers. Recognizing the role of each family member and consulting with them about what matters to the family with regard to treatment goals and selection will build respect, trust, and enhance adoption. Once strong relationships are formed and the family feels heard, collaborative partnerships develop, and the behavior analyst will be better positioned to explore other goals and priorities that lead to long lasting positive and generalizable effects on the child's education and overall health.

CONSIDERATION #2: THE NATIVE LANGUAGE OF THE HOME

This consideration specifically addresses the linguistic culture of the family and community, when attempting to communicate with family members, share latest evidence-based practices, and select goals and treatment approaches. Knowing how to read or translate words into a different language is not synonymous with being an expert in the nuances of the language, culture, or home environment, nor does it guarantee an equal understanding of the intended meaning. This is why it is critical to use the language that is understood by the family members, that meets each at their level of understanding, and attempts to build upon shared common grounds for the modality of communication (i.e., non-verbal and verbal communication skills), including word and sentence choices, intonation, the types of examples used, and facial and body gestures.

For example, the Arabic language has rich and complex ways to convey word meanings whereby one word may have multiple meanings that are socially and contextually dependent. The meaning of "punishment" is contextually bound and is an accepted way to address problem behaviors. Introducing the idea and concept of positive reinforcement as a new approach to establish behaviors is a challenge that requires shaping (i.e., pairing procedures, opportunities for contacting positive outcomes, etc.).

To address this challenge, when conveying discipline-specific information to families, try to avoid jargon and use words that are easily understood, even by non-native speakers. Also, if possible, include a multilingual translator who has an understanding of the family's culture who can help convey the meaning of words to facilitate ongoing conversation. However, it is important to recognize that while a knowledge of the client's language may facilitate communication, cultural knowledge may be insufficient. As practitioners, we know that sometimes communication breakdowns can occur even when the practitioner and family speak the same native language. If we hope to effectively seek a family's investment in our goals and treatments, we need to obtain culturally relevant linguistic knowledge and sensitivity to effectively explain relevant treatment approaches.

CONSIDERATION #3: SOCIAL, ECONOMIC, AND POLITICAL CONTEXTS

This consideration pertains to influences across these contexts: individual, family, social-economic within the broader community, and government policy. Our biases and stereotypes towards other cultures should not influence our decision-making process and color social judgments of families and individuals we work with. The cultural social environment within which a family lives may influence, but does not dictate, the customs they choose to abide by within their home. For example, while a family might live within a conservative religious broader community, they may not necessarily abide by those rules and norms in their home. On the other hand, a family who lives in an open social society may consider a simple handshake offensive or refusing/opposing the professional's suggestions disrespectful. Therefore, practitioners need to educate themselves on the cultural norms of each family before entering their homes.

Considering the social-economic contexts of families is critical in helping the practitioner gain a better understanding of the variables that drive families' choices around educational and health issues. Families are under a great deal of internal and external pressures while helping their child cope and become a productive member of their community. These stressors may be a function of lack of resources and support (i.e., financial, family, healthcare providers, education, material) in addition to social demands/expectations, and the broader political landscape. These stressors may contribute to the family's choices of non-effective and sometimes harmful treatment options. For instance, a culture that stigmatizes individuals with disabilities may prevent the family from seeking help and early diagnosis, hindering or delaying access to available treatment options. Also, access to resources may be bound to cultural social-economic factors. Culturally appropriate and relevant resources may be unavailable or not accepted by the community at large, such as assessment modalities, data collection procedures, tools and technology systems, language used, socially acceptable means of managing resources, and treatment approaches.

Political context can also contribute to awareness around the prevalence, core characteristics, and effective treatment for individuals with autism. Education and health ministries may have inadequate, incomplete, or inaccurate information and may not abide by acceptable standards of care. In countries where awareness around ASD is emerging, policy changes are lagging behind. As practitioners we must act as "first responders" and information providers to families. It is our responsibility to help, support, and inform the public and stakeholders of the latest evidence-based practices and effective treatments while respecting the CLD background of the families and clients we serve.

To address these challenges, the practitioner should demonstrate empathy and compassionate care to help the family seek necessary support systems within the boundaries of their cultural norms. Practitioners can demonstrate positive compassionate social behaviors, such as active and empathic listening, asking and attending to the families' stories, feelings and concerns, and accepting without judgment. For example, speaking less and listening more, and using comforting non-verbal behaviors such as reassuring facial expressions and gestures (e.g., nodding head in acknowledgement). Practitioners can rely on observable behaviors following a data-driven objective approach which drives the decision-making process, simultaneously providing guidance and support to families. This will increase opportunities for the family to contact positive outcomes and celebrate successes, empowering families to advocate best practices for their child. During this process, the practitioner–family relationship can be strengthened by displaying: (a) cultural humility to better understand the conditions that may contribute to disparities in accessing evidence-based practices, health and outcomes; (b) an open mind to learn how the family approaches and seeks relevant information, and how they successfully access effective treatments; and (c) respect for the family being the expert of their child and acknowledging their part in the therapeutic relationship. In other words, listening to the family and following their lead while learning along the way from shared experiences, enhances building strong bonds which forges trusting practitioner–family relationships and empowers families to become strong advocates for their child.

CONCLUSION

There is a global need for increased awareness of available, scientifically validated, effective treatment approaches and resources for ASD. Cultural considerations are important to reduce the dangerous influences of pseudoscience and facilitate access to effective treatment. Adopting cultural responsiveness, humility, and culturally aware practices will foster trusting relationships and promote selection of effective, scientifically validated treatment.

Given the need for the field of ABA to promote standards of excellence in culturally aware and responsive practices when working with CLD families, it is necessary to develop educational and training programs that address teaching repertoires that promote culturally aware, responsive, and competent practices.

On a final note, we should keep our behavior analytic hats firmly on as we learn more about different cultures. Believing in broad generalizations and stereotypes and placing individuals into shallow cultural boxes would only give rise to new forms of prejudice. All knowledge at the cultural sub-group level should be considered as a mere possibility, and not as a conclusion about every individual within that group. While awareness and appreciation for diversity is important, relying on observable behaviors in individuals is our vaccine against prejudice.

REFERENCES

Behavior Analyst Certification Board. (2020). *BACB certificant data.* https://www.bacb.com/bacb-certificant-data

Bishop, S. R., Lau, M., Shapiro, S., Carlson, L., Anderson, N. D., Carmody, J., Segal, Z. V., Abby, S., Speca, M., Velting, D., & Devins, G. (2004). Mindfulness: A proposed operational definition. *Clinical Psychology: Science and Practice, 11*(3), 230–241. https://doi.org/10.1093/clipsy/bph077.

Brodhead, M. T., Durán, L., & Bloom, S. E. (2016). Cultural and linguistic diversity in recent verbal behavior research on individuals with disabilities: A review and implications for research and practice. *The Analysis of Verbal Behavior, 30,* 75–86. https://doi.org/10.1007/s40616-014-0009-8

Brodhead, M. T., & Higbee, T. S. (2012). Teaching and maintaining ethical behavior in a professional organization. *Behavior Analysis in Practice, 5,* 82–88.

Dennison, A., Lund, E. M., Brodhead, M. T., Mejia, L., Armenta, A., & Leal, J. (2019). Delivering home-supported applied behavior analysis therapies to culturally and linguistically diverse families. *Behavior Analysis in Practice, 12*(4), 887–898. https://doi.org/10.1007/s40617-019-00374-1.

Fong, E. H., Catagnus, R. M., Brodhead, M. T., Quigley, S., & Field, S. (2016). Developing the cultural awareness skills of behavior analysts. *Behavior Analysis in Practice, 9,* 84–94. https://doi.org/10.1007/s40617-016-0111-6

Fong, E. H., & Tanaka, S. (2013). Multicultural alliance of behavior analysis standards for cultural competence in behavior analysis. *International Journal of Behavioral Consultation and Therapy, 8,* 17–19.

Hayes, S. C., & Plumb, J. C. (2007). Mindfulness from the bottom up: Providing an inductive framework for understanding mindfulness processes and their application to human suffering. *Psychological Inquiry, 18*(4), 242–248. https://doi.org/10.1080/10478400701598314.

Hook, J. N., Davis, D., Owen, J., & DeBlaere, C. (2017). *Cultural humility: Engaging diverse identities in therapy.* American Psychological Association.

Maenner, M. J., Shaw, K. A., Baio, J., Washington, A., Patrick, M., DiRienzo, M., Christensen, D. L., Wiggins, L. D., Pettygrove, S., Andrews, J. G., Lopez, M., Hudson, A., Baroud, T., Schwenk, Y., White, T., Rosenberg, C. R., Lee, L., Harrington, R. A., Huston, M., . . . & Deitz, P. M. (2016). Prevalence of Autism Spectrum Disorder among children aged 8 years—Autism and Developmental Disabilities Monitoring Network, 11 sites, United States, 2016. *Surveillance Summaries 2020, 69*(4), 1–12. https://dx.doi.org/10.15585/mmwr.ss6904a1

Mosher, D. K., Hook, J. N., Captari, L. E., Davis, D. E., DeBlaere, C., & Owen, J. (2016). Cultural humility: A therapeutic framework for engaging diverse clients. *Practice Innovations, American Psychological Association, 2*(4), 221–233. 2377–889X/17/$12.00 http://dx.doi.org/10.1037/pri0000055

Neely, L., Gann, C., Castro-Villarreal, F., & Villarreal, V. (2019). Preliminary findings of culturally responsive consultation with educators. *Behavior Analysis in Practice, 13*(1), 270–281. https://doi.org/10.1007/s40617-019-00393-y

Sopaul, A. (2019). An interpretative phenomenological analysis of families affected by autism in Dubai. *Dubai Medical Journal, 2,* 82–89. https://doi.org/10.1159/000501770

Sue, S. (1998). In search of cultural competence in psychotherapy and counseling. *American Psychologist, 53*(4), 440–448. https://doi.org/10.1037/0003-066X.53.4.440

Taylor, B. A., LeBlanc, L. A., & Nosik, M. R. (2018) Compassionate care in behavior analytic treatment: Can outcomes be enhanced by attending to relationships with caregivers? *Behavior Analysis in Practice.* Published online. https://doi.org/10.1007/s40617-018-00289-3

14

CULTURE

A Cultural Behavioral Systems Science Perspective on the Struggle for Social Justice

Traci M. Cihon and Kyosuke Kazaoka

INTRODUCTION

Wright (2019), in "The Story of 2019: Protests in Every Corner of the Globe," noted that protests were being held in numerous countries, across six continents, aptly naming 2019 the year of protests. The Carnegie Endowment for International Peace estimates that since 2017 there have been over 100 anti-government protests worldwide, resulting in nearly 30 governments or leaders who have fallen (Carnegie Endowment for International Peace, 2020, September 1). Thus far in 2020, the US alone has experienced at least three categories of protests (e.g., coronavirus lockdown, prison, and police brutality; carnegieendowment. org, 2020). The 2020 protests regarding police brutality have involved more than 1 million protesters, have lasted for more than 100 days; and, the protests are still active (Carnegie Endowment for International Peace). Clearly, Wright was correct in anticipating that "protest movements will almost certainly be a feature of 2020" (para. 12).

The recent protests against police brutality,[1] starting after the death of George Floyd, raised voices against the use of excessive force and systemic violence toward people of color, especially toward Black and African Americans. Although different groups have different perspectives on this matter, one unifying argument stems from a social and environmental justice perspective – equities and inequities are social problems resulting from unjust distributions of power, money, and resources (Marmot et al., 2008). Moreover, the issue of systemic violence by police is only one element of the rampant social injustices currently facing humanity. The gender pay gap, health inequities, economic disparities, and differential access to education, as well as countless forms of discrimination still plague the world, leaving one questioning whether or not protests are sufficiently powerful to change such an unjust world.

Individual protesters and groups who are organizing movements to produce social change encounter numerous barriers, many of which would seemingly result in a deceleration of such efforts, especially from a radical behaviorist perspective. Protesters often encounter aversive contingencies such as tear gas, rubber bullets, physical assaults, arrests, and more. However, contrary to what encountering these contingent aversives might predict, the protests continue and, in many cases strengthen. In Portland, for example, following the arrival of federal troops armed in riot gear, using crowd-control weapons, we saw more community members join the protest (e.g., groups like the wall of moms, the wall of vets, and dads with leaf blowers), who engaged in mutually supportive prosocial behaviors including the provision of food and medical supplies.

---

1 This is not intended to suggest that the police brutality against people of color is a recent phenomenon. The US has a long history of systemic oppression and countless citizens have fought against such oppressive systems through active demonstrations (e.g., protests and boycotts) and symbolic gestures (e.g., raising black-gloved fists or kneeling down during the national anthem) for generations.

With the momentum for social change growing, a closer examination of strategic nonviolent action from a radical behaviorist perspective, complemented by with recent advances in culturo-behavior science (e.g., Cihon & Mattaini, in press; Mattaini, 2013), could offer both a more coherent explanation as to how such efforts to disrupt unjust systems persist in the face of aversive contingencies as well as ways to mobilize such efforts to produce systemic change. In this chapter, we discuss nonviolent struggles and briefly introduce culturo-behavior science before we summarize how the combination of the two can support the disruption of unjust systems and the construction of more socially – and environmentally-just societies.

NONVIOLENT STRUGGLE

Gene Sharp, a prominent political scientist and founder of the Albert Einstein Institute, posited that using violence against oppressors was likely to fail (e.g., Sharp, 2012). Oppressors are more likely to possess superior power such as military/police personnel and equipment; and even when violent uprisings are successful, the government of the formerly oppressed begin to fear another violent uprising. Thus, they fortify, further strengthening their power, and the result is often that one oppressor is simply replaced by another.

Chenoweth and Stephan (2011) analyzed over 300 "violent and nonviolent resistance campaigns between 1900 and 2006 . . ." showing that "nonviolent resistance campaigns were nearly twice as likely to achieve full or partial success as their violent counterparts" (p. 22). Traditional methods of the use of violence against oppressors are declining; people are beginning to use methods of civil disobedience such as mobilizing the masses to maximize the power of the people, coinciding with the increasing number of protests around the world (Chenoweth & Stephan, 2011).

Important to understanding Chenoweth and Stephan's (2011) analysis of nonviolent resistance campaigns is Sharp's (2005, 2016; see also Helvey, 2004) pluralistic model of power. Contrary to earlier monolithic models of power that suggest that power is applied by the oppressor to the oppressed in a unidirectional manner, Sharp (2005, 2016) suggests that the sources of power instead reside in the population and that a government's ability to exercise its power depends on the population's consent. Sharp (2005) identified six sources of what he termed "political power": authority, human resources, skills and knowledge, intangible factors, material resources, and sanctions. Authority refers to the population's perception of the legitimacy of the government; this collective perception determines the degree to which the government relies on cooperation or obedience to exercise its power to control. Using human resources, including specialized skills and knowledge, intangible factors such as psychological and institutional beliefs (e.g., religion and cultural norms), material resources (e.g., natural, financial, infrastructural, and resources to maintain theses), and sanctions (i.e., punishments or pressures the government uses to achieve cooperation or obedience), the government exercises its power. Political power, therefore, provides a government with the means to control the population.

Sharp's (2005) pluralistic model of power helps one identify the sources of the government's power, or the institutions that serve as "pillars of support" (p. 35). Examples of such institutions include police, military, civil servants, media, the business community, youth, laborers, religious organizations, and non-governmental organizations (Helvey, 2004). For example, the police provide the means by which the government controls the population (e.g., the police may arrest people who engage in illegal activities). The business communities provide the money, in the form of taxes, to fund the police. Both the police and the business communities further depend on other institutions to maintain their functions. The business communities are dependent upon the population for their income – both the laborers (often the oppressed) and those who support such oppressive practices (often the business owners; see also Ulman, 1986). Sharp's (2005, 2016) pluralistic model of power provides insights as to how the government uses its power and the sources by which it acquires and sustains its power, illustrating how political power resides in the relationships among the government, the institutions, and the population.

Sharp (2005), emphasizing that the population holds the power to affect change, classified 198 methods of nonviolent action (Helvey, 2004; Sharp, 2012) into three categories. The first category, actions to send a message, focuses on actions that seek to change the attitudes and opinions of others and includes 54 strategies that are largely symbolic peaceful demonstrations such as marches and vigils. Actions to suspend cooperation and assistance, the second category, moves a step further, and includes 103 strategies related to active noncooperation with social, economic, and political relationships such as labor strikes and boycotts. The third category, methods of disruption, includes 41 strategies such as nonviolent occupation and alternative transportation systems (e.g., carpools organized by community leaders during Montgomery Bus Boycott), strategies that emphasize more direct intervention to change given conditions.

In *Strategic Nonviolent Power: The Science of Satyagraha*, Mattaini (2013) suggests that the application of cultural and behavioral systems analysis to nonviolent struggle "has unique contributions to make not only to the study of resistance movements themselves but also, and especially, to the practice of effective resistance" (p. 2). However, before detailing Mattaini's analysis, it is important to briefly introduce culturo-behavior science (CBS) as an emerging specialization within behavior analysis.

CULTURO-BEHAVIOR SCIENCE

Bridging concepts from General System(s) Theory (e.g., von Bertalanffy, 1968) and ecological systems science (e.g., Mattaini, 2019, in press), Behavior Systems Analysis (e.g., Krapfl & Gasparotto, 1982), and cultural selection (e.g., Glenn, 2004; Skinner, 1981), CBS brings together those behavior analysts who seek to understand both Skinner's (1981) third "kind" of selection (i.e., cultural selection) and those working toward applications of behavior science to cultural and community change (e.g., Community Behavioral Psychology; e.g., Fawcett, 1991). Readers are encouraged to explore CBS in more detail (see for example Cihon & Mattaini, in press and Emerging Cultural and Behavioral Systems Science, 2019) as here we highlight just two concepts from CBS: metacontingencies (cf., Glenn, 2004; Glenn et al., 2016) and system interdependencies (cf. Walonick, 1993).

METACONTINGENCIES

In its simplest form the metacontingency is the "contingent relation between (1) recurring interlocking behavioral contingencies having an aggregate product and (2) selecting environmental events or conditions" (Glenn et al., 2016, p. 13).[2] Nonviolent struggle and actions require the

---

2   Others (e.g., Houmanfar et al., 2010) have offered an expanded definition of the metacontingency that includes five terms: the cultural–organizational milieu → socio-interlocked behaviors → AP → consumer practices → group-rule generation.

coordinated behaviors of many individuals to be effective. Considering the events in Portland, the metacontingency may provide some explanation as to why, when met with stronger aversive contingencies, the protests grew in strength rather than dissipating. In addition to the operant consequences that would likely function as a punisher, an additional consequence (i.e., a cultural consequence), such as activists from other cities showing solidarity with Portland activists, may have served to strengthen the interlocking behavioral contingencies (i.e., the coordinated behaviors among various groups of protesters; IBCs) and aggregate products (e.g., resistance against the federal agents, food and medical support; APs), supporting the recurrence of these events (i.e., the IBCs and corresponding APs, also termed the culturant; Hunter, 2012; also see Borba et al., 2017 for a discussion of ethical self-control).

SYSTEM INTERDEPENDENCIES

According to systems theory, a system is more than the sum of its parts. It is insufficient to understand only the elements of the system, as the relations among the elements of the system are important in order to gain a complete understanding of the system (von Bertalanffy, 1968). The relations among the elements of the system are interdependencies, like Sharp's (2005) pillars of support. Therefore, attempts to understand only one element of a system such as the police or military, will not provide a full understanding of the state of affairs; instead, the relations among these pillars must also be considered to understand the whole (i.e., how the pillars work together to sustain the governmental power and control). Recall that in Sharp's (2005) pluralistic model of power, a government relies on other institutions for the sources of its power; thus, the relations among these institutions, the interdependencies, function collectively to determine the government's use of its political power to control the population. The source of the government's power then can only be understood, then, if the interdependencies are also understood.

STRATEGIC NONVIOLENT POWER

Mattaini (2013) conceptualized the relations within and among the pillars of support as interlocking networks of contingencies in his application of CBS to Sharp's (2005, 2016) analyses of nonviolent struggle. The interlocking networks of contingencies that are formed among the pillars of support provide the inputs an institution needs to exercise its power (i.e., output). Returning to police as an example, we are reminded again that the police require several inputs including human resources, money, equipment, etc., to sustain its function(s). These inputs, however, are provided by other institutions, such as the business community, local government, local community, and so on. The confluence of these institutions, their inputs, outputs, and the interdependencies among them, create the networks of contingencies that sustain the police. Often considered important in the formation of an understanding of complex social issues and undesirable cultural practices, such analyses of the networks of contingencies, or matrix analyses (see also Aspholm & Mattaini, 2017; Biglan, 1995) can serve as an important initial step toward disrupting oppressive institutions and practices (Mattaini, 2013). It is important to emphasize, however, that understanding the power relations and the pillars of support, along with strategic planning efforts (Helvey, 2004; Sharp, 2005, 2016) are critical for the success of such organized movements (Mattaini, 2013).

Mattaini (2013) reorganized Sharp's (2005) categories of nonviolent actions into six categories based on their functionalities. We provide a brief description of these categories in order to illustrate how they might be incorporated into function-based strategic planning efforts, that strengthen the probability that collective, nonviolent action will disrupt the contingencies sustaining oppressive systems.[3]

Protest (often by way of negative reinforcement) and persuasion (generally through positive reinforcement) focus on changing direct-acting contingencies, equivalence relations (e.g., all criminals are bad vs. some crimes are committed for survival), establishing rules (e.g., communities will be strengthened if resources supporting police are redistributed to other community sectors) and relational frames, as well as shifting networks of interdependent contingencies. Persuasive actions are advantageous when conditions require a change in the perspective of community members and/or controlling agencies (see also Todorov & Lemos, in press) to garner support for a new way of thinking about things.

Disruptive noncooperation and resource disruption involve intentionally withholding or withdrawing something the opponent group wants or needs to sustain its power such as cooperation or resources (i.e., extinction). Resource disruption requires an understanding of the resources and motivating conditions that the opponent group requires to maintain their activities. Recalling that governments require the cooperation of and the resources garnered from other institutions, disruptive noncooperation and resource disruption function to disrupt these inputs, thereby reducing the government's power and control. If an entity no longer receives the same level of inputs (e.g., labor), it can no longer sustain the same level of outputs (e.g., financial support to another institution). This strategy is often accompanied by setting up alternative contingencies (e.g., labor will return to previous levels if X conditions are met).

Retaliation serves to reduce the specific behaviors an opponent group engages in through the use of aversive contingencies (i.e., punishment). Because retaliation rests on the use of coercive strategies, Mattaini (2013) cautions that retaliation strategies be carefully considered before implementation as the use of coercive strategies can result in further retaliation from the recipient thereof, and even cycles of countercontrol (cf. Sidman, 1989); therefore, they should be used as a last resort.

Mattaini (2013) emphasizes that constructive noncooperation may be the most desirable (and powerful) strategic nonviolent action, though the least understood. Constructive noncooperation focuses on making changes within the activism group (e.g., constructing new operant contingencies, IBCs, metacontingencies, such that new systems interdependencies [i.e., networks of contingencies] are formed), rather than attempting to change the behaviors of the opponent groups (see also Goldiamond, 1974/2002; Mattaini & Atkinson, 2011; Roose & Mattaini, in press). As efforts continue to identify alternatives to policing, we may see more opportunities to employ constructive noncooperative strategies, forming new patterns of coordinated responding within and among different community sectors, working together to create more equitable and just societies (e.g., restorative justice movements; Umbreit et al., 1994).

---

3   Readers are strongly encouraged, however, to read Mattaini (2013) in its entirety to gain a more comprehensive understanding of what is only briefly summarized here within.

MOVING FORWARD

Human behavior is at the core of the unjust distribution of resources and the creation of more just and equitable distributions. Behavior scientists can bring the concepts and principles of behavior science and an emerging CBS to activist and advocacy efforts (see also Ardila-Sánchez et al., in press), providing the science and tools thereof to mobilize such efforts to bring change to the long history of social injustices that have long-plagued humanity. Perhaps, following the year of protests, is the ideal time to study the methods of nonviolent struggle in order to contribute to the further development of effective nonviolent strategic action, disrupting the unjust networks of contingencies and the sources of social injustices, to make the world a little better place.

REFERENCES

Ardila Sánchez, J. G., Richling, S. M., Benson, M. L., & Rakos, R. F. (in press). Activism, advocacy, and accompaniment. In T. M. Cihon & M. A. Mattaini (Eds.), *Behavior science perspectives on culture and community*. Springer.

Aspholm, R. R., & Mattaini, M. A. (2017). Youth activism as violence prevention. In P. Sturmey (Ed.), *The Wiley handbook of violence and aggression*. John Wiley & Sons.

Biglan, A. (1995). *Changing cultural practices: A contextualist framework for intervention research*. Context Press.

Borba, A., Tourinho, E. Z., & Glenn, S. S. (2017). Effects of cultural consequences on the interlocking behavioral contingencies of ethical self-control. *Psychological Record, 67*(3), 399–411. https://doi.org/10.1007/s40732-017-0231-6

Carnegie Endowment for International Peace (2020, September 1). *Global protest tracker*. https://carnegieendowment.org/publications/interactive/protest-tracker

Chenoweth, E., & Stephan, M. J. (2011). *Why civil resistance works: The strategic logic of nonviolent conflict*. Columbia University Press.

Cihon, T. M., & Mattaini, M. A. (Eds.) (in press). *Behavior science perspectives on culture and community*. Springer.

Emerging Cultural and Behavioral Systems Science (2019). [special section]. *Perspectives on Behavior Science, 42*(4).

Fawcett, S. B. (1991). Some values guiding community research and action. *Journal of Applied Behavior Analysis, 24*(4), 621–636. https://doi.org/10.1901/jaba.1991.24-621

Glenn, S. S. (2004). Individual behavior, culture, and social change. *The Behavior Analyst, 27*(2), 133–151. https://doi.org/10.1007/BF03393175

Glenn, S. S., Malott, M. E., Andery Benvenuti, M., Houmanfar R. A., Sandaker, I., Todorov, J. C., Tourinho, E. Z., & Vasconcelos, L. (2016). Toward consistent terminology in a behaviorist approach to cultural analysis. *Behavior & Social Issues, 25*, 11–1. https://doi.org/10.5210/bsi.v25i0.6634

Goldiamond, I. (1974/2002). Toward a constructional approach to social problems: Ethical and constitutional issues raised by applied behavior analysis. *Behaviorism, 2*, 1–84. https://doi.org/10.5210/bsi.v11i2.92

Helvey, R. L. (2004). *On strategic nonviolent conflict: Thinking about the fundamentals*. The Albert Einstein Institution.

Houmanfar, R. A., Rodrigues, N. J., & Ward, T. A., (2010). Emergence & metacontingency: Points of contact and departure. *Behavior and Social Issues, 19*, 78–103. https://doi.org/10.5210/bsi.v19i0.3065

Hunter, C. S. (2012). Analyzing behavioral and cultural selection contingencies. *Revista Latinoamericana de Psicología, 44*(1), 43–54.

Krapfl, J. E., & Gasparotto, G. (1982). Behavioral systems analysis. In L. W. Fredericksen (Ed.), *Handbook of organizational behavior management*. Wiley.

Marmot, M., Friel, S., Bell, R., Houweling, T. A., Taylor, S., & Commission on Social Determinants of Health (2008). Closing the gap in a generation: Health equity through action on the social determinants of health. *The Lancet, 372*(9650), 1661–1669. https://doi.org/10.1016/S0140-6736(08)61690-6

Mattaini, M. A. (2013). *Strategic nonviolent power: The science of satyagraha.* AU press.

Mattaini, M. A. (2019). Out of the lab: Shaping an ecological and constructional cultural systems science. *Perspectives on Behavior Science, 42*(4), 713–731. https://doi.org/10.1007/s40614-019-00208-z

Mattaini, M. A. (in press) Cultural systems analysis: An emerging science. In T. M. Cihon & M. A. Mattaini (Eds.), *Behavior science perspectives on culture and community.* Springer.

Mattaini, M. A., & Atkinson, K. (2011). Constructive noncooperation: Living in truth. *Peace and Conflict Studies, 18*(1), 3–43.

Roose, K. M. & Mattaini, M. A. (in press). Challenging violence: Toward a 21st century, science-based "Constructive programme." In T. M. Cihon & M. A. Mattaini (Eds.), *Behavior science perspectives on culture and community.* Springer.

Sharp, G. (2005). *Waging nonviolent struggle: 20th century practice and 21st century potential.* Extending Horizons Books.

Sharp, G. (2012). *From dictatorship to democracy: A conceptual framework for liberation.* Serpent's Tail.

Sharp, G. (2016). *Civilian-based defense: A post-military weapons system.* The Albert Einstein Institution.

Skinner, B. F. (1981). Selection by consequences. *Science, 213*, 501–504. https://psycnet.apa.org/doi/10.1126/science.7244649

Todorov, J. C. & Lemos, R. F. (in press). Applying behavioral science to large scale social changes. In T. M. Cihon & M. A. Mattaini (Eds.), *Behavior science perspectives on culture and community.* Springer.

Ulman, J. (1986). Working class strategies for world peace. *Behavior Analysis & Social Action, 5*(1–2), 36–43.

Umbreit, M., Coates, R. B., & Kalanj, B. (1994). *Victim meets offender: The importance of restorative justice and mediation.* Criminal Justice Press.

von Bertalanffy, L. (1968). *General system theory.* George Braziller.

Walonick, D. S. (1993). General systems theory. http://www.statpac.org/walonick/systems-theory.htm

Wright, R. (December, 2019). The story of 2019: Protests in every corner of the globe. *The New Yorker.* https://www.newyorker.com/news/our-columnists/the-story-of-2019-protests-in-every-corner-of-the-globe

15

THE DO BETTER MOVEMENT

The Science of Togetherness

Megan Miller and Jennifer Phelps

Sometimes in our society, whether it be in our professions or our personal relationships, there's a common misconception that if you spend too much time looking at the past, you can't get to what the future might hold. This is partially true. Living in the past, behind you, doesn't allow you to move forward to what's in front of you. That being said, there's no denying that, especially as behavior analysts, we learn from past actions. That's why we take that information, analyze it and focus on what from the past we will honor, talk about, and even integrate into a new vision or idea. It's how we get where we're going without constantly or consistently making the same mistakes over and over again.

And, to put it frankly, it's how we DO BETTER.

This is why the *Do Better Movement* was created. It is a professional development initiative for behavior analysts and other professionals who want to be better practitioners and inspire change. The initiative revolves around teaching topics of clinical relevance, providing continuing education courses, and community involvement opportunities. *Do Better* is a collective enterprise with a common purpose. We want each community member to experience a sense of alliance with people who share a passion for disseminating quality training and the common goal to simply Do Better in their personal and professional life.

Over the past three years, the *Do Better Movement* has organically established itself as a community of practice. Communities of practice consist of three characteristics: domain, community, and practice (Wenger-Trayner, 2015). We are motivated by Etienne Wegner who said, "Communities of practice are groups of people who share a concern or a passion for something they do and learn how to do it better as they interact regularly."

Domain refers to community members having a shared interest. The domain provides a common ground for members of the community to be inspired to engage in meaningful action-based learning. The domain for *Do Better* is a shared commitment to engaging in lifelong learning focused on developing humane, culturally competent, and compassionate interventions for consumers of behavior analytic services.

Community means that members engage in collective learning by sharing information, building relationships, engaging in problem-solving opportunities, having discussions, and participating in joint learning activities all focused on the shared domain of interest. In a strong community, ample opportunities are provided for interaction and members are encouraged to give space and take space for their ideas. Members of the *Do Better* community engage in collective learning through webinars, podcasts, live discussions on topics, activities posted within the community, and conference events.

The last characteristic, practice, means the members of the community practice within the domain of interest. The core of collective knowledge within the community is developed around the practice of the community. The *Do Better* community primarily consists of behavior analysts and related professionals who directly provide behavior analytic services or work on multi-disciplinary teams where behavior analysis is a utilized service.

But why create a movement? Hasn't there been a drive amongst professionals in all fields to do better at what they do? We created the *Do Better Movement* to promote bringing in a diverse group of individuals who are passionate about cultivating the power of questioning everything, the art of facilitating hard and uncomfortable discussion, and the disciplined practice of continuously observing our environment to identify potential problems, opportunities, emerging techniques and ideas. We are building a community of like-minded professionals that are dedicated to understanding, connecting, and exploring the edges of applied behavior analysis, and it is aimed at letting therapists break free of the chains of rigid, cookie-cutter commercial assessments and programs and grow their skillset, such as how to fluently make moment to moment decisions based on the current context and learner responding.

The field of behavior analysis is growing rapidly to meet a high demand for behavior analytic services (Behavior Analyst Certification Board, 2019). Graduate level training in the science of behavior analysis provides a minimum competency for practicing, leaving most practitioners yearning to learn more and continue to develop their skill sets as they embark on their career. After providing international consultation and supervision for several years, clear trends emerged within these skill sets that were lacking consistently across the globe for behavior analytic students, new behavior analysts, and even some seasoned behavior analysts. These trends led to the creation of a list of online presentations to conduct for supervisees and clients. It was taking far too long to train individuals one by one on these critical content areas and it was impossible to find the time to host the presentations. Because of this, pen was set to paper and public commitments were made to provide professional development content on a monthly basis and the movement was formed. Say-do correspondence is a very powerful tool (Bevill-Davis et al., 2004).

The first year of the movement consisted of one free webinar per month on one of the critical topic areas and focused on presenting content in easily consumable format that left attendees with resources to use to apply in practice. The second year of the movement consisted of starting an online community and inviting emerging experts in the field of behavior analysis to disseminate their work and practice with the rest of the community. For the third year of the movement, it was clear that the community was large and motivated to continue to learn. An open invitation for presentations resulted in at least two webinars per month presented by members of the community. This year has been the most unique in that we are all learning from each other and connecting with areas of practice that we didn't even know we needed to access in order to Do Better.

Surprisingly to us, this community has grown into something we could have never have foreseen. With more than 8,000 people representing 99 countries, the *Do Better Movement* consistently receives feedback from members of the community regarding career changing improvements in their practice and skill sets after participating in *Do Better* learning opportunities. The *Do Better Movement* has hosted more than 50 webinars on a variety of topics within the field of behavior analysis, created the *Do Better* Podcast, hosted an online conference, and provided other educational experiences online. All focused on creating opportunities to learn how to *Do Better*. As part of this inclusive community, avenues have been created for analysts and therapists to have true dialogue amongst themselves, which has allowed them to address hard topics and subjects.

One avenue for people to *Do Better* is through our Ambassador program. BCBA's use what they have learned from our webinars, workshops and the *Do Better* Podcast, and use it to mentor other BCBAs, therapists and analysts. The Ambassador program provides mentorship in a range of topic areas: ethics consultation, problem-solving barriers to learning, and precision teaching to name a few.

The *Do Better Movement* is also set to revolutionize the conference experience. Too often when attending a conference, there is an exorbitant amount of new information learned and gleaned, but once returning home to practice it, there's very little application of new skills. And there's always the value of connecting with colleagues and networking during conferences. The *Do Better* Couch to Camp experience flips the conference experience by having the learning experience occur online with the opportunity to receive coaching for several months after the conference to put learning into practice. The event culminates with a camp to bring everyone together in person to focus on further application of content and provide opportunities for networking and self-care.

Recent research published within the field has also called for improvements in behavior analysts' skill sets in the areas of cultural humility and engaging in multi-disciplinary practices (Beaulieu et al., 2019; Miller et al., 2019; Taylor et al., 2019; Wright, 2019). The *Do Better Movement* is focusing on disseminating information to behavior analysts about how to engage in dialogue from a place of curiosity and a willingness to learn multiple perspectives.

As the *Do Better Movement* continues to look to the future to continue to do better, we realize that, like any behavior, it will need to be adaptive in services, outreach and perspective. Therapy and practices need to be creative and innovative, staying away from the rigidness that sometimes can be overwhelming and dull within an intervention setting.

And how do we do that? By starting where behavior analysts start: graduate programs. We also do this by working with companies to adopt the content being taught instead of just relying on individuals to go through the motions in graduate courses and apply the information in practice.

The *Do Better Movement* will also create avenues that recognize people who are doing the work to DO BETTER and who will stay committed to improving their practices with lifelong learning techniques and practices. And focus will also have to be on inclusion of diverse and expanded content and perspectives from marginalized communities.

The Do Better Movement has risen to embrace the challenges of our time enabling and facilitating cutting-edge courses, workshops, and discussions for behavior analysts who strive to create lifelong change for their clients and practice methods.

But how, right now, can you DO BETTER?

Start by asking yourself: what are those in my speciality, company or professional community afraid to do or talk about? Then do that!

From there, unlock your creativity and passion and use it as a force for positive change. Don't be afraid to think or act outside your own comfort zone, but be careful with your words because words matter. They can embody leadership and have the power to open doors, build bridges, inspire vision, and engage the world.

Share, share, Share! Share all of this and the knowledge you know because, more than likely, you know more than you think you know and should share it with your peers and colleagues. We are in the field of studying behavior and analyzing it. We should share as much information as we can with each other. In the end that will make us all *Do Better*.

Recognize the role your learning history plays in how you engage with others and commit to learning how to engage in difficult discussions with colleagues, friends, and clients. Recent publications within the field of behavior analysis provide an initial starting point for doing better in having culturally informed, constructive, compassionate, and humble dialogue (e.g., Beaulieu et al., 2019; Miller et al., 2019; Taylor et al., 2019; Wright, 2019). Developing an understanding of various communication methods used in counseling and conflict resolution can also deepen our ability to *Do Better* engaging with others from a place of curiosity, empathy, and perspective taking. Choose an article, book, or course to complete in the areas of non-violent communication, compassionate listening, and/or motivational interviewing (e.g., Dore, 2017; Klimecki, 2019; Museux et al., 2016; Rubak et al., 2005; Tschaepe, 2018).

And, lastly, we have to understand and come to terms with the fact that we don't know what we don't know. No one, ever, has learned something they already knew. So we have to be flexible and open to developing new skills, leaning into learning more about interventions that are different from our initial training history, and work to make impactful change. That takes commitment. It's a lifelong commitment to learning and to changing, especially if the new information you encounter doesn't fit with your style and approach. Be curious, reflect on whether it should be incorporated into the work you are doing and how you can use the information to *Do Better*.

REFERENCES

Beaulieu, L., Addington, J., & Almeida, D. (2019). Behavior analysts' training and practices regarding cultural diversity: The case for culturally competent care. *Behavior Analysis in Practice, 12*(3), 557–575.

Behavior Analyst Certification Board. (2019). US employment demand for behavior analysts: 2010–2018. Author.

Bevill-Davis, A., Clees, T. J., & Gast, D. L. (2004). Correspondence training: A review of the literature. *Journal of Early and Intensive Behavior Intervention, 1*(1), 13.

Dore, J. (2017, September 11). *The four processes of motivational interviewing*. Psych Central Professional. https://pro.psychcentral.com/the-four-processes-of-motivational-interviewing/

Klimecki, O. M. (2019). The role of empathy and compassion in conflict resolution. *Emotion Review, 11*(4), 310–325.

Miller, K. L., Re Cruz, A., & Ala'i-Rosales, S. (2019). Inherent tensions and possibilities: Behavior analysis and cultural responsiveness. *Behavior and Social Issues, 28*(1), 16–36.

Museux, A. C., Dumont, S., Careau, E., & Milot, É. (2016). Improving interprofessional collaboration: The effect of training in nonviolent communication. *Social work in health care, 55*(6), 427–439.

Rubak, S., Sandbæk, A., Lauritzen, T., & Christensen, B. (2005). Motivational interviewing: A systematic review and meta-analysis. *British Journal of General Practice, 55*(513), 305–312.

Taylor, B. A., LeBlanc, L. A., & Nosik, M. R. (2019). Compassionate care in behavior analytic treatment: Can outcomes be enhanced by attending to relationships with caregivers?. *Behavior Analysis in Practice, 12*(3), 654–666.

Tschaepe, M. (2018). Cultural humility and Dewey's pattern of inquiry: Developing good attitudes and overcoming bad habits. *Contemporary Pragmatism, 15*(1), 152–164.

Wenger-Trayner, E., & Wenger-Trayner, B. (2015, April 15). *Introduction to communities of practice*. Wenger-Trayner.com. https://wenger-trayner.com/introduction-to-communities-of-practice/

Wright, P. I. (2019). Cultural humility in the practice of applied behavior analysis. *Behavior Analysis in Practice, 12*(4), 805–809.

16

EQUITABLE EDUCATION

The Role of Behavior Analysts in Providing Equitable Services for Clients in Public Schools

Nicole Hollins and Stephanie Peterson

Many families struggle to gain access to an equitable education for their children. For some, this struggle may include attending countless school meetings, making daily phone calls to further understand school policies on busing, or even attending frequent meetings with teachers and administrators to address behavioral concerns. Over two decades of research indicates that access to education early on (i.e., preschool) directly impacts a student's academic achievements, cognitive abilities, and behavioral outcomes (Barnett, 1995; Hamre & Pianta, 2001). As such, advances in equitable education include numerous laws (e.g., the Individuals with Disabilities Education Act [IDEA], 2004) and programs (e.g., Head Start) aimed at ensuring both access to and fair treatment in education. Nonetheless, the fight for equitable education continues for many students with and without disabilities. Given that behavior analysts have expertise in motivation, learning, and social behavior, they can also contribute consultation services to teachers and families in educational settings. Behavior analysts obtain either a master's or doctoral degree, and they primarily provide evidence-based services to increase desired behaviors (i.e., functional communication, daily living skills, social skills, and academic learning skills) and decrease undesired or aberrant behaviors (i.e., severe problem behaviors) (BACB, 2014). As such, behavior analysts could play an integral role in ensuring equitable education for clients in public schools.

In this chapter, we discuss two big ideas that may increase the probability of *all* students receiving access to equitable education. These are: (a) an acknowledgment of and action to limit exclusionary discipline practices, and (b) the use of effective, evidence-based teaching practices. It is beyond the scope of this chapter to extensively review the research on these variables; thus, readers are referred to helpful literature reviews cited in this chapter. Instead, we discuss the intersection of these variables and how behavior analysts can contribute to equitable service delivery for their clients in public schools.

Students with developmental disabilities who are enrolled in public schools are legally entitled to an appropriate education (IDEA, 2004). According to IDEA (2004), an equitable education for students with developmental disabilities includes (a) a free appropriate public education, (b) identification and evaluation to determine the need for special education services, (c) an individualized education program (IEP) that describes specific educational goals, (d) education that occurs in the least restrictive environment, (e) adherence to due process safeguards, and (f) the involvement of parents and students during the decision making process. Despite these legal protections for students with disabilities under IDEA, exclusionary practices persist, causing students without disabilities to be excluded from educational settings at a higher rate than their peers (Wesley & Ellis, 2017). It seems clear that we have not yet achieved equitable education for all and that further conversation and action is warranted.

Individuals with disabilities are not the only individuals who experience inequities in their education. The disparities of minority representation in school discipline data has been documented consistently for more than 25 years (Krezmien et al., 2016). Investigators have found consistent evidence of significant minority overrepresentation in office referrals (Lietz & Gregory, 1978), suspensions (Cooley, 1995; Costenbader & Markson, 1998; Skiba et al., 2003), and expulsions (Gilliam & Shahar, 2006; Skiba et al., 2002). For example, research shows that minority preschool students (i.e., 5 years and under) are being expelled and suspended at four times the rate compared to their peers in K-12 community and private programs (Gilliam & Shahar, 2006; Neitzel et al., 2018; US Department of Education, 2016). Similarly, researchers also suggest that students with emotional and behavior disorders (EBD) or emotional impairments (EI) have substantially higher rates of suspensions than students with other disabilities (Zhang et al., 2004). Thus, these exclusionary practices place minority children at a greater risk of being identified as having a disability (Connor et al., 2019).

As such, when discussing equitable education, there may be value to attending to minority status in analyses of problem behavior for both students with and without developmental disabilities, as minorities account for many of the suspensions and expulsions (Gilliam & Shahar, 2006). Some variables that may contribute to minorities being expelled and suspended at higher rates than their peers may include teachers and other school leaders engaging in bias-based behavior (De Houwer, 2019) and a lack of evidence-based teaching practices (Kestner et al., 2019). Furthermore, as students/clients have the right to effective treatment (Van Houten et al., 1988), school-based behavior analysts are ethically obligated to advocate for their clients by including relevant variables in their analyses throughout the duration of service provision (BACB, 2014).

De Houwer (2019) appropriately defines biased-based behavior or implicit bias as a behavioral phenomenon. That is, implicit bias is something that people *do* rather than something that people *possess* as an innate characteristic. Further, bias is behavior that is influenced in an implicit manner by subtle cues that function as indicators for the social group to which others belong. Adopting a behavioral perspective toward a concept that many find difficult to both define operationally and measure (i.e., bias) places behavior analysts in a position to be part of the solution. Behavior analysts are often adept at objectively defining and measuring variables, and therefore, should be able to include behaviors that may be indicative of bias in their analyses to better serve their clients. Furthermore, as race is a variable that has shown to affect teacher–student interactions (Eddy & Easton-Brooks, 2011; Fitzpatrick et al., 2015), the analysis of teacher–student interactions between different racial groups in the classroom may be valuable.

When consulting in classroom settings, it is important for the behavior analyst to assess different environmental conditions that might evoke appropriate or inappropriate behaviors, such as the rate of reprimands the teacher delivers, praise statements the teacher makes, and demands the teacher places on students in the classroom (Kestner et al., 2019). The behavior analyst could examine whether there are any differences in these variables for students of color in comparison to their white peers as a measure of potential bias. This might serve as an objective measure to evaluate variables related to potential bias and may allow behavior analysts to better serve their clients. Rather than anecdotally reporting teacher–student interactions with a white peer appeared to differ from those with a student of color, behavior analysts might adopt a more empirical approach. For example, a consulting behavior analyst may say, "*During the large group, Susan (Black student) received 13 reprimands and Brittney (White student) received 2 reprimands when there weren't any noticeable differences in their behaviors. Let's talk about how we can provide more consistent delivery of behavior-specific statements to all students, which might increase class wide engagement during large group instruction.*" By adopting this model, the problem is clearly identified, subjectivity is removed, and the solution is directly presented.

As behavioral skills training is an effective method for teaching various skills (Parsons et al., 2012), the behavior analyst may also work collaboratively with the teacher to explicitly provide behavior-specific statements to increase appropriate behaviors and decrease inappropriate behaviors during a period where inappropriate behaviors are more likely to occur. The use of behavior-specific statements can be conceptualized as using classroom evidence-based practices. Evidence-based classroom practices include embedding frequent active student responding and opportunities to respond during instruction (see reviews Common, 2020; MacSuga-Gage & Simonsen, 2015), providing behavior-specific praise statements (see review Floress et al., 2017; Zoder-Martell et al., 2019), giving clear signals for the onset of transitions between activities or settings (Embry & Biglan, 2008), and embedding group contingencies into the lessons (see review Maggin et al., 2017). There is a robust body of literature to support the effectiveness of embedding evidence-based classroom practices into instruction. Applying these technologies consistently across *all* children can be a powerful way to impact students from all backgrounds with and without developmental disabilities, from preschool to college educational settings. Taken together, the behavior analyst may first carefully analyze all relevant variables in the classroom, identify if bias exists, then provide the teacher feedback about any variable teacher–student interactions that exist, and follow such conversations with behavioral skills training on evidence-based classroom practices to increase the generalization of the functional alternative behaviors across the school day. For example, a consulting behavior analyst may say, *"Remember yesterday when we spoke about consistent delivery of behavior-specific statements? That same concept applies during large group. I suggest you clearly state your expectations and provide examples and non-examples of target behavior."*

Navigating service provision in a school setting is no easy job, especially for behavior analysts who are in a consultative role. In this role, the behavior analyst is an outsider, which can make it difficult to have sensitive conversations with teachers. Nonetheless, when asked to assess a client's behavior, the role of the behavior analyst is to collect data about motivational operations, antecedents, behaviors, and consequences in the context of their daily occurrence (Fong et al., 2016). While these variables are important to analyze as part of behavioral consultation services, it may be equally important for the behavior analyst to collect data on teacher–student interactions, attending to behaviors that may vary across students. Specifically, the behavior analyst may need to attend to whether teacher behavior varies by minority background of their students and their use of effective evidence-based classroom practices. By operationally defining and measuring all relevant variables, behavior analysts can address disparities in access to services for culturally and linguistically diverse populations (Neely et al., 2020) and improve the overall classroom environment (Simonsen et al., 2008) for *all* children. Doing so will be an important step in achieving equitable education for all students.

REFERENCES

Barnett, W. S. (1995). Long-term effects of early childhood programs on cognitive and school outcomes. *The Future of Children, 5*(3), 25–50.

Behavior Analyst Certification Board. (2014). *Professional and ethical compliance code for behavior analysts.* BACB.

Common, E. A., Lane, K. L., Cantwell, E. D., Brunsting, N. C., Oakes, W. P., Germer, K. A., & Bross, L. A. (2020). Teacher-delivered strategies to increase students' opportunities to respond: A systematic methodological review. *Behavioral Disorders, 45*(2), 67–84.

Connor, D., Cavendish, W., Gonzalez, T., & Jean-Pierre, P. (2019). Is a bridge even possible over troubled water? The field of special education negates the overrepresentation of minority students: A DisCrit analysis. *Race, Ethnicity and Education, 22*(6), 723–745.

Cooley, S. (1995). Suspension/expulsion of regular and special education students in Kansas: A report to the Kansas State Board of Education.

Costenbader, V., & Markson, S. (1998). School suspension: A study with secondary school students. *Journal of School Psychology, 36*(1), 59–82.

De Houwer, J. (2019). Implicit bias is behavior: A functional-cognitive perspective on implicit bias. *Perspectives on Psychological Science, 14*(5), 835–840.

Eddy, C. M., & Easton-Brooks, D. (2011). Ethnic matching, school placement, and mathematics achievement of African American students from kindergarten through fifth grade. *Urban Education, 46*(6), 1280–1299.

Embry, D. D., & Biglan, A. (2008). Evidence-based kernels: Fundamental units of behavioral influence. *Clinical Child and Family Psychology Review, 11*(3), 75–113.

Fitzpatrick, C., Cote-Lussier, C., Pagani, L. S., & Blair, C. (2015). I don't think you like me very much: Child minority status and disadvantage predict relationship quality with teachers. *Youth and Society, 47*(5), 727–743.

Floress, M. T., Beschta, S. L., Meyer, K. L., & Reinke, W. M. (2017). Praise research trends and future directions: Characteristics and teacher training. *Behavioral Disorders, 43*(1), 227–243.

Fong, E. H., Catagnus, R. M., & Brodhead, M. T. (2016). Developing the cultural awareness skills of behavior analysts. *Behavior Analysis Practice, 9*(1), 84–94.

Gilliam, W. S., & Shahar, G. (2006). Preschool and childcare expulsion and suspension. *Infants and Young Children 19*(3), 228–245.

Hamre, B. K., & Pianta, R. C. (2001). Early teacher-child relationships and the trajectory of children's school outcomes through eighth grade. *Child Development, 72*(2), 625–638.

The Individuals with Disabilities Education Act [IDEA] for Children with Special Educational Needs. (2004). Section 504 of the Rehabilitation Act, and the Americans with Disabilities Act (ADA). CRS Report for Congress (R40123).

Kestner, K. M., Peterson, S. M., Eldridge, R. R., & Peterson, L. D. (2019). Considerations of baseline classroom conditions in conducting functional behavior assessments in school settings. *Behavior Analysis in Practice, 12*(2), 452–465.

Krezmien, M. P., Leone, P.E., & Achilles, G. M. (2016). Suspension, race, and disability: Analysis of statewide practices and reporting. *Journal of Emotional and Behavioral Disorders, 14*(4), 217–226.

Lietz, J., & Gregory, M. (1978). Pupil race and sex as determinants of office and exceptional educational referrals. *Education Research Quarterly, 3*(2), 61–66.

MacSuga-Gage, A. S., & Simonsen, B. (2015). Examining the effects of teacher-directed opportunities to respond on student outcomes: A systematic review of the literature. *Education and Treatment of Children, 38*(2), 211–239.

Maggin, D. M., Pustejovsky, J. E., & Johnson, A. H. (2017). A meta-analysis of school-based group contingency interventions for students with challenging behavior: An update. *Remedial and Special Education, 38*(6), 353–370.

Neely, L., Gann, C., & Castro-Villarreal, F. (2020). Preliminary findings of culturally responsive consultation with educators. *Behavior Analysis Practice, 131*(1), 270–281.

Neitzel, J. (2018). Research to practice: Understanding the role of implicit bias in early childhood disciplinary practices. *Journal of Early Childhood Teacher Education, 39*(3), 232–242.

Parsons, M. B., Rollyson, J. H, & Reid, D. H. (2012). Evidence-based staff training: A guide for practitioners. *Behavior Analysis in Practice, 5*(2), 2–11.

Simonsen, B., Fairbanks, S., Briesch, A., Myers, D., & Sugai, G. (2008). Evidence-based practices in classroom management: Considerations for research to practice. *Education and Treatment of Children, 31*(3), 351–380.

Skiba, R. J., Michael, R. S., Nardo, A. C., & Peterson, R. (2002). The color of discipline: Sources of racial and gender disproportionality in school punishment. *The Urban Review, 34*(4), 317–342.

Skiba, R., Simmons, A., Staudinger, L., Rausch, M., Dow, G., & Feggins, R. (2003, May). *Consistent removal: Contributions of school discipline to the school-prison pipeline.* Paper presented at the School to Prison Pipeline Conference, Harvard University, Cambridge, MA.

U.S. Department of Education Office of Civil Rights. (2016). *2013–2014 Civil rights data collection a first look: Key data highlights on equity and opportunity gaps in our nation's public schools.* U.S. Department of Education.

Van Houten, R., Axelrod, S., Bailey, J. S., Favell, J. E., Foxx, R. M., Iwata, B. A., & Lovaas, O. I. (1988). The right to effective behavioral treatment. *Journal of Applied Behavior Analysis, 21*(4), 381–384.

Wesley, L., & Ellis, A. L. (2017). Exclusionary discipline in preschool: Young Black Boys' Lives Matter. *Journal of African American Males in Education, 8*(2), 22–27.

Zhang, D., Katsiyannis, A., & Herbst, M. (2004). Disciplinary exclusions in special education: A 4-year analysis. *Behavioral Disorders, 29*(4), 337–347.

Zoder-Martell, K. A., Floress, M. T., Bernas, R. S., Dufrene, B. A., & Foulks, S. L. (2019) Training teachers to increase behavior-specific praise: A meta-analysis. *Journal of Applied School Psychology, 35*(4), 309–338.

17

FEMINISM

We Can Shatter Glass: An Optimistic Reminder to Behavior-Analytic Feminists

Natali Wachtman Perilo and Julie Ackerlund Brandt

Who are your role models in behavior analysis? If you are like many in our field, some names that come to mind quickly might include: B.F. Skinner, Don Baer, Todd Risley, Montrose Wolf, Jack Michael, Tony Cuvo, Brian Iwata, Wayne Fisher, Greg Madden, and Greg Hanley. There's nothing wrong with this list; these are all prestigious men . . . we repeat *men*. If this list was equitable, it would also include Betty Hart, Beth Sulzer-Azaroff, Cathleen Piazza, Dorothea Lerman, Linda LeBlanc, Linda Hayes, Amy Odum, Sigrid Glenn, Ruth Anne Rehfeldt, and Bridget Taylor. I must admit, even as a woman in this field, coming up with a list of ten prestigious women "off the top of my head" took longer than the preceding list of ten prestigious men. This is not necessarily surprising given that a list of the "10 most prolific authors" in behavior analysis only included three females, and they were included in the lower 40% (e.g., 6th, 8th, and 10th; Dixon et al., 2018). In fact, this issue is likely an example of the lingering effects of how sexism, and related issues of racism (notice that 95% of the individuals listed are white . . .) have affected behavior analysis and the way our founders/important figures are presented and portrayed.

We're all familiar with challenges associated with sexism that women face throughout society; and, remembering the overt and covert examples of sexism within the field of behavior analysis is important to allow for growth and progress (Baires & Koch, 2020; Li et al., 2018). These examples include differences in pay, leadership representation, and difficult social interactions that range from unwanted flirtations to sexual harassment (Baires & Koch, 2020; DeFalice & Diller, 2019; LeBlanc, 2015; Li et al., 2018; Taylor, 2015). These are issues that many of us have either encountered, or have had close friends and colleagues encounter. Additionally, there are also more subtle issues such as attitudes regarding females as less educated, being overly emotional, or less competent/skilled in research and publication when compared to their male counterparts (McSweeney, 2018; Petursdottir, 2015). The personal accounts and examples of these situations have been published for years; and although potentially disheartening, awareness of this history and having examples of how to deal with and potentially overcome these issues and attitudes can be instrumental for young women just starting out in the field. Because this isn't an "old school" problem, females are still working to be as represented and respected as males in our field.

Culturally based behaviors, such as sexism, have evolved over time and are rooted in relational frames regarding stimuli and positions associated with success and power that have been reinforced continually (Barnes-Holmes et al., 2010; Matsuda et al., 2020; Szabo, 2020). Behavior analysis is in a prime position to help work toward the development and adoption of new – or at least more varied – relational frames to increase equality and diversity through research on derived relational responding (DRR; Arhin & Thyer, 2004; Barnes-Holmes et al., 2020; Dixon et al., 2018). Although not currently studied directly regarding gender biases and sexism, some of the previous research on cultural biases and racism may be generalizable to a new wave of feminist research and progress (de Carvalho & de Rose, 2014; Dixon et al., 2006; Levin et al., 2016; Mizael et al., 2016). For example, there are studies demonstrating some promising research regarding the malleability of children's relational frames (de Carvalho & de Rose, 2014; McGlinchey & Keenan, 1997), at least compared to the relative permanence of adult's frames which have had a longer history of reinforcement (Dixon et al., 2006; Strand & Arntzen, 2020; Watt et al., 1991; for further description of research on DRR regarding racism biases see Matsuda et al., 2020). DRR research provides a potential method to evaluate and shift sexist attitudes and biases to a more equitable state.

The continued effects of sexism should not be confused with a lack of feminist progress and understanding overall. If lists similar to those presented here were presented 30 years ago, the differences would likely not only include time taken to produce the second list, but potentially an inability to do so without consulting journal articles and university faculty rosters. The notion of the list being presented 50 years ago is almost ludicrous, because the likelihood of an author – who would most likely be male (Iwata & Lent; 1984; Li et al., 2018; McSweeney & Parks, 2002; Poling et al., 1983; Simon et al., 2007) – even considering the importance of women in behavior analysis, would have been substantially less than now. *BUT*, in light of these statements, an important difference can also be noted in the progressive increases in the representation of women within behavior analysis as represented by authorship & editorship, organizational leaders, faculty, and practitioners (Baires & Koch, 2020; DeFalice & Diller, 2019; Li et al., 2018, 2019; Nosik et al., 2018; Sundberg et al., 2019). This progress is something to be highlighted and celebrated – and reinforced – or it may decrease or cease to exist altogether (Szabo, 2020).

One of the most often researched topics regarding women in behavior analysis is the number of women as authors of empirical manuscripts and membership on editorial boards, which has shown the disparity between the percentage of male and female authors has generally and progressively narrowed as of 2017 (Baires & Koch, 2020; Dixon et al., 2018; Iwata & Lent, 1984; Li et al., 2018; McSweeney et al., 2000). If one concentrates on authors of the *Journal of Applied Behavior Analysis* (*JABA*), the difference between the average number of female authors increased from 26% in 1978 to 57% in 2017 (i.e., Li et al. 2018). Although this is a considerable and encouraging increase in authorship over the past 40 years; female sole-authorship is still a less-observed phenomenon (DeFalice & Diller, 2019; Li et al., 2018; Szabo, 2020), and similar trends have been observed in editorial board analyses (DeFalice & Diller, 2019). Whereas women only comprised 34% of the *JABA* editorial board in 1995, the current JABA board includes 52% female members (Wiley Online Library, 2020). In addition, the editor in chief is female and 43% of the associate editors are also female (Wiley Online Library, 2020). These percentages are promising and deserve to be celebrated – and again, reinforced!

One may wonder how we can capitalize on this progress and ensure that it continues to be the pattern within the academic realm of our field. There are two recommendations provided to encourage these patterns: recruitment (Odum, 2000), and mentorship (Rehfeldt, 2018). Recruitment has especially been discussed as an important variable for increasing the number of women representatives in the experimental analysis of behavior (EAB) realm (Odum, 2000). Examples can include recruitment of female undergraduate students who may otherwise be unaware of opportunities in EAB or Applied Behavior Analysis (ABA).

Following recruitment, the retention of females across realms of behavior analysis is an additional concern. Although 88% of BCBA certificates are female; as the degree increases (i.e., master to doctoral level), the proportion of females decreases (Nosik et al., 2018). Mentorship is an important variable in the retention of females and has been cited as important and valued experiences by many (Rehfeldt, 2018); however, the mentor does not always have to be another female, there have been many males who have served as influential mentors and affected the trajectory of many females' careers (Rehfeldt, 2018; Taylor, 2015).

The misguided assumption that only women are involved or concerned with femi-nism is common but incorrect; feminism is the overall movement to eliminate sexism – defined as stereotypes or discrimination based on gender (often, but not always, towards females) – and ensure equity for all genders in terms of social, economic, and political rights (DeFalice & Diller, 2019). It is important to remember the men who work tirelessly to encourage and mentor women; for example, I (Julie) don't believe I would have con-tinued in my academic journey if not for two men that mentored me during undergrad. Dr. Gregory Madden and Dr. Kevin Klatt were the first to encourage me and tell me that I had potential. In fact, they pushed me at a time in my life when I had to decide whether I should pursue graduate training, or stay in the familiar setting of my hometown to become an elementary-school teacher. If it weren't for these men, I would have taken that "easy" and safe path; however, their insistence that I showed promise so early in my career (and *continued* reminders during graduate training), were instrumental in my pursuit of a doctoral degree and career in academia. Of course, I was also lucky to have amazing female mentors on my journey, Dr. Claudia Dozier and Dr. Ruth Anne Rehfeldt were huge impacts on my doctoral and masters level training, respectively. They were examples of intelligent, strong, successful women in behavior analysis, and I will always be thankful for their guidance (and *continued* support).

Mentorship is key and should occur across settings; not simply in academia, it should occur within organizations such as the Association for Behavior Analysis International (ABAI) and clinical settings as well (Sellers et al., 2016; Sundberg et al., 2019). Mentor-ship opportunities within organizations such as ABAI began as early as 1942 with the National Council of Women Psychologists, and has grown and progressed to include the Association for Women in Psychology, the American Psychological Association's Wom-en's Program office and Society for Women in Psychology (Division 35), and the annual Women in Behavior Analysis (WIBA) conference (DeFalice & Diller, 2019; Szabo, 2020). These organizations and conferences present opportunities for women to network and connect with other women who have survived or observed similar concern including sex-ual harassment, pay discrepancies, and achieving a work/life balance (Sundberg et al., 2019). Through these connections, women are able to mentor each other, and promote strategies to ensure the progress that has been made in terms of equality is maintained and continues to grow.

Mentorship in the clinical realm of our field is also key to ensuring a continuation of strong female representation within behavior analysis. In fact, it is within the clinical realm that female behavior analysts may be able to make the largest strides in affecting societal change regarding feminism as females make up over 80% of BCBAs (Nosik et al., 2018). Additionally, through collaboration with schools and the general public, BCBAs may be able to reach a large number of impressionable children and adoles-cents and have the opportunity to provide an environment of education and training in issues regarding equality (Baires & Koch, 2020). A key to continuing the feminist agenda of equality for all genders is through continued support of other women and encour-agement of children to develop associations between female, male, and non-binary individuals.

Please don't mistake the optimistic tone of this chapter with naïveté or a "Pollyanna-type" ignorance; because there is no denying the evidence provided showing the presence – at least previously – of a glass ceiling in behavior analysis (Li et al., 2018, 2019; McSweeney et al., 2000; McSweeney & Parks, 2002; Nosik & Grow, 2015; Petursdottir, 2015). In fact, as female authors, we have both experienced examples of sexism, which have included comments regarding last names, hiring practices based on family status, suggestive comments regarding clothing or appearance, and expectation to flirt with senior faculty to name just a few, so we do not mean to discredit or discount that history. Additionally, we recognize that the issues faced by women of minority status and LGBTQ+ individuals face a myriad of additional concerns and hurdles based on intersectionality, the multidimensional experience that comes with multiple personas such as being a Black woman or Lesbian woman (Beene, 2019; Cirincione-Ulezi, 2020). To many, progress likely feels small or non-existent, but generalization of the strides made by white (mainly) women to our minority siblings is possible! Furthermore, our goal can't simply be to increase the numbers of women and minorities into groups; we need to change the environment and behavior patterns such that the value of all individuals is evident through our cultural and societal practices (Buzzanell, 1995) Through committed actions such as continued conversations and interactions with diverse individuals and groups; evaluating practices, policies, and agreements to ensure equity and inclusion across gender and race; creating and participating in safe spaces to engages in conversation and collaboration. Finally, by challenging and clarifying biases and our own rule-governed behavior, we can continue to help others make similar progress to feeling recognized as equal (Baires & Koch, 2020; Beene, 2019). Admittedly, we all still have work to do and progress to make; however, our hope is that through continued committed actions of feminist behavior analysts, the past will not be forgotten, previous progress will be maintained, and additional progress will grow. Together, we won't just move mountains, we'll smash (glass) ceilings!

REFERENCES

Arhin, A., & Thyer, B. A. (2004). The causes of racial prejudice: A behavior-analytic perspective. In J. L. Chin (Ed.), *The psychology of prejudice and discrimination: Bias based on gender and sexual orientation* (pp. 1–20). Greenwood.

Baires, N. A., & Koch, D. S. (2020). The future is female (and behavior analysis): A behavioral account of sexism and how behavior analysis is simultaneously part of the problem and solution. *Behavior Analysis in Practice, 13*(1), 253–262.

Barnes-Holmes, D., Barnes-Holmes, Y., & McEnteggart, C. (2020). Updating RFT (more field than frame) and its implications for process-based therapy. *The Psychological Record, 1*(20). https://doi.org/10.1007/s40732-019-00372-3

Barnes-Holmes, D., Murphy, A., Barnes-Holmes, Y., & Stewart, I. (2010). The implicit relational assessment procedure: Exploring the impact of private versus public contexts and the response latency criterion on pro-white and anti-black stereotyping among white Irish individuals. *The Psychological Record, 60*, 57–79. https://doi.org/10.1007/BF03395694

Beene, N, (2019). Letter to the editor: One perspective and diversity in ABA. *Behavior Analysis in Practice, 12*(2), 899–901.

Buzzanell, Patrice. (1995). Reframing the glass ceiling as a socially constructed process: Implications for understanding and change. *Communication Monographs, 62*, 327–354.

Cirincione-Ulezi, N. (2020). Black women and barriers to leadership in ABA. *Behavior Analysis in Practice.* https://doi.org/10.1007/s40617-020-00444-9

de Carvalho, M. P., & de Rose, J. C. (2014). Understanding racial attitudes through the stimulus equivalence paradigm. *The Psychological Record, 64*, 527–536. https://doi.org/10.1007/s40732-014-0049-4

DeFalice, K. A., & Diller, J. W. (2019). Intersectional feminism and behavior analysis. *Behavior Analysis in Practice, 12*(2), 831–838.

Dixon, M. R., Belisle, J., Rehfeldt, R. A., & Root, W. B. (2018). Why we are still not acting to save the world: The upward challenge of a post-Skinnerian behavior science. *Perspectives on Behavior Science, 41*, 241–267. https://doi.org/10.1007/s40614-018-0162-9

Dixon, M. R., Rehfeldt, R. A., Zlomke, K. R., & Robinson, A. (2006). Exploring the development and dismantling of equivalence classes involving terrorist stimuli. *The Psychological Record, 56*, 83–103. https://doi.org/10.1007/BF03395539

Iwata, B. A., & Lent, C. E. (1984). Participation by women in behavior analysis: Some recent data on authorship of manuscripts submitted to the journal of applied behavior analysis. *The Behavior analyst, 7*(1), 77–78.

LeBlanc, L. A. (2015). My mentors and their influence on my career. *The Behavior Analyst, 38*, 237–245.

Levin, M. E., Luoma, J. B., Vilardaga, R., Lillis, J., Nobles, R., & Hayes, S. C. (2016). Examining the role of psychological inflexibility, perspective taking, and empathic concern in generalized prejudice. *Journal of Applied Social Psychology, 46*, 180–191. https://doi.org/10.1111/jasp.12355

Li, A., Curiel, H., Pritchard, J., & Poling, A. (2018). Participation of women in behavior analysis research: Some recent and relevant data. *Behavior Analysis in Practice, 11*, 160–164.

Li, A., Gravina, N., Pritchard, J., & Poling, A. (2019). The gender pay gap for behavior analysis faculty. *Behavior Analysis in Practice, 12*(4), 743–746.

Matsuda, K., Garcia, Y., Catagnus, R., & Brandt, J. A. (2020). Can behavior analysis help us understand and reduce racism? A review of the current literature. *Behavior Analysis in Practice*, 1–12. https://doi.org/10.1007/s40617-020-00411-4

McGlinchey, A., & Keenan, M. (1997). Stimulus equivalence and social categorization in Northern Ireland. *Behavior and Social Issues, 7*(2), 113–128. https://doi.org/10.5210/bsi.v7i2.310.

McSweeney, F. K., Donahoe, P., & Swindell, S. (2000). Women in applied behavior analysis. *The Behavior Analyst, 23*, 267–277.

McSweeney, F. K., & Parks, C. D. (2002). Participant by women in developmental, social, cognitive, and general psychology: A context for interpreting trends in behavior analysis. *The Behavior Analyst, 25*, 37–44.

Mizael, T. M., de Almeida, J. H., Silveira, C. C., & de Rose, J. C. (2016). Changing racial bias by transfer of functions in equivalence classes. *Psychological Record, 66*, 451–462. https://doi.org/10.1007/s40732-016-0185-0

Nosik, M. R., & Grow, L. L. (2015). Prominent women in behavior analysis: An introduction. *The Behavior Analyst, 38*(2), 225–227. https://doi.org/10.1007/s40614-015-0032-7

Nosik, M. R., Luke, M. M., & Carr, J. E. (2018). Representation of women in behavior analysis: An empirical analysis. *Behavior Analysis: Research and Practice, 19*(2), 213–221. https://doi.org/10.1037/bar0000118

Odum, A. (2000). Reflections on the glass ceiling: Women in the experimental analysis of behavior. *The Behavior Analyst, 23*, 279–283.

Petursdottir, A. I. (2015). Influences on my early academic career. *The Behavior Analyst, 38*, 255–262.

Poling, A., Grossett, D., Fulton, B., Roy, S., Beechler, S., & Wittkopp, C. J. (1983). Participation by women in behavior analysis. *The Behavior Analyst, 6*, 145–152.

Rehfeldt, R. A. (2018). Lessons from a female academician: Some further reflections on a glass ceiling. *Behavior Analysis in Practice, 11*(1), 181–183.

Sellers, T. P., Valentino, A. L., & LeBlanc, L. A. (2016). Recommended practices for individual supervision of aspiring behavior analysts. *Behavior Analysis in Practice, 9*, 274–286.

Simon, J. L., Morris, E. K., & Smith, N. G. (2007). Trends in women's participation at the meetings of the Association for Behavior Analysis: 1975–2005. *The Behavior Analyst, 30*, 181–196.

Strand, R. C., & Arntzen, E. (2020). Social categorization and stimulus equivalence: A systematic replication. *The Psychological Record, 70*(1), 47–63. https://doi.org/10.1007/s40732-019-00364-3

Sundberg, D. M., Zoder-Martell, K. A., & Cox, S. (2019). Why WIBA? *Behavior Analysis in Practice, 12*(2), 810–815.

Szabo, T. (2020). Equity and diversity in behavior analysis: Lessons from Skinner (1945). *Behavior Analysis in Practice, 13*(1), 375–386.

Taylor, B. A. (2015). Stereo knobs and swing sets: Falling in love with the science of behavior. *The Behavior Analyst, 38*, 283–292.

Vargas, T. (2018, March 1). She coined the term 'glass ceiling.' She fears it will outlive her. *Washington Post*.

Watt, A., Keenan, M., Barnes, D., & Cairns, E. (1991). Social categorization and stimulus equivalence. *The Psychological Record, 41*, 33–50. https://doi.org/10.1007/BF03395092

Wiley Online Library. (2020, September 13). *Journal of applied behavior analysis editorial board*. https://onlinelibrary.wiley.com/page/journal/19383703/homepage/editorialboard.html

18

GENDERED LANGUAGE
Moving toward a Compassionate Gender Expansive Society

Arin R. Donovan

INTRODUCTION

Step back in time nearly 600 years ago, prior to anyone of European descent stepping foot on present-day America. This land you enter is inhabited by hundreds of unique tribes of Indigenous people. Each tribe has their own individual differences and are vastly different from your own understanding of culture and society. Within this space, humans exist with flexible gender roles around labor, spirituality, and leadership (Bronski, 2011). Gender expands beyond the limited binary classification system of man and woman. Many of the tribes have third or fourth gender categories which embrace the fluidity of gender expression, behavior, and sexuality. And rather than these gender expansive individuals being shunned to the margins of society, they are held up in the center as transcendent, spiritual leaders. They are honored, valued, and protected.

This brief depiction of gender within Indigenous groups existed prior to European settler colonization of present-day America. In fact, gender variation and expansion existed in more than 300 Indigenous tribes prior to European colonization (Janiewski, 1995). Among the things Europeans/Puritans brought with them to present-day America was a rigid classification of gender which was enforced with legal and religious doctrine. Their ideology simultaneously resulted in the marginalization and oppression of all women and led to the erasure of gender non-conforming individuals who were previously respected and revered in their communities.

It is important to note from the outset, that the issue isn't with the existence of gender, but rather the deeply rooted gender binary system, created and maintained by the patriarchy (Moane, 2011). The gender binary system and the language used within it harms individuals with expansive gender identities through rejection and exclusion. This chapter will provide an overview of gender in a historical and current context, the harmful impact of the gender binary system, and ways to move toward a compassionate gender expansive society.

THE GENDER BINARY SYSTEM

The current gender system was established through patriarchal, heteronormative colonization and has resulted in a binary (man and women) system. These socially constructed categories are defined by cultural standards, norms, and roles, typically aligned with a physical sex assigned at birth. Everyone exhibits some level of gender performativity, behaving in accordance with society's social standards based on their physical sex assigned at birth (Butler, 1990). Gender social categories carry significant social weight and often establish and maintain harmful and discriminatory stereotypes (Drake et al., 2018).

Understanding the development of the patriarchy provides valuable insight into the establishment of gender binary stereotypes and norms. Historically, women held political, religious, and economical power, but around 2,000 B.C. women increasingly became excluded from those arenas (Learner, 1986). The recognition of reproduction as a valuable commodity and eventual control of women's reproduction is viewed as one of the core factors in societal exclusion of women and the development of the patriarchy. Legal codes began to define women by their relationship to men (fathers, husbands, etc.) and their social and class status was defined by their sexual status. Shifts in religion from polytheism to monotheism (one male deity and male religious leaders) led to exclusions for positions of power in religious institutions and served as a primary means to control women. Altogether, colonial systems of domination including control, exclusion, fragmentation, and violence led to the patriarchal system which continues to persist and uphold cultural norms, stereotypes, and behavior. A more recent example can be found in the biomedical theory of gender and sex.

In 1959, scientists from the field of psychology and embryology posed a biomedical model to explain masculine and feminine behavior as an effect of differentiated hormones on the brain development of males and females (Van Den Wijngaard, 1997). According to this theory, the presence of male hormones defines masculinity and results in, "sexual initiative, action intelligence, and an interest in career," and the *absence* of male hormones defines femininity which results in "sexual receptiveness, passivity, a preoccupation with pretty clothes, and motherhood" (Van Den Wijngaard, 1997, p. 41). The development of this theory and the scientific evidence for biological gender differences was developed on the foundation of paternal and colonial dualistic system of gender and sex during that time. In other words, this theory was developed by white, cisgender, heterosexual men and based on their prejudicial, self-focused perspective of gender and sex which would ensure the continuation of patriarchal ideals and groups that directly benefit from those ideals.

Feminists such as Germaine Greer and Margaret Mead, rejected biomedical models of sex and gender (Van Den Wijngaard, 1997). Mead, an anthropologist in the early to mid 20th century, conducted cross-cultural research and found that human behavior among sexes varies drastically across different cultures. Genetic and hormonal sex differences were not the result of specific "gendered" behavior, but rather the environment and learning context of an individual.

Despite the scientific efforts and evidence produced by Mead and others, the biomedical model of sex and gender armed society with power in the form of "scientific" evidence that gender is biological and therefore, any individual who identifies beyond the binary gender and sex of male and female must be defective in some natural way. In the 1960s, a survey indicated that a majority of medical professionals rejected procedures such as "sexual reassignment surgery" for transexual individuals due to their moral, ethical, and religious beliefs (Green, 1969). If rejection from medical professionals was not enough, these defects were regarded as mental pathology and were categorized as a gender identity disorder published in the Diagnostic and Statistical Manual by the 1980s (Drescher, 2010). To address pathological gender incongruences, reparative therapies were prescribed to correct these incongruences. Highly regarded behavior therapies such as Applied Behavior Analysis have also published data in which the researcher "trained" gendered play into children, labeling play associated with the opposite as "deviant sex-role behaviors" (Rekers & Lovaas, 1974). The cycle of coercion and control continues, not only in direct reparative therapies, but also in the interpretation of data. GNC individuals experience an increase in mental health issues such as; anxiety, depression, and suicidality and rather than interpreting these data as an effect of social exclusion and risk of violence within the environment, the biomedical model has used these effects of harm to suggest gender and sexual disorders. And despite data and personal narratives as evidence of harm caused by reparative therapies, as of 2020, 24 states and 4 territories of the United States have zero policies or laws banning conversion therapy (https://www.lgbtmap.org/equality-maps/conversion_therapy).

The biomedical model of sex and gender has led to the societal rejection and exclusion of anyone identifying outside of the binary male and female. The development of the minority stress model (Meyer, 2003a) paints a different empirical picture that emboldens the stressful impact minority's experience when identifying beyond the colonial and patriarchal binary gender system (Hendricks & Testa, 2012).

GNCT INDIVIDUALS AND MINORITY STRESS

It can be challenging to identify and analyze structural discrimination barriers such as those experienced by GNC individual from a gender binary system on an individual level (Link & Phelan, 2001). In order to assess the impact of prejudice stemming from institutional barriers, group level of analysis can be beneficial (Meyer, 2003b). One way to conceptualize this impact is through minority stress. Minority stress involves a combination of proximal and distal stressors which result in cumulative and additive stressors based on social stigmatization and prejudice (Meyer, 2003a). The minority stress model is based on three assumptions. First, the stress experienced by minorities is unique and not experienced by all members, especially those that occupy dominant spaces. Second, the stress is a product of societal structures and therefore, is ongoing and chronic. Third, the stress is a direct result of social institutional structures and beyond the control of the individual's control. With those three factors in mind, gender non-conforming (GNC) issues can be discussed in the minority stress framework. It is important to note that often, gender expansive identities in scientific literature and research are discussed within a binary transgender context, leaving out identities beyond the binary (Lefevor et al. 2019). Not only are there differences in the experiences that lead to stress between GNC individuals and their binary transgender counterparts, the focus on transgender experiences and identities in a binary context adds to the exclusion and erasure of GNC people.

Minority stress for gender non-conforming and transgender individuals (GNCT) individuals can present in a variety of ways. For GNCT individuals, especially those whose gender expression does not match their assumed physical sex, their identity is in constant question by society. Questions such as "are you a boy or are a girl?" are directly asked by children who lack the social awareness that pointed questions regarding someone's personal identity are inappropriate. In fact, gender stereotyping can be observed in children as young as 2.5 years old (Gelman et al., 2004). Being approached with seemingly innocent questions of this nature can result in more than potential apprehension and anxiety. Questions of this nature can place a GNCT individual in a position of answering in a variety of ways, none of which are simple. One individual may respond in a manner that avoids the topic of gender expansive identities and results in conforming to and reinforcing a gender binary system. Others may choose to educate individuals about gender expansive identities which requires emotional labor and causes stress for the GNCT individual. Regardless of how someone chooses to respond, the context in which the question is asked plays a significant role. Choosing to "out" oneself may place that individual in a life or death situation.

The need to place individuals in a gender box is not isolated to children. Over time, the innocent questions of children become hidden stares and whispers of teens and adults as they attempt to identify what genitalia may be hiding under an incongruent exterior. Stares, while seemingly harmless can turn into whispers which then turn into verbal statements of harassment. According to the 2015 U.S. Transgender Survey (James et al., 2016), 46% of GNCT experienced verbal harassment within the year prior to the survey due to their identity. For those in kindergarten through 12th grade, 54% were verbally harassed because others thought they were GNCT. Verbal harassment can lead to physical and sexual violence, or in some cases, murder. In the past years, violent murders of GNCT have been on the rise according to tracking data from the Human Rights Campaign. Between 2015 and 2019, there have been 21, 23, 29, 26, and 27 murders of GNCT individuals, respectively. As of the summer of 2020, 26 trans and gender non-conforming individuals have been murdered and the majority of these deaths have been Trans Women of Color. Aside from homicide, suicidality is another risk of living within the current gender system. In 2015, the rate of attempted suicide for the GNCT population (46%) was nine time higher that the U.S. population (4.6%) (James et al., 2016).

As mentioned above, examining the impact on minority groups can provide a broader picture of the issues GNCT individuals face. We live in a world where gender and trans-phobic biases can be confirmed with a quick online search that leads to a wealth of information suggesting that GNCT individuals suffer from mental health issues due to gender incongruence and psychopathology. However, the same institutions and systems that produce those sources are also part of the same institutions and systems that uphold cisgender and heteronormative standards as dominant. In fact, there are data to indicate that there is no difference in the prevalence of mental health of GNCT children and cisgender children when the GNCT children's gender identity are supported and affirmed by their family and community (Olson, 2016). One can choose to cling to information that confirms prejudicial biases and stereotypes that perpetuate minority stress that has well documented effects on health and well-being. Or one can choose to critically analyze and reject that information to move toward a more compassionate, gender expansive society.

MOVING TOWARD A COMPASSIONATE GENDER EXPANSIVE SOCIETY

For many Americans our public and/or private educations have been based on a white-washed version of U.S. History in which genocide and erasure of historically marginalized groups has been downplayed, if not, eliminated completely (Kendi, 2016). It centers white, cisgender and heteronormative ideology while subtly, and often blatantly, aligning histor-ically marginalized groups with negative stereotypes that run rampant in current society. Moving towards a more compassionate society begins with interrogating your assumptions of the truth. This chapter has given an extremely brief introduction into the exclusion and erasure of TGNC individuals that existed peacefully prior to colonization. If needed, use this chapter as a springboard to create your own independent understanding of history by reading accounts and narratives from voices that are not present in mainstream education. Throughout the process, ask yourself whose experience is being centered, whose voice is being left out, and who serves to benefit from the current narratives. Perspective taking and empathy are also key factors in this process. It is suggested that perspective taking can reduce instances of attributing someone's behavior to an internal attribute (fundamental attribution error) (Hooper et al., 2015). By avoiding the fundamental attribution error, an individual's behavior can be viewed as a result of the environment. To make a clear connection to gender related issues, consider the high rate of mental health risks associated with the TGNC community. The fundamental attribution error would lead one to view anxiety and depression as a result of internal conflict. Active perspective taking can assist in seeing the environment (gender binary system and resulting minority stress) as a cause of the anxiety and depression.

Interrogation of your assumptions does not stop with an external analysis of the world. Moving toward a compassionate gender expansive society involves continued analysis of your biases, prejudices, and behaviors that uphold harmful systems. You are not immune to the gender system. It permeates every part of our existence, from the language we use, our immediate and implicit associations, to the overt actions we make each day. It is the product of living in a colonized world. However, once you know, you can't unknow. In the famous words of Maya Angelou, "Do the best you can until you know better. Then when you know better, do better." You can continue upholding the same systems you now know are harmful or tear down those systems by any means necessary. In this context specifically, closely examining how gender is embedded into society reveals the complexity and seemingly overwhelming task of moving towards a gender expansive society. Start by identifying the individual behaviors you engage in that reinforce that system and then actively work to move in a more compassionate direction. A good place to start is "degendering" your language. Gendered language limits the analysis of gender (Butler, 1990). Consider replacing gendered terminology and stereotypes with neutral words and phrases. For example, the next time you see a stranger who physically presents as female or male, use the term "person" instead of making the assumption that they identify as a "man" or "woman." Furthermore, the media is rife with gender stereotypes and social media is one avenue in which we can actively reinforce those stereotypes. Before you share a post, picture, or meme on social media, analyze it for gender stereotypes. Does the post only refer to mother-parents who homeschool their children? Does the language in your post uphold gender stereotypes such as connections of boys and rough and tumble play or girls and princesses? Also, consider how you uphold gendered cultural practices such as gender reveal parties. These practices can be harmful to GNCT individuals and in fact, the creator if the gender reveal party regrets doing so and now speaks out about the harm those events cause to GNCT individuals (Ehrlich, 2020).

In 1977 the Combahee River Collective stated, "The personal is political" (BlackPast, 1977). It is impossible to remove the person from the political system that governs their life. If laws and policies exist that actively uphold systems of oppression and fail to protect all humans equally, then we must use our power and agency to change the system. For individuals who hold power that comes with dominant identities (white, cisgender, heterosexual, abled-bodies etc.), there is an obligation to leverage that power and activate for justice and equity. If you are not actively working to dismantle oppressive systems, then you are, even through silence and inaction, actively upholding those systems that inflict harm (Freire, 1970).

Gender stereotypes are so heavily ingrained into our society that anyone expanding beyond those binary boxes seem to threaten the very truth and nature of humanity. But that threat is not an actual threat to humanity but rather, a threat to the colonial ideology of power and control on which the binary gender system was built. In 1990, Butler asked, "If gender is constructed, could it be constructed differently, or does constructedness imply some form of social determinism, foreclosing the possibility of agency and transformation?" (p. 7). We do not have to remain constrained to the system into which we were born. A gender expansive world does not jeopardize our humanity, it uplifts humanity through compassionate validation of all humans.

REFERENCES

BlackPast, B. (2012, November 16) (1977). *The Combahee River Collective Statement*. Blackpast.org. https://www.blackpast.org/african-american-history/combahee-river-collective-statement-1977/

Bronski, M. (2011). *A queer history of the United States*. Beacon Press.

Butler, J. (1990). *Gender trouble: Feminism and the subversion of identity*. Routledge.

Drake, C. E., Primeaux, S., & Thomas, J. (2018). Comparing gender stereotypes between women and men with the implicit relational assessment procedure. *Gender Issues, 35*, 3–20.

Drescher, J. (2010). Queer diagnoses: Parallels and contrasts in the history of homosexuality, gender variance, and the diagnostic and statistical manual. *Archives of Sexual Behavior, 39*, 27–460.

Ehrlich, B. (2020, September 10). *Creator of gender reveal parties speaks out against the practice (again) on 'The Daily Show'*. Rolling Stone. https://www.rollingstone.com/tv/tv-news/gender-reveal-daily-show-1057436/

Freire, P. (1970). *Pedagogy of the oppressed*. 30th anniversary edition. Continuum

Gelman, S. A., Taylor, M. G., & Nguyen, S. P., Leaper, C., & Bigler, R. S. (2004). *Mother-child conversations about gender: Understanding the acquisition of essentialist beliefs*. Wiley.

Green, R. (1969). Attitudes towards transsexualism and sex-reassignment procedures. In R. Green & J. Money (Eds.), *Transsexualism and sex reassignment* (pp. 235–251). The Johns Hopkins University Press.

Hendricks, M. L., & Testa, R. J. (2012). A conceptual framework for clinical work with transgender and gender nonconforming clients: An adaptation of the minority stress model. *Professional Psychology: Research and Practice, 43*, 460–467.

Hooper, N., Erdogan, A., Keen, G., Lawton, K., & McHugh, L. (2015). Perspective taking reduces the fundamental attribution error. *Journal of Contextual Behavioral Science, 4*, 69–72.

Human Rights Campaign. (n.d.) Retrieved from: https://www.hrc.org/resources/violence-against-the-trans-and-gender-non-conforming-community-in-2020

James, S. E., Herman, J. L., Rankin, S., Keisling, M., Mottet, L., & Anafi, M. (2016). *The Report of the 2015 U.S. Transgender Survey*. National Center for Transgender Equality.

Janiewski, D. (1995). Gendering, racializing, and classifying: Settler colonization in the United States, 1590–1990. In Stasiulis, D. & Yulva-Davis, N. (Eds.) Unsettling settler societies: Articulations of gender, race, ethnicity, and class. London: SAGE Publishing.

Kendi, I. X. (2016). *Stamped from the beginning: The definitive history of racist ideas in America*. Nation Books.

Learner, G. (1986). *The creation of the patriarchy*. Oxford University Press.

Lefevor, G. T., Boyd-Rogers, C. C., Sprague, B. M., & Janis, R. A. (2019). Health disparities between genderqueer, transgender, and cisgender individuals: An extension of minority stress theory. *Journal of Counseling Psychology, 66*(4), 385–395

Link, B. G. & Phelan, J. C. (2001). Conceptualizing stigma. *Annual Review of Sociology, 27*, 363–385.

Meyer, I. H. (2003a). Prejudice, social stress, and mental health in lesbian, gay, and bisexual populations: Conceptual issues and research evidence. *Psychological Bulletin, 129*, 674–697.

Meyer, I. H. (2003b). Prejudice as stress: Conceptual and measurement problems. *American Journal of Public Health, 93*(2), 262–265.

Moane, G. (2011). *Gender and colonialism: A psychological analysis of oppression and liberation*. Palgrave Macmillan.

Olson, K. R., Durwood, L., DeMeules, M., & McLaughlin, K. A. (2016). Mental health of transgender children who are supported in their identities. *Pediatrics, 137*(3), e21053223.

Rekers, G. A, & Lovaas, O. I. (1974). Behavioral treatment of deviant sex-role behaviors in a male child. *Journal of Applied Behavior Analysis, 7*(2), 173–190.

Van Den Wijngaard, M. (1997). *Reinventing the sexes: The biomedical construction of femininity and masculinity*. Indiana University Press.

19

GLOBAL IMPACT

Standing for Science Takes a Village – An International One

David Celiberti, Maithri Sivaraman, and Lina Slim

When the first author was a Rutgers University graduate student in the late 1980s and worked at the Douglass Developmental Disabilities Center, he was immediately struck that only a tiny percentage of students with ASD were receiving the lion's share of the expertise and resources. This disparity was particularly troubling after realizing that scores of other children with ASD, in fact, the vast majority, were receiving "generic" special education services which did not yet incorporate state-of-the-art, science-based intervention. He also learned that outdated and unsupported models of treatment (e.g., psychoanalytic play therapy) were still popular in certain areas of the United States. Over time, conditions improved in the United States with more and more children with autism able to access interventions that, to varying degrees, were science-based (with the notable exception of rural communities). Furthermore, here in the United States, there has been an exponential increase in the number of credentialed behavior analysts.

Sadly, this evolution has not been the case internationally. Outside the United States, many children with autism reside in countries where human resources to carry out the very best that science has to offer are scarce. Systems and laws to support quality intervention may be lacking, and the cultural, societal, and religious practices of these countries may pose unique challenges. It is beyond the scope of this short chapter to detail these challenges in a manner that does them justice; however, we would like to highlight some of our efforts to promote the global dissemination of science-based autism treatment. We believe these efforts may better position communities to consider and incorporate science-based treatment, and to be less susceptible to the dangerous byproducts of pseudoscience (e.g., potential harm, poor outcomes, depletion of precious resources, and distrust in the professional community).

There are many barriers to the dissemination and adoption of evidence-based practice that we highlight below. Simply being aware of these barriers does not necessarily mean that one is able to address them directly or even has the resources to do so; however, the first step is recognizing where the challenges lie. When you embrace the notion that it "takes a village," it compels you to embody the role of change agent while respecting the reality that efforts of others are needed for synergy to take place. It is in that spirit that we wanted to provide information about our work through the Association for Science in Autism Treatment (ASAT).

Since its creation in 1998, ASAT has been committed to the promotion of evidence-based practices for individuals with autism. Sadly, a simple Google search for "autism treatments" yields almost 50 million results. Some showcase evidence-based interventions while the vast majority do not. Whereas the sheer number of treatments available can be both daunting and frustrating for consumers and providers, it has become our mission to offer a clearer path toward effective treatment. It would be unfortunate if our efforts only aided families in the United States; therefore, ASAT's goal is to ensure that consumers across the globe, both savvy and inexperienced, are familiar with appropriate, effective, and evidence-based treatments.

How does one attempt to promote evidence-based practices (EBPs) in other parts of the world? Disseminating science-based treatments in international communities is tantamount to sailing uncharted waters with no sextant. We believe that recognizing barriers to effective treatment and making successful inroads must occur on many levels (e.g., at the level of family, community, and the political system).

Some family-level considerations in international dissemination could involve linguistic and cultural factors. To illustrate, a family in France may view 40 hours per week of Early Intensive Behavioral Intervention (EIBI) delivered to a 4-year-old child as torturous because all intervention is perceived as "work." A family in India may find that having a child learn to write letters and numbers, and to participate in a general education classroom might seem more important than being toilet trained or independently putting on a shirt. A family who abides by Muslim religious values and norms may prioritize goals that will help the child participate in religious prayer practices over academic tasks.

A culturally competent behavior analyst must recognize, respect, and address these considerations (Dennison et al., 2019) through education, training, supervision, consultation, and collaboration, and yes, even trial-and-error learning. However, cultural responsiveness alone may not even be enough; having cultural humility may enhance understanding of how each family accesses and receives information within their communities. For example, a family in India receiving services from a board-certified behavior analyst (BCBA) based in the U.S. may benefit from learning both (a) how to access reliable information, and (b) how to approach autism treatment by seeking models of other families within or outside their communities, who were faced with similar challenges and succeeded at making strides in their child's progress.

If we take a step back from the level of the family, we start to observe barriers at the community level. Perhaps most palpable is the deluge of misinformation within the community: media representations are fraught with click baits and articles exalting harmful treatments. "Stem cell therapy breathes life into 12-year autistic girl" and "adjunctive (circus arts) therapies providing positive results for autism" are just two recent examples from India and Australia, representing an abundance of pseudoscience (The Hans Times, 2016; Singh, 2016). Similarly, at the provider level in many countries, providers often lack education and training in evidence-based practices even when they recognize that science-based interventions are more impactful than generic, pseudoscientific, or otherwise poor-quality interventions. This is coupled with a dearth of credentialed behavior analysts. Although the United States and Canada account for only 4.7% of the world's population, more than 95% of BCBAs live in these countries (BACB, 2020). On the other hand, Lagos, Nigeria has a population of 21 million people. Based on the most recent global ASD estimate (i.e., 1%) (Maenner, 2020), this translates to 210,000 individuals with autism; yet the BACB's certificant registry lists only 2 behavior analysts in all of Nigeria at this time.

Several system-level barriers also exist. Through ASAT's interviews with professionals around the world, we have learned that there is often no recognition for behavior analytic providers in most parts of the world. As a specific example, BCBAs cannot practice in Belgium and Italy unless they are also certified as a clinical psychologist. There are no applied behavior analysis (ABA) training programs in many parts of Asia and Africa. Additionally, there is no insurance coverage for ABA services, and the short supply of trained ABA professionals results in prohibitively high treatment costs for families. Parent advocates have worked tirelessly in Canada to have autism included in Medicare coverage, but sadly, lost at the Supreme Court of Canada. Unfortunately, the supply demand disconnect brings many unique challenges. These include, but are not limited to, providers charging exorbitant fees, having excessive caseloads, and working outside of their areas of expertise; all of which create a situation in which low-resource families are unable to access services.

We recognize that a dearth of qualified professionals can be directly addressed by an increased number of trained and credentialed behavior analysts (BCBAs or their equivalent) and the establishment of local training programs. However, building awareness about evidence-based practices within a community is a crucial step as well. One critical aspect for raising awareness is that a *need* or motivation exists within the community. For example, a Chinese American subscriber contacted the first author for permission to translate ASAT's article on "Recurrence of Autism in Families" into Mandarin because she felt the need for this information in her homeland. Similar connections have prompted other translation efforts carried out by ASAT. A second critical aspect to making inroads within a community has involved including members from the community itself. Community members often have invaluable experience and knowledge about the grassroots-level issues. For example, ASAT Extern Amanda Bueno, based in Brazil, has been instrumental in disseminating science-based treatment options and dispelling the myths that are prevalent in her community. Amanda translated our treatment summary about bleach therapy as this was a method garnering popularity in her native country of Brazil. Many of these efforts have been possible through ASAT's volunteering and externship program (detailed below) that is open to anyone across the world interested in promoting science-based treatment.

In the next section of this chapter, we focus specifically on ASAT's efforts most relevant to international dissemination. Our efforts are broadly consistent with evidence-based practices recommended for global dissemination (e.g., Healey et al., 2017). These include partnering with members in the community, conducting a needs assessment with stakeholders in the community, and making changes to the service delivery process by adapting the language and content as required.

Several decades of scientific support indicate that applied behavior analysis lays the groundwork for an effective treatment for people with autism. ASAT has supported the work of behavior analysts outside the United States in myriad ways: 1) to serve as a resource and 2) to help and guide the families they serve to be less susceptible to the dangerous influences of pseudoscience.

The published articles in *Science in Autism Treatment*, our monthly publication, continually address the full range of the autism spectrum and stress the importance of asking questions to assess provider competency, adequate experience, credential verification, and goodness of fit. We currently have almost 13,000 subscribers from over 100 countries. We explain treatment concepts using nontechnical language, which is particularly important as English may not be the primary language of many of our readers. With respect to content, we are mindful of our global audience. In addition to showcasing diverse applications of ABA in our Clinical Corner column, we have recently focused on topics such as bilingualism and telehealth that are particularly relevant within the global community.

ASAT has interviewed international experts to identify strategies that were successful, and strategies that encountered barriers, in their respective countries. We interview prominent behavior analysts from across the globe around common themes of service delivery, dissemination, and access to behavior analytic treatment. Some recent interviews have included Mickey Keenan, Eitan Elder, Paul McDonnell, Pooja Panesar, and Francesca degli Espinosa. We have also shared parental perspectives of parent advocates outside the United States such as Nicole Rogerson, Jane McCready, Andrew Kavchak, and Beverly Sharpe. These interviewees share their trials and tribulation as they generously discuss their journeys. In fact, the 2nd author's recent interview with Dr. Degli Espinosa is a perfect example of how we strive to share the expertise of individuals outside the United States (this interview highlighted innovative ways in which some BCBAs in Italy adapted home-based services in the face of the COVID-19 pandemic). Overarching, recurring themes addressed by our interviewees include: empowering families with information, consulting with families and their community to enhance cultural sensitivity, and awareness of the contextual environment to ascertain effective treatment selection, collaboration with allied professionals and stakeholders (i.e., community resource groups, government support), building advocacy groups and partnering with parents, and above all, being persistent in their efforts. Our interviews have also addressed the barriers to credentialing in other parts of the world and supporting a multilingual community to providers and families.

Through our Media Watch letters, we respond to accurate and inaccurate representations of autism treatment, including, but not limited to applied behavior analysis (ABA). Many of our letters address ABA outside of the United States, including countries like India, Australia, China, South Africa, Israel, UAE, and Canada. We remain committed to not just address ABA as it is applied in other countries but to combat the pseudoscience that separates individuals with autism from the very best that science has to offer. It is important to note that accurate portrayals are encouraged, and inaccuracies in representations are directly challenged while offering alternative, accurate information.

Our 150-hour externship program is one of many volunteer opportunities that offer valuable experiences for beginning and seasoned professionals alike. ASAT has long included volunteers from around the world. We have had several externs from outside the U.S. including Canada, Australia, Ireland, Brazil, India, and UAE join our efforts. Each Extern has the opportunity to work on three individualized goals over the course of their experience and to gain experience in sharing information about science-based treatment. Many of these goals are tied to international dissemination and embrace the very title of this short chapter.

In an attempt to address linguistic barriers, we are promoting the field of ABA worldwide by making our website content available in over 80 languages. This feature is prominently displayed at the top of the homepage of our website (www.asatonline.org.). We have created and translated one-page flyers showcasing our newsletter and website offerings in over 12 languages and uploaded these to our website so they can be printed and shared. We regularly provide articles and resources that can be shared by providers of behavior analytic services, some of which have been translated into other languages. Again, this is achieved through active collaboration with individuals from around the world wanting to partner with us.

Finally, we maintain active social media pages (Facebook, Instagram, and Twitter) to help parents, other family members, and providers outside of North America better understand the scope of evidence-based practice regardless of their country of origin, and to join a global community that shares those values.

Although much of this chapter has described ASAT's efforts, we recognize this is not just a unilateral transmission of information. There is so much to learn about, with, and from one another with respect to international dissemination (e.g., research published in other languages likely contains valuable information that can enhance our work). We are open and willing to listen to all members from around the world with their own perspectives and needs, and will offer support to the extent we have the resources to do so. For instance, although our Media Watch initiative will continue to address and respond to media representations of autism and its treatment across the globe, it is important for everyone to monitor representations in the media; we hope you consider ASAT as a model for that.

As we embrace the reality that we are part of a shared global community, we recognize our responsibility to establish strong international ties that build robust support systems and promote learning and growth for all involved. Acknowledging that a one-size-fits-all approach is not applicable, we will continue working together in a dynamic and ongoing manner to promote the adoption of culturally sensitive, science-based practices that celebrate the diversity each person brings while advancing the notion that science matters – no matter where you live!

REFERENCES

Behavior Analysis Certification Board. (2020). *Certificant data.* BACB. https://www.bacb.com/bacb-certificant-data.

Dennison, A., Lund, E. M., Brodhead, M. T., Mejia, L., Armenta, A., & Leal, J. (2019). Delivering home-supported applied behavior analysis therapies to culturally and linguistically diverse families. *Behavior Analysis in Practice, 12*(4), 887–898. https://doi.org/10.1007/s40617-019-00374-1

The Hans India. (2016, June 9). Stem cell therapy breathes life into 12 year old autistic girl. Andhra Pradesh Breaking News, Telangana News, Hyderabad News Updates, Coronavirus Updates, Breaking News. https://www.thehansindia.com/posts/index/Hans/2016-06-08/Stem-cell-therapy-breathes-life-into-12-year-old-autistic-girl/233700#:~:text=The%20family%20of%20the%20city,brought%20about%20to%20the%20child.

Healey, P., Stager, M. L., Woodmass, K., Dettlaff, A. J., Vergara, A., Janke, R., & Wells, S. J. (2017). Cultural adaptations to augment health and mental health services: A systematic review. *BMC Health Services Research, 17*(1), 8. https://doi.org/10.1186/s12913-016-1953-x

Maenner, M. J., Shaw, K. A., Baio, J., Washington, A., Patrick, M., DiRienzo, M., Christensen, D. L., Wiggins, L. D., Pettygrove, S., Andrews, J. A., Lopez, M., Hudson, A., Baroud, T., Schwenk, Y., White, T., Rosenberg, C. R., Lee, L.-C., Harrington, R. A., Huston, M . . . & Dietz, P. (2020). Prevalence of autism spectrum disorder among children aged 8 years—Autism and Developmental Disabilities Monitoring Network, 11 sites, United States. *Surveillance Summaries, 69*(4), 1–12. http://dx.doi.org/10.15585/mmwr.ss6904a1

Singh, L. (2016, February 4). Adjunctive therapies providing positive results for autism and other conditions. *The Sydney Morning Herald.* https://www.smh.com.au/healthcare/adjunctive-therapies-providing-positive-results-for-autism-and-other-conditions-20160203-gmkjls.html

20

HIGHER EDUCATION
Evidence-Based Teaching in Culturally Responsive Higher Education

Lauren K. Schnell and April N. Kisamore

Student populations in colleges and universities are diversifying across race, culture, and generation. It is now commonplace to teach in a higher education classroom that is multiracial, multicultural, and multigenerational.

In fact, Hinton and Seo (2013) reported that 1 in 5 *undergraduate* students at four-year colleges identify as non-white, with 53% of undergraduate college learners identifying as non-Hispanic white, 21% identifying as Hispanic, 15% identifying as Black, and 8% identifying as Asian. Additionally, the Institute of International Education (2016) reported that 362,228 international students joined graduate programs in the U.S. as of 2016 adding diversity to the culture of the classroom, and diversity in learning histories.

Students with racially and culturally diverse backgrounds may bring learning histories wrought with experiences of oppression or marginalization which influence their overt participation in class due to past experiences of being silenced from sharing in traditionally white spaces. Relatedly, many cultures disapprove of or prohibit individuals from speaking out or contradicting a professor, or individual assumed to be in power. Therefore, culturally diverse students may have a history of contacting punishment for behaviors such as participation, question-asking, or debating prior to arriving in the college or university classroom (Wagner, 2005).

Additionally, *graduate* students over the age of 24 are now represented as the majority when compared to the total number of students enrolled in graduate programs; thus, representing generational diversity. As of 2019, the typical college classroom included learners across at least three or four different generations (e.g., baby boomers, generation X, millennials, and generation Z) all who attend with varying strengths and deficits in their learning repertoires (Online College Students, 2019).

Adult learners (those over the age of 24) bring complex learning histories, including educational and life experiences, that differ from pre-adult college learners (Caruth, 2014). For example, baby boomers (those born between 1944 and 1964) typically present as independent thinkers and clear communicators with a strong commitment to hard work as a tribute to the cultural variables in their history (e.g., World Wars I and II, Civil Rights movement) (Cekada, 2012). This history varies greatly from millennials (those born between 1985 and 2002) whose members are considered to be the most educated and technologically literate, and have a tendency to expect instant gratification or quick responses from their teachers and colleagues (Cekada, 2012).

With this continued increase in diversity, higher education professors need to build inclusive learning communities while being cognizant of their own *and* their students' learning histories. Culturally relevant education (CRE) is a conceptual framework that recognizes the importance of including learners' cultural backgrounds, age, socio-economic status, ability, language, interests, and lived-in experiences (i.e., learning histories) while also affirming racial, and cultural identities, preparing students for rigorous learning, creating student-centered learning environments, cultivating critical thinking, and developing students' abilities to connect with others in the classroom (Ladson-Billings, 1995).

DEVELOPING CULTURAL COMPETENCE

Cultural competence is a system of behaviors, beliefs, and policies that enable teachers to work effectively with students in cross-cultural situations (e.g., diversity across generation, race, culture, ability, socio-economic status). Cultural competence in higher education includes instruction that centers around self-awareness, ethics, cross-cultural application, diverse work environments, and language diversity (Conners, 2020); as well as purposeful action to confront cultural bias, understand cultural identity, and develop both interpersonal and personal awareness of the intersection of culture and treatment methods (Fong et al., 2016).

Often, students in higher education classrooms present with diverse backgrounds that differ from the instructor (e.g., race, age). In these cases, instructors must first evaluate their own cultural influences while accepting that culture does make a difference in teaching and learning (Dennison et al., 2019). Assessments such as the Diversity Self-Assessment Tool (Montgomery, 2001) or the Multicultural Sensitivity Scale (Jibaja-Rusth et al., 1994) can be used for self-evaluation by instructors. Results of these assessments might be useful in supporting one's own acknowledgement of implicit biases and aid in reflections of their own culture and how that might impact their behavior when teaching in the classroom (Salend & Taylor, 2002).

Awareness of implicit biases can also aid professors in creating "brave spaces" where students feel comfortable sharing their experiences with racial and ethnic tensions (Arao & Clemens, 2013). Teaching and learning from a culturally responsive framework is likely to evoke emotional responses as professors and students might have a learning history in which such material was conditioned as aversive. Because of this, the professor and students must be prepared for an emotionally charged atmosphere and must develop strategies to tolerate these responses rather than avoid them (Wagner, 2005).

Developing a Culturally Responsive Classroom

The culturally responsive classroom is one in which there are clear and academically challenging expectations for all students. This means that as professors design their courses, they must consider how to incorporate strategies that make expectations clear and create learning opportunities that are relevant such that every student, regardless of race, culture, or generation learns target skills such as: identifying, defining, and applying concepts and principles, engaging in critical thinking and problem solving, communicating clearly and effectively with others, and actively engaging in conflict resolution.

PROMOTE CONTINGENCIES

To make expectations in a CRE classroom clear, the professor can add a diversity statement to the course syllabus that indicates the professor's commitment to and expectation for equity and diversity in the class. This statement promotes accountability by the professor and students particularly when the professor outlines actionable items that will occur throughout the semester to (a) encourage equity through antecedent events and (b) respond to instances of discrimination through consequence events. Several resources are available to support faculty in creating a diversity statement (e.g., KU Center for Teaching Excellence, [Creating an Inclusive Syllabus]).

To be successful in creating a culturally responsive classroom, professors must be ready to instruct and engage students using empirically-sound interventions. For example, research in teaching and learning outcomes has demonstrated that teaching procedures that encourage overt student responding produce higher test scores than those involving only covert responding (e.g., reading, listening) (Alba & Pennypacker, 1972; Miller & Malott, 1997; Yoder & Hochevar, 2005). To ensure the participation of marginalized students (e.g., Black, Indigenous, People of Color, cultural minorities, adult learners) who might otherwise remain silent in traditionally white, young, spaces such as the college classroom, instructors may establish an expectation for participation (Wagner, 2005). Tactics in the college and university classroom that increase overt student participation should be identified and implemented to (a) maximize learning opportunities, (b) allow for ongoing assessment of learning across all students with diverse learning histories, and (c) demonstrate to all students that their presence is of value to the class (Hinton & Seo, 2013).

Create Adequate Learning Opportunities

Active student responding (ASR) refers to techniques used to evoke observable responses from students in the classroom (Heward, 1994). Using ASR as a teaching tactic in the college and university classroom allows professors to identify students who are learning and those who are not. With this information, professors can determine when it is necessary to modify learning opportunities to meet the needs of all students. For example, *Student A* may rarely respond accurately during ASR opportunities, alerting the professor that additional tactics are necessary to increase *Student A*'s learning. For example, the professor may provide additional supports for *Student A* by sharing guided notes prior to lecture delivery.

Interaction amongst students allows for diversity awareness in the classroom and students consider interaction to be a hallmark feature of a diverse classroom (Maruyama et al., 2000). More so, critical consciousness through pedagogy, a hallmark of CRE, refers to an emphasis in student engagement such that students learn to think critically while developing relationships with peers and with their professors. There are a number of ways to incorporate active responding, and opportunities for interaction and collaboration into the classroom. Some examples are discussed below.

WRITING AND DISCUSSION EXERCISES

In-class writing exercises associated with class material have been demonstrated as effective tools for increasing student responding (Butler et al., 2001; Harton et al., 2002). These exercises, designed to be short in length and followed by a small group discussion, can involve writing down responses to instructor posed questions or completing in-class writing activities in response to readings or topic reviews. Students can then be organized into pairs or small groups to review their written responses with each other prior to sharing again in a large group discussion. These exercises allow students to draft thoughts and share ideas from their own experiences then review them in smaller, and potentially safer groups, prior to sharing with the large group. Aside from increasing self-awareness and self-reflection, this technique also fosters interaction and support amongst smaller groups of students.

In the CRE classroom, writing and discussion exercises should be focused around readings that incorporate diverse authorship, multiple examples from various cultures (Wang et al., 2019), and applications of content with culturally diverse populations (Hinton & Seo,

2013). Professors might also provide writing prompts to students, while in small groups, that include multiculturalism and diverse content (Fuentes, in press; Pope et al., 2019). During small group writing and discussion exercises, instructors may encourage students to interact with students who are racially, culturally, or generationally different from themselves (Hinton & Seo, 2013) in an effort to increase opportunities for learning and collaboration as students themselves can learn from each other. For example, students who are of the baby boomer generation may be able to teach millennials about professionalism or model strong work ethic, all of which are commonalities in their learning histories. Similarly, millennial students may be able to teach baby boomers how to use technology in and out of the classroom to access supplemental materials and information. Additionally, allowing students to share their culturally relevant experiences in short-writes or small groups may establish the motivating operations needed to engage in open dialogue that has a previous history of punishing consequences.

INTERTEACHING

During interteaching, students are provided with a preparation guide, prior to the class period, that contains questions designed to lead or guide them through a reading assignment. Students answer the questions before the class period and prepare to discuss their answers with fellow students in class. Then students work in pairs to review their completed preparation guides while the instructor moves around the room answering questions and guiding student discussions. Once students finish working together, they complete a record sheet in which they list items they would like the instructor to elaborate on or discuss at the start of the next class period (Boyce & Hineline, 2002). Interteaching has been shown to lead to higher exam grades and higher rates of class satisfaction when compared to traditional lectures (Saville et al., 2011). Much like the writing and discussion exercises, interteaching allows students to practice learning from each other and developing collaborative relationships while also engaging in conflict resolution, if they have differing answers.

In the CRE classroom, interteaching may allow for purposeful collaboration across student populations and similar to the materials selected during writing and discussion exercises, readings used in interteaching should incorporate diverse authorship, multiple examples from various cultures (Wang et al., 2019) and applications of content with culturally diverse populations (Hinton & Seo, 2013).

RESPONSE CARDS

Response cards are cards or signs that students simultaneously hold up indicating their response to an instructor delivered question (Shabani & Carr, 2004). Numerous studies have demonstrated the success of using response cards to increase the frequency and accuracy of student responding (Narayan et al., 1990), increase scores on quizzes and tests (Maheady et al., 2002), and reduce disruptive behavior (Armendariz & Umbreit, 1999) across students with diverse learning histories including moderate and severe disabilities (Berrong et al., 2007), university students (Shabani & Carr, 2004), inner-city Black students (Gardner et al., 1994), and students with limited English proficiency (Davis & O'Neill, 2004). Response cards may be preprinted or blank, or they can be small whiteboards that students can write on with dry-erase markers. Following student responding, the college or university professor states the correct answer and provides an elaboration if the majority of the students responded incorrectly.

In the CRE classroom, response cards allow for non-vocal participation. This may be a benefit to those students who do not have a reinforcing history with speaking in class. Additionally, response cards allow the professor to assess student learning and identify students who might benefit from additional supports such as guided notes, a study group, or more interteaching time.

CONCLUSION

As the landscape of the college and university classroom continues to diversify, instructors must commit to cultural responsiveness all while implementing the most up-to-date, evidence-based teaching procedures. This chapter suggests ways in which college and university instructors can create a learning environment that infuses culturally relevant education into pedagogy and curriculum while building learning communities that account for the importance of learners' histories.

REFERENCES

Alba, E., & Pennypacker, H. S. (1972). A multiple change score comparison of traditional and behavioral college teaching procedures. *Journal of Applied Behavior Analysis, 5*(2), 121–124. doi.org/10.1901/jaba.1972.5-121

Arao, B., & Clemens, K. (2013). From safe spaces to brave spaces: A new way to frame dialogue around diversity and social justice. In L. Landreman (Ed.), *The Art of Effective Facilitation*. Stylus Publishing.

Armendariz, F., & Umbreit, J. (1999). Using active responding to reduce disruptive behavior in a general education classroom. *Journal of Positive Behavior Interventions, 1*(3), 152–158. 10.1177/109830079900100303

Berrong, A. K., Schuster, J. W., More, T. E., & Collins, B. C. (2007). The effects of response cards on active participation and social behavior of students with moderate and severe disabilities. *Journal of Developmental and Physical Disabilities, 19*(3), 187–199. 10.1007/s10882-007-9047-9047

Boyce, T. E., & Hineline, P. N. (2002). Interteaching: A strategy for enhancing the user- friendliness of behavioral arrangements in the college classroom. *The Behavior Analyst, 25*(2), 215–226. doi.org/10.1007/BF03392059

Butler, A., Phillmann, K. B., & Smart, L. (2001). Active learning within a lecture: Assessing the impact of short, in-class writing exercises. *Teaching of Psychology, 28*(4), 257–259. doi.org/10.1207/S15328023TOP2804_04

Caruth, G. D. (2014). Meeting the needs of older students in higher education. *Participatory Educational Research, 1*(2), 21–35. doi.org/10.17275/per.14.09.1.2

Cekada, T. L. (2012). Training a multigenerational workforce. *Professional Safety, 57*(3), 40–44.

Conners, B. M., & Capell, S. T. (2020). An introduction to multiculturalism and diversity issues in the field of applied behavior analysis. In *Multiculturalism and Diversity in Applied Behavior Analysis: Bridging Theory and Application* (pp. 1–3). Routledge. doi.org/10.4324/9780429263873-1

Davis, L. L., & O'Neill, R. E. (2004). Use of response cards with a group of students with learning disabilities including those for whom English is a second language. *Journal of Applied Behavior Analysis, 37*(2), 219–222. 10.1901/jaba.2004.37–219

Dennison, A., Lund, E. M., Brodhead, M. T., Mejia, L., Armenta, A., & Leal, J. (2019).Delivering home-supported applied behavior analysis therapies to culturally and linguistically diverse families. *Behavior Analysis in Practice, 12*(4), 887–898. doi.org/10.1007/s40617-019-00374-1

Fong, E. H., Catagnus, R. M., Brodhead, M. T., Quigley, S., & Field, S. (2016). Developing the cultural awareness skills of behavior analysts. *Behavior Analysis in Practice, 9*(1), 84–94. doi.org/10.1007/s40617-016-0111-0116

Fuentes, M. A., Zelaya, D. G., & Madsen, J. W. (In press). Rethinking the course syllabus: Considerations for promoting equity, diversity and inclusion. *Teaching of Psychology*.

Gardner, R., Heward, W. L., & Grossi, T. A. (1994). Effects of response cards on student participation and academic achievement: A systematic replication with inner-city students during whole-class science instruction. *Journal of Applied Behavior Analysis, 27*(1), 63–71. 10.1901/jaba.1994.27–63

Harton, H. C., Richardson, D. S., Barreras, R. E., Rockloff, M. J., & Latané, B. (2002). Focused Interactive Learning: A tool for active class discussion. *Teaching of Psychology, 29*(1), 10–15. doi.org/10.1207/S15328023TOP2901_03

Heward, W. L. (1994). Three "low-tech" strategies for increasing the frequency of active student response during group instruction. In R. Gardner III, D. M. Sainato, J. O. Cooper, T. E., Heron, W. L. Heward, J., Eshleman, & T. A. Grossi (Eds.), *Behavior analysis in education: Focus on measurably superior instruction* (pp. 283–320). Brooks/Cole.

Hinton, D., & Seo, B. I. (2013). Culturally relevant pedagogy and its implications for retaining minority students in predominantly white institutions (PWIs). In D. M. Callejo Perez, J. Ode (Eds), *The stewardship of higher education: Re-imagining the role of education and wellness on community impact* (pp. 133–148). Sense Publishers. doi.org/10.1007/978-994-6209-6368-363_8

Institute of International Education. (2016). Number of international students in the US hits all-time high. https://www.iie.org/Why-IIE/Announcements/2019/11/Number-of-International-Students-in-the-United-States-Hits-All-Time-High

Jibaja-Rusth, M. L., Kingery, P., & Holcomb, J. D., Buckner, W. P., & Pruitt, B. E. (1994). Development of a multicultural sensitivity scale. *Journal of Health Education, 25*(6), 350–357. 10.1080/10556699.1994.10603060

Kansas University Center for Teaching Excellence. (n.d.). *Creating an inclusive syllabus*. https://cte.ku.edu/creating-inclusive-syllabus

Ladson-Billings G. (1995). Toward a theory of culturally relevant pedagogy. *American Educational Research Journal, 32*(3), 465–491. https://doi.org/10.3102/00028312032003465

Maheady, L., Michielli-Pendi, J., Mallette, B., & Harper, G. F. (2002). A collaborative research project to improve the academic performance of a diverse sixth grade science class. *The Journal of the Teacher Education Division of the Council for Exceptional Children, 25*(1), 55–70. https://doi.org/10.1177/088840640202500107

Maruyama, G., Moreno, J. F., Gudeman, R. H., & Marin, P. (2000) Does diversity make a difference? Three research studies on diversity in college classrooms. American Council on Education and American Association of University Professors.

Miller, M. L., & Malott, R. W. (1997). The importance of overt responding in programmed instruction even with added incentives for learning. *Journal of Behavioral Education, 7*(4), 497–503. https://doi.org/10.1023/A:1022811503326

Montgomery, W. (2001). Creating culturally responsive, inclusive classrooms. *Teaching Exceptional Children, 33*(4), 4–9. 10.1177/004005990103300401

Narayan, J. S., Heward, W. L., Gardner, R. III, Courson, F. H., & Omness, C. (1990). Using response cards to increase student participation in an elementary classroom. *Journal of Applied Behavior Analysis, 23*(4), 483–490. https://doi.org/10.1901/jaba.1990.23-483

Online College Students. (2019). https://www.learninghouse.com/knowledge-center/research-reports/ocs2019-research-report.

Pope, R. L., Reynolds, A. L., & Mueller, J. A. (2019). "A change is gonna come": Paradigm shifts to dismantle oppressive structures. *Journal of College Student Development, 60*(6), 659–673. https://doi.org/10.1353/csd.2019.0061

Salend, S. J., & Taylor, L. S. (2002). Cultural perspectives: Missing pieces in the functional assessment process. *Intervention in School and Clinic, 38*(2), 104–112. https://doi.org/10.1177/10534512020380020601

Saville, B. K., Lambert, T., & Robertson, S. (2011). Interteaching: Bringing behavioral education into the 21st century. *The Psychological Record, 61*(1), 153–166

Shabani, D. B., & Carr, J. E. (2004). An evaluation of response cards as an adjunct to standard instruction in university classrooms: A systematic replication and extension. *North American Journal of Psychology, 6*(1), 85–100.

Wagner, A. E. (2005). Unsettling the academy: Working through the challenges of anti-racist pedagogy. *Race Ethnicity and Education, 8*(3), 261–275. 10.1080/13613320500174333

Wang, Y., Kang, S., Ramirez, J., & Tarbox, J. (2019). Multilingual diversity in the field of applied behavior analysis and autism: A brief review and discussion of future directions. *Behavior Analysis in Practice, 12*(4), 795–804. /10.1007/s40617-019-00382-1

Yoder, J. D., & Hochevar, C. M. (2005). Encouraging active learning can improve students' performance on examinations. *Teaching of Psychology, 32*(2), 91–95.

21

HUMANITY OF ABA

ABA as a Humane Approach

David Celiberti, Kirsten Wirth, and Kate McKenna

INTRODUCTION

Since the inception of Lovaas' model of applied behavior analysis (ABA) for autism intervention (1987), we have seen criticisms of the scientific rigor and replication used in studies, misconceptions of practitioners and the science, and more recently, concerns from some adults who identify as autistic. In our (ABA scientists' and practitioners') endeavor to adhere to the tenets of behavior analysis (Baer et al., 1968), follow strict procedures, use data for decision-making, and offer technological descriptions that do not resort to mentalism, we have at times lost the ability to effectively communicate with our consumers and colleagues outside of our discipline. In this chapter, we will attempt to address some of those challenges by highlighting the humanity and heart of ABA.

A common misconception likely stems from outdated language used in the 70s and 80s involving a "cure" for autism, that ABA is used to make individuals with autism as normal as possible. The ultimate goal for any behavior analyst is (or should be) to help all clients (not solely individuals with autism – another misconception!) reach their full potential by being as independent and successful as possible. We know from research (Horlin et al., 2014) that the cost of not providing effective intervention includes increased behaviors that interfere with learning and relationship development, increased financial costs to families, decreased employment for families, increased dependence on others, and more. Individuals deserve to learn and achieve the greatest level of happiness, independence, self-determination, and self-advocacy possible, and access the most effective teaching we know to get them there (Walsh, 2011). Most of us are in this line of work because we care about people and are committed to using our best evidence to help them achieve their potential. We use data and strictly adhere to procedures to maximize potential, but we do so with the end goal of independence, rather than normalcy.

The Behavior Analyst Certification Board (BACB, 2020) was established in 1998 to standardize practices by behavior analysts and protect its consumers. Many behavior analysts were already governed by separate regulatory bodies (e.g., licensed psychologists, speech-and-language pathologists, social workers); however, many were not, and unfortunately some practitioners claimed to provide ABA services without appropriate training or credentials. Currently, the BACB® has certified over 40,000 practitioners, maintains a searchable BACB certificant registry, and assists in the development of state laws to ensure licensure and further protection for the public. Most importantly, the BACB® developed a code of ethics by which we must abide. This code helps to protect us all from perceived overgeneralizations that poor implementation (based on incompetence, misapplication, or unethical behavior) is a valid reflection of all of us. This code is similar to others' (e.g., American or Canadian code of ethics for psychologists) in that it includes guidelines related to conflicts of interest, welfare of the client(s), informed consent, research practices, collaborating with others, etc. The ethics code also goes beyond those standards to include the fundamental tenets of the science of ABA (e.g., data-based decision-making, specification of evidence-based practices, use of least restrictive procedures to avoid restraint and aversive practices as much as possible, and focus on interventions based on reinforcement). We believe that competent behavior analysts who carry out their work consistent with the *Professional and Ethical Compliance Code for Behavior Analysts* have much to be proud of and demonstrate their humanity through their work in a myriad of significant ways as described below.

Behavior Analysts Show their Humanity by Offering Evidence-based Interventions

Against a backdrop of hundreds of treatments that lack scientific validity, it is humane to ensure that those we serve receive treatments with a proven track record of success to maximize their potential. That's why we do not use non evidence-based "treatments" that waste precious time and resources. The alternative for providers to simply use procedures they like irrespective of scientific validation should be unacceptable, may be harmful, and is certainly not humane. Furthermore, using evidence-based interventions can reduce reliance on medications or the need for more restrictive environments for the client. Careful and concerted efforts to lessen the need for medication and reduce the need for more restrictiveness further exemplifies our humanity.

Behavior Analysts Show their Humanity by Individualizing Intervention at Every Level

Whether it is matching treatments to underlying function, constantly assessing and using the individual's most powerful motivators, or choosing targets based on the needs of individuals and their families, the commitment to individualization permeates everything we do. A cookie-cutter approach that ignores client characteristics, needs, culture, and values may reflect the practice of some behavior analysts but, fortunately, it is not the norm. The current ethical code is replete with guidelines that support our careful individualization and provide a framework in which it can take root.

Behavior Analysts Show their Humanity by Letting the Data Speak

Objectivity is far more humane than subjectivity when it comes to measuring outcomes and justifying the many important decisions that need to be made. The significant time we invest in data collection means that we are not wasting the time of those we serve. It provides us with a clear way to assess improvement, even when such improvement is small. Using the data to guide and inform our decisions ensures that our commitment to individualization continues throughout our work with the client. The ongoing collection of data enables us to determine if the adjustments prompted by our analysis lead to a desired outcome. This level of care associated with the efforts taken to both collect and use data is something that should be undertaken by all providers regardless of discipline. We use data to make the most of our clients' time as a way of showing we care. We care about their time and resources, and want them to achieve the most in the least amount of time. Providers who are not as committed to continuous data collection are not as well positioned to objectively benefit and avoid wasted time. Intervention choices should be about the science, not our egos or comfort levels. If an intervention does not show results, we use the principles of our science to make necessary adjustments.

Behavior Analysts show their Humanity in the Manner in which Goals are Conceptualized and Ultimately Selected

It is humane to recognize that our goal selection is resume building for those we serve. Individuals are given functional and appropriate skills to be *more successful* within their *current* life and environment (by considering each individual's input to the extent possible, parent or caregiver input, and applying cultural sensitivity). Individuals are taught skills to achieve *future* success in *less restrictive* environments (anticipatory goal selection and programming) by creating new repertoires of skills which make new environments and levels of self-determination more possible. Part of that humanity is the versatility that enables us to both focus on small skills and look at the broader picture. These two vantage points can occur simultaneously and are compatible. This framework compels behavior analysts not to be shackled to goals that merely target deficits or give the appearance of normalcy but rather promote broader goals such as independence, self-determination, and access to new opportunities.

Behavior Analysts Have Shown their Humanity by Decades of Recognition that Parents are Partners

Historically, some therapeutic orientations have put forth untested and invalid notions that parents caused their children's autism. As one can imagine, such a viewpoint can be upsetting and disempowering for parents of newly diagnosed children. Behavior analysts have long embraced the idea that parents and other family members are significant agents of change, and decades of parent training efforts reflect that investment and recognition. As our field has evolved, our humanity has compelled us to deeply, meaningfully, consensually, and frequently engage family members in all aspects of intervention – not just implementation. This includes appreciating the cultural differences represented within the communities we serve. Certainly, this partnership extends to other providers involved with the individuals we serve (e.g., case workers).

Behavior Analysts Show their Humanity in the Very Careful and Transparent Way they Carry Out Interventions

Behavior analytic interventions are delivered in a transparent and detailed manner such that others could implement them in the same way. For skill acquisition efforts with more challenged learners, this delivery breaks down learning into easily attainable goals using structure, consistency, and repetition. Our humanity is further demonstrated when individual programs are carefully designed to work toward a larger set of goals related to self-determination, independence, and higher quality of life.

Behavior Analysts Show their Humanity Through their Commitment to Reinforcement

With respect to the use of reinforcement, four points cannot be overstated: (a) behavior analysts recognize that if desired changes would happen in the absence of reinforcement, they would already be happening. It is indeed humane to provide the individual with access to abundant experiences that will increase their motivation (e.g., to participate in their family and community, gain life skills and independence). Therefore, considerable effort is placed on layering in reinforcement strategically and intentionally; (b) reinforcement selection is individualized by embracing flexibility, creativity, and in the case of behavior reduction efforts, is carefully matched to function; (c) reinforcer selection is a journey and continually adjusted; (d) pairing is essential. A reinforcing relationship between the provider and learner (i.e., rapport) is the soil in which learning can take root.

Behavior Analysts Show their Humanity when the Celebration of Outcome is Rooted in Evidence of Endurance and Carryover

Behavior analysts strive for lasting change that persists over time without prompt dependence or the necessity of others being present for desired behaviors to be demonstrated. The ultimate testament to treatment success is carryover across settings, situations, and people. Each skill should come with a unique set of litmus tests that could be the end goal (e.g., persistence and generalization across people for a skill, fluency and generalization across settings).

Behavior Analysts Show their Humanity in how Challenging Behaviors Are Viewed, Understood, and Addressed

Although it is commonplace to hear terms such as "maladaptive" or "dysfunctional," behavior analysts recognize that challenging behaviors are actually quite adaptive and functional for some individuals who strive to get their needs met. Functional assessments – including functional analyses – enable identification of the underlying communicative intent of challenging behaviors. In other words, determining motivations that underlie the behavior are important first steps. An adequate and reliable functional assessment enables behavior analysts to respect the communicative goals of the behavior, while helping the individual develop other ways to meet those goals. As a result, a comprehensive and functionally relevant behavior plan provides individuals with more acceptable tools for negotiating their environment, getting their needs met, communicating their needs, or learning a competing or coping response.

We hope we have been successful in highlighting how behavior analysts demonstrate their humanity. As behavior analysts, we are always learning. As the efficacy and efficiency of our field continue to evolve and advance, we must advance along with it. We must continue to adhere to the *Professional and Ethical Compliance Code for Behavior Analysts*, to continuously evaluate our competencies, and to ensure that clients' needs and skills for independence and self-determination are the foundation of our interventions. In the final section of this chapter, we wanted to outline some concrete ways the humanity of ABA described above can shine through our work.

FINAL THOUGHTS

Behavior analysts seek to effect meaningful change in the lives of our clients. For our work to be effective and lasting, that change must be meaningful for the individual and those around them. Our work with clients requires not only our technical skills but also good interpersonal skills, including the promotion of open communication and relationship building, that are often grown in practice rather than taught in our graduate programs. They are skills that we should practice in responding compassionately to the people with whom we work. Behavior analysts should endeavor to:

- *Be a team player:* We do not do our work in isolation, but in concert with a team that includes family members and caregivers, educators, and related service providers. How we communicate and relate to team members will influence the opinions that they form about ABA. Relying on data and evidenced-based procedures is at the core of what we do; however, when explaining the rationale for treatment decisions, be aware of your presentation in body language and tone of voice; avoid suggesting that others are "doing it wrong."

- *Avoid jargon:* This reminder bears repeating as one of the common misperceptions about behavior analysts is that we use technical vocabulary instead of language that is easily understood by clients, caregivers, and members of the treatment team. Clear concise explanations in "everyday" language are critical to developing respectful relationships with clients and their families. This can result in their active participation in the process of setting goals and designing interventions. Furthermore, because we often rely on others to carry out our suggestions, it is critical that such recommendations are accessible and understood.

- *Be both receptive and responsive to feedback:* Openly listening to feedback and suggestions from other clients, caregivers, team members, and supervisors is critical to both building relationships with clients and colleagues and continuing to acquire new skills and develop as a professional. It is equally important to be responsive to feedback, to change your behavior in response to constructive feedback, or to compromise when appropriate with caregivers and team members.

- *Ensure that the lens of social validity anchors our work with families:* Social validity refers to the significance of the target behavior, the importance of the outcomes, and the appropriateness of the strategies and the procedures for the client (Hanley, 2010). In planning programs for skill development or behavior change, we ask these questions of our clients – Is this important to you? Will the procedures we are recommending be convenient for you to implement? Do you feel that I have heard your concerns and answered your questions? Are you satisfied that the acquired skills have resulted in meaningful change? This requires engaging in ongoing conversations with clients to gather information related to social validity so that the elements of social validity are at the center of planning educational programs and behavioral interventions.

- *Be relationship-based:* Working and interacting with a behavior therapist should be reinforcing for clients, caregivers, and team members. Apply what you have learned about pairing to yourself and your professional relationships. Research indicates that skills related to listening, collaboration, and conveying empathy and compassion are highly valued by clients and caregivers (Taylor, et al., 2019). Demonstrate concern and respect by asking questions and listening empathetically without becoming defensive.

- *Design interventions that will work within the context of the client's daily circumstances and environment:* Apply what you know about the client's daily circumstances and environment in your planning. Interventions that ask too much of caregivers or that are designed without client collaboration have little chance of success. It is important to recognize that agreed upon priorities and environmental variables can shift over time, another reason why ongoing conversation with clients is critical when planning interventions.

CONCLUSION

The commitment to excellence, transparency, individualization, and accountability inherent in behavior analysis may be easily overlooked by our clients and colleagues, and sometimes ourselves. Embracing these attributes gives us much to be proud of and we hope this short chapter serves as a reminder that we are all works in progress. The success of our work is based on our use of evidenced-based practices, a commitment to the principles of social validity, and our belief that clients can acquire skills that will open their lives to new experiences. When we embrace and highlight the humanity of applied behavior analysis, we are communicating what is at the heart of our science – *working with others* – to create significant, maintainable, and lasting positive change in the lives of others.

REFERENCES

Baer, D. M., Wolf, M. M., & Risley, T. R. (1968). Some current dimensions of applied behavior analysis. *Journal of Applied Behavior Analysis, 1*(1), 91–97.

Behavior Analyst Certification Board. (2020, September 14). BACB. https://bacb.com

Hanley, G. P. (2010). Toward effective and preferred programming: A case for the objective measurement of social validity with recipients of behavior-change programs. *Behavior Analysis in Practice, 3*(1), 13–21.

Horlin, C., Falkmer, M., Parsons, R., Albrecht, M. A., & Falkmer, T. (2014). The cost of autism spectrum disorders. *PLOS One, 9,* e106552.

Lovaas, O. I. (1987). Behavioral treatment and normal educational and intellectual functioning in young autistic children. *Journal of Consulting and Clinical Psychology, 55*(1), 3–9. https://doi.org/10.1037/0022-006X.55.1.3

Taylor, B. A., LeBlanc, L. A., & Nosik, M. R. (2019). Compassionate care in behavior analytic treatment: Can outcomes be enhanced by attending to relationships with caregivers? *Behavior Analysis in Practice, 12*(3), 654–666.

Walsh, M. B. (2011). The top 10 reasons children with autism deserve ABA. *Behavior Analysis in Practice, 4*(1), 72–79.

22

INCLUSIVITY

"We've Tried Nothing and We're All out of Ideas!": Disruptive Behavior and Faith-based Congregations

Bobby Newman

INTRODUCTION

In 2009, I produced a small book for use with Unitarian Universalist congregations called *The Inherent Worth and Dignity of ALL Individuals*. While written for UUs, the ideas were meant to be applicable in any faith-based group. The aim of the book was to provide a perspective and basic ideas to guide congregations when faced with issues related to difficulties caused by the interaction of individuals who engage in behavior that others may regard as upsetting to other members of congregations. The book grew out of experiences within four aspects of my life:

1. Difficulties a particular congregation was facing with a congregant who would horde food and touch all food items on the table at "coffee hour" and use racial slurs against other congregants.
2. The "Caring Congregations" training of the Unitarian Universalist Association, which is meant to help congregations to address such issues and to provide help to individuals who require it.
3. My Applied Behavior Analytic work with individuals diagnosed on the Autism Spectrum.
4. My history working with crime victims assistance and the New York Police Department and police departments around the world.

Each of the above experiences will be folded into our examination of key issues below. We will begin with a case study taken from a story that appeared on the Internet and has been verified with local authorities. As we will see again and again, we are often considering conflicting rights of individuals. It is a given that any two individuals have equal rights to attend worship services. But what happens if one individual engages in behavior that encroaches on the rights of others to attend in peace, as in the example noted above? To take just one additional example to make this conflict concrete, what if one individual is diagnosed with Post-Traumatic Stress Disorder and sudden, loud noises are extremely anxiety-provoking, and another congregant engages in loud and sudden vocal tics we might associate with Tourette's Syndrome? These conflicts are not minor. Such misunderstandings have led to police involvement, physical assaults, and even death (e.g., Maqbool, 2018; Newman, 2020; Schlikerman & Ford, 2018; Treisman, 2020).

CASE STUDY OF THE CONFLICT

A teenager diagnosed with Autism Spectrum Disorder was barred from his local church. This was not done lightly. The situation was a difficult one all around. It led to gun-toting deputies enforcing court orders and culminated in a legal injunction, one that was upheld against the family's appeal.

As stated above, this decision was not made lightly by the church. The teen in question was quite large (reportedly over six feet tall and weighing over 200 pounds) and the behaviors in question were considered disruptive and dangerous by the church and its congregants. The reported behaviors in question included:

1. Spitting and urinating in the sanctuary during services.
2. Pulling a teenage girl into his lap and not releasing her (according to one account, for over 15 minutes).
3. Nearly knocking elderly people over while bolting from church.
4. Starting and revving cars of parishioners, without first obtaining their permission to enter or turn on the car.
5. Noise-making during worship.

The church faced a serious liability issue. If they knew a dangerous situation existed and did nothing to address it and then someone suffered a serious injury, the church could potentially be held legally liable. Other congregants might also stop attending due to perceived danger, or situations could suddenly escalate out of control (e.g., when the teen pulled the girl into her lap and did not release her, what if others physically intervened to free her?). From the family's side, the basic question was a simple one: "If our son cannot be welcome in church, then where can we ever think he will be welcomed and accepted?"

The teen's family tried to address this situation. They sat with their son and attempted to redirect his behavior and even attempted to physically prevent some of the behavior described above. The church also attempted to address the situation, offering private sacraments and a closed-circuit system for watching services from within the church building. His family did not feel such exclusion was acceptable. The conflict finally landed in the courts and the church's position was upheld. The situation culminated with law enforcement intervening to keep the teen from entering the church.

WAS BARRING FROM CHURCH THE ONLY OPTION?

When the only proposed solution is barring an individual from a setting, my mind immediately goes back to the episode of *The Simpsons* where they explain in flashback how the Ned Flanders character developed his personality. He was being raised by Beatnik parents who did not believe in saying "no" or providing redirection or rules. As Ned trashed the psychiatrist's office, Ned's mother was heard to say, "We've tried nothing and we're all out of ideas!"

Was barring from church the only option? As a behavior analyst, the emphatic answer to the above question is a definite NO. It is a basic tenet of Applied Behavior Analysis that all behavior has a function, which is to say that there is a reason the person is engaging in the behavior; the behavior is achieving some end for the individual. If we can understand those functions through a process known as Functional Analysis, we can design treatment plans to address those behaviors and hopefully teach alternate behavior that would not lead to conflict with others. Let's take just two examples from the reported behavior that led to the conflict with between the teen, his family and the church:

1. Noise-making: Individuals diagnosed with Autism Spectrum Disorder often engage in such behavior, sometimes referred to in the clinical research literature as "non-contextual vocalizations." There is a wide research literature suggesting how such

behavior can be addressed, depending on the function of the behavior. In a simplest scenario, a "Differential Reinforcement of Other behavior" (DRO) can be used to reinforce the absence of the behavior. In this case, the individual receives reinforcing consequences for progressively longer and longer periods of not engaging in the behavior targeted for reduction until the behavior is no longer displayed.

2. Pulling the teen girl into his lap: Again, depending on the function of the behavior, a treatment plan to avoid recurrences could be designed. To take a very common function for such behavior, the individual diagnosed on the Autism Spectrum is actually seeking physical pressure rather than a social interaction. The teen girl in this case might actually just be serving as a source of weight/pressure. If that was determined to be the function, supplying some other source of physical pressure (e.g., a sandbag) could eliminate the potentially dangerous behavior.

The particulars of what the treatment plans might consist of would of course vary, depending on what the functions of the behaviors are determined to be. Progress might also not be immediate, and a certain amount of understanding would have to be sought while the treatment plans are given time to work and adjusted for maximum effectiveness. Nonetheless, there is no reason to believe that the behaviors could not be addressed, given appropriate time and resources. I was not personally involved in this particular situation and only read about it in Internet news reports, but would have loved an opportunity to intervene.

IS SITTING QUIETLY IN CHURCH THE ONLY WAY TO PARTICIPATE IN A FAITH-BASED COMMUNITY?

If it is, please tell me so I can seek a new one. Forgive the glibness, but if a faith tradition does not include behavior other than sitting quietly in services, I seriously have to question the point. I would hope that any faith-based congregation would have other, more physical and less verbal ways to act out their faith. Let's take another case study, this one I was actually involved with.

As a late teen, I helped out a local Jewish Synagogue, volunteering with some of their activities. One particular afternoon, I found myself paired with a young man I will call Michael for the purposes of this flashback sequence. Michael was a young man who truly enjoyed being at Temple. He was developmentally disabled, functioning near the borderline of mild to moderately Intellectually Disabled. He loved sitting with the other men at the "learning" sessions that preceded afternoon prayers. He was not able to participate on a very deep level in the discussion of Torah and Talmud, but attempted to do so, and was particularly interested in the ethics discussions.

On the day in question, Michael and I were putting together Passover packages, boxes of the foods necessary for the ritualistic Seder meal, for delivery to those who could not otherwise afford these necessities. Michael was in his element. He could work enthusiastically and excessive language was not needed. We worked together, loading items into boxes and then the boxes onto hand trucks that were then brought to delivery vehicles. As fate would have it, however, at one point Michael worked just a bit too enthusiastically. He put his box on the hand truck with a bit too much force and the jars in the box shattered, making a rather large mess.

Time froze. Michael's lips began to quiver and tears welled in his eyes. One could almost perceive a thought bubble over Michael's head. "They are going to be very mad at me. They are not going to allow me to come to Temple or to help anymore!"

There was clearly only one thing to do. I picked up the box I was loading and put it down on top of Michael's shattered one with force equal to that he had used, with similar results. If I may steal a joke from Buddy Hackett, I went back through the thousands of years of lore and knowledge of my people and said, "Sorry dude, I broke your box." (Ok, as I always say at this point, I am sure Maimonides never actually said "Sorry, dude," but I am claiming a little artistic license). Michael was very generous with me. He replied, "You didn't break it, it broke." So, it was no one's fault. His relief was palpable as we cleaned our mess. He was not in trouble and he was much more careful from that point forward and never was there a more enthusiastic volunteer who took more pleasure in what he was doing.

My point here obviously has nothing to do with broken jars, but rather with how we are going to put our faith-based ideas into action. Perhaps sitting and listening to a homily and standing and sitting and reciting lines on cue is not really the key to the whole thing. Perhaps we are called to engage in some other behaviors, ones that perhaps may match our individual skills and proclivities a bit more closely.

As I conclude this section, I wish to clarify a point. I have suggested alternate ways of participating in faith-based communities in addition to the behavior training that might help the person to participate in more traditional services. I suggest alternate ways as an option, but certainly not the only one or a prescribed option. I feel it is necessary to include this proviso, as sometimes people think that providing such options is a slippery slope that means people will just jump on an opportunity to "eliminate the problem" by excluding an individual. I ask that this not be the take-away point.

When I teach ethics classes in ABA, on night one, there are two "conversation stoppers" that I ask people to avoid. These are behaviors that make it impossible or too unpleasant to continue an otherwise productive conversation:

1. Not to think and speak in bumper stickers. A great many conclusions are possible in ethics discussions, but those conclusions must be based on critical analysis and not slogans. Most importantly, one must be able to answer the "and then what" implications of their final conclusions.
2. Assume good intentions. It is easy to vilify those who disagree. In the vast, vast majority of cases, no offense was intended but may be taken by someone else.

Let me provide an example of the second conversation-ender. I own a tank top (my preferred type of shirt) that reads, "I like my whiskey straight. My friends can go either way." Both of the statements on the shirt are true. I do enjoy whiskey, and do drink it straight ("neat," for purists). I also go along with Paul Newman, who wrote something to the effect that when you think about all the things that are really interesting about a person, what they do with their private parts is so low down on the list that it really isn't significant.

I have to admit, I have been surprised that the shirt has drawn a few negative comments. It did not come from the corner you might expect, but rather from individuals who were upset that the shirt reads *either* way rather than *any* way (i.e., upset that it seems gay or straight are the only options, seemingly excluding people who are bisexual, or pansexual or asexual or any of a number of characterizations). I would bet anything that such exclusionary ideas were never in the mind of the shirt's creators. They were certainly never in mine. Yet, conversation-ending offense has sometimes been taken. It is precisely that sort of emotional reaction where insult was never intended that I wish to avoid in our current discussion.

CONCLUDING THOUGHTS

There is an inescapable idea that we have to accept. There are certain behaviors that no matter how understanding we ask people to be, are never going to be allowed in society. In my own career, I have been asked to intervene by families or legal authorities and provide assistance when individuals engaged in such behavior. A very small sample includes:

1. Physically assaulting elderly strangers while standing on line for the movies.
2. Running and screaming in the aisles of an airplane.
3. Grabbing, opening and eating food in the supermarket.
4. Touching strangers or younger people without consent.
5. Throwing rocks and bottles at trains that were perceived to be off-schedule or cars that were perceived to be playing their radios too loudly.

Given that there are behaviors that will never be acceptable in society, any individual that engages in the behavior is vulnerable to being forcibly excluded. In this brief essay, I have attempted to demonstrate that exclusion is not the only option, certainly not if your stance is "We've tried nothing and we're all out of ideas." There is a science, Applied Behavior Analysis, that exists to help us in understanding and addressing such behavior. Through the application of this science, we can help all people to meaningfully participate in faith-based communities, one way or another. If I were a deity, ABA is just the sort of gift I would want to bestow on my creation.

REFERENCES

Maqbool, A. (2018, October 4). *Don't shoot, I'm disabled.* BBC News. https://www.bbc.com/news/stories-45739335

Newman, B. (2002). Cautionary vignettes. In P. Schaefer Whitby (Ed.), *Cases on teaching sexuality education to individuals with autism* (Advances in Early Childhood and K-12 Education). IGI Global.

Schlikerman, B., & Ford, L. (2018, September 5). Teen with autism shot to death by police. chicagotribune.com. https://www.chicagotribune.com/news/ct-xpm-2012-02-02-ct-met-calumet-city-shooting-20120202-story.html

Treisman, R. (2020, September 9). 13-year-old boy with autism disorder shot by Salt Lake City police. NPR.org. https://www.npr.org/2020/09/09/910975499/autistic-13-year-old-boy-shot-by-salt-lake-city-police

23

INCOME INEQUALITY
Understanding the Needs of Economically Disadvantaged Children and Families

Margaret Uwayo, Mya Hernandez, and Denise Ross

INTRODUCTION

By definition, economically disadvantaged families in the United States are families with annual incomes equal to or below the federal poverty level[1] (Fontenot et al., 2019; U.S. Department of Health and Human Services, DHHS, 2020). Families that meet the federal guidelines for being low-income, poor, and/or experiencing poverty, are described as *economically disadvantaged*. Economic disadvantage has been correlated with outcomes such as: academic underperformance, increased school dropout rates, higher infant mortality, higher levels of obesity, increased likelihood of emotional and behavioral challenges, and overall less stability at home (Haider 2014; National Center for Education Statistics, 2019; Russell et al., 2016; Sheridan & McLaughlin, 2016). Given that approximately 11% of American adults and 16% of children live in poverty (Children's Defense Fund, 2020), there is an urgent need to discover ways in which practitioners can increase successful outcomes and quality of life for economically disadvantaged populations. In this chapter, we seek to describe the needs of economically disadvantaged populations, barriers and challenges that behavior analysts may experience in efforts to serve clients who are economically disadvantaged, and potential solutions for addressing the social and cultural needs of these clients.

DEMOGRAPHICS OF ECONOMICALLY DISADVANTAGED CHILDREN AND FAMILIES

In 2019, 10.5% of individuals in America lived below the poverty level (United States Census, 2020). Children under 18 were 30.4% of individuals in poverty (United States Census, 2020). While poverty rates were slightly lower in 2019 for most age and racial groups when compared to 2018 (United States Census, 2020), poverty levels in the United States are still higher than many other developed countries, which impacts the educational and health outcomes of U.S. children (Organization for Economic Cooperation and Development, OCED, 2018, 2019). Table 23.1 displays selected characteristics of individuals in poverty in the United States.

IMPACT OF ECONOMIC DISADVANTAGE ON CHILDREN AND FAMILIES

Health. As previously noted, economic disadvantage is associated with negative health outcomes in children including their physical and mental health. We define *health* as a child or

---

[1] Poverty is defined as having a family income at or below the federal poverty level. In 2020, a family of four with an income of $26,200 or lower was in poverty (U.S. Department of Health and Human Services, 2020).

Table 23.1 Percentage of population below poverty level by selected characteristics

Characteristic	Percentage
Race/Ethnicity[1] (within group)	
American Indian/Alaska Native	23.0
Black	21.2
Other race	18.3
Hispanic	17.2
Pacific Islander/Native Hawaiian	16.5
Multiracial	15.2
Asian	9.6
White	9.0
Age[1]	
Under age 18	30.4
18 to 59	51.5
60 and older	18.1
Educational Attainment[2]	
No high school diploma	23.7
High school, no college	11.5
Some college	7.8
College degree	3.9

[1] Adapted from *Poverty status in the past 12 months by race and age, 2019, U.S. Census Bureau, American Community Survey, Table B-17.* Race, Age, and Poverty in the United States: 2019.

[2] Adapted from *People in poverty by selected characteristics: 2018 and 2019, U.S. Census Bureau, Current Population Survey, 2019 and 2020 Annual Social and Economic Supplements (CPS ASEC), Table B-1.* Income and Poverty in the United States: 2019.

parent's physical, mental, and emotional health. Generally, individuals with lower socioeconomic statuses have lower health outcomes than individuals from higher socioeconomic statuses (American Psychological Association, 2010). These outcomes include significantly higher rates of obesity (Levine, 2011), diabetes (Gaskin et al., 2014), asthma (Cardet et al., 2016), and psychological stress (APA, 2010) among economically disadvantaged children and their families. Chaudry and Wimer (2016) suggest that health disparities exist because of a lack of access to resources, psychological stress, and the length of time in poverty. Since physical, mental, and emotional health interact during child development, understanding the physical and mental health effects of poverty can better prepare behavior analysts to address the needs of economically disadvantaged children and families (Yoshikawa et al., 2012).

Education. In the U.S., poverty remains a serious challenge that impacts individuals and their communities. Research indicates that income status begins to impact children's literacy outcomes even before formal schooling begins – in part because of the importance of prerequisite vocabulary skills before reading instruction begins and their lack of access to resources that promote literacy such as books and parental literacy (Aikens &

Barbarin, 2008; van Bergen et al., 2016; Chetty et al., 2016; Henning et al., 2010; Washbrook & Waldfogel, 2011). Economically disadvantaged children who do not read proficiently by third grade are four times more likely to drop out of high school and are less likely to attain gainful employment which, consequently, perpetuates their SES status (APA, 2020; Doerschuk et al., 2016; Hernandez, 2012; National Center for Educational Statistics, 2019; Reardon et al., 2013).

Employment and Earnings. Unemployment and underemployment both contribute to SES; however, poverty has a reciprocal impact on employment and earnings. For instance, job accessibility is key to gaining and maintaining employment but those living in poverty face challenges when commuting to employment. While high income workers have more choices in residency due to having more financial resources at their disposal for commuting (e.g., they can live long distances from their employer), those in poverty often must rely on public transportation or other means of transportation. Additionally, those living in poverty often earn significantly less. Poverty-level wages are widely prevalent in the U.S. and partly account for why working families continue to live in poverty. A poverty level wage is an hourly wage that still leaves a full-time, full-year worker below the federal poverty level for their family size. According to U.S. census data in 2017, more than one in nine workers are being paid a poverty-level wage which is, ultimately, too little to allow families to escape poverty (Cooper, 2018).

BARRIERS TO EFFECTIVE SUPPORT OF ECONOMICALLY DISADVANTAGED POPULATIONS

Behavior Analysis works toward improving the human condition through the analysis of environmental factors that impact behavior change. Because the majority of behavior analysts (77.72%) practice within the realm of developmental disabilities and autism, there have been limited applications of behavior analytic practices in other areas of social significance such as poverty, child welfare, and social justice (Behavior Analyst Certification Board, 2020). The following is a list of barriers within the field derived from the authors' experiences and the published work of researchers and practitioners:

- In spite of impressive outcomes with special populations like individuals with autism, many findings have yet to be applied to mainstream society (Friman, 2010; Poling, 2010).

- Instruction, training, and research on the application of behavior analytic principles to other populations is not the norm. Additionally, the most fruitful careers are in this area as well (Normand & Kohn, 2013).

- Few graduate programs in behavior analysis prepare students for work in a field other than autism (Poling, 2010). The handful of graduate programs that focus on topics aligned with the concerns of mainstream society (literacy, training, health, or safety practices) are specialized programs at lone institutions. This may not offer access to a wider graduate student body (Normand et al., 2013).

- Practitioners are not prepared to practice with diverse populations and, instead, practice within their cultural comfort zone (Normand et al., 2013; Poling, 2010).

- A majority of research in ABA is published exclusively in the field's flagship journals (Friman, 2010).

- The field focuses on the implementation of effective practices with individuals rather than large scale implementation, which does not translate effective findings to mainstream society (Biglan, 2015; Normand et al., 2013).

Along with barriers within the field that prevent the dissemination and implementation of behavior analytic principles, there are barriers outside the field that present additional challenges:

- Funding opportunities for psychological research is limited. For instance, only 3.2% of the nation's federal budget for research went to psychological research in 2016 (Stamm et al., 2017).
- Program interventions may not be sustained by non-behavior analytic practitioners once behavior analytic support ends.
- Misguided notions about learning by non-behavior analytic practitioners drive their use of behavior analytic practices (e.g. every student learns differently, teachers do not need to measure student performance, or drill and practice stifle student creativity and limits their understanding) (Heward, 2003).
- Misguided notions about behavior analytic practices also result in a lack of adherence (e.g., ABA therapy involves punishing practices, ABA therapy eliminates what makes children unique, ABA therapy is only for children with autism).
- A lack of dissemination of behavior analytic practices due to limited publication in non-behavior analytic journals.

RECOMMENDATIONS FOR PRACTICE WITH ECONOMICALLY DISADVANTAGED CHILDREN AND FAMILIES

Understand that poverty is complex. Poverty affects not only those experiencing it, but also society at large (Biglan, 2015). Examining and understanding the various contextual factors that make poverty more likely for individuals may be one way that practitioners can improve their cultural sensitivity, become effective in their practices, and serve as agents of change in society. Rather than just an issue of financial ability, poverty may be viewed as a co-occurring set of complex events (i.e., education, mental and physical health, academic attainment, personal choice) that may be situational, occurring at different points in time, or generational, and affecting individuals from all countries and races (Payne, 2013). Put simply, poverty is a combination of factors that may be defined as "the extent to which an individual does without resources" (Payne, 2013, p. 11) or even as setting events that affect the way individuals interact with their environments. By analyzing, understanding, and ultimately planning for inevitable contextual factors, practitioners can develop responsive, practical, and sustainable intervention for disadvantaged individuals.

Spend time in communities and families impacted by poverty. Due to limited training programs that prepare behavior analysts for work in a variety of settings, the authors recommend that practitioners spend time in communities and working with families impacted by poverty. By spending time in these communities, practitioners can have a better understanding of the environment and the barriers many of these families face. Additionally, they can build rapport with these communities and be better prepared to build and maintain trusting relationships. Poverty is a large scale issue in the U.S. that warrants a behavior analytic analysis.

However, if behavior analysts are not prepared to work in these communities, there is little impact they can have despite the development of effective practices.

Understand the intersectionality between race and class. When examining issues of race and class, it is clear that non-White populations are disproportionately economically disadvantaged. However, it is also important to not assume that a member of a specific ethnic or racial group is economically disadvantaged. In an effort to be culturally relevant, behavior analysts are encouraged to treat clients as individuals. Knowing one's client can help determine their needs.

Collaboration and interdisciplinary partnerships. Behavior analysts should also look to partner with practitioners from other fields (e.g., doctors, social workers, teachers). Through collaboration in applied work or research, behavior analysts can expand their scope of practice and potentially expand career opportunities for future practitioners in the field. Research conducted in partnership can gain visibility in other fields when published in non-behavior analytic journals as well.

Examine their experiences with social class. Liu (2012) in his description of his Social Class World Model (SCWM), a model of teaching designed to help students learn about classism, begins training on social class by having students examine their own experiences through a series of questions intended to examine your own views of social class. First, how are your views of social class different or similar to others in your same socioeconomic class? Which behaviors are expected as a part of that class? Next, which socialization messages have you received about social class and how did you receive them? What are your own prejudices, and feelings about discussing social class (e.g., do you think that discussing social class is taboo)? Finally, how does your social class affect how you view others (e.g., what is appropriate behavior for a child) and how have you been the target of classism or demonstrated classism to others?

Pursue retraining and supervision to expand your scope of practice. Training and supervision in social class should take place after discussions about one's own experiences. As a practitioner, part of your training is to recognize your role in breaking down systems that maintain inequality while also recognizing that practitioners may contribute to those systems. During training, explicit examples of classism should be discussed. Further, training in social class should emphasize factors that produce stress for economically disadvantaged clients. Iceland (2013) suggests that practitioners be trained on the demographics of poverty, rate of poverty over time, economic gaps and their impacts on an individual's life, relationship of poverty to national trends in work and education, and issues of access to resources such as health care.

In addition to readings for training, Liu (2012) suggests that the most effective way to teach trainees about clients from ED backgrounds is in supervision settings with clients who have differing social class backgrounds. In these settings, trainees provide services to a particular population under the supervision of a socially competent supervisor (e.g., homeless population). The supervisor helps the trainee understand clinical practice with the population, but the ultimate goal is that they learn about themselves and their values related to social class. Supervisors should look for trainees to replace their own worldview with responsive clinical practice that does not contain social bias.

CONCLUSION

The purpose of this chapter was to describe some of the conditions that affect individuals who are economically disadvantaged, the barriers that impact practice with economically disadvantaged populations, and considerations for behavior analysts to work with children and families who need support. Lower economic conditions are associated with a number of life conditions that can impact the psychological and physical lives of individuals who experience them, including poor health conditions (Gupta et al., 2007), lack of affordable housing, underemployment, limited financial resources, and inconsistent transportation (Lange et al., 2017). Yoshikawa and colleagues (2012) notes that these correlates of poverty such as lower levels of education, impoverished neighborhoods, and fewer food resources relate to psychological stress for children and families. For example, during the current global pandemic, a lack of digital resources to access school was a stressor for some economically disadvantaged parents and families. This stressor may have intersected with other factors such as disability, race, and gender. To support families experiencing these and other conditions that are an outcome of lower SES, the authors of this chapter recommend that behavior analysts expand their scope of competence to include economically disadvantaged families and children.

REFERENCES

Aikens, N. L., & Barbarin, O. A. (2008). Socioeconomic differences in reading trajectories: The contribution of family, neighborhood, and school contexts. *Journal of Educational Psychology*, *100*(2), 235–251. https://doi.org/10.1037/0022-0663.100.2.235

American Psychological Association. (2010). *Children, youth, families, and socioeconomic status.* https://www.apa.org/pi/ses/resources/publications/children-families

American Psychological Association. (2018). *Inclusion of social class in psychology curricula.* https://www.apa.org/pi/ses/resources/publications/social-class-curricula

Behavior Analyst Certification Board. (2020a). *Certificant data.* BACB. https://www.bacb.com/bacb-certificant-data/

Biglan, A. (2015). *The nurture effect: How the science of human behavior can improve our lives and our world.* New Harbinger Publications.

Cardet, J. C., King, T. S., Louisias, M., Weschler, M., Israel E., & Phipatanakul, W., (2016). Income is an independent risk factor for worse asthma outcomes. *The Journal of Allergy and Clinical Immunology*, *137*(2). https://doi.org/10.1016/j.jaci.2015.12.029

Chaudry, A. C., & Wimer, C. (2016). Poverty is not just an indicator: The relationship between income, poverty, and child well-being. *Academic Pediatrics*, *16*(3), 23–29. https://doi.org/10.1016/j.acap.2015.12.010

Chetty, R., Hendren, N., Lin, F., Majerovitz, J., & Scuderi, B. (2016). Childhood environment and gender gaps in adulthood. *American Economic Review*, *106*(5), 282–88.

Children's Defense Fund. (2020). The state of America's children. https://www.childrensdefense.org/wp-content/uploads/2020/02/The-State-Of-Americas-C hildren-2020.pdf

Cooper, D. (2018, June 15). *One in nine U.S. workers are paid wages that can leave them in poverty, even when working full time.* Economic Policy Institute. https://www.epi.org/publication/one-in-nine-u-s-workers-are-paid-wages-that-can-leave-them-in-poverty-even-when-working-full-time/

Doerschuk, P., Bahrim, C., Daniel, J. R., & Kruger, J. (2016). Closing the gaps and filling the STEM pipeline: A multidisciplinary approach. *Journal of science Education and Technology*, *25*(4). https://doi.org/10.1007/s10956-016-9622-8

Fontenot, B., Uwayo, M., Avendano, S. M., Ross, D. (2019). A descriptive analysis of applied behavior analysis research with economically disadvantaged children. *Behavior Analysis in Practice, 12*, 782–794. https://doi.org/10.1007/s40617-019-00389-8

Friman, P. C. (2010). Come on in, the water is fine: Achieving mainstream relevance through integration with primary medical care. *The Behavior Analyst*, *33*(1), 19–36. https://doi.org/10.1007/BF03392201

Gaskin, D. J., Thorpe, R. J., Jr, McGinty, E. E., Bower, K., Rohde, C., Young, J. H., LaVeist, T. A., & Dubay, L. (2014). Disparities in diabetes: The nexus of race, poverty, and place. *American Journal of Public Health, 104*(11), 2147–2155. https://doi.org/10.2105/AJPH.2013.301420

Gupta, R. P., de Wit, M. L., & McKeown, D. (2007). The impact of poverty on the current and future health status of children. *Paediatrics & child health, 12*(8), 667–672. https://doi.org/10.1093/pch/12.8.667

Haider, S. J. (2014). Racial and ethnic infant mortality gaps and socioeconomic status. *Focus, 31*, 18–20. http://www.irp.wisc.edu/publications/focus.htm

Henning, C., McIntosh, B., Arnott, W., & Dodd, B. (2010). Long term outcome of oral and phonological awareness intervention with socially disadvantaged preschoolers: The impact on language and literacy. *Journal of Research in Reading, 33*(3), 211–246

Hernandez, D. J. (2012). (rep.). *Double jeopardy: How third-grade reading skills and poverty influence high school graduation* (pp. 1–24). https://files.eric.ed.gov/fulltext/ED518818.pdf

Heward, W. L. (2003). Ten faulty notions about teaching and learning that hinder the effectiveness of special education. *The Journal of Special Education, 36*(4), 186–205.

Iceland, J. (2013). *Poverty in America: A handbook.* University of California Press.

Lange, B. C. L., Dau, A., Goldblum, J., Alfano, J., & Smith, M. (2017). A mixed methods investigation of the experience of poverty among a population of low-income parenting women. *Community Mental Health Journal, 53*(9), 1–10. https://doi.org/10.1007/s10597-017-0093-z

Levine J. A. (2011). Poverty and obesity in the U.S. *Diabetes, 60*(11), 2667–2668. https://doi.org/10.2337/db11-1118

Ming Liu, W., Alt, M. C., & Pittsinger, R. F. (2013). The role of the social class worldview model in the assessment, diagnosis, and treatment of mental and physical health. In F. A. Paniagua & A.-M. Yamada (Eds.), *Handbook of multicultural mental health* (pp. 111–125). Elsevier. https://doi.org/10.1016/b978-0-12-394420-7.00006-0

National Center of Education Statistics. (2017). *The conditions of education.* NCES. https://nces.ed.gov/pubs2019/2019144.pdf

Normand, M. P., & Kohn, C. S. (2013). Don't wag the dog: Extending the reach of applied behavior analysis. *The Behavior Analyst, 36*(1), 109–122. https://doi.org/10.1007/BF03392294

Organization for Economic Cooperation and Development (OECD). (2018). *Policy brief on child well-being – Poor children in rich countries: Why we need policy action.* OECD https://www.oecd.org/els/family/Poor-children-in-rich-countries-Policy-brief-2018.pdf

Organization for Economic Cooperation and Development (OECD). (2019). *Society at a glance 2019: OECD social indicators.* OECD Publishing. https://doi.org/10.1787/soc_glance-2019-en

Payne, R. K. (2013). *A framework for understanding poverty: A cognitive approach.* Aha process Inc.

Poling, A. (2010). Looking to the future: will behavior analysis survive and prosper? *The Behavior Analyst, 33*(1), 7–17. https://doi.org/10.1007/BF03392200

Reardon, S. F. (2013, May). The widening income achievement gap. http://www.ascd.org/publications/educational-leadership/may13/vol70/num08/The-Widening-Income-Achievement-Gap.aspx

Russell, A. E., Ford, T., Williams, R., & Russell, G. (2016). The association between socioeconomic disadvantage and attention deficit/hyperactivity disorder (ADHD): A systematic review. *Child Psychiatry and Human Development, 47*, 440–458. https://doi.org/10.1007/s10578-015-0578-3

Semega, J., Kollar, M., Shrider, E. A., & Creamer, J. F. (2020). *Income and poverty in the United States: 2019.* U.S. Government Publishing Office. https://www.census.gov/library/publications/2020/demo/p60-270.html

Sheridan, M. A., & McLaughlin, K. A. (2016). Neurological models of the impact of adversity on education. *Current Opinion in Behavioral Sciences, 10*, 108–113. https://doi.org/10.1016/j.cobeha.2016.05.013

Stamm, K., Christidis, P., & Lin, L. (2017, April). How much federal funding is directed to research in psychology? *Monitor on Psychology, 48*(4). http://www.apa.org/monitor/2017/04/datapoint

U.S. Department of Health and Human Services (2020). U.S. Poverty Guidelines for 2020. https://www.hhs.gov/sites/default/files/2019-annual-report.pdf

van Bergen, E. V., van Zuijen, T., Bisop, D. V. M., & deJong, P. F. (2016). Why are home literacy environments and children's reading skills associated? What parental skills reveal. *Reading Research Quarterly.* https://doi.org/10.1002/rrq.160

Washbrook, E. V., & Waldfogel, J. (2011). *On your marks: Measuring the school readiness of children in low-to-middle income families.* Resolution Foundation.

Yoshikawa, H., Aber, J. L., & Beardslee, W. (2012). The effects of poverty on the mental, emotional, and behavioral health of children and youth implications for prevention. *American Psychologist, 67*(4), 272–284.

24

INDIGENOUS RIGHTS

Finding the Trail: Indigenous Considerations for Decolonizing
Research and Clinical Work

Louis Busch and Angela Levasseur

INTRODUCTION

We all know the story about the man who sat by the trail too long, and then it grew over, and
he could never find his way again. We can never forget what has happened, but we cannot go
back. Nor can we just sit beside the trail.

Pitikwahanapiwiyin (Chief Poundmaker, 1842–1886)

Indigenous peoples are the descendants of the original inhabitants of lands that have been
subject to the destructive force of European colonization. In North America, there are more
than 600 distinct groups of Indigenous peoples, each with unique histories, cultural, and
spiritual practices, languages, education programs, governance structures, social systems,
and worldviews. The relationship between Indigenous peoples and settlers has been strained
by centuries of colonial violence, racism, and systemic discrimination in policy and practice.
One of the primary barriers that continue to impede progress and the development of collaborative relationships between Indigenous and non-Indigenous people, is a lack of understanding of these oppressive systems and their ongoing impact on Indigenous peoples today.
In an effort to inform non-Indigenous clinicians and researchers who may interact with
Indigenous peoples and their communities, this chapter will (a) explore historic and ongoing
injustices perpetrated against Indigenous peoples; (b) provide examples of harms done in
the name of science, medicine, and social work; (c) discuss the processes of decolonization
and self-determination in research and clinical practice; and (d) suggest individual and group
behaviors which may lead to progress in the form of respectful partnerships.

INJUSTICE THEN AND NOW

Colonization is the settlement of one group onto the homelands of another, typically resulting in exploitation of resources, displacement of the Indigenous group, and the forced impo-
sition of the colonizer's culture, laws, language, religion, and way of life upon the land's
original inhabitants (Gareau & Baer, 2020). Through colonization, Indigenous peoples
across North America are denied even the most basic of human rights afforded to mainstream society. This deliberate system of oppression repeated across generations (and active
in the present day), has greatly impeded the ability of Indigenous peoples to exercise self-
sufficiency, self-government, self-determination, and to heal from its precipitating harms.
Indigenous peoples have survived multiple attempts at race-based physical and cultural
genocide in the form of overt mass violence (e.g. Massacre at Wounded Knee, Cypress Hills
Massacre), a disproportionate rate of deaths at the hands of the police (see the murders of
J.J. Harper, Lawrence Wegner, Rodney Naistus, Neil Stonechild, Dudley George and their
resulting inquiries) (Linden, 2005), institutional complacency and negligence in preventing
or responding to violence against Indigenous peoples (e.g. National Inquiry into Missing and
Murdered Indigenous Women and Girls, 2019), forced relocation and dispossession of lands

(e.g. the Trail of Tears and the reserve/reservation system); biological warfare (e.g. intentional transmission of smallpox along Indigenous trade routes) (Patterson & Runge, 2002), tyrannical assimilation policy (e.g. Canada's Indian Act, American Indian Termination Policy) (Lavoie et al., 2010; Ulrich, 2010), abusive education directives (e.g. Indian residential schools and day schools), racist social programs (e.g. child welfare system, mass apprehension and adoption initiatives) (Blackstock, 2016; Johnston, 1983), legal suppression of Indigenous ceremonies and spiritual practice (e.g. criminalization of the Sun Dance and Potlatch ceremonies) (MacDonald, 2013) discriminatory policing and judiciary practices (e.g. deaths in custody, failure to investigate Indigenous deaths and disappearances, extreme overrepresentation of incarcerated Indigenous men, women, and youth, and freezing deaths by police "starlight tours") (Chartrand, 2019; Drache, Fletcher, & Voss, 2016; Reifenberg, 2018), and a disproportionate burden of pollution and environmental degradation (e.g. heavy metals released while mining, flooding and water contamination from hydro-electric dams, and neurotoxins associated with oil spills and dispersants) (Fernández-Llamazares et al., 2020).

The objectives of many of these racist and archaic policies and programs were often made explicit by government officials, such as Richard Henry Pratt's commitment to "Kill the Indian, Save the Man" (Silburn, 2005) or the objective of the Canadian government to "Kill the Indian in the Child" (Harper, 2008); both state-sanctioned mandates of cultural genocide. The devastating effects of these repeated instances of colonial violence have been collectively experienced, intergenerationally damaging, and remain overwhelmingly unresolved today (Coates, 2008). Although it is not possible to explore the many facets of systematic oppression faced by Indigenous peoples in the space of this chapter, an examination of the residential school system is a necessary first step in understanding the ability of colonial processes to persist in injury and destruction across generations and into the everyday lives of Indigenous people today.

The Indian residential school system (referred to as boarding or industrial schools in the United States) has had long-lasting and severely detrimental effects, not only on the survivors of these schools but also intergenerationally. The first Canadian residential school, the Mohawk Institute, opened in Branford, Ontario in 1831, with the last school, Gordon Residential School in Punnichy, Saskatchewan, not closed until 1996. Parallel events occurred to the south, with Carlisle Indian Industrial School opened in Pennsylvania in 1879, where more than 60,000 children were enrolled in off-reserve boarding schools across the USA through 1970 (Native American Advancement Foundation, 2013). As a result of government policy, children were forcefully removed from their homes as young as 4 years of age, with their parents threatened with starvation and imprisonment for any protest or resistance (Rheault, 2012). Many children spent the majority of their childhoods away from their parents, grandparents, and extended families; as well as their traditional homelands. This prolonged familial separation and surrogate supervision by teachers, dormitory supervisors, school administrators, and clergy was wholistically damaging to the children who attended residential schools, particularly as Indigenous cultures place great emphasis on the role of the extended family and the inclusion of grandparents in child-rearing (National Collaborating Centre for Indigenous Health, 2019).

The upset of these cultural systems has been devastating for Indigenous families and has widely contributed to a multitude of social issues that continue to plague Indigenous communities today. Many survivors have shared graphic and horrifying accounts of how they endured physical, sexual, mental, and emotional abuse at the hands of school staff and clergy (Truth and Reconciliation Commission, 2015). Children were physically beaten for perceived insubordination, for speaking their Indigenous languages, for practicing their culture, for making mistakes, for looking at clergy members, and oftentimes for no reason at all. As stated by Milloy and Coates (1999) "discipline was the curriculum and punishment the pedagogy" (p. 44). Children were often underfed and malnourished during their time at residential school; many faced starvation. Survivors detail substandard living conditions and exposure to diseases such as mumps, measles, and tuberculosis, without appropriate medical treatment.

In Canada, it is estimated that as many as 6,000 children died while at residential schools as a result of these horrific conditions. The American government has not yet made an effort to account for the number of children who did not return home from its boarding schools. However, what is known is that approximately 83% of Indigenous children in the USA were placed in boarding schools by 1926 and held under conditions that are now equated to torture (EagleWoman & Rice, 2016).

Being reared in abusive, foreign, and highly institutionalized environments destroyed the transmission of positive parenting skills between generations. Unlike the pedagogy of the Residential school system, traditional Indigenous parenting approaches did not include corporal punishment and often emphasized child autonomy, honesty, personal responsibility, and community belonging. Residential schools suppressed the development of healthy family and community relationships, impeded opportunities to learn effective coping skills, and obstructed the ability to develop or maintain one's self-esteem, self-worth, or a sense of belonging. The physical, mental, emotional, and spiritual ramifications of 165 years of residential schools have resulted in widespread intergenerational trauma, collective trauma, the proliferation of adverse childhood experiences, and the development of adverse community environments in First Nations communities.

HARMS DONE IN THE NAME OF SCIENCE, MEDICINE, AND SOCIAL WORK

In addition to the destructive impacts of the residential school system, many harms have been done in the name of science, medicine, and social work. Unfortunately, Indigenous people were not afforded relief from the gradual elimination of residential schools. In the 1960s, as governments began to close the schools, authorities fashioned a new child apprehension scheme in the guise of social service programs to ensure the continued and prolonged perpetuation of cultural genocide against Indigenous peoples in the form of the so-called "Sixties Scoop" in Canada and the "Indian Adoption Program" in the USA. The Sixties Scoop refers to the time period between 1960 and 1980 when thousands of Indigenous children were taken from their homes and adopted out to Caucasian families all over Canada, throughout the United States, and even as far as Europe.

Thousands of Indigenous children endured familial separation, culture, and language loss, identity confusion, and widespread physical, sexual, mental, emotional, and spiritual abuse. It was not uncommon for non-Indigenous families to adopt Indigenous children who had been stolen from their families, as a source of labor and to access the stipends provided by the government. In today's child welfare system, Indigenous children continue to be apprehended, removed from their families, communities, and cultures, and placed in non-Indigenous households at disproportionate rates. Sadly, it seems the "Sixties Scoop" has simply evolved into the "Millennium Scoop" (Sinclair, 2007, p. 67) with Indigenous children 15 times more likely to be placed in child welfare than non-Indigenous children (Blackstock et al., 2016). In fact, there are three times more children in the child welfare system today than there were in attendance in residential schools at its peak (Blackstock, 2016). In this way, the legacy of cultural genocide that has targeted the Indigenous family unit that began with the residential school system has been perpetuated into the present day, with North American governments either indifferent or actively fighting accountability in the courts (Elliott, 2019).

Between 1942 and 1952, government-funded programs in Canada, including the Hospital for Sick Children (now SickKids Hospital in Toronto), carried out medical experiments on Indigenous children without the knowledge or consent of their families. The experiments involved the testing of various chemicals and supplements on Indigenous children facing starvation at residential schools, with the experiments continuing even as the children died of malnutrition (Talaga, 2018; MacDonald et al., 2014; Mosby, 2013). In the 1950s, under the guise of accessing much needed medical treatment, Alaska Natives and Inuit (including children and pregnant women) were recruited for government-funded experiments requiring the ingestion of radioactive isotopes to test the role of the thyroid gland in human acclimatization to cold weather. The procedures resulted in permanent damage by destroying cells in the thyroid glands with no medical follow-up made available for participants (Hodge, 2012).

A modern-day eugenics program in the form of coerced sterilizations (e.g. tubal ligations and hysterectomies) has been an ongoing practice applied against Indigenous women across North America. In many of these cases, medical staff and social service workers coerced women to get the procedures following childbirth against the threat of apprehending their children or terminating social assistance payments (Stote, 2015; Torpy, 2000). Another common practice is sterilization without the knowledge or consent of Indigenous women while they are undergoing another procedure, such as an appendectomy. In reviewing cases of sterilization of Indigenous women in the U.S., Hodge (2012) found that even when consent forms were signed, they were often "inadequate or illegally obtained" (p. 433). Sadly, like the residential school system and child welfare abuses, and the harms of colonial research practices, the practice of sterilization of Indigenous women is not ancient history, but an alarmingly recent practice. In 2019, more than 100 Indigenous women filed a class-action lawsuit following experiences of coerced sterilizations occurring in the province of Saskatchewan alone over the last 30 years; the most recent incident on record occurred in 2017 (Dhaliwal, 2019).

A LASTING LEGACY OF TRAUMA

Indigenous peoples across North America have been collectively wounded by their experience of colonial violence as manifested in a myriad of deleterious socioeconomic and health issues. Many Indigenous communities now face extreme housing shortages, overcrowding, unemployment, and disproportionate rates of chronic health conditions, incarceration, substance dependence, mental health challenges, suicide, and violence. Communities are plagued by chronic underfunding of social, education, and healthcare programs, resource exploitation, and the lasting impact of environmental pollution. These issues have in turn, led to a disproportionate level of Indigenous children, youth, and adults reporting adverse childhood experiences, perpetuating a vicious cycle of revictimization that crosses generations and further aggravates pre-existing health disparities between Indigenous communities and mainstream communities. Unsurprisingly, Indigenous peoples hold a disproportionate burden of disease and chronic health conditions across North America.

DECOLONIZING RESEARCH AND CLINICAL WORK

Perhaps as a result of these disparities and the associated social challenges, Indigenous peoples are among the most researched population in the world, while also enjoying almost no benefit of that research. *Helicopter research* refers to the practice of non-Indigenous researchers dropping into Indigenous communities, conducting research with little or no consultation or input from community members, and then leaving without sharing the results, benefits, or credit for the research conducted (Campbell, 2014). A similar phenomenon could be referred to as *helicopter consulting*, in which non-Indigenous clinicians and mental health practitioners conduct assorted consultations, training, and psychological assessments (often at exorbitant costs to the communities) and simply leave with no regard to the suitability or sustainability of those assessments and interventions. Researchers and clinicians with little knowledge of the communities and cultures they are infiltrating have regularly applied disrespectful methodologies and published in a way that intensifies stigmatization (e.g. disproportionate amount of research on Fetal Alcohol Spectrum Disorder compared to other common neurodevelopmental disorders or an excessive focus on substance use disorders). Indigenous people are often viewed by clinicians, researchers, and academics as a "problem to be solved" and as "passive objectives requiring assistance from external experts" (Cochrane, 2008, p. 22). In both Canada and the USA, dishonesty, and exploitation by researchers in relationships with Indigenous communities have been commonplace over the last century. For example, in the 1970s, and 1980s, researchers harvested blood samples from the Havasupai and Nuu-chah-nulth peoples under the guise of researching treatments for diabetes and arthritis, with blood samples instead being sent abroad without permission, used to establish ancestry, and applied for a variety of other clinical research studies for which consent was not provided (Cochrane, 2008; Hodge, 2012). Likely as a result of these experiences, some Indigenous organizations now view western research as an "implicitly political process" and an "instrument of oppression and colonialism" (Campbell, 2014, p. 41).

RESILIENCE, RESISTANCE, AND THE DECOLONIZATION OF RESEARCH AND CLINICAL WORK

In spite of a centuries-long campaign of ethnic cleansing, eugenics, assimilation, and institutional violence and racism, Indigenous peoples have resisted and successfully protected their cultures, languages, and communities from colonial annihilation. By nourishing ethnocultural identity, reclaiming political empowerment, and resisting systems of centralized bureaucratic domination by colonial government entities, Indigenous peoples are gaining ground in self-determination in the areas of education, social services, healthcare, research, economic development, and land and resource management. In this way, Indigenous peoples are working to heal and rebuild from the effects of colonization. The cornerstone of this decolonization work is Indigenous control of all things that impact Indigenous lives. Non-Indigenous researchers and clinicians can be allies in this work.

In the context of research and clinical work, much can be done to promote respectful partnerships with Indigenous peoples and to recover from the damage done by colonial research and clinical practices of the past and present. First, researchers and clinicians must account for the unique context of each community and its history. A *pan-Indigenous* perspective views Indigenous identity and culture as generic and uniform, instead of recognizing the diversity that exists across hundreds of unique nations and thousands of unique communities; a harmful practice that "can thwart local expressions of cultural identity" and leave communities vulnerable to "control and manipulation by [non-Indigenous] society" (Kirmayer et al., 2000, p. 117).

Second, professionals must be well informed of the methods and harms of colonization, both historical and present, and understand it as a setting event, an ever-present contextual variable, in the lives of Indigenous peoples. Third, researchers and clinicians must be prepared to relinquish control of endeavors related to Indigenous peoples. In practical terms, this may mean sharing status as principal investigator, partnering in the design of research methodology, arranging for joint-control of funding decisions, provision of fair and respectful authorship rights in all publications, and taking a participatory and community involved approach to the design and execution of a research project from the point of inception (when considering a an application for funding and before any research begins). Researchers should seek out local Indigenous Research Ethics Review Committees within First Nations communities (Sahota, 2009) and adhere to existing guidelines for self-determination applied to research, such as the First Nations Information Governance Centre's Ownership, Control, Access and Possession (OCAP) (Mecredy et al., 2018) and Chapter 9 of the Tri-Council Policy Statement on Ethical Conduct for research Involving Humans (CIHR, 2018). Researchers should work to eliminate tokenism in partnerships with Indigenous peoples, such as the practice of including Indigenous components on grant requests in an apparent attempt to increase its attractiveness to funders, seeking Indigenous collaborators in signature alone, and then neglecting meaningful engagement, collaboration, and credit-sharing thereafter.

Fourth, academic institutions and clinical training programs must prioritize the cultural competence of faculty, students, and staff and insist on the provision of culturally safe services. Cultural competency is defined as "a set of congruent behaviors, attitudes, and policies that come together to enable effective work in cross-cultural situations . . . competence implies having the capacity to function effectively within the context of cultural beliefs, behaviors, and needs presented by consumers and their communities" (Office of Minority Health, 2001, p. 4). Cultural safety from an Indigenous context, "means that the educator/practitioner/professional, whether Indigenous or not, can communicate competently with a patient in that patient's social, political, economic and spiritual realm" (Baba, 2013, p. 4). and "considers the social, political, and historical contexts of health care" including "the difficult concepts of racism, discrimination, prejudice and unequal power relations" (Hart-Wasekeesikaw & Gregory, 2009, p. 24). In practical terms, this may mean including cultural competence and culturally safe practice as prerequisites to graduation and requiring an evaluation of those competencies for professional certification or licensure of healthcare practitioners. It may also mean a shift in thinking beyond cultural competency, to *cultural humility* (Greene-Moton & Minkler, 2020). Researchers and clinicians who want to interact with Indigenous communities must work to "develop knowledge, understanding, and respect for cultural traditions, practices, rituals, and ceremonies and their impact on health" (Baba, 2013). This includes recognizing that comprehensive Indigenous frameworks for wellness already exist (e.g. First Nations Mental Wellness Continuum Framework; Health Canada and Assembly of First Nations, 2015) as do Indigenous frameworks for research and program evaluation (Chilisa, 2019; Wilson, 2008).

Fifth, clinicians must evaluate the suitability of their service delivery models in the context of working with Indigenous peoples and communities. Many clinical service delivery models (including the behavior analytic tiered service delivery and mediator models) were developed in the context of resource-rich urban centers and powered by graduate students in academic institutions. Adaptation of the tiered service or mediator service delivery model to the geography, social structures, political, and culture of remote or urban Indigenous communities may pose a unique challenge (Cotton et al., 2014). In rural communities, this mismatch is compounded by limited infrastructure, exorbitant costs of food and travel, and political issues and a possible incongruence in the values, knowledge, perspectives, and experiences of the communities and service providers. An effective model of clinical care considers the context of those services from the onset of planning and development and leverages the knowledge and expertise of the individuals living within that context in its design.

Finally, each helping profession as a collective must engage in a radical process of reconciliation. As described by Blackstock (2016) in her review of social work practices that have contributed to the harm of Indigenous people,

> social work must look in the professional mirror to see its history from multiple perspectives including that of those who experienced the harm. We must look beyond our need to not feel blamed so we can learn and change our behavior . . . As the doers of good we have not been trained to stand in the shadow of our harmful actions so we ignore or minimize them . . . We must courageously redefine the profession using reconciliation processes and then move outwards to expand the movement into society.
>
> (p. 35)

The same could be extended to behavior analysts, psychologists, psychiatrists, nurses, and other helping professionals; many of whom have yet to meaningfully reflect on the harmful practices of their professions. At the individual level, this means an examination of one's own culture, history, and values and its impact on the care they provide. At the group level, it means a collective examination of a discipline's harmful practices, both current and historical, while moving forward with reconciliation efforts.

It is our hope that this chapter serves as a starting point for practitioners who are currently working with, or are considering working with Indigenous peoples and communities. It is also our hope that this work prompts practitioners to dive deeper and wider, to do the uncomfortable work of understanding and confronting the harmful practices leveraged against the marginalized peoples by academic and clinical institutions, to explore collaborative solutions that uphold and respect the voices, so that together, we may remember and find our way back to the trail.

REFERENCES

Baba, L. (2013). *Cultural safety in First Nations, Inuit and Métis public health: Environmental scan of cultural competency and safety in education, training and health services.* Prince George, Canada: National Collaborating Centre for Aboriginal Health.

Blackstock, C. (2016). The complainant: The Canadian human rights case on First Nations child welfare. *McGill Law Journal, 62*(2), 285–328.

Campbell, T. D. (2014). A Clash of Paradigms? Western and indigenous views on health research involving Aboriginal peoples. *Nurse Researcher, 21*(6), 39–43. https://doi.org/10.7748/nr.21.6.39. e1253

Canadian Institutes of Health Research, Natural Sciences and Engineering Research Council of Canada, and Social Sciences and Humanities Research Council of Canada, Tri-Council Policy Statement: Ethical Conduct for Research Involving Humans, December 2018.

Chartrand, V. (2019). Unsettled times: Indigenous incarceration and the links between colonialism and the penitentiary in Canada. *Canadian Journal of Criminology and Criminal Justice, 61*(3), 67–89.

Chilisa, B. (2019). *Indigenous research methodologies.* Sage Publications.

Coates, K. (2008). *The Indian Act and the Future of Aboriginal Governance in Canada.* National Centre for First Nations Governance. http://fngovernance.org/ncfng_research/coates.pdf

Cochran, P. A., Marshall, C. A., Garcia-Downing, C., Kendall, E., Cook, D., McCubbin, L., & Gover, R. M. (2008). Indigenous ways of knowing: Implications for participatory research and community. *American Journal of Public Health, 98*(1), 22–27. https://doi.org/10.2105/ajph.2006.093641

Cotton, M. E., Nadeau, L., & Kirmayer, L. J. (2014). Consultation to remote and Indigenous communities. In *Cultural consultation* (pp. 223–244). Springer.

Dhaliwal, R. K. (2019). Settler colonialism and the contemporary coerced sterilizations of Indigenous women. *Political Science Undergraduate Review, 4*(1), 29–39.

Drache, D., Fletcher, F., & Voss, C. (2016). What the Canadian public is being told about the more than 1200 missing & murdered Indigenous Women and First Nations issues: A content and context analysis of major mainstream Canadian media, 2014–2015. Available at SSRN: https://ssrn.com/abstract=2758140 or http://dx.doi.org/10.2139/ssrn.2758140

EagleWoman, A., & Rice, G. W. (2016). American Indian children and US Indian policy. *Tribal law journal, 16,* 1–29.

Elliott, A. (2019, October 9). Canada doesn't care about Indigenous children. *Washington Post.* https://www.washingtonpost.com/opinions/2019/10/09/canada-doesnt-care-about-Indigenous-children/

Fernández-Llamazares, Á., Garteizgogeascoa, M., Basu, N., Brondizio, E. S., Cabeza, M., Martínez-Alier, J., McElwee, P., & Reyes-García, V. (2020). A state-of-the-art review of Indigenous Peoples and environmental pollution. *Integrated Environmental Assessment and Management, 16*(3), 324–341.

Gareau, P., & Baer, T., (2020). Indigenous Canada: Colonization [Lecture]. University of Alberta. https://www.ualberta.ca/admissions-programs/online-courses/Indigenous-canada/index.html

Greene-Moton, E., & Minkler, M. (2020). Cultural competence or cultural humility? Moving beyond the debate. *Health Promotion Practice, 21*(1), 142–145.

Harper, S. (2008). Statement of apology to former students of Indian residential schools. *Canada. Parliment: House of Commons. House of Commons Debates (Hansard), 142*(110), 1515–1525.

Hart-Wasekeesikaw, F., & Gregory, D. M. (2009). *Cultural competence and cultural safety in First Nations, Inuit and Métis nursing education: An integrated review of the literature.* Aboriginal Nurses Association of Canada.

Hodge, F. S. (2012). No meaningful apology for American Indian unethical research abuses. *Ethics & Behavior, 22*(6), 431–444.

Johnston, P. (1983). *Native children and the child welfare system.* James Lorimer & Co.

Kirmayer, L. J., Macdonald, M. E., & Brass, G. M. (2000). The mental health of Indigenous peoples. Proceedings of the Advanced Study Institute "The Mental Health of Indigenous Peoples," McGill Summer Program in Social & Cultural Psychiatry and the Aboriginal Mental Health Research Team, 29–31.

Lavoie, J. G., Forget, E. L., & Browne, A. J. (2010). Caught at the crossroad: First Nations, health care, and the legacy of the Indian Act. *Pimatisiwin: A Journal of Aboriginal and Indigenous Community Health, 8*(1), 83–100.

Linden, R. (2005). Policing first nations and Metis people: Progress and prospects. *Saskatchewan Law Review, 68,* 303.

MacDonald, D. B. (2013). Reconciliation after genocide in Canada: Towards a syncretic model of democracy. *AlterNative: An International Journal of Indigenous Peoples, 9*(1), 60–73.

MacDonald, N. E., Stanwick, R., & Lynk, A. (2014). Canada's shameful history of nutrition research on residential school children: The need for strong medical ethics in Aboriginal health research. *Paediatrics & Child Health, 19*(2), 64.

Mecredy, G., Sutherland, R., & Jones, C. (2018). First Nations data governance, privacy, and the importance of the OCAP® principles. *International Journal of Population Data Science, 3*(4). https://doi.org/10.23889/ijpds.v3i4.911

Milloy, J. S. (1999). *A national crime: The Canadian government and the residential school system, 1879 to 1986.* Winnipeg: University of Manitoba Press.

Milloy, J. S., & Coates, K. (1999). A national crime: The Canadian government & the residential school system, 1879 to 1986. *The American Review of Canadian Studies, 29*(4), 692.

Mosby, I. (2013). Administering colonial science: Nutrition research and human biomedical experimentation in Aboriginal communities and residential schools, 1942–1952. *Histoire sociale/Social history, 46*(1), 145–172.

National Aboriginal Health Organization. (2008). *Cultural competency and safety: A guide for health care administrators, providers and educators.* National Aboriginal Health Organization.

National Collaborating Centre of Aboriginal Health. (2015). *Family is the Focus-Proceedings Summary.* National Collaborating Centre for Aboriginal Health.

National Inquiry into Missing and Murdered Indigenous Women and Girls. (2019). *Reclaiming power and place: Final report of the national inquiry into missing and murdered Indigenous women and girls.*

Patterson, K. B., & Runge, T. (2002). Smallpox and the Native American. *The American Journal of the Medical Sciences, 323*(4), 216–222.

Reifenberg, K. (2018, December 31). *The starlight tours sustaining settler-colonialism in Canada.* https://journals.uvic.ca/index.php/onpolitics/article/view/19419

Rheault, D. (2012). Solving the "Indian Problem" – Assimilation Laws, Practices, and Indian Residential Schools. Special Edition of Feathers In the Wind. Ontario Métis Family Records Center (OMFRC). https://www.omfrc.org/2017/03/solving-indian-problem-indian-residential-schools/ on 9/17/2020

Sahota, P. C. (2009). Research regulation in American Indian/Alaska Native communities: Policy and practice considerations. *Policy Research Center Tribal Research Regulation Toolkit,* 1–20.

Silburn, S., Zubrick, S., Lawrence, D., Mitrou, F., Demaio, J., Blair, E., Cox, A., Bailie, J., Dalby, R., Pearson, G., & Hayward, C. (2006). The intergenerational effects of forced separation on the Social and emotional wellbeing of Aboriginal children and young people. *Family Matters, 75,* 10–17.

Sinclair, R., (2007). Identity lost and found: Lessons from the Sixties Scoop. *First Peoples Child and Family Review, 3*(1), 65–82.

Stote, K. (2015). *An act of genocide: Colonialism and the sterilization of Aboriginal women.* Fernwood Publishing.

Talaga, T. (2018). *All our relations: Finding the path forward.* House of Anansi.

Torpy, S. J. (2000). Native American women and coerced sterilization: On the Trail of Tears in the 1970s. *American Indian Culture and Research Journal, 24*(2), 1–22.

Ulrich, R. (2010). *American Indian nations from termination to restoration, 1953–2006.* University of Nebraska Press.

Truth and Reconciliation Commission of Canada. (2015). *Honouring the truth, reconciling for the future: Summary of the final report of the Truth and Reconciliation Commission of Canada.* Truth and Reconciliation Commission of Canada.

Wilson, S. (2008). Research is ceremony. *Indigenous research methods.* Fernwood.

25

ISLAMOPHOBIA

Behavior Analysis and Islamophobia: A Behaviorist Point of View

Wafa Attallah Aljohani

INTRODUCTION

Like many others, I remember exactly where I was on September 11, 2001, at home in Jeddah, Saudi Arabia. A friend called, panicked, and asked me to check the news. I watched in fear as the news unfolded; at first, I did not know what it was; I was heartbroken, knowing that I was actively witnessing another world tragedy. I watched the reports on different channels, in English and Arabic, trying to get a bigger picture of what was happening. I felt sick knowing that the majority of the attackers shared the same nationality, ethnicity, and faith as me. I was – and still am – confused that someone would intentionally harm others. To me, growing up Muslim meant that I do no harm, think of others and treat everyone with kindness, dignity, and respect. So, I spent a lot of my time interacting with people on social media – with my younger and not as fluent English-speaking self – as an attempt to learn more. I saw how our interactions turned into verbal attacks as soon as they knew my background. Being in my early teenage years, these conversations were a key factor in shifting my interests from political history to the desire to understand how and why people behave. During my first international trip after 9/11, I had my first-hand real-life experience with Islamophobia. That was the first time I felt scared about something I had little hand in changing my identity. In the following few sections, I'll share my thoughts on Islamophobia, from a behaviorist point of view, acknowledging my personal history as an Arab, Middle Eastern, Muslim woman.

ISLAMOPHOBIA AND ANTI-MUSLIM PREJUDICE

To better understand Islamophobia, it would be important to put a historical context to how it originated. One of the earliest uses of the term was in 1925 by Nasreddine Dinet, a French painter, and Sliman Ben Ibrahim, an Algerian intellect, who documented their observations of Europe's hostility towards the Islamic faith and Arabic culture. At that time, Islamic and Arabic cultures were perceived in an orientalist view as "others" who were inferior to the West (Said, 1979). The term and its meaning transformed from a dislike towards Muslims and Arabic cultures to extreme fear and social anxiety with a rejection of cultures and the religion itself (Runnymede Trust, 1997; Stolz, 2005), which was reinforced by a number of critical historical, political, and social events (i.e., Jyllands-Posten cartoon, 9/11, Muslim Mapping, the Muslim ban, and the *Charlie Hebdo* shooting amongst others).

Interestingly, this behavior does not only impact Muslims and Arabs but also extends to individuals who are perceived – typically by their physical appearance – to be within the same culture (i.e., South Asians) or faith (i.e., Sikhism, Jainism) based on prejudice and stereotypes. As a definition, Islamophobia can be explained as the hatred of the Islam faith and Muslims. Since Muslims can identify with many cultures, Islamophobia can also include the assumption that all Muslims come from one race or ethnicity (i.e., Arabic). Islam is a culturally-based belief rather than a faith with a set of religious practices. There are many historical, political, and social factors that play a role in our understanding of Islamophobia, which only gives a small glimpse to the complexity of their behavior.

In 1997, a report titled "Islamophobia: a challenge for us all" presented two distinct ways to view Islam; an open view and a closed view. Both views described how non-Muslims see Muslim cultures. The open view of Islam included eight features:

1. Viewing Islam as a diverse culture
2. Recognizing the shared commonalities between Islam and other faiths and cultures
3. Respecting that Islam's differences are equally worthy of respect
4. Considering Muslims as partners in finding solutions for everyday problems
5. Accepting Islam as a genuine religious faith
6. Debating criticism of the West instead of rejecting it
7. Not justifying discrimination against Muslims
8. Viewing inaccurate criticism of Islam as unfair and problematic.

While the closed view of Islam included these eight features:

1. Viewing Islam as intolerant to deliberation and static
2. Not seeing any shared values with other cultures
3. Considering Muslims cultures as irrational and inferior to the West
4. Seeing Islam as violent and threatening
5. Considering Muslims as manipulative with political ideology
6. Defending racial discrimination
7. Rejecting Muslim criticism of secularism
8. Accepting anti-Muslim hostility.

The features identified in the closed view of Islam and the behaviors that come as a result of these perceptions are often expressed by individuals that would engage in Islamophobic behaviors (Runnymede Trust, 1997). Currently, limited behavior analytic explanations are available to understand complex social behavior such as Islamophobia. Therefore, it would be helpful to start with the simplest explanations, analyze commonalities with other behaviors (i.e., xenophobia, racism), and draw parallels to build a behavior analytic foundation. A good starting point is to evaluate the consequences in the environment both outside of the skin (i.e., overt behaviors) as well as within the skin (i.e., covert behaviors; Skinner, 1986, 1965), as well as contingencies of reinforcement and punishment. In the book *Beyond Freedom and Dignity*, Skinner (1971) described how certain values are associated with a group of people, and that could be identified by the people who practice it, without the need for geographical or racial isolation. He further explained that cultures could evolve and survive when these values are reinforced. If we think of Islamophobia and how it shifted from a patronizing orientalist view of culture, to more aggressive behaviors towards Muslims or people perceived to be Muslims, it becomes evident how these new practices are evolving as a result of effective and powerful reinforcers.

Unfortunately, these reinforcers may not be simple or clear ones to identify. It may take several attempts to analyze this social behavior and its related variables accurately. None-theless, taking steps to identify social justice issues is within the applied realm of behavior analysis (Pritchett et al., 2020). It is time to challenge our norms, and dive into social justice issues, apply new contingencies, shape forward-thinking, and impactful behaviors.

ISLAM AND MUSLIM MISREPRESENTATIONS

Over 300 million Muslims live in countries where Islam is not the dominant religion. Muslims are often represented to be within a particular racial and ethnic group. In behavior analytic terms, a neutral stimulus can become conditioned punishers (i.e., Arab sounding names, sights of veiled women, Muslim call of prayer) if repeatedly paired with aversive stimuli (i.e., loud sounds or visuals). As much as these learned behaviors are hurtful and inaccurate, many Muslims see these patterns of systematic discrimination and come in contact with them with increasing regularity. The overlap between Islam and cultures is another layer that adds to this complexity. For example, people who identify with the closed view of Islam might think Arabs and individuals from the Middle East comprise the majority of Muslims globally, when in fact, 60% of the Muslim population lives in Asia. Only 20% of Muslims are in the Middle East and Northern Africa (Pew Research Center, 2017). This assumption stems from the repeated misrepresentations of Islam and Muslims in mainstream media.

There are countless examples of patronizing and dehumanizing Muslims and their cultures. One of my earliest experiences with Islam and Muslims misrepresentations was at an early age. Aladdin was released in 1992 around the same time when I developed an interest in learning English. I used to sing along to songs to learn new vocabulary. So, there I was singing along to Aladdin's "Arabian Nights," and I caught myself saying some words that I knew held a negative connotation. I paused, reread them, and could not comprehend how we are portrayed in a Disney's children's classic film. The lyrics read, "I come from a land where they cut off your ear if they don't like your face, it's barbaric, but hey, it's home." These words were later altered, but not entirely, just enough to avoid public criticism. I later realized many more misrepresentations in that cartoon (i.e., mixing Arabic and Indian cultures). I began to see a clear pattern of that behavior; many were subtle such that if you are not from that culture, you may not recognize the associations forming. For example, the sound of Muslim's call of prayers – Adhan with the words "Allahu Akbar," "Allah is great," paired with bombing and terrorist acts, despite the call of prayer often holds a warm and comforting feeling for Muslims. It was also clear how many of these systematic misrepresentations also reinforced the idea of a white savior (Mastro, 2016), which to me, goes back to the colonial mentality and orientalist view that is erroneously accepted throughout the world.

These examples are additional indicators that normalizing prejudice and discrimination have been rooted in societies for many years. Nonetheless, behavior analysts can evaluate their behaviors and begin the change towards a more inclusive society. Many notable efforts have been made in behavior analysis to provide practical solutions to solve these issues (i.e., ABAI's special interest group on Culture and Diversity, Behavior Analysis in Practice Journal).

Similar to other religions, there are variations as to how individual Muslims practice their faith. Many of the set principles in Islam are action-based (i.e., praying at certain times a day, fasting Ramadan). Every Muslim can practice the way that aligns with their upbringing, how strong their beliefs are, and the level of exposure to other cultures, just to list a few of these variables. For example, some Muslims pray five times a day, fast the month of Ramadan, while others don't. Knowing these variations and how followers of Islam can practice their faith in a variety of ways, may help behavior analysts when working with Muslim colleagues to not jump to conclusions and fall into inaccurate stereotypes.

Additionally, the varying histories of reinforcement and punishment Muslims practice can explain the way Muslims interact with other behavior analysts. A person might avoid working in places when they don't see anyone similar to them in that environment, or if they fail to navigate the communication and language barriers. In an interview with a Muslim behavior analyst, she reported that when interacting with colleagues, she makes an effort to refrain from using Arabic words such as "Besm Allah," or "Allah Akbar" as these words might be associated with negative connotations. She expressed that by refraining from using specific words, her non-Muslim colleagues might feel safer, which might create a better working environment. She also described how some overt behaviors, such as wearing the hijab or refraining from drinking alcohol (even when others are not observing), could be challenging concepts to explain. If we closely observe, we find that many Muslim behavior analysts working in less-diverse workplaces attempt to change their behavior to accommodate and create a less-threatening environment. This might be effortful but would result in greater consequences, feeling accepted and less isolated.

ISLAMOPHOBIA AND HEALTH

The negative effects of discrimination and systematic racism on physical and mental health is well documented within racial minorities (i.e., African Americans). A number of studies showed that repeated experiences of racism and discrimination were linked to symptoms of anxiety, higher levels of depressions, and general mental illness (Barnes & Lightsey, 2005; Broman et al. 2000; Soto et al., 2011). Although Islamophobia is not always racially defined, Muslims who repeatedly experience microaggressions may suffer similar health issues.

Physical Health. Perceived racial and cultural discrimination has been shown to affect physical health. In 2008, Brondolo and colleagues (2008) measured ambulatory blood pressure (ABP) in a sample of 357 American-born English-speaking black and Latinx adults. The results showed that perceived racism increases the risks of displaying unexpected and variable blood pressure patterns and cardiovascular health. In 1990, Krieger evaluated racial and gender discrimination in a sample of 51 black and 50 white women. The findings showed that gender discrimination was not associated with high blood pressure in white respondents, while black women had an increase in risk factors for elevated blood pressure.

Mental Health. Islamophobia can negatively affect the mental health of a person. Samari and colleagues (2016) conducted a systematic literature review on the effects of Islamophobia on health. The findings showed that poor mental health was consistent with discrimination experiences among Muslims and that depression was higher in those responders "highly visible as a Muslim" (e.g., a woman wearing a headscarf, a man wearing thobe). The same report also showed that Muslims who sought healthcare experienced discrimination.

Gender Discrimination. Muslim women experience additional gender-based stressors, which increases their health risk factors. In particular, Muslim women who wear the hijab may deal with preconceived notions related to freedom and oppression. They may also face additional challenges in forming relationships with peers in professional environments. For example, when I first started my postgraduate degree in the United States, I was wearing the headscarf. I could feel how uncomfortable and eliminating it was to interact with others while visibly looking different. I distinctly remember the first colleague who initiated a conversation with me, an African American gay woman. Other than being a good friend, her behavior showed high levels of compassion and empathy, possibly as she might have been at the receiving end of similar types of discrimination, and was familiar with the feelings of isolation and rejection that often come with being different.

MUSLIMS IN BEHAVIOR ANALYSIS

With the increased social justice challenges and in behavior analysis, in particular, it is critical to be active agents in creating new progressive realities that respect differences, promote
equality, and rejects all forms of discrimination. Behavior analysts have the tools to recognize the signs and decrease behaviors associated with Islamophobia. Behavior analysts can
engage in several practices that would promote healthier and more inclusive environments
for Muslim colleagues. The following suggestions are not exclusive to those working with
Muslim individuals; they can also be used to create a more inclusive and safer work environments for other marginalized groups as well:

1. Behavior analysts should recognize the different cultures their colleagues identify
    with and how it can affect communication and social interaction.
2. Behavior analysts should monitor their own biases and consider how the environ-
    ment plays a big part in how they view and work with others.
3. Behavior analysts should establish work environments that are safe and welcoming
    to different people, especially marginalized communities (i.e., African American
    Muslims, first-generation immigrants).
4. Behavior analysts should evaluate their verbal behavior, including non-vocal behav-
    ior, when interacting with others who may not share the same background, lan-
    guage, race, and identity.
5. Behavior analysts should be active agents in changing discriminatory behavior at
    workplaces and education, and understand the emotional, physical, and psycholog-
    ical effects discriminatory behaviors have on marginalized individuals.
6. Behavior analysts should consider how political, social, and cultural changes can
    directly impact their colleagues' behavior and well-being. (i.e., a Muslim colleague's
    well-being after a mosque shootings).
7. Behavior analysts should practice compassion and kindness towards others.
8. Behavior analysts should develop the skills to engage in healthy discussions regard-
    ing sensitive social justice issues and recognize the long-term benefits of having
    these skills.
9. Behavior analysts should develop the skills to recognize mistakes and engage in
    behaviors to correct them.
10. Behavior analysts should conduct ongoing cultural competency training to ensure
    that every colleague is well represented and feels safe to express their different
    opinions.
11. Behavior analysts should advocate for legislation that would directly benefit mar-
    ginalized groups (i.e., access to lectures during religious observance).

Behavior analysis is a science that can and should be used to improve human behavior,
including social justice issues. The progressive nature of science should not be taken for
granted (Leaf et al., 2016). As the number of people trained in behavior analysis increases,
it would be naive to minimize the importance of having fair and inclusive environments that
treat every person with respect. This chapter provides an initial explanation of Islamophobia, as seen in a behavioral analytic world view, which is shaped by my personal learning
history. My hope is that we continue to engage in healthy discourse and navigate complex
social justice behaviors while staying true to the science of applied behavior analysis.

REFERENCES

Barnes, P. W., & Lightsey, O. R., Jr. (2005). Perceived racist discrimination, coping, stress, and life satisfaction. *Journal of Multicultural Counseling and Development, 33*(1), 48–61. https://doi.org/10.1002/j.2161-1912.2005.tb00004.x

Barrios, B. A., & Shigetomi, C. C. (1980). Coping skills training: Potential for prevention of fears and anxieties. *Behavior Therapy, 11*(4), 431–439. https://doi.org/10.1016/S0005-7894(80)80061-X

Broman, C. L., Mavaddat, R., & Hsu, S. Y. (2000). The experience and consequences of perceived racial discrimination: A study of African Americans. *Journal of Black Psychology, 26*(2), 165–180.

Brondolo, E., Libby, D. J., Denton, E. G., Thompson, S., Beatty, D. L., Schwartz, J., Sweeney, M., Tobin, J. N., Cassells, A., Pickering, T. G., & Gerin, W. (2008). Racism and ambulatory blood pressure in a community sample. *Psychosomatic Medicine, 70*(1), 49–56. https://doi.org/10.1097/PSY.0b013e31815ff3bd

Gottschalk, P., & Greenberg, G. (2018). *Islamophobia and anti-Muslim sentiment: Picturing the enemy.* Rowman & Littlefield.

Krieger, N. (1990). Racial and gender discrimination: risk factors for high blood pressure?. *Social Science & Medicine, 30*(12), 1273–1281.

Leaf, J. B., Leaf, R., McEachin, J., Taubman, M., Ala'i-Rosales, S., Ross, R. K, Smith, T., & Weiss, M. J. (2016). Applied behavior analysis is a science and, therefore, progressive. *Journal of Autism and Developmental Disorders, 46*(2), 720–731.

Mastro, M. A. (2016). The mainstream misrepresentation of Muslim women in the media. Pew Research Center. (2018, January) https://www.pewresearch.org/fact-tank/2018/01/03/new-estimates-show-u-s-muslim-population-continues-to-grow/

Pritchett, M., Ala'i, S., Re Cruz, A., & Cihon, T. (2020). Social justice is the spirit and aim of an applied science of human behavior: Moving from colonial to participatory research practices. https://doi.org/10.31234/osf.io/t87p4

Runnymede Trust. (1997). *Islamophobia: A challenge for us all.* Runnymede Trust.

Samari, G. (2016). Islamophobia and public health in the United States. *American Journal of Public Health, 106*(11), 1920–1925.

Said, E. W. (1979). *Orientalism.* Vintage.

Sirin, S. R., & Gupta, T. (2009). Muslim, American, and immigrant: Integration despite challenges. In A. Masten, K. Liebkind, & D. J. Hernandez (Eds.), *Realizing the potential of immigrant youth* (pp. 253–278). Cambridge University Press. https://doi.org/10.1017/CBO9781139094696.013

Skinner, B. F. (1965). *Science and human behavior* (No. 92904). Simon & Schuster.

Skinner, B. F. (1971). *Beyond freedom and dignity.* Knopf/Random House.

Skinner, B. F. (1986). The evolution of verbal behavior. *Journal of the Experimental Analysis of Behavior, 45*(1), 115.

Soto, J. A., Dawson-Andoh, N. A., & BeLue, R. (2011). The relationship between perceived discrimination and generalized anxiety disorder among African Americans, Afro Caribbeans, and non-Hispanic Whites. *Journal of Anxiety Disorders, 25*(2), 258–265.

Stolz, J. (2006). *Explaining Islamophobia. A test of four theories based on the case of a Swiss city.* https://www.academia.edu/3578146/Explaining_Islamophobia_A_test_of_four_Theories_Based_on_the_Case_of_a_Swiss_City_2006_SZS_31_547_566

26

CRIMINAL JUSTICE

The Implications of Dissemination of Applied Behavior Analysis in the Criminal Justice System

Bree Lutzow

The use of the term "corrections" when referring to the criminal justice system in the United States began around the 1960s (Holland, 1978). It would be assumed that a correctional facility would lend its name and do just that, correct stimuli or behavior in order to prevent reoffending. However, overwhelming research has shown that the current criminal justice model is largely unsuccessful with decreasing repeat offenders, thereby increasing crime rates, exhausting budgets, and perpetuating an ineffectual system (Alpher et al., 2018; Bonta et al., 2003; Fazel & Wolf, 2015).

The mid 1960s introduction of the "War on Crime" movement created a foundation for policy changes focused on punitive measures that lacked evidentiary support like, increased policing and tougher sentencing, consequences implemented as a result of crime that already occurred rather than antecedent manipulations and behavior change to prevent further crime (Dölling et al., 2009; Kearney et al., 2014). Further initiatives continued into the 1990s with "the tough on crime" mentality that lacked evidence of its efficacy in decreasing criminal behavior (Kearney et al., 2014). Data collected through the decades showed that since the 1960s, reported crime skyrocketed until about 1993, when rates began to steadily decrease. Despite these decreases in reported crime, incarceration rates increased exponentially until very recently (Alpher et al., 2018; Gramlich, 2019; Kearney et al., 2014).

While it may seem that a decrease in reported crime and incarceration implies effective contingencies, they are not reflective of actual decreasing trends in criminal behavior. The United States Bureau of Justice Statistics National Crime Victimization Survey indicates that in 2018, only 43% of violent crime and 34% of property crime were actually reported, meaning well over half of crime is not being reported or detected (Gramlich, 2019). The relationship between reported crime rates and incarceration rates is one that is weak and shows little causation. According to Roeder et al. (2015), the recent decrease in incarceration rate is correlated more with policy changes reclassifying charges and sentence reductions rather than actual improvements in criminal behavior. That is to say, it is the change in contingencies decreasing these rates rather than behavior change. While reducing incarceration has individual, familial, and economic benefits, they do not instill behavior change within an individual (Roeder, et al., 2015).

Despite reported decreases in these trends, when comparing the rates of incarceration in the United States to the rates of other countries, the United States continues to compromise about 24% of the global prison population. With only 4.7% of the total global population, this is a huge discrepancy. Relative to social validity, this accounts for 0.7% of the United States population and 1.07% of working age adults (Sawyer & Wagner, 2020). While that number may seem small, that represents about 2.3 million people. In 2017, the care of these 2.3 million people cost United States taxpayers $37 billion (Hyle, 2018). The personal impact of incarceration also results in lost or reduced wages, difficulty finding employment, and disrupted family structures, to name a few. Faulty models for behavior also impose a risk to family members evidenced by 52% of incarcerated youth reporting an immediate family member with a history of incarceration thereby sustaining the cycle (Smith, 2020).

A primary goal of criminal justice is the rehabilitation of offenders and prevention of reoffending. This means, the system in place should act as an effective punisher for criminal behavior while facilitating the acquisition of replacement behaviors. The most widely used indicator of a system's success is recidivism rate, or the act of reoffending. This broad definition does not offer specific measurements or standards for a follow-up period or for the inclusion/exclusion of offenses (Bonta et al., 2003). A study conducted by Alpher et al. (2018), followed adults in a United States federal corrections facility for a nine-year period. Of the offenders released in this period, 83% were arrested again where 44% of these arrests occurred within the first year.

If punishment is a consequence following a behavior that decreases future instances of that behavior, then ideally incarceration as a punishment procedure should result in lower recidivism rates. The inability of the current criminal justice system to deter crime can easily be explained using the science of behavior. The inflated rates of recidivism are evidence of a weak punishment contingency. This is not to say that the potency of the punishing consequence should increase, but rather, a treatment package including antecedent/environmental manipulations, and reinforcement for alternative behaviors, in addition to effective punishment contingencies should be considered.

In a utopian society, risk factors for delinquency would not exist and a criminal justice system would not be needed. However, knowing this is not realistic in the current environment, what can behavior analysis do? If we are looking to prevent delinquency at a primary (for all populations) or secondary level (for individuals at risk of delinquency), interventions to prevent risk factors to criminal behavior are key (Burchard, 1987). Risk factors may include: poverty, victimization of abuse or neglect, witnessing abuse, substance abuse, poor family relationships, and family members with a history of criminal behavior (Smith, 2020). A large majority of crime committed is for economic gain or, in behavioral terms, functioning for access to tangibles (Holland, 1978).

Burchard (1987) made distinctions between therapeutic and sociopolitical contingencies. Therapeutic contingencies are those that are designed by and can be directly delivered by a behavior analyst. In contrast, social/political contingencies are the legislative decisions creating laws and policies regarding what behavior is criminal and the consequences delivered following those behaviors. Sociopolitical contingencies are not typically designed with behavior analytic principles. They exert control over a person's environment and have the potential to cause adverse effects on behavior with the potential to increase criminal behavior. While behavior science technologies using therapeutic contingencies are evidence based in changing an individual's behavior, they are not able to achieve the environmental changes needed to reach a broader array of individuals. Creating more opportunities for at risk individuals to contact reinforcement in a socially acceptable manner could reduce many of these risk factors. For instance, education programs with more focus on vocational and skills training could lead to more expansive employment opportunities and decrease the risk of poverty. Programs combining functional reinforcement and punishment would also be more effective. Schools using the Positive Behavioral Interventions and Supports framework, and evidence based interventions (Positive Behavioral Interventions and Supports, 2019) have shown improvements in attendance, behavioral problems, and student/teacher satisfaction (Johnson et al., 2013). Aiding families and individuals in accessing resources for other indicators of risk such as substance abuse, domestic abuse, healthcare, etc. could also eliminate barriers and reduce the likelihood of a feedback loop continuum and the need for tertiary interventions which are applied to offenders already in the system.

In accordance with using the least restrictive procedures possible, Burchard (1987) examined the effects of juvenile offenders in different environments, least restrictive being at home with supervision (probation), and most restrictive being a criminal justice institution. Using a cost benefit analysis, at home supervision is significantly more economical than institutionalization. According to Hyle (2018), the cost for intensive probation for an adult is below $3,000 a year while the cost for housing an adult in a federal prison is over $35,000 a year. If more intensive behavioral services were provided in the least restrictive environments possible, it would still cost less than it does to institutionalize somebody. This is especially true when factoring the empirical evidence supporting behavior analysis and effective behavior change, versus the typical non-behavioral programming provided in a facility.

Other environmental changes to consider are those necessary after release from the criminal justice system. Oftentimes, offenders are released from a facility with just enough money for a meal and a ride home. The likely response is for them to return to the environment they came from, which holds the same reinforcement system they accessed before being incarcerated. While there are some re-entry programs providing assistance with housing, employment, and drug counseling, very few individuals are able to access these programs due to low funding and high prison populations (Seiter & Kadela, 2003). Without the development of appropriate replacement behaviors while in the system, we cannot expect these contingencies to not continue to function as discriminative stimuli.

Facilitating an enhanced skill repertoire that can be generalized to the community environment and serve as behavioral cusps allow the individual to access a wider array of reinforcement contingencies. Another problem with returning to the original physical environment is the likelihood of returning to the same social environment. According to Megens and Weerman (2011), individuals are more likely to commit crime if they contact reinforcement for crime-related behavior in their social environment. Additionally, juveniles are more likely to commit crime if their peers have. In 2009, Kirk conducted a natural study on individuals from New Orleans after Hurricane Katrina impacted the area in 2005. Many of the individuals who were released after the hurricane were unable to return home and moved to Texas or other neighboring areas. When compared to individuals who stayed in New Orleans, recidivism rates were significantly lower for those who moved away, attributed to being removed from their previous social environment acting as a discriminative stimulus for criminal behavior.

Even though effective policy and legislative change is largely out of the control of the behavior analyst, the application of behavioral interventions on the individual or facility wide is within our scope. As previously indicated, the most common indicator of criminal justice system success is recidivism rate. A breadth of studies have looked at recidivism rates, but few have looked at the comparison of those rates between specific types of interventions. Lipsey (2009), conducted a meta-analysis using 548 studies on juvenile interventions. Lipsey categorized interventions into two philosophies: external control and therapeutic interventions.

External control interventions focus on discipline (i.e. boot camps), deterrence (i.e. Scared Straight), and surveillance (i.e. probation) Therapeutic interventions include restorative programs (i.e. restitution or mediation), skill-building (i.e. vocational training, behavioral therapy, cognitive behavioral therapy), counseling (i.e. family, group), and multi-service (a combination of individualized and group programming). When just comparing external control and therapeutic interventions as groups, therapeutic interventions were more successful with lower recidivism rates. Discipline and deterrence programs were the most ineffective and actually increased recidivism rates. Surveillance programming exhibited better results than the other external control interventions, but the results were nominal when compared to therapeutic interventions. The largest therapeutic groups compromised skill-building and counseling programs. Of the skill-building programs, behavioral therapy and cognitive behavioral therapy were the most successful with 23% and 27% reductions in recidivism, respectively.

Other skill-building interventions including social skills programming, academics, and vocational programming also showed improvements between 6% and 14%. Programs with the most success exhibited more contact hours with the program practitioner and longer session durations. Risk level for recidivism was also a factor. Those who already exhibited a low risk of recidivism showed marginal results, while those who indicated a higher risk showed vast improvements. This suggests that targeting higher risk juveniles with more intensive services would be a better use of resources and services. Cohen and Piquero (2009) estimated that intervention of high-risk youth at 14 years old saved $2.6–5.3 million in the youth's lifetime. While counseling interventions showed recidivism rates comparable to skill-building interventions, the risks of counseling programs are greater. Group therapy could re-traumatize individuals and provide aversive consequences in the future like bullying or coercion. Also, relying on peers or family for counseling creates additional barriers. These other participants may not be motivated to participate, and it may be unknown if these individuals are discriminative stimuli or stimuli signaling punishment. The risks with counseling are important to consider as they are typically the most widely used intervention in criminal justice systems and receive larger funding than other interventions (Gaines, 2008).

A similar meta-analysis by Redondo et al. (2001) compared 32 treatment programs throughout Europe. They evaluated additional environmental factors like facility type, size, and amount of security. Follow-up periods for recidivism were also accounted for. The studies averaged a 26.4-month follow-up period. The different intervention models included in the analysis were non-behavioral therapy, educational/informative programs, behavioral therapy, cognitive behavioral therapy, classical penal therapy, diversion programs, and community therapy. Behavioral therapy compromised 19% of the total interventions and showed the greatest reduction in recidivism at 23.1% compared to the control groups. When compared to the other intervention models, behavioral therapy had nearly two times the success rate of all others combined at 12%.

While recidivism rates measure the success of a program at its conclusion, there is little data analyzing the effects of programming within the system. French and Gendreau (2006) conducted a meta-analysis examining the efficacy of treatment for reducing inmate misconduct as well as misconduct as an indicator of recidivism. Misconduct was defined as assault, theft, and non-compliance. The most effective interventions in not only decreasing prison misconduct but also recidivism were those addressing criminogenic needs. Criminogenic needs are stimuli that could serve as motivating operations and include interpersonal relationships, education, employment, substance abuse, recreation, and mental health (Andrews & Bonta, 2003). Of the studies examined, 38% implemented programs that had behavioral science components including cognitive behavioral therapy, radical behavior programming, and social learning while 30% were non-behavioral in nature (diet, group therapy, and nondirective).

The remaining programs did not implement any treatment interventions. Programs using behavioral science components showed more robust results compared to non-behavioral interventions with a 26% decrease in misconduct. Behavioral programs targeting more criminogenic needs allow inmates to contact more reinforcement and showed greater improvements compared to approaches that did not address criminogenic needs behaviorally. These results correlated with a decrease in recidivism rates suggesting generalization into the community. Of the studies showing decreases in recidivism rates as a result of treatment, 92% utilized behavioral treatments (French & Gendreau, 2006). The notion that prison misconduct is a proxy for recidivism not only shows that these interventions were effective within, but outside of the prison walls as well.

While intensive behavior analysis treatment packages may not be common within the criminal justice system, specific behavior analysis technologies have been implemented with success. One of the most common is the use of a token system as an antecedent modification. The majority of these token systems are facility wide and focus on reducing problem behaviors using punitive response costs. A landmark study by Phillips in 1968, incorporated a token system with additional strategies including corrective feedback, behavior specific praise, response cost, and threats of deductions. Results indicated that a combination of strategies rather than just response cost were more effective in reducing aggressive statements and improving completion of tasks and homework, and punctuality. Other behavioral science technologies used on a facility or individual level have also shown favorable results. Group reinforcement contingencies have shown to decrease disruptive behaviors and increase transitions within juvenile facilities (Brogan et al., 2017; McDougale et al., 2018). Implementation of Behavior Skills Training with staff as well as incarcerated juveniles has improved staff satisfaction, decreased problem behaviors, and improved staff/juvenile relationships (Edgemon et al., 2020; McDougale et al., 2018).

The potential social impact behavior analysis can impose is only limited because of societal barriers, not because of its inability to create change. The dissemination of applied behavior analysis within the criminal justice system, a system so established and resistant to change, requires remedies that perhaps only a behavior analyst can repair. By understanding what we already know of the issues within the criminal justice system, be they primary, secondary, or tertiary, we can move forward with creating solutions and abolishing ineffective policies and practices.

REFERENCES

Alpher, M., Durose, M. R., & Markman, J. (2018). *2018 update on prisoner recidivism: A 9-year follow-up period (2005–2014)*. United States of America, Bureau of Justice Statistics, Office of Justice Programs.

Andrews, D. A., & Bonta, J. (2003). *The psychology of criminal conduct* (3rd ed.). Anderson.

Bonta, J. L., Dauvergne, M., & Rugge, T. (2003). *The reconviction rate of federal offenders*. Solicitor General Canada. https://www.csc-scc.gc.ca/research/err-19-02-en.shtml.

Brogan, K. M., Falligant, J. M., & Rapp, J. T. (2017). Interdependent group contingencies decrease adolescents' disruptive behaviors during group therapy: A practitioner's demonstration. *Behavior Modification, 41*(3), 405–421. https://doi.org/10.1177/0145445517693812

Burchard, J. D. (1987). Social policy and the role of the behavior analyst in the prevention of delinquent behavior. *The Behavior Analyst, 10*(1), 83–88. https://doi.org/10.1007/bf03392410

Cohen, M. A., & Piquero, A. R. (2009). New evidence on the monetary value of saving a high risk youth. *Journal of Quantitative Criminology, 25*(1), 25–49. https://doi.org/10.1007/s10940-008-9057-3

Dölling, D., Entorf, H., Hermann, D., & Rupp, T. (2009). Is deterrence effective? Results of a meta-analysis of punishment. *European Journal on Criminal Policy and Research, 15*(1–2), 201–224. https://doi.org/10.1007/s10610-008-9097-0

Edgemon, A. K., Rapp, J. T., Brogan, K. M., Richling, S. M., Hamrick, S. A., Peters, R. J., & O'Rourke, S. A. (2020). Behavioral skills training to increase interview skills of adolescent males in a juvenile residential treatment facility. *Journal of Applied Behavior Analysis.* https://doi.org/10.1002/jaba.707

Fazel, S., & Wolf, A. (2015). A systematic review of criminal recidivism rates worldwide: Current difficulties and recommendations for best practice. *PLOS One, 10*(6). https://doi.org/10.1371/journal.pone.0130390

French, S. A., & Gendreau, P. (2006). Reducing prison misconducts: What works! *Criminal Justice and Behavior, 33*(2), 185–218. https://doi.org/10.1177/0093854805284406

Gaines, T., Barry, L. M., & Cautilli, J. (2008). A new view: Behavioral coaching for prevention of delinquency and recidivism implications for public policy. *The Journal of Behavior Analysis of Offender and Victim Treatment and Prevention, 1*(4), 14–28. https://doi.org/10.1037/h0100453

Gramlich, J. (2019, October 17). *5 facts about crime in the U.S.* Pew Research Center. https://www.pewresearch.org/fact-tank/2019/10/17/facts-about-crime-in-the-u-s/

Holland, J. G. (1978). Behaviorism: Part of the problem or part of the solution. *Journal of Applied Behavior Analysis, 11*(1), 163–174. https://doi.org/10.1901/jaba.1978.11-163

Hyle, K. (2018). *Annual determination of average cost of incarceration* (United States of America, Bureau of Prisons, Office of General Counsel). Washington, D.C. https://www.govinfo.gov/content/pkg/FR-2018-04-30/pdf/2018-09062.pdf.

Johnson, L. E., Wang, E. W., Gilinsky, N., He, Z., Carpenter, C., Nelson, C. M., & Scheuermann, B. K. (2013). Youth outcomes following implementation of universal SW-PBIS strategies in a Texas secure juvenile facility. *Education and Treatment of Children, 36*(3), 135–145. https://doi.org/10.1353/etc.2013.0019

Kearney, M. S., Harris, B. H., Jacome, E., & Parker, L. (2014, May). *Ten economic facts about crime and incarceration in the United States.* The Hamilton Project. https://www.hamiltonproject.org/papers/ten_economic_facts_about_crime_and_incarceration_in_the_united_states.

Kirk, D. S. (2009). A natural experiment on residential change and recidivism: Lessons from Hurricane Katrina. *American Sociological Review, 74*(3), 484–505. https://doi.org/10.1177/000312240907400308

Lipsey, M. W. (2009). The primary factors that characterize effective interventions with juvenile offenders: A meta-analytic overview. *Victims & Offenders, 4*(2), 124–147. https://doi.org/10.1080/15564880802612573

McDougale, C. B., Coon, J. C., Richling, S. M., O'Rourke, S., Rapp, J. T., Thompson, K. R., & Burkhart, B. R. (2018). Group procedures for decreasing problem behavior displayed by detained adolescents. *Behavior Modification, 43*(5), 615–638. https://doi.org/10.1177/0145445518781314

Megens, K. M., & Weerman, F. M. (2011). The social transmission of delinquency. *Journal of Research in Crime and Delinquency, 49*(3), 420–443. https://doi.org/10.1177/0022427811408432

Phillips, E. L. (1968). Achievement place: Token reinforcement procedures in a home-style rehabilitation setting for "pre-delinquent" boys. *Journal of Applied Behavior Analysis, 1*, 213–223. https://www.ncbi.nlm.nih.gov/pmc/articles/PMC1311003/pdf/jaba00085-0023.pdf.

Positive Behavioral Interventions and Supports. (2019). *Classroom PBIS.* Center on Positive Behavioral Intervention and Supports. https://www.pbis.org/topics/classroom-pbis

Redondo Illescas, S., Sánchez-Meca, J., & Garrido Genovés, V. (2001). Treatment of offenders and recidivism: Assessment of the effectiveness of programmes applied in Europe. *Psychology in Spain, 5*(1), 47–82. http://www.psychologyinspain.com/content/reprints/2001/6.pdf.

Roeder, O., Eisen, L. B., & Bowling, J. (2015, February). *What caused the crime decline?* Brennan Center for Justice. https://www.brennancenter.org/our-work/research-reports/what-caused-the-crime-decline

Sawyer, W., & Wagner, P. (2020, March). *Mass incarceration: The whole pie 2020.* Prison Policy Initiative. https://www.prisonpolicy.org/reports/pie2020.html.

Seiter, R. P., & Kadela, K. R. (2003). Prisoner reentry: What works, what does not, and what is promising. *Crime & Delinquency, 49*(3), 360–388. https://doi.org/10.1177/0011128703049003002

Smith, E. (2020). *Selected findings of the FBI's Uniform Crime Reporting Program.* (U.S. Department of Justice, Office of Justice Programs, Bureau of Justice Statistics. Retrieved from https://www.bjs.gov/content/pub/pdf/sffucrp.pdf.

27

LGBTQ2IA

Supporting Ontogenic and Cultural Compassion Building for the
LGBTQ2IA Community

Worner Leland, August Stockwell, and Janani Vaidya

INTRODUCTION

LGBTQ2IA Terminology Formation

Although the terms *lesbian, gay, bisexual, transgender, queer, questioning, two-spirit, intersex, asexual,* and *aromantic* are often grouped together under the LGBTQ2IA acronym, these terms serve different functions in describing components of the human experience. Concepts encapsulated in this acronym include phylogenic selection of reproductive and sexual biology (*intersex*), covert behavior of self-identity (*transgender, queer, questioning, two-spirit*), covert biological behavior of attraction and desire occasioned by others' biology and self-identity behaviors (*lesbian, gay, bisexual, queer, questioning*), and phylogenic selection of variable attraction experiencing (*asexual, aromantic*). Additionally, these are only a small fraction of the terms used to identify one's experience of these concepts.

These identities do not exist in a vacuum. They are each one natural form of variability in the concept classes in which they fall under (and are collectively oppressed by groups holding traits in these concept classes that have been culturally selected as privileged traits, and often exist in an oppositional binary). *Intersex* biological experiences are ones oppressed in favor of biological binary sex development (*male* and *female*). *Transgender, queer, questioning,* and *two-spirit* self-identities are ones oppressed in favor of "typical" *cisgender* binary experiences (of being a *cisgender man* or *cisgender woman*). *Lesbian, gay, bisexual, queer,* and *questioning* experiences of attraction are ones oppressed in favor of "typical" *heterosexual* experiences of attraction to a binary "opposite" sex. *Asexual* and *aromantic* experiences of variable or no sexual or romantic attraction are ones oppressed in favor of *allosexual* and *alloromantic* attraction. Even more broadly, although imperfectly, the term *queer* may be used to describe this overarching experience of oppression based on these concept classes, and may be used additionally as a political identity in the movement toward liberation.

OPPRESSION AND HARM

Oppression of those who hold LGBTQ2IA identities ranges from micro interpersonal harms of invalidation to macro interpersonal harms and systemic harms, up to and including death. As of 2020, at least six countries actively implement capital punishment for consensual and private same-sex sexual behavior, and that capital punishment is legalized in five others (Human Dignity Trust, 2020), and additional "semi-legal" killings, torture, and harassment by police and extra-judicial killings, torture, and harassment by citizens continue to occur throughout the world (Ungar, 2000). As of 2020, an additional 70–77 countries currently criminalize consensual male same-sex sexual behavior, 38–44 countries currently criminalize consensual female same-sex sexual behavior, and 15 countries currently criminalize transgender identity or expression (Human Dignity Trust, 2020; Human Rights Watch, 2020). Worldwide nonconsensual intersex genital mutilation (IGM) continues to occur (Monro et al., 2017; Smith & Hegarty, 2020), and to a lesser degree intersex infanticide continues to occur (Ghattas, 2013). Nonconsensual, forced, and coercive sterilization of transgender and intersex bodies continues to occur (Honkasalo, 2019; Rowlands & Amy, 2018).

"Corrective" rape and assault of asexual, transgender, and homosexual individuals continues to occur (Doan-Minh, 2019). Conversion therapy attempts to change one's gender identity or sexual orientation remain legal in much of the world (Alempijevic et al., 2020; Mallory, et al., 2019). Access to consensual gender affirming medical intervention is still frequently denied or made inaccessible for transgender and gender nonconforming people (Ashley, 2019).

LGBTQ2IA individuals are also likely to be disparately affected by oppression via medical care and other helping professions care pathologization and mistreatment, financial insecurity, housing insecurity, harassment and gatekeeping in school and work spaces, harassment and gatekeeping in gendered and non-gendered community spaces, inaccessibility of and harassment in washrooms, and mistreatment and violence throughout various forms of interaction with government institutions and the carceral state. They are also likely to be impacted by societal and interpersonal macro and microaggressions including: denial that their identities or biology exists, incorrect use of names or pronouns, presumptuous and often gendered use of labels or terminology, stereotyping, asking invasive questions, and beyond (Castro-Peraza et al., 2019; Deutsch, 2018; James et al., 2016; Nadal, 2013; Ungar, 2000). It is also widely noted that these disproportionate experiences are even more heavily experienced by those who hold other intersecting identities which are targeted for oppression (e.g., race, country of birth, class, disability or neurotype difference).

Indigenous and culturally specific sexual identities and gender identities continue to be erased, even within the framework of affirmation, due to the impacts of colonization (Driskill, 2010; Picq, 2020; Pyle, 2019). Additionally, behavioral attempts at distancing oneself from oppression exist within the LGBTQ2IA community as well, through the creation of internal hierarchies which afford privilege and power along a spectrum of assimilation which privileges behaviors or other identities that align more closely to dominant norms (Ungar, 2000).

Acting in solidarity with LGBTQ2IA people is not a one-issue consideration given the interlocking structures of harm present in society. People who are queer and/or transgender also hold multiple other identities, which create a unique lived experience that may involve both axes of privilege and oppression. Thus, it is important to remember that LGBTQ2IA justice is inextricably linked with racial justice, disability justice, reproductive justice, housing justice, economic justice, and other paths of advocacy for equity and liberation from coercive contingencies.

FUNCTIONAL COMPASSION BARRIERS VIA SELECTIONISM

Compassion for the LGBTQ2IA community requires acknowledgement of individual and systemic oppression of individuals who hold LGBTQ2IA identities and who engage in correlated behaviors (such as engaging in sexual behavior with a person of the same gender, or engaging in behaviors which affirm one's gender but which are socially considered antithetical to the gender one was assigned at birth by the dominant verbal community). To acknowledge that oppression exists is to acknowledge that oppressing behaviors are selected and maintained by consequences which in some way must have been historically contextually adaptive for the individuals or groups who engage in those oppressive behaviors. That is to say, those who actively engage in oppression of others (or those who are in-grouped based on shared characteristics with those who engage in oppression, such as sharing a common skin color, nation of origin, sexuality, gender, neurotype, etc.) benefit from privileges afforded to them by their shared identity, many of which include freedom from being the target of oppression based on the characteristics selected for targeting.

To put it plainly, to be heterosexual and cisgender in our current context affords one some degree of privilege to not be a target of oppression based on their gender or sexuality. This intersects with similar privileges afforded for being white, for speaking English, for being upwardly ranked in a class or caste hierarchy, for being neurotypical, and for being non-disabled. Giving up this hierarchical power may elicit phylogenetically selected feelings of vulnerability, distress, and anxiety. It is behavior which requires response effort. And it is behavior which has the potential to make one a target of oppression by proxy. As such, many in positions of privilege may engage in avoidance of anti-oppressive behaviors, even if they are not actively engaging in targeted oppressive behaviors.

Separately, to engage in anti-oppression behaviors may be values-aligned for individuals or groups; however, it is important to note that holding a value of anti-oppression does not guarantee that one's behaviors are anti-oppressive. In the field of Behavior Analysis, it is often asked "why we are not acting to save the world" (Skinner, 1987) with our science and its post-Skinnerian advancements (Dixon et al., 2018). However, our belief in the efficacy of our science often leads to Behavior Analytic Saviorism – the promotion of behavior analytic science and skill sets to "help" or "save" people or groups who hold oppressed identities, without addressing the active systemic oppression and systemic barriers faced by the actually impacted (Gingles & Preudhomme, 2020).

These philanthropic behaviors may be maintained in a behavior analyst or other compassionate helper's repertoire through positive reinforcement in the form of praise, social, political, and academic advancement, financial compensation for the work, and biobehavioral covert responding of positive self-regard. They may also be maintained by negative reinforcement in the biobehavioral form of guilt alleviation. However, these philanthropic behaviors are often ones which occasion changes in the environment different than the changes being called for by actually impacted groups, and which do little to dismantle cultural contingencies of oppression or to promote actual justice as identified by the oppressed group.

BUILDING COMPASSION CAPACITY THAT MOVES TOWARD LIBERATION

When considering how a person can act in compassionate solidarity with LGBTQ2IA people, centering self-determination and promoting the autonomy and freedom of those directly impacted is critical. Goldiamond's (1965, 1976) clinical work involving a nonlinear analysis of behavior stressed that freedom from coercion involves more than simply ensuring that people have access to valued resources; it also requires expanding a network of that person's degrees of freedom (i.e., the number of response options available to access reinforcement in a given context). Whereas a situation involving only one response option is defined as a coercive contingency because there is no real choice available to a person, a focus on expanding the number of response options available increases the degrees of freedom available to a person. That is, the richer the behavioral alternatives are to effectively interact with the environment, the more free a person is (Baum, 2016). Working to increase choice is paramount to respecting the autonomy and dignity of LGBTQ2IA people. Stated another way, the goal is liberation where a person is free to engage in responding based on their individual values, not simply assimilation into the dominant societal contingencies involving limited available options. And LGBTQ2IA liberation is directly intertwined with liberation and freedom from coercive contingencies for all.

Behavior Analytic values and skill sets can absolutely impact LGBTQ2IA compassion building when they center actively engaging in anti-oppressive practices that minimize harm and move in the direction of harm eradication. At the ontogenic level, individuals may use skill building, and especially fluency building measures, to increase knowledge about LGBTQ2IA identities. Antecedent practices which can be employed to minimize interpersonal oppression include functional replacement behaviors for oppressive norms such as the use of non-presumptuous non-gendered language (e.g., replacing relational gendered terms like "ladies and gentlemen" with "everyone", "mother and father" with "parents," "boyfriend and girlfriend" with "significant other" or "partner") until proper stimulus control has been established in the form of verbal confirmation (i.e., a person telling you or modeling for you the language that is accurate for them). Additionally, this involves not using presumptuous gendered pronouns (such as "he" or "she") when speaking about someone until proper stimulus control has been established in the form of verbal confirmation (i.e., a person telling you or modeling for you the pronouns that are accurate for them).

We can also practice actively unpairing topographic stimuli from our concepts of identity. There is no one way to look LGBTQ2IA, and it is inaccurate and harmful to assume that visual stimuli (such as someone's style of dress, haircut, mannerisms, body shape, etc.) are generally indicative of identity. As such, these replacement behaviors should be universally applied to all we interact with, and we should be cautious to not allow them to come under faulty stimulus control. Similarly, we should not require that someone perform their identity by shifting these topographies in order to be believed about that held identity. We may also eliminate generalization statements or presumed shared experiences based on shared identities or shared topography (i.e., not all women menstruate; not all people with breasts also have vulvas; not all people with partners experience sexual attraction) and aim for more precision in our language.

At the consequent level, we must shift our ability to receive error correction with gratitude. When we fail to engage in antecedent behaviors of harm reduction, or when we find that those behaviors were not functional in either a broad or a specific single-subject context, and are told that we are causing harm or engaging in oppressive behavior, it is crucial not to defensively attempt to punish this feedback behavior. Instead through a lens of cultural humility (Tervalon & Murray-Garcia, 1998; Wright, 2019), we may utilize these new data to pivot and shift our behavior such that it continues to align with our values of affirmation and anti-oppression. Feedback giving is an act of hope, and feedback implementation is an act of care.

It is crucial that we also acknowledge systemic power imbalances, and work to dismantle structures of oppression at the level of cultural change. Actively addressing these inequalities at the institutional level, as well as at the individual level, is consistent with the value of cultural humility (Fisher-Borne et al., 2015). At the cultural level, we may engage in anti-oppressive shifts through shifting our collective modeling and education. As we move away from teaching inaccurate frames-of-opposition based binary concepts, we can instead focus on a reliance on scientific understanding of variability and complexity in sex, sexuality, and gender, and can model valuing and uplifting these differences. We must continue to engage in error correction of oppressive behaviors, and the reinforcement of behaviors rooted in justice and affirmation. Although we may like to assume that a move toward anti-authoritarian values would inherently include LGBTQ2IA affirmation, data indicate that in spaces moving toward democracy, there is often still political scapegoating which falls on marginalized communities, and that LGBTQ2IA targeted legal violence, semi-legal violence, and extra-judicial violence as a form of counter-control maintains (Ungar, 2000). To engage in LGBTQ2IA affirming cultural shifts requires not just passive value holding, but concrete political action to shape rule governed behavior on a wider systemic level.

While engaging in social and political action, it is important for behavior analysts to seek out guidance from those most directly impacted and to act from a place which centers the interconnectedness of our liberation. That is to say that racism, colorism, xenophobia, sexism, classism, and ableism are LGBTQ2IA issues, and vice versa. When providing support at the social and political action level, behavior analysts must be cautious not to move into a place of saviorism, and instead of launching initiatives or engaging in research which may miss crucial components of one's lived experience and actual needs, we should be solely engaging from a place that is community participatory (Pritchett et al., 2020) or directly community led. Instead of engaging in anti-oppression from a framework of charity, we must engage from a framework of queer autonomy, queer autonomous spaces, and mutual aid (Ackelsberg, 2013; Brown, 2011; Piepzna-Samarasinha, 2018) which centers and is led by those actually impacted.

In the absence of clear data, and in the presence of continually changing cultural contexts, there is no clear rapid or single path toward collective liberation. To engage in social or political action in an ongoing effort. In aiming to shift this behavior into habitual action, it may be beneficial to first analyze one's own strengths and capacities, as well as boundaries, and to find a space for practice and a cluster of activist behaviors where one wants to choose to focus their time. It may be useful to actively practice these skill sets to fluency, as fluency building promotes retention, endurance, and capacity for application (Binder, 1996). It may also be beneficial to find queer-led modeling and mentorship while growing these skill sets, and to provide course correction such that the behavior is resulting in consequences which are actually beneficial to harm reduction and liberation.

Finally, it is important to build skill sets of sitting with one's own discomfort. One space of discomfort which may lead us to enact harm on LGBTQ2IA individuals is in the variety of tactics in the struggle for liberation. In structures of incredible violence, reactionary practices may be culturally framed as extreme or as violent by those in positions of power, while tacitly ignoring the state-sanctioned and culturally-sanctioned violence which these behaviors push back against. When discomfort with other's liberatory tactics arises, we must be careful to examine, with curiosity, where it comes from and what may have shaped this discomfort in our repertoires. We may also experience discomfort regarding our own behaviors toward anti-oppression and liberation. Discomfort may occur around the growth required to build skill sets for cultural action. Discomfort may occur around accepting corrective feedback, especially when that feedback is impassioned. Discomfort may occur around the lack of clarity of a path forward or the magnitude of both the problem and the struggle toward a better world. Instead of letting these thoughts occasion avoidance or rigidity, we can instead choose to actively strengthen our psychological flexibility (Hayes et al., 2012; Kashdan & Rottenberg, 2010) and allow it to assist in the ongoing movement in the direction of our values.

REFERENCES

Ackelsberg, M. A. (2013). *Resisting citizenship: Feminist essays on politics, community, and democracy.* Routledge.

Alempijevic, D., Beriashvili, R., Beynon, J., Birmanns, B., Brasholt, M., Cohen, J . . . & Fincanci, S. K. (2020). Statement on conversion therapy. *Journal of Forensic and Legal Medicine,* 101930.

Ashley, F. (2019). Homophobia, conversion therapy, and care models for trans youth: Defending the gender-affirmative approach. *Journal of LGBT Youth,* 1–23.

Baum, W. M. (2016). Understanding behaviorism: Behavior, culture, and evolution. John Wiley & Sons.

Binder, C. (1996). Behavioral fluency: Evolution of a new paradigm. *The behavior analyst, 19*(2), 163–197.

Brown, G. (2011). Amateurism and anarchism in the creation of autonomous queer spaces. In J. Heckert & R. Cleminson (Eds.), *Anarchism & sexuality: Ethics, relationships and power.* Routledge.

Castro-Peraza, M. E., García-Acosta, J. M., Delgado, N., Perdomo-Hernández, A. M., Sosa-Alvarez, M. I., Llabrés-Solé, R., & Lorenzo-Rocha, N. D. (2019). Gender identity: The human right of depathologization. *International Journal of Environmental Research and Public Health, 16*(6), 978.

Deutsch, T. (2018). Asexual people's experience with microaggressions (Doctoral dissertation). City University of New York.

Dixon, M. R., Belisle, J., Rehfeldt, R. A., & Root, W. B. (2018). Why we are still not acting to save the world: The upward challenge of a post-Skinnerian behavior science. *Perspectives on Behavior Science, 41*(1), 241–267.

Doan-Minh, S. (2019). Corrective rape: An extreme manifestation of discrimination and the state's complicity in sexual violence. *Hastings Women's LJ, 30,* 167.

Driskill, Q. L. (2010). Doubleweaving two-spirit critiques: Building alliances between native and queer studies. *GLQ: A Journal of Lesbian and Gay Studies, 16*(1–2), 69–92.

Fisher-Borne, M., Cain, J. M., & Martin, S. L. (2015). From mastery to accountability: Cultural humility as an alternative to cultural competence. *Social Work Education, 34*(2), 165–181.

Ghattas, D. C. (2013). *Human rights between the sexes: A preliminary study on the life situations of inter* individuals.* Heinrich-Böll-Stiftung.

Gingles, D., & Preudhomme, K. (2020, June 3). Behavior analysts: Behavior analytic saviorism is revealing itself [Infographic]. Beautiful Humans Change. https://www.beautifulhumanschange.com/resources

Goldiamond, I. (1965). Justified and unjustified alarm over behavioral control. In O. Milton (Ed.), *Behavior disorders: Perspectives and trends* (pp. 237–261). J. B. Lipincott.

Goldiamond, I. (1976). Protection of human subjects and patients: A social contingency analysis of distinctions between research and practice, and its implications. *Behaviorism, 4,* 1–41.

Hayes, S. C., Strosahl, K. D., & Wilson, K. G. (2012). *Acceptance and commitment therapy: The process and practice of mindful change* (2nd ed.). The Guilford Press.

Honkasalo, J. (2019). In the shadow of eugenics: Transgender sterilization legislation and the struggle for self-determination. In R. Pearce, I. Moon, & D. L. Steinberg (Eds.), *The emergence of trans: Cultures, politics and everyday lives* (pp. 17–33). Routledge.

Human Dignity Trust. (2020). *Map of countries that criminalise LGBT people.* https://www.humandignity trust.org/lgbt-the-law/map-of-criminalisation/

Human Rights Watch. (2020). *World Report 2020 event of 2019.* https://www.hrw.org/sites/default/files/world_report_download/hrw_world_report_2020_0.pdf

James, S. E., Herman, J. L., Rankin, S., Keisling, M., Mottet, L., & Anafi, M. (2016). *Executive summary of the report of the 2015 U.S. transgender survey.* National Center for Transgender Equality.

Kashdan, T., & Rottenberg, J. (2010). Psychological flexibility as a fundamental aspect of health. *Clinical Psychology Review, 30*(7), 865–878.

Mallory, C., Brown, T. N., & Conron, K. J. (2019). Conversion therapy and LGBT youth-update. https://escholarship.org/content/qt0937z8tn/qt0937z8tn.pdf

Monro, S., Crocetti, D., Yeadon-Lee, T., Garland, F., & Travis, M. (2017). Intersex, variations of sex characteristics, and DSD: The need for change. Research report. University of Huddersfield.

National Association of Social Workers. NASW code of ethics. https://www.socialworkers.org/About/Ethics/Code-of-Ethics/Code-of-Ethics-English

Nadal, K. L. (2013). Contemporary perspectives on lesbian, gay, and bisexual psychology. That's so gay! Microaggressions and the lesbian, gay, bisexual, and transgender community. *American Psychological Association.*

Picq, M. L. (2020). Decolonizing indigenous sexualities: Between erasure and resurgence. In M. J. Bosia, S. M. McEvoy, & M. Rahman (Eds.), *The Oxford handbook of global LGBT and sexual diversity politics.* Oxford University Press.

Piepzna-Samarasinha, L. L. (2018). *Care work: Dreaming disability justice.* Arsenal pulp press.

Pritchett, M., Ala'i, S., Re Cruz, A., & Cihon, T. (2020, August 19). Social justice is the spirit and aim of an applied science of human behavior: Moving from colonial to participatory research practices. *Behavior Analysis in Practice.*

Pyle, K. (2019). "Women and 2spirits": On the marginalization of transgender Indigenous people in activist rhetoric. *American Indian Culture and Research Journal, 43*(3), 85–94.

Rowlands, S., & Amy, J. J. (2018). Preserving the reproductive potential of transgender and intersex people. *The European Journal of Contraception & Reproductive Health Care, 23*(1), 58–63.

Skinner, B. F. (1987). Why we are not acting to save the world. *Upon Further Reflection,* 1–14.

Smith, A., & Hegarty, P. (2020). An experimental philosophical bioethical study of how human rights are applied to clitorectomy on infants identified as female and as intersex. *Culture, Health & Sexuality,* 1–16.

Tervalon, M., & Murray-Garcia, J. (1998). Cultural humility versus cultural competence: A critical distinction in defining physician training outcomes in multicultural education. *Journal of Health Care for the Poor and Underserved, 9*(2), 117–125.

Ungar, M. (2000). State violence and lesbian, gay, bisexual and transgender (LGBT) rights. *New Political Science, 22*(1), 61–75.

Wright, P. I. (2019). Cultural humility in the practice of applied behavior analysis. *Behavior Analysis in Practice, 12*(4), 805–809.

28

MICROAGGRESSIONS

Addressing Microaggressions in the Workplace Using
Acceptance and Commitment Therapy

Shaneeria Persaud and Stephanie Bolden

WHAT ARE MICROAGGRESSIONS?

Racism was coined by Ruth Benedict in 1942 as "the dogma that one ethnic group is condemned by nature to congenital inferiority and another group is destined to congenital superiority" (p. 87). This is summarized as one racial group having superiority or supremacy over all other racial groups. To maintain this power imbalance, racist behavior must dehumanize, demoralize, humiliate, and cause physical, mental, emotional, or spiritual harm to individuals of the marginalized group. The narrative of racism is deeply rooted into world history.

The instances in which we are familiar with are very overt instances of racism, for example: slavery of African Americans, lynching of African Americans in America, and the genocide of European Jews in Germany to name a few. However, over time the acts of racism have shifted to becoming less overt and more subtle. Though racist acts are more commonly subtle, they still cause the same physical, mental, and emotional harm as overt racism. These subtle actions can be referred to as microaggressions. Sue and colleagues (2007) described microaggressions as daily cursory, routine, deliberate, or inadvertent humiliations, whether verbal, behavioral, or environmental, that convey aggressive, disparaging, or pessimistic racial insults toward people of color. In the workplace, microaggressions contribute to the glass ceiling effect for Black employees by sending messages of exclusion with expectations of failure, and by zapping their psychological and spiritual energies in the workplace (Miller & Travers, 2005).

In behavior analytic terms, microaggressions positively reinforce racism, racial hostility, and unhealthy and unstable work environments. Additionally, microaggressions act as an abolishing operation for culturally responsive and humble workplaces. Microaggressions have an abative effect on behavior that promotes racial equity and inclusivity in the workplace.

HOW ARE MICROAGGRESSIONS COMMITTED AND MAINTAINED IN THE WORKPLACE?

Sue and colleagues (2007) identified that microaggressions can be divided into three subcategories: microassaults, microinsults, and microinvalidations. Microassaults are explicit racial derogations emitted through verbal or nonverbal attacks that are intentional in causing harm to a person. This can be using a racial slur or engaging in deliberate discriminatory behavior. Microinsults are communications that convey rudeness, insensitivity, and demeans a person's racial heritage or identity. Microinsults are subtle, and can occur unbeknownst to the perpetrator, such as, sarcastically joking about a cultural stereotype. Microinvalidations are communications that exclude, negate, or nullify the psychological thoughts, feelings, or experiences of a person of color. Regardless of the type of microaggression committed, the act is damaging and has sustaining effects. In order to address how to decrease these harmful actions, their function and common contingencies must be identified.

Microaggressions are shaped through operant conditioning via socially mediated positive reinforcement (attention) or socially mediated negative reinforcement (escape) (Cooper et al., 2020). Microaggressions that result in attention from others (e.g., head turns, facial expressions) may increase the likelihood of microaggression behavior in the future, if said behavior is attention seeking. Behaviors are also maintained due to their effectiveness in terminating or postponing aversive events (e.g., using a racial slur and in turn the individuals remove themselves from the environment). Both the function of the microaggression and its consequences will maintain the behavior over time. While identifying *why* the behavior occurs, it is also important to note antecedent events that *trigger* the occurrence of the behavior. Below are some examples of possible three-term contingencies of microaggression behavior.

PERSONAL NARRATIVES

"We Need a BCBA"

I encounter microinsults frequently in my position; however, there is one particular instance that is still quite vivid to me. In this incident, I had a client that was engaging in severe

Table 28.1 Microassault

Antecedent	Behavior(microassault)	Consequence	Hypothesized Function
Black therapist assigned in-home session	Caregiver has confederate flag displayed as the therapist enters the home *(since this symbol has become a conditioned stimulus to acts of hatred and violence, and promotion of the enslavement of Black people, its presence within a session is a microassault)*	Therapist is removed from case **OR** Therapist is prompted to ignore the behavior and remain on case	*(social negative reinforcement)* Caregiver escapes working with Black therapist **AND/OR** (social positive reinforcement) Caregiver gains access to continue to display microassaults towards therapist

Table 28.2 Microinsult

Antecedent	Behavior (Microinsult)	Consequence	Hypothesized Function
Black BCBA successfully provides large group training	Afterwards, a White colleague approaches the BCBA and says "you were so articulate and well spoken"*(the hidden message is that the Black BCBA was not anticipated to be well spoken because they are Black, or that they may not be as articulate as their White colleague)*	Black BCBA ignores the "compliment"	*(social positive reinforcement)* White colleague wants attention for acknowledging intelligence of Black colleague

Table 28.3 Microinvalidation

Antecedent	Behavior (Microinvalidation)	Consequence	Hypothesized Function
A Black colleague telling a trusted colleague about a recent microaggression experience	Colleague says "I'm sure that they didn't mean it like that. It sounds like you're reading too much into it."	Black colleague no longer talks to their colleague about their racist experiences	(social negative reinforcement) White colleague escapes uncomfortable discussion of microaggression
A Black colleague telling a trusted colleague about their emotional response following the murder of George Floyd	Colleague says "Yeah, that really sucks. Maybe they should've called another police officer."	Black colleague no longer expresses their cultural trauma	(social negative reinforcement) White colleague escapes uncomfortable discussion of racism and social injustice

behaviors that were not being managed by the assigned staff. The parents were frustrated and they sought an attorney. I was brought in to complete a Functional Behavior Assessment (FBA) and correlating Behavior Intervention Plan (BIP) (which had to be reviewed by all stakeholders for approval to implement). Because of the nature of this case, the attorney was to review the documents prior to our meeting to familiarize himself with the contents and come prepared with questions and/or comments. During the meeting while reviewing the documents, the attorney says to me, "That was a very well written document. However, the family has requested to have a Functional Behavior Assessment and Behavior Intervention Plan completed by a Board Certified Behavior Analyst."

Wow. I was in absolute shock! The document clearly indicated my credential as a Board Certified Behavior Analyst (BCBA). While the comment may seem innocent in nature, there was an underlying message: How could *you* be the *BCBA*? How could *you* be smart enough? Articulate enough? Have enough tenacity to be worthy of such a credential? His microinsult was a microaggressive attack on *my* intelligence. It was assumed that I should be inferior to someone else who is perceived to have more knowledge, experience, and expertise than me, based on my being a *Black woman.*

"I Like Your Hair Straight"

Being an African American and Guyanese woman, I have a head full of beautiful curly, kinky hair. However, the idea that my hair is beautiful is a fairly new concept to me. Prior to 2013, the appearance of a Black woman wearing her hair in its natural state (whether that was curly, kinky, dreaded, etc.) was considered unprofessional or uncouth. Of course, this bias is rooted in the Caucasian standard of a workplace, as Caucasian hair is naturally straight and fine. This is one of the many reasons why Black women constantly damage their hair with harsh chemicals, so that it could resemble the straight texture of a Caucasian woman's hair; as that is what was considered a "professional" look. In the same stance, for Black men it was also not (and in some cases still may not be) acceptable to wear their hair in its natural state.

There are times when I occasionally straighten my hair, and ironically, it's those times I get a slew of questions asking, "Why don't you wear your hair like this more often?" Minuscule to most, the question is still damaging as it indirectly assumes that my hair is "better" in the straightened state rather than its natural curly/kinky state.

A quick Google search for "women's professional hairstyle" will reveal what the current expectations are for women's professional hairstyles. Results include predominantly White women with long, straight hair. Similarly a Google search for "women's unprofessional hairstyle" will include predominantly Black women with kinky/curly hair, braids, dreads, and other styles that keep Black hair in its natural state. These results can easily be setting events to microaggression behaviors in the workplace.

APPLICATIONS FOR DECREASING MICROAGGRESSIONS IN THE WORKPLACE

Microaggressions reinforce White privilege, reduce the psychological and physical health of offended person(s), and undermine inclusive culture. Throughout this paper, we have identified the origin of microaggressions and provided examples as to how this type of behavior appears in the workplace. Similarly, we must identify actionable steps to reduce microaggressions. The literature does not offer research on how to remediate offender behavior nor are there published research articles on how to mitigate the effects of microaggressions for the victim. However, there have been several promising and effective studies using Acceptance and Commitment Therapy (ACT; also referred to as Acceptance and Commitment Training, ACTr) to reduce racial bias of offenders. ACT interventions target six processes: present moment awareness, values, committed actions, defusion, self as context, and acceptance; to increase psychological flexibility while teaching mindfulness and attending to the present moment so that one can engage in behaviors that are in line with their personal values. In terms of microaggressions, remaining in contact with the present moment helps the offended person to be flexible, acknowledge that the moment is happening, and affords the offended person the opportunity to discriminate between behaviors (i.e., committed actions) that are in line (e.g., correcting the offender in an effort to educate them on their microaggression) or not in line (e.g., remaining silent) with their values.

Research has shown that being present in the moment can decrease stress levels and reduce implicit racial bias (Lueke & Gibson, 2015). Research also suggests that interventions based on acceptance facilitate coping skills and reduce stress levels (Gould et al., 2018). One may postulate that the use of acceptance based-procedures could benefit both the victim of a microaggression as well as the perpetrator to reduce current stress levels and de-escalate the encounter more quickly. Accepting that each party has a different history of learning and reinforcement that influences their behavior allows for perspective taking and mindful interactions with aversive stimuli. This reduction in tension would allow each party to effectively communicate their points of view while remaining in the present moment.

Cognitive *defusion* allows us to assess our private events (e.g., covert verbal behavior) and notice them for what they are (e.g., just thoughts) without becoming engulfed by those events. Defusion allows us to accept our private behaviors and move through them, responding only to the direct properties of the environment. For example, defusion allows for individuals to notice the emotional response to the microaggression but to only respond to the outer environmental antecedents as they are experienced. This allows for each party to interact in the present, accepting the other's experience and interacting on environmental antecedents in lieu of private events. The defusion process has been successfully used to reduce racism (Lillis & Hayes, 2007).

Self as a context makes way for perspective taking, to be able to observe ourselves within our own experience without judgment, the labels we give ourselves, or the roles we may be fused with. Self as a context sets the occasion for understanding the vantage points of the speaker and the listener, and facilitates a more flexible experience with empathy and compassion for ourselves and others.

Each of the aforementioned ACT processes pave the way for values to guide behavior. Values are our motivators, the who and what we want to be about. When dealing with microaggressions, a value may be, "I want to respect individuals from other cultures and practice cultural humility." This may lead to committed actions, whereby steps are taken to embrace and learn about other cultures (e.g., reading, traveling, taking classes). The authors suggest that ACT can be used to help victims of microaggressions deal with the negative thoughts and feelings that arise from these experiences.

ACT has been effective in reducing biases and can also be applied to the dissolution and reduction in the complex social problem of microaggressions, microinvalidations and microinsults. Further research is needed on the combination of ACT and traditional behavior principles to determine the most effective intervention for reducing microaggressions in the workplace. Until such research has been completed, it is recommended by the authors that ACT be practiced within the workplace on both the personal and organizational levels to mitigate the occurrences of microaggressions.

REFERENCES

Benedict, R. (1942). *Race and racism*. G. Routledge & Sons.

Cooper, J. O., Heron, T. E., & Heward, W. L. (2020). *Applied behavior analysis*. Pearson Education.

Gould, E. R., Tarbox, J., & Coyne, L. (2018). Evaluating the effects of acceptance and commitment training on the overt behavior of parents of children with autism. *Journal of Contextual Behavioral Science, 7*, 81–88. https://doi.org/10.1016/j.jcbs.2017.06.003

Lillis, J., & Hayes, S. C. (2007). Applying acceptance, mindfulness, and values to the reduction of prejudice: A pilot study. *Behavior Modification, 31*, 389–411

Lueke, A., & Gibson, B. (2015). Mindfulness meditation reduces implicit age and race bias: The role of reduced automaticity of responding. *Social Psychological and Personality Science, 6*, 284–291.

Miller, G. V. F., & Travers, C. J. (2005). The relationship between ethnicity and work stress. In A.-S. G. Antoniou & C. L. Cooper (Eds.), *New horizons in management: Research companion to organizational health psychology* (pp. 87–101). Edward Elgar Publishing.

Sue, D. W., Capodilupo, C. M., Torino, G. C., Bucceri, J. M., Holder, A. M. B., Nadal, K. L., & Esquilin, M. (2007). Racial microaggressions in everyday life: Implications for clinical practice. *American Psychologist, 62*(4), 271–286. https://doi.org/10.1037/0003-066x.62.4.271

29

MINDFULNESS

Skills and Lessons Learned during the 2020 Pandemic: A Behavior Analytic View of Honing Mindfulness, Awareness, and Kindness

Jessica L. Fuller

INTRODUCTION

The 2020 pandemic has been an earthshaking setting event affecting individuals across the globe. Many were facing strict lockdowns for months on end without being in touch with other human beings or any resemblance of normality. Many lost their jobs, limiting their incomes, and were forced to make unimaginable life changes. It tested our patience, ability to cope, and our ability to care for ourselves in a wholesome way.

Many of us increased our use of technology by integrating remote technology into our work and personal life. The presence on social media increased with the lack of connection to the physical outside world. With that rise in time spent online, we learned new perspectives, connected with new people, had access to much more information than ever before, and often fell victim to self-judgment when comparing ourselves to others and how they portrayed their edited lives on a screen.

Personally, motivation lacked those first few weeks the pandemic began. Old patterns of anxiety arose, fear-driven thoughts affected my sleep, and my overall ability to see life in a positive scope diminished. I inadvertently created establishing operations (EO) for sleeping longer and abolishing operations (AO) for meditation. I noticed my happiness quickly depleting. Just last December, I was strolling the streets of Copenhagen on a study abroad trip studying human happiness. Little did I know that this hype I had created about honing happiness and self-awareness would be put to test three short months after that.

And then, one morning, as I listened to a webinar on Acceptance and Commitment Therapy (ACT), I heard the words "you must take care of yourself first in order to take care of others." These were the words that changed my outlook and snapped me back to having my feet on the ground with my head back in the present moment. I quickly realized how I was inadvertently affecting those around me and how in order to make sure my child and husband were okay, I needed to make sure I was okay first.

Mindfulness is a perfect way to achieve balance, self-care, and psychological flexibility. While lack of motivation, stress, and fear may all be internal events, they are behaviors too, and there are ways to address these, even as behavior analysts. As Skinner said in his book *Science and Human Behavior* (1965), "thoughts and feelings ARE behavior."

The concept of happiness is quite arbitrary and may look quite different between individuals. It is a concept that may be difficult to quantify and measure. Nevertheless, it is a critical indicator of well-being. Although this may be a particular topic for another field, such as positive psychology, what we learn from this may give us great insight into topics and issues we should be addressing within our field of study. Singh et al. (2004) studied happiness in individuals with disabilities by teaching direct care staff about mindfulness's philosophy throughout a tailored mindfulness training. The results of this study found that teaching direct care staff about mindfulness correlated with an increase in the happiness levels of the individuals they worked with. Although happiness can be challenging to measure, there were evident changes in observable and measurable behavior that serve as happiness indicators.

When looking at mindfulness as a skill, one can create an operational definition of observable and measurable behaviors. Mindfulness is the skill or ability to be fully aware and present of the here and now, the present moment. Human beings are fully capable of honing present moment awareness through practice, consistency, and commitment, just as we prescribe behavior treatments and interventions to our clients within applied behavior analysis (ABA).

This became quite clear to me as I observed my son's behavior. Even though his world had drastically shifted, he took every moment in the day to be present in the moment. Next time you are around a child, take a moment to observe their interactions with their environment. You may notice how they see things that we may take for granted (like the tiniest ant walking on the sidewalk). This ability to see the world in a slow, detailed, and meticulous manner sounds like a skill every behavior analyst should have, being that we too are observing our client's environments regularly. A question that arises is, do we maintain this skill (power of observation) after we take our behavior analyst hat off? Once we are home and being regular human beings? As behavior analysts, have we learned to generalize our observation skills we are so fluent in within our profession to the many areas of our lives?

If we look at mindfulness as a necessary skill for success, we may begin to generalize the idea of attending to the present moment as a necessary skill to improve our well-being and happiness. Yes, two words that can be quite mentalistic, but when defined correctly, could be observed and measured to create socially significant behavior change for ourselves and those around us. It can be a useful tool that allows us to interact with our environment effectively and compassionately.

A skill is defined as having the ability to do something to mastery. In other words, doing something really well. When looking back at the concept of human happiness, mindfulness directly relates in various ways. When we prioritize our well-being and self-care, we can create meaningful change in our life, regardless of the circumstances. ABA is a powerful science that addresses socially significant behaviors, and through evidence-based practices aids in the decrease of maladaptive behaviors and the creation of socially significant skills. Through the lens of ABA, there are simple yet effective tools that not only helped me get back to a mindful way of being in the midst of our ever-changing world, but that can help anyone bring mindfulness and happiness into their everyday life.

GOAL SETTING

Once you have decided to master the skill of mindfulness, take a moment to decide on what your goals are. Goals may aid in predicting well-being by increasing the probability of contacting reinforcement (Ramnerö & Törneke, 2015). Goals can present themselves quite differently across individuals. Maybe it is to be more present during playtime with your kids or to listen with curiosity when your partner is giving you their point of view on a political matter. It may even be to help you fall asleep easier at night or to remember to think before giving an opinion. Regardless of what your goal may be, set an intention and objectively define the behavior. You may even want to use a post-it somewhere visible as a reminder of why you decided to start this journey. It is incredibly important to remember to be kind to yourself throughout this process. Just as you would not expect to head to the gym for the first time in years and bench press a 200-lb weight, you cannot expect to be able to sit for an extended period of time and gain all the beneficial effects from meditation on the very first day. As mentioned above, it is vital to set sustainable and attainable goals. Be kind to yourself and practice patience, and just as you do not compare the goals you set between clients, do not compare yourself to others. This practice is for you, and your growth will be achieved through individualized planning and goal setting.

Break down of Goals

Breaking down your goals allows space for improvement and sets you up for success. Just as you would when creating an intervention for a client, make sure you are setting clear short and long-term goals. There is some variance in the recommended time that is needed to benefit from meditation. While some authors recommended that the average time to engage in daily meditation is 20 minutes, a study by Zeng et al. (2017) concluded that short yet regular practice may increase present moment attention. If you have never meditated before, 20 minutes of sitting in silence can be a lot, so this can be your long-term goal. Setting short-term goals will be entirely individualized and can be completed after taking some baseline data of what is right for you.

Self-monitoring

Self-monitoring can be described as keeping an active record of a particular behavior as a means to achieve behavior change in ourselves. The field of behavior analysis uses self-evaluation techniques to compare past performance to current performance and compare current performance to a long-term goal (Cooper et al., 2007). Once we identify the behaviors we want to address and have objectively defined them, self-monitoring can be an excellent tool to track behavior. In mindfulness, we achieve this level of present moment awareness through consistency and active practice of meditation.

Sanitize the Environment

Carve out some time and a quiet space to engage in your practice. Find an area free of clutter where you can sit in silence for a few minutes per day. This could be in your living room, bedroom, outside, anywhere where you can be free from interruptions. You do not need to have a fancy pillow or Zen area to do this practice. Look at your environment and use what you have (e.g., a chair, the floor, or the edge of your bed). Make some environmental modifications if needed to simply sanitize the environment from external factors that may distract you (i.e., silence your phone).

Antecedent Interventions

We all have days in which we struggle to get through our goals. That is why antecedent manipulations are so important in setting up your practice and being successful. An antecedent manipulation is a behavior change strategy (Cooper et al., 2007) that may help decrease the possibility of engaging in behaviors that will lead to not completing your practice (e.g., procrastination) and that may increase the probability of you engaging in it. You can set reminders on your phone, add it to your to-do list, or even establish a behavioral contract to ensure you are meeting your goals. A behavioral contract can be particularly useful if having others cheer you on and provide social reinforcement is a significant motivation for you.

Data

Data is a crucial component of how we make decisions, and tracking mindfulness and meditation is not the exception. By collecting data, you will be able to create sustainable behavior change as you will be able to set the criteria for your goals based on your successful completion of prior established goals. For example, if you collect data on your very first day of meditation, you may find that your baseline is 2 minutes. Now you know that you need to work your way up from that (slowly! We don't want any ratio strain). Continue to take data for a few more days, then decide what your next goal is. Maybe it's 3 minutes, then 4, then 5. Just as long as you are consistent and you are taking data, you will be able to make changes when needed and modify your intervention to set your practice up for success.

Reinforcement

Of course, there had to be reinforcement added here as we know using this principle aids in successful completion and creation of new skills. Create a system where you can access a preferred activity, for instance, after achieving a goal you set (e.g., eating your favorite snack following your meditation practice). Reinforcement is a global principle that applies to all of us, not just our clients.

Our ever-changing world continues to push our boundaries, present us with new information, and we are bombarded by tons of information daily. Whether we look at our social media, turn on the news, or look at a newspaper, we are exposed to many different critical issues of our society and our world. As mentioned above, mindfulness can create behavior patterns such as psychological flexibility, compassion, empathy, and perspective-taking, amongst other things. Although these are not targeting one topic in particular, there is a clear connection between the positive effects and the potential to create a space of empathy within our communities.

Going back to that statement I heard in the webinar I attended a few months back, *"you must take care of yourself first in order to take care of others"* – it is now more than ever that we must take action to create behavior change within ourselves in order to be able to support and fight for the causes we are so passionate about. It is crucial to first create a culture of self-care and mindful awareness of our behaviors to serve those around us, from relationship building within your own home, working with a client, and fighting for social justice.

According to hundreds of studies, mindfulness-based interventions have been proven to effectively strengthen immune functions, increases attention, memory and cognition, promotion of personal development such as: self-compassion, empathy, perspective-taking, increased happiness, and decreased anxiety amongst many other positive outcomes that we all need during these trying times and hopefully can generalize past the 2020 global pandemic. The idea that we can make a real impact on our world can begin by applying the same principles we use with our clients to create positive behavior change in ourselves. Our founding father, B.F. Skinner believed we had the necessary tools and technologies to change the world with behavior analysis, and maybe, just maybe, if we put a little focus on ourselves, we may tap into his vision to save the world by making it a little kinder, starting with ourselves.

REFERENCES

Cooper, J. O., Heron, T. E., & Heward, W. L. (2007). *Applied behavior analysis* (2nd ed.). Pearson.

Ramnerö, J., & Törneke, N. (2015). On having a goal: Goals as representations or behavior. *The Psychological Record, 65*, 89–99. https://doi.org/10.1007/s40732-014-0093-0

Singh, N. N., Lancioni, G. E., Winton, A. S. W., Wahler, R. G., Singh, J., & Sage, M. (2004). Mindful caregiving increases happiness among individuals with profound multiple disabilities. *Research in Developmental Disabilities, 25*(2), 207–218. https://doi.org/10.1016/j.ridd.2003.05.001

Zeng, X., Chio, F. H., Oei, T. P., Leung, F. Y., & Liu, X. (2017). A systematic review of associations between amount of meditation practice and outcomes in interventions using the four immeasurables meditations. *Frontiers in psychology, 8*, 141. https://doi.org/10.3389/fpsyg.2017.00141

30

ORGANIZATIONAL BEHAVIOR MANAGEMENT
Promoting a Compassionate Culture within an Organization

Jacob A. Sadavoy and Michelle L. Zube

The days of working for a company for 25 years, getting a watch to commemorate your service, and retiring from a one company career are behind us. In 2018, US companies had an average turnover rate of 22%, with 15% of employees leaving voluntarily; of them 81% left for better job opportunities. Canada was on par with an average rate of 21% of which 12% constituted voluntary turnover (Catalyst, 2020). Perhaps some of these changes can be attributed to the entrance of the millennial generation into the workforce. Hershatter and Epstein (2010), sought to find ways in which college-educated millennials approach work. Their findings suggest that millennials seek structure and reassurance. These qualities may be attributed to them being "trophy kids"; however, this generation was brought up in an educational and societal system that fostered their need for approval and clear expectations. They find feedback is critical to their understanding that they are moving along a progressive path towards success. As behavior analysts, this is par for the course in our practice of ongoing monitoring of behavior, providing clear expectations, feedback, and reinforcement. Additionally, the authors found that millennials care about employee–employer relationships and they seek companies that support a positive environment, ideally one in which they feel challenged (but not overwhelmed) and are doing work in the service of others. When it comes to company loyalty, millennials will be loyal to employers who reciprocate that loyalty.

OBM utilizes the principles of applied behavior analysis (ABA) and applies them to organizational problems and challenges (Skinner, 1953; Skinner, 1981). The main purpose is to create motivating work environments that help people reach their potential and improve employee and business outcomes (Lotfizadeh et al., 2014; Michael, 1982). Oftentimes, the application of behavior analysis is applied to an individual; however, when looking at an organization, system analysis remains the primary focus. The outcomes of that analysis are applied to those within the organization and for stakeholders outside the organization and, through this analysis, common components of work performance have been shown to be feedback and reinforcement. It is essential for an OBM practitioner to understand both the theory and philosophy of behaviorism in order to be successful and practice earnestly (Duncan & Lloyd, 1982). The field of OBM continues to provide invaluable contributions to consulting practice areas such as: culture change, innovation, leadership, quality assurance, performance improvement, safety, training and development, and essentially any other organizational structure that involves human interaction with others or technology (Daniels, 1989; Daniels & Daniels, 2004; Dickinson, 2001; Diener et al., 2009; Frazier et al., 2013; Ivancevich et al., 2014; Mawhinney; 1984; McSween, 1995; Shook et al., 1978).

An organization's ability to thrive is contingent upon its ability to meet environmental demands by targeting and maintaining behaviors that achieve a common goal. An organization can be viewed as a behavioral system of employee interactions and the manner by which those behaviors relate to the environment (Ludwig & Houmanfar, 2009). The field of OBM is tasked with making socially significant environmental changes at the organizational level to improve business performance and to yield positive outcomes. The field of OBM can be divided into three main areas of practice: Performance Management (Austin, 2000; Binder, 1998; Daniels & Daniels, 2004; Daniels & Rosen, 1982; Diener et al., 2009; Gilbert, 1978),

Behavioral Systems Analysis (McGee & Crowley-Koch, 2019; McGee & Diener, 2010), and Behavior-Based Safety (Frazier et al., 2013; Wiegand & Geller, 2005; McSween, 1995; Wilder et al., 2009). All three areas of practice are different in scope, however they have all been heavily applied to a variety of industries, researched extensively, and have accumulated enough evidence that the principles of applied behavior analysis can result in socially significant improvement of behaviors within an organization.

The term "organization" has several meanings. As a noun, it is an administrative and functional structure (e.g., business) or the personnel within such a structure; as an adjective it is complete conformity to the standards and requirements of an organization (Merriam-Webster, n.d.). Glenn and Malott (2004) describe organizations as cultural entities that may or may not "have characteristics peculiar to themselves over and above their inclusion in the general categories of operant behavior and cultural things" (p. 89). Thus, "organization" can refer to societies, corporations, or essentially any group or body of people that shares a common purpose or mission. Organizational behaviors then are the behaviors of individuals within an organization and the behavior of an organization as a whole. Aubrey Daniels (2009) acknowledges a key variable that drives all organizational outcomes is human behavior: "If management practices, systems, and processes are not designed on the basis of known facts about behavior, no organization can expect to create a workplace where all employees consistently give their best" (p. 7).

Similarly, the word "culture" has various topographies. As a noun it describes the customary beliefs, social forms, and material traits of a group or the characteristic features of everyday existence shared by people in a place or time; shared attitudes, values, goals, and practices that characterizes an institution or organization; or the set of values, conventions, or social practices associated with a particular field, activity, or societal characteristic (https://www.merriam-webster.com). Glenn (2003) offered, ". . . cultures are nothing more than learned behavior and its physical products . . ." (p. 223). Baum (2000) stated, "Culture consists of behavior. The units are practices shared by members of a group and acquired as a result of membership in the group" (p. 181); and added ". . . cultural change constitutes an evolutionary process" (p. 182). Organizational culture is critical to the evolution, success, and sustainability of any organization. Organizations rely on staff performance for productivity and the overall success of the organization. In order for organizations to evolve and thrive, expectations for employee performance must align to meet the ever-changing needs of the organization. The Society for Human Resource Management (SHRM) states, "the key to a successful organization is to have a culture based on a strongly held and widely shared set of beliefs that are supported by strategy and structure" (SHRM, 2020). A weak culture that is devoid of leadership, values, and purpose can have detrimental effects not only for the entity but for the individual employees as well. Fortunately, culture, like behavior, is not static and can change to adapt to and ameliorate the environment in which it exists.

In order for organizations to thrive, they must be outcome driven and have a strong sense of purpose or "why." It is imperative for organizations to value engaging in good practices to meet the needs of prospective and current employees who place importance on purpose and meaningful work. A 2020 Harvard Business Review reported that prospective employees are seeking places of work that align with their personal values and where the culture maintains alignment to the vision, purpose, and goals of the organization (Baumgartner, 2020). This may seem daunting especially for larger organizations or organizations that serve a large geographic area. The reality is that when it comes to organizational culture, organizations can be proactive and reinforce greater consistency and alignment by deriving specific measurable work outputs and behavior and extrapolate small incremental gains to larger operations or organizational structural changes (Binder, 1998).

It is apparent that we are living in challenging times and the mental health crisis is rampant. The World Health Organization (WHO) reports that globally, an estimated 264 million people suffer from depression and that a negative work environment can compound the symptoms of depression and related conditions (e.g., anxiety). The benefits of a healthy work environment that helps employees to deal with a myriad of private events can have significant benefits. For example, a WHO-led study estimated that for every US$ 1 put into treatment for common mental disorders, there is a return of US$ 4 in improved health and productivity (WHO, n.d.). Organizations have the capacity to value the creation of nurturing environments that can mitigate many of the issues that permeate the work environment (e.g., outside stressors, absenteeism, low productivity, burnout, job dissatisfaction, indifference, etc.) and provide interventions that can enrich the work environment. According to Biglan (2019), "behavioral science has fortunately pinpointed the kind of environment needed to ensure the development of prosociality and prevent virtually the entire range of common and costly societal problems" (p. 18).

OBM practitioners can take advantage of interventions informed by Acceptance and Commitment Therapy (ACT) to bring far reaching benefits for organizations with employees demonstrating greater behavioral and psychological flexibility. A major tenant of ACT is the importance of contacting values. Values transcend across one's personal and professional lives, and the need for organizations to facilitate a community founded on the basis of shared purpose with its employees. The effects of creating organizations that not only improve employee performance but also employee well-being, can have collateral effects on society at large. Hayes and colleagues (2004), demonstrated the use of ACT and a value-declaration exercise to reduce burnout amongst substance abuse therapists when compared with a control group. *The Mindful and Effective Employee* discusses the prevalence and the impact of psychological distress in the workplace. The authors provide a rationale for employers to support employees increasing psychological flexibility and values-guided behavioral effectiveness and suggest that there are practical benefits of psychological flexibility that can be applied across all areas of one's life. They contend that training mindfulness and values-based goal setting are easy to disseminate and implement in the workplace. Additionally, the implementation of the six core processes of ACT aligns with recent trends in the occupational health policy and practice (Flaxman et al., 2013).

To date, there is little in the way of compassion and empathy in the workplace in OBM literature which is likely the result of both concepts being "too subjective to examine experimentally or teach" (Taylor et al., 2018, p. 664). Similar to the challenge of addressing concepts such as values which are not associated in our verbal behavior as representing either reinforcing or punishing properties of a stimulus; compassion and empathy make reference to attending to another's suffering, empathically feeling another's pain, and acting in a manner intended to ease said suffering (Herbst & Houmanfar, 2009; Lilius et al., 2008; Miller, 2007). Taylor and colleagues (2018) postulate that the field, "must individually and as a profession interrogate the assumption that concepts such as compassion and empathy are too nebulous or metaphorical to command either our scientific attention or the tools of our discipline" (p. 664). The authors argue that this is paramount during this period of our lives, where we are confronted by two concurrent pandemics; one relating to health and the other race. As practitioners set out to promote better work environments, this current landscape that challenges all employees requires an onus on organizations to support the health, security, and joy of their employees. Atkins and Parker (2012), propose that organizations that focus on promoting mindfulness and improved employee psychological flexibility (and reduced inflexibility) will result in an increased compassionate response that includes: noticing, appraising, feeling, and acting. Conceptualize an organization that encourages thoughtful personal conversations, seeks to improve employee psychological flexibility (while reducing psychological inflexibility), provides a forum to discuss values while making value-oriented decisions, reinforces perspective taking and active listening, and celebrates identity and diversity. Behavior analysis can realize all those goals through reinforcement and environmental manipulations. It is the authors' belief that doing so will presuppose a compassionate workplace culture.

By fostering more nurturing environments and creating an organizational culture that has a shared sense of purpose with a community centered around a shared verbal repertoire (i.e., values-based, mindfulness, present moment), we can begin to envision a workplace akin to *Walden Two* (Skinner, 1948). Abernathy (2009) suggests four recommendations to improve organizations using Skinner's (1948) concepts. These include: incorporating utopian ideas into existing organizations in lieu of creating new communities, applying the advances in performance measurement and performance pay to refine *Walden Two*'s work "credit" system, addressing the problem of poor performing members via performance management, and refining *Walden Two*'s self-management "code" and general administration. Abernathy stated, "Traditionally, Organizational Behavior Management has focused many of its efforts on improving the interaction between the supervisor and the subordinate through better prompting, feedback, and reinforcement. It is argued that this was not Skinner's ultimate vision of how to improve society" (p. 192). So perhaps it's best to look to Skinner (1987) for further explanation, ". . . by allowing natural consequences to take control whenever possible, we generate behavior that is more likely to be appropriate to any occasion upon which it may occur again, and in doing so we promote the survival of the individual, the culture, and the species" (Skinner, 1987, p. 177). This further supports the need to cultivate environments within organizations that increase the likelihood of prosocial behaviors.

In light of this text, as we look upon our science and our field to progress forward into unchartered territories towards a more compassionate and productive society, we can look to areas such as OBM to not only guide us in this process but also assist us with determining how we can expand the scope of OBM. Further enhancements are possible through Prosocial (Atkins et al., 2019) (see conclusion chapter by Dr. Szabo for additional information) and the application of Ostrom's 8 Core Design Principles (Ghezzi et al., 2021; Ostrom, 1990). Prosocial extends OBM's practices of determining group values and increases the efficacy of group dynamics by maintaining fair and equitable distribution of resources, and determining parameters for conflict resolution. These are all factors that can increase the viability of an organization while teaching members of the group to work together in harmonious collaboration. These practices can have collateral effects that extend beyond the organization and become ingrained in everyday life.

While OBM has largely focused on the growth of business and productivity through employee performance (e.g., McGee & Crowley-Koch, 2019; Frazier et al., 2013; Austin, 2000), we offer that creating a setting with the proper contingencies in place will afford individuals the opportunity to contact reinforcement while creating the capacity to live a values directed life. Often individuals seek out a variety of ways to combat the human condition such as therapy, yoga, meditation, or spirituality. While these methods may work for some, outside sources of support may come with barriers (e.g., time and money restraints). But what if organizations could offer a breeding ground for mindfulness, flexibility, and values-based behaviors? Workplaces can provide their employees opportunities to develop these skills for mutually beneficial relationships between professional development and personal development. It can be anticipated that these behaviors will generalize outside the work environment due to a likelihood of these behaviors coming into contact with reinforcement (improved relationships and self-contentment). Human beings engaging in more mindfulness, flexibility, and value-based decision-making would be a nice foundational step to reaching the terminal goal of a utopian workplace with an opportunity for societal generalization.

REFERENCES

Abernathy, W. B. (2009). *Walden two* revisited: Optimizing behavioral systems. *Journal of Organizational Behavior Management, 29*(2), 175–192. https://doi.org/10.1080/01608060902874567

Atkins, P. W. B., & Parker, S. K. (2012). Understanding individual compassion in organizations: The role of appraisals and psychological flexibility. *Academy of Management Review, 37*, 524–546.

Atkins, P. W. B., Wilson, D. S., Hayes, S. C., & Ryan, R. M. (2019). *Prosocial: Using evolutionary science to build productive, equitable, and collaborative groups.* Context Press.

Austin, J. (2000). Performance analysis and performance diagnostics. In J. Austin and J. E. Carr (Eds.), *Handbook of applied behavior analysis* (pp. 321–349). Context Press.

Baum, W. M. (2000). Being concrete about culture and cultural evolution. In F. Tonneau and N. S. Thompson (Eds.), *Perspectives in ethology.* Perspectives in Ethology, vol. 13. Springer. https://doi.org/10.1007/978-1-4615-1221-9_7

Baumgartner, N. (2020, April 8). Build a culture that aligns with people's values. *Harvard Business Review.* https://hbr.org/2020/04/build-a-culture-that-aligns-with-peoples-values

Biglan, A. (2019). *The nurture effect: How the science of human behavior can improve our lives & our world.* New Harbinger.

Binder, C. (1998). The six boxes™: A descendent of Gilbert's behavior engineering model. *Performance Improvement, 37*(6), 48–52. https://doi.org/10.1002/pfi.4140370612

Catalyst. (2020, April 16). *Turnover and retention: Quick take.* https://www.catalyst.org/research/turnover-and-retention/

Daniels, A. C. (1989). *Performance management.* Performance Management Publications.

Daniels, A. C. (2009). *Oops! 13 management practices that waste time and money (and what to do instead).* Performance Management.

Daniels, A. C., & Daniels, J. E. (2004). *Performance management: Changing behavior that drives organizational effectiveness.* Performance Management Publications.

Daniels, A. C., & Rosen, T. A. (1982). *Performance management: Improving quality and productivity through positive reinforcement.* Performance Management Publications.

Dickinson, A. M. (2001). The historical roots of organizational behavior management in the private sector. *Journal of Organizational Behavior Management, 20*(3–4), 9–58. https://doi.org/10.1300/j075v20n03_02

Diener, L. H., McGee, H. M., & Miguel, C. F. (2009). An integrated approach for conducting a behavioral systems analysis. *Journal of Organizational Behavior Management, 29*, 108–135.

Duncan, P. K., & Lloyd, K. E. (1982). Training format in industrial behavior modification. In R. M. O'Brien, A. M. Dickinson, & M. Rosow (Eds.), *Industrial behavior modification* (pp. 87–404). Pergamon Press.

Flaxman, P. E., Bond, F. W., & Livheim, F. (2013). *The mindful and effective employee: An acceptance & commitment therapy training manual for improving well-being and performance.* New Harbinger Publications.

Frazier, C. B., Ludwig, T. D., Whitaker, B., & Roberts, D. S. (2013). A hierarchical factor analysis of a safety culture survey. *Journal of Safety Research, 45*, 15–28. https://doi.org/10.1016/j.jsr.2012.10.015

Geller, E. S. (2005). Behavior-based safety and occupational risk management. *Behavior Modification, 29*(3), 539–561. https://doi.org/10.1177/0145445504273287

Ghezzi, E. L., Funk, J. A., & Houmanfar, R. A. (2021). Restructuring law enforcement agencies to support prosocial values: A behavior-scientific model for addressing police brutality. *Behavior Analysis in Practice.* https://doi.org/10.1007/s40617-020-00530-y

Gilbert, T. F. (1978). *Human competence: Engineering worthy performance.* McGraw Hill.

Glenn, S. S. (2003). Operant contingencies and the origin of cultures. In K. A. Lattal and P. N. Chase (Eds.), *Behavior theory and philosophy.* Springer. https://doi.org/10.1007/978-1-4757-4590-0_12

Glenn, S. S., & Malott, M. E. (2004). Complexity and selection: Implications for organizational change. *Behavior and Social Issues, 13*(2), 89–106. https://doi.org/10.5210/bsi.v13i2.378

Hayes, S. C., Bunting, K., Herbst, S., Bond, F. W., & Barnes-Holmes, D. (2006). Expanding the scope of organizational behavior management. *Journal of Organizational Behavior Management, 26*(1–2), 1–23. https://doi.org/10.1300/j075v26n01_01

Hayes, S. C., Bissett, R., Roget, N., Padilla, M., Kohlenberg, B. S., Fisher, G., Masuda, A., Pistorello, J., Rye, A. K., Berry, K., & Niccolls, R. (2004). The impact of acceptance and commitment training and multicultural training on the stigmatizing attitudes and professional burnout of substance abuse counselors. *Behavior Therapy, 35,* 821–835.

Herbst, S., & Houmanfar, R. (2009). Psychological approaches to values in organizations and organizational behavior management. *Journal of Organizational Behavior Management, 29,* 47–68. https://doi.org/10.1080/01608060802714210

Hershatter, A., & Epstein, M. (2010). Millennials and the world of work: An organization and management perspective. *Journal of Business and Psychology, 25*(2), 211–223. https://doi.org/10.1007/s10869-010-9160-y

Ivancevich, J. M., Konopaske, R., & Matteson, M. T. (2014). *Organizational behavior & management* (10th ed.). McGraw Hill.

Lilius, J. M., Worline, M. C., Maitlis, S., Kanov, J., Dutton, J. E., & Frost, P. (2008). The contours and consequences of compassion at work. *Journal of Organizational Behavior, 29*(2), 193–218. https://doi.org/10.1002/job.508

Lotfizadeh, A., Edwards, T., & Poling, A. (2014). Motivating operations in the journal of organizational behavior management: Review and discussion of relevant articles. *Journal of Organizational Behavior Management, 34,* 69–103. https://doi.org/10.1080/01608061.2014.914010

Ludwig, T. D., & Houmanfar, R. (2009). Behavioral systems: Understanding complex contingencies in organizations. *Journal of Organizational Behavior Management, 29*(2), 85–86. https://doi.org/10.1080/01608060902874518

Mawhinney, T. C. (1984). Philosophical and ethical aspects of organizational behavior management. *Journal of Organizational Behavior Management, 6*(1), 5–31. https://doi.org/10.1300/J075v06n01_02

McGee, H. M., & Crowley-Koch, B. (2019). Using behavioral systems analysis to improve large scale change initiatives in autism service organizations. *Perspect Behav Sci 42,* 931–954.

McGee, H. M., & Diener, L. H. (2010) Behavioral systems analysis in health and human Services. *Behavior Modification, 34*(5), 415–442. https://doi.org/10.1177/0145445510383527

McSween, T. E. (1995). *The values-based safety process: Improving your safety culture with a behavioral approach.* Wiley.

Merriam-Webster. (n.d.). Organization. In *Merriam-Webster.com dictionary.* Retrieved November 18, 2020, from https://www.merriam-webster.com/dictionary/organization

Michael, J. L. (1982). Distinguishing between discriminative and motivational functions of stimuli. *Journal of the Experimental Analysis of Behavior, 37,* 149–155.

Miller, K. I. (2007). Compassionate communication in the workplace: Exploring processes of noticing, connecting, and responding. *Journal of Applied Communication Research, 35,* 223–245.

Ostrom, E. (1990). *Governing the commons: The evolution of institutions for collective action.* Cambridge University Press.

SHRM. (2020, July 29). *Understanding and developing organizational culture.* SHRM. https://www.shrm.org/resourcesandtools/tools-and-samples/toolkits/pages/understandinganddevelopingorganizationalculture.aspx.

Shook, G. L., Johnson, C. M., & Uhlman, W. F. (1978). The effect of response effort reduction, instructions, group and individual feedback, and reinforcement on staff performance. *Journal of Organizational Behavior Management, 1*(3), 207–215. https://doi.org/10.1300/j075v01n03_05

Skinner, B. F. (1948). *Walden two.* Macmillan.

Skinner, B. F. (1953). *Science and human behavior.* Macmillan.

Skinner, B. F. (1981). Selection by consequences. *Science, 213*(4507), 501–504. https://doi.org/10.1126/science.7244649

Skinner, B. F. (1987). *Upon further reflection*. Prentice Hall.

Taylor, B. A., LeBlanc, L. A., & Nosik, M. R. (2018). Compassionate care in behavior analytic treatment: Can outcomes be enhanced by attending to relationships with caregivers? *Behavior Analysis in Practice, 12*(3), 654–666. https://doi.org/10.1007/s40617-018-00289-3

Wiegand, D. M., & Geller, E. S. (2005). Connecting positive psychology and organizational behavior management. *Journal of Organizational Behavior Management, 24*(1–2), 3–25. https://doi.org/10.1300/j075v24n01_02

Wilder, D. A., Austin, J., & Casella, S. (2009). Applying behavior analysis in organizations: Organizational behavior management. *Psychological Services, 6*(3), 202–211. https://doi.org/10.1037/a0015393

World Health Organization. (n.d.). *Mental health in the workplace*. WHO | World Health Organization. https://www.who.int/teams/mental-health-and-substance-use/mental-health-in-the-workplace

31

NEPANTLA

Finding Spirit: The Pedagogy of Nepantla

Shahla Ala'i and Alicia Re Cruz

WE LIVE IN A TIME WITHOUT SPIRIT

It has become clearer and clearer that there is a global divide concerning the well-being of the earth's population. Some members of our planet live in excess, using resources at the expense of others. The pandemic of 2020 places the precarity of the situation in crystalline focus. The challenges faced by already marginalized people are unequal. For example, all children experienced disruptions in education, but the children of privileged families have been able to marshal and continue their education with hi-tech resources and learning pods tapping expertise, while others have languished, separated from access to learning. The same is true in healthcare. The majority of the credentialed wealthy have the luxury of isolation and remote work and of receiving advanced health care and interim support to navigate their illnesses. Housing security is unstable and contingent on reliable incomes and safety nets not available to those living in poverty. Food security is as perilous. The number of under resourced humans grows each day.

These are not new problems. They are exposed injustices. The caste systems that serve as understructures to our modern world are unveiled and challenged (Wilkerson, 2020). The gravity of this situation is communicated to us through painful visual images in social media and growing discourse in all segments of society. Black Americans are disproportionately murdered, Latino children are in cages, the lands, and the bodies of indigenous people are polluted, women are at the bottom rung of all the atrocities. Anger and accusation mount in every corner. And the corners signal that race, gender, religion, income, and ethnicity are made the intersecting and dividing lines.

These lines are part of an ancient history of hierarchical organization (Wilkerson, 2020) and in the more recent millennia the foundations of colonialism (Quijano, 2000), deeply rooted in the symbiotic relationship of racism, capitalism, and patriarchy (Lugones, 2010). These processes set in motion and mark the long legacy of systemic divisions that reach us today. Racism, the codification of race, a social construct, reinforces the dividing line between dominant and subservient groups of society; while the control of labor, it's resources and outcomes reinforce the economic and political control of the dominant group (Quijano, 2000). And colonial impositions of values and expectations on gender reinforces a systemic pattern of power that marks the subordinated position of women and people with differing gender identities (Lugones, 2010). These forces produce gross inequities supported by laws, terror, greed, religious and supremist rationalizations, and dehumanization (Wilkerson, 2020).

Lives are not cherished with equal measure. And in our world, death plays a political role in the control of vast populations forced to live under infrahuman conditions, in the status of living death (Mbembé, 2013). Our legacy is based on systems that create and maintain contingencies of coercion and harmful schedules of attraction to ownership and power, limiting degrees of response freedom and opportunity for much of the world's population. And the stimulus control is well established.

As the disparities and suffering rise, so do the voices of dissent. Sociologists are unpacking difficulties within science and technology and helping us learn how to stop the perpetuating cycles of systemic racism (Benjamin, 2013). Feminist and queer scholars tell us there are under-recognized ways of knowing that will be critical to human progress (Anzaldua, 1987; 2002). Indigenous teachers tell us that there are spiritual alternatives to capitalism and Marxism (Means, 1980). Psychologists tell us there is a need for an integrated view of individual and global progress that honors the human rights of all (Mustakova-Possardt, 2004). Youth are uprising and protesting systemic injustices. They ask for something more.

As behavior analysts we are part of this system. Take for example, one of our most active areas of research and practice, early intervention. There is over 50 years of evidence indicating that a particular configuration of treatment is more likely to lead to dramatic changes in the life of a child with autism (e.g., Howard et al., 2014; Lovaas, 1987; McEachin et al., 1993; Wolf et al., 1964). Yet, the majority of this knowledge was designed, implemented, reviewed, approved, and directed by a discipline positioned in a global north, capitalist, and largely male led context (Miller et al., 2019). This is similar to patterns discussed within most of the applied sciences (e.g., Henrich et al., 2010).

A diagnosis of autism involves identifying that a person is experiencing significant difficulties with social, communication and activity repertoires (APA, 2013). These are three fundamental areas of human interaction and quickly position exposure to cultural tensions and injustices. From infancy, children and parents from different cultures interact in different ways (e.g., Keller et al., 2004) and respond to the formula of early intervention programs in different ways. In fact, a growing number of studies have suggested that there are disparities in access to behavior analytic interventions and that many of our services are incongruent and sometimes repellant to people from the non-dominant culture (e.g., Angell et al., 2018; Angell et al., 2016; Broder-Fingert et al., 2020; Durkin et al., 2017; Ennis-Cole et al., 2013).

It is unsettling to think we are inaccessible, unresponsive, or undesirable. Applied Behavior Analysis is a discipline anchored in social importance (Baer et al., 1968) and if we are not aimed toward social justice and responsiveness, perhaps we are out of step with our stated mission (Pritchett et al., 2020). In addition to pointing out the marks of our hegemonic structures and improving our areas of practice and research, is there more we can contribute to the well-being of humanity? We firmly believe that Applied Behavior Analysis can be a powerful motor of critical social transformation, centering the values of community and the diversity of ways of knowing to combat the dehumanizing effects of oppression, marginalization, and discrimination.

WE CAN BECOME COMMUNITIES OF SOCIAL TRANSFORMATION

In considering quickly growing knowledge bases in multiple forms of endeavor, Boland and Tenkasi suggest that, "The stronger and more well developed a community's perspective is, the more useful a conduit model of communication and feedback becomes" (1995, p. 355). In this context, they were talking about perspective understanding and exchanges that have been required to tap multiple, diverse, and seemingly opposing knowledge bases to create unknown technologies, such as smartphones. Here we speak of joining with the multiple knowledge bases required to imagine and create a *humanity* that is just, that counters dehumanization and marginalization.

We (Alicia and Shahla) have different professional and epistemological trajectories. Alicia is an anthropologist who initiated her work with indigenous Mayas in the Yucatan and continued with immigrants and asylum seekers in Texas, with an emphasis on the experiences of women. Her work is largely qualitative. Shahla is an applied behavior analyst and her work centers on intervention support for children and families who are under resourced and from the non-dominant culture. Her work is primarily experimental. In spite of our differences, there are common threads in our lives. Being young mothers in academia brought us together. For more than two decades our friendship has been survival and healing in an institution that does not have a place to accommodate motherhood nor structures that validate gender equality. Similarly, our "applied" mission facilitates conversations that cross-disciplinary and pedagogical borders, keeping our concrete aim at social justice. These conversations are the inspirational motor for our adventurous epistemological and pedagogical exercises that center on the transformative potential of crossing disciplinary borders and building a community that intentionally invites different ways of thinking and being. Over the years, for example, we have collaborated with our students on projects related to culturally responsive relationship development with families (Thompson, 2012), human trafficking prevention (Sayles, 2012), cultural perceptions of autism (Mandell et al., 2009; Otwori, 2017), participatory research practices (Pritchett et al., 2020), increasing social empathy (Love, 2020), and the process of collective shaping towards social justice understanding (Morris, 2020; Perez-Glendon, 2020).

This brief mention of our lived experiences, fragments of the narrative of our lives is intentional. We wish to emphasize the critical role of our positionality, not only as authors of this chapter, but also as indicative of the fallacy embedded in the claim that all scholarly and scientific products can be presented as depersonalized, objective products (England, 1994). Communication cannot be divorced from the identity of the speaker. It only appears this way when all speakers and listeners share the same dominant position. Here we underline the importance of enunciating positionality as a way of expanding our objectivity and inviting the community to understand the context for our social justice activism, research, and scholarship products.

Behavior analysis, as a field, has been largely devoted to dissemination, promoting our conceptualizations and practices for what we perceive as the greater good. We are beginning to question our own fundamental structures and methods and learn new ways to listen and respond to the voices of society that have been marginalized, oppressed, or silenced. Perspective making, understanding, and communicating the unique contributions of one community of knowledge and perspective taking, listening to the perspectives of other sources of knowledge for a common effort or goal is a requirement of synthesized and accelerated progress (Boland & Tenkasi, 1995). In the case of behavior analysis, and its aims towards socially just research and practice we offer that there must be intentional perspective learning spaces in our discipline. These spaces would include and amplify the voices of diverse parts of society, including the people rising, the marginalized and those left out of decision making (Pritchett et al., 2020).

A Western, scientific paradigm tells us we need to be objective, divorced from our emotional and spiritual selves. At the same time, we search for a way to fight the alienation of our humanity. There is a movement, a resurgence, a growth, and an expansion of notions related to spirituality and away from materialism.

> Being is a spiritual proposition. Gaining is a material act. Traditionally, American Indians have always attempted to be the best people they could. Part of that spiritual process was and

is to give away wealth, to discard wealth in order not to gain. Material gain is an indicator of false status among traditional people, while it is "proof that the system works" to Europeans. (Russel Means, in a Speech to the 1980 Black Hills International Survival Gathering)

WHAT IS SPIRIT?

Spiritual practices are built around understanding this. Womanists describe the idea that we are sacred to one another, linked to the spiritual realm and to the earth, and that tending to this sacred interconnectedness is essential to our survival (Maparyan, 2012; Walker, 2003). The spiritual realm is the metaphysical, the things beyond the material, our physical events. This type of knowing allows and welcomes investigation and practice to learn what can link us. Spirit learning involves practices that develop compassion, respect, truthfulness, curiosity, generosity, forgiveness, patience, justice, and many more treasures. Encompassing all is love.

Acknowledging spirit is a value. Scientific practices are embedded in structures that nourish and maintain (or discourage and punish) different sets of values. We live in a time that requires we examine those values. Those values can influence our actions (Hayes, 2016). If our metavalue is to be social justice, a spiritual goal, it will require an understanding of what that means and how to learn love for all humanity.

Despair seems inevitable. Our liberation from this old way of being and into well-being is inextricably bound to one another (e.g., Assembly, 1948; Maparyan, 2012; Wilkerson, 2020). How do we move out of this? How do we transform? How can we change and learn to be human beings that are repelled and convulse when our fellow humans suffer, that move all of us towards a life built and supported by spiritual dimensions?

The efforts will be many and dimensional. As individuals, and as behavior analysts, we can be part of the efforts. We suggest here that we begin by stepping into the *Nepantla*, a pedagogy for learning in these urgent times. Anzaldua (1987) first introduced the idea of *Nepantla*, a Nahuatl concept describing the space between two bodies of water, as a metaphor for learning in transformative states. It is a ". . . site of transformation, the place where different perspectives come into conflict and where you question the basic ideas, tenets and identities . . . where you struggle to find equilibrium (Anzaldua, 2002, p. 548). The transformational power of this pedagogical metaphor has been explored in the field of education, particularly working with Latinx students struggling in the context of living in another culture, with other ways of existing.

Our times are characterized by merging contexts and uncertainty. This asks for a pedagogy of uncertainty, a way of transformation into the unknown. It calls for intentional and reflective inductive methods, respect for different ways of knowing and active listening to a diversity of voices. That means to navigate through cultural, emotional, and conceptual borderlands. It also means to put aside for the moment the conviction that we have "The" answer. To listen and learn from others, to share and reflect, to act and reflect. To become comfortable with different ways of talking, conceptualizing, and acting. It requires that all knowing is provisional and open to transformation. It asks we choose values aligned with love and universal well-being and that those values guide each decision point along our unfolding path. Our focus is on the process of building collective understanding and action toward the common good.

Barrera and Kramer (2009) suggest we pursue *third choices*. If your way versus my way is the only choice, one will be excluded, one will dominate. "When only two contradictory choices seem feasible, it is not possible to be truly responsive to choices different than our own. (p. 110)". This requires moving through conviction and fear and searching for what connects us, what allows us to create a new, unimagined, meaningful community for all (hooks, 2003).

Part of entering the learning space of *Nepantla* means inviting ways of knowing that have been excluded from Western science. Entering this space also requires courage to dismantle the organizing principles of a seemingly orderly universe. Being in *Nepantla* forces us into a hard and painful process of critical analysis, awareness of a need for change, and search for the tools to initiate the struggle for transformation. One entry into this process is referred to as *Conocimiento* (Anzaldua, 1987) and involves alternative ways of knowing, feeling, and acting upon the world, that are, ". . . rooted in the lived experience of survival, community building, intimacy with the natural environment, health, healing, and personal growth among everyday people from all walks of life, and articulated primarily but not exclusively by women of color from around the world . . ." (Maparyan, 2012, p. 33). Ways of knowing and approaches to spirituality practiced by communities of women and indigenous peoples will be foreign and uncomfortable to many behavior scientists.

Nepantla is an in-between place of transformation and discomfort. It is a place of stickiness and uncertainty. For applied behavior analysts, holding both spirit and emotions *and* objectivity and physical events will be a great source of tension. At the same time, this is not a new concept to us (Wolf, 1978); finding heart was present at the birth of our applied discipline. Wilkerson (2020) tells humanity that it will be necessary, for the "heart is the last frontier" (p. 370).

Our conceptualizations suggest that the process of entering *Nepantla* will break some stimulus controls and structures; we willingly enter an environment of collective shaping that includes many ways of knowing. *Nepantla* allows space for inclusion, inspiration, the development of different values, and imagination. The life of the spirit and ancient wisdom may have a place in our frames. We can begin to deemphasize evangelical dissemination and emphasize dialectical praxis.

More than our disparate professional positionality has informed our work. Our ethnicities are different, can be confusing and our lived experiences can be misunderstood. We come from cultures that have colonized and been colonized, there are different accents and spices sprinkled throughout our beloved and extended families. But, together, we have watched responses to our beautiful children of complicated ancestry. We have witnessed the grace and the vileness the world is capable of offering. Both personally and professionally, we have moved forward as sisters; agreeing, disagreeing, angering, forgiving, consoling, and praying together. It is this relationship that keeps us returning to the *Nepantla* classroom. We have seen firsthand third choices that emerge from our tensions and sharing, from our commitment to the direction of love.

WE LIVE IN A TIME OF SPIRIT TRANSFORMATION

Our future lies in entering *Nepantla* and learning in the unknown territories. We can enter that portal, the transition, knowingly, willingly and with the intention of transformation, into a more just and loving world, or we will be pushed into entry, attempting a (futile) commandeering of dominion and force (Roy, 2020). As we do so, we shake free of identities and experiences confined by binary worlds and words, (us or them, man or woman, north or south, rich or poor, white or color, polychronic or monochronic, behaviorist or mentalist) but as expanded and fluid members of a community beautiful in our diversity within the whole.

Entering *Nepantla*, focused on a common set of directional values and principles, allows us to work with others and begin to imagine that larger rhythm, a world that is inclusive and transformed. Entrance into that world will be full of contradictory tensions and unfamiliar ways of knowing and acting. It will set the occasion for fear and a lot of discomfort. It will require values and reinforcers attached to the life of the spirit. Scholar and activist, bell hooks reminds us that, "Love will always move us away from domination in all its forms. Love will always challenge and change us" (p. 137, 2003). There is a place for behavior science in this unfolding period of civilization. Our task is to move away from the need to dominate, and into a provisional, directional, and collective effort.

REFERENCES

American Psychiatric Association. (2013). *Diagnostic and statistical manual of mental disorders* (5th ed.). American Psychiatric Publishing.

Angell, A. M., Frank, G., & Solomon, O. (2016). Latino families' experiences with autism services: Disparities, capabilities, and occupational justice. *OTJR: Occupation, Participation and Health, 36*(4), 195–203. https://doi.org/10.1177/1539449216666062

Angell, A. M., Empey, A., & Zuckerman, K. E. (2018). A review of diagnosis and service disparities among children with autism from racial and ethnic minority groups in the United States. *International Review of Research in Developmental Disabilities*, 145–180. https://doi.org/10.1016/bs.irrdd.2018.08.003

Anzaldua, G. & Keating, A. L. (2002). *This bridge we call home: Radical visions for transformation*. Routledge.

Anzaldua, G. (1987). *Borderlands/La frontera: The new mestiza*. Aunt Lute.

Assembly, U. N. (1948). *Universal declaration of human rights*. UN General Assembly, *302*(2). https://doi.org/10.4337/9781845428297.00024

Baer, D. M., Wolf, M. M., & Risley, T. R. (1968). Some current dimensions of applied behavior analysis. *Journal of Applied Behavior Analysis, 1*(1), 91–97. https://doi.org/10.1901/jaba.1968.1-91.

Barrera, I., & Kramer, L. (2009). *Using skilled dialogue to transform challenging interactions: Honoring identity, voice, & connection*. Paul H. Brookes.

Benjamin, R. (2013). *People's science: Bodies and rights on the stem cell frontier*. Stanford University Press.

Boland, R. J., & Tenkasi, R. V. (1995). Perspective making and perspective taking in communities of knowing. *Organization Science, 6*(4), 350–372. https://doi.org/10.1287/orsc.6.4.350

Broder-Fingert, S., Mateo, C. M., & Zuckerman, K. E. (2020). Structural racism and autism. *Pediatrics, 146*(3). https://doi.org/10.1542/peds.2020-015420

Durkin, M. S., Maenner, M. J., Baio, J., Christensen, D., Daniels, J., Fitzgerald, R., & Imm, P. (2017). Autism spectrum disorder among US children (2002–2010): Socioeconomic, racial, and ethnic disparities. *American Journal of Public Health, 107*, 1818–1826. https://doi.org/10.2105/AJPH.2017.304032

England, K. V. L. (1994). Getting personal: reflexivity, positionality, and feminist research. *The Professional Geographer, 46*(1), 80–89. https://10.1111/j.0033–0124.1994.00080.x

Ennis-Cole, D., Durodoye, B. A., & Harris, H. L. (2013). The impact of culture on autism diagnosis and treatment: Considerations for counselors and other professionals. *The Family Journal, 21*(3), 279–287. https://doi.org/10.1177/1066480713476834

Hayes, S. C. (2016). Acceptance and commitment therapy, relational frame theory, and the third wave of behavioral and cognitive therapies – republished article. *Behavior Therapy, 47*(6), 869–885. https://10.1016/j.beth.2016.11.006

Henrich, J., Heine, S. J., & Norenzayan, A. (2010). The weirdest people in the world? *Behavioral and Brain Sciences, 33*(2–3), 61–83. https://doi.org/10.1017/s0140525x0999152x

hooks, b. (2003). *Teaching community: A pedagogy of hope*. Taylor & Francis.

Howard, J. S., Stanislaw, H., Green, G., Sparkman, C. R., & Cohen, H. G. (2014). Comparison of behavior analytic and eclectic early interventions for young children with autism after three years. *Research in Developmental Disabilities, 35*(12), 3326–3344. https://doi.org/10.1016/j.ridd.2014.08.021

Keller, H., Lohaus, A., Kuensemueller, P., Abels, M., Yovsi, R., Voelker, S., Jensen, H., Papaligoura, Z., Rosabal-Coto, M., Kulks, D., & Mohite, P. (2004). The bio-culture of parenting: Evidence from five cultural communities. *Parenting, 4*(1), 25–50. https://doi.org/10.1207/s15327922par0401_2

Lovaas, O. I. (1987). Behavioral treatment and normal educational and intellectual functioning in young autistic children. *Journal of Consulting and Clinical Psychology, 55*(1), 3–9. https://doi.org/10.1037/0022-006X.55.1.3.

Love, A. K. (2020). An evaluation of effects of collective shaping on perspective taking and social empathy statements related to social justice. University of North Texas, Denton, Texas. https://digital.library.unt.edu/ark:/67531/metadc1707351/: accessed September 28, 2020.

Lugones, M. (2010). The coloniality of gender. In W. Mignolo & A. Escobar (Eds.), *Globalization and the decolonial option* (pp. 369–390). Routledge.

Mandell, D. S., Wiggins, L. D., Carpenter, L. A., Daniels, J., DiGuiseppi, C., Durkin, M. S . . . & Kirby, R. S. (2009). Racial/ethnic disparities in the identification of children with autism spectrum disorders. *American Journal of Public Health, 99*(3), 493–498. https://doi.org/10.2105/AJPH.2007.131243

Maparyan, L. (2012). *The womanist idea: Contemporary sociological perspectives.* Routledge. https://doi.org/10.4324/9780203135938

Mbembé, A. (2013). Necropolitics. *Public Culture, 15*(1), 11–40. muse.jhu.edu/article/39984

McEachin, J. J., Smith T., & Lovaas, O. I. (1993). Long-term outcome for children with autism who received early intensive behavioral treatment. *American Journal of Mental Retardation, 97*(4), 359–391.

Means, R. (1980). For America to live Europe must die. https://theanarchistlibrary.org/library/russell-means-for-america-to-live-europe-must-die

Miller, K. L., Re Cruz, A., & Ala'i-Rosales, S. (2019). Inherent tensions and possibilities: Behavior analysis and cultural responsiveness. *Behavior and Social Issues, 28*, 1–21. https://doi.org/10.1007/s42822-019-00013-y

Morris, G. N. (2020). *Cultivating liberation: The effects of collective shaping on context and power dynamics within social justice narratives* (Thesis). University of North Texas, Denton, Texas. https://digital.library.unt.edu/ark:/67531/metadc1707279/

Mustakova-Possardt, E. (2004). Education for critical moral consciousness. *Journal of Moral Education, 33*(3), 245–269. https://doi.org/10.1080/0305724042000733046

Otwori, B. N. (2017). *It's going to be different, but it's going to be okay: Caregiver perspectives on autism, culture and accessing care* (Thesis). University of North Texas, Denton, Texas. https://digital.library.unt.edu/ark:/67531/metadc1062816/

Perez-Glendon, E. L. (2020). *Cultivating liberation within a verbal community: Evaluating the effects of collective shaping on written narratives and reflective statements about social issues* (Thesis). University of North Texas Denton, Texas. https://digital.library.unt.edu/ark:/67531/metadc1707343/

Pritchett, M., Ala'i, S., Re Cruz, A., & Cihon, T. (2020, August 19). Social justice is the spirit and aim of an applied science of human behavior: Moving from colonial to participatory research practices. *Behavior Analysis in Practice.* https://doi.org/10.31234/osf.io/t87p4

Quijano, A. (2000). Coloniality of power and Eurocentrism in Latin America. *International Sociology, 15*(2), 215–232. https://doi.org/10.1177/0268580900015002005

Roy, A. (2020). The pandemic is a portal. *Financial Times.* https://www.ft.com/content/10d8f5e8-74eb-11ea-95fe-fcd274e920ca

Sayles, T. P. (2012). *The effects of a human trafficking prevention workshop package on participant written and simulation responses* (Thesis). University of North Texas, Denton, Texas. https://digital.library.unt.edu/ark:/67531/metadc407816/

Thompson, M. J. (2012). *Improving family-provider relationships through cultural training and open-ended client interviews* (Thesis). University of North Texas, Denton, Texas. https://digital.library.unt.edu/ark:/67531/metadc115170/

Walker, A. (2003). *In search of our mothers' gardens: Womanist prose.* Mariner Books.

Wilkerson, I. (2020). *Caste: The origins of our discontents.* Random House.

Wolf, M. M. (1978). Social validity: The case for subjective measurement or how applied behavior analysis is finding its heart. *Journal of Applied Behavior Analysis, 11*(2), 203–214. https://doi.org/10.1901/jaba.1978.11-203

Wolf, M. M., Risley, T., & Mees, H. (1964). Application of operant conditioning procedures to the behaviour problems of an autistic child. *Behaviour Research and Therapy, 1*, 305–312. https://doi.org/10.1016/0005-7967(63)90045-7

32

NEURODIVERSITY & ABLEISM

From Accountant to Advocate: Ableism and
Neurodiversity in the Workplace

Thomas Iland

Full-time, permanent employment with benefits is a goal many strive to accomplish over their lifetime. The sense of financial freedom and independence and making a difference in an organization, gives one a sense of purpose and meaning. In the process, one becomes part of something bigger than oneself, plus has the potential to create change for the betterment of the individual, and the world.

In order to be most successful in employment, a certain degree of socialization and communication, be it with a colleague, a customer or client, or manager, is often a require-ment for the work to be done and for an organization to fulfill its objectives including, but not limited to, delivering value to its customers or clients.

It is currently perceived, and in many ways being realized, that this goal cannot be effec-tively fulfilled amongst individuals on the autism spectrum as autism, a social-communication disorder, can profoundly impact one's ability to obtain and retain permanent employment. For some it may present as incompetence or distractibility in an interview, becoming overwhelmed and melting down in a work environment, or saying the wrong thing at the wrong time to the wrong person. Individuals with autism have frequently been overlooked, underestimated, neglected, and terminated because of their diagnosis. As a result, over 90% of people with autism are currently unemployed or underemployed (Abrahams, 2016). This causes many to lose hope of ever accomplishing their goal of full-time, permanent employment with benefits.

My own journey to employment contains many stories of both success and failure. All of which have helped shape me into who I am today and put me on a path to a better life for myself.

From a very young age, I was fascinated with money. I still recall playing with a Fisher-Price cash register, sorting and rolling coins, and even walking around with my head down at museums, zoos, and other public places in search of loose change on the ground. My fascination with money, combined with my interest in Star Wars, led me to set my goal of becoming George Lucas's accountant. I'd heard accountants work with money and that's what I planned to do for him!

I let my parents know what I had in mind . . . and how they responded to this dream of mine made a world of a difference! Rather than saying or thinking, "That's a pipe dream!" or "You're not going to become that . . . look for something else!", my parents gave me . . . **a reality check!**

My parents explained to me that if I wanted to be George Lucas's accountant, I had to take special classes in college, take difficult exams, and find jobs at places before *Lucasfilm*. I could've quit my endeavor right then and there after being hit with the reality of my situa-tion . . . However, armed with what I call a "Batman mentality," in which I face my fears, don't give up, and eventually find a way, I told myself, "Challenge accepted!"

During my senior year in high school, I came across a Workability program that gave local jobs to students with autism and other learning differences. I was seeking work in the entertainment field, and was able to land a job working after school at my local *Hollywood*

Video store. My main job was re-shelving video tapes that had been returned by customers. This went on for a number of weeks and, one day, my mother asked my supervisor, "Are you going to give him other duties besides re-shelving videos?" The supervisor replied, "No, we figure students with disabilities can just re-shelve videos." Prior to even meeting me, it was clear that management had already assessed my potential and possibilities for growth which were grossly underestimated because they saw my disability, not my strengths. I left the position shortly thereafter.

After graduating from high school in 2002, I went to the local community college and began taking the introductory accounting courses needed to move towards my goal of being George Lucas's accountant. On the side, I looked for work that could help me earn some money and contribute to my parents' household expenses (I lived with my parents until age 25, which is when I graduated from a nearby university).

I applied for a position at my local movie theater where a classmate of mine was a supervisor and secured a job working at the concession stand. I was instructed to ask customers if they wanted to buy the featured popcorn-drink-candy combo. I made sure to begin EVERY transaction with that offer, sold a high number of combos, and was even recognized by the management for my efforts.

Unfortunately, my co-workers were both jealous and juvenile, and proceeded to bully me. One day, two of them got into a fight . . . and they "Punk'd" me (as in the Ashton Kutcher practical joke show) saying it was my fault that they were fighting. What's worse, a supervisor was also in on the joke. It was clear that I wasn't being respected at this job, which resulted in my resignation after approximately nine months.

I interviewed for my next position at a *Blockbuster Video* (staying with the entertainment/movie theme) where one of my former classmates was a manager. I got a job as a customer service representative . . . operating a cash register, assisting with store inventory counts, and updating advertising. In late 2004, the store announced that the entire *Blockbuster* company would be eliminating late fees on rented items returned late. From the get-go, I thought it was a bad idea and informed my manager and friend that we would be short on inventory and a large chunk of revenue would disappear. My manager responded, "Tom, who are people going to believe . . . the CEO of a Fortune 500 company . . . or a community college accounting major?" *Blockbuster* would eventually go on to file for bankruptcy and become defunct . . . so maybe that community college accounting major was onto something!

Before it went under though, I continued to serve customers in 2005 and explained to them that, while late fees were gone, if a customer kept an item for too long, it got sold to the customer with a charge to the customer's card on file. Customers came in day after day angry with the charges that they'd incurred and took that anger out on me. I couldn't reverse a charge without a manager override which hindered my independence and problem-solving on the job.

One day, a manager was on lunch and I was left to run the store. When I couldn't assist a customer without a manager present, the customer asked me, "Who do you call if there's an emergency?" Autism got the better of me and I responded, "The police?" She frowned and shot back, "Now you're just being a smartass." I remained calm until my manager returned and handled the situation. He actually ended up siding with me, even with my "smartass" comment, and did not write me up or penalize me for what had happened.

It still felt awful though . . . to not have any control over corporate policy, and having to take the heat from customers . . . which, in hindsight, resulted from a poorly planned and even more poorly executed policy which drove countless customers away. I believe this is one of the main reasons why *Blockbuster* went bankrupt and closed permanently.

When 2006 came, I had yet another choice to make . . . endure more customer anger and frustration for a couple of bucks an hour . . . or find something better for myself. I chose the latter, being at the point in my career where my biggest takeaway was that a job in retail was NOT for me.

My next job was working as a receptionist at a small accounting firm owned by a friend of a friend. I assisted with answering phones, accepting mail and deliveries, and cleaning the office area. I also received some valuable insight as to what accountants do during the day, what they talk about, and it provided a glimpse into the workplace culture. At the time, it looked like just the job I wanted and it motivated me to push through my university classes.

Also, while at my university, through its Accounting Association, I had the opportunity to tour local accounting firms, have mock interviews, and attend resume writing workshops. Having access to these opportunities to practice, make mistakes and REALLY get a taste for what my intended career required made ALL the difference for me and I continue to use information I learned from the Accounting Association to this day!

More people with autism need more access to more opportunities to help them get an idea of what kind of work they desire! Guessing or assuming 'what something would be like' won't cut it! It's experiencing it for themselves by themselves and being able to get their feet wet and even their hands dirty that will help them make better decisions. That will allow better decision-making so they can pursue more of what they want and avoid more of what they don't want.

In late 2007, I was nearing the end of my university experience, when a classmate of mine who worked for *Disney*, secured an interview for me with his supervisor! *Disney* was looking for paid property tax interns and THIS could be the foot in the door that I needed! I got the position and worked at *Disney* during my last semester and continued to work at *Disney* after graduating in 2008!

People often ask me, "How'd you get that through that interview? Did the employer know you have autism?" People then go on to say, "You have it easy! You don't look or sound autistic and you're not one to talk about autism matters!"

With the help of my Accounting Association practice, I felt and feel confident in an interview and do not usually bring up or have to bring up autism to an employer during that process. In fact, if you disclose your autism diagnosis during an interview, an employer might not hire you . . . and, by law, they can't ask you if you have a diagnosis nor can they say they didn't hire you because you have autism. In my experience, I've found that **self-disclosing after getting the job** and showing the employer that I'm "otherwise qualified" has been best for me.

Applying this to my *Disney* experience, after a few weeks of the internship, I found myself struggling to understand my duties. My manager had planned individual private sessions with each intern to ask how things were going. I took this opportunity to self-disclose my autism diagnosis to my manager. What's **MORE** important, I explained where I was struggling AND offered a remedy. For instance, I explained how I struggled with receiving a lot of spoken words at once and suggested that receiving my directions or procedures in writing would be better. Also, I found that I would sometimes ask the same question more than once and explained, "If you'll bear with me, the information will eventually stick."

My manager was open to the accommodations that I suggested, my work performance improved, and I even got promoted to Lead Intern, in which I supervised five interns, tracked their progress on over 500 tax returns, and even gave them a "how to" manual I'd written myself to improve their efficiency and effectiveness. As a result of these initiatives, the team set company department records for speed in which they completed their work which was attributed to my supervision!

After several tax seasons with *Disney*, no permanent job was made available to me. I went on to work at another internship at the Big 4 accounting firm, Deloitte, along with several temporary ("temp") accounting jobs. It was in these jobs that I discovered more and more what accounting entailed and I got more and more mentally exhausted. In late 2012, my manager at *Disney* recommended me for an entry-level position which I was able to secure! **My first permanent job with benefits EVER!** I was ecstatic to finally be at this point in my life!

As with *Disney*, I hadn't disclosed in the interview about my autism and immediately found the job difficult. I self-disclosed to my manager, feeling he, too, would be understanding and accommodating. Instead, he responded, **"You lied by omission in the interview. I don't have to help you and I'm not going to!"** Human Resources were immediately notified, I had a job coach going to bat for me, but the job coach could only help with the communication aspects of the job, not the technical skills needed. My mental health and happiness were deteriorating rapidly . . . I'd FINALLY gotten where I wanted to be jobwise . . . only to have my diagnosis thrown in my face. Out of respect for myself, my well-being, and in order for them to find someone more suited for the position, I resigned from the position after only four months. **This was the beginning of the end of my accounting career**.

Situations like these have the potential to not only destroy people with autism . . . but to define them. Oftentimes, the two go hand-in-hand. In my case, it took me being nearly destroyed mentally and emotionally in order to define myself, discover who I really am and embrace what I *really* needed to do . . . tell my story and show people **YOU HAVE THE POWER!** Sadly, too many people with autism may feel destroyed and are not able to pick up the pieces of their lives which are needed to define their *authentic* selves. **We need help picking up the pieces!**

People with autism are capable of so much more than we are given credit for . . . and yet society is unwilling or unable to do what is really necessary to help us see what we are truly capable of . . . particularly in an employment or job setting. Each and every one of us has a part to play to be inclusive and accepting of not only the problems and the perils of autism . . . but the potential and the possibilities of having someone with autism in the workplace.

Just like everyone else, we have the right to life, liberty and the pursuit of happiness . . . and yet these rights are being denied to us continuously on a daily basis. We deserve to find a place that allows us to work, earn our keep and be part of something bigger and greater than ourselves! That is what will make us become our **BEST SELVES!**

In closing, I've made it my life's work to live by example and show people that obstacles can be overcome, barriers can be broken, and ceilings can be shattered! When we work together to bring out the best in each other, the world becomes a better place . . . for everyone!

On a side note, it has been suggested that, as a result of my "Batman mentality," I have become (an) ableist. Let me assure you that **I am NOT an advocate for ableism . . . *I am an expert on EMPOWERMENT*** !

REFERENCE

Abrahams, A. (2016, September 24). You're autistic. You know you can do a good job, but will employers listen? https://www.washingtonpost.com/national/health-science/youre-autistic-you-know-you-can-do-a-good-job-but-will-employers-listen/2016/09/22/412956bc-4dca-11e6-a422-83ab49ed5e6a_story.html

33

PERSPECTIVE TAKING

A Relational Frame Approach to Understanding
Perspective-Taking in Compassion and Social Justice

Yors Garcia, Meredith Andrews, and Lisa Brothers

INTRODUCTION

Perspective-taking (PT) involves actively considering a particular situation or the world more generally from another person's point of view. Stated differently, it means putting yourself in another person's shoes. PT can be further divided in three sub-dimensions, visual or spatial PT, affective or emotional PT, and cognitive PT (Kavanagh et al., 2019a). Visual PT refers to the ability to see the world from another person's perspective, taking into account what they see and how they see it. In other words, spatial and social information are important elements to establish visual PT. Cognitive PT is defined as the skill to estimate correctly what another person thinks in a specific situation. Most of the research in cognitive PT has been conducted under the rubric of *theory of mind* (ToM). ToM is defined as the ability to infer mental states to oneself and others (Premack & Woodruff, 1978). Lastly, emotional PT corresponds to the ability to estimate how a person feels when the individual is in a certain emotional situation.

A variety of tools have been used to examine PT: self-report questionnaires (e.g., Toronto empathy questionnaire, basic empathy scale), performance-based tasks (e.g., comic strip task, deictic relations protocol), and neuroimaging measure (e.g., magnetic resonance imaging, event-related potentials) (Neumann et al., 2015). Research has shown that PT increases altruism (McAuliffe et al., 2020), promotes compassion toward another individual (Klimecki, 2019), helps to facilitate social interactions (Longmire & Harrison, 2018), reduces stereotyping and prejudice toward target's groups (Matsuda et al., 2020; Todd et al., 2011), increases the likelihood of out-group helping (Batson et al., 2002), and improves willingness to interact with stereotyped out-group members (Wang et al., 2014).

Behavior analysts have provided multiple conceptual reviews of PT using concepts such as: stimulus control (Schlinger, 2009), stimulus equivalence (Spradlin & Brady, 2008), PT continuum (DeBernardis et al., 2014), and relational frame theory (RFT) (Kavanagh et al., 2019a; Montoya-Rodríguez et al., 2017). Most of the behavior-analytic research has focused in teaching missing component skills such as tacting others' private events (Gould et al., 2011; Hahs, 2015; Welsh et al., 2019), deictic framing (Belisle et al., 2016; Montoya-Rodríguez & Molina-Cobos, 2019), and acquisition of an appropriate learning history (Charlop-Christy & Daneshvar, 2003; LeBlanc et al., 2003; Peters & Thompson, 2018). In this chapter we will focus exclusively on the RFT approach to PT.

RELATIONAL FRAME THEORY APPROACH TO PERSPECTIVE-TAKING

RFT is a contemporary behavior-analytic approach to human language and cognition (Hayes et al., 2001; Hughes & Barnes-Holmes, 2016). Simply stated, RFT proposes that the core unit in verbal behavior is relating stimuli or events in the world in new and untrained ways. Multiple behavioral patterns may emerge from this principle which are referred to as relational frames (Hughes & Barnes-Holmes, 2016). One of the simplest relational frames is coordination. Take for example, saying "cat" in front of a cat. In this case there is no physical similarity between the spoken word "cat" and the actual cat. Yet, the individual is able to respond to those two stimuli as similar. Responding to both stimuli as similar requires an extensive history of exemplar training using contextual cues such as "same as," "is," or "equal." From an evolutionary perspective this indicates that basic relational skills such as coordination framing emerge as a result of environmental pressures to cooperate between members of the same group (Hayes, & Sanford, 2014). More advanced relational frame repertoires such as comparison, causality, and hierarchical relations require additional behavioral skills, for example, social referencing, attending to others, joint attention, and PT.

In RFT, PT is another type of relational frame referred to as deictic framing. Unlike other types of relational frames, deictic frames are demonstrated relative to a specific perspective. In this case, from the speaker (Hughes & Barnes-Holmes, 2016). Research in RFT has indicated that there are three fundamental deictic relations that makes up PT: the interpersonal (I-YOU [other]), the spatial (HERE-THERE), and the temporal relations (NOW-THEN) (Kavanagh et al., 2019a). For example, the interpersonal relations, *I* and *YOU*, correspond to the speaker and listener position, respectively. The spatial *HERE* and *THERE* relations indicate the locations where events occur (e.g., home, theater, or restaurant). Lastly, *NOW* and *THEN* relations correspond to the time and moment when events and situations occur such as today or yesterday. All these relations interact resulting in a multitude of possible relational networks (e.g., I-HERE-NOW, YOU-THERE-THEN, I-THERE-THEN, and so on). For instance, "*I definitely know that could be frustrating. I can understand how YOU feel.*" In this situation, I can switch from I-HERE-NOW to I-THERE-THEN perspective.

Empirical evidence supports the utility of the deictic training protocol used for teaching PT skills (Montoya-Rodríguez et al., 2017); however, this protocol presents some important limitations. For example, it is explicitly designed for children and lacks specificity to clinical domains (Kavanagh et al., 2019a). To address some of these limitations RFT researchers have proposed the Implicit Relational Assessment Procedure (IRAP). The IRAP is a computer-based procedure that aims to assess the relative strength of previously established relational frames rather than their mere presence or absence in an individual's behavioral repertoire (Barnes-Holmes et al., 2020). Recently, RFT researchers have evaluated the utility of IRAP to assess deictic framing (Barbero-Rubio et al., 2016; Kavanagh et al., 2019b). Although results are promising, these IRAP studies do not help to distinguish between simple sense-making relations and PT (see Kavanagh et al., 2019a).

Furthermore, PT largely informs our understanding of compassion (Luciano et al., 2020; Luoma & Platt, 2015). In turn, compassion provides a framework from which we can address implicit biases (Greenwald & Banaji, 1995; Kang et al., 2014) and rule-governed behavior that drives social injustices (Mattaini & Rehfeldt, 2020; Pritchett et al., 2020). In the remainder of the chapter, the authors will provide some descriptions how PT skills improve compassion and socialization skills.

PERSPECTIVE-TAKING AND COMPASSION

Compassion is a multidimensional skill that consist of affective components, for example experiencing feelings and/or emotions of oneself and others, and cognitive components, such as awareness of self and others and problem solving, which motivate to alleviate or prevent suffering (Gilbert, 2019; Kirby, 2017; Klimecki, 2019; Preckel et al., 2018). Behaviorally speaking, compassion implies demonstrating an empathic response like, "*I can feel pain for another person*" while engaging in actions that help remove someone else's pain (Gilbert, 2019; Taylor et al., 2019). From an RFT account, however, compassion can be viewed as being aware of private events in oneself and others and relating those private events across context which functions to help others avoid or escape aversive stimuli. This definition has three distinct repertoires which we will examine more closely.

First, compassion consists of self-awareness which initially develops via simple discriminations. For instance, self-awareness starts as experiencing an emotion and tacting its presence (overtly or covertly). From an RFT approach, this involves establishing coordinated relations between private responses (feeling sad) and overt responses such as saying, "*I feel sad.*" In addition, an awareness of others develops when environmental stimuli (e.g., persons' words, facial expressions, actions) become discriminative stimuli for tacting others' private events (Skinner, 1981). In RFT terminology, I discriminate my own experiences from the perspective of I-HERE-NOW that is different from YOU-THERE-THEN. For example, "*I see YOU are doing a lot to help your local community.*"

Discrimination is important in the development of self-awareness. However, the notion of awareness within compassion is greatly expanded when we consider PT as a means of how respondent, perceptual, or operant functions transform across interpersonal, spatial, and temporal contexts (i.e., deictic framing) (Luciano et al., 2020; Luoma & Platt, 2015). As such, when one engages in verbal responses about painful stimuli (e.g., social injustice), it can elicit emotional responses (e.g., anger, distress, fear) even in the absence of direct contingencies (Vilardaga, 2009). Within compassion, this means one can experience an emotional response to someone else's pain by transforming functions from a YOU-THERE-THEN relation into an I-HERE-NOW relation. Moreover, this shared sense of perspective can develop into an US-THEM relation from which individuals form a group identity (Hayes & Sanford, 2014). Thus, PT enhances awareness of private events in oneself and others via relational responding.

The last, and arguably most important, part of the compassion definition is its function to help others avoid or escape aversive stimuli. This moves compassion from what is typically covert behaviors (i.e., privately tacting and relating) to meaningful overt behaviors which can be aimed at promoting social justice. For instance, this may be speaking against stereotyped comments or engaging in allyship. Compassionate behavior is often discussed at the individual level. However, in considering the role of compassion within social justice, there is a need to examine behavior at the cultural level (Davis, 2017).

PERSPECTIVE-TAKING AND CULTURE

Skills of PT and compassion can be shaped and strengthened through operant conditioning and higher-order processes such as relational framing (Kavanagh et al., 2019a; Luciano, et al., 2020). Taken together, these repertoires increase the probability of cooperative social interactions (e.g., Klimecki, 2019; Longmire & Harrison, 2018; Matsuda et al., 2020). When demonstrated across many social groups and contexts, PT and compassion can reasonably be expected to contribute to improved social relations within and between groups and cultures (see Davis, 2017; Wang et al., 2014)

An operant history of demonstrating PT and compassion, however, does not preclude the necessity for environments to be arranged which not only occasion these repertoires, but also extends them to *all* opposition. For example, an individual working in the same relevant contexts irrespective of individual or group differences. For example, one can demonstrate PT and compassion toward one group of people (e.g., heterosexuals), but fail to do so with another group (e.g., homosexuals). While not necessarily a skill deficit in deictic framing, the discriminated application of such skills to members of different social groups may occur for a variety of reasons. For example, in-group favoritism occurs because members of one group share the same values and identity (i.e., YOU-THERE-THEN are in a coordinated relation with I-HERE-NOW). However, out-group bias against another group may occur because US vs THEM are in an opposition frame (e.g., WE are smarter/better than THEM). Out-group favoritism also may occur, "US" prefer working with THEM, Afro-American individuals that are educated (Barnes-Holmes et al., 2020; Hayes, & Sanford, 2014).

The remainder of this chapter will focus on extending PT skills and compassion to multiple social contexts, especially with regard to issues of social justice. While social justice has been considered a cultural keyword due to the many different ways it can be perceived (Thrift & Sugarman, 2019), we offer a working definition of socially determined values, or conditioned reinforcers, related to matters of fairness and equality. In dealing with social issues, it becomes increasingly important to identify the myriad of concurrent contingencies across other levels of selection that influence the probability of engaging in component behaviors that lead toward fairness and equity (see Cihon, & Mattaini, 2019; Mattaini, 1996). This involves taking into account natural selection, behavioral selection, and cultural selection (Hayes, & Sanford, 2014; Skinner, 1981).

Just as contingencies of reinforcement are responsible for selecting operants that comprise individual repertoires (e.g., behavioral selection), interlocking behavioral contingencies (IBCs) develop between members of a group or culture when their individual behaviors interact to produce an aggregate product (AP; Glenn et al., 2016). The IBC/AP unit has been termed a culturant (Hunter, 2012). At the level of cultural selection, the culturant is the unit that may then be selected by events or conditions that benefit the group (Glenn et al., 2016). While it is possible that these selecting consequences align with those which function as reinforcers at the individual level, it is also possible for them to be in a frame of company with members from different ethnic, cultural, and gender groups, although interacting with these individuals may be in a frame of opposition (US vs THEM), all individuals engage in the same activities to produce an AP.

Complying may be in this individual's best "self-interest," but may also result in a number of aversive social consequences from members of this group if the rules are disobeyed. Since consequences for the group may be delayed, they often require verbal contingencies to link the individual behaviors to the desired cultural-level outcome (dos Reis Soares et al., 2018). Rules may be thought of as the basic unit of selection at the sociocultural level (Aguiar et al., 2019). The importance of including this level of analysis to issues of social justice cannot be understated, as selection at the cultural level is *in addition* to behavioral selection, not alternative (Borba et al., 2017).

CONCURRENT CONTINGENCIES

Figure 33.1 provides one example of the types of concurrent contingencies at each level that, in combination, may influence the probability of an operant that perpetuates issues of social injustice (e.g., racial discrimination exhibited by a police officer). The role of PT is embedded within the antecedents as part of the context which may reveal prejudicial beliefs (e.g., Levin

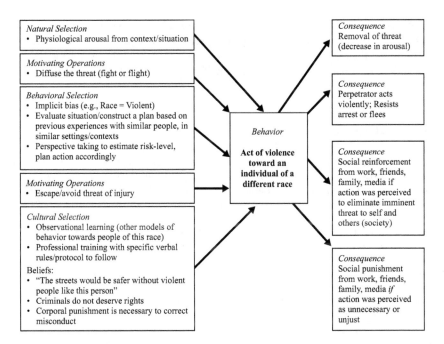

Figure 33.1 Example of concurrent contingencies incorporating each level of selection

et al., 2016; Matsuda et al., 2020). As covert verbal behavior (e.g., thinking silently), such beliefs can have discriminative functions as stimuli evoking operant behavior (see Tourinho, 2006). As shown in Figure 33.1, a single behavior is likely occasioned by variables at the level of natural selection (e.g., physiological arousal), in addition to learning history at the operant level (e.g., implicit bias, PT), as well as many different networks of IBCs that have been selected at the cultural level (e.g., verbal rules). Considering the wide range of variables that may comprise concurrent contingencies for any given behavior, the role of PT and compassion is highlighted here for selection at the individual *and* cultural level. The skills of PT and compassion can be shaped through the verbal community by identifying each individual's role in IBCs and linking those to outcomes they are contributing to (e.g., verbal contingencies), whether deemed positive or negative for the survival of the culture (Davis, 2017; Klimecki, 2019).

CONCLUSION

In summary, the literature on deictic relational frames has demonstrated the operant nature of PT skills and our ability to develop them at the individual and group levels. A behavior-analytic conceptualization of compassion helps inform the use of PT skills to take meaningful actions. A more comprehensive analysis of the types of concurrent contingencies involved across behavioral and cultural levels of selection can help us identify social contexts and cultural consequences that may at present be responsible for selecting culturants incompatible with empathy and compassionate behavior (e.g., discrimination and prejudice).

At the time of publication, the estimated population in the United States alone exceeded 330 million people (U.S. Census Bureau). By arranging for selection of prosocial behaviors

(e.g., indiscriminative PT, compassion) at both the individual and cultural levels, the repertoires of far more individuals can be shaped to promote social justice at a noticeable level.
If we are to use the contributions of our science to impart lasting change for the benefit of
groups and society on a grander scale, selection of more prosocial behaviors at the sociocultural level will be crucial.

REFERENCES

Aguiar, J. C., Oliveira-Castro, J. M., & Gobbo, L. (2019). Rules as basic units of sociocultural selection.
Perspectives on Behavior Science, 42, 851–868. https://doi.org/10.1007/s40614-019-00201-6

Barbero-Rubio, A., López-López, J. C., Luciano, C., & Eisenbeck, N. (2016). Perspective-taking measured by implicit relational assessment procedure (IRAP). *The Psychological Record, 66*(2), 243–252.
https://doi.org/10.1007/s40732-016-0166-3

Barnes-Holmes, D., Harte, C., & McEnteggart, C. (2020). Implicit cognition and social behavior. In
R. A. Rehfeldt, J. Tarbox, & M. Fryling (Eds.), *Applied behavior analysis of language and cognition* (pp. 264–
280). New Harbinger.

Batson, C. D., Chang, J., Orr, R., & Rowland, J. (2002). Empathy, attitudes, and action: Can feeling
for a member of a stigmatized group motivate one to help the group? *Personality and Social Psychology
Bulletin, 28*(12), 1656–1666. https://doi.org/10.1177/014616702237647

Belisle, J., Dixon, M. R., Stanley, C. R., Munoz, B., & Daar, J. H. (2016). Teaching foundational
perspective-taking skills to children with autism using the PEAK-T curriculum: Single-reversal "I–
You" deictic frames. *Journal of Applied Behavior Analysis, 49*(4), 965–969. https://doi.org/10.1002/
jaba.324

Borba, A., Tourinho, E. Z., & Glenn, S. S. (2017). Effects of cultural consequences on the interlocking
behavioral contingencies of ethical self-control. *The Psychological Record, 67*, 399–411. https://doi.
org/10.1007/s40732-017-0231-6

Charlop-Christy, M. H., & Daneshvar, S. (2003). Using video modeling to teach perspective taking to
children with autism. *Journal of Positive Behavior Interventions, 5*(1), 12–21. https://doi.org/10.1177/1
0983007030050010101

Cihon, T. M., & Mattaini, M. A. (2019). Emerging cultural and behavioral systems science. *Perspectives
on Behavior Science, 42*(4), 699–711. https://doi.org/10.1007/s40614-019-00237-8

Davis, M. H. (2017). Empathy, compassion, and social relationships. In E. M. Seppälä, E. Simon-
Thomas, S. L. Brown, M. C. Worline, C. D. Cameron, & J. R. Doty (Eds.), *The Oxford handbook of
compassion science* (pp. 299–315). Oxford University Press.

DeBernardis, G. M., Hayes, L. J., & Fryling, M. J. (2014). Perspective taking as a continuum. *The Psychological Record, 64*(1), 123–131. https://doi.org/10.1007/s40732-014-0008-0

dos Reis Soares, P. F., Rocha, A. P. M. C., Guimarães, T. M. M., Leite, F. L., Andery, M. A. P. A., &
Tourinho, E. Z. (2018). Effects of verbal and non-verbal cultural consequences on culturants. *Behavior and Social Issues, 27*(1), 31–46. https://doi.org/10.5210/bsi.v27i0.8252

Gilbert, P. (2019). Explorations into the nature and function of compassion. *Current Opinion in Psychology,
28*, 108–114. https://doi.org/10.1016/j.copsyc.2018.12.002

Glenn, S. S., Malott, M. E., Andery, M. A. P. A., Benvenuti, M., Houmanfar, R. A., Sandaker, I . . . &
Vasconcelos, L. A. (2016). Toward consistent terminology in a behaviorist approach to cultural analysis. *Behavior and Social Issues, 25*(1), 11–27. https://doi.org/10.5210/bsi.v25i0.6634

Gould, E., Tarbox, J., O'Hora, D., Noone, S., & Bergstrom, R. (2011). Teaching children with autism
a basic component skill of perspective-taking. *Behavioral Interventions, 26*, 50–66. https://doi.
org/10.1002/bin.320

Greenwald, A. G., & Banaji, M. R. (1995). Implicit social cognition: Attitudes, self-esteem, and stereotypes. *Psychological Review, 102*, 4–27. https://doi.org/10.1037/0033-295X.102.1.4

Hahs, A. D. (2015). Teaching prerequisite perspective-taking skills to children with autism. *International
Journal of Psychology and Behavioral Sciences, 5*(3), 115–120.

Hayes, S. C., & Sanford, B. T. (2014). Cooperation came first: Evolution and human cognition. *Journal of Experimental Analysis of Behavior, 101*(1), 112–129. https://doi.org/10.1002/jeab.64

Hayes, S. C., Barnes-Holmes, D., & Roche, B. (2001). *Relational frame theory: A post-Skinnerian account of human language and cognition.* Plenum.

Hughes, S., & Barnes-Holmes, D. (2016). Relational frame theory: Implications for the study of human language and cognition. In R. D. Zettle, S. C. Hayes, D. Barnes-Holmes, & A. Biglan (Eds.), *The Wiley handbook of contextual behavioral science* (pp. 179–226). Wiley-Blackwell.

Hunter, C. S. (2012). Analyzing behavioral and cultural selection contingencies. *Revista Latinoamericana de Psicología, 44*(1), 43–54.

Kang, Y., Gray, J. R., & Dovidio, J. F. (2014). The nondiscriminating heart: Lovingkindness meditation training decreases implicit intergroup bias. *Journal of Experimental Psychology: General, 143*(3), 1306–1313. https://doi.org/10.1037/a0034150

Kavanagh, D., Barnes-Holmes, Y., & Barnes-Holmes, D. (2019a). The study of perspective-taking: Contributions from mainstream psychology and behavior analysis. *The Psychological Record.* Advanced online publication. https://doi.org/10.1007/s40732-019-00356-3

Kavanagh, D., Matthyssen, N., Barnes-Holmes, Y., Holmes, D., McEnteggart, C., & Vastano, R. (2019b). Exploring the use of pictures of self and other in the IRAP: Reflecting upon the emergence of differential trial type effects. *International Journal of Psychology and Psychological Therapy, 19*(3), 323–336.

Kirby, J. N. (2017). Compassion interventions: The programmes, the evidence, and implications for research and practice. *Psychology and Psychotherapy: Theory, Research and Practice, 90*(3), 432–455. https://doi.org/10.1111/papt.12104

Klimecki, O. M. (2019). The role of empathy and compassion in conflict resolution. *Emotion Review, 11*(4), 310–325. https://doi.org/10.1177/1754073919838609

LeBlanc, L. A., Coates, A. M., Daneshvar, S., Charlop-Christy, M. H., Morris, C., & Lancaster, B. M. (2003). Using video modeling and reinforcement to teach perspective-taking skills to children with autism. *Journal of Applied Behavior Analysis, 36,* 253–257. https://doi.org/10.1901/jaba.2003.36-253

Levin, M. E., Luoma, J. B., Vilardaga, R., Lillis, J., Nobles, R., & Hayes, S. C. (2016). Examining the role of psychological inflexibility, perspective taking, and empathic concern in generalized prejudice. *Journal of Applied Social Psychology, 46,* 180–191. https://doi.org/10.1111/jasp.12355

Longmire, N. H., & Harrison, D. A. (2018). Seeing their side versus feeling their pain: Differential consequences of perspective-taking and empathy at work. *Journal of Applied Psychology, 103*(8), 894–915. https://doi.org/10.1037/apl0000307

Luciano, C., Gil-Luciano, B., Barbero, A., & Molina-Cobos, F. (2020). Perspective taking, empathy, and compassion. In M. Fryling, R. A. Rehfeldt, J. Tarbox, & L. J. Hayes (Eds.), *Applied Behavior Analysis of Language and Cognition: Core Concepts and Principles for Practitioners.* (pp. 281–289). New Harbinger Publications.

Luoma, J. B., & Platt, M. G. (2015). Shame, self-criticism, self-stigma, and compassion in acceptance and commitment therapy. *Current Opinion in Psychology, 2,* 97–101. https://doi.org/10.1016/j.copsyc.2014.12.016

Matsuda, K., Garcia, Y., Catagnus, R., & Brandt, J. A. (2020). Can behavior analysis help us understand and reduce racism? A review of the current literature. *Behavior Analysis in Practice, 13,* 336–347. https://doi.org/10.1007/s40617-020-00411-4

Mattaini, M. A. (1996). Envisioning cultural practices. *The Behavior Analyst, 19*(2), 257–272. https://doi.org/10.1007/BF03393168

Mattaini, M. A., & Rehfeldt, R. A. (2020). Editorial: Rendezvous with truth and discovery. *Behavior and Social Issues.* Advanced online publication. https://doi.org/10.1007/s42822-020-00034-y

McAuliffe, W. H., Carter, E. C., Berhane, J., Snihur, A. C., & McCullough, M. E. (2020). Is empathy the default response to suffering? A meta-analytic evaluation of perspective taking's effect on empathic concern. *Personality and Social Psychology Review, 24*(2), 141–162. https://doi.org/10.1177/1088868319887599

Montoya-Rodríguez, M. M., & Molina-Cobos, F. J. (2019). Training perspective taking skills in individuals with intellectual disabilities: A functional approach. *Journal of Contextual Behavioral Science, 14,* 1–10. https://doi.org/10.1016/j.jcbs.2019.08.003

Montoya-Rodríguez, M. M., Molina, F. J., & McHugh, L. (2017). A review of relational frame theory research into deictic relational responding. *The Psychological Record, 67,* 569–579. https://doi.org/10.1007/s40732-016-0216-x

Neumann, D., Chan, R., Boyle, G. J., Wang, Y., & Westbury, R., (2015). Self-report, behavioral, and neuroscientific approaches to measuring empathy: A multidisciplinary perspective. In: Boyle, G. J., Saklofske, D. H. (Eds.), *Measurement of Personality and Social Psychological Constructs* (pp. 257–289). Elsevier, Chennai.

Peters, L. C., & Thompson, R. H. (2018). How teaching perspective taking to individuals with autism spectrum disorders affects social skills: Findings from research and suggestions for practitioners. *Behavior Analysis in Practice, 11*(4), 467–478. https://doi.org/10.1007/s40617-018-0207-2

Preckel, K., Kanske, P., & Singer, T. (2018). On the interaction of social affect and cognition: Empathy, compassion and theory of mind. *Current Opinion in Behavioral Sciences, 19,* 1–6. https://doi.org/10.1016/j.cobeha.2017.07.010

Premack, D., & Woodruff, G. (1978). Does the chimpanzee have a theory of mind? *Behavioral and Brain Sciences, 1,* 515–526. https://doi.org/10.1017/S0140525X00076512

Pritchett, M., Ala'i, S., Cruz, A. R., & Cihon, T. (2020). Social justice is the spirit and aim of an applied science of human behavior: moving from colonial to participatory research practices. *Behavior Analysis in Practice.* Advanced online publication. https://doi.org/10.31234/osf.io/t87p4

Schlinger, H. D. (2009). Theory of mind: An overview and behavioral perspective. *The Psychological Record, 59*(3), 435–448. https://doi.org/10.1007/BF03395673

Skinner, B. F. (1981). Selection by consequences. *Science, 213,* 501–504. 10.1126/science.7244649

Spradlin, J. E., & Brady, N. (2008). A behavior analytic interpretation of theory of mind. *International Journal of Psychology and Psychological Therapy, 8*(3), 335–350.

Taylor, B. A., LeBlanc, L. A., & Nosik, M. R. (2018). Compassionate care in behavior analytic treatment: Can outcomes be enhanced by attending to relationships with caregivers? *Behavior Analysis in Practice, 12*(3), 654–666. https://doi.org/10.1007/s40617-018-00289-3

Thrift, E., & Sugarman, J. (2019). What is social justice? Implications for psychology. *Journal of Theoretical and Philosophical Psychology, 39*(1), 1–17. https://doi.org/10.1037/teo0000097

Todd, A. R., Bodenhausen, G. V., Richeson, J. A., & Galinsky, A. D. (2011). Perspective taking combats automatic expressions of racial bias. *Journal of Personality and Social Psychology, 100*(6), 1027–1042. https://doi.org/10.1037/a0022308

Tourinho, E. Z. (2006). Private stimuli, covert responses, and private events: conceptual remarks. *The Behavior Analyst, 29*(1), 13–31. https://doi.org/10.1007/BF03392115

U. S. Census Bureau. (n.d.). *U.S. and World Population Clock.* Retrieved September 18, 2020, from https://www.census.gov/popclock/

Vilardaga, R. (2009). A relational frame theory account of empathy. *International Journal of Behavioral Consultation and Therapy, 5*(2), 178–184.

Wang, C. S., Kenneth, T., Ku, G., & Galinsky, A. D. (2014). Perspective-taking increases willingness to engage in intergroup contact. *PloS One, 9*(1), e85681. https://doi.org/10.1371/journal.pone.0085681

Welsh, F., Najdowski, A. C., Strauss, D., Gallegos, L., & Fullen, J. A. (2019). Teaching a perspective-taking component skill to children with autism in the natural environment. *Journal of Applied Behavior Analysis, 52*(2), 439–450. https://doi.org/10.1002/jaba.523

34

PREJUDICE AND OPPRESSION

Addressing Societal Issues of Prejudice and Oppression: How Can Behavior Analysis Help?

Lauren A. Goodwyn

From its inception, behavior analysis has been a field interested in addressing issues of social importance. To accomplish this, we must identify what is socially important and for whom. In doing so, we must first be cognizant that what is socially important for one group of people may not be of concern to others and that there are underlying biases which impact how people view the concerns of society. These biases can lead to prejudices and prejudices lead to oppression within those groups that require the most assistance to overcome the societal constructs that result in their oppression. As a science, behavior analysis is equipped with principles and interventions that may be helpful in mitigating issues of prejudice.

PREJUDICE AND OPPRESSION

Prejudice is a "preconceived judgment or opinion," "an adverse opinion or leaning formed without just grounds or before sufficient knowledge" (Merriam-Webster, n.d.). Prejudice is often formed toward a group other than the group the individual belongs to and can be based on a myriad of differences including but not limited to: race, age, sexual orientation, sexual identity, religious beliefs, mental health, socioeconomic status, and dis/ability. From an evolutionary perspective, prejudice promotes an us-versus-them mentality where people categorize others based on how they differ from themselves, thus when faced with diminished resources, the individual can identify who should and should not receive resources based on whether they belong to the same group as the individual (e.g., Comas-Díaz, 2000; Nario-Redmond, 2020). Oppression can stem from that prejudice, for example, when resources are not allocated based on need but instead on inclusion in the group that controls the resources. In the field of social work, oppression is often defined as "a system of domination that denies individuals dignity, human rights, social resources, and power" (Dominelli, 2008, p. 10). According to Merriam-Webster.com (n.d.), oppression is "unjust or cruel exercise of authority or power." Those who have the power are typically those who also control the resources.

No one is without prejudice or bias, but it is when that prejudice negatively impacts the person or others that it becomes a societal concern. Prejudice and oppression of underrepresented populations has been ever-present in society. Native Americans were oppressed by white colonists (e.g., Brave Heart & DeBruyn, 1998; Brave Heart et al., 2011;), Africans were brought to America and enslaved (e.g., Davis, 2020; Parish, 2018), women weren't permitted the right to vote until 1920, individuals with disabilities are often stereotyped as incompetent (Kallman, 2017; Nario-Redmond, 2020), and transwomen are murdered at alarmingly high rates with little to no investigation or prosecution of the offenders (see Stotzer, 2009 and Wirtz et al., 2020 for a review). Prejudice occurs across environments including the primary, secondary, and higher education classroom (e.g., Bal, 2018; Little & Tolbert, 2018; Osa, 2007), in academia (e.g., Martin, 2018; Price 2009), the workplace (e.g., equal pay for equal work), the proverbial board room (e.g., lack of promotions for underrepresented populations), housing, social environments, and the physician's office (McBride et al., 2014).

Considering the impact prejudice can have across all facets of life, it seems that behavior analysis, a science focused on socially relevant behaviors, has the technology and techniques to take action against prejudice although behavior analytic literature addressing these issues is scarce. However, fields of psychology (e.g., Bogart & Dunn, 2019; Gonzalez et al., 2015; O'Donohue, 2016), social psychology (e.g., Rohmer & Louvet, 2012), counseling psychology (e.g., MacLeod, 2013), anthropology (Allen & Jobson, 2016; Miller et al., 2019), and social work (e.g., Dominelli, 2008) have a much larger breadth of research in this area. It is suggested that behavior analysts look to those fields as guidance on how behavior analytic principles can be applied to identify, study, and reduce prejudices.

A BEHAVIOR ANALYTIC ACCOUNT OF PREJUDICE

To identify ways behavior analysis can help mitigate prejudices, it is important to evaluate how prejudice originates. From a behavior analytic perspective, prejudice may develop due to direct contingencies (Matsuda, 2020), verbally governed behavior or, most likely, a combination of the two (Catania, 2018). With direct contingencies, behavior is shaped through direct contact with contingencies as opposed to verbally governed behavior which develops due to "rules" that have been taught or self-learned. Direct contingency processes can be broken down into respondent conditioning, operant conditioning, and stimulus generalization (Matsuda, 2020). Respondent conditioning of prejudice may arise if an initially neutral stimulus (NS), for example, a black male, is paired with a scary situation (UCS), such as a home invasion, and becomes a conditioned stimulus (CS) resulting in a newly conditioned response (CR) of fear. A later encounter with a black male, unrelated to the home invasion, may elicit a response of "black men are scary," and result in prejudiced behaviors. Prejudice can also develop via operant conditioning. Consider a student who emits a derogatory remark toward a gay classmate which results in laughs and positive attention from their peers. Through contingencies of reinforcement, the student is likely to continue making such remarks. Prejudices also arise through stimulus generalization. For example, a college student may observe that a classmate with a learning disability is permitted more time to take tests and is noted to be doing well in the class. The student may perceive the extra time to take tests as 'special treatment' and may be upset that they are not permitted extra time, especially if they are doing poorly in the class. They may characterize any success of the student with a disability as being 'given' and not 'earned' which may generalize to prejudices toward other individuals with disabilities in the future.

Prejudiced behaviors that are verbally governed, develop due to verbal histories of hearing about a specific group and behaving in a particular way based solely on what one has heard or has been self-generated and not based on any direct contact with someone from that group. For example, when a child overhears their parents speaking in a derogatory way about someone's sexual orientation. The child may then act differently toward someone at school who shares the same or similar sexual orientation even though the child had no previous interaction with that student.

Studies in relational frame theory (RFT) offer an analysis of how prejudices can develop and how they can be changed, although the latter is more difficult to accomplish (e.g., Dixon & Lemke, 2007). An RFT perspective evaluates prejudice as a function of derived relational responding (DRR) (Critchfield et al., 2018). Briefly, DRR refers to emergent learning about a new class based on its relationship with previously established classes and results in differential behavior toward the new class in the absence of direct contingencies shaping the behavior (see Critchfield et al., 2018; Dixon et al., 2018; and Rehfeldt, 2013 for a more detailed review). Rule-governed behavior likely plays a critical role in the generalization of behaviors to this novel class. Analyzing emergent relations can provide a framework to study, as to how complex interactions between multiple classes can develop and how they can be taught and changed. For example, Dixon and colleagues (e.g., Dixon et al., 2009; Dixon et al., 2003; Dixon & Lemke, 2007; Dixon, Rehfeldt, et al., 2006; Dixon, Zlomke et al., 2006) have conducted extensive research using relational frame theory to study and alter Americans' prejudices toward middle eastern individuals and symbols.

So where does behavior analysis currently stand in the fight against prejudices? Most behavior analytic research on prejudices focuses primarily on racism (e.g., Arhin & Thyer, 2004; Briggs & Paulson, 1996). However, findings from those studies could apply to other areas of prejudice. Prejudice is a complex behavior and there is little behavior analytic research studying this phenomenon, thus, it can be challenging to identify ways behavior analysis can address this societal issue.

BARRIERS TO ADDRESSING PREJUDICES AND POTENTIAL SOLUTIONS

Prejudice is a pervasive issue that continues to plague society. As such, there are many barriers which can make addressing these issues challenging. Below are a few of those barriers and a brief discussion on how the principles of behavior analysis can help minimize those barriers.

Prejudice Persists Through Time and Across Contexts

As previously reviewed, prejudices and oppressive structures have been around for some time and are ingrained in our culture both directly and inadvertently. On a societal level for example, prejudice is evident in laws against gay marriage and the disproportionate killing of blacks at the hands of law enforcement (Hitchens, 2017; Nordberg et al., 2016; Whitesel, 2017). On an individual level, prejudice may manifest itself as failing to hire someone with a disability because they are viewed as less competent (e.g., Kallman, 2017) or identifying middle eastern men as "scary" (e.g., Dixon et al., 2009; Dixon & Lemke, 2007). Prejudices that exist within the individual and across society can be difficult to address because they have existed for so long, with such a dense learning history across generations and are embedded in the laws that govern society.

People Are Often Unaware of Their Own Prejudices

To mitigate an issue, it must first be identified and defined. However, people are often unaware of their own biases and prejudices. People may believe they are not prejudiced toward a certain group but their nonverbal behavior toward that group is incongruent with their verbal behavior. For example, a teacher may report that she treats all of her students the same yet reprimands her black male students disproportionately more often than their white peers (Knochel et al., 2020). Colleges and universities may advertise a commitment to diversity but lack diversity among faculty or in the content of their courses. If an individual is unaware of their biases and prejudices, they cannot actively address them and moreover could be unknowingly perpetuating those prejudices.

People Tend to Avoid Talking About Prejudice

People do not have enough conversations addressing prejudices. Aside from those who may be unaware of their own prejudices, those who are aware of them, are likely to avoid talking about them because prejudice is often viewed as a pejorative term (Catania, 2018). People do not want to be deemed harsh or viewed in a negative light, and therefore they often avoid discussing prejudices, which exacerbates the issue. Conversations about prejudices can be uncomfortable (e.g., Sue, 2004). Social constructs often make having conversations about prejudice, and particularly racism, challenging. For example, addressing topics of prejudices, racism, and white privilege is discouraged because our society has established rules that topics that are of a potentially oppressive and uncomfortable nature should be avoided. Moreover, our society has also fostered a sense of "color-blindness" where we are encouraged not to recognize differences in race, which only further minimizes the struggles and oppression of marginalized groups (see Sue, 2013, for further discussion).

Naming Can Lead to Boundaries

Naming as a verbal repertoire can result in categorizations that set bounds indicating where inclusion in one group begins and inclusion in another group ends. Some categories are traditionally viewed as a dichotomy, for example skin color (i.e., black vs white) and gender (i.e., female vs male). Others are viewed as consisting of multiple categories, for example religion (e.g., Christianity, Islam, Hinduism, Judaism, etc.) and sexual orientation (e.g., lesbian, bisexual, pansexual, etc.). These boundaries, however, ignore the continuum which exists within all these societal constructs suggesting that an individual is included in one group at the exclusion of another group along the same continuum. The verbal categories used to divide and subdivide people into separate groups does little if anything to reduce prejudices. These verbal categories or constructs will likely become less functional as people from different populations continue to overlap creating more diverse continua.

Prejudice is a Complex Phenomenon

Prejudice is a phenomenon developed through complex interactions of verbal and nonverbal behavior. Complex verbal repertoires influenced by individual learning histories can result in the creation of interwoven concepts between numerous stimulus relations (Dixon et al., 2018). Repertoires that emerge as a result of these interactions can be difficult to study due to the often covert nature of how these stimulus relations form and how additional relations are derived. Therefore, we may be able to observe prejudiced behaviors but may not have access to how those prejudices developed or have the technology to determine their function.

STRATEGIES TO ADDRESS PREJUDICE AND OPPRESSION

The first step in addressing prejudice is on an individual level. As behavior analysts we must become aware of biases and assumptions about behavior that exist within our own skin. Being open and acknowledging our own biases allows space for others to come forward to share and discuss their biases (Sue, 2013). We must foster more than a superficial discussion about prejudices and its underpinnings by encouraging our students, colleagues, and other professionals to engage in conversations about their values, concerns, and perspectives as they relate to societal issues, in the absence of judgment (Fong et al., 2016; Fong et al., 2017; Miller et al., 2019). Developing cultural awareness and a focus on cultural humility and responsiveness can give behavior analysts confidence in facilitating these conversations in an effective manner, where all participants of the dialogue have a voice that is respected and can learn from each other's' experiences.

In addition to developing cultural awareness of self, Fong and colleagues (2016) recommend developing cultural awareness of clients. Doing so, can allow behavior analysts to obtain important cultural information to guide the development of interventions which take into consideration cultural differences and identify any potential cultural barriers to service delivery. Behavior analysts should incorporate strategies to promote cultural awareness in their practice, model this behavior for their staff and supervisees, and share resources and strategies with their colleagues to encourage a practice of seeking new experiences as a means of learning about different cultures (Fong et al., 2016; Miller et al., 2019). Cultivating genuine relationships, both personal and professional, with people of diverse backgrounds will likely lead to a better understanding of cultural differences and is a starting point toward mitigating prejudices.

On an organizational and institutional level, prejudice can be addressed by implementing cultural awareness training and supervision practices at each level within an organization (Fong et al., 2016). The same applies for graduate training programs. Content on cultural awareness, cultural humility, and cultural responsiveness should be included in behavior analytic courses. Additionally, professors should strive to promote diversity within their courses by including content from professionals within the field with diverse backgrounds, experiences, and cultures. This requires a decolonization of academia such that the traditional constructs of education as previously established by the dominant culture of society are restructured in favor of offering a more diverse approach which better represents the multicultural world we live in.

Behavior Analytic Principles and Technologies that Can Help

Reinforcement is one the most powerful tools we use as behavior analysts to encourage behavior change. Reinforcement can be used to increase anti-prejudiced behavior and encourage interactions among diverse groups (e.g., Hauserman, 1973). Modeling is another effective tool to reduce prejudices (e.g., Arhin & Thyer, 2004). Self-monitoring in combination with performance feedback has been found to be effective at decreasing prejudiced behaviors (e.g., Knochel et al., 2020). Self-monitoring and performance feedback could be applied to other professionals such as professors, physicians, CEOs, policy makers, and law officers as a means of increasing people's awareness of their own biases and lead to more equitable treatment among the individuals with whom they interact and service.

Multiple exemplar training can also be an effective strategy to mitigate prejudices (e.g., Dixon et al., 2009). For example, professors' syllabi should contain content which speaks to the contributions of researchers from diverse backgrounds. Focused discussions about diversity within their respective fields should be thoughtfully incorporated into class discussions and assignments. This is particularly important in the field of behavior analysis which until recently has been dominated by cisgender white male researchers publishing most of the research that exists in the field although there is an increasing number of women first authors within the last decade (Kranak, et al., 2020). The use of multiple exemplars could also serve the function of exposing students to counter-stereotypical examples (Lai et al., 2016; Matsuda et al. 2020). It may be possible to disrupt students' negative biases about a certain group by exposing them to leaders in their field, people whom they would presumably hope to emulate, from that group.

MOVING TOWARD A MORE CULTURALLY CONSCIOUS SOCIETY

It seems now, more than ever, there is a need for behavior analysts to reflect upon Wolf (1978) and help the field of applied behavior analysis find its heart. It is our responsibility as behavior analysts to focus our efforts on issues that are socially significant; issues which include prejudice and oppression. Prejudices continue to persist through time, permeate a variety of environments, and impact marginalized groups. The application of behavior analysis to societal problems such as prejudice and oppression is necessary. Behavior analysts should advocate for underserved populations, advocate for the application of behavior analysis outside the scope of autism spectrum disorder to those populations who would benefit (e.g., incarcerated individuals), and collaborate to develop structured trainings teaching behavior analysts to effectively work with people from diverse populations (Miller et al., 2019).

Issues of prejudice and oppression are beginning to receive more attention in behavior analytic research (Fong et al., 2016; Fong et al., 2017; Matsuda, 2020; Miller et al., 2019), as focus in the field is beginning to shift toward a more culturally conscious approach. Still, more research is necessary to identify effective strategies for measuring prejudices, identifying functions of prejudices, and implementing effective strategies to mitigate prejudices with lasting changes.

The field of behavior analysis should also work toward branching into areas where it has traditionally been absent. If behavior analysts are going to have a larger impact on the decisions that govern society, we need a seat at the table. Behavior analysts should strive to contribute in areas of public health, social justice reform, law enforcement, and politics. More research is required in these areas to determine effective means of applying behavior analytic principles to change behavior, biases, and ultimately prejudices to address the oppressive constructs of our society.

REFERENCES

Allen, J. S., & Jobson, R. C. (2016). The decolonizing generation: Race and theory in anthropology since the eighties. *Current Anthropology, 57*(2), 129–148. https://doi.org/10.1086/685502.

Arhin, A., & Thyer, B. A. (2004). The causes of racial prejudice: A behavior analytic perspective. In J. L. Chin (Ed.), *The psychology of racial prejudice and discrimination, Racism in America* (Vol. 1, pp. 1–19). Praeger.

Bal, A. (2018). Culturally responsive positive behavioral interventions and supports: A process-oriented framework for systemic transformation. *The review of education, pedagogy, and cultural studies, 40*(2), 144–174. https://doi.org/10.1080/10714413.2017.1417579

Bogart, K. R., & Dunn, D. S. (2019). Ableism special issue introduction. *Journal of Social Issues, 75*(3), 650–664. https://doi.org/10.1111/josi.12354

Brave Heart, M. Y. H., & DeBruyn, L. M. (1998). The American Indian Holocaust: Healing historical unresolved grief. *American Indian and Alaska Native Mental Health Research, 8*(2), 60–82. https://doi.org/10.5820/aian.0802.1998.60

Brave Heart, M. Y. H., Chase, J., Elkins, J., & Altschul, D. B. (2011). Historical trauma among indige-nous peoples of the Americas: Concepts, research, and clinical considerations. *Journal of Psychoactive Drugs, 43*(4), 282–290. https://doi.org/10.1080/02791072.2011.628913

Briggs, H. E., & Paulson, R. I. (1996). Racism. In M. A. Mattaini & B. A. Thyer (Eds.), *Finding solutions to social problems: Behavioral strategies for change* (pp. 147–177). American Psychological Association.

Catania, A. (2018). A behavior analytic perspective on discrimination and prejudice. *En análisis de la conducta en México: Investigación y aplicaciones 2018* (pp. 11–28). Sociedad Mexicana de Análisis de la Conducta.

Comas-Díaz, L. (2000). An ethnopolitical approach to working with people of color. *American Psycholo-gist, 55*(11), 1319–1325. https://doi.org/10.1037/0003-066X.55.11.1319

Critchfield, T. S., Barnes-Holmes, D., & Dougher, M. J. (2018). Editorial: What Sidman did -- Historical and contemporary significance of research on derived stimulus relations. *Perspectives on Behavioral Science, 41*(1), 9–32. https://doi.org/10.1007/s40614-018-0154-9

Davis, P. E. (2020). Painful legacy of historical African American culture. *Journal of Black Studies, 51*(2), 128–146. https://doi.org/10.1177/0021934719896073

Dixon, M. R., & Lemke, M. (2007). Reducing prejudice towards Middle Eastern persons as terrorists. *European Journal of Behavior Analysis, 8*(1), 5–12. https://doi.org/10.1080/15021149.2007.11434269

Dixon, M. R., Belisle, J., & Stanley, C. R. (2018). Derived relational responding and intelligence: Assessing the relationship between the PEAK-E pre-assessment and IQ with individuals with autism and related disabilities. *The Psychological Record, 68*(4), 419–430. https://doi.org/10.1007/s40732-018-0284-1

Dixon, M. R., Branon, A., Nastally, B. L., & Mui, N. (2009). Examining prejudice towards Middle East-ern persons via a transformation of stimulus functions. *The Behavior Analyst Today, 10*(2), 295–318. https://doi.org/10.1037/h0100672.

Dixon, M. R., Dymond, S., Rehfeldt, R. A., Roche, B., & Zlomke, K. R. (2003). Terrorism and rela-tional frame theory. *Behavior and Social Issues, 12*(2), 129–147. https://doi.org/10.5210/bsi.v12i2.40

Dixon, M. R., Rehfeldt, R. A., Zlomke, K. R., & Robinson, A. (2006). Exploring the development and dismantling of equivalence classes involving terrorist stimuli. *The Psychological Record, 56*(1), 83–103. https://doi.org/10.1007/BF03395539

Dixon, M. R., Zlomke, K. M., & Rehfeldt, R. A. (2006). Restoring Americans' nonequivalent frames of terror: An application of relational frame theory. *The Behavior Analyst Today, 7*(3), 275–289. https://doi.org/10.1037/h0100153.

Dominelli, L. (2008). *Anti-racist social work* (3rd ed.). Palgrave Macmillan.

Fong, E. H., Catagnus, R. M., Brodhead, M. T., Quigley, S., & Field, S. (2016). Developing the cul-tural awareness skills of behavior analysts. *Behavior Analysis in Practice, 9*(1), 84–94. https://doi.org/10.1007/s40617-016-0111-0116

Fong, E. H., Ficklin, S., & Lee, H. Y. (2017). Increasing cultural understanding and diversity in applied behavior analysis. *Behavior Analysis: Research and Practice, 17*(2), 103–113. http://dx.doi.org/10.1037/bar0000076

Gonzalez, K. A., Riggle, E. D., & Rostosky, S. S. (2015). Cultivating positive feelings and attitudes: A path to prejudice reduction and ally behavior. *Translational Issues in Psychological Science, 1*(4), 372–381. http://dx.doi.org/10.1037/tps0000049

Hauserman, N., Walen, S. R., & Behling, M. (1973). Reinforced racial integration in the first grade: A study in generalization. *Journal of Applied Behavior Analysis, 6*(2), 193–200. https://doi.org/10.1901/jaba.1973.6-193

Hitchens, B. K. (2017). Contextualizing police use of force and black vulnerability: A response to Whitesel. *Sociological Forum, 32*(2), 434–438. https://doi.org/10.1111/socf.12338

Kallman, D. (2017). Integrating disability: Boomerang effects when using positive media exemplars to reduce disability prejudice. *International Journal of Disability, Development and Education, 64*(6), 644–662. https://doi.org/10.1080/1034912X.2017.1316012

Knochel, A. E., Blair, K.-S. C., Kincaid, D., & Randazzo, A. (2020). Promoting equity in teachers' use of behavior-specific praise with self-monitoring and performance feedback. *Journal of Positive Behav-ior Interventions.* https://doi.org/10.1177/1098300720951939

Kranak, M. P., Falligant, J. M., Bradtke, P., Hausman, N. L., & Rooker, G. W. (2020). Authorship trends in the *Journal of Applied Behavior Analysis:* An update. *Journal of Applied Behavior Analysis,* 1–9. https://doi.org/10.1002/jaba.726

Lai, C. K., Skinner, A. L., Cooley, E., Murrar, S., Brauer, M., Devos, T., Calanchini, J., Xiao, Y. J., Pedram, C., Marshburn, C. K., Simon, S., Blanchar, J. C., Joy-Gaba, J. A., Conway, J., Redford, L., Klein, R. A., Roussos, G., Schellhaas, F. M. H., Burns, M, Hu, X., . . . & Nosek, B. A. (2016). Reducing implicit racial preferences: II. Intervention effectiveness across time. *Journal of Experimental Psychology: General, 145*(8), 1001–1016. https://doi.org/10.1037/xge0000179

Little, S. D., & Tolbert, L. A. (2018). The problem *with* black boys: Race, gender, and discipline in Christian and private elementary schools. *Christian Education Journal, 15*(3), 408–421. https://doi.org/10.1177/0739891318805760

MacLeod, B. P. (2013). Social justice at the microlevel: Working with clients' prejudices. *Journal of Multicultural Counseling and Development, 41*(3), 169–184. https://doi.org/10.1002/j.2161-1912.2013.00035.x

Martin, J. L., & Beese, J. A. (2018). Disappearing feminists: Removing critical voices from academe. *Forum on Public Policy Online, 2018*(1), 1–22. https://search.proquest.com/docview/2155999360?accountid=166077

Matsuda, K., Garcia, Y., Catagnus, R., & Brandt, J. A. (2020). Can behavior analysis help us understand and reduce racism? A review of the current literature. *Behavior Analysis in Practice, 13*(3), 336–347. https://doi.org/10.1007/s40617-020-00411-4

McBride, S., Durso, L. E., Hussey, H., Gruberg, S., & Robinson, B. G. (2014). *We the people: Why Congress and U.S. states must pass comprehensive LGBT Nondiscrimination protections.* Center for American Progress. https://cdn.americanprogress.org/content/uploads/2014/12/24121649/LGBT-WeThePeople-report1.pdf?_ga=2.244963149.915410043.1600294795-2100578883.1600294795

Merriam-Webster. (n.d.). Oppression. In *Merriam-Webster.com dictionary.* Retrieved September 18, 2020, from https://www.merriam-webster.com/dictionary/oppression

Merriam-Webster. (n.d.). Prejudice. In *Merriam-Webster.com dictionary.* Retrieved September 18, 2020, from https://www.merriam-webster.com/dictionary/prejudice

Miller K. L., Cruz, A. R., & Ala'i-Rosales, S. (2019). Inherent tensions and possibilities: Behavior analysis and cultural responsiveness. *Behavior and Social Issues, 28*(1), 16–36. https://doi.org/10.1007/s42822-019-00010-1

Nario-Redmond, M. R., (2020). *Ableism: The causes and consequences of disability prejudice.* Wiley Blackwell.

Nordberg, A., Crawford, M. R., Praetorius, R. T., & Hatcher, S. S. (2016). Exploring minority youths' police encounters: A qualitative interpretive meta-synthesis. *Child and Adolescent Social Work Journal, 33*(2), 137–149. https://doi.org/10.1007/s10560-015-0415-3

O'Donohue, W. T. (2016). Oppression, privilege, bias, prejudice, and stereotyping: Problems in the APA Code of Ethics. *Ethics & Behavior, 26*(7), 527–544. https://doi.org/10.1080/10508422.2015.1069191

Osa, J. O (2007). The pervasiveness of racial prejudice in higher education in the U.S.: Raising awareness and solution. *Forum on Public Policy Online,* 3. Retrieved from: https://files.eric.ed.gov/fulltext/EJ1099150.pdf

Parish, P. J., (2018). *Slavery: History and historians.* Taylor & Francis.

Price, E. G., Powe, N. R., Kern, D. E., Golden, S. H., Wand, G. S., & Cooper, L. A. (2009). Improving the diversity climate in academic medicine: Faculty perceptions as a catalyst for institutional change. *Academic Medicine, 84*(1), 95–105. https://doi.org/10.1097/ACM.0b013e3181900f29

Rehfeldt, R. A. (2013). Toward a technology of derived stimulus relations: An analysis of articles published in the *Journal of Applied Behavior Analysis,* 1992–2009. *Journal of Applied Behavior Analysis, 44*(1), 109–119. https://doi.org/10.1901/jaba.2011.44-109

Rohmer, O., & Louvet, E. (2012). Implicit measures of the stereotype content associated with disability. *British Journal of Social Psychology, 51*(4), 732–740. https://doi.org/10.1111/j.2044-8309.2011.02087.x

Stotzer, R. L. (2009). Violence against transgender people: A review of United States data. *Aggression and Violent Behavior, 14*(3), 170–179. https://doi.org/10.1016/j.avb.2009.01.006

Sue, D. W. (2004). Whiteness and ethnocentric monoculturalism: Making the "invisible" visible. *American Psychologist, 59*(8), 761–769. https://doi.org/10.1037/0003-066X.59.8.761

Sue, D. W. (2013). Race talk: The psychology of racial dialogues. *American Psychologist, 68*(8), 663–672. https://doi.org/10.1037/a0033681

Whitesel, J. (2017). Intersections of multiple oppressions: Racism, sizeism, ableism, and the "illimitable etceteras" in encounters with law enforcement. *Sociological Forum, 32*(2), 426–433. https://doi.org/10.1111/socf.12337

Wirtz, A. L., Poteat, T. C., Malik, M., & Glass, N. (2020). Gender-based violence against transgender people in the United States: A call for research and programming. *Trauma, Violence, & Abuse, 21*(2), 227–241. https://doi.org/10.1177/1524838018757749

Wolf, M. M. (1978). Social validity: The case for subjective measurement or how applied behavior analysis is finding its heart. *Journal of Applied Behavior Analysis, 11*(2), 203–214. https://doi.org/10.1901/jaba.1978.11-203

35

PRIVILEGE

Read, Reflect, Resist: Deconstructing Privilege

Sanyukta Bafna

INTRODUCTION

It's 7 pm on a Tuesday evening and I am marveling at the beautiful sunset over the Arabian Sea from my 16th floor apartment in a well-known neighborhood in Mumbai, India. This, while my country's economy is crumbling, unemployment is at an all-time high, and COVID-19 seems to have caused havoc all over the world. The 2020 pandemic has clearly highlighted the inequities of the world we live in today. More than tens of thousands of Indian migrant laborers walked home to their villages whereas a certain Indian billionaire went from being the eighth richest to the sixth richest person in the world (Kamdar, 2020). Almost every night at dinner, my family talks about how thankful they are to be *privileged* enough to have a safe home during this time. They are absolutely right, we are privileged. While they continue to compare what's happening in the news to our lives, I am thinking about the many layers of privilege and how we can use it to make the world a better place.

Pre-pandemic, I spent a significant part of my career trying to deconstruct my privilege and understand how it impacts the kind of educator I am. Up until I started teaching, I never thought too much about it because where I am from, you do not question privilege if you have it. I am grateful for having a job that forced me to acknowledge my privilege and think about what it means to use it productively. Although I am still on the journey of learning and deconstructing it everyday, I have picked up a few tools along my journey that helped me grow. In this essay, I will talk about the three Rs: read, reflect, and resist that helped me deconstruct my privilege. I will describe how these helped me create an open and engaging environment for my students and teacher colleagues (hooks, 2014).

According to the *Oxford English Dictionary* (2020), privilege is "a special right, advantage, or immunity granted or available only to a particular person or group." It is a complex socio-political structure that is constantly evolving and shifting depending on your identity and location (Samuels & Ross-Sheriff, 2008). Able-bodied, upper class, Hindu, cis men are immune to privilege as described in the dictionary because their lives are considered *normal* and everyone outside of it, in the margins, are seen as "the others." Even though one might be aware of the advantages one has when growing up with privilege, people are largely unaware of the disadvantages and limited opportunities for *the others* (Johnson, 2006; Kendall, 2006). My story is no different. My family's class privilege enabled me to live in a bubble for 20 years of my life. Bursting this bubble allowed me to understand just how complicated privilege is, and how one must constantly engage in learning more about it.

I became a teacher at the age of 20, soon after graduating from college as part of a national fellowship program that took the *brightest minds from top institutions* and put them up for a challenge in government and low-income private schools. I took on this endeavor with the hope to *transform* the lives of the students I would teach. I was naive to say that nothing in my life before had prepared me for the difficulty of this job. This was largely because of how different my life was from the students I was trusted to teach. Living in Mumbai where slums and skyscrapers cohabitate and share a pin code, I assumed I would know more about their lives, but my knowledge was superficial. I have come to terms with the reality that I did not transform the lives of my first batch of students in any way. However, my work led me to a path of understanding the relationship between power and privilege (Johnson, 2006). The last ten years of wrestling with different kinds of privileges related to gender, sexuality, class, caste, religion, location, and ability has transformed my own life and taught me to be more sensitive, aware and accepting. On many days, I wish I had been more aware when I was growing up. The good news is, that it is never too late to start and there are multiple ways in which you can unravel your privilege. In the following sections, I share some of my experiences that aided my process of becoming socially aware and suggest actions that will help individuals interested in participating in the process of deconstructing their privilege.

READ (FROM THE MARGINS)

When I think about how dominant discourses influence the way we think about "the others," an image that comes to my mind is a group of male politicians sitting around a table and making decisions about women's bodies. This often makes me cringe, and I find myself wondering, what do they really know about the female body? Where did they learn it? How could women not have more agency in deciding how to live their lives? It seems kind of obvious that women should be involved in making decisions about their lives, yet in many parts of the world that is not a reality yet. This also applies to other groups of people who are fighting discrimination and inequity because of a social group they belong to. Ideas about who they are and what they need is determined by hegemonic forces (Apple, 2004). Hegemony supposes the control of something that is truly total and at such a depth that it constitutes as common sense for most people under its sway. It saturates the consciousness and emphasizes the value of dominant systems, meanings and values (Apple, 2004). While we have not reached that sweet spot of many groups of people having control over decisions related to their lives, it is time for us to make more of an effort to understand the lives of *the others* from their perspective.

For years, official knowledge in textbooks and curriculums has been postured as essential facts that are developmentally appropriate and significant to learn while growing up. What we often do not realize is that knowledge is political (Apple, 2004). Irrespective of which part of the world we are in, school structures, curriculum, books, and media is designed around social capital that privileges the norm and benefits those in power (Apple, 2004). We never question where the knowledge comes from, or whose knowledge is it. This widens the gap between those who have power and those who do not. Power and knowledge are impossible to separate (Foucault, 1978). If we truly want an inclusive society where people from different identities have a voice, we must shift the power dynamics and hear from people in the margins. By letting only those with privilege decide what knowledge is important, we are painting tainted images of *the others* that are arbitrarily constructed and rarely consider the many dimensions of people's lives (Sensoy & Marshall, 2010).

For instance, children's literature plays a big role in helping young people understand the world and the many different communities in it. One such popular book is *The Bread-winner* by Deobrah Ellis, which paints pictures of Muslim girls from the east as "vulnerable, naive, ignorant, uncivilised, and in need of rescue from the efforts, good will, and knowledge of the educated, modern" West (Sensoy & Marshall, 2010). Such books have been written by Western authors for consumers in the West who do not consider their own role in understanding the challenges faced by Muslim girls in the east. They also assume a single image of everyone who comes from the east, as though their identity is unidimensional (Mohanty, 2003). If one wants to understand the reality and struggles of those who were historically denied access to opportunity because of their gender, sex, class, caste, religion, or ability, we must engage directly with them. One way to do that is to seek literature written and produced by people belonging to these groups. This will allow you to truly understand their perspective as opposed to just learn about them. Learning about people who have been marginalized from those in power does not allow us to deconstruct our assumptions and leaves us believing that we need to "save" them and "provide" for them at best (Freire, 2018). Our education system is designed by people in power so we only receive knowledge that will maintain the status quo. If we want the status quo to change, it is important to amplify the voices of those in the margins. You have to work slightly harder to find these because systems including search engines are designed to promote hegemony and dignify those in power (Apple, 2004).

REFLECT (ON WORDS AND ACTIONS)

When I worked in a government school, my family always described my work to people they knew as *teaching underprivileged children*. Something about this made me feel really uncomfortable but it was hard for me to pinpoint exactly what the issue was. Upon reflection and conversations with others that did similar work, I realized that the language used to describe the students I taught classified them solely on the basis of their socioeconomic class. It did not consider other aspects of their identity that made them complex, multifaceted human beings (Mohanty, 2003). Additionally, it also suggested that all of them led similar lives with the exact same opportunities and challenges, which I had learned was not true. This process of making meaning of language helped me understand the power of words and its implications. It also helped me engage my family in understanding realities of people that are different from them, and the most appropriate ways to talk about them.

For the purpose of using reflection to understand one's privilege and its implications on society, I define it in terms of unearthing cultural assumptions with the intention of bringing about change (Fook & Askeland, 2007). If one wants to use their privilege positively, it is important to constantly engage in reflection where you confront what you know, how you know, and think about what you would like to change (Banks, 2015). In my experience, this process is uncomfortable to begin with. However, it pushes you to want to do things differently. For example, over the course of my career, I have had the opportunities to work with many groups of young girls to deconstruct patriarchy, so that they have greater agency over their lives (Kabeer, 2005). Through these engagements, we often critiqued practices in our homes and communities, asked difficult questions and suggested actions that would change the dominant narratives (Mohanty, 1989). The process was not always straightforward and worked differently in different schools. For some of these girls, going home and questioning age old traditions involved angering their parents who wanted to revoke their access to education. I spent a lot of time reflecting on what was appropriate to do in a situation like this. After asking some critical questions to both myself and others who worked with me, we realized the best thing to do was to involve their parents in the conversation regarding patriarchal systems and how it deters their daughters' lives. This allowed for more open and honest conversation, letting both the girls and their parents share different perspectives that led to thoughtful and healthy decisions.

RESIST (THE NORM)

On a random Monday morning when I was finding it hard to drag myself out of bed, I received an email from someone who had met one of my student's at a dinner party. She wrote to me about how my student talked to her about gender being a spectrum and the need to resist societal gender norms. I sprung out of my bed in excitement, because I knew that this small victory would go a long way in the future. If we need more equity in society, I argue that it is important to resist social norms. This process begins with questioning language, attitudes and behaviors in our current social settings.

Hans Rosling (2019) asserts that the world is doing much better than it was decades ago. Contrary to popular belief, lesser people live in poverty, life expectancy around the globe has increased, and young and girls have more access to education than before. He is right. We are doing better on the more obvious indicators of development but for greater change to take place we need to shake up privilege and undo the more subtle and covert hints of difference in society. You do not need to be an activist, politician, or social worker to resist power and create change. We can start by resisting power through organic ways in our immediate settings (Apple, 2014). Actions that seem small but can go a long way in transforming society include, but are not limited to denouncing toxic masculinity in the workplace, calling out bigotry or racist remarks at family events, standing up for a classmate who is being bullied because of their ability, questioning media for its stereotypical depiction of marginalized groups, and many more. Although change is slow, we must use our privilege and voice to support it wherever we can (Paechter, 2001). Resistance and power are inseparable, and wherever there are relations to power, resistance plays an important role in refusing normative scripts and allowing subjectivity of experiences (Mohanty, 1989; Paechter, 2001).

CONCLUSION

On many days I still carry around the guilt of my privilege and feel like I need to be doing more with all this awareness. I constantly ask myself what I could be doing differently, and what more could society be doing to make our communities more inclusive. I wonder what my life would be like without my privilege – would the discomfort make me work harder? Would I just accept the fate of society and tell myself that this is how things have always been? In moments like these, I am reminded of my students from different years across different settings. All of them have participated in processes of undoing privilege and conceptualizing a better world with me. These moments from my classrooms fill me with hope for a better tomorrow. A tomorrow that is more accepting and respectful of *the others*. As I continue to marvel at the sunset over the Arabian Sea from my apartment, I am thinking of my students and the journey we are on to read, reflect, and resist. I highly recommend you join us.

REFERENCES

Apple, M. (2004). On analyzing hegemony: Systems management and the ideology of control. In M. Apple (ed.) *Ideology and curriculum* (3rd ed.), pp. 1–23. Routledge.

Apple, M. (2014). Regulating official knowledge: Whose curriculum is it anyway? In M. Apple (ed.) *Official knowledge* (3rd ed.), pp. 67–97. Routledge.

Banks, J. A. (2015). *Cultural diversity and education: Foundations, curriculum, and teaching.* Routledge.

Fook, J., & Askeland, G. A. (2007). Challenges of critical reflection: 'Nothing ventured, nothing gained'. *Social Work Education, 26*(5), 520–533.

Foucault, M. (1978). *The history of sexuality.* Pantheon.

Freire, P. (2018). *Pedagogy of the oppressed.* Bloomsbury.

hooks, b. (2014). *Teaching to transgress.* Routledge.

Johnson, A. G. (2006). *Privilege, power, and difference* (2nd ed.). McGraw Hill.

Kabeer, N. (2005). Gender equality and women's empowerment: A critical analysis of the third millennium development goal 1. *Gender & Development, 13*(1), 13–24.

Kamdar, B. (2020). India's rich prosper during the pandemic while its poor stand precariously at the edge. *The Diplomat.*

Kendall, F. E. (2006). *Understanding white privilege: Creating pathways to authentic relationships across race.* Routledge.

Mohanty, C. T. (1989). On race and voice: Challenges for liberal education in the 1990s. *Cultural Critique, 14,* 179–208.

Mohanty, C. T. (2003). "Under western eyes" revisited: Feminist solidarity through anticapitalist struggles. *Signs: Journal of Women in culture and Society, 28*(2), 499–535.

Oxford English Dictionary. (2020). Privilege. https://www.lexico.com/definition/privilege

Paechter, C. (2001). Using poststructuralist ideas in gender theory and research. *Investigating gender: Contemporary Perspectives in Education,* 41–51.

Rosling, H. (2019). *Factfulness.* Flammarion.

Samuels, G. M., & Ross-Sheriff, F. (2008). Identity, oppression, and power: Feminisms and intersectionality theory. *Affilia, 23*(1), 5–9.

Sensoy, Ö., & Marshall, E. (2010). Missionary girl power: Saving the 'Third World' one girl at a time. *Gender and Education, 22*(3), 295–311.

36

RACISM

Applying Behavior Analysis to Dismantle Racism:
From Ideas to Action

Kozue Matsuda, Yors Garcia, Robyn Catagnus, and Julie Ackerlund Brandt

INTRODUCTION

Racism is a complex cultural phenomenon that is revealed through the behaviors (Arhin & Thyer, 2004; Elliott-Cooper, 2018) of a dominant group in relation to the oppressed (Adair & Howell, 1988). It is "the exclusion that occurs when the critical consequence is the use of the institutions of society to deny a group or group member the opportunity, means or benefits for any available alternative that is available to others in the society" (Robbins & Layng, 2012, p. 5). Despite hundreds of years of resistance to racism, it continues to this day (Nelson et al., 2013).

Various researchers have described the upholding of *systemic* racism by societal and governmental policies as a particularly urgent crisis (see Feagin, 2010, Preface). Racism has dire outcomes for those who experience it: increased risk of mental and physical health problems (Williams et al., 2019), bullying (Xu et al., 2020), hindered employment prospects (Hicks et al., 2020), exclusionary school discipline (Sondel et al., 2019), conflicts with police (Pierson et al., 2020; Siegel et al., 2019), and violence and death (Guerin, 2005). Even so, behavior analysis (BA) has been used as the basis for surprisingly little racism research (Li, 2020; Matsuda et al., 2020; Melendez et al., 2020). This chapter briefly reviews the existing research, and it challenges the field to move from ideas toward actual dismantling of racism.

BA accounts for complex human behaviors, including bias, prejudice, and overt racism (Dixon et al., 2018; Matsuda et al., 2020). However, early studies of race and racial integration (cf. Hauserman et al., 1973) were followed by little further BA research (see Li, 2020; Matsuda et al., 2020; Melendez et al., 2020). As a result, the field's contributions to equity include several articles featuring traditional behavior-analytic accounts of how racial prejudice is learned and mitigated and studies of implicit bias based on derived relational responding (see Matsuda et al., 2020).

This paucity of research in itself presents a challenge, in that the field lacks shared technical definitions for the relevant phenomena. For now, we define racial *prejudice* as "unreasoned dislike, hostility, or antagonism towards, or discrimination against, a race . . . or other class of people" (Oxford English Dictionary, 2019). Discriminatory behaviors, including verbal ones, directed at members of an ethnic group (Guerin, 2005; Lai et al., 2016) may be defined as "the distancing of a group or group member by removing oneself from that group or individual" (Robbins & Layng, 2012, p. 5). In vernacular speech, *bias* is often a synonym for prejudice and can be overt or unintentional; however, bias need not be negative. Patterns of biased responding can consistently lead to unfair outcomes for a group. Most BA bias research relates to behaviors that are implicitly and unintentionally influenced by cues related to race or ethnicity (De Houwer, 2019), studied though a conceptual lens of derived relational responding (DRR; Critchfield et al., 2018), which is closely related to BA. A brief summary of both lines of research – traditional BA and DRR research – follows.

BEHAVIOR-ANALYTIC ACCOUNT OF BIAS

A behavior-analytic account of bias relies on basic behavioral principles to explain how prejudice and racism develop through direct relations: respondent learning, operant learning, observational learning, and stimulus generalization. *Respondent learning* occurs when a neutral stimulus (NS) is paired with an unconditioned stimulus (UCS) such that it becomes a conditioned stimulus (CS). It elicits a conditioned response (CR), topographically similar to the unconditioned response (UCR) elicited by the UCS. For example, when seeing a black person (NS) is paired with seeing a violent action, such as looting (UCS), the UCS might elicit feelings of anger or fear (UCR). Pairing the NS with the UCS may subsequently result in the sight of another black person (CS) eliciting fear or anger (CR). *Operant learning* through direct reinforcement or punishment contingencies may also account for the development of bias (Arhin & Thyer, 2004). For example, when a white child bullies an Asian child and peers laugh or join in the teasing, if the peers' social responses are reinforcing, then bullying is likely to occur again as overt acts of racism.

Conversely, *observational learning* involves learning through indirect contingencies such as watching others' racist behaviors (Skinner et al., 2019). For example, when teachers punish students of color more severely than white students (Nowicki, 2018), white students learn to treat others inequitably. They may also be learning that they, as white students, can engage in some behaviors that students of color cannot. Bias may also develop via *stimulus generalization*, when control of a behavior extends beyond identical stimuli to stimuli that are similar to those that were initially learned. Consider representations of minority groups in news outlets, social media, and entertainment, which often focus on negative or narrow stereotypical portrayals (Ramasubramanian & Oliver, 2007). With repeated exposure to such media, a person may speak, think, or behave as if everyone in that group is similar, even in different contexts or with varied individuals.

Unfortunately, BA conceptual analyses of racism have not led to experimentally validated interventions through behavior-analytic approach alone. It could be argued that traditional BA has neglected the conceptual account of racism and related interventions despite the potential for innovative, systemic, or community-changing mitigation strategies derived from our science.

Interestingly, many behavior-analytic procedures have been researched in other disciplines, such as education, and found to be effective alternatives to discriminatory practices. For example, a number of alternatives to racially inequitable zero-tolerance policies in schools, such as reinforcing and praising positive behavior, video modeling, and social skills instruction, are drawn from or researched in behavior science (De Jesús et al., 2016; Diffey & Mignone, 2017). However, as behavior analysts, we still are not using these to reduce inequities, and we feel uncomfortable or unprepared to do so (Henry et al., 2020). At the time of this writing, the authors know of only one published, applied experimental BA study specifically designed to impact racial inequity (Knochel et al., 2020).

DERIVED RELATIONAL RESPONDING (DRR) ACCOUNT OF BIAS

Over the past two decades, functional contextualists have developed a more robust line of experimental and conceptual research that explains racism as DRR. To this end, studies have examined the acquisition of prejudicial beliefs (Watt et al., 1991), social categorization (McGlinchey & Keenan, 1997), and racial attitudes related to skin color (de Carvalho &

de Rose, 2014; Mizael et al., 2016). Although this research overlaps or may integrate with traditional behavioral principles (Critchfield et al., 2018), it is conceptually underpinned by relational frame theory (RFT) and differs in its account of racism.

RFT explains human language and cognition in terms of patterns of generalized responding, from exposure to reinforced exemplars or an extended history of these (Barnes-Holmes et al., 2010). Moreover, it purports that traditional BA may not fully explain how bias develops (Critchfield et al., 2018; de Carvalho & de Rose, 2014; Dixon et al., 2009; McGlinchey & Keenan, 1997) without an account of DRR (de Carvalho & de Rose, 2014; Dixon et al., 2009). For example, a person who watches the news may learn an arbitrary relation between black skin (Stimulus A) and depictions of poverty (Stimulus B) (Dixon, 2017). When the media then depict those who live in poverty as lazy and dependent on government welfare (Stimulus C), these pairings could lead to the conclusions "Poor people are black" or "Black people are lazy and dependent on welfare," despite real-world evidence to the contrary. When this learning repeatedly occurs across a society, other problematic racist relational responses can emerge – and persist – without direct exposure to reinforcement contingencies (for more on DRR and stimulus equivalence, see Critchfield et al., 2018; Stewart et al., 2013).

HOW RACISM PERSISTS: STIMULUS EQUIVALENCE

DRR research confirms that people learn biased and prejudiced behaviors. Along with studying the development of racism, functional contextualists have experimentally measured[1] and examined bias mitigation. The limited evidence from these studies suggests that when biases and prejudices are relations that already exist, it is difficult to establish and construct new relations. Not surprisingly, racism has proven difficult to eradicate, and DRR studies have indeed confirmed that biased responding is persistent. For example, in Northern Ireland, where religious disputes are prominent social issues, researchers found that well-established relations affected the learning of new relations. Specifically, Catholic participants failed to demonstrate positive equivalence relations in the presence of Protestant symbols (Strand & Arntzen, 2020; Watt et al., 1991).

However, another experiment suggests that children's learning of new, positive relations may be more malleable than that of adults (McGlinchey & Keenan, 1997). This difference has been replicated (de Carvalho & de Rose, 2014), and it speaks to the importance of learning histories over time: Adults likely have longer histories in which their biases were reinforced than children do. Changing racial bias and prejudice is made difficult by pre-established relations and long learning histories (Dixon, Rehfeldt, et al., 2006; Dixon, Zlomke, & Rehfeldt, 2006), but DRR researchers nevertheless attempt to change problematic bias.

DRR RESEARCH ON CHANGING BIAS OR PREJUDICE

DRR researchers have examined whether it is possible to shift biases by teaching new relations between stimuli. For example, in one study where U.S. college students were asked to

---

1   Interested readers can learn more about implicit bias measurement based on DRR in studies on the implicit relational assessment procedure. See Barnes-Holmes et al. (2010); Drake et al. (2015); De Houwer (2019).

rate Middle Eastern males, American males, and everyday objects using a Likert-type scale ranging from 1 (*evil*) to 10 (*good*), participants demonstrated a bias toward rating Middle Eastern males as *evil* during pretesting. However, following match-to-sample training, they rated similar images as being more *good* – demonstrating the power of relational training for affecting preexisting prejudice functions. In another study, children who demonstrated negative biases relating to faces with black skin were able to learn new equivalence relations that reduced their biased responding (Mizael et al., 2016). Perhaps helping people learn new relations between stimuli that cue race, either through training or social interventions, can reduce racism.

Functional contextualists have also evaluated the utility of Acceptance and Commitment Training (ACTr), which is conceptually based on RFT, to reduce racism (Levin et al. 2016; Lillis & Hayes, 2007). The few prejudice reduction studies most closely related to BA have investigated ACTr interventions, which include the use of strategies such as mindfulness, acceptance, and committed action to align with personal values (Hayes et al., 2013). ACTr procedures such as *perspective-taking interventions, values clarification exercises*, and *mindfulness* might help decrease bias for those who suffer from bias. *Perspective-taking* interventions, or active viewing of others' experience, has been shown to reduce stereotyping, prejudice, and intergroup bias toward multiple ethnic groups (Adida et al., 2018; Galinsky & Ku, 2004; Galinsky & Moskowitz, 2000; Todd et al., 2011; Vescio et al., 2003). *Value clarification* has been shown to reduce stigma associated with racial minorities (Lillis & Hayes, 2007; West et al., 2013) and to clarify values (Cohen et al., 2006).

Behavior analysts commonly define *mindfulness* in relation to specific covert and overt behaviors (Andrews et al., 2020; Wolfgang et al., 2020) of contact with the present moment as one component of the ACT model (Hooper et al., 2010). Mindfulness has been found to cause a decrease in implicit race bias (Hooper et al., 2010; Lueke & Gibson, 2015; Proulx et al., 2018). Although ACTr was developed more than three decades ago (Hayes et al., 2013), it is only recently that behavior analysts have shown an interest in using this technology to decrease racism and prejudice (e.g., Matsuda et al., 2020; Melendez et al., 2020). The following section suggests several ways in which interested readers can explore racism and take action for change.

APPLYING IDEAS TO ACTION

Our world faces an entrenched problem of unfair, prejudicial behaviors of dominant groups toward oppressed ethnicities and races. Despite advocacy and resistance, racism has persisted for hundreds of years, across generations and cultures, and BA has done little to change these behavioral patterns. How, then, can we even begin to address so intractable a social problem?

The few BA and ACTr racism articles are either non-experimental or focused on implicit bias, but they do include numerous *ideas* for applied interventions. Accordingly, we hope that the field will waste no time in applying the science of BA to dismantle racism in support of social justice. Previously, we published a detailed list of ways in which behavior analysts can act to mitigate racism, including cultural self-reflection, community racism interventions, prejudice reduction, organizational management strategies, and studying the experiences of racism in our own field (Matsuda et al., 2020). We also enumerated ideas proposed by other BA and DRR researchers, such as reinforcing interracial socializing, altering listener behavior, punishing overt racism and modeling of racism, fostering intercultural relationships, using counter-reasoning, and providing behavioral training in cooperative learning (Arhin & Thyer, 2004; Flannelly & Flannelly, 2000). Guerin (2005) is another excellent source of detailed ideas for prejudice and racism interventions based on contextual and functional analyses of specific discriminatory behaviors.[2] Furthermore, nonlinear contingency analyses of the behaviors and emotions of racism may lead us in new directions (Robbins & Layng, 2012). Interestingly, an upcoming issue of one behavior-analytic journal is expected to focus on reducing systemic racism, thus expanding the BA literature base and likely offering still more ideas.

As we write this chapter, we are suffering from a viral pandemic during a time also described by the president of the American Psychological Association as a "racism pandemic" (American Psychological Association, 2020). We must confront society's increasing division by making effective efforts to enhance the science of behavior with a view to rejecting such divisions. The field has recently been inspired toward social justice, and we hope that with increased dialogue about racism and possible solutions (Sylvain et al., 2020), we can maintain this momentum, together harnessing the rage, anger, and sadness associated with racism to dismantle it altogether (Catagnus et al., 2020).

REFERENCES

Adair, M., & Howell, S. (1988). *The subjective side of politics, breaking old patterns, weaving new ties: Alliance building, and democracy at work.* Tools for Change.

Adida, C. L., Lo, A., & Platas, M. R. (2018). Perspective taking can promote short-term inclusionary behavior toward Syrian refugees. *Proceedings of the National Academy of Sciences of the United States of America, 115*(38), 9521–9526. https://doi.org/10.1073/pnas.1804002115

American Psychological Association. (2020). "We're living in a racism pandemic," says APA president [Press release]. https://www.apa.org/news/press/releases/2020/05/racism-pandemic

Andrews, M., Garcia, Y., Catagnus, R. M., & Gould, E. (2020). A survey of mindfulness-based interventions and clinical practice by behavior analysts [Manuscript submitted for publication].

Arhin, A., & Thyer, B. A. (2004). The causes of racial prejudice: A behavior-analytic perspective. In J. L. Chin (Ed.), *The psychology of prejudice and discrimination: Bias based on gender and sexual orientation* (pp. 1–20). Greenwood.

Barnes-Holmes, D., Barnes-Holmes, Y., & McEnteggart, C. (2020). Updating RFT (more field than frame) and its implications for process-based therapy. *The Psychological Record, 1*(20). https://doi.org/10.1007/s40732-019-00372-3

Barnes-Holmes, D., Murphy, A., Barnes-Holmes, Y., & Stewart, I. (2010). The Implicit Relational Assessment Procedure: Exploring the impact of private versus public contexts and the response latency criterion on pro-white and anti-black stereotyping among white Irish individuals. *The Psychological Record, 60*, 57–79. https://doi.org/10.1007/BF03395694

Catagnus, R., Umphrey, B., & Griffith, A. (2020). Anger, fear, and sadness: How emotions could help us end a pandemic of racism [Manuscript submitted for publication].

Cohen, G. L., Garcia, J., Apfel, N., & Master, A. (2006). Reducing the racial achievement gap: A social-psychological intervention. *Science, 313*(5791), 1307–1310. https://doi.org/10.1126/science.1128317

---

2 Guerin, who was trained as an experimental social psychologist, teaches social and community behavior interventions (among related topics) in Australia. He has had extensive training and experience with BA and incorporates many of its principles in his community-based research, which sometimes addresses racism and often focuses on partnerships with indigenous, refugee, and immigrant communities. Interested readers are encouraged to read his interdisciplinary work for actionable ideas for mitigating racism.

Critchfield, T. S., Barnes-Holmes, D., & Dougher, M. J. (2018). What Sidman did: Historical and contemporary significance of research on derived stimulus relations. *Perspectives on Behavioral Science, 41*, 9–32. https://doi.org/10.1007/s40614-018-0154-9

de Carvalho, M. P., & de Rose, J. C. (2014). Understanding racial attitudes through the stimulus equivalence paradigm. *The Psychological Record, 64*, 527–536. https://doi.org/10.1007/s40732-014-0049-4

De Houwer, J. (2019). Implicit bias is behavior: A functional-cognitive perspective on implicit bias. *Perspectives on Psychological Science, 14*, 835–840. https://doi.org/10.1177/1745691619855638

De Jesús, A., Hogan, J., Martinez, R., Adams, J., & Hawkins Lacy, T. (2016). Putting racism on the table: The implementation and evaluation of a novel racial equity and cultural competency training/consultation model in New York City. *Journal of Ethnic & Cultural Diversity in Social Work, 25*(4), 300–319. https://doi.org/10.1080/15313204.2016.1206497

Diffey, L., & Mignone, J. (2017). Implementing anti-racist pedagogy in health professional education: A realist review. *Health Education and Care, 2*, 1–9. https://doi.org/10.15761/HEC.1000114

Dixon, M. R., Belisle, J., Rehfeldt, R. A., & Root, W. B. (2018). Why we are still not acting to save the world: The upward challenge of a post-Skinnerian behavior science. *Perspectives on Behavior Science, 41*, 241–267. https://doi.org/10.1007/s40614-018-0162-9

Dixon, M. R., Branon, A., Nastally, B. L., & Mui, N. (2009). Examining prejudice towards Middle Eastern persons via a transformation of stimulus functions. *The Behavior Analyst Today, 10*, 295–318. https://doi.org/10.1037/h0100672

Dixon, M. R., Rehfeldt, R. A., Zlomke, K. R., & Robinson, A. (2006). Exploring the development and dismantling of equivalence classes involving terrorist stimuli. *The Psychological Record, 56*, 83–103. https://doi.org/10.1007/BF03395539

Dixon, M. R., Zlomke, K. M., & Rehfeldt, R. A. (2006). Restoring Americans' nonequivalent frames of terror: An application of relational frame theory. *The Behavior Analyst Today, 7*, 275–289. https://doi.org/10.1037/h0100153

Dixon, T. L. (2017). A dangerous distortion of our families: Representations of families, by race, in news and opinion media. Color of Change. https://colorofchange.org/dangerousdistortion

Drake, C. E., Kramer, S., Sain, T., Swiatek, R., Kohn, K., & Murphy, M. (2015). Exploring the reliability and convergent validity of implicit racial evaluations. *Behavior and Social Issues, 24*, 68–87. https://doi.org/10.5210/bsi.v24i0.5496

Elliott-Cooper, A. (2018). Conceptualizing racism: Breaking the chains of racially accommodative language. *Ethnic and Racial Studies, 41*(3), 586–588. https://doi.org/10.1080/01419870.2017.1334941

Feagin, J. R. (2010). *The white racial frame: Centuries of racial framing and counter-framing*. Routledge.

Flannelly, L. T., & Flannelly, K. J. (2000). Reducing people's judgment bias about their level of knowledge. *The Psychological Record, 50*(3), 587–600. https://doi.org/10.1007/BF03395373

Galinsky, A. D., & Ku, G. (2004). The effects of perspective-taking on prejudice: The moderating role of self-evaluation. *Personality and Social Psychology Bulletin, 30*(5), 594–604. https://doi.org/10.1177/0146167203262802

Galinsky, A. D., & Moskowitz, G. B. (2000). Perspective-taking: Decreasing stereotype expression, stereotype accessibility, and in-group favoritism. *Journal of Personality and Social Psychology, 78*(4), 708–724. https://doi.org/10.1037//0022-3514.78.4.708

Guerin, B. (2003). Combating prejudice and racism: New interventions from a functional analysis of racist language. *Journal of Community & Applied Social Psychology, 13*, 29–45. https://doi.org/10.1002/casp.699

Guerin, B. (2005). Combating everyday racial discrimination without assuming "racists" or "racism": New intervention ideas from a contextual analysis. *Behavior and Social Issues, 14*, 46–70. https://doi.org/10.5210/bsi.v14i1.120

Hauserman, N., Walen, S. R., & Behling, M. (1973). Reinforced racial integration in the first grade: A study in generalization. *Journal of Applied Behavior Analysis, 6*(2), 193–200. https://doi.org/10.1901/jaba.1973.6-193

Hayes, S. C., Levin, M. E., Plumb-Vilardaga, J., Villatte, J. L., & Pistorello, J. (2013). Acceptance and commitment therapy and contextual behavioral science: Examining the progress of a distinctive model of behavioral and cognitive therapy. *Behavior Therapy, 44*(2), 180–198. https://doi.org/10.1016/j.beth.2009.08.002

Henry, K. K., Catagnus, R. M., Griffith, A. K., & Garcia, Y. A. (2020). Ending the school-to-prison pipeline: Perception and experience with zero-tolerance policies and interventions to address racial inequality [Manuscript submitted for publication].

Hicks, C., Kibibi, N., & Thomson, W. (2020). 137 A meta-analysis assessing the outcome of occupational injury by minority employee race. *Injury Prevention, 26* (suppl. 1), A47.3–A48. https://doi.org/10.1136/injuryprev-2020-savir.120

Hooper, N., Villatte, M., Neofotistou, E., & McHugh, L. (2010). The effects of mindfulness versus thought suppression on implicit and explicit measures of experiential avoidance. *International Journal of Behavioral Consultation and Therapy, 6*, 233–244. https://doi.org/10.1037/h0100910

Knochel, A. E., Blair, K. C., Kincaid, D., & Randazzo, A. (2020). Promoting equity in teachers' use of behavior-specific praise with self-monitoring and performance feedback. *Journal of Positive Behavior Interventions*, 1098300720951939. https://doi.org/10.1177/1098300720951939

Lai, C. K., Skinner, A. L., Cooley, E., Murrar, S., Brauer, M., Devos, T., Calanchini, J., Xiao, Y. J., Pedram, C., Christopher K., Marshburn, C. K., Simon, S., Blanchar, J. C., Joy-Gaba, J. A., Conway, J., Redford, L., Klein, R. A., Roussos, G., Schellhaas, F. M. H., Burns, M . . . & Nosek, B. A. (2016). Reducing implicit racial preferences: II. Intervention effectiveness across time. *Journal of Experimental Psychology: General, 145*, 1001–1016. https://doi.org/10.1037/a0036260

Levin, M. E., Luoma, J. B., Vilardaga, R., Lillis, J., Nobles, R., & Hayes, S. C. (2016). Examining the role of psychological inflexibility, perspective taking, and empathic concern in generalized prejudice. *Journal of Applied Social Psychology, 46*, 180–191. https://doi.org/10.1111/jasp.12355

Li, A. (2020). Solidarity: The role of non-black people of color in promoting racial equity. *Behavior Analysis and Practice*. Advance online publication. https://doi.org.10.31234/osf.io/pmqhn

Lillis, J., & Hayes, S. C. (2007). Applying acceptance, mindfulness, and values to the reduction of prejudice: A pilot study. *Behavior Modification, 31*, 389–411. https://doi.org/10.1177/0145445506298413

Lueke, A., & Gibson, B. (2015). Mindfulness meditation reduces implicit age and race bias: The role of reduced automaticity of responding. *Social Psychological and Personality Science, 6*(3), 284–291. https://doi.org/10.1177/1948550614559651

Matsuda, K., Garcia, Y., Catagnus, R., & Brandt, J. A. (2020). Can behavior analysis help us understand and reduce racism? A review of the current literature. *Behavior Analysis in Practice*, 1–12. https://doi.org/10.1007/s40617-020-00411-4

McGlinchey, A., & Keenan, M. (1997). Stimulus equivalence and social categorization in Northern Ireland. *Behavior and Social Issues, 7*(2), 113–128. https://doi.org/10.5210/bsi.v7i2.310.

Melendez, J. L., Tan, I. M. C., Lau, J. C., & Leung, J. (2020). Practical resources for talking to children with autism about systemic racism. *Behavior Analysis and Practice*. Advance online publication. https://doi.org/10.31234/osf.io/jkh4b

Mizael, T. M., de Almeida, J. H., Silveira, C. C., & de Rose, J. C. (2016). Changing racial bias by transfer of functions in equivalence classes. *Psychological Record, 66*, 451–462. https://doi.org/10.1007/s40732-016-0185-0

Nelson, J. C., Adams, G., & Salter, P. S. (2013). The Marley hypothesis: Denial of racism reflects ignorance of history. *Psychological Science, 24*(2), 213–218. https://doi.org/10.1177/0956797612451466

Nowicki, J. M. (2018). *K–12 education: Discipline disparities for black students, boys, and students with disabilities: Report to Congressional Requesters (GAO-18-258)*. U.S. Government Accountability Office. https://www.gao.gov/products/GAO-18-258

Oxford English Dictionary. (2019). Prejudice. https://www.lexico.com/definition/prejudice

Pierson, E., Simoiu, C., Overgoor, J., Corbett-Davies, S., Jenson, D., Shoemaker, A., Ramachandran, V., Barghouty, P., Phillips, C., Shroff, R., & Goel, S. (2020). A large-scale analysis of racial disparities in police stops across the United States. *Nature Human Behaviour*, 1–10. https://doi.org/10.1038/s41562-020-0858-1

Proulx, J., Croff, R., Oken, B., Aldwin, C. M., Fleming, C., Bergen-Cico, D., Le, T., & Noorani, M. (2018). Considerations for research and development of culturally relevant mindfulness interventions in American minority communities. *Mindfulness, 9,* 361–370. https://doi.org/10.1007/s12671-017-0785-z

Ramasubramanian, S., & Oliver, M. B. (2007). Activating and suppressing hostile and benevolent racism: Evidence for comparative media stereotyping. *Media Psychology, 9*(3), 623–646. https://doi.org/10.1080/15213260701283244

Robbins, J., & Layng, R. R. (2012). *Toward a new consequentialism: Nonlinear contingency analysis and the understanding of behavior* [Paper presentation.] Association for Behavior Analysis International Conference on Theory and Philosophy, Santa Fe, NM, United States.

Siegel, M., Sherman, R., Li, C., & Knopov, A. (2019). The relationship between racial residential segregation and black-white disparities in fatal police shootings at the city level, 2013–2017. *Journal of the National Medical Association, 111*(6), 580–587. https://doi.org/10.1016/j.jnma.2019.06.003

Skinner, A. L., Olson, K. R., & Meltzoff, A. N. (2019). Acquiring group bias: Observing other people's nonverbal signals can create social group biases. *Journal of Personality and Social Psychology.* Advance online publication. https://doi.org/10.1037/pspi0000218

Sondel, B., Kretchmar, K., & Hadley Dunn, A. (2019). "Who do these people want teaching their children?" White saviorism, colorblind racism, and anti-blackness in "No Excuses" charter schools. *Urban Education.* https://doi.org/10.1177/0042085919842618

Stewart, I., McElwee, J., & Ming, S. (2013). Language generativity, response generalization, and derived relational responding. *The Analysis of Verbal Behavior, 29,* 137–155. https://doi.org/10.1007/BF03393131

Strand, R. C., & Arntzen, E. (2020). Social categorization and stimulus equivalence: A systematic replication. *The Psychological Record, 70*(1), 47–63. https://doi.org/10.1007/s40732-019-00364-3

Sylvain, M. M., Knochel, A. E., Gingles, D., & Catagnus, R. M. (2020). ABA while Black: The impact of racism and performative allyship on Black behaviorists. [Manuscript submitted for publication].

Todd, A. R., Bodenhausen, G. V., Richeson, J. A., & Galinsky, A. D. (2011). Perspective taking combats automatic expressions of racial bias. *Journal of Personality and Social Psychology, 100,* 1027–1042. https://doi.org/10.1037/a0022308

Vescio, T. K., Sechrist, G. B., & Paolucci, M. P. (2003). Perspective taking and prejudice reduction: The mediational role of empathy arousal and situational attributions. *European Journal of Social Psychology, 33*(4), 455–472. https://doi.org/10.1002/ejsp.163

Watt, A., Keenan, M., Barnes, D., & Cairns, E. (1991). Social categorization and stimulus equivalence. *The Psychological Record, 41,* 33–50. https://doi.org/10.1007/BF03395092

West, L. M., Graham, J. R., & Roemer, L. (2013). Functioning in the face of racism: Preliminary findings on the buffering role of values clarification in a Black American sample. *Journal of Contextual Behavioral Science, 2*(1–2), 1–8. https://doi.org/10.1016/j.jcbs.2013.03.003

Williams, D. R., Lawrence, J. A., Davis, B. A., & Vu, C. (2019). Understanding how discrimination can affect health. *Health Services Research, 54,* 1374–1388. https://doi.org/10.1111/1475-6773.13222

Wolfgang, H., Catagnus, R. M., & Garcia, Y. (2020). Should behavior analysis include mindfulness? A systematic literature review [Manuscript submitted for publication].

Xu, M., Macrynikola, N., Waseem, M., & Miranda, R. (2020). Racial and ethnic differences in bullying: Review and implications for intervention. *Aggression and Violent Behavior, 50,* 101340. https://doi.org/10.1016/j.avb.2019.101340

37

RURAL ACCESS

Rural Access to Ethical and Appropriate Behavior Analytic Treatment in Schools

R. Nicolle Carr

INTRODUCTION

I have met some of the most passionate and dedicated teachers and administrators in some of the smallest and most rural schools here in Oklahoma. There truly are many wonderful aspects of rural education from the dedication of the teachers to the all-hands-on-deck attitude of the administration. All 50 states have rural areas as defined by the USDA-Economic Research Service (USDA-ERS, 2019); no state is immune. With rural school districts often comes smaller budgets, lack of expert personnel/resources and cultural stigmas to overcome.

OKLAHOMA

Oklahoma is the 20th largest state in the United States with about 69,900 square miles and a population of 3,930,864 (US News, 2019). We are estimated to have about 36% of our land considered rural with the Oklahoma City Metro, Norman, Edmond, and Tulsa Metro serving as the largest cities. In that nearly 4 million people, we have 140 BCBA/BCBA-Ds currently on the BACB registry (12 BCBA-Ds, 128 BCBAs). Of those behavior analysts serving the vast need in Oklahoma – from schools to clinics – just under 30% live outside these metro areas (BACB, 2020a). The difficulties seen in rural areas with increased poverty rates as indicated by the percentage of students eligible for free and reduced lunch (e.g., 62.5% for Oklahoma) (NCES, 2017), school based BCBAs can start to run into seemingly impenetrable barriers.

ETHICAL BARRIERS

A survey sent to all members of the state affiliate of ABAI called Oklahoma Association of Behavior Analysts (OKABA) found Multiple Relationships and Conflict of Interest (1.11), Supervisory Competence and Supervisory Volume (4.2/4.3) and Boundaries of Competence (4th Core Principle) to be the codes most violated from the *Ethics Code for Behavior Analysts* (furthermore known as the BACB Code; BACB, 2020b). Of course, Oklahoma is not the only state with low numbers of BCBAs finding themselves in unique ethical situations. As Young-Pelton and Dotson (2017) note, the truth of the matter may not be the codes violated most often in rural versus urban or metro areas but in how they are avoided or remediated.

Multiple relationships was the number one reported violation for BCBAs in smaller communities. Small towns breed close knit families, inter-tangled friend groups, gossip, and hearsay. Where one goes to church, what they do on Saturday night, and parent marital happiness may be information a clinician has going into a case in the schools – information usually unknown when working with a client/student. In this case, multiple relationships for the behavior analyst can occur in many forms. A clinician may know the parents well, the teacher may be a good friend, or the client may even play on the same sports team as the clinician's child. In some instances, the dilemma comes down to determining if it is better to refer a child out to another provider or keeping a case. Considerations include; if there are other providers available, the severity of the problem behavior if there is a waiting list, and the degree of relationship between the provider and the potential client (to name only a few).

[*A favorite response I give my students is – It Depends. It depends because if you are the aunt to a child referred to you – it is probably best to find a new provider. If you are the best friend of the child's mom's cousin and you have hung out at the same church picnics – this may be a case you can take. It depends. In small towns, a provider may run into a client at the grocery store. Or church. Or any other public location. A provider may be best friends with the teacher. If a clinician lives and works in the same rural area, it is near impossible to not receive a referral for a potential client with more than one connection. It is important to determine if unbiased treatment can be provided, if it is safe to refer to a waiting list and what changes need to occur to the current relationship until the treatment is provided or terminated.*]

The second ethical issue providers in states with limited numbers of BCABs may face is finding supervision and receiving appropriate education due to their location. For example, of the 140 BCBAs in Oklahoma, only 64 are noted to have taken the supervision training and are willing to train others. Of those, only 10% live outside the metro area making it near impossible to cover all students needing supervision outside these parameters. Teachers (or anyone with a daytime job) needing supervision, for example, find it extremely difficult to fulfill the required hours without using tele-supervision, moving, or quitting their job. In a state with low rates of certified teachers, that just creates a new set of problems if certified teachers are taken out of a classroom so they can receive supervision in behavior analysis.

Luckily, there are many BCBAs willing to supervise across the United States who are competent. In some cases, it is all they do. Facebook and Social Media groups have lists of tele-supervision resources. Finding en-vivo experiences can be difficult for the more rural areas – but continued dedication on the part of the student is important. One can reach out to local universities and ask for resources. Find the state affiliated ABAI group or other Special Interest Groups and make connections. Finding someone willing to work with a supervisee in a rural area can be accomplished but it takes dedication to finding that person. Once options become available, the potential supervisee should be sure to ask how many other supervisees the supervisor has had previously, how many they currently have, and how many times, if any, they can observe in person (or will it all be video recordings, etc.). Use of behavior skills training and behavior specific praise from a supervisor is what will make or break, oftentimes, a new supervisee. Finding a good fit for both people is imperative to the relationship working. The time spent interviewing each other at the start will be worth it in the long term.

Finally, boundaries of competence can easily be violated in rural areas. Behavior analysts are asked to make tough choices daily. Prioritize behaviors to treat. Prioritize cases to take. Triage the self-injurious cases and aggressive cases to clinicians who have prior experience. Give the feeding issues to those with that background. But what happens when the closest person with that background is three hours away with a waiting list? A clinician may decide to take the case.

There is not currently a standard on how the BACB or ABAI determine what is and is not in a BCBAs boundary of competence – only what is in their scope of practice as outlined in the task list (Brodhead et al., 2018). Webinars, podcasts, and journal articles on the topic may be a good place to start, but going to work with someone who specializes in that area is the ultimate method to obtain understanding of the topic. Many working adults are unable to take off work and from family obligations to travel elsewhere to engage in an internship-like learning opportunity; however, reaching out to those cited in the literature and finding a mentor in the area to help you with the case is highly advised if referring out is not in the best interest of the client.

Rarely does one BCBA/BCBA-D have a boundary of competence and experience that can fulfill all areas of need. However, it comes back to *It Depends*. Is a mentor available in the state which might allow one to take the case with continued mentorship while seeking out education on the topic? Or, is it safer to put the child on a waiting list for the next BCBA who might have that area of specialty in the near vicinity and have availability? Each situation is unique. As Brodhead and others discuss (2018), the BACB does not currently define what our competences are or how they are obtained. Due to this, a gray area on this ethical code remains and the behavior analyst must determine the best way to do no harm to the potential client while remaining within his/her boundaries.

RESOURCES

A lack of resources permeates rural education. That might be in the form of staff, money, time, or knowledge. Many rural schools operate with volunteer staff helping in classrooms and in offices. Couple that with teachers in some states receiving emergency certification to teach and a perfect storm of ineffective strategies and interventions may be at play in a classroom. When going into a rural situation, an evaluation and balancing act of what SHOULD be done has to be compared to what CAN be done. Asking a single teacher to take frequency data on a high rate behavior in a classroom with ten other students with autism might be the best data collection program. However, if it is not a feasible option for that teacher, a partial interval recording or permanent product data collection program may be needed. Or, can they train the parent volunteer who often works in the library to take data? Or, can two teachers swap out part of their planning period one day to take data on a student in each other's class. There might not be an ideal way to handle a situation when a lack of staff is the issue, but being creative can sometimes lead to a few extra hands when needed.

A lack of funding can lead to a host of issues from not being able to pay for outside consultants (a BCBA included) for the number of hours or the amount of services needed. Consider what the school can do and work within it. This might include an intense training for two hours for various staff versus two hours of data collection that cannot be turned into an intervention to be implemented due to a lack of funds. Similarly, do not recommend a school buy program XX for a student without also providing a low – tech/less expensive option that could have similar benefits. Telling a district that only a specific program will help them with a specific issue is not likely to get funded. However, finding ways to bring in parts of that program or showing alternative methods that can be made with supplies already at the school based on our science might get funded.

When barriers are the result of a lack of knowledge in a topic – for the teacher, staff, or administration at a school – work with the administration to have a future Professional Development day target those areas. Or, a behavior analyst can host a training for school staff willing to invest their time. Providing a large scale training prior to the start of the school year can also help teachers have the knowledge from day one. Investing effort to teach the science of our field to those willing to listen can reap more benefits than working with individual teachers only during times of crisis.

OTHER THOUGHTS: BUY-IN

Since staffing is often low, getting buy-in from the staff is critical. Going into a classroom with an air of importance will destroy the olive branch the teacher may be willing to give. This goes so far as to what one wears to a classroom. For example, when I go to my rural schools, I will leave the suit at home. Most of my teachers are in jeans and a t-shirt. I will put on jeans, a white t-shirt, and a blazer, at most. No heels. Why? Because I need to get on the floor with the students and the teacher and show that I am in it to help. I am willing to get bitten. I am willing to have snot wiped on my arms too. I am not better than anyone else in that classroom and I have to show those who are there that I am in the trenches with them for that day. It is the small things that will help you with buy-in from school staff.

A second consideration and possibly more important is the culture of rural areas. Often, punishment in the form of spankings/time out are a default 'discipline technique' used without hesitation. There may be an appeal for the behavior analyst to also use punishment initially or quickly within a program. The ethical code does not allow for such hair trigger use of punishment so a full disclosure to the parent/teacher may be needed on the steps one may attempt first before moving to a more restrictive procedure, if needed. Careful steps are to be taken here as this is one more place where the olive branch can be rescinded. Acknowledging the need and desire for a quick change in behavior is important and a middle ground both parties can usually agree on. It is the delivery, however, that can make or break the relationship between analyst and consumer.

CONCLUSION

A fundamental lack of resources is often the issue when violations to the code and appropriate treatment occur. The lack of time, people, knowledge, and money are often the root cause with the lack of money to pay for knowledgeable people at the crux of many ill attempts to provide quality treatment. This combination results in piecemeal treatment plans, too large a caseload, or an analyst limping through a case outside their boundary of competence. All of which, of course, can lead to ineffective treatment.

It is not the case that most people who violate the ethical code or provide lackluster treatment do so intentionally or with ill-will toward those whom they are treating. Rather, one wakes up and realizes they are knee deep in a treatment plan without the right people or support to do it optimally. How they handle the slippery slope they have somersaulted to the bottom of is where adherence to the code and a potentially successful outcome are found. One step at a time, one barrier at a time – effective treatment can reach rural school districts and provide effective and evidence-based interventions.

REFERENCES

Brodhead, M. T., Quigley, S. P., & Wilczynski, S. M. (2018). A call for discussion about scope of competence in behavior analysis. *Behavior Analysis in Practice, 11*(4), 424–435. https://doi.org/10.1007/s40617-018-00303-8

Behavior Analyst Certification Board. (2020a) *Certificant registry*: Oklahoma. https://www.bacb.com/services/o.php?page=101135

Behavior Analyst Certification Board. (2020b). *Ethics code for behavior analysts*. Author.

National Center for Education Statistics (NCES). (2019, April). Table 204.10. Number and percentage of public school students eligible for free and reduced price lunch, by state: selected years, 2000–01 through 2016–17. https://nces.ed.gov/programs/digest/d18/tables/dt18_204.10.asp

United States Department of Agriculture/Economic Research Service (USDA-ERS). (2019, October 23). Rural classification: Overview. https://www.ers.usda.gov/topics/rural-economy-population/rural-classifications/

US News and World Report. (2019). Best states: Oklahoma. https://www.usnews.com/news/best-states/oklahoma

Young-Pelton, C. A., & Dotson, T. D. (2017). Ethical issues in rural programs for behavior analysis for students with disabilities. *Rural Special Education Quarterly, 36*(1), 38–48. https://doi.org/10.1177/8756870517703407

38

SEXUAL HARASSMENT

Sexual Harassment in the Modern Era

Connie B. Newman and Kim Templeton

INTRODUCTION

Sexual harassment is deeply rooted in society and influenced by long-standing social norms that sexualize and objectify women and assume that women and sexual or gender minorities hold inferior status. It occurs in educational institutions, housing, on the street, and in diverse workplaces including healthcare, law, government, the military, food services, retail, and film.

The definition of sexual harassment encompasses sexual coercion, unwanted sexual attention, and gender harassment or bias. Gender harassment manifests as insulting and hostile attitudes and behaviors towards members of one gender, whether men, women, or non-binary individuals. Harassment usually indicates a desire to exert power, rather than sexual attraction. Consequences for the victim include depression, anxiety, burnout, lower productivity, loss of confidence, and slower career advancement. Fears of retaliation lead to fewer reports.

Strategies to address sexual harassment include vocal support and actions, commitment to change by leadership, anti-harassment policies, training, safe reporting procedures, investigation of complaints, and corrective actions. Ending sexual harassment necessitates a profound change in culture and attitudes. Addressing this issue is essential and should not be delayed until more women are promoted to leadership positions. Women and men must continue to speak against this behavior, which can have negative and profound professional and personal impact, and work together to eliminate sexual harassment from the workplace.

Equity for women in the United States during the 20th century is evident from ratification of the 19th amendment in 1920, giving women the right to vote, and passage of Title VII of the Civil Rights Act of 1964, which prohibits discrimination and harassment (including sexual harassment) in many, but not all, workplaces (Loria, 2017; Turk, 2016). Yet, despite Title VII, sexually harassing behavior continues in the workplace, and in many instances is not reported for fear of retaliation or that nothing would be done. In 2006, Tarana Burke coined the phrase "MeToo" to raise awareness of sexual harassment in the workplace, and in 2017 the hashtag #MeToo went viral on social media. Women all over the world began to acknowledge that they too had been victims.

Sexual harassment has nothing to do with sexual attraction but is an attempt to maintain the status quo. It occurs in educational institutions, housing, and in diverse workplaces such as academia, medicine and healthcare, law, the government, the military, and multiple industries including food services, retail, manufacturing, hospitality, film, music, sports, and media. Sexual harassment can be targeted at peers, students or trainees, and, in the case of healthcare professionals, at patients. This essay will discuss the definition of sexual harassment, historical antecedents, prevalence, consequences for the victim and perpetrator, and potential strategies for prevention and intervention.

DEFINITIONS

While the term "sexual harassment" is frequently thought of as rape, sexual assault is the least common but most egregious form of harassment. The definition of sexual harassment has evolved and become more inclusive, now also including comments or acts that reflect gender bias or discrimination. Legal definitions of sexual harassment comprise both "quid pro quo" harassment, in which an opportunity or positive evaluation related to a job, a profession, or education is contingent upon one or more sexual acts, and those acts that result in a hostile work environment (U.S. Equal Employment Opportunity Commission, n.d.). A hostile work environment may be created by one or more of the following: using crude language to address women, belittling statements, objectification of women as sexual objects, or posting pictures of a sexual nature in the office or in a work-related email. Psychologists have broadened the definition of sexual harassment to include sexual coercion, unwanted sexual attention, and gender harassment or bias. The term gender harassment is defined as behaviors that show insulting, hostile, and/or derogatory attitudes towards members of one gender, whether men, women, or non-binary individuals (Fitzgerald et al., 1995; Rotundo et al., 2001).

Sexual harassment is not always targeted toward women, although women more commonly are the victims. Perpetrators are more often men. The most common type of sexual harassment is gender harassment or bias (National Academies of Sciences, Engineering, and Medicine, 2018), which indicates hostility towards women (Leskinen et al., 2011), especially those who do not conform to gender roles (Berdahl, 2007). Gender harassment permeates the culture of an institution or organization. As such, it may not be directed toward a specific person but can be seen in the attitudes, language, hiring and promotion practices, and even in the pictures or posters displayed. The perception and impact of sexual harassment may vary by race, ethnicity, sexual preference, and other social factors (Collins, 2015). Women of color, for example, may perceive sexual harassment as both gender discrimination and race discrimination. While harassment is frequently reported among those earlier in their training or careers, this is an issue that can be faced by women of any age; those who are older may become victims of harassment by those who resent the positions of authority that women achieve, using harassment to attempt to level the playing field. Older women in the workforce also face bias based on both gender and age (Templeton et al., 2020).

Street harassment is a form of sexual harassment which occurs in public, and is commonly directed towards women, or sometimes gay men, who are walking either alone or in a group. It may involve verbal and non-verbal behavior, and may include humiliating comments, objectionable language, and threats (Thompson, 1994). It can make some women feel powerless and embarrassed. They may be afraid to react, for fear of rape or murder. Street harassment can occur regardless of how a woman is dressed but the blame is frequently placed on the victim, rather than the perpetrator (Thompson, 1994). One effect of street harassment is that women stay home where they feel safe, which can impact their ability to work and unfortunately, reinforce the notion that a woman's place is in the home, rather than in public.

HISTORICAL ATTITUDES TOWARDS WOMEN

Sexually harassing behavior is deeply rooted in human society and has a complex etiology. Today, evidence suggests that sexually harassing behavior is not primarily the result of sexual attraction which has a biological basis, but rather motivated by a desire (unconscious or conscious) to exert power over women, placing women at all levels of an organization, including those in leadership roles, at risk (McLaughlin et al., 2012).

Although testosterone is responsible for libido, and along with estrogen, influences brain development, there is little evidence to show that testosterone levels within a normal range correlate with aggression. Stereotypical gender roles, however, appear to influence harassing behavior. For centuries, women were believed to be inferior to men in intellect, but necessary for reproduction, and suited to roles in the home as mothers and caregivers. In contrast, men were considered powerful, aggressive, suited to public life, and the "breadwinners." In marriage, a woman was expected to be subservient to her husband, who controlled all property, except, in some cases, property acquired by the woman prior to marriage.

The influence of gender stereotypes can be seen in early Roman history, when women did not have individual names, and used the family name modified by female endings. In the Roman Republic (509 BC to 27 BC), women were under the control of men, whether a guardian or a husband (Nguyen, 2006). A Latin word for "rape" did not exist, but forced sex, seduction, attempted seduction, abduction, adultery, or ravishment were punishable by law, in the case of freeborn women, in an effort to protect family property from illegitimate heirs. Women of lower social classes (slaves, prostitutes, foreigners) did not have legal protection. Rape of women during war was acceptable behavior. In the Common Era, middles ages, and subsequent centuries, sexual harassment and violence continued. Married women were considered to be "property" of their husbands, and often did not have the agency to say "no" to sex. Intimate partner violence was deemed acceptable. Mary Wollstonecraft, regarded as one of the first feminist philosophers and best known for her book *A Vindication of the Rights of Women* (1792), argued that women were not inferior and deserved education and a public life. Wollstonecraft was influenced by her early experiences at home, where she would routinely attempt to protect her mother from domestic violence (Todd, 2000).

Intimate partner violence (IPV) sometimes involves sexual coercion and continues to be a problem today in poor and affluent countries. IPV against women in the U.S. declined by 53% between 1993 (the year before the Violence in Women Act [VAWA] was approved) and 2008. (Modi et al., 2014). Regrettably, VAWA is not a permanent law and must be reauthorized every five years.

Workplace harassment is more common today than in previous centuries, because widespread employment of women outside of the home is a relatively recent phenomenon. In the U.S., various state's laws banned outside employment for married women in the 19th and 20th centuries (Way, 2018); by the 1930s 26 states still had such laws (Turpin, 2010). This obvious discrimination was related to the societal expectations of women as mothers and caregivers. Workplace harassment that has ensued as more women entered the workforce is usually intended to discourage women from working or at least from achieving positions of leadership.

PREVALENCE

Reliable data on the prevalence of sexual harassment or its identifying behaviors is limited. Sexual harassment is under-reported because of fears of reprisal, that nothing would be done to punish the perpetrator, or because the victim may not recognize certain behaviors as sexual harassment. A 2018 survey in the U.S. with a 78% response rate found that of 6,251 adults, 51% of women and 27% of men reported they were subjected to unwanted sexual advances and sexually harassing comments or behavior both inside and outside of work (Graf, 2018). A 2003 meta-analysis of multiple surveys, with more than 86,000 responses, found that 58% of women reported sexual harassment at work, with prevalence varying from 43 to 69% depending upon occupation (Ilies et al., 2003). A 2019 survey found a high rate (over 90%) of sexual harassment of sexual minorities (LGBTQ2IA), which usually began in middle school or high school (Smith et al., 2020). Official complaints of sexual harassment are far less than what is reported in anonymous surveys, and comprised 10% of complaints to the Equal Employment Opportunity Commission in 2018 and 2019 (U.S. Equal Employment Opportunity Commission, n.d.). The vast majority of these complaints were from women.

Sexual harassment in the medical profession is a significant problem (Newman et al., 2020), and may cause women trainees to doubt their ability to become a doctor and fear retaliation if they report the incident (Binder et al., 2018). A 2011 review of multinational studies reporting sexual harassment in 30,000 medical students, interns and residents, found that sexual harassment was reported by 33% of students and 36% of residents. Most of the reports were from women (Fnais et al., 2014). A survey of graduating medical students in 2017 found that 14.8% reported unwanted sexist comments and 4.3% unwanted sexual advances by faculty, staff, nurses, residents, or other students (American Association of Medical Colleges All Schools Summary Report, 2017). Less than one-quarter of the medical students who had experienced sexual harassment or other offensive behavior reported these incidents to the medical school faculty or administration (Binder et al., 2018).

In a 1995 study, 52% of women faculty at an academic medical institution reported sexual harassment, compared to 5% of men (Carr et al., 2000). In a 2014 survey of medical school faculty with career development awards, 30% of women and 4% of men reported having experienced unwanted sexual comments, attention or advances by a colleague or superior (Jagsi et al., 2016). The reported prevalence of sexual harassment of women is even higher among those in surgery, a field still primarily composed of men. Almost 70% of women in some studies report being victims of sexual harassment (Bruce et al., 2015; Freedman-Weiss et al., 2020) with no significant differences between those in practice and those still in training (Whicker et al., 2020). One might envision that sexual harassment would not be a problem for senior women physicians. Yet, in a survey of women physicians, average age 70 years old, who attended medical school in the 1960s and 1970s, 10% of those in the late stages of their careers reported current sexual harassment, although it occurred infrequently (Templeton et al., 2020).

The challenges of sexual harassment in the medical field became more visible in 2018, when women healthcare professionals formed TIMES Up Healthcare (TUH) (Choo et al., 2019). The goal of TUH is to achieve equity in the health professions and prevent sexual harassment in the medical workplace. Their signature program includes medical and nursing schools, medical centers and hospitals who agree to prevent sexual harassment and gender inequity, support equal opportunity and compensation, and track sexual harassment.

INDIVIDUAL AND ORGANIZATIONAL CONSEQUENCES

Sexual harassment has negative effects on the physical and mental health of the victim. Sexual coercion can lead to post traumatic stress disorder and other adverse psychological effects. Other sexually harassing behaviors have also been associated with depression, anxiety and loss of sleep. A survey of over 7,500 employees in Denmark found a doubling of depressive symptoms associated with sexual harassment by clients, customers, colleagues, supervisors, or subordinates (Friborg et al., 2017). Sexual harassment has been found to increase the risk of burnout among women trainees (Hu et al., 2019) and physicians. This behavior reflects the underlying issue with burnout: a lack of connection between the values of the individual and those of the workplace or place of education.

Sexual harassment may be associated with lower productivity, absence from work, and less career/job satisfaction. This may lead to a change in job or a change in career (Fitzgerald et al., 1995; Lim & Cortina, 2005; National Academies of Sciences, Engineering, and Medicine, 2018). In the medical profession, sexual harassment has been linked to slower academic advancement (National Academies of Sciences, Engineering, and Medicine, 2018). In the aforementioned 2014 survey of medical school faculty who had received career development awards, women reported that sexual harassment made them feel less confident as physicians; about half said that sexual harassment adversely impacted their career advancement (Jagsi et al., 2016). Harassment of women physicians may have negative consequences for patient care, as it can interfere with education of trainees and make it difficult for physicians and other healthcare professionals to work effectively in teams.

There are usually few consequences for the perpetrator. Victims, especially women, are unlikely to file a report for a variety of reasons discussed earlier, but especially because of the fear of retaliation, which makes it seem unwise to risk their career. In a survey of orthopaedic surgeons and trainees, Whicker and colleagues (2020) found that only 15% of victims reported the incident, usually to someone outside of medicine; only about 5% of victims reported this to someone in authority in their departments. The rates of reporting harassment are not significantly different between those who are victims or those who witness harassing behavior (secondary victims); unlike men, women may suffer negative consequences whether they are the primary or secondary victim of harassment, likely because of how this behavior is reflected in their culture at work. Even when harassment is reported, it is unlikely that action will be taken to address the concern (Bruce et al., 2015). Espinoza & Hsiehchen (2020) found that of faculty accused of sexual harassment, only 20% were terminated and about 10% faced sanctions, supporting the concerns expressed by victims who do not report. This lack of action can lead to perpetrators who recurrently target victims over time (Espinoza & Hsiehchen, 2020).

STRATEGIES FOR PREVENTION AND INTERVENTION

Ending sexual harassment in society will necessitate a profound culture change, which is difficult to achieve in the short term. Changes in the workplace, however, are feasible. The first step is to acknowledge that this behavior exists. For interventions to be effective, it is important to understand prevalence at the local level, to be able to track the impact of interventions, and change over time. It is critical that workplace leaders publicly and proactively support anti-sexual harassment initiatives. Practical solutions to reduce or eliminate sexual harassment in the workplace include development of an anti-harassment policy that is disseminated by leadership, as well as clear processes for reporting, training, adjudication of complaints, and corrective actions that can stop serial harassers. The success of these initiatives has not been adequately studied.

Training is not without hazards and must be done appropriately to avoid backlash against women (Tinkler et al., 2013). Research has found that for women, training may be associated with a feeling of disempowerment (Tinkler et al., 2015), and for men, a female trainer as compared to a male trainer may increase unconscious bias (Tinkler et al., 2013). Training sessions should address all types of sexual harassment, and explain policies and procedures, including safe reporting. Interactive sessions are recommended. Multiple sessions within the first year, with annual refresher courses are suggested although the frequency of training sessions has not been adequately studied. Managers require additional training about responding to employees with complaints. Bystander (or "upstander") training is helpful to teach responses and interventions to witnessed situations where a colleague is the recipient of sexually suggestive, or hostile comments or behaviors.

Procedures for safe reporting are essential. Although the identity of the recipient is needed to adjudicate a complaint, the availability of anonymous reporting in addition might help uncover more instances of potential harassment. One of the challenges for the recipient of harassing behavior is lack of proof when there are no witnesses. Keeping a written log of episodes of harassment, conversations and other interactions with the harasser, and keeping all written and email communications may be helpful. Reporting and participating in these cases can be traumatic, and victims need to be afforded necessary support and counseling during the process.

Some data suggests that reporting is associated with worse job, psychological and health outcomes. However, it has been hypothesized that these adverse outcomes may be caused by organizational minimization or possibly retaliation (Bergman et al., 2002). Although retaliation may be prohibited by the workplace, it is not easily prevented outside of the workplace. In academic medicine, for example, the alleged perpetrator may strike back through professional colleagues outside of the medical center. This can result in fewer invitations to lecture, join committees, or receive awards.

Workplaces must develop a standard process or a policy for investigation and resolution of complaints of sexual harassment, and corrective actions. Unfortunately, perpetrators of harassment are frequently more senior and influential in the workplace, and there may be few consequences to their behaviors, even if they are found guilty after investigation. The practice of passing the perpetrator on to another institution or place of employment without full disclosure is not just, and merely perpetuates the problem, as those who engage in this behavior are frequently serial harassers. For healthcare professionals who are found guilty of sexual harassment, especially when this includes sexual favors or acts, clear discipline regarding their license to practice may protect future victims, both those in healthcare as well as patients.

While policies and protocols need to be adopted to address sexual harassment, a fundamental change in culture is needed that advances equity for women, so that they are no longer seen as targets for harassment and are supported and accepted in their career advancement. Strategies that can lead to change in the climate of an organization – and society – include support and advancement of women of all backgrounds and age to leadership positions, empowerment of women, and recruitment of male allies for vocal support. Fear of being accused of harassment cannot be used as an excuse to refrain from mentoring women (Leopold, 2019).

CONCLUSIONS

Sexual harassment today is rooted in beliefs dating back centuries. The overarching question is how to change long-standing social norms that sexualize and objectify women, and assume that women and sexual or gender minorities hold inferior status. Harassment is an attempt to return women to that presumed inferior status and maintain the status quo of *cis* male dominance. Laws and organizational policies are a component of change, but will likely be insufficient by themselves without a fundamental shift in culture. Public announcement of a new norm will not be effective; and while public discussions and deliberations may spur reform, this might take generations (Bicchieri et al., 2014). However, actions to address this issue can lead to change in the short term and may eventually modify attitudes and beliefs.

There is reason for optimism. In the past one hundred years women achieved the right to vote in the United States and the right to employment, including in professional positions requiring higher education. These advances towards equity were the result of outspoken efforts that took place over many years and offer hope for an end to sexual harassment. To achieve this vision, we must continue to shine a light, speak out against this injustice, and show by our actions, especially those in positions of leadership, that sexually harassing behavior will not be tolerated.

REFERENCES

American Association of Medical Colleges. *Medical student graduation questionnaire. All schools summary report 2017.* https://www.aamc.org/system/files/reports/1/2017gqallschoolssummaryreport.pdf

Berdahl, J. L. (2007). The sexual harassment of uppity women. *Journal of Applied Psychology, 92*(2), 425–437.

Bergman, M. E., Langhout, R. D., Palmieri, P. A., Cortina, L. M., & Fitzgerald, L. F. (2002). The (un)reasonableness of reporting: Antecedents and consequences of reporting sexual harassment. *Journal of Applied Psychology, 87*(2), 230–242. https://doi.org/10.1037/0021-9010.87.2.230

Bicchieri C., & Mercier H. (2014). Norms and beliefs: How change occurs. In M. Xenitidou & B. Edmonds (Eds.), *The complexity of social norms.* Computational Social Sciences. Springer. https://doi.org/10.1007/978-3-319-05308-0_3

Binder, R., Garcia, P., Johnson, B., & Fuentes-Afflick, E. (2018). Sexual harassment in medical schools. *Academic Medicine, 93*(12), 1770–1773. https://doi.org/10.1097/acm.0000000000002302

Bruce, A. N., Battista, A., Plankey, M. W., Johnson, L. B., & Marshall, M. B. (2015). Perceptions of gender-based discrimination during surgical training and practice. *Medical Education Online, 20*(1), 25923. https://doi.org/10.3402/meo.v20.25923

Carr, P. L., Ash, A. S., Friedman, R. H., Szalacha, L., Barnett, R. C., Palepu, A., & Moskowitz, M. M. (2000). Faculty perceptions of gender discrimination and sexual harassment in academic medicine. *Annals of Internal Medicine, 132*(11), 889. https://doi.org/10.7326/0003-4819-132-11-200006060-00007

Choo, E. K., Byington, C. L., Johnson, N., & Jagsi, R. (2019). From #MeToo to #TimesUp in health care: Can a culture of accountability end inequity and harassment? *The Lancet, 393*(10171), 499–502. https://doi.org/10.1016/s0140-6736(19)30251-x

Collins, P. H. (2015). Intersectionality's definitional dilemmas. *Annual Review of Sociology, 41*(1), 1–20. https://doi.org/10.1146/annurev-soc-073014-112142

Espinoza, M., & Hsiehchen, D. (2020). Characteristics of faculty accused of academic sexual misconduct in the biomedical and health sciences. *JAMA, 323*(15), 1503–1505. https://doi.org/10.1001/jama.2020.1810

Fitzgerald, L. F., Gelfand, M. J., & Drasgow F. (1995). Measuring sexual harassment: Theoretical and psychometric advances. *Basic and Applied Psychology, 17*(4), 425–444.

Fnais, N., Soobiah, C., Chen, M. H., Lillie, E., Perrier, L., Tashkhandi, M., Straus, S. E., Mamdani, M., Al-Omran, M., & Tricco, A. C. (2014). Harassment and discrimination in medical training. *Academic Medicine, 89*(5), 817–827. https://doi.org/10.1097/acm.0000000000000200

Freedman-Weiss, M. R., Chiu, A. S., Heller, D. R., Cutler, A. S., Longo, W. E., Ahuja, N., & Yoo, P. S. (2020). Understanding the barriers to reporting sexual harassment in surgical training. *Annals of Surgery, 271*(4), 608–613. https://doi.org/10.1097/sla.0000000000003295

Friborg, M. K., Hansen, J. V., Aldrich, P. T., Folker, A. P., Kjær, S., Nielsen, M. B., Rugulies, R., & Madsen, I. E. (2017). Workplace sexual harassment and depressive symptoms: A cross-sectional multilevel analysis comparing harassment from clients or customers to harassment from other employees amongst 7603 Danish employees from 1041 organizations. *BMC Public Health, 17*(1). https://doi.org/10.1186/s12889-017-4669-x

Graf, N. (2018, April 4). *Sexual harassment at work in the era of #MeToo.* Pew Research Center's Social & Demographic Trends Project. https://www.pewsocialtrends.org/2018/04/04/sexual-harassment-at-work-in-the-era-of-metoo/

Hu, Y., Ellis, R. J., Hewitt, D. B., Yang, A. D., Cheung, E. O., Moskowitz, J. T., Potts, J. R., Buyske, J., Hoyt, D. B., Nasca, T. J., & Bilimoria, K. Y. (2019). Discrimination, abuse, harassment, and burnout in surgical residency training. *New England Journal of Medicine, 381*(18), 1741–1752. https://doi.org/10.1056/nejmsa1903759

Ilies, R., Hauserman, N., Schwochau, S., & Stibal, J. (2003). Reported incidence rates of work-related sexual harassment in the United States: Using meta-analysis to explain reported rate disparities. *Personnel Psychology, 56*(3), 607–631.

Jagsi, R., Griffith, K. A., Jones, R., Perumalswami, C. R., Ubel, P., & Stewart, A. (2016). Sexual harassment and discrimination experiences of academic medical faculty. *JAMA, 315*(19), 2120. https://doi.org/10.1001/jama.2016.2188

Leopold, S. S. (2019). Editorial: Fears about #MeToo are no excuse to deny mentorship to women in orthopaedic surgery. *Clinical Orthopaedics and Related Research, 477*(3), 473–476. https://doi.org/10.1097/corr.0000000000000654

Leskinen, E. A., Cortina, L. M., & Kabat, D. B. (2011). Gender harassment: Broadening our understanding of sex-based harassment at work. *Law Hum Behav., 35*(1), 25–39.

Lim, S., & Cortina, L. M. (2005). Interpersonal mistreatment in the workplace: The interface and impact of general incivility and sexual harassment. *Journal of Applied Psychology, 90*(3), 483–496. https://doi.org/10.1037/0021-9010.90.3.483

Loria, L. (2017). The 19th Amendment. *Encyclopaedia Britannica.*

McLaughlin, H., Uggen, C., & Blackstone, A. (2012). Sexual harassment, workplace authority, and the paradox of power. *American Sociological Review, 77*(4), 625–647. https://doi.org/10.1177/0003122412451728

Modi, M. N., Palmer, S., & Armstrong, A. (2014). The role of Violence Against Women Act in addressing intimate partner violence: A public health issue. *Journal of Women's Health, 23*(3), 253–259. https://doi.org/10.1089/jwh.2013.4387

National Academies of Sciences, Engineering, and Medicine. (2018). *Sexual harassment of women: Climate, culture, and consequences in academic sciences, engineering, and medicine.* The National Academies Press. https://doi.org/10.17226/24994.

Newman, C., Templeton, K., & Chin, E. L. (2020). Inequity and women physicians: Time to change millennia of societal beliefs. *Permanente Journal, 24*(3), 11–16.

Nguyen, N. L. (2006). Roman rape: An overview of Roman rape laws from the Republican period to Justinian's reign. *Michigan Journal of Gender and Law, 13*(1), 76–112.

Rotundo, M., Nguyen, D. H., & Sackett, P. R. (2001). A meta-analytic review of gender differences in perceptions of sexual harassment. *J Appl Psychol., 86*(5), 914–922.

Smith, D. M., Johns, N. E., & Raj, A. (2020). Do sexual minorities face greater risk for sexual harassment, ever and at school, in adolescence?: Findings from a 2019 cross-sectional study of U.S. Adults. *Journal of Interpersonal Violence.* https://doi.org/10.1177/0886260520926315

Templeton, K., Nilsen, K. M., & Walling, A. (2020). Issues faced by senior women physicians: A national survey. *Journal of Women's Health, 29*(7), 980–988. https://doi.org/10.1089/jwh.2019.7910

Thompson, D. M. (1994). The woman in the street: Reclaiming the public space from sexual harassment. *Yale Journal of Law and Feminism, 6*, 313–348.

Tinkler, J. E. (2013). How do sexual harassment policies shape gender beliefs? An exploration of the moderating effects of norm adherence and gender. *Social Science Research, 42*(5), 1269–1283. https://doi.org/10.1016/j.ssresearch.2013.05.002

Tinkler, J., Gremillion, S., & Arthurs, K. (2015). Perceptions of legitimacy: The sex of the legal messenger and reactions to sexual harassment training. *Law & Social Inquiry, 40*(01), 152–174. https://doi.org/10.1111/lsi.12065

Todd, J. M. (2000). *Mary Wollstonecraft: A revolutionary life*. Weidenfeld & Nicolson.

Turk, K. (2016). Equality on trial: Gender and rights in the modern American workplace. University of Pennsylvania Press.

Turpin, A. L. (2010). The ideological origins of the women's college: Religion, class, and curriculum in the educational visions of Catharine Beecher and Mary Lyon. *History of Education Quarterly, 50*(2), 133–158. https://doi.org/10.1111/j.1748-5959.2010.00257.x

U.S. Equal Employment Opportunity Commission. (n.d.). *Data visualizations: Sexual harassment charge data*. https://www.eeoc.gov/statistics/data-visualizations-sexual-harassment-charge-data

Way, M. M. (2018). Family economics and public policy, 1800s-Present: How laws, incentives, and social programs drive family decision-making and the US economy. Springer.

Whicker, E., Williams, C., Kirchner, G., Khalsa, A., & Mulcahey, M. K. (2020). What proportion of women orthopaedic surgeons report having been sexually harassed during residency training? A survey study. *Clinical Orthopaedics & Related Research*. Publish Ahead of Print. https://doi.org/10.1097/corr.0000000000001454

Wollstonecraft, M. (2015). *A vindication of the rights of woman with strictures on political and moral subjects*. Forgotten Books.

39

SOCIAL CATEGORIZATION & STEREOTYPES

Stop Judging a Person by Their Cover:
How Stereotypes Limit Our Connection with Others

Jacob A. Sadavoy

Social categorization is described as a cognitive process in which we place individuals into social groups (Allport, 1954). An individual's social category is a part of their identity and culture and is commonly one of the descriptors (that follow one's name) when asked to tact or expressively label oneself (Haslam et al., 1996). Zentall and colleagues (2002) defined "a category as a class of stimuli that occasion common responses in a given context. Such classes include; stimuli involved in an explicit learning history plus, potentially, novel stimuli to which the fruits of this history may transfer" (p. 238). This allows humans to make connections with previously learned material and use categorical responding to transfer stimuli without formal teaching based on categorical generalization. Through a social categorization lens, this process can lead to stereotyping; the overgeneralization, and a learning history bias directed at a social group or identity. In this chapter, I will discuss social categorical formations, biases around ingroups and outgroups based on learning history, stereotyping and social identity suppression or withdrawal, and ways in which behavior analysis can address this social discord via stimulus equivalence, relational frame theory (RFT), and compassion.

In social categorization there are ingroups and outgroups (Tajfel et al., 1971). You are a member of your ingroup which plays an important role in the development of the verbal behavior of your self-concept, and by way of comparison, how others are tacted or labeled outside your social category – the outgroup (Johnson et al., 2000). It has been widely documented that children have formed explicit and implicit preferences based on people's gender, race, and linguistic group (Dunham & Emory, 2014; Renno & Shutts, 2015). Aboud (1988) demonstrated that children as young as 4 and 5 years old identified their own group accurately 80% of the time and that number jumps to 100% by ages 6 and 7. Further, 5-year old children had learned cultural norms corresponding to typical behaviors deemed masculine and feminine while developing stereotypes around age, race, and physical attractiveness (Bigler & Liben, 2006). Our stereotypes and prejudices are learned through many different processes which allow for confirmation across multiple media contexts and thus, generalization occurs, and the bias maintains. Stereotypes can be formed in children's conversations with parents and peers (Aboud & Doyle, 1996), from the behaviors as seen pictured in the media (Brown, 1995), and largely the social context in which one lives. As we get older, we can learn about our implicit biases by being culturally introspective. This can be catalyzed by completing a cultural responsiveness self-assessment (a favorite of mine is the *Central Vancouver Island Multicultural Society's Cultural Competence Self-Assessment Checklist*).

Social categorization, to some, is believed to be innate, but attributing stereotypical judgments about an outgroup is most definitely learned (Aboud, 1988; Dunham & Emory, 2014; Renno & Shutts, 2015). We have the ability to categorize objects, acknowledging that a fork and a spoon are both within the category of eating utensils; however, one can discriminate which one is used for soup versus linguine. After all, a fork and spoon are different. Similarly, the notion that all humans are the same is inherently false. Therefore, when one says that they do not see color, gender, sexual orientation, ability, race, socioeconomic status, amongst other categories, are they denying social categorization? Are they attempting to proclaim inclusivity? Are they aware that saying "I don't see _____" can be interpreted as "I don't see you."

McGlinchey and Keenan (1997) discussed group allegiance and detailed the strong division in Northern Ireland between Protestants and Catholics across beliefs, surnames and names of schools, place of residence, type of sport one watches or plays, flags, and more. Bias shifted to prejudice which culminated in conflict and the horrific 1969 Northern Ireland riots. They postulated "that children may learn to behave with prejudice as a result of social contingencies maintained by members of their religious group" (McGlinchey & Keenan, 1997, p. 114). Thus, the formation of a stimulus class taught and reinforced through "stereotyped cues" promoted *outgroup homogeneity* which is the phenomenon in which we place greater similarities of the relations within the outgroup than one's ingroup (Ostrom & Sedikides, 1992). This overgeneralization is reinforced because we will find ways to demonstrate agreement across our stereotypical beliefs, and not attend to observations that reject these beliefs (Fyock & Stangor, 1994; Snyder et al., 1977; Word et al., 1974). It might be described as selective attending; noting corroborating evidence and ignoring evidence that conflicts with the belief. Phelan and Rudman (2010) noted that once we possess the stereotypical view that men make better leaders than other genders, men will be given more opportunities and will have more success in leadership positions, whereas, other genders have to overcome the fact that they are assumed to have inferior leadership abilities. In other words, there are also elements of self-fulfilling prophecy. Simply, individuals use learned stereotypes as cognitive shortcuts to navigate a complex social world. These shortcuts allow one to sort and categorize information so that it is interpreted more efficiently, but at the cost of accuracy and poor decision-making about other people (Cuddy et al., 2007).

Weinstein and colleagues (2008) noted that by examining social context, social categorization can lead to stereotyping, prejudice and discrimination by categorizing ingroups against outgroups in terms of social preferences, empathic responding, and resource distribution. There exists a tendency to view our ingroup as more similar and those in the outgroup as being a separate entity (Allport, 1954; Liberman et al., 2017). Social identity theory posits that outgroup homogeneity is reinforced to maintain an individuals' positive sense of self and uniqueness (Tajfel et al., 1971). There exists a natural tendency to view positively one's own ingroup compared to a less desirable outgroup, especially if the ingroup represents the majority (Johnson et al., 2000). Johnson and colleagues noted that "auto-stereotyping" and "self-hatred" can exist amongst individuals at early ages before they are aware of their ethnic identity. They went on to conclude, "negative stereotypes that have developed through cognitive, information-based processes may not be easily undermined by the sudden realization that one is a member of that group" (Johnson et al., 2000, p. 2).

This concept is evident in politics. Rothschild et al. (2018) conducted an open-ended survey which demonstrated effects of social identity on partisan identification but also "suggest[ed] strong connections between partisan social identity, trait-based thinking, and mass-level polarization" (p. 439). The results demonstrated that Democrats describe their ingroup (co-partisans) as "caring" and "open-minded," while labeling Republicans as "prejudiced" and "closed-minded." Republicans view their ingroup as "honest" and "individualist," while describing their outgroup as "lazy" and "unrealistic." With outgroup homogeneity, there is a greater sense that all members of the outgroup behave in this stereotypical manner and any observation in line with that assessment reinforces this stereotypic belief (Huddy et al., 2015). Imagine entering a conversation with an individual that supports an alternative partisan group with the anticipation that they will be prejudiced/closed-minded or lazy/unrealistic; those biases could limit an opportunity to have an open-minded conversation.

"Thus, thinking of party affiliation as a social identity in and of itself should relate to larger differences in how the parties are perceived, as well as more extreme opinions among mass-level partisans" (Rothschild et al., 2018, p. 427).

Social categorizations are not static. We move, marry, and grow older and all these occurrences can alter one's ingroup (Johnson et al., 2000). As we age, some may attribute common stereotypes to aging that may be in line with ageism which has a negative impact on their health and quality of life. This is compounded and reinforced by societal ageism which is the stereotyping, prejudice, and discrimination of the general public against others based on age (Burnes et al., 2019). Therefore, it is understandable why some people are resistant to grow older and embrace an elderly self-identity. The LGBTQ2IA community faces ongoing hardships, stigmas, and challenges that suppress their self-identity and, as such, many in the community conceal their sexual orientation to avoid entering the marginalized LGBTQ2IA ingroup (Corrigan & Matthews, 2003; Rasmussen, 2004). It is critical for those in marginalized outgroups to find their community to build their self-identity; it is equally critical for the ingroup majority to recognize the benefits and the need for inclusivity and recognize their natural stereotypical tendencies.

SOCIAL CATEGORIZATION, STEREOTYPING, AND RELATIONAL FRAME THEORY (RFT)

There exists a strong conceptual and growing empirical relationship between language and derived stimulus relations (Hayes et al., 2001). This empirical relationship does not indicate that derived stimulus relations depend upon language or that such relations are mediated by language. An individual's current derived responses along with their learning history of relational responding provides the basis of their Derived Relational Responding (DRR) performance (Barnes et al., 2017). One can demonstrate DRR by assessing the relations of x, y, and z where if x is less than y, and y is less than z if the untaught derivatives of z being greater than y and x and x being less than z is known. According to Hayes and colleagues (2001), "prejudice involves a derived transformation of the functions of individuals based on a direct or verbal contact with the functions of a few members of conceptualized groups" (p. 202) where transformation is the phenomenon in which there exists a transfer of stimulus function.

I am a huge fan of the Hamilton Tiger-Cats football team and as such, their provincial rivals, the Toronto Argonauts are incredibly aversive and without any conditioning history, I have transformed that aversive function to other things related to the Argonauts (e.g., the color blue or their 'A' logo) and to the few individuals who are supporters of that football team. In 2007, Illinois state senator, Barack Hussein Obama announced he will run for office in the hopes of being the next President of the U.S.A. Obama's middle name is the same as Iraqi President, Saddam Hussein and Obama is also a black man. For White Homogenous City, U.S.A, Obama is a black man with a first and last name that is atypical to that population (x). That name matches the name of a proclaimed enemy-of-the-state and all exemplars of past presidents have been white men (y). Lastly, one culture is associated with violence and anti-American values (e.g., World Trade Center attacks, Gulf War, *Black Hawk Down*, *Iron Man*) and the other is associated with crime and violence (e.g., Jim Crow, the television show *COPS*, local media differentiating mental illness for white murders but depicting black murders as thugs, gang members, products of their environment) (z). The derived relational account would suggest that Obama (x) might be associated with violent traits with a "hidden agenda" to destroy Americans and their values (z). Just as easily, however, an individual could pair Barack Hussein Obama with being a Harvard Law graduate, born in Hawaii, or a Chicago White Sox fan. We pair constructs based on our learning histories, our environment, and the social context created by the conversational community. Thus, the socially-mediated consequences of our verbal behavior will shape the likelihood of our opinion of Obama as being positive or negative based on our contact with punishment or reinforcement contingent on the verbal community and the attributes of Obama they select.

Weinstein et al. (2008) looked at the social categorization of obese versus thin people and accounted for the negative effects weight shaming has on those who see themselves as obese [e.g., 91% feeling ashamed of their weight, 96% having negative experiences at school, 90% having feelings of being humiliated in school, and, after completing school obese woman earn 12% less than non-obese woman (Irving, 2000; Neumark-Sztainer, et al., 1998; Register & Williams, 1990)]. Weinstein et al. (2008) sought to use a brief conditioning history to demonstrate the existence of transformation of a learned bias to arbitrary stimuli. Therefore, the participants, of various weights, who likely have had years of experiential learning equating obesity as undesirable, were able to relate their bias to a random, unrelated stimuli (Weinstein et al., 2008). The implications of these results is the possibility that RFT could provide a technology to help to overcome stereotypical beliefs. For further or additional information on RFT, please refer to the chapter in this text by Dr. Garcia and colleagues.

SOCIAL CATEGORIZATION, STEREOTYPING, AND STIMULUS EQUIVALENCE

One such solution to this engrained social reality is to reduce observed bias related to a stereotype using stimulus equivalence. Stimulus equivalence is generally defined as the interchangeability of stimuli within a class (Arntzen et al., 2006; Sidman, 1971; Sidman, 2009). A positive demonstration of stimulus equivalence would require reflexivity, symmetry, and transitivity (Sidman & Tailby, 1982). For example, if shown a picture of a tiger with two other non-tigers and asked to match; reflexivity would be a correct response in the absence of training and reinforcement. Symmetry would be taught to select a tiger from an array of non-tigers with the spoken word *tiger* and, without additional training and reinforcement, the learner responds with the tact, spoken word *tiger* when presented with a tiger picture. Finally, transitivity would be the introduction of the written word tiger and for the learner to be able to relate the word tiger with spoken word tiger and a picture of the tiger without teaching and reinforcement. The learner effectively demonstrated that written tiger, tiger image, and the spoken word *tiger* "are equivalent." With respect to racial social categorization, it has been demonstrated that when presented with a black face without emotion; it was labeled as angry more often than a face that was white. Similarly, when presented with an angry, racially ambiguous face, participants were more likely to label the face as black (Hugenberg & Bodenhausen, 2003, 2004). De Carvalho and de Rose (2014) and Mizael, de Almeida et al. (2016) conducted studies that examined participants' bias related to skin color, to create equivalence classes with "positive" symbols and human faces of color. Mizael et al. (2016) found that participants demonstrated class formation among these stimuli, but that the stimulus equivalence training, and resulting class formation, reduced the stereotypical beliefs related to skin color. Further applications of such findings could be used for shaping and replacing stereotypic views from young individuals who are just beginning to formulate stereotypical biases from environmental observation, social interaction, and messaging from media and movies to law enforcement officers and teachers where implicit bias limits the safety and potential of marginalized populations. For further or additional information on stimulus equivalence, please refer to the chapter in this text by Dr. Albright and colleagues.

SOCIAL CATEGORIZATION, STEREOTYPING, AND COMPASSION

Kristin Neff (2003) wrote, "compassion involves being open to and moved by the suffering of others, so that one desires to ease their suffering. It also involves offering others patience, kindness, and non-judgmental understanding, recognizing that all humans are imperfect, and make mistakes" (p. 224). Taylor and colleagues (2019), provided an outline of critical skills related to compassion, empathy, collaboration, and positive social interaction for practitioners to embody with vulnerable clients. An extrapolation of their work is to bring this sense of compassion and empathy to one's social interactions. A way to combat engrained, unintended stereotypical beliefs is to approach each other human with honesty and genuine interest in who they are and their story. The term "sonder" was coined by John Koenig and is the realization that each random passerby is living a life as vivid and complex as your own (Bowman, 2015). Each person has a unique learning history made up of consequences that has shaped their being. I will never be black, Vietnamese, gay, autistic, a single mother, or First Nations and to assume otherwise, would be committing a fallacy. Therefore, in an effort to relate to someone else, especially someone with a different identity than my own, I must be present not to overgeneralize my experiences and identity onto another. By being compassionate and empathic in all interactions, one can focus not on who they are in a social exchange (or their ingroup) but learn, listen, and appreciate another for who they are, and their unique point of view shaped by their own learning history. Taylor and colleagues (2019) outline several ways in which one can make a stand for compassion such as: confirming emotional response in a non-judgmental manner, offering supportive comments, engaging in active listening, demonstrating perspective taking, verifying emotional responses, and having present moment awareness throughout interactions. When interacting with anyone, but especially a person whose social category is different than yours, being compassionate could effectively mitigate one's natural stereotypical beliefs. For further or additional information on compassion, please refer to the chapter in this text by Dr. LeBlanc and colleagues.

Additional research is required with respect to social categorization, stereotyping, and behavior analysis. RFT and stimulus equivalence provide a likely framework to replace stereotypical beliefs. Utterances like "I don't see color," "Merry Christmas and Happy Holidays are the same thing," "I don't understand gay marriage, but you do you," are harmful. They further marginalize outgroups and inhibit their ability to express their self-identity. The author suggests demonstrating greater compassion and empathy with others as an alternative intervention; which will require those of privilege to abandon contingencies that provide them a social, political, and economical advantage over marginalized groups. As a white, cisgender male it is effortless to promote connecting to outgroups because my ingroup is not marginalized. This would be significantly more taxing for those that are in marginalized ingroups, who experience being challenged to ignore or conform to systemic injustices that impede their rights. The "challenge" I will face, being a member of the privileged ingroup, is finding ways in which promoting inclusivity provides similar or greater reinforcement compared to our current political, social, and economical patriarchal culture which is designed by and for white, cisgender men to win at the expense of others. This text was born from our current reality that there is rampant social injustice. We are not utilizing an "experimental attitude towards everything" in an effort to improve the human condition (Skinner, 1948). Overthrowing systemic injustice in favor of an inclusive and supportive societal culture which embraces all of us equally and celebrates our unique diverse backgrounds can be realized. I believe by being more compassionate, listening before responding, and demonstrating empathy with a sincere interest to learn about and love our marginalized outgroups would be a step in that direction. Step one is admitting that you have biases and being proactive and introspective in learning what they are. Through understanding and compassion we can see past our biases which are inherently misleading and limit connections with amazing human beings.

REFERENCES

Aboud, F. E. (1988). *Children and prejudice*. B. Blackwell.

Aboud, F. E., & Doyle, A. B. (1996). Parental and peer influences on children's racial attitudes. *International Journal of Intercultural Relations, 20*, 371–383.

Allport, G. W. (1954/1979). *The nature of prejudice*. Doubleday.

Arntzen, E. (2006). Delayed matching to sample: Probability of responding in accord with equivalence as a function of different delays. *The Psychological Record, 56*(1), 135–167.

Barnes-Holmes, D., Finn, M., McEnteggart, C., & Barnes-Holmes, Y. (2017). Derived stimulus relations and their role in a behavior-analytic account of human language and cognition. *Perspectives on Behavior Science, 41*(1), 155–173.

Bigler, R. S., & Liben, L. S. (2006). A developmental intergroup theory of social stereotypes and prejudice. In R. V. Kail (Ed.), *Advances in child development and behavior* (Vol. 34, pp. 39–89). Elsevier.

Bowman, D. (2015). On sonder. *Medical Humanities, 41*(2), 75–76.

Brown, R. (1995). *Prejudice: Its social psychology*. Blackwell.

Burnes, D., Sheppard, C., Henderson, C. R., Jr, Wassel, M., Cope, R., Barber, C., & Pillemer, K. (2019). Interventions to reduce ageism against older adults: A systematic review and meta-analysis. *American Journal of Public Health, 109*(8), e1–e9.

Corrigan, P. W., & Matthews, A. K. (2003). Stigma and disclosure: Implications for coming out of the closet. *Journal of Mental Health, 12*, 235–248.

Cuddy, A. J. C., Fiske, S. T., & Glick, P. (2007). The BIAS map: Behaviors from intergroup affect and stereotypes. *J. Pers. Soc. Psychol., 92*(4), 631–648.

de Carvalho, M. P., & de Rose, J. C. (2014). Understanding racial attitudes through the stimulus equivalence paradigm. *The Psychological Record, 64*(3), 527–536. https://doi.org/10.1007/s40732-014-0049-4

De Rose, J. C., Hidalgo, M., & Vasconcellos, M. (2013). Controlling relations in baseline conditional discriminations as determinants of stimulus equivalence. *Psychological Record, 63*(1), 85–98.

Dunham, Y., & Emory, J. (2014). Of affect and ambiguity: The emergence of preferences for arbitrary groups. *J Soc Issues., 70*(1), 81–98.

Fyock, J., & Stangor, C. (1994). The role of memory biases in stereotype maintenance. *British Journal of Social Psychology, 33*(3), 331–343.

Haslam, S. A., Oakes, P. J., & Turner, J. C. (1996). Social identity, self-categorization, and the perceived homogeneity of ingroups and outgroups: The interaction between social motivation and cognition. In *Handbook of motivation and cognition: The interpersonal context* (Vol. 3, pp. 182–222). The Guilford Press.

Hayes, S. C., Barnes-Holmes, D., & Roche, B. (eds.). (2001). *Relational frame theory: A post-Skinnerian account of human language and cognition*. Plenum Press.

Huddy, L., Mason, L., & Aarøe, L. (2015). Expressive partisanship: Campaign involvement, political emotion, and partisan identity. *American Political Science Review, 109*(1), 1–17.

Hugenberg, K., & Bodenhausen, G. V. (2003). Facing prejudice: Implicit prejudice and the perception of facial threat. *Psychol. Sci., 14*, 640–643.

Hugenberg, K., & Bodenhausen, G. V. (2004). Ambiguity in social categorization: The role of prejudice and facial affect in race categorization. *Psychol. Sci., 15*(5), 342–345.

Irving, L. (2000). Promoting size acceptance in elementary school children: The EDAP puppet program. *Eating Disorders: The Journal of Treatment & Prevention, 8*, 221–232.

Johnson, C., Schaller, M., & Mullen, B. (2000). Social categorization and stereotyping: 'You mean I'm one of "them"?' *The British Journal of Social Psychology, 39*, 1–25.

Liberman, Z., Woodward, A. L., & Kinzler, K. D. (2017). The origins of social categorization. *Trends in Cognitive Sciences, 21*(7), 556–568. https://doi.org/10.1016/j.tics.2017.04.004

McGlinchey, A., & Keenan, M. (1997). Stimulus equivalence and social categorization in Northern Ireland. *Behavior and Social Issues, 7*(2), 113–128. https://doi.org/10.5210/bsi.v7i2.310

Mizael, T. M., de Almeida, J. H., Silveira, C. C., & de Rose, J. C. (2016). Changing racial bias by transfer of functions in equivalence classes. *The Psychological Record, 66*(3), 451–462.

Neff, K. D. (2003). The development and validation of a scale to mea-sure self-compassion. *Self and Identity, 2*, 223–250.

Neumark-Sztainer, D., Story, M., & Faibisch, L. (1998). Perceived stigmatization among overweight African-American and Caucasian adolescent girls. *Journal of Adolescent Health, 23*, 264–270.

Ostrom, T. M., & Sedikides, C. (1992). Out-group homogeneity effects in natural and minimal groups. *Psychological Bulletin, 112*(3), 536–552.

Phelan, J. E., & Rudman, L. A. (2010). Prejudice toward female leaders: Backlash effects and women's impression management dilemma. *Social and Personality Psychology Compass, 4*(10), 807–820.

Rasmussen, M. (2004). The problem of coming out. *Theory Into Practice, 43*(2), 144–150.

Register, C. A., & Williams D. R. (1990). The wage effects of obesity: A longitudinal study. *Social Science Quarterly, 71*, 130–141.

Renno, M. P., & Shutts, K. (2015). Children's social category-based giving and its correlates: Expectations and preferences. *Dev Psychol., 51*(4), 533–543.

Rothschild, J. E., Howat, A. J., Shafranek, R. M., & Busby, E. C. (2018). Pigeonholing partisans: Stereotypes of party supporters and partisan polarization. *Political Behavior, 1*(2), 423–443.

Sidman, M. (2009). Equivalence relations and behavior: An introductory tutorial. *The Analysis of verbal behavior, 25*(1), 5–17. https://doi.org/10.1007/BF03393066

Sidman, M. (1971). Reading and auditory-visual equivalences. *Journal of Speech and Hearing Research, 14*, 5–13.

Sidman, M., & Tailby, W. (1982). Conditional discrimination vs. matching to sample: An expansion of the testing paradigm. *Journal of the Experimental Analysis of Behavior, 37*(1), 5–22. https://doi.org/10.1901/jeab.1982.37-5

Skinner, B. F. (1948). *Walden two*. New York: Macmillan

Snyder, M., Tanke, E. D., & Berscheid, E. (1977). Social perception and interpersonal behavior: On the self-fulfilling nature of social stereotypes. *Journal of Personality and Social Psychology, 35*(9), 656–666.

Tajfel, H., Billig, M. G., Bundy, R. P., & Flament, C. (1971). Social categorization and intergroup behavior. *European Journal of Social Psychology, 1*, 1–39.

Taylor, B. A., LeBlanc, L. A. & Nosik, M. R. (2019) . . . Compassionate care in behavior analytic treatment: Can outcomes be enhanced by attending to relationships with caregivers? *Behav Analysis Practice, 12*, 654–666.

Weinstein, J. H., Wilson, K. G., Drake, C. E., & Kellum, K. K. (2008). A relational frame theory contribution to social categorization. *Behavior and Social Issues, 17*(1), 40–65.

Word, C. O., Zanna, M. P., & Cooper, J. (1974). The nonverbal mediation of self-fulfilling prophecies in interracial interaction. *Journal of Experimental Social Psychology, 10*(2), 109–120.

Zentall, T. R., Galizio, M., & Critchfield, T. S. (2002). Categorization, concept learning and behavior analysis: An introduction. *J Exp Anal Behav., 78*, 237–248.

40

SOCIAL JUSTICE
An Overdue and Urgent Topic for Behavior Analysis

Mary Jane Weiss

Social justice is being increasingly referenced and has become ubiquitous in conversations about societal woes in 2020. Dictionary.com defines social justice as, "fair treatment of all people in a society, including respect for the rights of minorities and equitable distribution of resources among members of a community." Merriam Webster defines it as, "a state or doctrine of egalitarianism." Indeed, the themes commonly embedded into discussions of social justice in society echo these threads of equity, of equal access, and of universal respect for human rights.

In the wake of multiple and repeated instances of police brutality toward African American citizens, there has been a significant and undeniable realization of systemic inequity and systemic racism. It has become clear that there is not fair treatment of all people within society, and that resources are allocated extremely unfairly. Indeed, as the lens widens to examine many aspects of society, the injustice becomes more visible. In nearly every area of life-education, economic opportunity, health care, incarceration, etc.- the same pattern is seen. Furthermore, the trend appears to be accelerating, and the disparities are increasing. The United Nations (2006) has noted that social injustice has increased, as the disparity of wealth continues to increase and the opportunities to improve one's economic stature have declined and are not equitably available.

BEHAVIOR ANALYSIS AND SOCIAL JUSTICE

One of the core tenets of behavioral analysis is the ability to improve the circumstances and reduce the challenges for individuals and for groups. There is also a strong focus on examining environmental factors that promote positive individual and communal outcomes, and an optimism about how we can alter environments for individuals and for the broader community (Sidman, 2001; Skinner, 1948; 1953; 1961; 1987). In these ways, issues of fairness, equity, and equal opportunity seem entirely congruent with the foundational principles and early efforts of behavior analysis. In other ways, behavior analysis has yet to be fully extended to these issues, and is potentially (at least partially) untapped to address them (Baer et al., 1968).

There are a number of areas for an expanded focus within ABA that have received more attention in recent years. For instance, the field has grappled recently with what some have noted as compassionate care skills, which comprises the behaviors that convey compassion, respect, and understanding. Taylor and colleagues (2018) noted weaknesses in compassionate care skills among behavior analysts working with individuals with autism. In surveying parents served by behavior analysts, these researchers discovered areas for improvement, including the extent to which behavior analysts checked in on the family, engaged in active listening, or acknowledged treatment mistakes. The implications of these deficits are clear; clients who do not feel heard, understood, or supported are likely to have lesser treatment outcomes. Additionally, the impression that is formed of the field of behavior analysis might suffer, as clinicians might be experienced as lacking in warmth, empathy, and concern.

These skills have been undervalued and underemphasized in the training of behavior analysts (LeBlanc et al., 2019). It is interesting to speculate on why such skills have not been emphasized in the teaching and training of behavior analysts. It is likely, in part, because of the clear separation of ABA from psychology which defined the early years of the field. Moreover, the challenge in defining such skills is formidable. How does one define compassion, teach an individual to engage in compassionate behavior, measure compassionate care, or provide feedback on whether it was demonstrated? As a science concerned with the use of evidence-based practices, data-based decision making, and the use of procedures that can be defined and reliably measured, behavior analysis may have struggled to embrace the need to tackle these clinical challenges from a measurement perspective.

Similar to the recent spotlight on compassionate care skills, recent articles have highlighted the need for more nuanced training in cultural humility (Wright, 2019). Cultural humility has been defined as 'a framework used by other professional disciplines to address both institutional and individual behavior that contributes to the power imbalance, the marginalization of communities, and disparities in health access and outcomes" (Wright, 2019). Miller, Re Cruz, and Ala'i Rosales (2019) emphasized the importance of cultural responsivity in clinical intervention, and highlighted how our improvements in it could increase both outcomes and understanding.

More researchers have noted that these skills are not emphasized in the education and training of behavior analysts (Beaulieu et al., 2019). These researchers found that behavior analysts express confidence in delivering culturally responsive intervention, despite the lack of exposure to it and training in it. Encouragingly, dialogue is increasing, and efforts are being made to operationally define, measure, and provide feedback to clinicians on the demonstration of skills including compassionate care, interprofessional collaboration, and cultural humility (Conners et al., 2019; Fong et al., 2016). Furthermore, efforts are increasing towards diversity in behavior analysis as a field (Fong et al. 2017).

Interestingly, other fields have been emphasizing compassionate care and cultural humility for many years. One can find examples of the emphasis in compassionate care across the fields of nursing, counseling, social work, and other helping professions. Similarly, cultural humility has received attention from multiple other professions for many years. As a field, behavior analysts have embraced the need to define these skills and refine our approaches to include them. Efforts to learn from other fields and to explore the level of need within our own field have increased. This has accelerated the momentum with which these issues are being discussed and referenced, in conceptual, research, and clinical contexts. In a similar way, behavior analysis may be able to learn from allied fields in the area of social justice.

HUMAN SERVICE PROFESSIONS AND SOCIAL JUSTICE

Perhaps the human service profession with the largest focus on social justice is social work, where it is embedded into all aspects of the field. In the *Social Work Dictionary*, Social justice is defined as, "an ideal condition in which all members of society have the same basic rights, protection, opportunities, obligations, and social benefits." Social work has basic values articulated in their ethical code: Service, Social Justice, Dignity and Worth of the Person, The Importance of Relationships, Integrity, and Competence. The value of Social Justice is associated with the Ethical Principle, *Social workers challenge social injustice*. The code goes on to say," Social workers pursue social change, particularly with and on behalf of vulnerable and oppressed individuals and groups of people. Social workers' social change efforts are focused primarily on issues of poverty, unemployment, discrimination, and other forms of social injustice. These activities seek to promote sensitivity to and knowledge about oppression and cultural and ethnic diversity. Social workers strive to ensure access to needed information, services, and resources; equality of opportunity; and meaningful participation in decision making for all people." Social workers, clearly and explicitly, tackle injustice, seek to rectify it, and are committed to changing unjust systems. They also seek to educate the community about oppression and about the need for societal change.

Psychology also tackles social justice, albeit in a more indirect and less action-oriented manner. Like social work, psychology identifies general ethical principles that serve as core values: beneficence and non-malfeasance, fidelity and responsibility, integrity, justice, and respect for people's rights and dignity. The Justice principle states that

> Psychologists recognize that fairness and justice entitle all persons to access to and benefit from the contributions of psychology and to equal quality in the processes, procedures, and services being conducted by psychologists. Psychologists exercise reasonable judgment and take precautions to ensure that their potential biases, the boundaries of their competence, and the limitations of their expertise do not lead to or condone unjust practices.

In this context, we see a slightly narrower definition of justice, in the context of psychological services access. We also, however, see that there is an emphasis on how psychologists are obligated to ensure that they do not unwittingly participate in or condone unjust practices. They are urged to examine their biases, ensure they practice in the bounds of their competence, and recognize their limitations or need for expanding their skills and understanding. This focus on the evolution of the skill set, in a continual sense, is consistent with a humble approach to serving others, and mirrors much of the thinking across disciplines about cultural humility.

In 2011, the Presidential Address at the APA Conference (Munsey, 2011; Vasquez, 2012) focused on social justice, and spoke to the ways in which psychology research has advanced social justice. Melba Vasquez pointed out that psychological research had influenced the prohibition of life without parole sentences for juveniles in criminal cases, persuaded legislators to permit state adoption by gay individuals, and convinced courts that prison crowding was detrimental to the mental health of inmates. She also cited statistics regarding the income gap, poverty, homelessness, health status and access disparities, and other systemic challenges to equity. The focus of psychology, she suggested, must be to address these issues with research, innovation, and a commitment to bettering the lives of all those we encounter. She also highlighted the need for more diversity in professional guild organizations, highlighting a source of injustice within the field.

In the years since, a number of other psychologists have called for a broad commitment to social justice, and have explored philosophical and theoretical foundations of it within psychology (Arfken & Yen, 2014). Psychology research and practice have been posited as related to social justice, even when such a link is not explicit (Louis et al., 2014). Walsh and Gokani (2014) argue that there has been a long standing desire of psychologists to address social injustice, and to strive to improve social inequity.

Jost and Kay (2010) define several elements of social justice, including *distributive, procedural,* and *interactional* justice. Distributive justice refers to the allocation of blessings and burdens. In a just society, benefits and struggles should be shared and equitable. Procedural justice refers to laws and procedures being applied fairly across all of society's members. Examples of contexts that should be fairly represented include norms, rights, liberties, and entitlements. Interactional justice refers to how individuals are treated by authorities and by fellow citizens. In a just society, all members are treated similarly, and are afforded respect and dignity in all interactions.

BEHAVIOR ANALYSIS AND SOCIAL JUSTICE

Social justice issues can be examined in many ways. Unlike many of our allied fields, behavior analysis has been slow to recognize the impact of social justice in micro and in macro ways. In recent years, the disparities (in socioeconomic, race, and other areas) between those served and those who are in the field has been identified and discussed. Indeed, even in research contexts, it appears that behavior analysts have identified few demographic characteristics when describing research participants (Jones et al., 2020). Certain demographics appear to be woefully under-reported, such as socioeconomic status, which was reported in only 2% of studies. This seems to be a serious omission in describing the participants. In addition, the underreporting of other characteristics, such as cultural heritage, limits our ability to study how culture impacts treatment, which also potentially reduces the generalizability of findings.

On a macro level, behavior analysis has been turning its attention increasingly to issues of broad humanitarian concerns. Specifically, there has been a recent call for a recognition of power imbalances and a commitment to advancing social justice, including racial justice (Matsuda et al., 2020; Pritchett et al., 2020). These authors call for a paradigm shift, in which compassionate care is delivered to alleviate human suffering. Indeed, the authors note, social justice can be considered the "applied spirit of the science."

What are the barriers to exploring social justice on individual and on larger levels? What are the changes we need to be making? First, in the same way we analyze other contingencies, we must look at how systems perpetuate injustice, privilege, and marginalization. Second, we need to shift these skills to priorities within coursework and supervised experience. In this way, the next generation is introduced to these concepts and principles early in their careers. Third, within research contexts, we must commit to reporting and studying the impact of demographic variables, analyzing the impact of culturally sensitive approaches, and obtaining social validity data on how our procedures and interactions impact individuals, families, and systems, including in the context of remediating injustices.

THE FUTURE OF BEHAVIOR ANALYSIS

Behavior analysis has been concerned with the betterment of humanity since its inception. It is entirely congruent with its foundational principles and historical applications to focus on social justice. Furthermore, it is inextricably linked to social validity; we seek to have our work valued and for the changes that occur to be indicated as meaningful by those we serve to assist (Kazdin; 1977; Wolf, 1978). Behavior analysts need to broaden their lens to include social justice in the analysis of individual and social problems and in the training of the next generation of behavior analysts. Like other newer areas receiving intense attention in the field, such as compassionate care, interprofessional collaboration, and cultural humility, social justice is an essential focus. Much of the work that has been done in allied fields serves as instruction for us, and our own field's rich demonstrations of effectiveness provides confidence that we can learn more about this as well. As Skinner (1948) said, "It is not a question of starting. The start has been made. It's a question of what's to be done from now on"

(p. 257). As we strive to understand and change the world, we will be echoing the optimism of our predecessors and expanding the range of impacts behavior analysis has had on all of humanity.

REFERENCES

Arfken, M., & Yen, J. (2014). Psychology and social justice: Theoretical and philosophical engagements. *Journal of Theoretical and Philosophical Psychology, 34*(1), 1–13. https://doi.org/10.1037/a0033578

Baer, D. M., Wolf, M. M., & Risley, T. R. (1968). Some current dimensions of applied behavior analysis. *Journal of Applied Behavior Analysis, 1*(1), 91–97. https://doi.org/10.1901/jaba.1968.1-91.

Baer, D. M., Wolf, M. M., & Risley, T. R. (1987). Some still-current dimensions of applied behavior analysis. *Journal of Applied Behavior Analysis, 20*(4), 313–327. https://doi.org/10.1901/jaba.1987.20–313.

Beaulieu, L., Addington, J., & Almeida, D. (2019). Behavior analysts' training and practices regarding cultural diversity: The case for culturally competent care. *Behavior Analysis in Practice, 12*(3), 557–575. https://doi.org/10.1007/s40617-018-00313-6

Conners, B. & Johnson, A., Duarte, J., Murriky, R., & Marks, K. (2019). Future directions of training and fieldwork in diversity issues in applied behavior analysis. *Behavior Analysis in Practice, 12*(4), 1–10. https://doi.org/10.1007/s40617-019-00349-2

Fong, E. H., Catagnus, R., Brodhead, M., Quigley, S., & Field, S. (2016). Developing the cultural awareness skills of behavior analysts. *Behavior Analysis in Practice, 9*, 84–94. https://doi.org/10.1007/s40617-016-0111-6.

Fong, E. H., Ficklin, S., & Lee, H. Y. (2017). Increasing cultural understanding and diversity in applied behavior analysis. *Behavior Analysis: Research and Practice, 17*(2), 103–113. http://dx.doi.org/10.1037/bar0000076

Jones, St. Peter, C. C., & Ruckle, M. M. (2020). The reporting of demographic variables in the Journal of Applied Behavior Analysis. *Journal of Applied Behavior Analysis, 53*, 1304–1315. https://doi.org/10.1002/jaba.722

Jost, J. T., & Kay, A. C. (2010). *Social justice: History, theory, and research.* In S. T. Fiske, D. T. Gilbert, & G. Lindzey (Eds.), *Handbook of social psychology* (pp. 1122–1165). John Wiley & Sons. https://doi.org/10.1002/9780470561119.socpsy002030

Kazdin, A. E. (1977). Assessing the clinical or applied importance of behavior change through social validation. *Behavior Modification, 1*(4), 427–452. https://doi.org/10.1177/014544557714001

LeBlanc, L., Taylor, B., & Marchese, N. (2019). The training experiences of behavior analysts: Compassionate care and therapeutic relationships with caregivers. *Behavior Analysis in Practice.* https://doi.org/10.1007/s40617-019-00368-z

Louis, W. R., Mavor, K. I., La Macchia, S. T., & Amiot, C. E. (2014). Social justice and psychology: What is, and what should be. *Journal of Theoretical and Philosophical Psychology, 34*(1), 14–27. https://doi.org/10.1037/a0033033

Matsuda, K., Garcia, Y., Catagnus, R., & Brandt, J. A. (2020). Can behavior analysis help us understand and reduce racism? A review of the current literature. *Behavior Analysis in Practice*, 1–12. https://doi.org/10.1007/s40617-020-00411-4

Miller, K. L., Re Cruz, A., & Ala'i-Rosales, S. (2019). Inherent tensions and possibilities: Behavior analysis and cultural responsiveness. *Behavior and Social Issues, 28*, 1–21. https://doi.org/10.1007/s42822-019-00013-y

Munsey, C. (2011) And social justice for all. *APA Monitor, 42*, 30.

Pritchett, M., Ala'i, S., Re Cruz, A., & Cihon, T. (2020, August 19). Social justice is the spirit and aim of an applied science of human behavior: Moving from colonial to participatory research practices. *Behavior Analysis in Practice.* https://doi.org/10.31234/osf.io/t87p4.

Sidman, M. (2001). *Coercion and its fallout* (2nd ed.). Authors Cooperative.

Skinner, B. F. (1953). *Science and human behavior.* Macmillan.

Skinner, B. F. (1961). The design of cultures. *Daedalus, 90*(3), 534–546.

Skinner, B. F. (1987). Why we are not acting to save the world. In B. F. Skinner, *Upon further reflection* (pp. 1–14). Prentice Hall.

Skinner, B. F. (1948). *Walden two*. Hackett Publishing.

Taylor, B. A., LeBlanc, L. A., & Nosik, M. R. (2018). Compassionate care in behavior analytic treatment: Can outcomes be enhanced by attending to relationships with caregivers? *Behavior Analysis in Practice, 12*(3), 654–666. https://doi.org/10.1007/s40617-018-00289-3

United Nations. (2006). Social justice in an open world: The role of the United Nations. United Nations.

Vasquez, M. J. T. (2012). Psychology and social justice: Why we do what we do. *American Psychologist, 67*(5), 337–346. https://doi.org/10.1037/a0029232

Walsh, R. T. G., & Gokani, R. (2014). The personal and political economy of psychologists' desires for social justice. *Journal of Theoretical and Philosophical Psychology, 34*(1), 41–55. https://doi.org/10.1037/a0033081

Wolf, M. M. (1978). Social validity: The case for subjective measurement or how applied behavior analysis is finding its heart. *Journal of Applied Behavior Analysis, 11*(2), 203–214. https://doi.org/10.1901/jaba.1978.11-203

Wright, P. I. (2019). Cultural humility in the practice of applied behavior analysis. *Behavior Analysis in Practice, 12*(4), 805–809. https://doi.org/10.1007/s40617-019-00343-8

41

SOCIAL MEDIA
A Global Social Tool or Dilemma?

Ryan L. O'Donnell

INTRODUCTION

The Definition and Scope of Social Media

Social media is defined by the Oxford English Dictionary as "websites and applications that enable users to create and share content or to participate in social networking" (Oxford English Dictionary, n.d.). The most active social media platforms in today's global society, based on the number of users, includes:[1]

- Facebook – over 2.6 billion users[2] (Clement, 2020)
- YouTube – over 2 billion logged-in users visit YouTube each month and with over 1 billion hours of video watched every day and billions of views. (*YouTube by the numbers* 2020)
- Instagram – over 1 billion users (Clement, 2020)
- TikTok – over 800 million users (Clement, 2020)
- LinkedIn – over 700 million users (*Linked In About Us*, 2020)
- Reddit – over 430 million users and over 2.3 million subreddits (Frontpage Metrics, 2020)
- Pinterest – over 367 million users and over 2 Billion searches every month (Clement, 2020) with 600 million of those are visual searches (Sehl, 2020)
- Twitter – over 326 million users (Clement, 2020) and approximately 10% of those make up 80% of all tweets (Wojcik & Hughes, 2020)
- Snapchat – over 238 million users and more than 4 billion snaps are created each day (Noyes, 2020)

Some have suggested that certified behavior analysts stay off these platforms entirely (John S. Bailey, personal communication, September 13, 2018) and suggested ways certified behavior analysts can engage with social media (O'Leary et al., 2015). While ethical discussions must continue, the ubiquitous use of these platforms calls for a larger discussion on their influence and role for individual behavior analysts and the field. The Pew Research Center (2020) has seen American adults engaged in at least one social media platform increase from

---

1   I have purposefully left out messaging platforms and some lesser known apps which may operate in some similar ways as the more well-known above. The points made in this chapter are based on knowledge and understanding of the first list. If you'd like to investigate them on your own, please consider starting with: WhatsApp – over 2 billion users; Facebook Messenger – over 1.3 billion users; Weixin/WeChat – over 1.2 billion users; QQ – over 694 million users; Sina aWeibo – over 550 million users; QZone – over 517 million users; Kuaishou – Over 400 million users.

2   What other industries call their consumers "users?"

5% in 2005 to 72% in 2019. Since the advent of the Internet, socially mediated contingencies many experience daily have shifted topography due to private businesses creating these social media platforms, but also due to a fundamental change in what they sold – precise behavioral prediction and influence.

In the late 1990s and early 2000s, as the Internet became widely adopted, influencing others was further democratized and human behavior became much more accessible to commoditize. Social media users gain access to features of a platform in exchange for their information. Conversely, the social media platform provides society with the ability to reach audiences that we once knew (e.g., past classmates, ex-lovers, co-workers) or audiences we wish to reach (e.g., groups based on your interests and hobbies, new business customers via micro-targeted ads or influencers). The development of social media platforms fundamentally changed the way in which our society functions, as anyone with an Internet connection can be heard without having to transcend or play by the rules in hopes of being chosen by the traditional gatekeepers (e.g., physical publishers, media networks, media executives, and agents). The exact amount of democratization users experience remains unclear as the people behind the decisions of how social media platform features work to amplify user voices is largely unknown. The complex algorithms and terms of service of each social media site are still determined by a relatively small group of decision makers within the private business sector (i.e., the gatekeepers may just be changing).

To be abundantly clear, the opportunity provided in a country like the United States of America where anyone with an idea has the possibility to create a functioning private business is something that I whole-heartedly believe in (later I'll discuss one of the major contingencies that I see as needing correction). However, the questions should be to what extent and at what expense? While the information that you provide is almost always written such that you are licensing your content (that is, your data is still your data legally and the platforms are just hosting it on your behalf), they now have access to the keys of the gate to your behavioral data.

As behavior analysts we know behavior is at the root of everything that we do, know, and understand. Every click, scroll, picture, video, link, reaction, ad, argument, tagged post, purchase (on and off-site), etc. is subject to measurement and analysis at levels our field's founders (Kantor, 1975; Skinner, 1953) only dreamed of having in their labs. Couple this with A/B testing (also known as split testing or bucket testing) where users are randomized into two variants (each provided with a version of an interface to engage with) and automation and social media platforms have the ability to experimentally test and optimize experiences for their viewers individually in real time.

In a matter of years, a small group of entrepreneurs leveraged the benefits of a democratized infrastructure that the Internet provided and created the conditions for global experimentation. That influenced us to opt-in and agree to them in exchange for free access, and then we provided them with the data they required to carry out arguably the most elaborate human experiment ever. Now this doesn't mean that the discussions of O'Leary & colleagues (2015) or the concerns of Bailey (personal communication, September 13, 2018) are not warranted, but for a field that proclaims "to predict-and-influence [behavior], with precision, scope, and depth, whole organisms interacting in and with a context considered historically and situationally" (Hayes et al., 2012, p. 4). I believe the first and foremost discussion required into exploring social media requires a discussion of what it is; an operant chamber on a unprecedented scale.

How Social Media Platforms Work

Social media platforms operate from a historically novel business model for the technology industry: user-generated content. Everything we provide and how we behave on a platform can be measured with rigor. While these are all behaviors, I will classify them as:

- Information we directly upload (e.g., email address, name, age, date of birth, location data, personal photos, personal videos, links)
- Behaviors we engage in (e.g., what we like and follow, share, where the information derives from that we share, who we follow and don't engage with, how long we stay on a page, which advertisements we click on, and what political content we interact with)

Most social media platforms are designed to gather and predict our behavior in one of two ways:

1. We sign up and provide them with this user-generated content slowly, in which they can build an understanding of who we are through what we like, dislike, etc. (e.g., Facebook, LinkedIn)
2. We sign up and provide very little of this info explicitly, but they learn much of what interests us and keeps us engaged and on the platform through providing us with content right away (e.g., YouTube, TikTok).

These platforms are largely based in Silicon Valley, California with the claimed ethos of bringing people together to connect and achieve "great things." While technologies may allow this ethos to be achieved, the same technologies can divide people in ways we may not be able to immediately identify (Green, 2019; Green, 2020; Jacoby et al., 2018; Noujaim & Amer, 2019; Orlowski 2020). For example, in 2019, *The Great Hack*, shared a glimpse of how Cambridge Analytica, a small company residing in Great Britain, had influenced more than 200 elections around the world between 2013–2018 (Noujaim & Amer, 2019). Cambridge Analytica bragged that it had 5,000 data points on every American voter that they used to target "persuadables" – undecided voters in key voting precincts who might go either way if shown the right propaganda to vote for now President Donald Trump.

Jacoby et al. (2018) are one of many who highlighted how the Internet Research Agency (based in Russia) attempted to create division by forming meetups that were known to be in opposition with one another. Heart of Texas, a Russian-controlled Facebook group that promoted Texas secession amassed hundreds of thousands of followers, ran an ad on Facebook announcing a rally on May 21, 2016 to "Stop Islamification of Texas." Simultaneously, another Russian-sponsored group, United Muslims of America, advertised a "Save Islamic Knowledge" rally for the same place and time. These are two terrifying examples with no clarity, as to what extent social media had actually influenced human behavior and at what cost.

Social media is a way to amplify your message; however, the megaphone is dynamic and it can change in size based on who you are, your message, and how well the post is performing. When we provide a social media platform with information or create content to host on their platform it is amplified to your audience (e.g., friends, followers, and sometimes even audiences related to them). When user-generated content performs in ways that human-designed algorithms select, then it may be down ranked (shown to fewer people), or further boosted to more screens around the world. This dynamic relationship is important to understand. As behavior analysts who uphold empiricism and data-based decision making, these platforms have embedded within them the ability to make real-time data-based decisions for each behavior you engage in on the social media platform (via each click, pause, replay, share, etc.). In the case of Cambridge Analytica, content posted quickly can lead to outcomes such as persuading voters on candidate choices without their explicit awareness. However, the same algorithms can help connect you to fellow colleagues around the globe or provide you with that Internet meme that hits just the right way after a long and arduous day of service delivery. Again, we come back to the question . . . at what cost?

Social media business models primarily thrive off ad-based revenue; resulting in contingencies that appear to be aligned to encourage longer engagement times (perhaps even addiction) by its users. Coincidentally, longer durations of engagement lead to more they can learn about a user and effectively markets towards them (e.g., new content, advertisements). A post that performs well at keeping people on a platform (indirectly allowing for more advertisements towards you) is incentivized by the social media site to be shared with more similar users, creating a situation where content can quickly accelerate to more screens (but at the helm of the algorithms the developers deploy to gauge which human behaviors its appropriate for). This primary revenue of advertiser revenue provides some unique situations.

First, there is a clear model in which you can "pay to play." For example, anyone that has a Facebook account can set up a Facebook business account and begin running advertisements. While there are some laws around special categories such as political ads, housing advertisements, etc. there is also controversy around the ability of businesses to micro-target consumers as highlighted previously with Cambridge Analytica and the Internet Research Agency (Jacoby et al., 2018; Noujaim & Amer, 2019; Orlowski, 2020). However, these social media platforms provide extreme value for users trying to reach a particular audience. For example, the author of this chapter used this strategy to place his behavior analytically oriented Facebook videos to behavior analysts in geographical locations during behavior analytic conferences for the first two years of his business. In addition, he has also helped agencies communicate their values and attract top talent through YouTube advertisements. This strategy is relatively cheap compared to older models such as conference advertising models, but it requires knowledge of social media, content creation, storytelling, etc.

Success on social media is defined by the ability for a social media campaign to articulate goals, create a strategy, leverage resources, and usually pay to get it to the right people at the right time through advertisements or dark posts. Dark posts are targeted ads on social media; however, unlike boosted and organic posts, they don't appear on a personal or business timeline. Rather, they show up as sponsored content in the feeds of users you're specifically targeting. For wholesome and relatively safe content, this may not be of much concern.[3] However in the case of Cambridge Analytica or the Internet Research Agency this is of great concern. Furthermore, what performs well may not be useful for a scientific enterprise like Behavior Analysis. For example, Vosoughi and colleagues (2018) found false news about terrorism, natural disasters, science, urban legends, and financial information that spreads up to six times faster on Twitter. What are the exact mechanisms that influence this? How ubiquitous is it? Are these phenomena avoidable? Questions such as these are still largely unknown and perhaps inaccessible due to the fact that these businesses operate in the private sector. For behavior analysts, one of the largest concerns appears to be when behavior analytic content from private accounts and business accounts has no checks and

---

3   This calls questions of who operationally defines this, and how we continue to evaluate necessary changes.

balances. A key tenet of our field is that relevant alternative perspectives are included, when verified as being effective and ethical.

Clarifying What Constitutes Behavior Analytic Content

With a sense of scale that these platforms play in influencing human behavior it's important to remind readers that as behavior analysts we subscribe to a set of philosophical assumptions. The behavior analytic worldview has been outlined as a form of contextualism (Hayes, et al., 1988). Contextualism is synthetic, meaning the whole is basic and the parts derived – that is an operant response is not described and identified by its parts (Sd + MO → R → C), but rather the ongoing act in context is our subject matter (e.g., the operant). Additionally, the truth criterion of contextualism is successfully working (Hayes et al., 1988). That is, a behavioral analysis of an event is scientifically true only in their relation to accomplishing a particular stated goal. Contextualism is also dispersive, meaning that "facts are related when they are found to be so, not by assumption" (Hayes et al., 1988, p. 98).

While there are various forms of contextualism such as the descriptive contextualism which forms Interbehaviorism (Kantor & Smith, 1975) or the work of Contextual Behavioral Science rooted in functional contextualism (Hayes et al., 2012), they are all synthetic and dispersive. It's important to underscore these assumptions as the value of any behavior analytic endeavor (e.g., research article, conceptual interpretation, social media campaign). Contextualism is determined based on whether it was first operating from these assumptions. Should it not be, it may still be of value to society; however, it may no longer be behavior analytic in nature. By now you hopefully have a sense of scale and understand the general workings of social media platforms so we can begin to explore how it can be leveraged by an individual or organization subscribing to the behavior analytic worldview.

WHICH PLATFORM IS BEST FOR SOCIAL INFLUENCE?

If you strip away the specific features and creator tools of each platform, social media platforms can be conceptualized as a unique social context in which behavior unique to that context occurs. Engaging content on one platform likely will not perform the same on other platforms as the context is determined by the history of the group's collective individual behavior on that platform. While these may shift over time or to new platforms, the context of each platform and what content performs well are not the same. Generally speaking, there are three types of content we can produce. While our field has far more knowledge and expertise in alternative communication modalities (e.g., Picture Exchange Communication System [PECS], Sign Language, Augmentative and Alternative Communication [AAC]) there are the three primary mediums in which content is created and consumed:[4]

- Written
- Auditory
- Imagery

---

4 There are a number of social media accounts outside the field of behavior analysis creating content for these alterna.

What used to be heard on the radio, is now consumed as podcasts. What used to be consumed via television, is now on-demand videos. What used to be in the newspapers, is now consumed as blogs, social media posts, or webpages (for more on these analogies see *Crushing It* by Gary Vaynerchuk). Additionally, there are three ways in which people largely behave on platforms:

- Consuming content (e.g., clicking, reacting, commenting, watching, sharing)
- Creating content (e.g., blogging, podcasting, posting videos)
- Curating content (e.g., sharing other's works to your own page)

In the contextualistic framework that behavior analysts operate within, these three media can be combined to form a unique content strategy through consuming, creating, and curating information for each platform to achieve personal, professional, or organizational goals. Questions that may help guide a behavior analyst in determining which social media platforms to allocate their efforts:

- What are your explicitly stated personal, professional, or organizational goals and how will you measure successful completion of the goal?
- Who are you trying to reach, and which social media platforms have their attention currently? This will help guide discussions for content, and where to host it.
- What value do people receive? What problem are you solving through your strategies?
- What ethical and legal concerns do you need to consider and solve in order to bring your social media campaign online and begin to influence?
- What skill sets are required for you to achieve your goal (e.g., storytelling, digital creation software, coding)?

Questions such as "Which platform is best?" is not something anyone can provide without answering questions like those described above and evaluating the data on the effectiveness of the strategies along with any known confounding variables. Consider this list as a starting point, with the tenets of the field (e.g., contextualism, empiricism, philosophic doubt, parsimony, determinism, experimentation, replication) as the guideposts for evaluation. Science is an endeavor aimed at increasing our contact with events in the natural world in a way that allows us to effectively interact with those events (Kantor, 1953; Skinner, 1953). Social media encompasses these events in a "digital world" and should be approached in a similar manner by behavior analysts.

General Considerations and Concerns

In 1988 Hayes, Hayes, & Reese stated, "Behavior analysis has always had significant conflicts with other psychological perspectives. At their most fundamental level, these conflicts are often philosophical, concerning such issues as the nature of the human and the purposes of science" (p. 97). Ironically this applies as much to the contemporary practice of Applied Behavior Analysis as it does to our difference with the psychological perspectives adjacent to us. The behavior analytic social media landscape shows as much connection and dissemination as it does in-fighting and arguments. The extent to which this occurs is hard to pinpoint and an area of much needed empirical investigation, as it is something frequently discussed by behavior analysts both on and off social media.

User-generated content is driven by contingencies like all other behavior. The data are most accessible to platform creators, but third-party analyses such as an empirical behavior analytic approach, is paramount. The "intentions" or "reasons" it is being created can be analyzed empirically as a series of non-linear contingencies (Goldiamond & Thompson, 1967, 2004). Unfortunately, influential issues occurring on social media occur behind the scenes and will likely continue to be inaccessible. This author is aware of reports of popular behavior analytic social media accounts and movements issuing threats of litigation and censorship to other behavior analytic creators. There are also reports of blatant errors and complete non-disclosed paid advertising (i.e., violating Federal Trade Commission guidelines and law). Others are being subjected to or instigating cancelation attempts, harassment, etc. While we may have the ability to look through the lens of a natural scientific approach, that doesn't mean we always do so and these platforms may also be sowing division within our own field . . . and again, at what expense and what cost?

One of the largest societal issues across the globe in today's social media age is this compounding of the democratization of information sharing and the lack of clearly communicated and validated influences for why someone is engaging in creating or curating content. If there is one single call to action for behavior analysis for social media, it would be for everyone to clarify their philosophical assumptions, state them publicly so they are known by others, to be held publicly responsible to live by them, and to note when their assertions have changed. I fear that the public perception of our field may be at risk without this, since it creates confusion to the consumer of online content as to what constitutes Behavior Analysis. Add this to the rapidly growing community of practitioners of Applied Behavior Analysis (Behavior Analyst Certification Board, 2020) and the issues discussed that drive the development and features of these platforms and I am afraid any valid concerns are just the beginning of a much larger discussions that calls for systematic changes for the field and world at large with respect to behavior occurring on social media.

Generally speaking, generating user content is susceptible to the same concerns of other forms of publishing (e.g., news outlets, radio stations, newspapers, peer-reviewed journals):

- It is subject to being influenced by economic incentives (e.g., paid ad placements, sponsored posts)
- It is subject to being influenced by external sources without consumer knowledge (e.g., unstated advertisers)
- It is subject to logical fallacies (e.g., reification, straw man arguments, the fallacy of incomplete evidence, appeals to emotion, Kafka trapping, arguments of popularity)
- It is subject to the repertoire(s), available resources, and history of those involved (i.e., confirmation bias, time, money)

Our field would benefit from asking questions of content creators on social media or when consuming content online to begin orienting our culture to the variables that may be affecting our public perception and dissemination. The value of a social media campaign in behavior analysis should be continually evaluated and upheld as an exemplar model to the degree to which it limits logical fallacies, states economic incentives clearly upfront to consumers, and corrects errors when they are pointed out by consumers or peers (i.e., skill deficits and logical fallacies). Even better will be a behavioral analysis of social media itself. Until then, and as a creator of behavior analytic social media content, I ask that creators uphold themselves to a higher standard with each post and that consumers continue to support those attempting to push the boundaries on science, communication, and dissemination. Finding a field such as behavior analysis that allows you to see the world through a pragmatic lens leads to a level of responsibility that has generated the ideas and calls to action in this book. What may bear even more responsibility is when you couple that knowledge with an online audience.

Considerations for Those Creating

This is in no way exhaustive or evaluated. But what I have learned from those that have mentored me directly and indirectly:

1. Social media platforms are designed to get the most from you presently, that they possibly can. They have leveraged the science in subtle ways, often unbeknown to the user.
2. Tread carefully. Create a review and support system around you to diligently observe signs that you identify as solely as your content, put off goals and values in service of views and clicks, or compromise yours or your loved one's privacy, security, and personal relationships.
3. The best time to start was yesterday, the second-best time is now (building an audience never gets easier).
4. Comments are a balance of modeling civil discourse and balancing when to respond and when to avoid feeding the trolls.
5. Creating at the expense of others is risky. It's far better to find another more prosocial approach.
6. If you find yourself in an influential position, free is the most expensive. People giving you free things, usually means there is an expectation of something in return. Establish clear expectations with any type of partnership.
7. Don't spoonfeed information. Provide just enough to keep people thinking.
8. Story structure matters more than what gear you have available to create with.
9. Bending and distorting the truth is enticing, but as scientists, we cannot succumb to it and should purposefully frame content to prevent misinformation from spreading. Sumner et al. (2014) found that information not carefully controlled for accuracy that made it into the hands of reporters drastically increased the chances of overextended inferences from humans to animal research and exaggerated causal claims.
10. What sets a creator apart on any platform is authentic and valuable content (memes only do our field so much . . .).
11. Obtaining information from one source, regardless of its form be it a peer-reviewed journal, book, social media platform, etc. is extremely risky.

Considerations for Those Consuming

". . . during a momentary lapse of reason, expressing one's opinion on a social media platform could have unintended and irreversible consequences" (Kelly et al., 2018, O'Leary et al., 2015). This statement should be acknowledged with each interaction on social media. Most errors are not worthy of threats of cancelation (in fact that's antithetical to the views of our field under most circumstances), but all posts, errors or not, are worthy of simple and clear feedback of what you appreciate and what you would consider doing differently and why. Furthermore, it's not going away. If you recall, these platforms have been and will continue to be a part of our lives (or those we serve). For those who have the expertise in online social media content, offer your skills, knowledge, and abilities and collaborate with content creators. It is much more likely to affect the change you want than the alternatives. At this point, the scale and impacts of social media may seem overwhelming to say the least . . . is there any silver lining?

The Sliver of Hope

As an avid reader of extremely esoteric behavioral science, it saddens me every time I see a question on social media that's been properly conceptualized or answered empirically, in our field (often decades ago) and pushed aside . . . Or when logical and empirical arguments are downplayed due to arbitrary factors such as the author or year completed that have no functional relation shown to be of concern in our literature. Or when world-views outside of our philosophical assumptions of contextualism are in conflict with what is being shared, recommended or adopted by someone (often unbeknownst to both parties). But we cannot forget our roots as behavior analysts, "the child [*sic*] knows best" (Lindsley, 1972). A social media post includes precisely what the current environmental conditions are evoking.

Morris (1985) stated that "If a scientific community does not arrange for contingencies that assure its survival, then so much the worse for that community, and for the rest of the culture at large" (p. 108). The first and most important consideration for anyone concerned with the role of social media in the behavior analytic community would be the coordination of our Verified Course Systems (VCS), the Behavior Analyst Certification Board (BACB®), professional and trade organizations (e.g., Association for Professional Behavior Analysts, Association for Behavior Analysis International, Behavioral Health Center of Excellence), our institutional training programs and universities, Approved Continuing Education (ACE) providers, independent content creators (e.g., podcasts, YouTube channels, filmmakers, designers), etc.

Kantor (1953) noted that any particular branch of science often found multiple answers for a single question, used alternative theoretical assumptions, or had general disagreement within the field. However, Kantor (1953) also proposed a solution. A logician of science: someone (or entity may be more appropriate) that could cohesively organize and synthesize the theoretical and empirical work of a field. What behavior analysis could benefit from is a cohesive approach to instilling, expecting, and assuring (to a degree) that our core tenets and assumptions are taught to mastery and disseminated with integrity. However, currently we are far too disorganized for this to begin. The first step is that we collectively value respect and humility for the scientific foundation of our field and emulate it in the ways that we behave in all aspects of our day-to-day interactions. Until that is solved, we will continue having issues that social media platforms purely magnify for us (and potentially the world) to see. Coupled with social media platforms that lean on ad-revenue contingencies to drive their content and we may very well be stuck in a vortex where opinion, errors and false news are far more likely to succeed. Talks of reform continue for social media platforms, and given it's been over 65 years since the concerns and propositions of Kantor (1953) in structuring our field to more accurately organize and communicate scientific information with little to no success due to lack of cooperation leaves me woefully optimistic. In the words of the great R. Buckminster Fuller, "Whether it is to be utopia or oblivion will be a touch-and-go relay race right up to the final moment" (Fuller, 1981, p. 36).

REFERENCES

Behavior Analyst Certification Board. (2020, September 15). *BACB Certificant Data*. BACB. https://www.bacb.com/bacb-certificant-data/

Clement, J. (2020, August 21). *Most used social media platforms*. Statista.com. https://www.statista.com/statistics/272014/global-social-networks-ranked-by-number-of-users/

Frontpage Metrics. (2020). *New subreddits by month: How Reddit grew over time*. Frontpagemetrics.com. https://frontpagemetrics.com/history/month

Fuller, R. B (1981). *Critical path*. St. Martin's Press.

Goldiamond, I., Thompson, D. M., & Andronis, P. T. (2004). *The blue books: Goldiamond & Thompson's functional analysis of behavior*. Cambridge Center for Behavior Studies.

Green, H. (2019). *An absolutely remarkable thing*. Dutton.

Green, H. (2020). *A beautifully foolish endeavor: A novel (the Carls)*. Dutton.

Hayes, S. C., Hayes, L. J., & Reese, H. W. (1988). Finding the philosophical core: A review of Stephen C. Pepper's *World Hypotheses: A Study in Evidence*. *Journal of the Experimental Analysis of Behavior, 50*, 97–111. https://doi.org/10.1901/jeab.1988.50-97

Hayes, S. C., Barnes-Holmes, D., & Wilson, K. G. (2012). Contextual behavioral science: Creating a science more adequate to the challenge of the human condition. *Journal of Contextual Behavioral Science, 1*(1),1–16. https://doi.org/10.1016/j.jcbs.2012.09.004

Jacoby, J., Bourg, A., Priest, D., & Robertson, M. (2018, October 29 and 30). The Facebook Dilemma (Season 2018; Episode 4) [TV series episode]. In M. & Chheng, L., Nolan, D (Executive Producer) *Frontline*. PBS Corp.

Kantor, J. R. (1953). *The logic of modern science*. Principia Press.

Kantor, J. R., & Smith, N. W. (1975). *The science of psychology an interbehavioral survey*. Principia Press.

Kelly, M. P., Martin, N., Dillenburger, K., Kelly, A. N., & Miller, M. M. (2018). Spreading the news: History, successes, challenges and the ethics of effective dissemination. *Behavior Analysis in Practice, 12*(2), 440–451. https://doi.org/10.1007/s40617-018-0238-8

Lindsley, O. R. (1972). From Skinner to precision teaching. In J. B. Jordan & L. S. Robbins (Eds.), *Let's try doing something else kind of thing* (pp. 1–12). Council on Exceptional Children.

LinkedIn. (2020). *About us*. LinkedIn Newsroom | LinkedIn. https://news.linkedin.com/about-us

Morris, E. K. (1985). Public information, dissemination, and behavior analysis. *The Behavior Analyst, 8*(1), 95–110. https://doi.org/10.1007/BF03391916

Noujaim, J., & Amer, K. (Directors). 2019. *The Great Hack* [Film]. The Othrs.

Noyes, D. (2020, August 3). *The top 10 valuable Snapchat statistics – Updated August 2020*. Zephoria Inc. https://zephoria.com/top-10-valuable-snapchat-statistics/

O'Leary, P. N., Miller, M. M., Olive, M. L., & Kelly, A. N. (2015). Blurred lines: Ethical implications of social media for behavior analysts. *Behavior Analysis in Practice, 10*(1), 45–51. https://doi.org/10.1007/s40617-014-0033-0

Orlowski, J. (Director). 2020. *The Social Dilemma* [Film]. Exposure Labs Argent Pictures The Space Program

Oxford English Dictionary. (n.d.) Social Media. Oxford Languages. Retrieved September 18, 2020, from https://www.lexico.com/definition/social_media

Pew Research Center: Internet, Science & Tech. (2020, June 5). *Demographics of social media users and adoption in the United States*. pewresearch.org. https://www.pewresearch.org/internet/fact-sheet/social-media/

Sehl, K. (2020, March 4). *23 Pinterest statistics that matter to marketers in 2019*. Social Media Marketing & Management Dashboard. https://blog.hootsuite.com/pinterest-statistics-for-business/

Skinner, B. F. (1953). *Science and human behavior*. Simon & Schuster.

Sumner, P., Vivian-Griffiths, S., Boivin, J., Williams, A., Venetis, C. A., Davies, A., Ogden, J., Whelan, L., Hughes, B., Dalton, B., Boy, F., & Chambers, C. D. (2014). The association between exaggeration in health related science news and academic press releases: Retrospective observational study. *British Medical Journal, 349*(dec12 7), g7666-g7666. https://doi.org/10.1136/bmj.g7666

Vosoughi, S., Roy, D., & Aral, S. (2018). The spread of true and false news online. *Science, 359*(6380), 1146–1151. https://doi.org/10.1126/science.aap9559

Wojcik, S., & Hughes, A. (2020, May 30). *How Twitter users compare to the general public.* Pew Research Center: Internet, Science & Tech. https://www.pewresearch.org/internet/2019/04/24/sizing-up-twitter-users/

42

STIGMA

Stigma Through a Behavioral Lens: A Kenyan Perspective

Pooja Panesar

WHAT IS STIGMA?

The *Oxford Dictionary* defines stigma as a mark of disgrace associated with a particular circumstance, quality, or person (Oxford Learner Dictionaries, 2020). *Webster's Dictionary* defines stigma as a set of negative and often unfair beliefs that a society or group of people have about something (Merriam Webster, 2020). According to these two definitions, one could extrapolate a component of stigma related to self, environment, and social community. Vogel and colleagues (2013) discuss public and self-stigma along with the short- and long-term effects on stigmatized individuals. Public stigma refers to the perceptions by the general population on different aspects as being socially unacceptable whereas self-stigma refers to an individual's perception of himself or herself as being socially unacceptable which leads to reduced self-esteem and self-worth. They also demonstrate how public stigma may lead to self-stigma.

DIFFERENT FACES OF STIGMA

Stigmas are ubiquitous and are observed across various groups, regardless of size and between individuals. On a larger scale, some prominent examples of stigma are stigmas across race, ethnicity, socioeconomic status, gender, cognitive ability, health status, and sexual preference. Stigmatization may be contingent upon the community you live in and/or where you come from. If the majority of people are of a certain age/gender/sexual preference, etc., a minority group is often the one who experiences stigmatization. Further, even what might be perceived as a "higher ability" (e.g., greater socioeconomic status) might be stigmatized by the majority group (e.g., lower socioeconomic status).

A prime example of this is how we perceive people with disabilities. In the general population, persons with developmental disorders are stigmatized as they are a minority group who has fewer rights and opportunities than the neurotypical population. We can even see stigma within this community itself – where individuals with fewer communication needs feel underrepresented and further stigmatized in their own community as well as within the general population (Autism Rights Movement, July 2020). Therefore, it is important to realize that within a stigmatized community one must be cognizant of all of its members as it is common for some to feel marginalized within their own stigmatized community.

During the COVID-19 pandemic, stigmatization has been more pronounced for the minority groups that have been affected. As this is a global pandemic, and anyone is susceptible to catching the virus – it is a virus (an organism that we are not yet able to control); and yet, as a people of this world, who are all equal in front of the virus, we have found a way to create stigma (Ramaci et al., 2020). During the initial stages of the pandemic, stigma was directed towards Chinese and others of Asian descent as they were regarded as the cause of the pandemic. This discriminated group then evolved towards minority or foreign groups within communities other than their own (Tiziana et al., 2020; UNESCO, 2020). In some countries (e.g. in the Kenyan slums), being tested for COVID-19 could lead to being shunned, even though citizens need to be tested to find work (Reuters, 2020).

BRINGING IT HOME

As a Kenyan woman running an organization for individuals with developmental disorders in Kenya and Tanzania, I have had the opportunity to see many facets of stigma within this community. Stigmas often stem from a lack of information and fear. Autism, for example, is unknown to the preponderance of Kenyans. Parents report they are unable to take their autistic child(ren) out into the community, to restaurants, the supermarket, to birthday parties, or other functions. They are accused of raising spoiled children, not teaching their children manners, and are branded ineffective parents. They keep their children inside until the children have developed the skills to cope in public settings, or the parents become confident in facing the stigma. This stigma stems from cultural myths and misconceptions in Africa around many disorders (Osman, 2016) and the parents feel it is not worth being ostracized.

One of the most common misconceptions is that disorders (which are considered a disease or illness) are contagious. Especially for seizure disorders, any fluids (e.g., saliva) passed during a seizure are considered to transmit the "disease" if someone comes into contact with them. For this reason, in rural areas, many individuals suffering from seizure disorders are kept away from the rest of the family (e.g., in an outhouse) and may be given their own set of dishes. The other common myths are that witchcraft and curses cause disorders. Typically, it is assumed the mother is cursed or the curse is carried from her family. This causes many families to separate and face ostracization from the community by being shunned. Other beliefs around the causes for disabilities include punishment for having premarital intercourse, if the mother's dowry is incomplete, or the family has received bad omens.

With perceived causes such as these, the first form of intervention is typically visiting traditional healers, seeking healers to perform exorcisms, and even traveling across countries to get potions and herbs to feed their children or bathe them in them to rid them of disease. It is challenging to let go of the cultural beliefs that have been ingrained within a culture for many generations.

As an organization, Kaizora hosts awareness events across different areas of the country in an effort to disseminate accurate information to communities. In June 2019, we held an event in Meru, a small town quite a distance from Nairobi. We selected a school for the "mentally challenged" as the setting. We conducted consultations and trainings for parents, students, and teachers. We visited a medical facility to train staff on autism spectrum disorder and cerebral palsy. Though our efforts were well appreciated, one of the hospital administrators said to us that we chose the wrong place to have the event. She said many people will not come to a school for the mentally handicapped because they will be seen in public and it will bring shame upon their family. Many families continue to remain in hiding and avoid seeking much needed help due to stigma. Another training was held at a reputable community temple and not a single person showed up!

In December 2019, we were looking for premises to expand our center in the city of Nairobi which is considered a cosmopolitan city with a well-educated population compared to other parts of the country. We were turned away from all the premises we approached when we explained the nature of our work. Excuses spanned from we would not afford the rent because of the population we serve or the families would not want such children to come to our establishment. Thoroughly offended, we confided in the parents of our clients during a get-together and they were not surprised at all. The hardship that they have faced over the years put our experiences (as professionals) as negligible. We will never understand as we have not walked in their shoes.

HOW STIGMA AFFECTS US

Marginalized groups who have been stigmatized can respond in a few ways. When a public stigma exists, not all individuals within that group are exposed in the same way. Each of these individual experiences can affect how a person internalizes an existing stigma and their subsequent reactions to it. This can be looked at from a behavioral perspective in terms of the functions of behaviors. For many, public stigma leads to fear of being personally stigmatized or they may have even experienced negative events while seeking opportunities (e.g., jobs, relationships). This could lead to avoidance behaviors which may result in missed opportunities due to anticipated discrimination for fear of seeking help as that would lead to judgment from others. This in turn leads to increased illnesses, hardships, poverty, and self-stigma.

We also see individuals within groups of marginalized people who may speak out towards an injustice leading to new opportunities or interactions with others within their same group. Being heard and recognized may reinforce the behavior of speaking out thus leading to the likelihood of this behavior increasing in the future. Ultimately, this results in advocating for their rights and for equality for their group. We have seen many movements build momentum over the years advocating for race, color, sexual preference or neuro-uniqueness (i.e., Black Lives Matter, LGBTQ2IA movement, etc.).

There are also groups who are indifferent to the stigma. They may encounter situations arising from stigma, but are able to continue with their journeys without being affected by either consequence. Maybe the experiences have been milder in nature or the individual's support system is able to cushion harsh experiences (see Figure 42.1).

HOW CAN WE DEAL WITH STIGMA?

Dealing with stigma makes me think of the famous saying – knowledge is power! Many stigmas stem from misconceptions and misunderstandings about a disorder, gender, ethnicity, and so on. For example, it is easy for many to assume that obesity is due to a lack of self-control, yet, underlying medical conditions or even the nature of many societies (marketing, access to healthy food, cost of food) may be the underlying cause. It is important for experts in these fields and individuals or groups who experience stigmas to educate the public. The more the public is educated, the less stigma individuals will face, and the less self-stigma will be experienced. The earlier this education is provided, the less people will continue to perpetuate the stigma (Watson & Larson, 2006).

In Kenya, through organizations I belong to, we have held numerous awareness and acceptance events for autism annually since 2010. These have had a huge impact in our community. Through free and accessible workshops, parents have been able to deal with

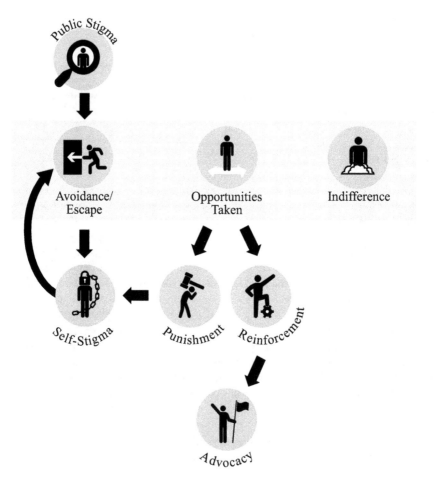

Figure 42.1 Public stigma can cause avoidance/escape behaviors which lead to a cycle of self-stigma and avoidance/escape. Opportunities taken that are punished can also lead to the cycle of self-stigma and avoidance/escape whereas opportunities reinforced bring about advocacy. A third group of individuals remain indifferent and are not as affected by stigma.

self-stigma and become more empowered. We typically have over 100 volunteers from local universities who often interact with children on the autism spectrum for the first time. This type of exposure is a positive experience that has led many to seek employment to better the lives of affected individuals (e.g., careers in behavior analysis and special education). This has spread awareness and acceptance. So many experiences stand out for me personally. For example, a mother of a 9-year-old girl came to me and said, "I thought all this time my child was being stubborn and annoying – I now realize she has autism"; a 38-year-old man came up to us after an event and quietly said "I now realize why I am different and shunned." When being publicly interviewed, I always pass on the message; to seek, to learn, and accept. Before inflicting your own judgment upon anyone, take a step back and learn first – it is amazing the knowledge we can gain through such experiences.

Many doctors and nurses still struggle to understand what autism is. How can we expect the general public, who do not have specialized training, to understand unless we help to impart that knowledge? It is our responsibility as global citizens to create an awareness and acceptance for any area of stigma we belong to, we share, or we can help with.

As a center, we have also encouraged visits and training sessions for other schools. We have some schools that bring grade 6 through 12 students (interested in psychology) for trips. This creates an opportunity, to have allistic students interact with our clients which concludes with an information session with staff. In these sessions, it is inspiring to hear the generations of tomorrow talk about wanting to make a difference. They now know better than to bully that one child who normally sits alone, and they feel the need to spread the word.

Most governments have clauses of equality in their constitutions; however, seeing this implemented is not always the case – as is in Kenya too. With our autistic youth, finding employment or even opportunities to volunteer or intern has proved to be exceedingly difficult. We have a wonderful telecommunication organization, *Safaricom*, which has taken in our clients as interns. However, this is one organization out of about 20 that we approached. At a salon, we were once told that their patrons would feel uncomfortable seeing our clients when they come for services! Nonetheless, we continue to push for employment. It would be beneficial for governments to implement reinforcement systems for organizations employing a minimum number of individuals with different needs and abilities. This would provide incentives for organizations while promoting equality. Educating businesses on the abilities and talents of people from marginalized groups would also be beneficial. It is not about disabilities; it is about looking at the abilities and placing individuals where they will thrive.

Acceptance and equality can come from an individual level, an organizational level, a community level, governmental level, and a global level. Each one of us can make a difference.

Acknowledging stigma is an important step in finding ways to beat it. Hamdani and colleagues (2017) discuss how acknowledgment of discrimination and emphasizing various ways of creating opportunities can create ways of participation to reduce stigma. During my trainings, I emphasize the importance of giving instructions in the form of what to do, rather than what not to do. I feel the same applies here. As people, we know we should not discriminate, we should not judge – but what do we do about that? It is important for each community, group of individuals, organization, government, and country to put relevant programs in place for what people **can** do to help, how to implement it, and where they can receive support if needed.

CONCLUSION

Stigma is something that exists all around us. Let's strive to seek knowledge, become aware, educate ourselves, and find a way forward on all levels, from personal to global; in doing so we have the opportunity to create a more tolerant world to live in.

REFERENCES

Autism Spectrum Disorder Fact Sheets. (2020, July 29). The Autism Rights Movement www.autism-help.org/points-autism-rights-movement.htm
Hamdani, Y., Ary, A., & Lusnky, Y. (2017). Critical analysis of a population mental health strategy: Effects on stigma for people with intellectual and developmental disabilities. *Journal of Mental Health Research in Intellectual Disabilities, 10*(2), 144–161.

Merriam-Webster Dictionary. (2020, July 28). Stigma. www.merriam-webster.com/dictionary/stigma

Osman, O. M. (2016, April 16). The taboo of mental illness in Kenya. *Al Jazeera*. www.aljazeera.com/indepth/features/2016/04/taboo-mental-illness-kenya-160406093345546.html

Oxford Learner Dictionaries. (2020, July 28). Stigma. www.oxfordlearnersdictionaries.com/definition/english/stigma?q=stigma.

Ramaci, T., Barattucci, M., Ledda, C., & Rapisarda, V. (2020). Social stigma during COVID-19 and its impact on HCWs outcomes. *Sustainability, 12*(9), 3834. https://doi.org/10.3390/su12093834

Tiziana, R., Massimiliano, B., Caterina, L., & Venerando, R. (2020). Social stigma during COVID-19 and its impact on HCWs outcomes. *Sustainability, 12*(9), 3834.

UNESCO (2020, May 25). COVID-19-related discrimination and stigma: A global phenomenon? Global Education Coalition. https://en.unesco.org/news/covid-19-related-discrimination-and-stigma-global-phenomenon

Vogel, D. L., Bitman, R. L., Hammer, J. H., & Wade, N. G. (2013). Is stigma internalized? The longitudinal impact of public stigma on self-stigma. *Journal of Counseling Psychology, 60*(2), 311–316. https://doi.org/10.1037/a0031889

Waita, E., & Njehia, J. (2020, May 27). Kenya rolls out testing in Nairobi slums, but some fear stigma. Thomson Reuters Foundation News. https://news.trust.org/item/20200527101501-3rorx/

Watson, A. C., & Larson, J. E. (2006). Personal responses to disability stigma: From self-stigma to empowerment. *Rehabilitation Education, 20*(4), 235–246.

43

STIMULUS EQUIVALENCE
A Derived Relational Account of Cultural Biases

Leif K. Albright, Bryan J. Blair, and Daniel M. Ferman

STIMULUS CLASSES

Human beings respond to stimuli in the environment, both internal and external, in a variety of ways (Michael, 2004). In some cases, stimuli elicit reflexive responding, as when a puff of air makes a person blink or when a leg swings up when the knee tendon is struck. In other cases, humans do not respond automatically in the presence of certain stimuli, such as when a person goes to the refrigerator only sometimes when they feel hungry or if a person ignores a phone call (Skinner, 1953). In addition to stimuli that are present before a behavior occurs, human behavior is controlled by other environmental changes such as stimulus changes that follow behavior (Keller & Schoenfeld, 1950), and individual biological or physiological stimulus conditions.

An antecedent stimulus class can be defined as a group of non-identical stimuli that each occasion a similar response. The main characteristic is mutual substitutability of class members within a given context (Zentall & Smeets, 1996). Stimulus classes can be loosely classified as similarity-based classes and nonsimilarity-based classes. Similarity-based classes (or perceptual classes, or feature classes) can be defined by the number of physical stimulus elements shared across the members of the class, or the degree to which an organism fails to discriminate between the members (Zentall & Smeets, 1996). Therefore, the central characteristic of nonsimilarity-based (or arbitrary) classes is that the members share a low number of stimulus elements, such that their relation is dependent on non-physical features. While the stimulus elements represent the particular members of a stimulus class, the defining characteristic of a stimulus class (regardless of the presence of shared features or not) is the similar response that each member occasions. It is this defining quality that differentiates a stimulus class from unrelated stimuli in the environment.

Members of stimulus equivalence classes are physically disparate, and cohere because of shared functional properties. Thus class-consistent responding is occasioned not by stimulus features but rather as a function of learning. With exposure to appropriate contingencies, these stimuli become interrelated or functionally substitutable with each other, and form an equivalence class. Therefore the presence of any member of a class, will occasion responding to other members of the same class (class-consistent responding). However, the formation of an equivalence class requires class-consistent responding to be demonstrated in the presence of any member, whether or not there was a direct learning history. It is the demonstration of these untrained and emergent relations that are necessary for the development of an equivalence class.

Research has demonstrated equivalence class formation with a wide range of stimulus modalities and topographies including verbal, gustatory (Annett & Leslie, 1995; Hayes et al., 1988), auditory (Dube et al., 1993), and tactile (Plaud, 1995). A consistent finding in the research is that equivalence classes are formed by individuals with established verbal repertoires within and across a wide range of stimuli (Plaud et al., 1998). Stimulus equivalence is considered a robust phenomenon (de Rose et al., 2013) and has been studied with an increasing breadth regarding both research topics and methodological components.

STIMULUS FUNCTIONS

Interest in applications of stimulus equivalence would be limited if the paradigm itself did not combine with other processes, particularly transfer of function. Hayes and colleagues (1991) described two types of functions that have been demonstrated in the literature, across a variety of topics, to transfer across members of an equivalence class: discriminative functions and consequential functions. The discriminative functions (e.g., behaving a certain way in the presence of a stimulus and not behaving in that way when the stimulus is not present) of the members within a class are altered through a series of systematically trained responses (e.g., selecting "Apple" in the presence of an apple and not in the presence of an orange). The function of apple is established as a discriminative stimulus, and apple's function is transferred from an SΔ to an SD. It can therefore be argued that the sole purpose of such training is to transfer discriminative function. Consequential functions refer to the excitatory or inhibitory effects on the future probability of a particular operant that preceded the specific consequence. A transfer of function in this regard would refer to the extent to which the members of a particular equivalence class can reinforce or punish a specific operant.

STIMULUS RELATIONS

Since Hayes and colleagues (1991), many stimulus-stimulus relations other than equivalence (e.g., greater than, less than, opposition) have been explored and combined into intricate networks of emergent relations. Additional processes such as stimulus generalization and contextual control combine with derived relational responding to form classes of almost unimaginable size and complexity. In the case of equivalence relations, the types of functions have been expanded to conditioned reinforcing functions (Hayes et al., 1988; Hayes et al., 1991), discriminative functions of public (Hayes et al., 1988) and private (DeGrandpre et al., 1992) stimuli, elicited conditioned emotional responses, extinction functions (Dougher et al., 1994), and sexual responses (Roche & Barnes, 1997). In the case of relations other than equivalence (e.g., opposition), demonstrations of the transfer of function are also increasingly available (Dymond & Barnes, 1994; Roche & Barnes, 1997).

As the library of studies documenting the transfer of stimulus function expands, the stimulus equivalence paradigm may provide a behavior analytic account into more contemporary and socially relevant concepts such as private events and mental disorders like anxiety or depression (Friman et al., 1998).

It has been suggested that anxiety disorders are the most common mental disorders and affect nearly 30% of adults at some point in their lives (Baxter et al., 2013). Despite the commonplace of this disorder, it is one that most behavior analysts have avoided in practice and research. As a research focus, the challenge of this disorder begins with its definition, as the DSM-V characterizes anxiety disorders as "excessive worry and apprehensive expectation that occurs more days than not for at least six months" (American Psychiatric Association, 2013). In the absence of overt and measurable behaviors, an operational definition is difficult to compose.

EXAMPLES OF TRANSFER/TRANSFORMATION OF STIMULUS FUNCTION

A behavior analytic perspective suggests that anxiety disorders primarily involve high-frequency avoidance or escape from events that may or may not have a direct or immediate relationship with punishment contingencies (Friman et al., 1998). These responses are most likely maintained by access to negative reinforcement, whether or not the aversive stimulus is real or perceived, public or private. As such a contingency may be formed between associated private events and labeled anxiety as the direct result of avoidance of an aversive event (Friman et al., 1998).

When anxiety-like responses cannot be traced to direct contingencies, additional processes could be in effect, such as stimulus function transformation. Take for example, an individual entering a novel social situation. The ascending reticular activating system in the brain is triggered, increasing heart rate and blood pressure as well as maximizing sensory alertness. This may result in a covert behavior commonly labeled as anxiousness. Hypothetically two classes may emerge: anxiety-producing contexts (class 1) comprising class members of covert and overt "anxious" behaviors; and social situations (class 2) comprising class members of novel contexts and settings, and covert and overt behaviors of others. These two classes may merge forming a bi-directional relationship (i.e. anxiety-producing contexts become related to social situations, and social situations become related to anxiety-producing contexts). As such, an aversive stimulus applied within the class of social situations extends to the members of the class of anxiety-producing contexts, thus leading future avoidance of novel social situations. Because of the merging of these two classes and the transformation of function, the avoidance response evoked from the aversive social situation now occurs in the presence of any anxiety-producing context. This merging of functions can create clinically debilitating response patterns especially if overt and covert behaviors emitted to avoid feeling anxiety are extended to those contexts that are common and naturally occurring throughout the typical day of the individual.

BIAS, DISCRIMINATION, AND RACISM

If a derived relational account can be applied to a concept such as anxiety, perhaps such an account can provide a partial explanation for prejudice, bias, discrimination, and even racism. However, any explanation must first begin with a definition, which is no easy feat when discussing a topic of such sociocultural significance and impact. A bias is a label toward or against someone often not based on actual knowledge or experience of the person or group. Bias is often manifested as stereotypes about people based on the group to which they belong and are often based on immutable physical characteristics, such as: gender, race, religion, ethnicity, and/or sexual orientation.

Given an individual's learning history, these biases may become members of their own equivalence classes. For example, if an individual is confronted for the very first time by someone with an ethnic name (A), and that individual has lived in a town where that ethnic name is associated with a different culture (B), and that culture is associated with descriptions of violent behavior from outside sources of information (C), then the derived relational account would suggest that this stranger (A) might be associated with violent traits (C). This example provides a very basic, yet relevant, demonstration of how some attitudes may form through derived relational responding. The reality is that this individual has likely established classes of direct and indirect relations with stimuli representing a variety of cultures which often run contrary to those biases. Yet, it might be the case that such biases may supersede what is predicted by class-consistent responding. Even though bias may not be based on actual knowledge or experienced contingencies, it still has the ability to interfere with behavior.

In Watt et al. (1991), equivalence classes using socially loaded stimuli relating to Catholic and Protestant symbols were attempted to be formed with Catholic and Protestant participants from Northern Ireland. The objective was to establish equivalence classes comprising a Catholic name and a Protestant symbol (A-C). None of the Protestant participants selected Protestant symbols conditionally on Catholic names as the trained relations predicted. Similarly, almost half of the Catholic participants also did not respond according to the trained relations. Watt et al.'s (1991) study reveals the degree to which socially loaded stimuli can impact the emergence of new equivalence relations. As such, this study provides some insight into how biases can interfere in the development of new classes.

De Carvalho and de Rose (2014) extended this line of research with an investigation with children from a community school in Brazil who were selected based on the results of a pre-screening assessment that demonstrated the presence of negative bias towards males of African descent. A series of conditional discriminations between positive symbols (A) and abstract symbols (B) and the abstract symbols (B) and pictures of men of African descent (C) were established, and the researchers presented a test to determine if the relation between men of African descent and positive symbols emerged (C-A). However, despite those baseline relations being demonstrated only one participant responded in a manner suggesting equivalence class formation. Only one participant demonstrated a reversal of the original bias demonstrated towards men of African descent from pretest to posttest. The other participants, however, maintained their biases despite responding to the baseline relations (i.e., A-B and B-C) in a class-consistent manner. As such, the results from de Carvalho and de Rose (2014) replicated the results of Watt et al. (1991) demonstrating the interference that socially loaded stimuli can have on the development of new relational classes.

In a follow-up study by Mizael et al. (2016) the authors manipulated training parameters to increase the yield of equivalence classes comprising relations contrary to the children's pre-experimental racial biases. Thirteen elementary-aged children who showed a pronounced negative bias toward faces of African descent as evidenced by several screening assessments pretest took part in the experiment. In this study children's evaluations of the faces of Caucasian individuals and individuals of African descent with the Self-Assessment Manikin (SAM) showed a distinct negative bias toward faces of individuals of African descent before training. Similar to de Carvalho and de Rose (2014), participants of Mizael et al. (2016) were taught a series of conditional discriminations between positive and negative symbols (A), abstract symbols (B), and pictures of faces of men of African and Caucasian descent (C). All 13 children showed equivalence class formation. In follow-up posttest assessments, the difference between evaluations of faces was no longer statistically significant. These findings suggest that procedures based on equivalence and transfer of functions could decrease racial biases.

These conflicting results warrant further analysis. Both studies assessed pre-existing biases. de Carvalho and de Rose (2014) used a matching-to-sample (MTS) procedure that evaluated whether the participant chose the negative or the positive symbols when either faces of African or Caucasian descent were displayed as samples. Mizael et al. (2016) used a similar procedure, but also included two additional assessment instruments (i.e., Self-Assessment Manikin and the Implicit Relational Assessment Procedure). The consistency of the results across all three assessment procedures in Mizael et al. (2016) suggest that the results are accurate. Had the MTS procedure used in Mizael et al. (2016) differed from the other assessment results, the argument might be made that the differing results across the studies could be the result of instrumentation. Such was not the case. In addition, the selection of participants in Mizael et al. (2016) was guided by a numerical value measuring bias. Only those participants scoring a value of at least +4 on the bias measure were included.

Since de Carvalho and de Rose (2014) did not use a similar measure it is possible that the participants in the latter study were simply less biased than those in the former study. Finally, the type of training and testing protocols used across both studies differed. de Carvalho and de Rose (2014) used a complex-to-simple methodology where both transitivity (AC) and a combined transitivity and symmetry (CA) relations were tested without any of the direct symmetrical relations (BA, CB) ever being assessed. It is possible that outcomes may have been different if these relations had been established. Because of the paucity of literature on these topics, additional research is necessary.

CONCLUSION

Racial and cultural biases appear to be, unfortunately, ubiquitous in most past and present societies. The function that those biases serve is for a different discussion; however, derived relational responding and the transformation of stimulus function offers some insight into how these biases may be formed. Past research has demonstrated the effect that these biases may have, specifically how they may interfere with future class development (de Carvalho & de Rose, 2014; Watt et al., 1991). This would suggest that a child raised in an environment where such biases are established might be less likely to form new classes contrary to those biases, regardless of whether the child has direct and reinforcing experiences with individuals of the biased groups.

But, thankfully all is not lost. The results of Mizael and colleagues (2016) demonstrated that pre-existing classes can be changed with direct training, resulting in the transformation of a class member, thus altering the function of the stimulus itself. What this suggests is a powerful alternative to the narrative that change is impossible. In other words, a child who is raised in that biased environment and derives certain stimulus functions can potentially have those biases and functions reversed. If the classes that constitute those beliefs and attitudes come in contact with an experience that contradicts their very foundation, it is possible that those classes can transform, and the biases mitigated or reduced. However, it is more likely that some form of systematic and repeated exposure, or even explicit training, might be necessary to achieve substantial change in responding. As such, we may have at least a partial solution, albeit theoretical, to the prejudices, bigotries, and racism that have long plagued society.

REFERENCES

American Psychiatric Association. (2013). *Diagnostic and statistical manual of mental disorders* (5th ed.). APA.

Annett, J. M., & Leslie, J. C. (1995). Stimulus equivalence classes involving olfactory stimuli. *The Psychological Record, 45,* 439–450. https://doi.org/10.1007/BF03395153

Baxter, A. J., Scott, K. M., Vos, T., & Whiteford, H. A. (2013). Global prevalence of anxiety disorders: A systematic review and meta-regression. *Psychological Medicine, 43,* 897–910. https://doi.org/10.1017/S003329171200147X

de Carvalho, M. P., & de Rose, J. C. (2014). Understanding racial attitudes through the stimulus equivalence paradigm. *The Psychological Record, 64,* 527–536.

DeGrandpre, R. J., Bickel, W. K., & Higgins, S. T. (1992). Emergent equivalence relations between interoceptive (drug) and exteroceptive (visual) stimuli. *Journal of the Experimental Analysis of Behavior, 58,* 9–18.

de Rose, J. C., Hidalgo, M., & Vasconcellos, M. (2013). Controlling relations in baseline conditional discriminations as determinants of stimulus equivalence. *The Psychological Record, 63,* 85–98.

Dougher, M. J., Augustson, E., Markham, M. R., Greenway, D. E., & Wulfert, E. (1994). The transfer of respondent eliciting and extinction functions through stimulus equivalence classes. *Journal of the Experimental Analysis of Behavior, 62,* 331–351. https://doi.org/10.1901/jeab.1994.62-331.

Dube, W. V., Green, G., & Serna, R. W. (1993). Auditory successive conditional discrimination and auditory stimulus equivalence classes. *Journal of the Experimental Analysis of Behavior, 59,* 103–114.

Dymond, S., & Barnes, D. (1994). A transfer of self-discrimination response functions through equivalence relations. *Journal of the Experimental Analysis of Behavior, 62,* 251–267. https://doi.org/10.1901/jeab.1994.62-251.

Frimanm, P. C., Hayesm, S. C., & Wilson, K. G. (1998). Why behaviour analysts should study emotion: The example of anxiety. *Journal of Applied Behavior Analysis, 32,* 137–156. https://doi.org/10.1901/jaba.1998.31-137.

Hayes, S. C. (1988). Contextualism and the next wave of behavioral psychology. *Behavior Analysis, 23,* 7–23.

Hayes, S. C., Kohlenberg, B. K., & Hayes, L. J. (1991). The transfer of specific and general consequential functions through simple and conditional equivalence classes. *Journal of the Experimental Analysis of Behavior, 56,* 119–137.

Keller, F. S., & Schoenfeld, W. N. (1950). *Principles of psychology: A systematic text in the science of behavior.* Appleton-Century-Crofts. https://doi.org/10.1037/11293-000

Michael, J. L. (2004). *Concepts and principles of behavior analysis.* Western Michigan University, Association for Behavior Analysis International.

Mizael, T. M., de Almeida, J. H., Silveira, C. C., & de Rose, J. C. (2016). Changing racial bias by transfer of functions in equivalence classes. *The Psychological Record, 66,* 451–462. https://psycnet.apa.org/doi/10.1037/11293-000

Plaud, J. J. (1995). The formation of stimulus equivalences: Fear-relevant versus fear-irrelevant stimulus classes. *The Psychological Record, 45,* 207–222.

Plaud, J. J., Gaither, G. A., Franklin, M., Weller, L. A., & Barth, J. (1998). The effects of sexually explicit words on the formation of stimulus equivalence classes. *The Psychological Record, 48,* 63–79.

Roche, B., & Barnes, D. (1997). A transformation of respondent conditioned stimulus function in accordance with arbitrarily applicable relations. *Journal of the Experimental Analysis of Behavior, 67,* 275–300.

Skinner, B. F. (1953). *Science and human behavior.* Free Press.

Watt, A., Keenan, M., Barnes, D., & Cairns, E. (1991). Social categorization and stimulus equivalence. *The Psychological Record, 41,* 33–50.

Zentall, T. R., & Smeets, P. M. (Eds.). (1996). *Stimulus class formation in humans and animals.* Elsevier Science.

44

URBAN PLANNING

Urban Planning through a Behavior Analytic Lens

May Chriseline Beaubrun

INTRODUCTION

Systemic racism and social injustice have played a significant role in the development and progress of the United States. We can trace the concerns within modern society back to specific points in history. For example, The Home Owners Loan Corporations, a federal agency, created "Residential Security" maps of major American cities (e.g., Atlanta, Detroit, Houston, and Philadelphia). These maps categorized city neighborhoods according to four grades: A (green), B (blue), C (yellow), and D (red). A (Green) was considered the best and mainly made up of businessmen. B (Blue) was considered desirable and mostly made up of White-collar workers. C (Yellow) was made up of working-class individuals and showed an "infiltration of a lower grade population." D (Red) were considered hazardous with an "undesirable population," namely Black people and other minorities (Madrigal, 2014). It was difficult and even impossible to buy or finance a home for individuals in redlined neighborhoods. As a result, landlords abandoned properties, city services, like transportation were unreliable, crime increased, and property values dropped significantly (Mitchell & Franco, 2018). The outcome was that suburbs flourished with White people, and it was legal to not sell homes to Black people. Residential security maps led to systematic mortgage discrimination. People from redlined neighborhoods were denied credit to purchase homes, as were real estate developers who wanted to build properties within these "hazardous" neighborhoods (Mitchell & Franco, 2018).

During the Civil Rights Movement, the Fair Housing Act (1968), banned discrimination based on race for an individual renting, buying a home, or applying for a home loan but it was rarely enforced. Unfortunately, the effects of systemic mortgage discrimination remain present today. For instance, homeownership creates wealth. Many of today's White American population reap the benefits of having relatives who had access to mortgages to build family wealth. Chetty et al. (2016) found that moving from a high-poverty neighborhood to a low-poverty neighborhood reduced teenage pregnancy, improved college attendance, and increased incomes by over 30%. Systemic mortgage discrimination also impacts education. Public schools are primarily funded through property taxes. With more properties or high valued properties, students have access to more resources, better facilities, and a higher quality of education. In neighborhoods with rental properties or lower valued properties, students have limited to no resources, poor facilities, and a lesser quality of education. These issues contribute to the school to prison pipeline.

The term *school to prison pipeline* is used to describe harsh school disciplinary practices that disproportionately affect Black students (Roberts, 2003). Black students are suspended three times more than their White counterparts. Students who have been suspended or expelled are less likely to graduate and more likely to enter into the juvenile system (Roberts, 2003). These statistics contribute to over-incarceration in the United States. Black people make up about 13% of the United States population but make up about 33% of the prison population (Sawyer, 2020). These disparities can be mitigated by providing access to living in better communities with more funding to schools.

Along with education, housing can also have major influences on health and wellness. As previously noted, the ramifications of redlining still exist today. Marginalized people continue to live in areas that were considered hazardous by the Home Owners Loan Corporations (Jan, 2018). Many of these homes are near industrial plants where residents are exposed to toxic fumes which lead to health conditions; including heart and lung diseases. These neighborhoods are far from grocery stores with fresh food and produce. Zhang & Debarchana (2016) use the term *supermarket redlining* to describe major supermarket chains avoiding opening stores in inner cities or low-income neighborhoods while relocating their existing stores to suburbs. With no alternative, people in redlined neighborhoods turn to processed foods high in sodium because they are more accessible. Take Detroit, for seven years in the mid-2000s, the city didn't have a large grocery chain (Meyersohn, 2020). Meyersohn (2020) reports that there are currently three major grocery chains (2 Meijer stores and a Whole Foods) in Detroit.

There are a number of other variables to consider. The water may be contaminated or not drinkable, like the 2014 Flint Michigan Water Crisis. Crumbling infrastructures of older homes may leave people at risk of lead exposure resulting in certain cancers, heart disease, asthma, and other health concerns (Krieger & Higgins, 2002). In addition, Black people are at higher risk for underlying conditions (i.e., asthma, hypertension, heart and lung disease, and diabetes) to begin with (National Academies of Sciences, Engineering, and Medicine, 2017). During the COVID-19 2020 Pandemic, the Black community are less likely to be able to engage in social distancing (because they are "essential" employees or rely on public transportation) and, as a result, are more likely to contract COVID-19 than White people (Bridges, 2020).

Black homes have far less access to tax-advantaged forms of savings, due in part to a long history of employment discrimination and other discriminatory practices (Hanks et al., 2018). With less wealth, there are fewer opportunities for upward mobility. This is compounded by lower income levels than their White counterparts as well as fewer opportunities to build wealth or to pass accumulated wealth down to future generations (Hanks et al., 2018). This translates into health and wellness concerns as well. Blacks, Hispanics, and some Asian populations seemingly have lower levels of health insurance coverage than White populations (Institute of Medicine, 2003). This is in part due to systemic racism and other social disadvantages. A research study revealed Black individuals with Medicare benefits were less likely than White individuals to receive commonly performed hospital procedures (McBean & Gornick, 1994).

Redlining has influenced law enforcement as well. Mesic et al. (2018) suggest that residential segregation manipulates implicit bias. Implicit bias is "behavior that is influenced in an implicit manner by cues that function as an indicator of the social group to which others belong" (De Houwer, 2019). An example is the stereotypes that associate Black people as being aggressive, dangerous, and violent (Spencer, 2016). For this reason, "Black" neighborhoods tend to be more heavily policed which contributes to racial profiling. Racial profiling is the use of discriminatory practices by the police of targeting individuals suspected of committing a crime based on their race, ethnicity, religion, or national origin. Racial profiling is illegal under the United States constitution (e.g., equal protection under the law to all and freedom from unreasonable searches and seizure) and also ineffective (Harris, 2003).

An important part of the training of Urban Planners is diversity, equity, and inclusion (Harris, 2015). Culturally competent planning can address the issues related to diverse communities (Agyeman & Erickson, 2012). Some important factors to good planning include being well prepared and having a positive impact on the urban economy (Melzer, 2013).

By activity planning for the future, city leaders can manage risks and connect short-term actions and long-term goals. Jobs within the city will attract investors that will generate economic activity. Culturally competent planning will be mindful of the distribution of economic activity (Melzer, 2013). Projects with strictly a financial benefit tend to have negative impacts on the marginalized individual within the community.

Gentrification, the influx of affluent residents and businesses into a city, can be beneficial but harmful as well (Florida, 2015). Areas that have undergone gentrification have less crime and increased property values. These areas also suffer from displacement through rent/price increases, the loss of affordable housing as well as homelessness. To reduce these disadvantages, there must be consideration of more inclusive public places for who and what is already in the city so that the needs of the culture are met.

So where does behavior analysis fit in? Through data analysis. Data is used to evaluate the effects of the intervention and to guide decision making (Cooper et al., 2020). To determine the effectiveness of urban planning data collection (i.e., economic data, sociodemographic information, events such as birth rates and causes of death) that are quantitative or qualitative (e.g., park amenities, streetscape elements, accessibility, etc.), or surveys and interviews can be analyzed (Acharya et al., 2018). Behavior analysts are not experts in urban planning, but they are experts in defining behaviors, collecting data, and interpreting data sets to promote effective interventions to replace societal structures that impede the Black community from thriving.

Implications for future research include Behavioral Community Psychology, the application of the principles of behavior analysis to problems within the community (Fawcett, 1980). Behavioral Community Psychology, similar to other behavioral sciences, breaks down large and complex behaviors into smaller components that can be operationally defined and measured (i.e., littering, tobacco use, compliance with traffic signs, etc.). Behavioral community psychology can be involved to ensure that children can walk and play outdoors safely without fear of crime, violence, or dangerous vehicular traffic and playground equipment (i.e., compliance with traffic signs) (Jason et al., 2019; Reynolds, 2018).

Behavior analysis is the science of human behavior. Behavior analysts should work closely with qualified professionals and continue to contribute to the literature providing function-based assessments and recommendations to work against social injustice and mitigate oppression and power imbalances such as those that influence housing and community affairs. Behavior analysts already utilize evidence-based interventions. Their knowledge and expertise to change behavior can be applied to address issues such as the social injustices described here.

REFERENCES

Acharya, K., Orleans, T., & Roerty, S. Z., (2018, July 13). Inclusive Health Places: A Guide to Inclusion & Health in Public Space. *Gehl Institute.* https://gehlinstitute.org/wp-content/uploads/2018/07/Inclusive-Healthy-Places_Gehl-Institute.pdf

Agyeman, J., & Erickson, J. S. (2012). Culture, recognition, and the negotiation of difference: Some thoughts on cultural competency in planning education. *Journal of Planning Education and Research, 32*, 358–366.

Bridges, K. (2020, June 11). The Many Ways Institutional Racism Kills Black People. *Time.* https://time.com/5851864/institutional-racism-america/

Chetty, R., Hendren, N., & Katz, L. F. (2016). The effects of exposure to better neighborhoods on children: New evidence from the Moving to Opportunity experiment. *American Economic Review, 106*(4), 855–902.

Cooper, J. O., Heron, T. E., & Heward, W. L. (2020). *Applied behavior analysis* (3rd ed.). Upper Saddle River, NJ: Pearson.

Davidoff, P. (1965). Advocacy and pluralism in planning. *Journal of the American Planning Association, 31*, 331–338.

De Houwer, J. (2019). Implicit Bias Is Behavior: A Functional-Cognitive Perspective on Implicit Bias. *Perspectives on Psychological Science*, 14. 174569161985563. https://10.1177/1745691619855638.

Fair Housing Act 1968, U.S.C. § 801.42.3601 (1968). https://www.justice.gov/crt/fair-housing-act-2

Fawcett, S. B., Mathews, R. M., & Fletcher, R. K. (1980). Some promising dimensions for behavioral community technology. *Journal of Applied Behavior Analysis, 13*(3), 505–518.

Florida, R. (2015). This is what happens after a neighborhood gets gentrified. *The Atlantic, 16.*

Gee, G. C., & Ford, C. L. (2011). Structural Racism and Health Inequities: Old Issues, New Directions. *Du Bois review: social science research on race, 8*(1), 115–132. https://doi.org/10.1017/S1742058X11000130

Hanks, A., Solomon, D., & Weller, C. E. (2018). Systematic inequality: How America's structural racism helped create the black-white wealth gap. *Washington: Center for American Progress.*

Harris, D. A. (2003). *Profiles in injustice: Why racial profiling cannot work*. The New Press.

Harris, K. E. (2015). Understanding the disposition of urban planning students toward social justice and equity themes. *SAGE Open, 5*(3), 2158244015607757.

Institute of Medicine (US) Committee on Understanding and Eliminating Racial and Ethnic Disparities in Health Care. (2003). *Unequal treatment: Confronting racial and ethnic disparities in health care*. Smedley, B. D., Stith, A. Y., & Nelson, A. R., (Eds.). National Academies Press.

Jan, T. (2018). Redlining was banned 50 years ago. It's still hurting minorities today. *Washington Post, 28.*

Jason, L. A., Glantsman, O., O'Brien, J. F., & Ramian, K. N. (2019). *Introduction to community psychology*. Rebus Community.

Krieger, J., & Higgins, D. L. (2002). Housing and health: Time again for public health action. *American Journal of Public Health, 92*(5), 758–768. https://doi.org/10.2105/ajph.92.5.758

Lawrence, K., Keleher, T. (2004). Structural racism. Presented in Race and Public Policy Conference. http://www.intergroupresources.com/rc/Definitions%20of%20Racism.pdf

Madrigal, A. C. (2014). The racist housing policy that made your neighborhood. *The Atlantic, 22.* https://www.theatlantic.com/business/archive/2014/05/the-racist-housing-policy-that-made-your-neighborhood/371439/

McBean, A. M., & Gornick, M. (1994). Differences by race in the rates of procedures performed in hospitals for Medicare beneficiaries. *Health Care Financing Review, 15*(4), 77.

Melzer. S., (2013, July 25). Ten reasons cities need urban planning. *Urban Times*. http://urbantimes. co/2013/07/ten-reasons-cities-need-urban-planning/

Mesic, A., Franklin, L., Cansever, A., Potter, F., Sharma, A., Knopov, A., & Siegel, M. (2018). The relationship between structural racism and black-white disparities in fatal police shootings at the state level. *Journal of the National Medical Association, 110*(2), 106–116.

Meyersohn, N. (2020, June 16). How the rise of supermarkets left out black America. *CNN Business*. https://www.cnn.com/2020/06/16/business/grocery-stores-access-race-inequality/index.html

Mitchell, B., & Franco, J. (2018, March 20). HOLC "redlining" maps: The persistent structure of segregation and economic inequality. NCRC. https://ncrc.org/holc/

National Academies of Sciences, Engineering, and Medicine. (2017). *Communities in action: Pathways to health equity*. National Academies Press.

Reynolds, R. (2018, November). Consortium to lower obesity in Chicago Children (CLOCC). In *APHA's 2018 annual meeting & expo (Nov. 10-Nov. 14)*. American Public Health Association.

Roberts, D. E. (2003). The social and moral cost of mass incarceration in African American communities. *Stan. L. Rev., 56*, 1271.

Sawyer, W. (2020, July 27). Visualizing the racial disparities in mass incarceration. Prison policy initiative. https://www.prisonpolicy.org/blog/2020/07/27/disparities/

Spencer, K. B., Charbonneau, A. K., & Glaser, J. (2016). Implicit bias and policing. *Social and Personality Psychology Compass, 10*(1), 50–63. https://doi.org/10.1111/spc3.12210

Wilhite, C. (2016, August 10). Behavior analysis and social justice: Aligning codes of ethics? *bSci21.* https://bsci21.org/behavior-analysis-and-social-justice-aligning-codes-of-ethics/

Zhang, M., & Debarchana, G. (2016). Spatial supermarket redlining and neighborhood vulnerability: A case study of Hartford, Connecticut. *Transactions in GIS: TG, 20*(1), 79–100. https://doi.org/10.1111/tgis.12142

45

WELLNESS

Wellness and the Use of Acceptance Commitment Training in the Workplace

Kate Elizabeth Harrison

Behavior analysts help individuals achieve independence across various aspects of life. They support families in working through behaviors in their natural environment. They work through challenging behaviors including those that impact an individual's safety. They collaborate with various professionals to ensure progress, and are responsible for staying up-to-date with best practice and research. In summary, behavior analysts spend their days working hard *helping others*. It's safe to say that most who enter the field of applied behavior analysis are not in it for the hefty paycheck but rather committed to helping others gain skills that are socially significant. While this is true, we could benefit from keeping this Dodinsky quote in mind: "Be there for others, but never leave yourself behind." Think about that, and let it sink in for a moment before reading any further.

Work-life balance is the term that refers to the relationship between work and non-work aspects of life, where achieving a satisfactory work-life balance is understood as restricting one part of the relationship to have more time for the other (Kelliher et al., 2018). This chapter offers a subjective perspective on the term work-life balance, understanding that there are individual perceptions of the relationship between work and non-work, and focuses primarily on the overt symptoms of a work-life imbalance that often result in employee burnout.

Burnout is a hot topic, especially as the World Health Organization added "burnout" to their 2019 revision of the International Classification of Diseases. According to the World Health Organization (WHO), burnout is "a syndrome that results from unsuccessfully managed workplace stress resulting in three dimensions: feelings of exhaustion, increased mental distance from or feelings of negativity about one's job, and reduced performance at work" (WHO, 2020). What is causing those who are in the helping field so much stress? The stressors likely vary from individual to individual, organization to organization, role to role. Still, some potential contributing factors may include: challenging relationships in collaboration and training attempts, large caseloads, unclear organizational policies, poor administrative communication, little feedback regarding performance, unpredictability in schedules, lack of boundaries relating to work calls, texts, and e-mails, and challenging cases. At the time of writing, the world is six months into the COVID-19 pandemic, which brought homeschooling, financial stressors, job insecurity, fear of getting sick, fear of loved ones getting sick, *in addition to* the previously mentioned potential stressors.

Whether looking at the previously mentioned stressors or reviewing a list relevant to individual experience, many, if not most, potential stressors can be simplified to six core misalignments that cause employees across industries to feel the effects of burnout. According to Maslach and colleagues (2001), the six core misalignments relate to:

1. An employee's workload
2. Control over the work that an employee does
3. The reward, or consequences, for the work
4. The community, or lack thereof

5. Fairness within a role and/or workload related to colleagues, and

6. Values – what or who is most important to the individual or the organization

Regardless of what specific stressor is present for an employee, it will likely align with one of these misalignments, making these critical for any leadership team to be familiar with when designing a work environment that stays ahead of workplace burnout.

These core misalignments within an organization set the occasion for common behaviors of an employee suffering from burnout including:

- Questioning of one's career choice
- Alienating oneself from work-related activities, like declining a coworker's offer to grab a coffee or skipping the holiday party
- Experiencing thoughts and feelings of dread about going to work
- Experiencing irritability with coworkers, perhaps snapping at minor miscommunications over email
- A decrease in productivity or work output, perhaps emitting more errors than usual in a treatment plan or completing fewer supervision sessions than is typical
- Thinking or talking about work non-stop, causing friends or family to roll their eyes

In some cases, there may even be an increase in the physical manifestation of symptoms, including headaches, stomach problems, and ongoing exhaustion. Leaders in organizations can be on the lookout for these behaviors amongst their teams and themselves. Every employee, regardless of role, is susceptible to burnout.

The statistics of workplace burnout should alarm anyone, especially those in leadership positions. In Gallup's 2018 burnout survey of 7,500 full-time employees, 23% reported feeling burned out more often than not, 44% reported feeling burned out sometimes, and 66% expressed dealing with burnout at some point throughout their work life (Wigert & Agrawal, 2020). Deloitte's 2015 Workplace Burnout Survey found that 77% of employees had experienced burnout at their current job, 91% reported having an unmanageable amount of stress negatively impacting the quality of their work, and that 70% felt their employers were not doing enough to prevent burnout within their organization (Fisher, 2020). While these statistics are scary enough alone, many organizations focus on prioritizing business results while ignoring the employee's well-being, intentional or not. It is a business, after all. But what if leaders were aware of the effect employee well-being has on their overall business results?

Applied behavior analysis is slowly expanding the scope of behavioral science to normalize the inclusion of emotions (Friman et al., 1998). A behavior analyst's role is to identify and predict relationships between events, so we must explore how the frightening burnout statistics above relate to observable and measurable results beyond the employee. Private events like stress, exhaustion, negative thoughts about work, and burnout lead to public problem behavior patterns such as absenteeism, turnover, frequent illness, and reduced quality of work, all of which lead to unnecessarily elevated business costs for organizations (Flaxman et al., 2013). While an organization *can* hire another employee, it will cost them. Not only do businesses lose money when losing an employee (Hall, 2019), they are also losing money when they hold on to disengaged employees—what's known as presenteeism (Hemp, 2014). These employees "show up" but produce a lower quality of work, which can result in clients taking their needs elsewhere. Just as an organization can hire a new employee, a client can always find another organization to suit their needs.

With employees spending upwards of 60% of their waking hours at work, likely increasing as a result of a rise of work from home jobs during the COVID-19 pandemic, the information surrounding burnout should urge leaders to prioritize their employees' well-being – now!

While there are many ways to prioritize employee's well-being while at work, this chapter will discuss one way to shape organization's and individual employee's work-life relationships. Acceptance and Commitment Training (ACTr) offers behavior analysts the tools to address private events in a way that the field has lacked for years (Hayes, 2019). Behavior analysts are discovering how fluency in ACTr can not only enhance their behavior analytic toolbox but, perhaps more importantly, their own lives. Just like Organizational Behavior Management (OBM) uses systems rooted in behavioral science to target an organization's productivity and financial gains, when used at the organizational level, ACTr can help an organization thrive by acknowledging and proactively addressing employee's mental well-being.

Briefly stated, ACTr involves a set of six core processes (Hayes et al., 1999): Present Moment Awareness, Values, Committed Actions, Self as Context (or viewing oneself flexibly), Cognitive Defusion (distancing from one's thoughts), and Acceptance (see Table 45.1). Each aims to teach the acknowledgment of thoughts without judgment and to act within personal, professional, or organizational values, rather than attempting to remove or change thoughts, feelings, or physical symptoms. Recall that list of stressors mentioned earlier. These may never change, but ACTr provides the mental tools to notice these stressors and take action by following personal and professional values anyway, what's known as psychological flexibility. Numerous research studies referenced in the book *The Mindful & Effective Employee* used various combinations of ACTr processes administered as treatment packages across organizations to improve staff well-being in the form of psychological flexibility, some showing improved ratings of "psychological distress" as well (Bond & Bunce, 2000; Brinkborg et al., 2011; Flaxman & Bond, 2010a; Flaxman & Bond, 2010b; Flaxman et al., 2013).

Table 45.1 ACTr in the Workplace

ACTr Core Process	Workplace Example
Present Moment Awareness	Taking deep breaths, listening, and noticing the meeting participants while feeling nervous *versus* thinking, "I screwed up that definition at the last meeting, what if I do it again?"
Values	The thought, "Growth and impact on children are important to me," *versus*, "I don't even know why I'm working with this client. She's too challenging for me!"
Committed Actions	Scheduling a meeting with a mentor to learn more about assessments *versus* saying, "I don't even know where to begin in trying to tackle this assessment."
Self as Context	Saying, "I'm a BCBA, I am right sometimes," *versus* saying, "I'm a BCBA, I am right."
Cognitive Defusion	Noticing, "I'm having the thought that I screwed up that report," *versus*, "I screwed up that report."
Acceptance	Thinking, "I am dreading this parent phone call, and I'm going to get it done now," *versus*, "I'm dreading this parent phone call. I'll do it next week."

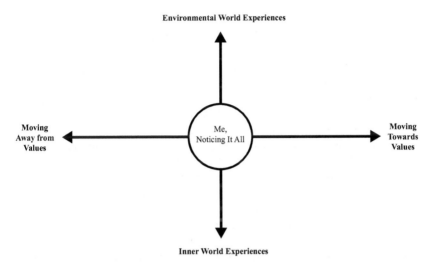

Environmental World Experiences

Moving
Away from
Values

Me,
Noticing It All

Moving
Towards
Values

Inner World Experiences

Figure 45.1 Adapted from The ACT Matrix (Polk & Schoendorf, 2014)

Chances are many people reading this may be struggling with thoughts like, "Am I in the right field?" "I am too stressed to do anything else but work." "All I do is work." "I have no boundaries!" You may be feeling some of the physical manifestations of stress as well. While there are many activities that one can explore to begin their psychological flexibility journey, I'll introduce one highly useful tool and can be used almost immediately upon learning.

The ACT Matrix (Polk & Schoendorff, 2014, see Figure 45.1) is a very simple visual used to help guide the discrimination between thoughts and feelings and our outer world experiences. It also helps identify behaviors that take us towards or away from who and what is essential in our lives or our organization. The ACT Matrix helps to visually sort through thoughts, feelings, behaviors, and values. Take a look at the Matrix shown below. The Matrix is composed of four quadrants, the top half representing the five-senses environment, including behaviors. The lower half represents an individual's inner world experiences, including thoughts, feelings, physical sensations, and values. Notice the vertical line separating the Matrix from right to left. The left side represents behaviors that move us away from our values, while the right side represents behaviors that take us towards our values.

When familiar and fluent with the ACT Matrix, walking yourself or a struggling employee through a matrix can be just one way a leader models the importance of well-being and helps realign their behaviors. Let's walk through what a Matrix could look like with a newly minted, stressed out BCBA, who is having difficulty finding a balance between work and personal life. It's crucial to catch employees like this early before the behavior patterns continue leading to burnout, health issues, and organizational impact.

The ACT Matrix can be worked in a variety of ways, but for this activity, we'll start in the lower-right quadrant and work clockwise until reaching the top-right quadrant. Before beginning, always be sure to ask the person if they would be interested in working through a matrix. This exercise requires some vulnerability, and people do not typically like to be surprised by that! Start by providing an overview of what the Matrix is, sharing the vertical line that separates workable versus unworkable behaviors and the horizontal line that separates public and private behaviors. Highlight the middle circle that symbolizes the employee by saying something like, "This is you; just noticing." Then, starting in the lower-right corner, the first question might be something like, "Can you tell me some important things to you? Who and what do you value most in life? What makes your heart feel happy?"

After they provide you with a list of the people and qualities of life that are most important to them, before moving on to the next quadrant, ask if they feel complete and are ready to move on. Then, move to the lower-left quadrant and ask a question that addresses their thoughts, feelings, and inner experiences (private events) that have been uncomfortable or difficult for them. For example, "So, you mentioned that you're feeling an imbalance between your job and your personal life outside of work. What are some thoughts that show up for you? Any physical symptoms show up when these thoughts pop into your mind? Where do you notice them?" Write everything down for the person, allow them to see what's pouring out while acknowledging how difficult these experiences must be. Before moving on to the next quadrant, consider thanking the person for sharing such difficulties—this isn't easy!

As you move above the horizontal line, to the upper left quadrant where the Matrix addresses environmental experiences, start by questioning what this person tends to do when these uncomfortable thoughts, feelings, and sensations show up. These are usually behaviors that may provide immediate relief from the discomfort of the lower-left quadrant and are likely behaviors that are out of alignment with their greater values. Often labeled as "away moves," the behaviors recorded in this quadrant may not *always* be moving them away from their values, but paying attention to what occurs in the body *before* these behaviors occur is critical in determining their workability. Some behaviors might even appear in both top quadrants! This is OK – but one must discern when the behaviors are problematic verses when they are helpful. Finally, when this box feels complete, invite the person to move to the upper-right quadrant. In this box, we're looking at "towards moves," or replacement behaviors that are in alignment with their values. Asking questions like, "What would/could the best version of yourself do?" "What would you do if those uncomfortable feelings magically disappeared?"

As you begin to wrap up the Matrix activity, point out the center "Me, Noticing" circle. Let the person know that the thoughts and feelings that show up in the lower-left quadrant are not likely to go away, but given this new sorting activity, they can begin to identify when they are engaging in behaviors that take them away from what is important to them (i.e., opening up the text during family dinner time), and pivot towards a behavior in the upper-right quadrant (i.e., feeling the tension in your chest as you ignore the text message alert while you're with your family). Finally, what's essential to notice throughout this activity is who is guiding it. As the facilitator, you're just asking the questions – the person who is responding is uncovering the information on their own.

The ACT Matrix is a brief glimpse into the impact that acceptance and commitment training might have if regularly incorporated into workplace wellness conversations (see Figure 45.2). Each of the six core processes are inexplicitly incorporated into the tool, and even someone who is unfamiliar with ACTr could see immediate value. Behavior analysts have the skill set to measure the individual efficacy of this tool, or at any level of a workplace wellness program, and on their overall business results.

Behavior analysts and those in helping fields have difficult jobs. Opportunities for burnout abound, and the consequences extend beyond those that directly affect the employee – burnout has direct, measurable effects on organizational success. Applied behavior analysis provides us with tools to create long-lasting, meaningful change. If we truly want to "save the world," we must begin by setting ourselves up for sustained success – an emphasis on wellness is paramount.

What are some things that you've been
doing that may not be working for you?

- Constantly check e-mail/texts
- Pull out laptop during a movie
- Avoiding things
- Complain
- Talking about work all the time

If you were the best version of
yourself, what would you do instead?

- Put work away at 6pm
- Ask friends and family what's
  going on in their lives
- Have tough conversations
- Walk my dog
- Ask for support

Moving Away from Values

Me, Noticing It All

Moving Towards Values

What thoughts, feelings, emotions
show up physically or emotionally?

- I'm stressed out
- I'm tired
- Tightness in my chest
- Tension in my shoulders
- I never get to "turn off"

What do you value?

- My career
- My clients
- My family and friends
- My health

Inner World Experiences

Figure 45.2 A sample matrix displaying work-life balance

REFERENCES

Bond, F. W., & Bunce, D. (2000). Mediators of change in emotion-focused and problem-focused worksite stress management interventions. *Journal of Occupational Health Psychology, 5*(1), 156–163. https://doi.org/10.1037/1076-8998.5.1.156

Brinkborg, H., Michanek, J., Hesser, H., & Berglund, G. (2011). Acceptance and commitment therapy for the treatment of stress among social workers: A randomized controlled trial. *Behaviour Research and Therapy, 49*(6–7), 389–398. https://doi.org/10.1016/j.brat.2011.03.009

Fisher, J. (2020, April 24). *Workplace burnout survey: Deloitte US*. Deloitte. https://www2.deloitte.com/us/en/pages/about-deloitte/articles/burnout-survey.html

Flaxman, P. E., & Bond, F. W. (2010a). A randomised worksite comparison of acceptance and commitment therapy and stress inoculation training. *Behaviour Research and Therapy, 48*(8), 816–820. https://doi.org/10.1016/j.brat.2010.05.004

Flaxman, P. E., & Bond, F. W. (2010b). Worksite stress management training: Moderated effects and clinical significance. *Journal of Occupational Health Psychology, 15*(4), 347–358. https://doi.org/10.1037/a0020522

Flaxman, P. E., Bond, F. W., & Livheim, F. (2013). *The mindful and effective employee an acceptance and commitment therapy training manual for improving well-being and performance*. New Harbinger Publications.

Friman, P. C., Hayes, S. C., & Wilson, K. G. (1998). Why behavior analysts should study emotion: The example of anxiety. *Journal of Applied Behavior Analysis, 31*(1), 137–156.

Hall, J. (2019, May 9). *The cost of turnover can kill your business and make things less fun*. Forbes. https://www.forbes.com/sites/johnhall/2019/05/09/the-cost-of-turnover-can-kill-your-business-and-make-things-less-fun/

Hayes, S. (2019). *A liberated mind: How to pivot toward what matters*. Avery.

Hayes, S. C., Strosahl, K., & Wilson, K. G. (1999). *Acceptance and commitment therapy: An experiential approach to behavior change*. Guilford Press.

Hemp, P. (2014, August 1). Presenteeism: At work-but out of it. *Harvard Business Review*. https://hbr.org/2004/10/presenteeism-at-work-but-out-of-it

Kelliher, C., Richardson, J., & Boiarintseva, G. (2018). All of work? All of life? Reconceptualising work-life balance for the 21st century. *Human Resource Management Journal, 29*(2), 97–112.

Maslach, C., Schaufeli, W. B., & Leiter, M. P. (2001). Job burnout. *Annual Review of Psychology, 52*(1), 397–422.

Polk, K. L., & Schoendorff, B. (2014). *The ACT matrix: A new approach to building psychological flexibility across settings and populations*. New Harbinger Publications.

Wigert, B., & Agrawal, S. (2020, August 4). Employee burnout, part 1: The 5 main causes. Gallup.com. https://www.gallup.com/workplace/237059/employee-burnout-part-main-causes.aspx

World Health Organization. (2020, September). *Mortality and morbidity statistics*. ICD-11. https://icd.who.int/browse11/l-m/en#/id.who.int/icd/entity/129180281

46

WHITE SAVIORISM
Lessons Learned and Continued Reflections

Whitney Hammel Anny

INTRODUCTION

It is important to note that this is a starting point to a conversation on white saviorism, as well as a snapshot in time, from the perspective of a white American woman who has worked outside of her home country for the past decade. Mistakes have been made over the years in international ABA dissemination work and this chapter is written from lessons learned and knowledge gained. In the field of Applied Behavior Analysis, philosophical doubt is one of the six attitudes of science which must be used to ask questions and seek the truth. This chapter does not claim to be everything one needs to learn about white saviorism, but it is a humble start and a call to action for additional research and input. This chapter will outline information about white saviorism and pose questions to help you challenge your preconceived views. It will discuss barriers to understanding white saviorism and share lessons and examples about individual and group behavior, with the goal of combating and preventing white saviorism in the world.

SAVING THE POOR PEOPLE OF THE WORLD, ONE INTERNATIONAL TRIP AT A TIME

White saviorism, or white savior complex, is a phrase that refers to a white person who engages in actions to help non-white people, that are self-serving rather than doing good for the community in which they are attempting to assist. Dr. Robin DiAngelo's article "No, I won't stop saying 'White supremacy.'" (2017) stated "White supremacy is not simply the idea that whites are superior to people of color (although it certainly is that), but a deeper premise that supports this idea – the definition of whites as the norm or standard for human, and people of color as an inherent deviation from that norm." White saviorism is birthed from white supremacy, where those from the Minority World, also known as western world or first world countries, engage in behaviors to help save the Majority World from itself. Majority World is a new, more accurate, term being used to describe countries that were derogatively referred to as developing world or third world countries. The Majority World countries label comes from the idea that these countries make up most of the population and therefore it is a reminder to those in the West that they are a minority in the world (Silver, 2015).

These countries are often depicted in American media as places of poverty, war, and famine. The idea of "West is best" is displayed in the media and presents the idea of white supremacy in the world. In 2017, only 42% of Americans held an active passport (Amos, 2018). Most people growing up in America do not travel extensively in their lifetime and therefore views of other countries and cultures are developed solely from television, movies, and print media. Yet the Majority World is not asking to be saved, especially by inexperienced and unqualified individuals, even if they do have good intentions. When an American watches something in our media that displays a "third-world country" as being impoverished and needing help, and then uses that inspiration to go on a trip to "help" or "save" a population group elsewhere, that is white saviorism.

You may be asking yourself, "What harm can come from white saviorism?" While that mission trip you took was "life altering" to you, what damages may have come from it? It is important to note here that the impact of one's actions are what matters, not the intentions. By building a house for a family how did your behavior impact the local economy? Did you take away opportunities for local contractors? Was the structure safe? How much money did you spend on the trip and could that money have built additional houses if donated? What about that time you volunteered in an orphanage overseas? Those children may have been smiling in your pictures but what emotional impact does it have for them to have a revolving door of people creating bonds and leaving? Are they truly orphans or were they removed from their family? Is the place they are living purposefully kept bare to encourage additional donations? While it is not comfortable to confront past behavior, I encourage you to be reflective and see the bigger picture behind the photo of a white person holding a smiling black child on their social media page.

BARRIERS IMPEDING UNDERSTANDING

Some barriers impeding understanding of white saviorism are: competing with societal praise for such behaviors, an individual's learned history, and lack of or resistance to personal confrontation of white privilege.

What is the function of white saviorism? Why do so many people engage in actions which are harmful to the people they are attempting to help? While there have not been formal ABA research articles published in this area, we can anecdotally look at examples of white saviorism to find proposed functions of the behavior. If we break down white saviorism to look for antecedents and consequences, we find that most often they point to functions of attention and automatic reinforcement. Why would a person want to change their white saviorism behavior when they are gathering positive praise from others for their actions? They are also likely feeling a sense of making an impact for the people they "helped" while the reality is that they did not make a significant impact and possibly caused harm. Some individuals may even gather extra attention online. For example, white saviors may use young brown or black children as props in their online dating profiles to portray themselves as a good catch who care about the world while the reality is that they are posing white saviors.

As mentioned in the above section, the media shapes a person's view of the majority world. One is unlikely to question something they only see portrayed one way. Chimamanada Ngozi Adichie (2009) mentions this concept in her TED talk "The Danger of a Single Story." If you have not traveled extensively, or before you did, what picture comes to mind when you think of Ethiopia? For myself growing up in a small, rural, predominantly white town, I can remember commercials on TV to raise funds for starving children with large bellies, suffering from malnutrition, with flies on their face. Is that truly what Ethiopia is about? Of course not! While speaking about the work in Ghana and sharing resources related to beliefs around autism by the community, I could easily share one story from a BBC documentary titled "The Worst Place in the World to Be Disabled?" (Seibel, 2016). That documentary tells about the belief of special needs children being "river children" and how they are viewed as demons who must be returned to their world. Yet that story does not depict a full or accurate picture of special needs in Ghana, especially to those who have never set foot in the country. By telling a single story, I have created a vision which displays savagery and horrors which may influence one's views of Ghanaians. It perpetuates a calling for white saviorism, whereas the story discussed above is one component of many views in a country of 30 million. It does not take into consideration the history of mental health in the country nor does it apply humility.

A final, and significant, barrier to impeding understanding of white saviorism is willingness to confront privilege. Confronting white privilege and the unwillingness to give up power associated with that privilege is not comfortable. White saviorism feels good, the praise you receive and the boost to one's ego is hard to compete against.

INDIVIDUAL BEHAVIORS THAT CAN LEAD TO PREVENTION OF WHITE SAVIORISM

What steps can you take as an individual to avoid engaging in white saviorism? The first step is to be open to growth. You may have made mistakes in the past, however, change in future behavior can be achieved by increasing your knowledge on this topic and confronting past behavior. You can start by reading this chapter with an open mind, free of defensiveness and taking next steps to continue learning. If you feel defensive, question from where that feeling is emerging, and do the work within yourself to be able to move past it, without burdening others.

You can engage in an exercise called flipping the script- ask yourself "Could I do this in my home country?" For example, is it possible to teach in the United States without a teaching credential? Should you take pictures of yourself with children you do not know and post them to your social media? If your answer is no, then do not engage in the behavior anywhere else either. There are real repercussions of white saviorism, and an extreme example is Renee Bach. Between 2010 and 2015, Ms. Bach posed as a doctor in Uganda where 105 children died under her care at a clinic that she had established to serve malnourished children (Aizenman, 2020). She was a 20-year-old high school graduate with no medical training. In July 2020, she settled a lawsuit and had to pay the families, however she faced no jail time. Could you imagine a Ugandan coming to the United States and engaging in similar behavior? Would they face the same consequences or harsher punishment?

Maybe you have valuable educational experience and skills that you're interested to authentically share through volunteering. If so, how can you go about volunteering abroad without engaging in white saviorism? When looking to volunteer with an organization in the Majority World, first do your research.

- Do your skills and educational background support the mission?
- Does the organization have local partners?
- If they are charging a fee to volunteer, where does the money go?
- Is the organization supporting local capacity or are they engaging in a revolving door of volunteers from the Minority World to keep the program afloat?
- Ask questions and do all you can to avoid supporting programs that are upholding white supremacy while presenting themselves as white saviors.

Once you find a program that is a good fit, schedule a call with the leadership on the ground to discuss a plan for the time you are volunteering.

- Create goals together with the organization to ensure that they align with their mission.

- Confirm that you can add to the organization's impact in a sustainable way, not drain their resources and waste your time.
- Inquire prior to your trip, how best to learn about the culture within the organization and if you can, connect with someone on the ground for advice on what to do and what not to do.
- If you do not find good answers to these questions, consider just traveling to the country of interest as a tourist, so your tourism dollars can contribute to the local economy, while actively avoiding white saviorism behaviors.
- Alternatively, if you find an organization you believe in, but you are not able to valuably contribute to their mission, consider donating rather than spending money on airfare and playing a savior.
- If you do find that you are able to add to the mission of an organization in an ethical way, then most importantly go willing to learn from that experience.

Once you are volunteering in a Majority World country, there are steps to take to avoid white saviorism and make an authentic impact. A quote from Sarita Hartz (2018) states, "Build relationships of mutual respect where the power dynamics do not rest on you 'saving' someone, but rather where you are learning and sharing your own problems as much as you are 'teaching'." Respect the agency of each individual, that they have the power and knowledge to solve their own problems and they have the capacity, knowledge and ability to change their own lives." By building relationships of mutual respect you learn to follow the lead of local partners while being humble and willing to learn. Be cognizant of your communication, both nonverbal and verbal. Avoid making comparisons to life back home as well as complaining. Be gracious and open to experiences in the culture in which you are working, which will help to build trust and respect. Expect that you will need a lot of support while there, as systems for doing things vary greatly from country to country and region to region. Just because you are comfortable with the "way we do things back home" does not make it the "best" or the "right way" to do something. Recognize when you have such thoughts, challenge yourself to grow in that moment – perhaps being more open to learning another way to do something and see its own merit.

When working, check in with local supervisors before giving input/feedback to others to understand any cultural differences. There may be ideas you want to share, however they do not generalize to real life for the client. You also do not have the full history of the client, including what has worked in the past and what has not. Know that no matter your experience, or years in a culture, you will never know what it truly means to be someone from that culture and should therefore avoid presenting yourself as an expert. When asked specific questions about the culture, connect people to local partners who can speak for themselves. Be ethical with your storytelling; gain informed consent for stories you may tell and avoid presenting yourself as the voice of the voiceless. All individuals have a voice; they may have been ignored or not had access to tell their stories, but you do not speak on their behalf. Create the platform to share their story without a white lens.

Dr. Victoria Farris, a researcher who developed an action-based guide to disrupting racism, discusses the need to first do the work within yourself to recognize racism before being able to dismantle it (Farris, 2019). It is your duty to expand your knowledge on racism, white supremacy, as well as white saviorism prior to working in the Majority World. If you see someone engaging in white saviorism, have a conversation with them. Share resources and help educate others about such behavior to make people question instead of praise white saviorism. Do the work within yourself to grow in your understanding as well as call out others for white saviorism.

One thing to note is that this chapter is focused on white saviorism in international work; however, white saviorism can and does occur in the US as well. Question your motives behind the intention to help, whether abroad or at home, and analyze the true impact of your behavior.

GROUP BEHAVIORS THAT CAN LEAD TO PREVENTION OF WHITE SAVIORISM

Organizations can also take steps to prevent being associated with or encouraging white saviorism by employees and volunteers. Group behaviors to consider include: representation, capacity building, setting equal staff salaries, training, and economic considerations.

For organizations considering working in the Majority World, representation is a must when creating a board as well as building a leadership team. The best person to work within any culture is someone who grew up in that culture, as they will have a full understanding of what works well and what does not.

One key goal of Minority World founders/leaders of an organization working internationally ought to be to work themselves out of a job. There are many ways to do this. The organization ought to have a plan for local staff to be leading the organization in the future. Create opportunities for growth and support continued education for your local staff. The work should be focused on making an ethical and sustainable impact that is not reliant on outsiders. If the organization is initially led by immigrants, what checks are in place to address cultural misunderstandings prior to implementation? For staff that are working in the organization, salary should be based on position and experience, not geographical home. Immigrants should make the same wage as the local employees of the same level. The goal should be to hire locally, but if not possible for specific reasons, then envision what you would pay a local employee and base salary on that figure. It is critical that what you do as an organization does not fall into the same commonplace cycles of systemic racism and oppression. Prior to bringing an immigrant to lead, work or volunteer in the organization, mandate training on cultural humility. Partner that person with local leaders on the ground and outline goals for their duration that address sustainable impact.

If an organization in the Minority World is wishing to share continued education opportunities to those in the Majority World while not perpetuating systematic racism and oppression, they should consider economic realities. How are you making conferences accessible to people worldwide? Are there online options for attendance to CEU events, and if so, is there a sliding scale based on GDP of the countries participating? Are sessions recorded to be able to be viewed at a different time for those in other time zones? How are you encouraging participation for research to be presented by Majority World researchers?

There are also a limited number of verified ABA courses available in Majority World countries. Most countries have none. How can universities that offer online ABA coursework break down economic barriers that currently uphold systematic racism and oppression? Could there also be a sliding scale available for coursework? If a Minority World organization or university is sending volunteers abroad, how are they training them to avoid white saviorism? Are they connected to local partners? Are the volunteer opportunities creating sustainable impact by building long lasting partnerships? What training is the organization offering prior to sending volunteers?

CALL TO ACTION

This chapter outlined questions to ask yourself, whether reflecting on the past or preparing for the future. This is a start to a conversation. Going forward, what next steps are you going to take to undo past conditioning and prevent white saviorism with yourself or your organization? What research needs to be done, and are you willing to tackle it? Let's change the narrative of the majority world and give back the platform to allow for experts from the majority world to speak for themselves.

REFERENCES

Adichie, C. N. (2009, October 7). *The danger of a single story | Chimamanda Ngozi Adichie.* YouTube. https://www.youtube.com/watch?v=D9Ihs241zeg

Aizenman, N. (2020, July 31). *U.S. missionary with no medical training settles suit over child deaths at her center.* NPR. https://choice.npr.org/index.html?origin=https://www.npr.org/sections/goatsandsoda/2020/07/31/897773274/u-s-missionary-with-no-medical-training-settles-suit-over-child-deaths-at-her-ce

Amos, O. (2018, January 9). *Is it true only 10% of Americans have passports?* BBC News. https://www.bbc.com/news/world-us-canada-42586638

DiAngelo, R. (2017, June 30). No, I won't stop saying "White supremacy." *Yes! Magazine.* https://www.yesmagazine.org/democracy/2017/06/30/no-i-wont-stop-saying-white-supremacy/

Farris, V. (2019). *DISRUPT course.* Farris Consulting. http://victoriafarris.com/disrupt-course/disrupt-course

Hartz, S. (2018, June 23). *4 ways to avoid the White savior complex in missions.* Sarita Hartz. http://www.saritahartz.com/4-ways-to-avoid-the-white-savior-complex-in-missions/

Seibel, I. (2016, June 11). BBC Documentary. *2015 The world's worst place to be disabled.* YouTube. https://www.youtube.com/watch?v=D9qF4gnXaDo

Silver, M. (2015, January 4). If you shouldn't call it Third World, what should you call it? NPR. https://choice.npr.org/index.html?origin=https://www.npr.org/sections/goatsandsoda/2015/01/04/372684438/if-you-shouldnt-call-it-the-third-world-what-should-you-call-it

CONCLUSION

Designing Organizations with Love: An ACT Prosocial Framework for Social Justice, Diversity, and Inclusion

Thomas G. Szabo

> It is important for all of us to appreciate where we come from and how that history has really shaped us in ways that we might not understand.
>
> (Sotomayor, n.d.)

DESIGNING ORGANIZATIONS WITH LOVE: AN ACT PROSOCIAL FRAMEWORK FOR SOCIAL JUSTICE, DIVERSITY, AND INCLUSION

This chapter is about two things seldom talked about in one sentence: design and love.

First, about design: behavior analysts do not subscribe to the view that humans design things entirely from scratch or build things with a unique, novel vision. Our stance in a behavioral world view is that when we design something that seems quite extraordinary, we are doing so because a class of responses that humans emitted at some point in our collective history is reselected in a current context or because novel contingencies generate equally novel forms of behavior (Skinner, 1953). When previously successful responses work in a presently challenging situation, onlookers that were not at hand in the past see behavior that appears creative, artistic, or ingenious. However, it is none of those things, really. It is as U.S. Supreme Court Justice Sonia Sotomayor suggests, our history coming to bear in a novel situation (Sotomayor, 2013).

Second, about love: behavior analysts examine the consequences of actions that seem to be selfish and those that appear to be selfless. In *Walden Two*, Skinner (1948) described powerful outcomes that came of Jesus' teaching to "love your enemies" (Skinner, 1948, p. 96). It appeared to be advice to an imprisoned people to bow in submission. Yet Jesus' message turned out to be a remarkable way of bringing about an end to the oppressive burden of hatred and a gateway to what he called "peace of mind" (Skinner, 1948, p. 97). According to Skinner, this was accomplished by the technique of practicing an opposing emotion, in other words, an incompatible behavior. Skinner suggested that phylogeny and ontogeny have prepared us to act with force and aggression, tactics that serve only the few, and work only in the short run. He argued that these tactics have led in the past to cultures being overthrown by those they are subduing with force, and he suggested that this will be the inevitable outcome that faces cultures that do not work to redesign themselves with the positive reinforcement practices he described in *Walden Two* as love (Skinner, 1953). To this end, Skinner wrote, "We are only just beginning to understand the power of love because we are just beginning to understand the weakness of force and aggression (Skinner, 1948, p. 97).

To design itself with love then, a group would need to do things that are both achievable and remarkable. Rather than create all its practices from scratch, the group would examine current contingencies, review what has worked in its own and other groups' remote histories and select from those alternatives a course of action that is inclusive of divergent voices, especially those that might disagree. This is no simple framework. But it is a structure with a function beyond preserving the status quo. The function of this framework is long-term survival of the group and reproduction of its most adaptive practices. In other words, diversity and inclusion seem central to Skinner's framework for cultural design.

Skinner recommended a cultural framework that both resembles and contrasts with that found in nonhuman species. In the natural world, evolutionary pressures select for group fitness by favoring species whose genes mutate with enough phenotypic diversity to respond to the challenges posed by a changing environment. Likewise, Skinner suggested that the fittest group will be the one with a large enough diversity of opinions to generate behavioral options for unforeseeable challenges. On the other hand, Skinner's framework involved establishing opportunities for members to develop their individual skills and harness the largest pool of potential positive reinforcers for themselves. This is important, because of the four operant contingency groups – negative and positive reinforcement and negative and positive punishment – of which all but positive reinforcement will bring behavior under aversive control. Rather than design the group with negative reinforcement and punishment contingencies, Skinner advocated that groups use positive reinforcement to generate cooperation among members and the experience of being free to choose from options carefully arranged to promote effective action. However, as his life came to an end, Skinner had only sketched this framework in interpretive works such as *Science and Human Behavior* (Skinner, 1953), *Walden Two* (Skinner, 1948) and *About Behaviorism* (Skinner, 1974). These works seemed to be a call for further research that behaviorists of his time were not yet ready to conduct. That fact may not have changed much to this day. For example, Luke et al. (2017) reported that the cumulative record of conceptual papers in *Behavior and Social Issues* is seven times that of the number of empirical papers (350, 50, respectively). As Don Baer, one of the founders of applied behavior analysis wrote, "We are not empowered to solve these bigger problems, we have not yet made an analysis of how to empower ourselves to try them, and we have not yet made the system-analytic task analyses that will prove crucial to solving those problems when we do empower ourselves sufficiently to try them" (Baer, 1987, p. 335).

Fortunately, a researcher of humble origins appeared in the late 20th century who would engage in naturalistic field studies that showed human groups attempting to organize themselves in a framework that was consistent with Skinner's suggestions. Elinor Ostrom was a resource biologist working with groups that shared the Los Angeles groundwater basins. Along an unrestricted passage that could have been a source of great tension among the businesses, Ostrom observed them doing something that caught her attention: they were cooperatively managing the commons. The practices she observed surprised Ostrom because they were the opposite to what ecologist Garrett Hardin wrote would be the inevitable outcome of social agreements among well-meaning collaborators. In *The Tragedy of the Commons*, Hardin imagined a plot of community land on which ten farmers living adjacent to the fields agree to forego both privatization and government regulation, and instead rely upon cooperation and public covenants to guide their actions. The farmers agree that the land can only sustain 100 head of cattle, so they each agree to have no more than 10 at any given time. This works well during rich economic cycles, when farmers are selling their livestock at a premium. But during lean cycles, when no one is buying and cows are cheap, a single farmer is likely to buy an extra ten cows, since after all, no one will know and just ten more cows are not likely to cause problems. But problems do ensue, because each of the farmers reacts to the situation in the same way, and in no time, there are 200 heads of cattle, the land is overgrazed, and the livestock perish. Interestingly, Hardin's thought experiment is recounted frequently by proponents of both privatization and government regulation alike.

Ostrom recognized that common-pool resource efforts of businesses sharing the Southern California groundwater basins contrasted with the oft cited prediction that given the opportunity, rational actors will exploit and pillage the ecosystem to their selfish advantage. Prevailing thought at the time was that either a laissez-faire political system allowing dominant businesses to overtake smaller ones and make better use of the land or top-down resource management regulations were needed to protect against the tragedy of the commons. Ostrom went on to investigate similar group self-design efforts in small shared resource communities across the globe. Over the course of 20 years, she generated a substantial body of evidence disproving the notion that groups cannot self-organize around a common purpose (Ostrom, 1990). She was awarded the Nobel Prize in Economics in 2009, notable in that she was the first woman to receive this honor.

Emerging from Ostrom's investigation of shared fisheries, waterways, and grazing lands was a thesis that caring for the commons required eight distinct functions to be organized from the ground up with involvement from enough diverse members of a group to create and sustain cooperative cultural norms. These functions, which she called "design principles" (Ostrom, 1990, p. 60), included:

1. Clearly defined common purposes
2. Equitable resource access
3. Collective choice arrangements
4. Monitoring of agreed upon expectations
5. Conflict-resolution procedures
6. Planned behavioral consequences
7. Self-organization of sub-groups
8. Scaled obligations to larger and outside entities

And here's where the story gets interesting to behavior analysts.

Presentation of the Nobel Prize in Economics to a woman caught the attention of David Sloan Wilson, an evolutionary biologist who had pioneered a model of multilevel selection (MLS; Wilson, 1975, 1976; Wilson & Sober, 1994). Wilson been working with behavior analyst and clinical psychologist Stephen C. Hayes at systemizing the empirical MLS evidence (e.g., Wilson, 1977, 1978; Wilson & Knollenberg, 1987) that dovetailed with Skinner's (1981) conceptual model of parallel natural, behavioral, and cultural selection. Specifically, Wilson and Hayes were studying the role of verbal relational behavior in MLS and cultural inheritance when Wilson read Ostrom's work. He immediately saw Ostrom's discoveries as data reflecting the utility of MLS approaches to cultural design. Wilson reached out to Ostrom, inviting her to join him in redrafting the eight design principles so that they could be used by schools, hospitals, churches, small businesses, and municipalities. Hayes, the founding developer of Acceptance and Commitment Therapy (ACT; Hayes et al., 1999/2012), suggested the creation of a workshop model for training these groups to use Ostrom's eight design principles. He asked for help from Kevin Polk, a Maine-based psychologist that had developed a simple instrument called the ACT matrix to be used with groups to induce behaviors associated with psychological flexibility (Polk & Schoendorff, 2014). Polk began writing a protocol for use of the matrix for helping groups develop a sense of lightness with each other as they discussed difficult issues. The group named the full approach that combined teaching multilevel group design and flexibility training ACT Prosocial, or simply, the Prosocial process.

If cultural problems can be addressed by organizations designing themselves with love (that is, if groups can learn from the remote past and use positive reinforcement to generate cooperative behavior in the present), the question remains as to how problems needing such solutions come to be in the first place. Skinner and others have not been silent on the issue. In the next section, I discuss evolutionary mismatch, the observation that as environments undergo changes, evolved traits become maladaptive. Specifically, I will address this phenomenon as it applies to organizations and cultural inheritance systems.

EVOLUTIONARY MISMATCH

Science and Human Behavior (Skinner, 1953) was Skinner's effort to generalize findings from the operant lab to problems of human culture. In one early passage, Skinner laid groundwork for interpreting the ways that human cultures go wrong by suggesting that as environments change, the capacity to be reinforced by a given event may have an evolutionary disadvantage. Skinner described sugar and sexual contact as reinforcing to most humans far beyond their current biological needs. His argument was that human susceptibility to reinforcement by sugar and sex was evolutionarily advantageous during epochs of famine and pestilence. Although modern conditions did away with these barriers to survival, the genetic endowment of the species has not yet changed in ways that meet the newly prevailing conditions of prosperity.

The notion that evolved traits become maladaptive as environments change and that new, adaptive patterns are slow to evolve has recently been termed evolutionary mismatch (Lloyd et al., 2011) but it was first described by Mayr as an evolutionary trap (Mayr, 1942). Yet Skinner went further to observe that similar to species, cultures reproduce themselves using patterns of behavior that have worked in recent times and that when faced with new scientific information, rapid environmental changes, and cultural upheavals, they are slow to adopt new forms that would be advantageous. For example, Western cultures have accepted determinism in some ways – we exonerate those who have committed crimes when they were unduly threatened, and we offer additional educational aids to those born with natural defects. At the same time, we have not let go of older, impoverished notions of individual willpower – we celebrate the heroism of soldiers without considering the inconspicuous sources of reinforcement that maintained their performance (Skinner, 1953). In other words, there is a cultural mismatch between older teachings and current knowledge that results in weak contingencies of reinforcement for desired performance.

Contemporary evolutionary theory posits similarly that unbridled natural selection often favors within-group competition over between-group cooperation because of the advantages that competition confers upon individuals for survival and reproduction (Wilson et al., 2013). However, between-group cooperation is needed for long-term survival and overall fitness of enough members of the group for its collective preparedness against predators and aversive conditions. Therefore, factors that limit selfishness without punishing self-preservation and which reward cooperation without punishing fair competition for equitable shares of common resources are both needed for a group's long-term viability. To the extent that individual fitness is favored via within-group competition over the group's long-term cooperation needs is a reflection of evolutionary mismatch, or within- and between-group selection imbalances (Biglan et al., 2020; Wilson et al., 2013).

Thus far, I have argued that 1) design is the application of previously successful strategies for self or others in novel situations where current repertoires are dysfunctional, 2) love is the use of positive reinforcement for less selfish and more cooperative actions that improve the long-term fitness of the group, and 3) unbridled evolutionary factors often favor the individual to the detriment of the group. Taken together, the implications are that humans are unlikely to survive unless new forms of social organization make use of remarkable but accomplishable strategies that bring about strategic balances of individual competition and group cooperation. Said differently, the levels of selection that Skinner (1953) and Wilson and Kniffin (1999) outlined as the known layers of multilevel selection may become imbalanced due to temporal lags in the evolutionary selection process. Therefore, human eusociality will likely benefit from proactive measures to bridge these gaps.

In the next section of this chapter, I will discuss the Prosocial framework used successfully by an international nongovernmental organization with limited resources during the West African Ebola epidemic of 2014–2016. The organization is Commit and Act (CAA), founded just a few years before the epidemic by a group dedicated to ending gender-based violence after the Sierra Leonean civil war. The Ebola epidemic was a global health crisis that was successfully contained at its epicenter in Sierra Leone, but not without devastating losses, vast global impact at the time, and profound new importance today in a world facing the COVID-19 pandemic at the time of this writing.

NUDGING SOCIAL JUSTICE, DIVERSITY, AND INCLUSION

Imagine that in your African village, you work as a subsistence farmer and sell a tiny share of your spoils in the marketplace so that you can send your children to school in the city. With your friends, you get together nightly at the pub, where a generator feeds electricity to the television, and you cheer on your favorite international football teams. The new government is maintaining a fragile peace, but it is well known that elected officials accept bribes and tell lies to maintain their power. Your nation is one of the poorest in the world, exploited for centuries for its wealth of precious metals and whose ports were once the hub of the global slave trade. Recently, friends and neighbors have died of inexplicable causes, and there is rumor that a new weapon has been unleashed as a means of spreading fear and controlling the vote in an upcoming election.

One day, strangers wearing plastic suits and gas masks appear in your village. They erect inflatable medical shelter tents and dig giant burial pits. Weeks before they had arrived, your auntie had gotten ill with the strange disease that had already claimed the lives of several neighbors and friends. When she died, you wrapped her in white cloth and laid her out in the parlor for loved ones to come and pay their respects. This is customary in your culture; it is how you honor your loved ones and express your grief at their loss. It is practiced widely, and your extended family expects this of you. The men in hazmat suits arrive at your door, remove your auntie, and place her body into one of the new giant burial pits. Then they take your children away and ask you to come with them to their tent, where they implore you to remain while they conduct tests to see if you are carrying the deadly virus. Tempers flare, but you go with the strangers. In quarantine, you recognize that the officials have no means to keep you there. You do not feel sick and long to be home with your family. They tell you that if you leave, you may endanger the lives of countless others. But neighbors and friends are saying that the virus is either a hoax, a demon that can be expelled with local remedies, or a government plot, and regardless of what it is, you should return to your home.

Ebola is one of a class of superviruses that attack the human immune system (Chowell & Nishiura, 2014). The Ebola virus is transmitted through contact with infected blood, other bodily fluids, or tissues; thus, customary burial practices in Sierra Leone exacerbated the rapid spread of the virus. The World Health Organization mobilized teams of aid workers that performed admirably and exactly as they had been trained. But customary practices and historical distrust of government in Sierra Leone produced a perfect storm of cultural mismatch between an ancient practice and current public health knowledge. In this context, the traditional international aid approach of quarantine and mass burial was slow to bring about changes in cultural practice (WHO, 2014).

It was against this backdrop that CAA began working in the villages and urban centers using a different strategy. Local community volunteers trained in the Prosocial approach met with schoolteachers and community leaders to find ways of stopping the virus without trampling important cultural observances. They met large groups in open air pavilions, provided information about the virus and how it is spread by unsuspecting humans, and gave people time to talk about the pain they and their communities were facing. The CAA workers then asked villagers to identify their most cherished personal and community values. Rather than imposing solutions from the outside, they asked villagers to brainstorm their own ideas for honoring loved ones in ways that would break the chain of transmission and save lives in their communities. A villager from one of the small towns outside Bo who was likely familiar with the Druze practice of kissing and embracing sacred trees (Dafni, 2007) suggested wrapping the trunks of banana trees with clothing from deceased loved ones and inviting the community to join together in washing, dressing, and embracing the effigy. A symbolic body could be adored in this way and sent off ceremoniously without endangering others. This idea immediately met with favor. The community decided as a group to try it and reconvened a week later to discuss ways to distribute banana tree trunks, get the word out, and manage potential opposition if it emerged. Leoneans who adopted this approach told others that they felt comfortable with this way of conveying their love and veneration and with help of CAA volunteers, the practice quickly spread throughout the Bo District. By November of 2015, the curve was flattened in the Bo District (Stewart et al., 2016). Figure 47.1 depicts a positive correlation between Prosocial efforts alongside that other workers in Bo compared to other districts with weakly coordinated efforts to stop the virus.

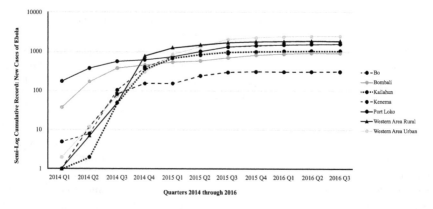

Figure 47.1 Transmission rates of the Ebola virus across eight districts in Sierra Leone 2014–2015. Prosocial workshops to address Ebola began in Bo District July 2014. The last reported case was in March 2016.

Adapted from World Health Organization, n.d. Retrieved, March 20, 2018 from https://apps.who.int/ebola/current-situation/ebola-situation-report-4-november-2015

A few key points are worth mention. First, the design of kissing and embracing a sacred tree was not new, though it may have appeared so to many who were unfamiliar with the ancient Druze practice. Consistent with known principles of behavior, this life-saving design innovation was a modification of a custom practiced elsewhere and retooled for use in the Leonean Ebola context. Second, CAA volunteers listened with love; that is, they positively reinforced community members' expressions of hurt, betrayal, confusion, and shame. Rather than telling people that they were wrong to feel these emotions, they willingly opened a space for what was discussed as being natural, given the circumstances. Third, rather than rushing to impose a solution or demand that the group uncover one, the CAA workers allowed the pain of the problem and discomfort of not having an answer to be present until members of the group themselves elected to begin brainstorming. Waiting in this way evoked a form of "creative hopelessness" (Hayes et al., 1999) that served to expose the underlying cultural mismatch. Lastly, the full inclusion of all members of the community honored tribal, religious and cultural diversity within the group.

Szabo (2020) suggested that diversity can be defined as a set of conditions that result in people with unique skill sets contributing to and gaining recognition within a group and that these conditions should include valuing, evoking, and reinforcing the novel contributions of members with uncommon skills. The practice of Prosocial in these Leonean focus groups meets this definition and offers a trail through the forests of injustice and social malaise.

PROSOCIAL AND THE STRUGGLE FOR SOCIAL JUSTICE

Social change movements encountering resistance from unjust systems sometimes struggle with conflicting internal pressures for nonviolent versus violent civil dissent (Boulard et al., under review). For example, during the American civil rights movement, internal conflicts over the use of force heightened when progress was thwarted by police and government. Infighting within the movement threatened to alienate key leaders from each other and their supporters (Alexander, 2010). Similar struggles over tactics were seen when Gandhi campaigned for India's independence from colonial rule (Wolpert, 2002).

Prosocial offers a unique lens from which to pursue agreement on tactics in a way that is socially just within the group itself. As it was used during the Leonean struggle to end Ebola, the Prosocial path to consilience between members during a conflict may involve listening with love to diverse viewpoints until a design emerges that all can live with. On such a path, members are encouraged to reflect whether things will be better than before for themselves and for others in the group (Atkins et al., 2019). A critical distinction is that in service of the group's broader aims, an individual may agree to cooperate wholeheartedly, even if they do not agree with the decision their colleagues have enacted. This sublimation of individual self-interest for the survival and reproduction of the group's vision is a central component of the Prosocial strategy for ameliorating within- and between-group imbalances. All are encouraged to voice their dissent but to first carefully consider whether they hold their opposition strongly enough to block the group or merely enough to go on record with their dissent while still offering their full engagement with the course to which the rest of the group has agreed (Owen & Buck, 2020).

To this end, it would be useful to define social justice. A behavioral definition of social justice suitable to the context of helping groups self-organize is that it is an ongoing practice of balancing the needs of the one, the few, the many, and the totality. The Prosocial process is a vehicle for pursuing social justice by acting with respect to the needs of individuals, groups, and groups of groups over both short- and long-term expanses of time.

IMPLEMENTATION PLANNING

Goals are easily listed during a spirited meeting when the group is aligned on its central purpose and the facilitator has evoked behavior that is psychologically flexible. But goals may be difficult to accomplish. They may require several sub-goals that the large group does not foresee needing or have time to identify during its early meetings. Particular goals may require the completion of others, and some of the early goals may need to be changed or terminated when the group examines them more carefully. A key variable in successful realization of aims established during a Prosocial planning process is the appointment or election of a team responsible for implementation planning.

Prosocial implementation teams are most effective when they are composed at least in part of senior representatives from each of the main stakeholder groups affected by the group's actions. Senior representatives should be selected because of their knowledge of systems in use and that could be used. However, it is important that members of the implementation planning team also include those with contacts among the group's most diverse constituents. A well-rounded team includes some with fresh perspectives and others with seasoned understandings of the complexities involved in the group's goal attainment. This extension of multilevel selection is relevant because the Prosocial process can unravel if it moves too slowly or too quickly. As Malott (2003) suggested, the process of organizational change involves both dynamic and static pressures that must be balanced over time.

To this end, a Prosocial implementation team is tasked with identifying parties responsible for getting work done, parties they are accountable to, estimates of task start and completion times, and lists of potential barriers. Barriers that a skilled implementation team might list could include both physical and cognitive-emotional impediments. Clear strategies for working through each barrier should also be listed and updated periodically. The implementation planning team should get together regularly to review progress, add new sub-goals, assign tasks, and celebrate milestones (Appendix Figure 47.2). Dashboard measures should be regularly graphed in ways that the entire organization can quickly glance at and perceive their status-to-date. These dashboards provide excellent motivation when progress is alternately slow or rapid (Szabo et al., 2012). Additional reinforcers for task completion can be used, but in at least two studies to date, readily visible dashboard metrics themselves have helped to maintain performance toward agreed upon goals (Lydon et al., 2012; Szabo et al., 2012) and have been used to mathematically ensure balanced performance (Abernathy, 2014).

An important benefit to establishing an implementation team is that the Prosocial facilitator is setting the stage to fade their involvement with the group. The team assumes full responsibility for its own execution of tasks, identification of problems and solutions, and program evaluation. As the Prosocial process becomes embedded within the culture of the group, the facilitator carefully fades their participation but remains available for consultation as needed.

CONCLUSION

Groups evolve much like species. Natural, behavioral, and cultural selection are parallel processes that may at times require active planning to achieve advantageous balance.

Within a species, natural selection to environmental exigencies generally occurs gradually, whereas ecosystem changes are sometimes abrupt. The environment often selects behavior that affords individuals with advantages, but this may be at the peril of the group. Groups generally advance in ways that serve them well, but this is at times at the expense of harmonious interaction with other groups. In each of these cases, selection pressures can produce conditions that are unbalanced. The Prosocial process is a way for groups to take into consideration their individual, group, and species needs over the course of days, years, and even epochs. At stake is the amelioration of potentially deadly evolutionary and cultural mismatches.

In a successful Prosocial planning process, all voices are heard. No one is left out. Not all voices need to have equal say and there may be times when groups make decisions that individuals find disagreeable. But throughout the Prosocial process, all participants are encouraged to bring their diverse experiences and repertoires to the table. New ideas are frequently found in the remote learning histories of the most junior or otherwise marginalized members of the team. Listening to and reinforcing their voices is a special kind of love that leads to greater harmony within and between groups. Listening with love offers the group a pathway for successful working that is richly inclusive. Balancing the needs of the one, the few, the many, and the totality leads to a remarkable and achievable kind of social justice.

REFERENCES

Abernathy, W. B. (2014). *The liberated workplace: Transitioning to Walden three.* Performance Management Publications.

Alexander, M. (2010). *The new Jim Crow: Mass incarceration in the age of colorblindness.* The New Press.

Atkins, P. W. B., Wilson, D. S., & Hayes, S. C. (2019). *Prosocial: Using evolutionary science to build productive, equitable, and collaborative groups.* Context Press.

Baer, D. (1987). Weak contingencies, strong contingencies, and too many behaviors to change. *Journal of Applied Behavior Analysis, 24,* 429–431. https://10.1901/jaba.1987.20-335

Biglan, A., Johansson, M., Van Ryzin, M., & Embry, D. (2020). Scaling up and scaling out: Consilience and the evolution of more nurturing societies. *Clinical Psychology Review, 81,* 101893. https://doi.org/10.1016/j.cpr.2020.101893

Boulard, C., Bethea-Miller, V., & Szabo, T. G. (2020). A behavioral analysis of police brutality and recommendations for social action. [Manuscript submitted for publication]. School of Behavior Analysis, Florida Institute of Technology.

Chowell, G., & Nishiura, H. (2014). Transmission dynamics and control of Ebola virus disease (EVD): A review. *BMC Medicine, 12,* 196. https://doi.org/10.1186/s12916-014-0196-0190

Dafni, A. (2007). Rituals, ceremonies and customs related to sacred trees with a special reference to the Middle East. *Journal of Ethnobiology and Ethnomedicine, 3,* 28. https://doi.org/10.1186/1746-4269-4263-28

Hayes, S. C., Strosahl, K. D., & Wilson, K. G. (1999/2012). *Acceptance and commitment therapy: An experiential approach to behavior change.* Guilford Press.

Lloyd, E., Wilson, D. S., & Sober, E. (2011). Evolutionary mismatch and what to do about it: A basic tutorial. *Evolutionary Applications, 2–4.* https://www.semanticscholar.org/paper/Evolutionary-Mismatch-And-What-To-Do-About-It-%3A-A-Lloyd-Wilson/a4f5acdfb7766761474a1d83c533f67496d94256

Luke, M. M., Roose, K. M., Rakos, R. F., & Mattaini, A. A. (2017). The history and current status of Behavior and Social Issues: 1978–2016. *Behavior and Social Issues, 26,* 111–127. https://doi.org/10.5210/bsi.v26i0.7728

Lydon, C. A., Szabo, T. G., Newsome, W. D., & Williams, W. L. (2012). Total performance service review in the smaller organization: The use of scorecards. *Journal of Rehabilitation Administration, 36*(2), 93–119.

Malott, M. E. (2003). *Paradox of organizational change: Engineering organizations with behavioral systems analysis.* Context Press.

Mayr, E. (1942). *Systematics and the origin of species, from the viewpoint of a zoologist.* Columbia University Press.

Ostrom, E. (1990). *Governing the commons.* Cambridge University Press.

Ostrom, E. (1992). Institutions and common-pool resources. *Journal of Theoretical Politics, 4*(3), 243–245. https://doi.org/10.1177/0951692892004003001

Owen, R. L., & Buck, J. A. (2020). Creating the conditions for reflective team practices: Examining sociocracy as a self-organizing governance model that promotes transformative learning. *Reflective Practice.* http://dx.doi.org.portal.lib.fit.edu/10.1080/14623943.2020.1821630

Polk, K. L., & Schoendorff, B. (2014). *The ACT matrix: A new approach to building psychological flexibility across settings and populations.* Context Press.

Skinner, B. F. (1948). *Walden two.* Prentice Hall.

Skinner, B. F. (1953). *Science and human behavior.* The Free Press.

Skinner, B. F. (1974). *About behaviorism.* Vintage Books.

Skinner, B. F. (1981). Selection by consequences. *Science, 213,* 501–504. https://doi.org/10.1126/science.7244649

Stewart, C., White, R. G., Ebert, B., Mays, I., Nardozzi, J., & Bockarie, H. (2016). A preliminary evaluation of Acceptance and Commitment Therapy (ACT) training in Sierra Leone. *Journal of Contextual Behavioral Science, 5*(1), 16–22. https://doi.org/10.1016/j.jcbs.2016.01.001

Szabo, T. G. (2020). Equity and diversity in behavior analysis: Lessons from Skinner, 1945. *Behavior Analysis in Practice, 13*(2), 375–386. https://doi.org/10.1007/s40617-020-00414-1

Szabo, T. G., Williams, W. L., Rafacz, S. D., & Newsome, W. (2012). Evaluation of the service review model with performance scorecards. *The Journal of Organizational Behavior Management, 32*(4), 274–296. https://doi.org/10.1080/01608061.2012.729408

WHO Ebola Response Team, Aylward, B., Barboza, P., Bawo, L., Bertherat, E., Bilivogui, P., Blake, I., Brennan, R., Briand, S., Chakauya, J. M., Chitala, K., Conteh, R. M., Cori, A., Croisier, A., Dangou, J. M., Diallo, B., Donnelly, C. A., Dye, C., Eckmanns, T., Ferguson, N. M . . . & Yoti, Z. (2014). Ebola virus disease in West Africa – the first 9 months of the epidemic and forward projections. *The New England Journal of Medicine, 371*(16), 1481–1495. https://doi.org/10.1056/NEJMoa1411100

Wilson, D. S. (1975). A general theory of group selection. *Proceedings of the National Academy of Sciences, 72,* 143–146.

Wilson, D. S. (1976). Evolution on the level of communities. *Science, 192,* 1358–1360. https://doi.org/10.1126/science.1273598

Wilson, D. S. (1977). Structured demes and the evolution of group-advantageous traits. *American Naturalist, 111,* 157–185. https://doi.org/10.1086/283146

Wilson, D. S. (1978). Structured demes and trait-group variation. *American Naturalist, 113,* 606–610. https://doi.org/10.1086/283417

Wilson, D. S., & Knollenberg, W. G. (1987). Adaptive indirect effects: The fitness of burying beetles with and without their phoretic mites. *Evolutionary Ecology, 1,* 139–59. https://doi.org/10.1007/BF02067397

Wilson, D. S., & Sober, E. (1994). Reintroducing group selection to the human behavioral sciences. *Behavioral and Brain Sciences, 17,* 585–608. https://doi.org/10.1017/S0140525X00036104

Wilson, D. S., & Kniffin, K. M. (1999). Multilevel selection and the social transmission of behavior. *Human Nature, 10,* 291–310. https://doi.org/10.1007/s12110-999-1005-x

Wilson, D. S., Ostrom, E., & Cox, M. E. (2013). Generalizing the core design principles for the efficacy of groups. *Journal of Economic Behavior & Organization,* 1–12. http://dx.doi.org/10.1016/j.jebo.2012.12.010

Wolpert, S. (2002). *Gandhi's Passion: The life and legacy of Mahatma Gandhi.* Oxford University Press.

APPENDIX

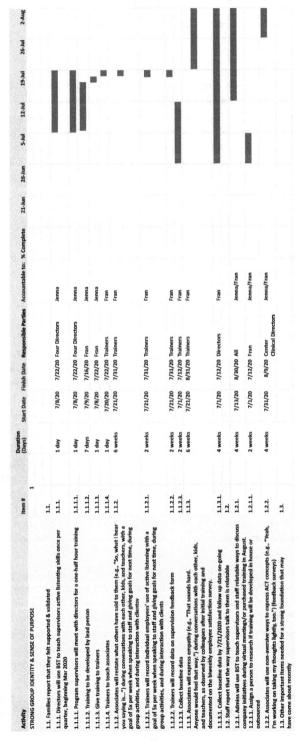

Figure 47.2 Example of Prosocial Implementation Plan, Core Design Principle #1, Strong Group Identity, and Sense of Purpose.

FINAL THOUGHTS

Michelle L. Zube

This text was born out of the idea of wanting to do more, do differently, and do better. The authors of these essays have demonstrated how the science of behavior analysis can be used to remediate issues that permeate society on all levels. Some may find this information interesting. Others may be inspired to explore new realms for the application of the science. It is our hope that many will see this as a call to action. And being in action to realize that outcomes in your life often require you to go beyond who and what you know yourself to be, and instead, to be in life as someone who is oriented around impacting the quality of life for other human beings.

In *The Nurture Effect*, Biglan (2015) discusses the way forward is through prevention and treatment using a behavioral science based approach to transform society beyond the individual level and to use the breadth of research available to evolve into a society that breeds compassion, prosocial behaviors, equality for all members. It is not enough to know that this is within our scope of practice. We must focus on the *applied* aspect and create pathways by which policy makers will begin to make evidenced based interventions available to all who need them. Not just who insurance companies deem appropriate and in need of services.

It is hard to unsee all that has happened and will continue to occur if we do not intervene. Marr (2006) points out that many of the major problems of the world (e.g., war, poverty, disease, genocide, etc.) are beyond the help of any science partially because political systems have never set up the proper contingencies to address these problems in a sustainable way. He suggests that even though the sciences can be used to mitigate some of these problems, without the science of behavior setting up the proper contingencies, very little will be accomplished.

The challenges addressed in this book, along with many others not detailed here, are systemic. Evolutionary biologist David Sloan Wilson asserts "Systemic problems require systemic solutions" (Biglan, 2020, p. 2). He suggests that we employ an evolutionary framework to problem solving with a focus on: establishing the target for selection, orienting variation around the target of selection, and the identification and replication of best practices. The identification and replication of best practices entails the collection and sharing of information in terms of scientific inquiry with an emphasis of replication being sensitive to context.

Similarly, Biglan (2020) proposes that change will be a top-down and bottom-up process. What will take place at the individual level will in turn bring forth changes across larger groups of people by cultivating the skills and values necessary for cooperation such that all who embrace them will benefit. Many have discussed the extent to which consequences have an impact not just at the individual level but on the greater environmental context. We can look to prosocial (Atkins et al., 2019) to better understand how to increase the efficacy of group dynamics so that problems are solved and all members of society are met with equality and justice.

When creating a movement, which is what we aspire, Biglan (2020) suggests we use our understanding of the human sciences and the influential factors on our political and economic systems to be our guide. The same understanding of how our societies and economies have evolved can be used to create a system that is beneficial for everyone. He urges, "We know what people need to thrive, and we know how to create the environments that nurture well-being" (p. 13). So what are we waiting for?

The contributors have offered a great deal of information that must continue to be explored, shared, replicated, and most importantly generalized. The call to action has cried out.

REFERENCES

Atkins, W. B., Wison, D. S., & Hayes, S. (2019). *Prosocial: Using evolutionary science to build productive, equitable, and collaborative groups.* New Harbinger.

Biglan, A. (2015). *The nurture effect: How the science of human behavior can improve our lives & our world.* New Harbinger.

Biglan, A. (2020). *Rebooting capitalism: How we can forge a society that works.* Values to Action.

Marr, M. (2006). Behavior analysis and social dynamics: Some questions and concerns. *Behavior and Social Issues, 15*(1). https://doi.org/10.5210/bsi.v15i1.345

INDEX

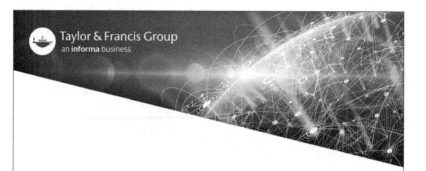

Printed in the USA
CPSIA information can be obtained
at www.ICGtesting.com
LVHW022031100923
757783LV00004B/36